Marcel Proust
and Spanish America

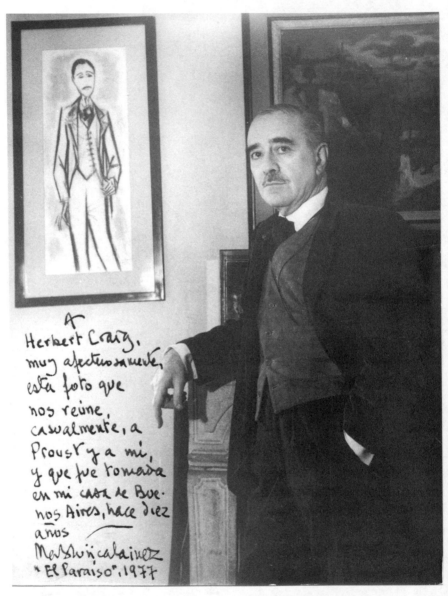

A
Herbert Craig,
muy afectuosamente,
esta foto que
nos reúne,
casualmente, a
Proust y a mí,
y que fue tomada
en mi casa de Bue-
nos Aires, hace diez
años
Manuel Mujica Láinez
"El Paraíso", 1977

Manuel Mujica Láinez in his home, photographed in front of a sketch of Proust.

Marcel Proust and Spanish America

From Critical Response to Narrative Dialogue

Herbert E. Craig

Lewisburg
Bucknell University Press
London: Associated University Presses

Associated University Presses
440 Forsgate Drive
Cranbury, NJ 08512

Associated University Presses
16 Barter Street
London WC1A 2AH, England

Associated University Presses
P.O. Box 338, Port Credit
Mississauga, Ontario
Canada L5G 4L8

The paper used in this publication meets the requirements of the American National Standard for Permanence of Paper for Printed Library Materials Z39.48–1984.

Library of Congress Cataloging-in-Publication Data
Craig, Herbert E.
    Marcel Proust and Spanish America: from critical response to narrative dialogue / Herbert E. Craig.
        p. cm.
    Includes bibliographical references and index.
    ISBN 0-8387-5485-6 (alk. paper)
    1. Proust, Marcel, 1871–1922—Appreciation—Latin America. 2. Proust, Marcel, 1871–1922—Influence. 3. Latin American literature—French influences. 4. Latin American literature—20th century—History and criticism. I. Title.
PQ2631.R63 Z5459865 2002
843'.912—dc21

2001043738

T

To the Proustians:
who read and discussed the *Recherche* with fervor,
   like Victoria Ocampo of Argentina
   or Yolanda Oreamuno of Costa Rica,
who wrote numerous articles on Marcel Proust,
   like Alone of Chile
   or Edmundo Valadés of Mexico,
who wrote novels as well as critical studies,
   like Jaime Torres Bodet of Mexico,
   Alejo Carpentier of Cuba,
   José Bianco of Argentina
   or Eduardo Caballero Calderón of Colombia,
who wrote long novels related to the *Recherche*,
   like Manuel Mujica Láinez of Argentina,
   José Donoso of Chile,
   Alfredo Bryce Echenique of Peru
   or Reinaldo Arenas of Cuba,
who studied the *Recherche* in depth and taught it,
   like Germaine Brée in Wisconsin
   or Philip Kolb in Illinois.

Contents

Acknowledgements

I WOULD LIKE TO THANK ALL OF THE AUTHORS WHOSE WORKS I HAVE cited, but most particularly those for which I needed to request special permission: *Rayuela* by Julio Cortázar, *El recurso del método* by Alejo Carpentier, and *Abaddón el exterminador* by Ernesto Sábato. These were received through the Agencia Literaria Carmen Balcells, S. A. (Barcelona), the Fundación Alejo Carpentier (Havana), and the Agencia Literaria Guillermo Schavelzon & Asociados (Buenos Aires), respectively.

Marcel Proust
and Spanish America

Point of Departure: An Intimate Conversation between an Aspiring French Writer and a Young Pianist Born in Venezuela

Among the readers and scholars of *A la recherche du temps perdu* [In Search of Lost Time], it is a well-known fact that the art song and opera composer, Reynaldo Hahn (1874–1947), was one of Marcel Proust's most intimate friends. Such Proustians are fully aware of the fact that two years before the publication of *Les plaisirs et les jours* [Pleasures and Days] (1896) its then unknown author met the nineteen-year-old pianist at the salon of Madeleine Lemaire, and the two young men began a spiritual and physical relationship that would last nearly thirty years, until Proust's death on 18 November 1922. They may also realize that Reynaldo, who was the only person outside of Marcel's family and domestic staff permitted to enter the dying man's bedroom, had been born in Caracas, Venezuela. But, they have little, if any, knowledge of the literary relation between Proust and the Spanish-speaking world, where the composer of "L'Heure exquise" [The Exquisite Hour] and *Ciboulette* spent his early years.

On the other hand, even though the readers and scholars of Spanish American literature may have heard that, like other modernist writers, Proust had a profound effect upon many of the novels of the Boom, they generally have no awareness of Reynaldo Hahn or of Proust's acquaintance with other Spanish Americans (e.g., the Argentine writer-diplomat Lucio V. Mansilla). Nor do they have a clear understanding of how, when, or where the *Recherche* was introduced into the New World, or in what way this literary relation has developed over time. The purpose of this study will be to enlighten both types of readers and scholars so that they can have a detailed knowledge of this very important personal and literary relation.

Indeed a few scholars and writers have carefully examined the friendship between Marcel Proust and Reynaldo Hahn. Philip Kolb published their letters in 1956, and this expert on Proust's correspondence and

Emmanuel Berl preceded these texts with a thoughtful introduction and preface. Additional information can be found in the complete *Correspondance de Marcel Proust* (1970–93), which Kolb also edited and published in twenty-one volumes. Proust's numerous biographers, especially since André Maurois and to include George D. Painter, Ghislain de Diesbach, and William C. Carter have traced this relationship over time, but they have largely ignored Hahn's place of birth. Painter, although very profuse in other details, was in this case so curt and careless as to say of Reynaldo, "He was a Jew, born at Caracas in Venezuela . . ." (1959, 1:170). Fortunately, Daniel Bendahan and other Venezuelan scholars have examined carefully Reynaldo's family and in particular his mother, who was truly a *caraqueña* and of the Christian faith.[1] Likewise they have shown that even though Reynaldo left his native land at an early age, he never forgot it nor its language.[2]

Curiously, one of the most interesting treatments of the relationship between Marcel Proust and Reynaldo Hahn appears in a play by the Venezuelan writer of Uruguayan origin, Ugo Ulive, rather than in a scholarly study. In *Reynaldo* (1985), the aspiring French novelist discusses his ideas with the younger pianist, and the latter performs for his friend the musical phrase which will be incorporated a few years later into *A la recherche du temps perdu*. The theatrical piece also depicts Hahn's relationship with his sister María, mother, and family, his memories of Caracas, the nature of his compositions, and his struggle to be accepted by the French musical community.

Without doubt the friendship between the author of the *Recherche* and the musician, composer, and eventual director of the Opera of Paris, was a very important one.[3] For Marcel's first book, *Les plaisirs et les jours,* Hahn composed four musical scores ("Portraits de peintres" [Portraits of Painters]), which appeared in its deluxe edition along with illustrations by Madeleine Lemaire. Proust began his second but later to be abandoned work, *Jean Santeuil,* while he and Reynaldo were spending two months together near Beg-Meil, Brittany. As Kolb pointed out, the young French writer intended to assign to his friend a predominant role, which he confessed in letter XXXV of their correspondence: "I want you to be always present, but like a God in disguise that no mortal can recognize" (1956, 53). This is, in fact, largely the case. Not only can one detect in the description of the Marquis de Poitiers Reynaldo's unique manner of simultaneously singing, smoking, and playing the piano, but also the name and initials of Jean's friend Henri de Réveillon allude directly to Hahn. Réveillon was precisely what Lemaire called her Marne region château (which was probably where the young men's physical intimacy began) and the letters "HR" constitute Hahn's initials in reverse order.[4] For Proust's most famous work, the *Recherche,* Hahn's excellent musical knowledge proved to be invaluable. According to various scholars, Proust sought his friend's counsel for the description of music and, in particular, for the elements used to create the *petite phrase* of Vinteuil.[5] Recent critics have suggested that Marcel's feelings for Reynaldo served as the basis for several aspects of Swann's love for Odette, including jealousy.[6]

The effects of this friendship also extended beyond Reynaldo himself. The French author wrote numerous letters to Reynaldo's sister María (who married in 1899 Raimundo de Madrazo, a Spanish painter and son of a famous portrait artist) and a few missives to Reynaldo's mother. Let me emphasize that the Hahn family maintained contact with the Venezuelan community in Paris and with a daughter who had stayed in Caracas.[7] In this regard, I should point out that Reynaldo's father, Carlos Hahn, had been a financial adviser to the Venezuelan president, Antonio Guzmán Blanco, and that, even after they had both moved to Paris, they remained on friendly terms. It is not entirely clear to what extent Proust came to know other Venezuelans, but there are a half dozen references in the *Correspondance de Marcel Proust* to Roberto Guzmán Blanco, who was a brother of the Duchesse de Morny, as well son of the former Venezuelan president.

In the *Recherche* itself can also be found a few remarks concerning South Americans. A particular family of such persons living in Paris closely resembles Reynaldo's. Discussing the vestiges of an immigrant family's original language, Proust wrote in *La prisonnière* [The Captive]:

> Dans une famille venue de l'Amérique du Sud et ne parlant plus que le français, ce sera un mot espagnol. Et à la génération suivante, le mot n'existera plus qu'à titre de souvenir d'enfance. On se rappellera bien . . . tel mot, mais les enfants ignorent ce que voulait dire au juste ce mot, si c'était de l'espagnol, de l'hébreux, de l'allemand. . . . (1954, 3:326)[8]

> [In a family originally from South America but no longer speaking anything but French, this will be a Spanish word. And for the members of the next generation, the word will only exist as a reminiscence of childhood. One will remember well . . . such a word, but the children are unaware what the word exactly means, whether it is from Spanish, Hebrew, German. . . .]

According to Alejo Santa-María (1971), with the assistance of Reynaldo Hahn, Pedro-Emilio Coll had the opportunity to visit Proust during his reclusion. Although there is little evidence as to when (or even if) this visit occurred, the Venezuelan writer-diplomat became familiar with Proust's work at an early date and attended his funeral at the small Parisian church of Saint-Pierre de Chaillot. A few days later, on 27 November 1922, Coll wrote of his impressions to a woman in Caracas, Elvira Zuloaga. In this letter (which was published twenty-five years later) with an almost prophetic voice, Coll called Proust "the first of the writers of contemporary France and one of the most extraordinary analysts of the human soul that has ever existed" (1947, 15). Here, due to the enthusiasm, I have found the hint of a possible influence worth examining. The same may be true for at least one other Venezuelan writer in spite of the fact that his principal works were published years before Proust's death.

Although it may appear coincidental that Mario Picón-Salas saw an affinity between Coll and Proust while Arturo Uslar Pietri found in the work of Manuel Díaz Rodríguez an anticipation of the *Recherche*, these two Venezuelan writers at times seem remarkably close to Proust.[9] The ideas of Díaz Rodríguez on involuntary memory, as found in the initial text of his second travel book *De mis romerías* [On My Pilgrimages] (1898), "Alma de viajero" [Soul of a Traveler], are surprisingly similar to those of Proust:

> El recuerdo de los sitios hermosos donde vivimos y de las cosas que en tales sitios amamos nos persigue y asedia. El menor suceso evoca, a veces, en nosotros multitud de imágenes, pálidas o vivas. Un olor cualquiera, que para los demás nada significa, puede en nostros despertar un gran número de sensaciones dormidas, apagadas casi muertas. (1982, 14–15)

> [The memory of the beautiful places where we lived and of the things that we love in such places pursues and besieges us. The slightest incident at times evokes in us a multitude of pale or vivid images. An ordinary scent, which for other persons means nothing, can awaken in us a great number of dormant, muffled, almost dead sensations.]

In this case, particularly given the early date, one can indeed consider the possibility of a common source. Pierre Loti, for example, described a few memory experiences in *Le roman d'un enfant* [The Novel of a Child] (1890) and Proust's classmate Fernand Gregh published in 1896 (*La Revue Blanche* [The White Review]) a curious text about this subject, which may have been inspired by young Marcel, "Mystères."[10] But it is also conceivable that Díaz Rodríguez, who lived in Paris intermittently from 1892 to 1901, read some of Proust's early texts as they were published in literary magazines (e.g., *La Revue Blanche*) or when they were collected in *Les plaisirs et les jours*."[11] Although Proust was not as explicit in these texts in his treatment of memory as he would be in the *Recherche* (1913–27), many of his ideas appeared in embryo form. In this way we can explain the remarks by Díaz Rodríguez in "Alma de viajero", as well as several brief memory experiences found in *Idolos rotos* [Broken Idols] (1901) and *Sangre patricia* [Patrician Blood] (1902). The same can be said for Pedro-Emilio Coll, who also spent time in Paris and London during the same years and used involuntary memory in at least two stories from *El castillo de Elsinor* [Elsinor Castle] (1901): "Opoponax" and "Borracho criollo" [A Drunk Creole].

I should note that concerning memory these two Venezuelans, who have been called *modernistas,* differ from their Spanish American contemporaries of the same movement. Unlike José Asunción Silva, who in a still Romantic mode used old, familiar objects to evoke the past in his poem "Vejeces" [Old Things] (1963, 76–77), and Manuel Gutiérrez Nájera, who likewise used as a stimulus previously heard music in "La serenata de Schubert" [The Serenade by Schubert] (1946, 2:95–97), Pedro-Emilio Coll and Manuel Díaz Rodríguez were much closer to Proust. Not only did they employ one of the five senses as had Baudelaire in "Parfum exotique" (1968, 56), but, unlike this great poet and more like Proust himself, they had the memory experiences begin involuntarily. This distance from other *modernistas* is especially evident in *Sangre patricia,* where Díaz Rodríguez used memory in a far more abstract way. A mere shade of green causes the protagonist to recall his beloved's eyes and the sea where her body was laid to rest. This spontaneous identification of similar sensations coincides in its technique with that of one of the texts from *Les plaisirs et les jours.* In "Vent de mer à la campagne" [Sea Wind in the Country], the violence of the wind and the shade of light on a particular day gave the narrator the impression of being at the seashore when he was actually in the inland region of Champagne. In this way, he was able to recover the past.

Already, like Marcel Proust and probably due to his example, Díaz Rodríguez was moving away from Spanish American *modernismo* and toward what we know today as Occidental modernism.[12] Although these two literary phenomena can trace their origins back to Charles Baudelaire, who, as early as 1846, first wrote about "la vie moderne" as a form of heroism against the traditional concept of art (1968, 259–61), and both combined the aestheticism of the Parnasse with the mystery of Symbolism, the modernists would be far more interested in the workings of the human mind than the *modernistas.* In this regard, Marcel Proust would play an predominant role. His subtle analysis of society and individual consciousness, of memory, time and art eventually allowed him to go beyond the apparent superficiality of his upper-class characters. But, this was not yet the case in *Les plaisirs et les jours,* and he would need to struggle for more than fifteen years to define his own unique form of modernism.

With the publication of the first two volumes of the *Recherche—Du côté de chez Swann* [Swann's Way] in 1913 and *A l'ombre des jeunes filles en fleurs* [Within a Budding Grove] in 1919—Proust's art of subjectivity, which we now identify with modernism, was firmly established. Thus, Spanish

American writers, like Pedro-Emilio Coll, saw Marcel Proust as a true and exciting alternative to the realist-naturalist models of the past. As we shall see, this French writer was able to show many Spanish Americans how they could transcend their simple observation of the world and penetrate beneath the surface of appearances. His poetic vision, his ideas on involuntary memory, and his method of psychological analysis would greatly affect the New World novel. Thus, with the aid of Marcel Proust and other modernists, such as James Joyce, Virginia Woolf, Franz Kafka, Thomas Mann, and William Faulkner, Spanish American narrative would be renewed and become itself quite modernist. This transformation began during the 1920s, but the new form of writing was not able to supplant the prevailing realist-regionalist tendencies until after 1940. The writers of the pre-Boom and Boom generations would use Proust and modernism as their literary base.[13] But, like the young writers in Europe and the United States, they would soon begin to question modernism and through their rebellion move toward what we know as postmodernism. Some rejected Proust's method of psychological analysis and cast doubt upon the exclusivity of involuntary memory, but the *Recherche* would remain a constant point of reference and a subject of debate. For this reason, even today Spanish Americans writers continue their relation with Proust.[14]

Indeed, Arturo Torres-Rioseco was accurate in stating years ago that Marcel Proust became and has remained the favorite twentieth-century French novelist for most Spanish American readers and writers (1963, 72). To this day, no one has replaced him in spite of the fact that he has had temporary rivals from Albert Camus and Jean-Paul Sartre to Alain Robbe-Grillet and Michel Butor.

From our perspective eight decades since Proust's death, it is possible to assert that this very important relation between the author of the *Recherche* and Spanish America began as an intimate conversation between two young men born on the opposite shores of the Atlantic Ocean: Marcel and Reynaldo.[15] Already, in their first encounter at Madeleine Lemaire's, we can discover some of the essential elements of Proust's vast novel. The presence of the two young men at her soirée implied their similar social aspirations. The performance of piano music that evening was an example of art, which brought the sensitive young men together.[16] Their meeting led to their friendship and love affair. Over time their bond changed as Hahn became more involved in his musical career and Proust explored other relationships. Years later, looking back upon his life, the French novelist examined such a process of change, but more importantly he attempted to recapture through memory and writing his experiences with Reynaldo and a host of other persons.

From this intimate conversation between the aspiring French novelist, Marcel Proust, and the young pianist of Venezuelan extraction, Reynaldo Hahn, there grew a multi-voiced dialogue which has spanned the Atlantic Ocean and continues yet today. This phenomenon can be examined in two distinct, but closely associated, ways. As Spanish Americans learned of Marcel Proust and read his monumental novel, they began to discuss the *Recherche* orally, in the sections on literature of their principal newspapers, in literary and academic magazines, and eventually in books. Moreover, during this same period many Spanish American writers, who had discovered in Proust's work new ideas and innovative techniques, tried to incorporate some of these examples of modernism into their own literary texts.

For the present study, I have chosen to examine these two facets and to demonstrate how they are inextricably bound. Not only have both literary critics and narrative writers paid attention to the same ideas and techniques found in the *Recherche*, but also some of the Spanish Americans who wrote about Proust used aspects of his work in their own short stories and novels. The interplay between theory and practice is often quite revealing.

As logic dictates, I will begin my study with the critical response by Spanish Americans to the *Recherche*. In chapter 1, I will show how Proust's work was first introduced into those countries most open to European literature, and how over time it gained acceptance in nearly all of the others. I will also explain how a tradition of Proustian criticism developed in Spanish America, and I will describe the nature and quality of its contributions. In itself this study can draw attention to a sorely neglected area.

In chapter 2, I will discuss how the literary relation between Proust's work and Spanish American narrative began and developed until the 1940s.[17] Citing specific examples, I will indicate how this connection became more precisely defined over time as Proust's readers, critics and scholars came to understand more fully all aspects of the *Recherche*. Here, I will also delineate the principal types of relations that exist: those that have been traditionally called influence and inspiration, plus more active exchanges which entail either a dialogue between a particular Spanish American work and Proust's text or a parody of the latter. In all cases, I will often rely upon brief textual fragments, along with personal testimony, because the words of the text can serve as concrete evidence or proof of the relation.[18]

In chapters 3 through 8, I will trace in a generally chronological order from the second period until the present specific themes or subjects found in Proust's text: high society (3); love, illness, and consciousness (4); the appreciation of art (5); time (6); involuntary memory (7); and the story of a literary vocation (8). By treating each of these subjects individually, I can explain their meaning in the *Recherche* and how particular Spanish American authors and works are related to Proust and to each other. In this way, I can also demonstrate the richness and diversity of Proust's relation with New World writers and prove that it encompasses far more than the *petite madeleine* episode and those texts derived from it.[19] This period, of course, includes the years that preceded the Boom, the Boom itself and those that have followed. Finally, inspired by Proust's own architectural design, I will draw together all of these themes and aspects and show how Proust's ideas on structure and his personal vision also affected numerous Spanish American writers of the twentieth century.

1

Reception and Critical Appreciation of *A la recherche du temps perdu* in Spanish America

ALTHOUGH MARCEL PROUST IS CONSIDERED TODAY AN OUTSTANDING modernist writer and one of the most important novelists of the twentieth century, his fame in France and around the world began slowly. His first book *Les plaisirs et les jours* (1896) received little attention from the critics even in Paris. Proust's translations of two of John Ruskin's books, *La Bible d'Amiens* (1904) and *Sésame et les lys* [Sesame and Lilies] (1906), were scarcely noticed. In broad terms, the critical appreciation of Proust's work began when he was forty-two years old and following the publication of *Du côté de chez Swann* (1913).

This, the first volume of *A la recherche du temps perdu,* was reviewed by a few well-known critics, such as Paul Souday in Paris and Francis de Miomandre in Brussels. Such reviews were generally favorable, but often entailed specific reservations because even the best critics were unable to appreciate certain aspects of Proust's originality. Only personal friends, like Lucien Daudet, were enthusiastic.

The actual literary fame of Marcel Proust did not begin until after the end of World War I, when his second volume *A l'ombre des jeunes filles en fleurs* could be published and when it was awarded the Prix Goncourt on 10 December 1919. Then, the number of articles greatly increased, and Proust was first cited as a major modern writer and was compared to the masters of French literature. In this case the critics also included Jacques Rivière and Edmond Jaloux, who introduced the *Recherche* to a much broader audience.

One can follow the evolution of Proustian criticism in French in several interesting studies. *Marcel Proust and His French Critics* (1940) by Douglas W. Alden listed for France, Belgium, and Switzerland a bibliography of 1,885 items (including newspaper articles) for the period 1895–1938 and featured a general appraisal of these texts. The more recent *Marcel Proust: The Critical Heritage* (1989) by Leighton Hodson provided in addition to a study of Proust's reception (1896–1931) a generous sampling of the critical texts themselves. In *La pudeur en crise: Un aspect de l'accueil d'A la recherche du temps perdu de Marcel Proust: 1913–30,* [Decency in Crisis: An Aspect of the Reception of In Search of Lost Time by Marcel Proust: 1913–30], Eva Ahlstedt focused her attention upon the reaction of the critics to some of the most controversial aspects of the *Recherche.*

Proust's work did, in fact, spark a considerable amount of controversy. After the first two volumes (which dealt with the youth of the protagonist and Swann's love affair and which in retrospect seemed quite innocent) came *Le côté de Guermantes I* [Guermantes' Way I] (1920), *Le côté de Guermantes II, Sodome et Gomorrhe I* (1921), and *Sodome et Gomorrhe II* (1922). These volumes not only depicted the exclusive milieus of the upper classes and studied the subject of snobbery, but the second and third also revealed the clandestine world of homosexuality, which, according to Proust, had been protected to some extent by upper-class privilege.

During this period, the critics of the *Recherche* became more openly divided between supporters and detractors. As each new volume was published, reviews and articles presented opinions from both sides. Following Proust's death in November 1922, the supporters were effusive in their praise and wrote for *La Nouvelle Revue Française* the famous "Hommage à Marcel Proust," which appeared in print on 1 January 1923. For a short time the general acceptance of the *Recherche* might have seemed a reality, but later in 1923 following the publication of *La prisonnière,* the attacks resumed. André Germain, for instance, became once again very critical of several facets of Proust's text, including its sentence structure and slow development, as well as the subject matter dealing with Albertine's presumed lesbianism.

The final volumes of Proust's work, *Albertine disparue* [Sweet Cheat is Gone or The Fugitive] and *Le temps retrouvé* [Time Regained], did not appear until 1925 and 1927, respectively. As Marcel never had the opportunity to review the end of his manuscript and to prepare the definitive text, this task was left to his brother, Robert, and other persons. These volumes were pieced together from Marcel's notebooks, and the decisions that were made have been disputed until nearly the present.[1]

The fame of Proust's work reached a high point after the publication of the final volume, where the author presented explicitly his ideas on time and memory and brought to its culmination the story of the protagonist's literary vocation. Proust's posthumous glory, however, was of brief duration because the positive assessments were soon contradicted by charges that Proust was a snob toward persons of his own social class, servile toward aristocrats and more than a disinterested observer of homosexuals.

During the 1930s there was a decline in Proust's prestige in France, which at the time of his study Alden believed to be definitive. In the 1940s this trend was reversed when new values were discovered in the

Recherche and when Proust's homosexuality became accepted almost as a condition for his originality. Scholars in France, as well as in Great Britain and the United States, devoted considerable effort to an elucidation of the *Recherche*. In 1949, André Maurois published his very important biography: *A la recherche de Marcel Proust* [In Search of Marcel Proust]. The posthumous publication of Proust's unfinished novel *Jean Santeuil* (1952) and of his critical essays *Contre Sainte-Beuve* [Against Sainte-Beuve] (1954) provided the scholars with new material to be examined. Interest was also expanded through the publication and study of Proust's voluminous correspondence, which made feasible even more detailed biographies, such as that of George D. Painter (1959).

Although Proustian criticism since 1940 has not been examined as carefully as for the previous period, *Les critiques de notre temps et Proust* [The Critics of Our Time and Proust] (1971) provides an interesting sampling of what was produced until 1970. Of particular interest are the studies by Maurice Blanchot, Jean Rousset and Gilles Deleuze. The book also suggests the role that New French Critics have played in the consecration of the *Recherche*, which began before the Proust Centennial in 1971 and has continued until nearly the present. In this regard, the studies by Rolland Barthes and Gérard Genette are very telling.[2]

For other languages besides French there have also been general studies of Proustian criticism. The most complete of these is the dissertation by John Newton Alley "English and American Criticism of Marcel Proust" (1959). Although Alley's organization is thematic rather than chronological, this work showcases the contributions of English-speaking scholars for the period that preceded it. There have also been articles on Proustian criticism in such countries as Italy, Sweden, Japan, Israel, and Brazil.

The bibliographies of Proustian criticism in French, English, and other languages have grown over the years since the one prepared by Léon Pierre-Quint, which can be found in *Comment travaillait Marcel Proust* [How Marcel Proust Worked] (1928), to Victor E. Graham's *Bibliographie des études sur Marcel Proust et son oeuvre* (1976). Although the latter does not include newspaper articles, it is extensive, being composed of more than 2,300 items. However, it is deficient for the language-speaking area where Reynaldo Hahn was born. For Spanish America it includes only twenty-seven.

In general, Proustian criticism from Spanish America has been sorely neglected. Alfonso Reyes observed this fact already in 1929 when he published "Proust en América" in *Libra* (Buenos Aires). Finding in Pierre-Quint's international bibliography no articles and only two reviews from Spanish America, Reyes suggested that its writers collect their own articles. Referring to Pierre-Quint, the Mexican scholar remarked:

And as he has expressed before his desire that the readers themselves help to rectify the omissions for a possible new edition, it is worthwhile for the writers of Spanish America, in their own interest, to come forward to fill in the gaps in the Proustian bibliography. (1929, 87)

Such neglect, which continued for the most part until I began to work on this project in the 1970s, was in no way suggested by Marcel Proust. He considered Spanish American readers like those of other countries. He wanted them also to have the opportunity to know the *Recherche*. Thus, he personally sought to insure that articles about his work be written and published in Spanish American literary magazines and newspapers. In the *Correspondance de Marcel Proust* can be found one letter to Gaston Gallimard in early January 1920 (1970–93, 19:43–44) and another to Paul Morand in February 1920 (19:129–30) where Proust refers specifically to M. García Calderón. The then recent Goncourt laureate wished to inform them that he had been in communication with this Peruvian writer (indubitably Ventura, instead of his brother Francisco) and had already sent him a personal photograph for *América Latina*. Proust's contact with García Calderón proved to be effective because in February 1920 this magazine (which was edited in Paris and London for Spanish Americans residing in Europe) included in its pages the said photograph of Proust, the Spanish version of an article by Edmond Jaloux and three brief selections from *A l'ombre des jeunes filles en fleurs*. Later, on 7 March and 18 July respectively, these same fragments entitled "Las jóvenes" [The Maidens], "Las flores" [The Flowers], and "Las sirenas" [The Mermaids] were reprinted in *Revista de Revistas* [Review of Reviews] of Mexico City and in *Orto* [Dawn] of Manzanillo, Cuba.

Although it may be impossible to know how these selections crossed the Atlantic, in the *Correspondance* we can observe how one of Proust's friends tried to disseminate knowledge of the *Recherche*. Paul Morand wrote to Proust on 6 May 1922, "I have had your books sent by way of M. de Vaulchier to M. Chezzeville [*sic*] who is going to publish a long study about you in the principal newspaper of Mexico City *Excelsior*" (1970–93, 21:172). Unfortunately in this case, such efforts appear to have been made in vain. Even though the French correspondent Jean Chuzeville published in *Excelsior* an article on new French writers on 14 July 1922, neither Philip Kolb nor I have been able to find the projected study on Proust.

In an attempt to compile for Spanish America a relatively complete bibliography and to provide a general study of the contribution of its critics and scholars to Proustian criticism, I have worked for many years (and in particular for two and a half) in the libraries of the United States and fourteen Spanish American countries.[3] The absence of indices and bibliographies has often meant examining the principal newspapers and literary magazines month-by-month. In this type of research one cannot be totally complete, but I have worked toward this goal and I have tried to be as objective and accurate as possible in reporting my findings.

I have chosen a chronological organization of the material in this chapter in order to show development, and I have focused my attention upon those subjects and critics linked to the dialogue between Proust and Spanish American narrative. Also, I will refer briefly to translations and editions of the *Recherche* and of Proustian criticism from Europe and the United States, and I will mention in notes other evidence of Proust's presence. In this way, I hope to illustrate the cultural impact of the French author and his work so that this chapter can serve as an introduction to all of those that follow.

THE INTRODUCTION OF MARCEL PROUST IN SPANISH AMERICA (1920–1928)

Although I have found no reference in Proust's *Correspondance* to Hahn's efforts to transmit knowledge of the *Recherche* across the Atlantic, it is feasible to surmise that he or a member of his family contacted someone in Paris or Caracas to do precisely that. In this way, we can explain why the earliest Spanish American article on Proust appeared in Venezuela. Just six weeks after *A l'ombre des jeunes filles en fleurs* received the Prix Goncourt and prior to the article and selection in *América Latina,* "Marcel Proust: El Prix Goncourt" was published in *El Universal* of Caracas on 23 January 1920.[4] In this case, the author was Francis de Miomandre, who had begun writing about the *Recherche* in 1914. His words were highly laudatory and allude to what would later be called Proust's modernist sense of consciousness:

> At the same time as M. Proust penetrates into the human soul, he immerses himself in that dark world full of subconscious life, of physiological life, and the most subtle of his cerebral digressions have an expectancy, a poetry, a captivating and instinctive beauty . . . the delightful nuances of the gaze of a being who suffers and who thinks. (1920, 5)

This article was soon followed by two others in the same newspaper. Angel Guerra (José Betancourt Cabrera, 4 March) also discussed the Prix Goncourt, but lamented the fact that Proust had won it. The article by Corpus Barga (28 May) had previously appeared in Spain (*El Sol* [The Sun], 27 March) and was one of the first texts on Proust there. Already at this time we can observe a pattern which would remain constant in *El Universal* and a few other newspapers during the 1920s. European correspondents from France or Spain, or Spanish Americans residing in Paris or Madrid would send original or translated articles to be published in the New World. The same was true following Proust's death in November 1922. Jean Tinaire discussed this loss in an article on 23 December of that year, and Corpus Barga's eulogy came out on 25 January 1923.

Likewise, in Buenos Aires, the first articles on Proust were written by foreign correspondents. At least one of these was the same, the one by Angel Guerra, which can be found in *La Nota* of 21 May 1920. Another by Alberto Insúa formed part of a series on new French writers. It was entitled "Un psicólogo: Proust" and was published in *La Nación* on 17 October 1920. This cosmopolitan newspaper would subsequently provide for its readers numerous articles on the *Recherche,* including reviews by Francis de Miomandre of three of Proust's works (7 August 1921, 11 May 1924, and 2 November 1924).

During the period immediately following Proust's death indubitably the outstanding publication on the *Recherche* in Argentina was an essay by José Ortega y Gasset. This famous text, whose French version was included in the New Year's day "Hommage à Marcel Proust" of the *Nouvelle Revue Française,* made its first appearance in Spanish in *La Nación* just two weeks later, on 14 January 1923. "Tiempo, distancia y forma en el arte de Proust" demonstrates the Spanish thinker's early interest in the *Recherche* and contains some of his controversial ideas about it. Focusing his attention on the minuteness of Proust's details, Ortega called this French author near-sighted and concluded that for him the structure of things was microscopic. The Spaniard also used the term "puntillismo" [point technique] to characterize the meticulous manner of the *Recherche.*

Such ideas elicited a strong reaction in Argentina and contributed to the early discussion of Proust's work there. Thus, unlike the Venezuelans, the Argentines themselves started quite early to discuss the *Recherche* in written form. In June 1923, a Spaniard who was living in Argentina, Antonio Herrero, began the discussion by suggesting in "La obra de Marcel Proust" (*Nosotros* [We]) that Ortega had merely emphasized the obvious concerning time and distance. Then, on 4 November 1923 in an article for *La Nación,* Manuel Gálvez refuted Ortega's idea that Proust was too near-sighted. The Argentine novelist asserted that the French author seemed to use a microscope in each eye "in such a way that he can draw attention to what is infinitely small, be it in the spiritual realm or among material things" (1924, 162). Shortly thereafter, Gálvez expanded "La literatura y el conocimiento: A propósito de Marcel Proust" [Literature and Knowledge: Concerning Marcel Proust] and placed its new version in his book *El espíritu de aristocracia y otros ensayos* (1924).[5]

The written discussion of Proust in Argentina, which then began to develop a body of Proustian criticism, can be compared to that of another South American country, Chile. But, the circumstances across the Andes were somewhat different. Perhaps because of the Chileans' greater distance from Europe, the press of Santiago did not rely so heavily upon foreign correspondents. The first articles on European literature were often written in the country itself, which fortunately benefited from the expertise of a former priest of French origin, Emile Vaïsse, who used the pseudonym, Omer Emeth. As the famous Chilean critic, Alone (Hernán Díaz Arrieta), would later explain, it was Omer Emeth, who initiated the discussion of Proust in Chile.[6] Curiously, this Franco-Chilean's first article was published so early that it predates any other critical text on the *Recherche* actually written in Spanish America. "Marcel Proust—¿En qué consiste la novedad de su arte?" [Marcel Proust—What Does the Newness of his Art Consist of?] appeared on 11 April 1921 in *El Mercurio* of Santiago. Here, besides discussing the values of the French novel, Omer Emeth spoke of the growing fame of its author and mentioned that even in England and Holland Proustian clubs were being established.

This Chilean article of 1921, as well as those by foreign correspondents published in Venezuela and Argentina during 1920, proves as groundless the claim by Alejo Carpentier at the time of the Proust Centennial that the *Recherche* was first known in Cuba.[7] According to my research, the earliest article in Havana was one by Alfonso Reyes, which was sent from Spain. It was entitled "Vermeer y la novela de Proust" and appeared in *Social* in February 1924. This was followed by an article that Enrique Gómez Carrillo wrote for *El Diario de la Marina* [The Marine Daily] (3 September 1926) and another by the Cuban José Antonio Ramos (*Social,* September 1928). Otherwise, Proust was only occasionally mentioned in Cuba during those years.[8]

Toward the end of 1925, a two-part study composed in French, "Marcel Proust: Essai d'une littérature introspective," appeared in *La Cruz del Sur* [The Southern Cross] of Montevideo. Its author, Alvaro Guillot Muñoz, would also provide for the same Uruguayan magazine in 1929 "De Rimbaud a Proust," which was intended to be part of a much longer study that was apparently never completed. The year 1925 also saw the first critical texts on Proust in Mexico, but these were written by foreign correspondents (e.g., Rose Lee, *El Universal Ilustrado,* 8 October).[9] Similarly in 1926 there appeared in Bogotá several articles by authors who were residing in Europe; these were José María Salverría (*El Espectador,* 24 January), Enrique Gómez Carrillo (*El Tiempo,* 17 October) and Paul Souday (*El Tiempo,* 14 November).[10]

The text by Gómez Carrillo, which was reprinted in Caracas (*El Universal,* 4 November) after appearing in Havana and Bogotá, must be singled out because of its negative impact. In "El calvario de un gran escritor" the famous Guatemalan *cronista* [columnist] expressed the first note of caution with regard to Proust. He suggested that interest in the *Recherche* was a mere fashion and was already beginning to wane in France. Gómez Carrillo's assessment of this work was largely unfavorable. For this reason, he used such terms as "soplo enfermizo" [sickly air] and "aliento morboso" [morbid breath] to describe Proust's manner. Although the Guatemalan did not attack the author of *Sodome et Gomorrhe* directly, his criticism apparently discouraged some Spanish Americans from reading and writing about the French novelist.[11] It does not seem by chance that following this article little more was published on Proust in Venezuela or Cuba and only a few articles can be found in Colombia during the late 1920s (e.g., "Recuerdos de Marcel Proust" [Memories of Marcel Proust] by León-Paul Fargue, *El Tiempo,* 6 October 1929).

For the years that preceded and immediately followed the posthumous publication of Proust's final volume, the cases of Argentina and Chile are radically distinct from these and are indeed fascinating. In both instances the reading of the *Recherche* constituted a rich cultural experience for the young intellectuals of the country.

In Buenos Aires following the publication of Ortega's essay, interest in Proust grew rapidly and spread to diverse sectors. One article in translation even appeared in *Nosotros* before Ortega's text: "Un casuista de almas: Marcel Proust" [A Casuist of Souls: Marcel Proust] by Arthur Symons (August 1922). This was followed in the same literary magazine by "La obra de Marcel Proust" by Edmond Jaloux in February 1923, and Francis de Miomandre devoted to the *Recherche* a lengthy portion of his "Crónica de la vida intelectual francesa" in April of the same year.

Quite early we can find in the vanguard literary review *Martín Fierro* texts associated with the *Recherche,* such as a translation of the famous "Ode à Marcel Proust" by Paul Morand (15 May 1924). A few years later critical texts about Proust appeared in the magazines of the opposing Boedo group (e.g., "Tolstoy en un atajo de Proust" [Tolstoy in a Brief Passage by Proust] by Manuel Kirschbaum, *Claridad,* 24 November 1928). One of the leftist leaders in particular, Roberto Mariani, became very interested in the French novelist. He composed "Introducción a Marcel Proust," which was a lecture that was subsequently printed in *Nosotros* in April 1927 along with an article by another Argentine writer Max Dickmann, "Por el camino de Proust" [Proust's Way]. Mariani pointed out the difficulty of the style, density and length of the *Recherche* but conceded, "And nonetheless, Marcel Proust is a marvelous spectacle because of the visual joy of the multicolored ensemble and precision of the interplay of its parts" (1927, 19).

During these years, there were several academic studies, such as "Du côté de chez Proust", where Carlos María Onetti considered in passing the relation between Henri Bergson and Proust (*Valoraciones,* September 1925), and "La sensación olfativa en Marcel Proust" by Aníbal Ponce (*Revista de Filosofía,* November 1925). Also Juan P. Ramos presented a lecture on Proust, which was printed in *Verbum* (September 1926). In particular, Ramos focused upon Proust's attitude toward love and the desire for possession. He pointed out that these feelings were related to the French author's essential subjectivity, but he also explained how through psychological analysis Proust was able to generalize and give the appearance of objectivity:

> Feeling, which in Proust, as in all human beings, is the determining factor for the majority of one's acts, acquires in this book the character of an objective reality, so firm, so deep, so impartial is his fierce analysis which he carries out in the core of his own soul. . . . (1926, 41)

As Julio Irazusta pointed out ten years later in "Proust, ayer y hoy" [Proust, Yesterday and Today] (*La Nación,* 22 November 1936), reading the *Recherche* during the late 1920s greatly affected young Argentines. For the actual reception of *Le temps retrouvé,* I would like to highlight two articles from the small and now forgotten literary magazine *Fiesta* because it was so closely identified with Proust.[12] In the first, "Marcel Proust y el momento actual" [Marcel Proust and the Present Moment] (30 August 1927), Arturo Seeber placed the French novel in its literary and philosophical context, which we have come to know as modernism, and concluded:

> *A la recherche du temps perdu* represents a culminating moment in the literary production of our time. Its personal vision of an inner world, and the independence of its innovative aesthetic criteria and the distinct characteristics of its style, mark it as one of the greatest creations of human ingenuity. (1927, 15)

The second, "El artista de la memoria" (15 October 1927), is also worthy of note because it proves that Seeber was so much *à la page* [up to date] that he could discuss Proust's final volume scarcely a month after it became available in France.

In Chile, during this same period, we can observe a similar growth but in some ways an even greater intensity. On 17 June 1923, Alone added to Omer Emeth's then solitary voice his own with his first article on Proust. Four others preceded the publication of *Le temps retrouvé,* and six months after this event a series of eight followed (March–August 1928). In these, Alone discussed various aspects of the *Recherche,* including the use of poetry and humor and the subjects of love, nature, immortality and time. The Chilean critic, who would eventually write more than 40 texts about Proust and his critics, ended this series with a daring examination of the French author's feminine temperament (*La Nación,* 9 August 1928). Although Alone used the stereotypes of his time, he considered valid a sensibility totally opposed to that of Rabelais, "el macho genial." Proust's manner of thought relied primarily upon intuition and penetrated deeply into human consciousness.

During the same year, 1928, one can find in *El Mercurio, La Nación* and *Atenea* a remarkable number of articles and notes on Proust.[13] Of special interest are Osvaldo Vicuña Luco's response to Alone in "Cartas acerca de Marcel Proust" [Letters about Marcel Proust] (*Atenea,* 30 May 1928) and Januario Espinosa's article "El Balzac del subconsciente" (*Atenea,* 31 October 1928).[14]

Looking beyond the critical texts themselves, one can determine the intensity of the Proustian fervor in Santiago through a satire of it by Jenaro Prieto. This text, which is quite famous in Chile, first appeared in *El Diario Ilustrado* on 18 July 1929. In "Una víctima de Proust" the Chilean humorist described the then current fashion of reading the *Recherche* and suggested that one had to be ill in order to find the time and patience to do so. Of the Proustians themselves, Prieto spoke of their honey-sweet voices and their warm encouragement to persevere. He finally concluded:

> The Proustians, in spite of the fact that they do not read Proust except when they are ill, are fearsome in a convalescent state. Proust's admirers have written so much about him, that it is not superfluous for the public to hear, at least once, the voice of one of his victims. (1973, 79)

Although the Mexicans, with the exception of Reyes, appear to have written little about Proust before *Le temps retrouvé* (perhaps only a review in *La Antorcha,* October 1925), in November 1928, they made an outstanding contribution to the Proustian criticism of Spanish America. The writers associated with the literary magazine *Contemporáneos* dedicated the issue of that month to Marcel Proust on the sixth anniversary of his death.

The leader of this homage, Jaime Torres Bodet, expressed his regret upon reaching the final page of the *Recherche,* but predicted that he and some of the members of his generation would never stop reading Proust's novel. At least, in his case, this proved to be true. Torres Bodet also responded to Ortega's "Ideas sobre la novela" (1925), where the Spaniard called the structure of the *Recherche* "paralítica." The Mexican poet-novelist said, "Only a superficial analysis would consider inert the attention paid to passionate, intensely dramatic events, which seethe in *A la recherche du temps perdu*" (1928, 288).

The other Mexican authors who participated in the "Aniversario de Proust" were Mariano Azuela, Genaro Estrada, Enrique González Rojo,

Bernardo Ortiz de Montellano, and Julio Torri. Among their remarks, those by Torri were the most profound. He saw in Proust a new Orpheus, who had descended to the realms of oblivion in search of his lost Euridice. One might notice in the list of Mexican writers the absence of Xavier Villaurrutia, who also was fascinated by Proust. But, he made his own contribution one year later when he translated for *Contemporáneos* a fine essay by Ramon Fernandez, a French critic of Mexican origin who had known Proust personally. In chapter 2, I will discuss narrative texts by both Torres Bodet and Villaurrutia because of their connection with the *Recherche*.

During the final years of the 1920s, one can also see the beginning of Proust's reception in a few other Spanish American countries. In *El Comercio* of Quito the *Recherche* was briefly discussed in the anonymous article "La novela moderna" (5 January 1927). Joaquín García Monge of Costa Rica reprinted in *El Repertorio Americano* on 9 June 1928 an article on Proust that Mario Santa Cruz had written for *El Universal Ilustrado* of Mexico. Although I have found only one or two brief references to Proust in *El Comercio* of Lima, José Carlos Mariátegui commented on his work in "El alma matinal" [The Morning Soul], which was first published in *Mundial* [World-wide] (3 February 1928).[15]

By this time, a few Spanish Americans had become aware of their contributions to the study of the *Recherche*. In the "Consultorio literario y artístico" of *La Nación* of Buenos Aires for 5 August 1928 one can read a partial summary of Argentine Proustian criticism of the period. After mentioning the studies by Juan P. Ramos, Manuel Gálvez and Roberto Mariani, to which I have already referred, the author of this note adds:

Another Argentine study about the author de "Les plaisirs et les jours" belongs to Dr. Agustín Urtubey and appeared in the literary supplement of *La Nación*. . . . The Argentine contribution to the bibliography also includes a poetic composition by Alvaro Melián Lafinur, bearing the title "Elegy to Marcel Proust." (1928, 15)

It was in this context that Alfonso Reyes, who had published a second article, "La última morada de Proust" [The Last Dwelling of Proust], in Argentina and Chile (*Valoraciones,* May 1928 and *Atenea,* 31 August 1928), decided to compile his Proustian bibliography for Spanish America and Brazil.[16] In *Monterrey* 1 (Jun. 1930), which he published in Rio de Janeiro, he repeated the request that he had made in *Libra* (see above). The section "Proust en América" also had entries in issues 2 (August 1930), 5 (July 1931) and 10 (March 1933). All together Reyes listed nearly two dozen Spanish American articles, along with five Brazilian texts. Furthermore, Raúl Silva Castro provided in *Monterrey* 7 (December

1931) his contribution: "Notas para la bibliografía chilena de Proust," which is comprised of more than another dozen titles.

FROM LOSING AS SUPERFICIAL PROUST TO GAINING A MORE PROFOUND ONE (1929–1949)

Shortly after the publication of *Le temps retrouvé* and the intense Proustian zeal expressed by Argentines, Chileans, and Mexicans in 1928, a negative reaction began to set in. I have already mentioned Jenaro Prieto's satire in Chile. Salvador Novo in Mexico was quick to predict the decline of Proust's fame. In his literary column "El cesto y la mesa" [The Basket and the Table] of *Revista de Revistas,* he wrote in May 1929 alluding to two locations described in *Sodome et Gommorhe:* "aside from Julio Torri and one or two others . . . I am certain that no one has continued immersing himself night after night in the inexhaustible and magnificent 'lake of delights of la Raspelière and of Balbec' " (1929, 5).

This ominous prediction about the fate of the *Recherche* was, of course, linked to what was already happening in Europe. As I suggested in the introduction to this chapter, the attacks on Proust had begun soon after the appearance of *Sodome et Gomorrhe,* but they became more personal as time elapsed and as Proust's intimate life became known. I already mentioned that Enrique Gómez Carrillo expressed considerable reserve about Proust even before the appearance of *Le temps retrouvé.*

One of the first articles in Spanish America to defend Proust explicitly was by the Spanish author Manuel Bueno. "El amor y el dolor de Marcel Proust" [The Love and Suffering of Marcel Proust] was reprinted in *La Razón* of Buenos Aires on 30 July 1929, after having appeared in *ABC* of Madrid (4 June 1929). Bueno dismissed the allusions to Proust's alleged depravity as "a legend that only those that have not read him can accept" or as "an invention of hostility." He also defended the author of the *Recherche* by saying, "he was a hypersensitive individual, or said in another way, a sensitive person. Everything affected him everything confused him" (1929, 7).

During the early 1930s we can ascertain in some of these countries a decrease in the number of articles about Marcel Proust. For Mexico I have found only two, but these appeared close in time: "La epopeya de los celos y el snobismo" [The Epic of Jealousy and Snobbery] by Julio Torri (*El Nacional,* 18 May 1933) and "Actualización de Marcel Proust" [Present Relevance of Marcel Proust] by Angel Dotor (*El Nacional,* 31 May 1933).

In contrast, both Argentines and Chileans still produced a considerable number of articles because of their sustained level of interest and desire to defend Proust. In Buenos Aires one of the younger members of the Florida group, Ulises Petit de Murat, published three articles in 1930–31. The best, "Concepción proustiana de la novela", came out in *Síntesis* in May 1930. Here, Petit de Murat explained how Proust had used the two principal social groups of his novel to unify it:

> In this way the upper middle class of Combray, so distant in the first volume from the milieu of the princes of Guermantes (royalist nobility), at the close of the Proustian social cycle in *Le temps retrouvé*, find themselves connected to this milieu due to plot events, which are characteristic of the the novelistic genre. (1930, 232)

Similarly, Enrique Anderson Imbert wrote at least two notes for the leftist newspaper *La Vanguardia* (16 September 1931 and 14 March 1937), and José Bianco published "Stendhal y Proust" in *La Nación* (9 April 1933). It is pertinent to remark that all three of these young Argentines would later write novels, some of which were related to Proust.

In Chile, a country of especially staunch Proustians, Alone continued to write about the *Recherche*. Two of his articles were published during the same month May 1931 in *La Nación:* "Marcel Proust, escritor místico" and "Proust y Montesquiou—sus cartas". Chile also saw the emergence of another devoted Proustian, whose very name recalls *Du côté de chez Swann:* Magdalena Petit. Her first article, "El estilo y la composición en la obra de Marcel Proust", can be found in *Atenea* (April 1930). This was soon followed by four others. Perhaps the most characteristic article by Magdalena Petit was "Proust, snob y servil", which appeared in Argentina and France instead of Chile (*Nosotros,* November 1932 and *Les Cahiers du Sud* [Southern Notebooks], August–September 1934). Here, Petit defended Marcel Proust, whose correspondence was then being harshly scrutinized. In response to the accusation that he was interested only in duchesses, she pointed out his careful analysis of the cook Françoise and his love for beautiful churches. Of the servile tone found in some of Proust's letters, the Chilean critic attributed this to his "special temperament" and to his being an "exceptional hyperaesthetic."

Another Chilean, Marta Vergara, defended Proust against his Marxist critics in "Nuevos ataques y nueva actualidad de Marcel Proust" [New Attacks and New Relevance of Marcel Proust] (*El Mercurio,* 13 December 1931). She summarized the prevailing communist assessment of the French author as "bourgeois, idle and decadent" and lamented the narrowmindedness of this conclusion. Vergara readily admitted the gulf that separated Proust's manner of life from that found in a workers' state, but, according to her, Proust's art and psychological acuteness were so universal that they transcended any system. For this reason, she predicted that the *Recherche* would survive whatever social changes might arise. In retrospect Vergara's article signals the beginning of a political debate over Proust in Spanish America.[17]

Across the Andes in Argentina, Marcel Proust also had ardent supporters, but their manner was less direct. The most notable among these was Victoria Ocampo. This wealthy woman of letters had become interested in Proust very early.[18] During the 1920s she discussed the *Recherche* in articles about other writers. For example, in "La alegría de leer a Rabindranath Tagore" (*La Nación,* 9 November 1924), she contrasted the joy of reading Tagore with the pleasure and anguish of reading Proust. She said that for her "Un amour de Swann" was as difficult as breathing under water. Fortunately, Ocampo learned how to alleviate that pain, and she came to love the French text dearly.

By the time that she founded the literary magazine *Sur* [South] (January 1931), Proust had become one of her favorite authors. Emblematically, in one of her first articles, "Palabras francesas" [French Words] she called upon the author of the *Recherche* to justify her attachment to the French language: "it is from Proust that I request assistence and whom I call upon in testimony of my truth" (1931, 14). In the same way that the narrator of *Le temps retrouvé* attributed a great importance to the first books that he had read during childhood (1954, 3:885), so did Ocampo, who had first learned to read in French. Quoting Proust, she explained, "In short, all of the words from the books of my childhood, those words that contain 'the brisk wind and brilliant sunlight that were present when we read them' were, for me, words in French."

As the principal sponsor of *Sur* (which became the most prestigious and cosmopolitan literary magazine of Spanish America and a disseminator of modernist texts), Victoria Ocampo encouraged the reading and discussion of the *Recherche*. She often mentioned Proust in her other articles (e.g., "Lecturas de infancia" [Readings of Childhood]). In response to the questionnaire that I prepared for her in 1977, she said of the literary group associated with her magazine: "Of Proust one has always spoken in Sur." In this regard, I must point out that the attitude toward Proust in the Sur group was never monolithic. Some of the members, such as José Bianco, sided with Ocampo, while others, most notably Jorge Luis Borges, were opposed. In chapter 2, I will return to this subject because these writers continued their discussion of the *Recherche* in their narrative texts.

Ostensibly, through the literary magazine itself, Victoria Ocampo promoted the reading and study of Proust's work. Besides several notes and a few articles, *Sur* provided in four installments the translation of a major critical study from France, *Marcel Proust: Sa révélation psychologique* by Arnaud Dandieu (September–December 1936). The value attributed to this book by the editorial staff is evident from the statement which announced it ("Una obra sobre la relevación psicológica de Proust"):

Starting with our next issue we will initiate the publication of one of the most extraordinary critical works brought forth by the work of Marcel Proust. It is the beautiful book by Arnaud Dandieu which bears the name of the author of *Du côté de chez Swann*. (1936, 125)

This publication seems to have had a considerable effect, which extended beyond the literary elite in Argentina. A few years later the translation of several other books at least partially devoted to the *Recherche* appeared in Buenos Aires: *Marcel Proust y Paul Valéry* (Losada, 1941) by Ernst Robert Curtius, two books by André Maurois, *Estudios literarios* (Hachette, 1942) and *Cinco rostros del amor* [Five Faces of Love] (Espasa-Calpe, 1942), and León Pierre-Quint's *Marcel Proust (Juventud-Obra-Tiempo)* [Marcel Proust (Youth-Work-Time)] (Santiago Rueda, 1944).

During these same years there began to appear throughout Spanish America studies by isolated Proustians. The Uruguayan novelist, Carlos Reyles, wrote "Marcel Proust y su mundo fantasmagórico y realísimo, surgido de la memoria del olvido" [Marcel Proust and His Phantasmagoric and Very Real World, Which Arose from the Memory of Forgetfulness] (*Incitaciones*, 1936). The Colombian, Bernardo Arias Trujillo, included in his *Diccionario de emociones* (1938) "Evocación fugaz de Marcel Proust" [Fleeting Evocation of Marcel Proust]. The then young Mexican poet, Octavio Paz, published in *El Popular* (25 November 1939) "Un mundo sin herederos" [A World without Heirs], which was part of a longer essay.[19] Among these, the two part study by the Venezuelan Gabriel Espinosa was the most ambitious. "La filosofía imaginativa de Marcel Proust: psicología estática y psicología dinámica" (*Revista Nacional de Cultura*, January–April 1941) is both abstract and original.

In contrast with this solitary phenomenon and in spite of the still reduced interest in Europe during these years, the intellectuals of one country, Cuba, began to discuss widely the *Recherche* for the first time. Already in April 1937 Luis Rodríguez Embil had published in Argentina (*Nosotros*) "La vivencia religiosa en la literatura contemporánea (Una nueva interpretación del caso Marcel Proust)" [The Religious Experience in Contemporary Literature (A New Interpretation of the Case of Marcel Proust)]. In 1939, Camila Henríquez Ureña delivered a perceptive lecture on Proust's novelistic theory that can be read in *Lyceum* (April–June), "Ideología literaria de Proust." Similarly in November 1942 Eva Fréjaville presented at the Círculo de Amigos de la Cultura Francesa "Marcel Proust desde el Trópico." This lecture was preceded by the note "Marcel Proust" in the magazine *La Verónica*, and its text was later printed as a pamphlet by the editorial firm of the same name. Let me point out that it was during this period that José Lezama Lima became interested in Proust. Although this poet-novelist never published an article or essay specifically about the *Recherche*, he often mentioned it in his letters and diaries, which have since been made available. Furthermore, he demonstrated his admiration for the French author by translating three poems from *Les plaisirs et les jours*. "Retratos de pintores: Alberto Cuyp, Antoine Watteau, Antoine Van Dyck" can be found in *Nadie Parecía* [No One Appeared] (March–April 1943).

Clearly during the early 1940s there was an appreciable shift in the attitude toward Marcel Proust, as the Spanish exile living in Argentina, Francisco Ayala, indicated in "Proust en la inactualidad" [Proust's Apparent Irrelevance]. In this text, which first appeared in *La Nación* of Buenos Aires (5 May 1940) and was later included in *Histrionismo y representación* [The Art of Acting and Representation] (1944), Ayala conceded that a few specific aspects of the *Recherche* seemed to be out of date. The French author's fascination with high society appeared superficial and old-fashioned. On the other hand, his deep psychological insight and keen understanding of time, memory and society were more relevant than ever. Thus, Ayala wrote, "How can one not recognize also in this curiosity toward the mechanism of social groups and toward the various ways of integrating them a trait that is very much of our time . . . ?" (1944, 144).[20]

Along with the publication of Spanish American articles on the *Recherche* and the translation of critical studies from Europe, I wish to mention the efforts to make Proust's narrative text available to those persons who did not know the French language. The peninsular translation by Pedro Salinas of the first two volumes, *Por el camino de Swann* (1920) and *A la sombra de las muchachas en flor* (1922), had been welcomed in Spanish America. Likewise the version by Salinas and José María Quiroga Pla of the two parts of the third volume *El mundo de Guermantes* was noticed soon after their publication in 1931–32.[21] But, no other volumes appeared for more than a decade.

In Chile, Alone considered the feasibility of making his own translation, but when he realized the difficulty of the task, he decided to create instead an anthology of texts from the version by Salinas. *Las mejores páginas de Marcel Proust* [The Best Pages of Marcel Proust] (Nascimento, 1933) was introduced by an essay and bibliography prepared by Alone. This Chilean sampling of the *Recherche* was followed in 1937 by an unauthorized edition of *A la sombra de las muchachas en flor* by Zig-Zag. Another edition of the prize-winning volume came out in Mexico in 1944 (Libros de México).

In precisely this same year an Argentine publisher began to make available for the first time in the Spanish language the entire text of *En busca del tiempo perdido*. Ironically this firm was not Sur, which had published many other European works, but rather Santiago Rueda, whose cultural agenda was far less pretentious.[22] Using the version by Salinas of the first two volumes, Rueda reprinted *Por el camino de Swann* and *A la sombra de las muchachas en flor* in 1944. Similarly *El mundo de los Guermantes* came out in 1945. For the remaining volumes, a new translator, the Argentine Marcelo Menasché, was hired. *Sodoma y Gomorra* and *La prisionera* were published in 1945 and *Albertina ha desaparecido* and *El tiempo recobrado,* in 1946. Menasché's translation was criticized, particularly in Madrid, for its argentinisms and for not being of the same quality as the version by Salinas, but we should observe that even in Spain no other edition of the final volumes appeared until 1952.[23]

The satisfaction of many Spanish Americans at being able to read Proust in their own language became immediately evident and has remained so. Not only did the Argentine edition receive wide distribution throughout Spanish America and can be found still today in the major libraries of the entire continent, but also Santiago Rueda discovered the economic value of providing a Spanish edition of nearly all of Proust's works. In 1946, he made available in a single volume using Bible-quality paper the complete text of *En busca del tiempo perdido*.[24] Menasché translated *El caso Lemoine* in 1946, and his versions of *Crónicas* and *Los placeres y los días* were published in 1947.[25]

After the end of World War II, the Europeans themselves rediscovered the value of Proust's novel and have henceforth considered it to be one of the outstanding works of the twentieth century. Curiously many Argentines had never lost this view since they learned of Proust during the 1920s. Years later, José Bianco recalled visiting France after the War and noticing that he and his countrymen were more familiar with the *Recherche* than the new generation of French writers. He wrote in "El ángel de las tinieblas" [The Angel of Darkness], "In París, after the second war, one spoke a great deal about existentialism and little or nothing about Proust. Young, intelligent writers boasted that they had never read him" (1977, 86).

During the late 1940s, one can find in the newspapers and literary magazines of Buenos Aires numerous articles on the *Recherche* and, in particular a few by young novelists, including the Uruguayan Juan Carlos Onetti and the Argentine Silvina Bullrich. To commemorate the 25th anniversary of Proust's death, both writers published articles on the same day, 16 November 1947. The Uruguayan, who would later be considered a herald for the Boom, asserted in *Clarín* that the elegant, exquisite Marcel Proust could be forgotten, but that the ailing French author in search of authenticity should be remembered:

> Then it is valuable to turn one's eyes toward him and to see him in his solitude inhaling with fatigue a warm, medicinal air, sweaty, disheveled and grotesque, remembering his past days, not to weep about them, but rather to force them truly to happen. . . . (1947, 4)

Although for different reasons, Alone (who had become so closely identified with Proust that he was depicted in satiric sketches carrying a volume of the *Recherche*) made a passionate defense of Proust's work in 1948. Using his alternate pseudonym, Pedro Selva, Hernán Díaz Arrieta tried to demonstrate the French author's search for transcendence in "El fondo místico de Proust" [The Mystical Grounding of Proust] (*Atenea*, March–April). In response to François Mauriac's criticism that God was absent from the *Recherche*, Pedro Selva affirmed the spiritual value of this work. He claimed that Proust's spirituality was directly related to his treatment of memory and art and involved an atemporal being found in man. The Chilean critic even suggested that this being might survive death.[26]

Sparked by the complete Argentine edition and evidence that many Europeans were returning to Proust, interest in his work began to expand to new areas of Spanish America. One of the best examples was Peru, where only slight attention had been paid to *Le temps retrouvé* in 1927. In Lima the literary magazine *Las Moradas* presented, in April 1948, a homage to Proust. The participants were comprised of the Peruvians César Moro, Emilio Westphalen, Aurelio Miró Quesada S., Honorio Delgado and the Mexican Francisco M. Zendejas. In "Marcel Proust y la penumbra anímica" [Marcel Proust and Mental Semi-darkness] Delgado emphasized the Frenchman's efforts to penetrate beneath the surface of appearances. In this regard the author of *A l'ombre des jeunes filles en fleurs* is compared to a deep-sea diver: "This work of a diver, in which Proust attains supreme mastery, is realized especially in particular conditions of introspection" (1948, 4). Such a fascination for Proust would continue in Peru during the 1950s and is most obvious in the university journal *Letras peruanas* and in two studies written by the French critic André Coyné, who was then residing in Peru.

Also, in Uruguay we can find evidence of a greater attention to the *Recherche*. Since the early 1940s notes on Proust had appeared in *Marcha*, but, as time elapsed, Emir Rodríguez Monegal and Mario Benedetti included more material about the French novelist. They presented se lections from the *Recherche*, letters by Proust and miscellaneous bibli ographical items. Rodríguez Monegal even mentioned the creation o the Société des amis de Marcel Proust et des amis de Combray ("El recuerdo de Marcel Proust" [Memory of Marcel Proust], 16 May 1947).

Likewise, Mexican critics and writers demonstrated in the late 1940s and early 1950s a renewed fascination for Proust. A Mexican translation of *Estudios literarios* by André Maurois (which is distinct from the Argentine version of a few years before) was published in 1948. The same French critic's biography *A la recherche de Marcel Proust* received special attention in "Revista Mexicana de Cultura", the Sunday supplement of *El Nacional* (17 April 1949). Similarly, "México en la Cultura" of *Novedades* [New Things] printed several articles, in particular three by Alfonso Alamán.

Indeed, Proust's partial eclipse was coming to an end, but that did not mean that resistance had disappeared. The Guatemalan leftist writer, Mario Monteforte Toledo, wrote "Marcel Proust, profundo superficial" for *Cuadernos Americanos* [American Notebooks] in 1949. Even though awareness of the *Recherche* was only starting to move from Mexico and Costa Rica to Guatemala and other Central American countries, some writers from the political left saw Proust's work to be almost a threat.[27] For this reason, Monteforte Toledo attempted to prove what other Spanish Americans had rejected nearly ten years before, that Proust's work was actually superficial in spite of its obvious profundity. In response, I would merely point out that the Guatemalan writer used as evidence only Proust's early texts and said nothing about the *Recherche* itself. Thus his conclusions about Proust as a novelist are invalid. I will return to Monteforte Toledo's article in Chapter 3 because his ideas signaled a narrative debate on the *Recherche* and on the desirability of its relation with the Spanish American novel.

ESTABLISHING A TRADITION OF READING AND WRITING ABOUT THE *Recherche* (1950–1970)

By 1950, educated Spanish Americans, particularly those living in the major capital cities, began to consider Proust's novel an essential component of their general intellectual culture. Even if students were not required to read long portions of the *Recherche* in school, persons interested in literature were expected to have some knowledge of it. The same can be said of other modernist works, such as *Ulysses* by James Joyce, which also received greater attention during the years that preceded the Boom.

During the 1950s, numerous studies on Proust appeared in Europe and the United States. Spanish Americans saw their own interest as an example of their participation in the intellectual life of the time. We read in the Argentine bibliographical publication *Libros de Hoy* [Books of Today] (May 1951) the following remark which precedes eight short reviews of new books on Proust: "Not a day goes by without our reading an essential study of the great French novelist" (J. A. 1951, 72–73). Similarly, Mario Lancelotti expressed in *La Nación* the attitude of the period in an article entitled precisely "Volviendo a Proust" [Returning to Proust] (23 November 1952):

> To the degree that we are are a small history, a storeroom of "lost time", we return necessarily to Proust, to live through the Guermantes, the Swanns, Albertine, Françoise or someone who could be our grandfather or our mother, a chronicle which, without ceasing to be that of Marcel, is also that of . . . our deep self. . . . (1952, 1)

In the literary sections or supplements of the principal capital city newspapers, beginning with *La Nación* and *La Prensa* of Buenos Aires and later to include *Excelsior* of Mexico City, *El Comercio* of Lima, etc., there appeared many articles about the *Recherche*. At times their number reflected the interest of a particular writer, such as Alejo Carpentier. He wrote more than a half dozen brief texts on Proust for his column "Letra y Solfa" [Letters and Music] of *El Nacional* of Caracas. He reviewed, for instance, the posthumously published version of Proust's unfinished novel *Jean Santeuil* (26 October 1951) and of his literary essays *Contre Sainte-Beuve* (5 January 1955). Furthermore, he discussed Proust's friendship and correspondence with Reynaldo Hahn and his sister María (16 August 1951 and 9 May 1956). These articles must have been of special interest to the *caraqueños*, who considered the Hahn family to be former residents of their city.

In general, these articles reflected a greater degree of specialization than those of an earlier period because the author nearly always assumed that the reader was somewhat familiar with Proust's life or work. Typical subjects included love and/or jealousy in the *Recherche*, Proust and psychology or medicine, Proust's ideas on literature or art, time and/or memory in the *Recherche* and visits to Illiers-Combray.

Likewise, in the literary and scholarly magazines of the 1950s and 1960s can be found numerous articles and essays about the *Recherche*, particularly in such countries as Argentina, Mexico, Peru and Uruguay. Proust's work was already considered a modern classic and was deemed worthy of a closer scrutiny. For this reason, we find during this period and the one that follows a larger number of texts that can truly be called essays because of the complexity of their subject matter and their greater length. In the previous decades there were only a few fully developed essays on the French writer, such as the introduction that Alone prepared for *Las mejores páginas de Marcel Proust*.

Examining in detail the essays since 1950, we can ascertain their greater depth and maturity. For example, the Uruguayan Gervasio Guillot Muñoz in "El bajo bosque proustiano" [Proustian Underbrush] (*Revista de la Facultad de Humanidades,* 1950) demonstrated a more thorough understanding of Proust's novel than his brother Alvaro had shown 25 years earlier. In a still more sophisticated manner, Mario Benedetti presented an original thesis and synthesis in his essay "Marcel Proust." This text first appeared in his book *Marcel Proust y otros ensayos* (1951) and has been reprinted several times in various collections, including *Sobre artes y oficios* (1968). Here, it was given a more descriptive title, "Marcel Proust y el sentido de la culpa" [Marcel Proust and His Sense of Guilt].

Although somewhat critical in its view of the French author, this essay presents several interesting ideas about him and his work. Benedetti cites evidence of a guilt complex in Proust's lengthy description and analysis of the night when the child protagonist of *Du côté de chez Swann* insisted upon waiting up for his mother. The narrator does, in fact, derive the weakness of his will from that incident, but, according to the Uruguayan writer, this and other alleged confessions were intended to mask a greater sense of guilt. Proust idealized the consciousness of his narrator and attributed his own questionable traits to other characters, most notably the homosexuals, Charlus and Jupien, and the supposed lesbian Albertine. In this way, Proust could punish these fictional persons for his own actions without appearing guilty to his readers. This attitude, of course, implied insincerity on his part and ultimately left him with a sense of remorse. For this reason, near the end of his life Proust confessed to André Gide his regrets for having taken from the homosexuals that he knew in life their best qualities so that he could enrich the young female characters in his novel. In doing so, he made the homosexuals seem worse than they actually were. Benedetti finally concludes that within the context of the novel this kind of transfer was justifiable and perhaps necessary. All of the elements in the text had to be subordinated to the whole, and the overriding truth was more important than any partial one.

Another outstanding essay of the period is "El taller de Proust" [Proust's Workshop] by the Argentine Enrique Anderson Imbert. It was first published in *Sur* (May–June 1957) and an expanded version of it later appeared in *Los domingos del profesor* [The Professor's Sundays] (1972).

The famous historian of Spanish American literature illustrates his interest and study of the *Recherche* and presents a somewhat audacious thesis. He claims that Proust's creative process is of greater value than his novel itself. Anderson Imbert notes in the *Recherche* several contradictions, irregularities, rigid theories and incongruities, but he hypothe-

sizes that these apparent flaws are useful because they suggest Proust's
method of creation and composition. In support of his thesis, the Argentine cites an example from *Le temps retrouvé* where the author attributed
to his character Robert de Saint-Loup the same traits and activities that
he had assigned to Legrandin in *Albertine disparue*. Such an oversight
indicates not only Proust's lapse in memory and inability to complete a
final revision before his death, but also how he developed his characters.
He borrowed incidents and traits from the lives of people that he knew
and then ascribed them to one character or another depending upon
his specific purposes.

Anderson Imbert also considers the complex relationship that exists
between Proust and his protagonist-narrator, but he avoids the error of
some critics or biographers. He does not transfer traits or incidents from
the life of one to that of the other. Instead the Argentine suggests that
one can discover Proust's professional secrets from a series of parallels
between his life and that of his principal characters:

> The first readings of the one who will prove to be the writer himself. Sources
> of literary apprenticeship. The art of reading. Emulation of an admired
> writer. Observations on the distinctive qualites of an impressionist style. The
> superiority of images over things in the perception of essential reality. Writing
> letters, writing literature, etc. (1972, 232)

This manner of reading Proust's work is most certainly of value. Although it cannot substitute for a more global understanding, it does
invite the audience to become involved in the creative process and to
consider how one's own life may be transformed into literature. Such
was indeed the case for Anderson Imbert, who wrote several novels, at
least one of which has a connection with the *Recherche,* as we shall see.

A third essayist of this time, who was also a novelist like Benedetti and
Anderson Imbert, was José Bianco. This Argentine, who began to write
about Proust during the 1930s, published two studies on the *Recherche*
during the 1950s. The first, "Proust y su madre", was simply a well-written
article for *La Nación* (3 June 1956), but the second was more ambitious.
Entitled "El sentido del mal en la obra de Proust" [The Sense of Evil in
the Work of Proust], this portion of a lecture on the French author's
interest in evil appeared in *La Torre* [The Tower] (San Juan, Puerto Rico,
January–March 1959). Years later ideas from both of these studies were
incorporated into "El ángel de las tinieblas" [The Angel of Darkness], an
essay which received the Premio Literario *La Nación* 1973. Its text appeared in three issues of this newspaper of Buenos Aires (27 January, 3
and 10 February 1974). It can now be read in *Ficción y realidad (1946–
1976)*. Although this essay on the complex relationship between Marcel
Proust and Paul Léautaud falls just beyond the period that we are study-

ing, I would like to discuss it here because it reflects in essay form a similar desire to make an original contribution to Proustian criticism.

Before any other critic, José Bianco attempted to explain why Proust held in low esteem Léautaud, even though this French contemporary of his was favorably impressed by a series of brief selections from the *Recherche*. In a letter that was never sent Proust called Léautaud, "the most foul being, the one most devoid of intelligence, style, grammar, originality . . . that exists. . ." (1977, 65–66).

After describing the morbidly tender relationship between Proust and his mother, Bianco suggests that the author of the *Recherche* was horrified by Léautaud's treatment of incest in *Le petit ami* [The Boyfriend]. Apparently, Proust found in the main character's feelings for his mother certain emotions which he himself had tried to repress. Furthermore, in order to speculate on what might have been Léautaud's reaction had he known more about Proust, the Argentine critic describes how the creator of Charlus had explored the world of sadism and cruelty to rats in order to enrich his narrative work. Bianco concludes that Léautaud might have considered Proust an angel of darkness in the same way that the latter held this opinion of Léautaud.

In addition to such essays which demonstrated the careful examination of the *Recherche* and its author, there appeared in Spanish America during the late 1960s three full-length books on Proust. These were entitled *Tiempo y memoria en la obra de Proust* (1967) by the Mexican Jaime Torres Bodet, *Un mito proustiano* (1968) by the Chilean Marta Rivas and *Proust* (1969) by the Venezuelan José Balza. These three books were the first on Proust to be written by Spanish Americans and were nearly the earliest to be produced in the Spanish language.[28] Only one peninsular study, *Marcel Proust o el vivir escribiendo* [Marcel Proust or To Live by Writing] by Carmen Castro (Madrid, 1952), had preceded them. In each case the subject and approach were different, but the references by all three authors to George D. Painter's *Marcel Proust: A Biography* suggest that this detailed study of Proust's life helped to inspire them. The date of the Spanish translation, 1967, seems to confirm this hypothesis.

Torres Bodet's book is the broadest in scope and reflects many years of reading and studying the *Recherche* and its critics. We recall that this Mexican writer led the homage to Proust that appeared in *Contemporáneos* in 1928. Understandably some of Torres Bodet's critical sources were from that period. Chapters I–IV and VI were originally presented as lectures at the Colegio de México during April 1967 and Chapter V was first published as an article in *Cuadernos Americanos* (July–August 1967).

After discussing at length Proust's life, Torres Bodet examines many of the principal themes of the *Recherche:* memory and forgetfulness, the struggle against time and the role of dreams and psychology. He also considers the composition of the *Recherche* and how its author tried to recover time. Admittedly, much of what the Mexican writer says about Proust had been stated previously by other critics or scholars, but his vast reading and careful selection of details are worthy of note. Torres Bodet also helps to situate Proust in his literary context by referring to other writers of the period. Let me point out that the Mexican author even discusses specific comments made by Marxist critics, such as Malaparte and Lunacharski. His responses to Ortega y Gasset are particularly original and his remarks on the issue of *Contemporáneos* place the contribution of his generation into a larger Proustian context. Furthermore, this book, like Torres Bodet's comments on Proust in his autobiographical text *Tiempo de arena* (1955), helps us to understand the relation between his narrative and Proust's.

In *Un mito proustiano,* which grew out of an academic thesis, Marta Rivas dealt with a more restricted subject: the Dreyfus Affair in the *Recherche.* For her documentation, she relied primarily upon Proust's text, but she also used Painter's biography, as she acknowledged.

According to Rivas, the Dreyfus Affair affected Proust personally more than any other historical event or phenomenon. Nonetheless, he treated it with great objectivity in his novel. He used the Affair often as a pretext in order to illustrate certain basis truths. Through it Proust showed the personality of his characters in specific social, political, psychological and moral situations and then deduced general psychological laws, which, from his modernist perspective, apply to all persons and at all times. The outstanding portion of this study is the one in which Rivas examines the reaction toward the Affair by each of Proust's major characters: Oriane, Basin, the Prince de Guermantes, Charlus, Swann, Odette, Mme. Verdurin and Bloch. Most of this analysis was already suggested in the original text, but it is helpful for the sake of comparison to see all of this material presented in an organized manner. This study is very thorough, but the conclusion that Proust was essentially a psychologist or a moralist is somewhat deceptive. To a large extent this assessment merely stems from the limited focus of the study itself.

The Venezuelan novelist, José Balza, wrote *Proust* early in his career and is obviously from a younger generation than either Jaime Torres Bodet or Marta Rivas. Although the first section of Balza's book involved considerable study using the biographies by George D. Painter, André Maurois, and Léon Pierre-Quint, this sketch of Proust's life is the least valuable part of the book. Perhaps for this reason the author chose to omit it in his later volume *Este mar narrativo* (1987), where we find only section II.

In this part, called "Mnemónica: paralelismos," José Balza sets forth an original theory concerning Proust's novel, which is provocative if not totally convincing. Unlike most Proustian scholars who have emphasized the importance of memory, Balza focuses his attention upon the structural elements found in the *Recherche,* and he calls these "paralelismos." He states his thesis in the following manner:

> this novel is built upon an exclusive technique which does not reside, as has been said, in the discoveries of the author about memory and introspection, nor in the writhing of a sensibility that restores time, but rather in the vital creation closest to the author: the belief in a type of parallelism underlying the forms of reality. (1969, 61)

In support of this thesis, Balza points out and explains a series of contrasting elements, which the reader of Proust's text must keep in mind in order to understand what happens later. Some of these are quite obvious, such as the two *côtés* [paths or ways], the differences between life and art, Gilberte and Albertine. But, others do not necessarily constitute binary poles: Odette and the soirée Sainte-Euverte or the death of Saint-Loup and that of the protagonist's grandmother.

Even though this reading of the *Recherche,* like Anderson Imbert's, is only partial and cannot substitute for an all-encompassing one, it draws attention to Proust's interest in narrative structure and even his anticipation of structuralism, both as a school of literary criticism and as a type of new narrative. As the reader can imagine, José Balza himself has reflected the latter to some extent in his own experimental texts, which approach the French *nouveau roman* and postmodernism. I note, however, that when such structural elements are found in Balza's stories or novels it is difficult to prove that they are of Proustian origin. For this reason, I have hesitated discussing them in this book.

Also, we can observe during the 1950s and 1960s a more generalized interest in the *Recherche* through the numerous translations of Proustian studies. For example, Zig-Zag of Santiago published in Spanish in 1956 *Correspondencia de Marcel Proust con su madre,* whose original had been prepared by Philip Kolb. Likewise, *En busca de Marcel Proust* [In Search of Marcel Proust] by André Maurois came out in Buenos Aires (Espasa Calpe) in 1958, and during the same year Claude Mauriac's book *Proust por él mismo* [Proust by Himself] appeared in Mexico City (Compañía General de Ediciones, S. A.). In Argentina a series of studies on the *Recherche* became available in 1969. This collection was entitled simply *Proust* (Editorial Jorge Alvarez, S. A.), and some of the authors were famous French critics: Pierre de Boisdeffre, Henri Peyre, R. M. Albérès, Gaeton Picon, Claude E. Magny, and Georges Poulet. Also worthy of note are several books partially devoted to Proust, many of which employed new literary theories or approaches. In this case, the then rapidly expanding Venezuelan press (especially Monte Avila) made the largest contribution. The titles include: *Mentira romántica y verdad novelesca* [Romantic Lies and Novelistic Truth] (1963) by René Girard, *El libro que vendrá* [The Book to Appear] (1969) by Maurice Blanchot, and *Eh Joe y otros escritos* [Oh Joe! and Other Writings] (1969) by Samuel Beckett.

Finally, I would like to assert that the interest of Cuban readers in Proust, which developed during the 1940s, continued after the triumph of Fidel Castro in 1959. Even though some Marxists considered the *Recherche* to be an example of decadent European literature, a few influential writers defended it. Thus, Virgilio Piñera was able to publish his revision of *Un amor de Swann* with the Editorial Nacional de Cuba in 1964.[29] For this, the first Cuban edition of any portion of Proust's work, Piñera also wrote a prologue and chronology of the French author's life. Later, he translated for the magazine of Cuban writers, *Unión,* an essay by the Soviet critic Anatoli V. Lunacharski, "Sobre Marcel Proust" (1966). Likewise, we find in the bulletin of the Unión de Escritores y Artistas de Cuba, *Mensajes* [Messages], the translation of a brief fragment from *Nouveaux mélanges* [New Miscellanies]: "Sobre el gusto" [On Taste] (October 1970).

FROM THE PROUST CENTENNIAL UNTIL THE RECENT PAST (1971–2000)

By the time of the one hundredth anniversary of Proust's birth (10 July 1871) there had developed at least a small group of Proustians in most of the Spanish American capital cities. These faithful readers of the *Recherche* were ready and eager to celebrate the Proust Centennial. Lectures to honor the greatly admired French novelist were delivered in at least two of the capitals, Santiago and Mexico City, and the principal newspapers and magazines throughout Spanish America published articles on Marcel Proust.[30]

These texts were of several types. *La Nación* of Buenos Aires presented on 11 July 1971 four articles by prestigious French critics: Henri Bonnet, Jacques de Lacretelle, Georges Piroué, and Georges Poulet. In contrast, *La Prensa* and *La Opinión* (also of Buenos Aires) printed articles by Argentines, who were not specialists on Proust (e.g., Raúl H. Castagnino, *La Prensa,* 4 July 1971). On the other hand, we can find in several newspapers articles by Spanish Americans who had studied the *Recherche* for many years. Alone, who had returned with great enthusiasm to Proust in the late 1960s after fifteen years of silence, participated in the homage of *El Mercurio* (4 July). Likewise, Eduardo Caballero Calderón, who had regularly used the pseudonym Swann in his columns, wrote a special article for *El Tiempo* of Bogotá (4 July). "En torno y en el contorno de Marcel Proust" [About and in the Environment of Marcel Proust] describes the Colombian author's experience of living in Paris almost next door to where Proust had resided before the death of his parents.

Other newspapers that published a series of articles to commemorate Proust's birth include: *El Comercio* of Lima, *Excelsior* and *Novedades* of Mexico City, *El Nacional* and *El Universal* of Caracas, *La República* of San José, *La Nación* and *La Prensa* of Santiago, and *El Espectador* of Bogotá. Even *El Caribe* and *Listín Diario* of Santo Domingo, *La Prensa* of Managua and *El Imparcial* of Guatemala City printed one or two articles apiece.

Of all of the Spanish American countries, Ecuador provided the most surprising case. Until this time few critical texts on the *Recherche* had ever appeared in this small Andean country. Then, as if to catch up for "lost time," *El Comercio* of Quito published six articles on Proust during July and August 1971. For this same period, I have also found others in *El Universo* and *El Telégrafo* of Guayaquil.

Various types of magazines also participated in the Centennial. The popular Argentine *Panorama* published an article by José Bianco (13–19 July), and Alberto Lleras wrote another for *Visión* (Mexico-Colombia, 25 July). *Ercilla* in Chile also made its contribution in the 28 July–3 August issue. Among the literary journals, I must single out *Marcha* of Montevideo, where in spite of its leftist orientation at that time and perhaps to justify its prior attention to the *Recherche,* Lucien Mercier chose to defend Proust (13 August). Also, particularly worthy of note, are the articles found in *Eco.* This fine Colombian literary review, which on more than one occasion since the 1960s had published texts dealing with Proust, offered a homage to him during the month of July. The first of its articles was by Ernesto Volkening, "Editorial: Marcel Proust."

Indubitably, the most complete homage in Spanish Amercia for the Centennial was the one that appeared in the literary supplement of *¡Siempre!* [Always!], "La Cultura en México" (14 July). Here can be found Miguel Capistrán's "Proust en México," which constitutes the best attempt to study the presence of Proust in a particular Spanish American country. (I am pleased to acknowledge what I learned from this text for the case of Mexico.) Other contributors to this homage included: Edmundo Valadés, Juan José Arreola, Juan García Ponce, Esther Seligson, and Alvaro Mutis.

The Proust Centennial represents a culmination of the discussion of the *Recherche* in Spanish America. Never before nor since have so many people had so much to say about Proust and his novel on the Western side of the Atlantic. (In this case, I am including Anglo America, as well as Spanish America, because it was then that I became fascinated with Proust.)

Also in this dialogue I must mention another voice even though it was heard in France itself. On 5 July 1971 Alejo Carpentier, who was then serving as a cultural advisor to the Cuban Embassy in Paris, delivered a formal lecture on Proust at the Collège de France. Along with the other presentations of that auspicious day, "Marcel Proust et l'Amérique latine" was later published in the *Bulletin de la Société des amis de Marcel Proust et des amis de Combray* (1972). An amplified version of it in Spanish can be found in *Casa de las Américas* (1971), and this was reprinted in *La Gaceta de Cuba* (December 1989).

In the lecture, Carpentier expressed his admiration for the *Recherche* and suggested that this French masterpiece had a revolutionary effect upon the Spanish American novel of those years. The Cuban author even claimed: "There is not presently any novelist on the other side of the Atlantic that does not owe him something" (1972, 1325).[31] Attempting to explain the nature of this literary relation, the Cuban novelist suggested that Proust had helped him and other Spanish American writers supercede their previous French model, Emile Zola. The author of the *Recherche* taught them how to use the novel as a means of inquiry to penetrate beneath the surface of appearances. Although Carpentier did not employ in this context a term that he had previously coined, "lo real maravilloso" [the marvelous real], he seemed to find the presence in Proust's work of a similar phenomenon. To describe what he and his companions felt when they discovered the *Recherche* in the mid 1920s, he said "It was a revelation, an overpowering experience". He even spoke of "nos yeux émerveillés" [our eyes filled with wonder] to express their admiration.[32] Likewise, he used similar terms to show what Proust's protagonist felt when he saw a clump of apple trees in *Sodome et Gomorrhe*:

> Marcel Proust experiences a type of marvel upon discovering the apple trees "in full bloom, with an unprecedented sumptuousness, having their feet in the mud and dressed for a ball, but taking no precaution to keep from ruining the most marvelous rose satin that anyone has ever seen and which the sun made shine. . . ." (1324)

In this regard, Carpentier emphasized how Proust had elevated common reality to the level of liturgy and magic. The Proustian protagonist saw, for example, in the exclusive milieu of the Guermantes family "all of the magic of the temple of the Grail" (1323).

Referring specifically to his own work, the Cuban novelist confessed that he had learned from Proust how to perceive in the early morning cries of street venders and in the sound of their instruments their long traditions and ancient religious origins. For Carpentier, such revelations by Proust in themselves had helped to transform the Spanish American novel. Thus, he concluded:

> I have insisted in particuliar upon a manner of seeing, defining, describing and making us penetrate into the essence of things, which is the basis of a true revolution in the world of the Spanish American novel. (1325)

In short, even though Carpentier did not refer to modernism or to any of Proust's contemporaries, he was suggesting that through his personal vision, Proust had helped him and other writers move beyond the objectivist approach of realism and naturalism.

A few years after Carpentier's lecture one scholar, Jaime Valdivieso, tried to apply in general terms the Cuban author's analysis of Proust's contribution to Spanish American narrative. The Chilean's study "Nuestra herencia de Proust o la Desconfianza de la mirada" [Our Proustian Legacy or the Distrusting Gaze] first appeared as an article in *Revista de la Universidad de México* (July 1978) and was later expanded to form part of his book *Bajo el signo de Orfeo: Lezama Lima y Proust* [Under the Sign of Orpheus: Lezama Lima and Proust] (1980).

Although Valdivieso stated some of his own ideas on Proust, he drew heavily upon the lecture by Carpentier. Like this novelist, for example, he emphasized Proust's attempt to search for true reality deeply within himself. Unfortunately, Valdivieso is not accurate when he suggests that Proust's gaze can be both scientific and intuitive at the same time. Even though the psychological analysis found in the *Recherche* might appear to be a continuation of the scientific manner of the nineteenth century, it was so closely tied to and dependent upon intuition that it was not at all positivistic. As for the French author's analysis of time and memory, this was not derived from science, but rather from introspection and a profound confidence in the value of deeply felt emotion. In current terms, Proust was a modernist and believed that he could generalize from a subjective point of view. Moreover, when Valdivieso attempted to describe the relation between Proust and specific Spanish American writers, he relied excessively upon verbal or situational coincidences, and he did not adequately focus his attention upon the essential themes and characteristics of the *Recherche*, which I will try to do later.[33]

Since the Proust Centennial, the continued, yet evolving, presence of the *Recherche* can be observed throughout Spanish America in several ways. First of all, new editions of *En busca del tiempo perdido* have been published to compete with the Alianza edition from Spain (1966–69). Symptomatically Ecuador, which began its relationship with Proust at the time of the Centennial, led the way. The Cromograf edition (Guayaquil, 1974–75), which bore the title *En busca del tiempo perdido,* but only included the first part *Por el camino de Swann*, was comprised of two small paperback volumes. Ana Bergholtz is listed as the translator, but she modified the version by Salinas only slightly. Benjamín Carrión wrote the prologue.

During the 1980s, there were three other popular editions of *Por el camino de Swann* which are nearly identical in appearance but which bear different imprints and cities of publication: Editorial Origen, S. A. (México, 1982), Editorial Oveja Negra (Bogotá, 1982), Hyspamérica Ediciones Orbis, S. A. (Buenos Aires, 1983). These two small, maroon, hardcover volumes also resemble the Orbis edition of Barcelona (1982). Perhaps more important than the physical similarity of these editions is their popular nature itself. Evidently, the general reading public in Spanish America wished to become familiar with at least the first part of Proust's work, as well as other modernist texts, which also appeared in similar editions. This was, likewise, the case in Cuba and Nicaragua where a joint popular edition of *Por el camino de Swann* came out in 1987.[34] I should further point out that Santiago Rueda of Buenos Aires reprinted its entire seven volume edition in 1979–80 and began to do likewise in 1990. The same text was also used for the more recent complete printings in Argentina by C. S. Ediciones (1995) and by Pluma y Papel (1999). But more importantly, the Argentine woman writer, Estela Canto, accomplished an important feat by creating an entirely new translation of Proust's first volume, which she renamed *Del lado de Swann* (Losada, 2000).[35]

Other translations or editions of selected portions of Proust's work encompass: Betty Ferber's study and anthology *En busca de sí mismo* [In Search of Himself] (México, 1972), *El caso Lemoine* (Buenos Aires, 1976), *Flaubert y Baudelaire* (Buenos Aires/Montevideo, 1978), *El indiferente* [The Indifferent One] (Buenos Aires, 1987), and an anthology prepared by the Spanish poet Luis Antonio de Villena, *La memoria involuntaria* (Buenos Aires, 1988). Most recently *Los placeres y los días* appeared in two distinct versions and editions (Buenos Aires, 1996 and México, 1999) and *Crónicas* in another (Buenos Aires, 1997). Fondo de Cultura Económica of Mexico also published in translation several studies on the *Recherche*, most notably *Proust* (1986) by Derwent May and *Sobre Proust* (1988) by Jean-François Revel.

Articles on the *Recherche* and related subjects have continued to appear in many of the same major newspapers as before. One can find, for example, in *El Mercurio* of Santiago and in *El Nacional* of Caracas during November 1982 articles to commemorate the sixtieth anniversary of Proust's death. In the former case, Carlos Ruiz Tagle described the Proustian cult that Alone established in Chile (14 November), while in the latter, José Balza ingeniously examined the various Novembers associated with Proust (21 November).

Of all of the Spanish American countries, Mexico has produced since the 1970s the largest number of notes and articles on the *Recherche,* its author and Proustian criticism. There are, for instance, reviews of recent studies in each of the literary supplements of the principal newspapers of Mexico City: "Diorama de la Cultura" (*Excelsior*), "México en la Cultura" (*Novedades*), "Revista Mexicana de Cultura" (*El Nacional*), "Revista de la Semana" (*El Universal*), and "El Heraldo Cultural" (*El Heraldo de México*). There have also been a large number of other critical texts. Luz Aurora Pimentel, who would later write a very interesting book on Proust in English, *Metaphoric Narration* (1990), examined an important modernist parallel in *Diálogos* 98 (March–April 1981): "Proust y Joyce: lectura y escritura de una realidad". Ernesto de la Peña published in "La Cultura en México" of *¡Siempre!* a series of fourteen articles under the general title "Proust, dueño del tiempo" [Proust, Owner of Time] (5 June–18 September 1991). Likewise, a Colombian writer living in Mexico, Marco Tulio Aguilera Garramuño, wrote nearly a dozen lengthy notes on the *Recherche* for "El Búho" of *Excelsior* (April 1993–January 1994). Finally, in the new supplement of *Excelsior,* "Arena", Sergio Nudelstejer began his series on twentieth century writers with first James Joyce and then Marcel Proust, 2 (14 February 1999).

One significant development of these decades has been the publication of a larger number of scholarly studies on the *Recherche* in the journals of various Spanish American universities. During the previous periods there had always been a few learned studies, particularly in magazines devoted to literature, philosophy or psychology.[36] However, since the Centennial, Proust's novel has been treated more frequently in academic literary studies. Lucía Fallas Chacón of the Universidad de Costa Rica, for instance, examined character development in the *Recherche* in three articles for *Káñina* (1977, 1980). Similarly, the Argentine professor Ana Galimberti has written several reviews and scholarly studies for *Revista Universitaria de Letras* (Mar del Plata). In this case, Galimberti's work has culminated in the creation of a book: *Marcel Proust: estudio de antecedentes, materiales estéticos y estilo en "La Recherche"* (Mendoza, Universidad Nacional del Cuyo, 1992).

Chapter 4, "Materiales estéticos", corresponds roughly to a previous article (October–November 1981). In both texts the author treats the fascinating subject of Proust's primary and secondary materials; that is, the discoveries by the protagonist that were *not* governed by will or intelligence and those that were. In the book itself, the author's attempt to link the artistic works by Vinteuil, Elstir, Bergotte, and la Berma to the memory experiences and dark impressions of the first category is especially valuable. Her other chapters deal, in particular, with diverse facets of the aesthetic atmosphere in which the *Recherche* was created. In this way Galimberti places in a broader context her in-depth study of Proust's aesthetic materials. Clearly, her knowledge of the works by Bardèche and other critics from Curtius to Ricoeur gave this study a solid foundation.

Some books and chapters from books have been more literary in orientation, while others were more scholarly.[37] The Mexican Proustian Edmundo Valadés, for instance, added a new literary article on the *Recherche* to six of his previously published texts to create *Por caminos de Proust* [Along Proustian Paths] (1974, 1983). Among these, probably the best is "Una caída de Gide" [A Lapse of Gide], where Valadés examined all of the references to Proust in André Gide's *Journal.*[38]

Several books have included at least one chapter on a particular aspect of the *Recherche*. In *El amor creación en la novela* (Buenos Aires, 1971), Federico Peltzer studied the connection between love and creation in the the novel by Proust, as well as in works by Stendhal, Dante, Cervantes and Durrell. A lecture by Jorge Dajes, "Entre Swann y Guermantes: Marcel Proust y el mundo judío", was given printed form in *Cuatro grandes escritores y el mundo judío* [Four Great Writers and the Jewish World] (Lima, 1983). Nodier Botero Jiménez included a study of the *Recherche* in two of his books: *El mito en la novela del siglo XX* (Bogotá, 1985) and *Crítica de la novela moderna* (Armenia, 1985).

Of the recent books themselves, *El olvido en la obra de Marcel Proust* (Medellín, 1986) is the most thorough study of a single subject. María Cristina Restrepo devotes her attention to the theme of forgetfulness, which has often been overshadowed by the germane theme of memory. Clearly, Restrepo's treatment is more complete than that of other Spanish Americans (e.g., Jaime Torres Bodet) because she studies forgetfulness in most of Proust's volumes. Understandably, she examines in detail *Albertine disparue,* where the narrator depicted the various stages of forgetting Albertine. However, her attention to *La prisonnière* is less justifiable. In her discussion of *Le temps retrouvé* she naturally emphasizes the connection between involuntary memory and forgetfulness because the latter preserves minute sensations, which are necessary for a recovery of the past to occur. This idea is evident from Proust's text, but Restrepo makes an interesting point when she tells how Albertine was recovered from the sound of water pipes.

In two distinct but comparable books, the Puerto Rican professor, Esteban Tollinchi, and the Argentine critic living in Spain, Blas Matamoro, examined Proust's view of reality using a phenomenological approach.[39] Both *La conciencia proustiana* [The Proustian Consciousness] (Río Piedras, 1978) and *Por el camino de Proust* (Barcelona, 1988) respectively, are organized by the principal themes of the *Recherche,* and the two authors explain Proust's ideas on the self, the other, and art. They have avoided as much as feasible narrative development and have focused their attention upon the ideas themselves. Tollinchi is more abstract and philosophical, while Matamoro, who uses a larger number of details from the novel, is more accessible to a general reader. Just the same, both authors have presented some valuable insights into Proust's patterns of thought. Such an approach is not common in Proustian scholarship and is otherwise absent from Spanish America. It is certainly justifiable because the narrator of the *Recherche* constantly alludes to his ideas and view of reality.

To demonstrate the differences between these two books, I have chosen the subject of love, which is discussed at length in both. Tollinchi first states what is generally accepted about Proustian love. It is a mental condition that often lacks well-founded support from the outside world. The other person serves as a mere screen for the lover's projection, etc. The Puerto Rican professor then speculates on the applicability of Proust's ideas to the real world and literature and concludes that the validity of this type of love is only apparent in Proust's novel itself. In contrast, Matamoro's analysis of Proustian love is more original, albeit more controversial. The Argentine refers specifically to all of the cases of love found in the *Recherche* and points out their numerous similarities. Clearly, some of Matamoro's ideas are debatable. He emphasizes, for example, the social and economic differences between the lover and the beloved and compares this relationship to the one that exists between masters and servants. To some extent, this point is well-taken, but I am not convinced that the feelings of the protagonist for the cook Françoise can serve as the archetype of love in the *Recherche.*

At the threshold of the twenty-first century, Spanish Americans are watching attentively the developments of Proustian criticism in France and the United States. They have not yet begun to produce detailed biographies, like that of Jean-Yves Tadié (*Marcel Proust,* 1996), or creative books, like that of Alain de Botton (*How Proust Can Change Your Life,* 1997), which seem to suggest that one of the greatest writers of the twentieth century, Marcel Proust, will also remain relevant in the twenty-first. But a few Spanish Americans, such as Odile Barón Supervielle, have reviewed these works (*La Nación* of Buenos Aires, 7 March 1999). Also I should underscore the significance of Estela Canto's new translation of Proust's first volume.

Looking back in time from the beginning of the new century, we can acertain how for approximately eighty years Spanish American critics, scholars and other readers of the *Recherche* have shown their interest in and careful study of this French masterpiece through the publication of articles, essays and books. I cannot claim to have found all of the critical texts on Proust's work that have been written by Spanish Americans or that have been published in the New World, but the bibliography which I offer as an appendix has more than 1100 items. Of these Argentina, Mexico and Chile have contributed the largest number (250, 250, and 175, respectively), but Colombia, Venezuela, Peru and Uruguay are also well represented (from 60 to 40 items each). These figures are by no means negligible, and the list includes more than a half dozen books of considerable quality. Unfortunately, because of the limited editions and inadequate distribution of these books, even those persons from Spanish America who have studied Proust are surprisingly unaware of all that has been produced. In "Lectores de Proust," which appeared in September 1991 (*Cuadernos Hispanoamericanos*), Blas Matamoro mentioned less than twenty Proustian studies published in Spain and Spanish America and concluded that Proustian criticism in the language of Cervantes has been "rather sparse and not consistent" (1991, 109). I hope that this chapter has dispelled any such notion. Numerous Spanish Americans (from Manuel Gálvez and Alfonso Reyes to José Balza and Blas Matamoro himself) have made valuable contributions to the study of the *Recherche*. Some, like Alone, Jaime Torres Bodet, José Bianco or Alejo Carpentier, have been passionately Proustian and have devoted much of their lives to reading and studying *A la recherche du temps perdu*. I will not argue that their critical texts have been as original as some of those published in France, England or the United States, but in recent years more innovative and daring approaches have been applied. Furthermore, such studies ought to be recognized in international bibliographies and should be known more thoroughly at least by Spanish Americans, if not by Proustian scholars in general.[40]

Moving beyond the critical texts themselves, I wish to draw attention to the importance of Proust as a cultural phenomenon in Spanish America, which has also been generally neglected.[41] Although most scholars acknowledge that, like other modernist writers, Proust has been widely read and admired in the New World, they have been extremely vague in citing examples. Besides the translation and publication of Proust's works in Argentina and other countries and the critical texts themselves, I would remind the reader of the various homages to Proust that have taken place over the years. In Mexico there have been two: the first in *Contemporáneos* in November 1928 and the second in "La Cultura en México" in July 1971. Also, the Peruvians conducted theirs in *Las Moradas* in April 1948 and the Colombians had another in *Eco* in July 1971. Furthermore, what we might call the Proustmania of 1928 in Chile and Argentina and to a lesser extent Mexico and the broad participation of

Spanish Americans in the Proust Centennial are certainly worthy of note. In a genuine sense, reading Proust helped to define one generation in Argentina, Chile and Mexico during the late 1920s and another in Uruguay, Peru and other countries during the late 1940s and early 1950s. Such an interest in Proust and other modernists helped to lay the foundations for the Boom whose effects, like those of the Proust Centennial, are still being felt today. In short, we can conclude that the reading, study and discussion of the *Recherche* have made an important contribution to the cultural life of Spanish America.

An essential component of the culture of the Spanish-speaking New World is, of course, the literature produced by its writers. From the numerous references to novelists and other creative authors in this chapter, it should already be evident how many Spanish American writers were also readers and students of the *Recherche*. Over time, many critics have suggested a literary relation between Proust and specific novelists from Argentina, Mexico, Cuba, etc., but only in a few cases have they attempted to define the relation carefully and almost no one has ventured beyond individual works or writers.[42] Using my examination of Spanish American Proustian criticism as an introduction to the presence of the *Recherche* in the New World and as a concrete point of reference, I will now procede to study in detail these literary relations. Again I cannot pretend to cover all cases, but I have tried to be as comprehensive as possible.

2
The Early Stages and a Definition of the Literary Relations between Proust and Spanish American Writers

THE SIGNIFICANT IMPACT OF *A la recherche du temps perdu* on twentieth century narrative has been generally accepted, but diversely interpreted. In France the Proustian revolution of the novel has in fact been re-defined by each new generation of writers and critics. Referring to the poetic vision that Proust contributed to modernism three decades before, Claude-Edmonde Magny, wrote in 1950:

> *A la recherche du temps perdu* represents a turning point in the evolution of a literary genre: it is with this book that the novel clearly assumes, for the first time, the mystical function that poetry had taken on more than a half century previously. . . . (1950, 169)

In 1966, R. M. Albérès (René Marill) observed alluding to Proust and his relation to the *nouveau roman:*

> by his influence, by the explosive intent of his work, he will be considered the first writer to transfer the interest of the literary artist, from the problems of the "content" of the work to the problems of sensation, vision, relativity, knowledge and description which, after him, in a continual manner through-out the 20th century, will shape the principal concern—and delight—of his innumerable successors. . . .(1966, 88)

At the time of the Proust Centennial, Jean Ricardou suggested how the *Recherche* had anticipated the type of novel of his generation:

> Far from concealing the text, the Proustian novel tends thus to make it arise from itself. In this way it forms part of those revolutions, at times miniscule, which overturn a traditional narration narrating a fiction to allow the arrival of a new fiction narrating its narration. (1971, 5)

In spite of such remarks, few critics besides Albérès have chosen to use the term influence to describe the French works that have followed the example of the *Recherche*. George Piroué even claimed that in spite of Proust's cult he did not have any disciples or imitators (*La Nación*, 11 July 1971). In *Proust et l'Amérique* (1982) Elyane Dezon-Jones studied the relation between the French novelist and fiction in the United States, but no one, to my knowledge, has done a comparable study for France. I suspect that the alleged lack of originality often associated with the term influence is in part responsible even though in the creative process there are only two major sources: one's life and one's readings.

Over the centuries, numerous literary theoreticians have attempted to explain the relation between two or more literary texts. Some have emphasized similiarities and have suggested that a particular author "imitated" or "borrowed" specific elements from an earlier writer. Therefore, it is said that the first author in time "influenced" the second or served as his source or model. It has even been alleged in some instances that one work is "derived from" an earlier one.

For some cases, the term influence is adequate because indeed the second author appears to follow closely the first, but in our modern world where originality is prized, few writers are willing to be merely someone else's son. To gain prestige, a greater sense of meaning or a place in history, each new writer naturally tries to be unique. According to Harold Bloom, there is a terrible stigma or anxiety attached to influence, and ambitious writers go to great lengths to escape from their precursors. To explain cases that are less extreme, where the second author follows the first but in a new and original way, some scholars have spoken of "inspiration." This term is pertinent because it suggests how a second work is infused by an earlier one, but is also mysteriously distinct.

In the twentieth century, some theoretical scholars made a considerable effort to take into account differences as well as similarities and have hypothesized what Mikhail Bakhtin called "dialogue." They have viewed intertextual literary relations as a type of conversation in which the second author does not merely "repeat" what the first author "said." He adds his own comments or even contradicts the earlier text. Tzvetan Todorov summarized Bakhtin's essential idea in the following way: "all discourse is in dialogue with prior discourses on the same subject, as well as with discourses yet to come, whose reaction it foresees and anticipates" (1984, x).[1]

This approach is both useful and workable because it allows the scholar to view literary relations like other forms of human communication and to avoid the difficult concepts implied in certain methodologies, such as Bloom's. It is easy to see, for example, how some writers question or answer earlier writers, or how they try to debate with them.[2] On the other hand, the idea of dialogue is so encompassing that it includes both the acquiescence of the most fawning disciple and the sharp, duplicity of the most rebellious student. This broad definition can lead to difficulties because the two extremes, which are generally called "influence" and "parody," have characteristics that are very distinct from those of the middle range (question, response or debate). Parody, for example, as Linda Hutcheon has amply shown in her study of this literary form, is tainted by irony, and its intentions can range from mere playfulness to destructive ridicule.

Although a few scholars may contend that all literary relations must be viewed *either* as a type of influence *or* as a type of dialogue, I would suggest that by using both of these terms plus the two complementary ones, inspiration and parody, it is possible to be more precise in defining the nature of a particular literary relation. Some authors have been relatively passive and conform more or less to the traditional concepts of influence and inspiration. Let us recall that for centuries imitation was considered good and even necessary for literary creation. In contrast, other authors have actively engaged a previous writer in a dialogue or have parodied one of his works and generally hope that their readers will be able to perceive the subtlety of what they have added to the first writer's utterance.

To illustrate, I would like to present a few examples from Marcel Proust's work, which evolved over time. In his early texts, which first appeared in literary magazines, such as *Le Banquet* [The Symposium] and *La Revue Blanche,* and were later collected to form his initial book *Les plaisirs et les jours* (1896), one can often see the influence of some of Proust's favorite authors, including Chateaubriand or Anatole France. For example, at the end of "La mort de Baldassare Silvande" (1924, 42–43) the protagonist hears the sound of church bells and recalls his mother and childhood much like Chateaubriand's narrator in *René* (1964, 150). But, also in Proust's first book, we can find a more original treatment of memory and observe how he was inspired by and surpassed his predecessors. As I noted above, in "Vent de mer à la campagne" the concept of memory is more abstract because the mere similiarity between the wind and light on two separate days allows the narrator to recover his past at the seashore.

As one can surmise, Proust's early texts already contained many of his characteristic themes such as memory, nature, high society, art, jealousy and music. According to the Spaniard Javier del Prado, *Les plaisirs et les jours* constitutes a type of "arqueología temática" for all of Proust's work.[3] Nonetheless, the reader must know the *Recherche* well in order to perceive what is typically Proustian. For this reason, the reviewers of *Les plaisirs et les jours* only saw in this work an intelligent example of the literature of its time.

In fact, it took Marcel Proust many years to develop his voice and to discover his own originality, which helped to create modernism. In his first and never finished novel, known today as *Jean Santeuil,* Proust tried to conform to the nineteenth century patterns of plot development and continued to use a third person narrator. Although each individual passage seems to cry out for its own independence and refuses to fit docilely into an orderly plot, Proust did not have the courage to break with the literary mold of his time. Furthermore, in spite of the fact that the subject of memory and the vocation of an artist are developed to a greater extent in *Jean Santeuil* than in *Les plaisirs et les jours,* Proust had not yet discovered how he could use these elements to create a new type of narrative structure. The repetition of scenes where one landscape recalls another merely shows his progress toward that goal.

In the years between the abandonment of his first novelistic attempt (*c.* 1899) and the conception of his masterpiece (1908–1909), Proust moved progressively toward a more active engagement with the writers that he knew. First of all, with the aid of his mother and Reynaldo's English cousin Marie Nordlinger, he translated two books by the British aesthete John Ruskin. Proust's versions, *La Bible d'Amiens* (1904) and *Sésame et les lys* (1906), cannot be considered merely literal. On the contrary, particularly in light of his prologues and notes, he offered a new interpretation. For example, unlike Ruskin, who believed that readers should simply admire and accept the ideas of a great writer, Proust insisted that an author's conclusions should serve primarily as a stimulus for one's own thought. The reader's wisdom begins where the author's ends.

Secondly, Proust studied very carefully the style of several major French writers, from Balzac and Flaubert to Renan and Regnier. He then composed a series of pastiches on a common subject, the so-called Lemoine affair. We can see in these stylistic imitations what Harold Bloom called the anxiety of influence. As Georges D. Painter suggested, Proust felt the need to exorcise the manner of these prestigious writers in order to free himself from their oppressive influence.[4] Through such exercises Proust increased his own stylistic versatility and sense of literary independence.

Proust's most obvious confrontation was with a critic rather than a novelist. In his posthumously published essays *Contre Sainte-Beuve,* Proust questioned the critical approach used by the famous nineteenth century French *arbiter* Charles Augustin Sainte-Beuve. After an introductory and very suggestive dialogue with his mother, he showed the weaknesses of a methodology that paid more attention to an author's life than to his actual work. Proust also denied the validity of Sainte-Beuve's negative assessment of his contemporaries Baudelaire and Balzac.

While preparing his vast novel *A la recherche du temps perdu,* Proust kept in mind some of his favorite authors but no longer as literary masters to be followed. Instead, he treated them as interlocutors in a dialogue. It is quite revealing that the protagonist of *La prisonnière* discusses with Albertine such writers as Thomas Hardy and Fedor Dostoevsky. Proust used their conversation to suggest what he wished to do on a novelistic level. The case of Balzac is perhaps the most obvious, but certainly not the only one.[5] The great nineteenth-century novelist wrote innumerable works, which constitute his *Comédie humaine.* For the protagonist (and Proust himself), the proportions of Balzac's work were admirable and worthy to be emulated, but the broad conception of the collective work was imperfect because it was added retrospectively after most of the novels had been written. In his own text, the Proustian protagonist hoped to take this idea a step further; he would begin with his plan for an enormous novel and then subordinate all of its elements to the whole.

In that search for unity, which would be based upon an individual consciousness, we can see how Proust's desire for originality led him toward what we call today modernism. As Malcolm Bradbury has pointed out "consciousness was both a psychological and aesthetic phenomenon" (1990, 139), and these features became essential characteristics of the modernist works by Marcel Proust and Virginia Woolf. The same critic adds: "The new vision deeply changed the form and construction of the modern novel, creating the art of subjectivity, inward perception and open form".[6]

Like Proust with regard to his predecessors and similar to many French writers following him, those Spanish American authors who admired the *Recherche* desired to enrich their own works by taking advantage of what they had learned from it. However, also in the manner of Proust, they have sought different types of relations. Some have allowed themselves to be influenced by him or have been inspired by a particular aspect of his novel, while others have tried to engage Proust in a dialogue or have written a pastiche of his manner or a parody of a facet of his work. After discussing several early examples, which can help us understand the various possible relations, I will explain in greater detail these four categories.

With this general orientation in mind, we can now proceed to the actual cases of the intertextual relation between Proust and Spanish American writers. In order to show how this connection began and developed over time, I will treat each work individually and chronologically. Later I will shift the focus to the specific themes or subjects found in the *Recherche.*

THE FIRST EXAMPLES: *El cántico espiritual* (1923) and
Ifigenia (1924)

Given the fact that Proust's great work was not known on the western
side of the Atlantic until *A l'ombre des jeunes filles en fleurs* received the Prix
Goncourt in December 1919, we might easily assume that no Spanish
American text could be related to this French novel until the early
1920s.[7] Literary critics and historians have in fact used this date, but no
one, to my knowledge, has dared to name the first works connected to
the *Recherche*. In his article on Proust published in 1934, Luis Alberto
Sánchez merely contended, "Proustian *capillas* [cliques] are installed in
our literature following 1920." Likewise, his definition of this relation is
very imprecise: "The imitators of Proust frequently stop time and convert into slowness his meticulousness, which are not the same thing"
(1934, 96–97).[8]

Searching for more complete information about the actual beginnings of the Proustian connection, I examined memoirs and other texts
by those persons who first wrote about the *Recherche* in the New World. In
this way, I discovered in the literary memoirs of the Argentine Manuel
Gálvez, *En el mundo de los seres ficticios,* his boastful claim of having been
influenced by Proust very early. Referring to the novels that he published
in 1922 and 1923, he said that this influence is evident "in portions of *La
tragedia de un hombre fuerte* and throughout *El cántico espiritual*" (1961,
361). Although I have found only a few isolated echoes of the *Recherche* in
the first of these books, there can be little doubt concerning Proust's
influence upon the second. By way of introduction, I would like to cite a
particular statement from Gálvez's essay on Proust because it seems to
me very suggestive: "His work is an immense storehouse of literary raw
materials, the most vast and well-supplied one that has existed in the
world" (1924, 154).

Obviously, Manuel Gálvez read carefully the early volumes of the *Recherche* and noted their very sensitive treatment of art, psychological
analysis and high society. Using his experience as a novelist of the realist
school, the Argentine attempted to follow these diverse facets of Proust's
work. To do so, he combined the story of an artist's life with the psychological study of a love affair. Although from the upper classes, the principal character Mauricio Sandoval instinctively appreciates beauty and art
and sacrifices his social position in order to be an artist. He first becomes
a painter, but an older colleague and his daughter convince him that,
because of his talent, he would be a better sculptor. The young woman,
whom he marries, plays a decisive role in the early stages of Mauricio's
career, but he eventually realizes that he must go beyond her traditional
concept of art if he is to discover his own originality. His search leads him

away from his wife and toward another woman who greatly inspires him, Susana.

Scattered throughout the early chapters of this novel we can find numerous Proustian echoes dealing with art and other subjects, yet the realism of Gálvez separates him from Proust's new type of novel. Even in the case of the love affair which follows, the distance between the Argentine realist and the French modernist is all too apparent. Perhaps the best example of this contrast can be seen in a passage involving music, love and memory. Like the protagonist of "Un amour de Swann", Mauricio associates a particular musical phrase with the woman that he loves. The similarities and differences can be observed through a juxtaposition of the following passages first by Proust and then by Gálvez:

> La petite phrase continuait à s'associer pour Swann à l'amour qu'il avait pour Odette . . . la petite phrase, dès qu'il l'entendait, savait rendre libre en lui l'espace qui pour elle était nécessaire, les proportions de l'âme de Swann s'en trouvaient changées. . . . (1954, 1:236)

> [The little phrase continued to be associated for Swann with the love that he had for Odette . . . the little phrase, as soon as he heard it, was able to free up in him the space that was needed for her; the proportions of Swann's soul were altered by it. . . .]

> Mauricio, desde este momento, unió esta música a la persona de Susana. Y durante toda su vida, no pudo oírla sin imaginar a su amiga. Por distraído que estuviese, por más preocupaciones que llenaran su espíritu, bastábale recordar mentalmente esas cuatro notas para tener ante sus ojos, como una presencia verdadera, la imagen de Susana. (1950, 155)

> [From this moment Mauricio associated this music with the person of Susana. And throughout his entire life, he could not hear it without imagining his friend. No matter how distracted he was or how many worries filled his mind, it was sufficient for him to recall mentally those four notes to have before his eyes, as a true presence, the image of Susana.]

Clearly these two passages are intertextually related, but we can observe an appreciable difference. Having heard a musical composition in the presence of a beloved woman, both male protagonists attempt to use a specific phrase from it in order to enrich their love. Although Swann and Mauricio only later realize how this association will be bound to memory, Gálvez's narrator already anticipates this fact. Also, we should note that the type of memory is obviously distinct in each case. Unlike Swann, who subsequently will be most deeply affected by the phrase when he hears it by chance at the soirée of Mme. de Saint-Euverte, Mauricio intentionally hums its four notes whenever he feels the need for Susana's presence. This contrast between the involuntary memory of the French author and the overtly conscious type of the Argentine writer suggests the gulf that separates them. Instead of allowing Proust's new variety of memory to help him escape from his traditional mold, Gálvez reduced memory to its merely realist proportions. Thus, it appears that in spite of his desire to take advantage of Proust's literary qualities, Gálvez at times found it difficult to comprehend thoroughly Proust's subtlety and true intentions.

To some degree, Manuel Gálvez also exemplifies the weakness that Sánchez attributed to the Spanish American writers of the 1920s. The Argentine did in fact slow down the pace of the text. This is particularly true when Gálvez attempted to follow Proust's psychological analysis of words and gestures. In chapter 16 of *El cántico espiritual,* the narrator devotes several pages to a simple conversation between Mauricio and Susana. We read, for instance:

> Susana había bajado la voz, pero no excesivamente, apenas lo necesario para revelar el sentido confidencial que daba a esas palabras. Mauricio, que la observaba, vio el cambio de actitud, y más que en el tono de la voz en la expresión que lo acompañaba. (72)

> [Susana had lowered her voice, but not excessively, scarcely enough to reveal the confidential sense that she gave to those words. Mauricio, who was observing her, saw the change in attitude, and more than in the tone of her voice in the expression which accompanied it.]

Gálvez emphasized his own psychological intention by attributing the same to his principal character: "Mauricio analizaba cada detalle de la conversación, cada mirada, cada silencio de Susana" [Mauricio analyzed each detail of the conversation, each glance, each silence of Susana]. Unfortunately the Argentine novelist did not penetrate into his characters' psyche in the manner of Proust, but remained on the surface. The text merely shows in detail what is obvious: the man and the woman find each other attractive.

Similarly, in another portion of *El cántico espiritual,* apparently influenced by Proust's famous analysis of Legradin's ambiguous greeting, Gálvez described profusely how Susana once smiled at Mauricio:

> Ella le miró a los ojos, como con reproche, pero al mismo tiempo de una manera bondadosa, suave, infinitamente suave, dijérase amorosa. Y sonreía con sonrisa forzada. Sonreía de sí misma, de aquella complicidad, de esas palabras y esas miradas que eran como mostrar un juego. (128–29)

> [She looked into his eyes, as in reproach, but at the same time in a kind manner, one that was gentle, infinitely gentle, one might even say lovingly. And she smiled with a forced smile. She smiled from her being, out of that

type of complicity, those words, those glances which seemed to reveal a game.]

Indeed, the Proustian passage is much longer because the narrator must explain the specific circumstances as well as analyze the meaning. Legrandin wished to greet the protagonist and his bourgeois family members without showing his aristocratic companion that he knew them. I will cite only the description of Legrandin's eyes:

> cherchant à compenser par l'intensité du sentiment le champ un peu étroit où il en circonscrivait l'expression, dans ce coin d'azur qui nous était affecté il fit pétiller tout l'entrain de la bonne grâce qui dépassa l'enjouement, frisa la malice; il subtilisa les finesses de l'amabiltié jusqu'aux clignements de la connivence, aux demi-mots, aux sous-entendus, aux mystères de la complicité; et finalement exalta les assurances d'amitié jusqu'aux protestations de tendresse, jusqu'à la déclaration de l'amour. . . . (1:125–26)

> [seeking to compensate through the intensity of his feelings for the rather narrow field in which he restricted their expression, in this blue corner of his eye which was reserved for us he caused to sparkle all of the warmth of his good grace which went beyond playfulness, bordered on mischievousness; he refined the artifice of his amiability to the point of winks of connivance, hints, hidden meanings, the mysteries of complicity; and finally he exaggerated his assurances of friendship to include the claims of affection and even a declaration of love. . . .]

In spite of the greater length of Proust's text, his numerous details are fully justifiable. They are important because of what they reveal about a specific person's feelings or intentions. The exaggeration and apparent contradiction in Legrandin's greeting suggest to the young protagonist the older man's snobbery. This flaw is surprising to the reader because the character would have denied it and the protagonist's family had not even suspected it. In contrast, the gestures of Gálvez's characters tell the reader almost nothing about them. They merely show that Susana has mixed emotions concerning the married man Mauricio, but these are never clearly defined. Such details and the analysis of them apparently have no other purpose than to seem profuse and subtle. Although Manuel Gálvez may be considered the first Spanish American writer to have clearly and openly chosen to follow Marcel Proust and to use the *Recherche* as a primary source for one of his novels, this combination was not very successful. His realist ideal of objectivity did not allow him to take advantage of Proust's modernist subjectivity. The fact that *El cántico espiritual* is one of Gálvez's least esteemed novels bears witness to this reality.

Another early Spanish American novel to be related to Proust was *Ifigenia* by Teresa de la Parra, but fortunately in her case she was able to benefit more fully from Proust's example. Her work, which bears the subtitle *Diario de una señorita que escribió porque se fastidiaba* [Diary of a Young Lady who Wrote because She Was Bored], appeared the very next year 1924 in Paris, where it received from the Casa Editora Franco-Iberoamericana first prize for New World fiction.

The literary connection between *Ifigenia* and the *Recherche* was suggested very early by the French critic of Argentine origin Max Daireaux. He wrote in an article published in *El Espectador* of Bogotá (15 July 1926),

> This book paints for us in a beguiling manner the life of a young woman from Venezuela, which makes one think of Marcel Proust. Because of the subtle precision of the analysis, the very rhythm of the phrase, the bewitching and mysterious charm of the style, this novel, in spite of being distinctly personal and original, is linked to the art of Swann. And it is . . . a rare and magnificent encounter. (1926, 10)

In spite of such arguments a major scholar on the Venezuelan writer, Velia Bosch (1979, 137), has denied the possible influence of Proust upon *Ifigenia* by saying that Teresa de la Parra could not have known the *Recherche* in Caracas when she began to write her novel in the early 1920s. However, the article by Francis de Miomandre published in January 1920, as well as two others from this same year that I mentioned in chapter 1, should dispel any such doubts.

As in *El cántico espiritual,* we find in *Ifigenia* numerous Proustian elements and even a slow pace of development, but as Marco Antonio Martínez suggested in his article "Proust y Teresa de la Parra," the *morosidad* [slow development] of *Ifigenia* is entirely appropriate and serves a valuable purpose. Unlike the Argentine realist, this woman writer, who was already beginning to display some of the characteristics of modernism, was very subtle, and all of the minute details found in her text fit very well with what she learned from Proust. To some extent the French novelist's own "feminine" temperament facilitated this type of blending. As we shall see, other women writers from Spanish America would also find in Proust a sensitive male author whom they could emulate.

On the one hand, even though Teresa did not intend to write a psychological novel in the manner of Proust (which was Gálvez's stated purpose), both her narrator María Eugenia and the intelligent laundrywoman Gregoria penetrated deeply into the motives of the other characters very much like Proust's narrator. Symptomatically, they examined with care the gestures of such persons. On the other hand, in spite of the fact that María Eugenia never chose to become a professional writer, she constantly demonstrates in her extensive letter and diary, which form the text of the novel, her intelligence, subtlety and poetic sense, which are in many ways akin to Proust's.

In this regard, the importance that María Eugenia attributes to her subjectivity and to apparently insignificant details firmly establishes her bond with the Proust and modernism. Like him, she considers physical sensations, such as odors, worthy of her attention, and she is very careful in her selection of such details when she describes persons and landscapes. At times, because of her Proust-like comparisons, Teresa de la Parra's narrator comes very close to the *Recherche*. Referring to the trip in her uncle's car from the Caribbean coast up to Caracas, she says of the palm trees near the beach,

> Cuando se va subiendo una montaña y se ven los cocoteros de arriba, sus cabezas desmelenadas sobre la finura del tallo parecen alfileres erizados en un acerico, que es la playa. Si el cocotero es uno solo y se mira a distancia . . . tiene la melancolía de un solitario que medita, y la inquietud de un centinela escudriñando en el horizonte, sus palmas desgajadas . . . parecen flores puestas en un búcaro de pie muy largo. (1991, 33)

> [When one is climbing a mountain and the coconut palms are seen from above, their unkempt heads over their slender stem seem like pins stuck into a pincushion, which is the beach. If the coconut palm is all alone and is viewed from a distance . . . it has the melancholy appearance of a loner who is meditating, and the uneasiness of a sentry guard scrutinizing the horizon, its detached fronds . . . seem to be flowers placed in a very long-stemmed vase.]

This passage reminds us of a specific portion of Proust's text because of the situation and the details chosen. While riding in Dr. Percepied's vehicle, the protagonist of "Combray" had been inspired to write his first literary text. Near the end, to describe the apparent movement of three church steeples he remarked:

> je les aperçus une dernière fois de très loin qui n'étaient plus que comme trois fleurs peintes sur le ciel au-dessus de la ligne basse des champs. Ils me faisaient penser aussi aux trois jeunes filles d'une légende, abandonées dans une solitude où tombait déjà l'obscurité . . . (1: 182)

> [I caught sight of them one last time from far away, and they were now only like three flowers painted on the sky above the low relief of the fields. They also made me think of three maidens in a legend who were abandoned in a solitary place just as the dark of night was falling. . . .]

I note in both texts the comparisons to flowers and to solitary persons viewed against the horizon. It is also apparent that Teresa de la Parra

discovered the value of Proustian comparisons and took full advantage
of them in the creation of her own text.

This Venezuelan novel comes closest to what might be called "the
essential Proust" when the protagonist-narrator describes two memory
experiences which transport her back to her childhood. In the first case,
upon receiving a letter from her best friend and feeling disappointed by
Cristina's cold indifference, María Eugenia remembers vividly specific
moments when they attended school together in southern France. This
type of memory experience might appear simply conventional because
of the common stimulus of a letter, but Teresa's narrator attributes to it a
Proust-like precision and mystery:

> Sobre el cristal de la tarde mojada, nítidamente, como en un espejo, recuerdo
> a Cristina, recuerdo su voz, recuerdo sus ojos azules . . . y me parece revivir
> aquella otra tarde nebulosa y fría del invierno europeo, cuando merendando
> juntas . . . me hizo en un instante su más íntima amiga, al hacerme su más
> íntima confidencia. (162)

> [On the windowpane of the wet afternoon, distinctly, as in a mirror, I remem-
> ber Cristina, I remember her voice, I remember her blue eyes . . . and I seem
> to relive that other misty, cold afternoon of a European winter, when having a
> snack together . . . she made me in an instant her most intimate friend when
> she confided in me her most intimate thoughts.]

Even though we do not find here a physical stimulus, which would be
typical of Proustian memory, María Eugenia suggests the second phase
of association: "¡Sí! . . . resumida en aquel misterio lejano, sobre el
cristal de la tarde: qué bien la siento pasar hoy toda mi infancia!" [Yes!
. . . condensed in that far away mystery on the windowpane of the afternoon, how well to I see today all of my childhood pass before me].
Proust's narrator says in a similar manner of the *madeleine* episode, where
he recovered an entire period of his past, "tout Combray et ses environs,
tout cela qui prend forme et solidité, est sorti, ville et jardins, de ma tasse
de thé" [all of Combray and its surroundings, all of those things that take
on shape and concreteness, have come forth, town and gardens, from
my cup of tea] (1:48).

Following this initial memory experience, María Eugenia recalls another episode involving memory; this one actually occurred in Europe
and is more Proustian than the first. At age eight during a dull mathe-
matics lesson with her governess, María Eugenia happened to spy in one
of the lenses of Miss Pitkin's glasses the reflection of a tree outside the
window. This visual image in combination with the woman's reference to
the one hundred apples of a math problem instilled in the young girl a

fervent desire for freshness, indolence and freedom. Her sensation in turn affected her memory:

> Y al punto mi pensamiento, como un pobre pajarito preso, comenzó a agitarse poco a poco en alas de sus deseos: revoloteó primero tímidamente; revoloteó luego con más brío; y por fin, emprendiendo un vuelo decidido hacia el pasado se perdió suavemente entre un boscaje de recuerdos vagos, imprecisos, llenos de virgiliana y bucólica dulzura . . . con mi vista siempre fija en el árbol . . . recordé dulcemente con algo de fruición y con mucho de melancolía aquellos días lejanos pasados en San Nicolás, la hacienda de Venezuela. . . . (165)

> [And immediately my thought, like a poor little captive bird, began to stir little by little on the wings of its desire: it fluttered at first timidly then it fluttered with greater verve; and finally undertaking a determined flight toward the past it became gently lost in a thicket of vague, imprecise memories that were full of Vergilian and bucolic sweetness . . . with my sight still fixed on the tree . . . I recalled sweetly with some pleasure and a great deal of melancholy those far-away days spent at San Nicolás, the country estate in Venezuela. . . .]

This memory experience is indeed quite Proustian because it is initially derived from a physical sensation in the present which brings to mind a similar sensation from the past. As in the case of the *madeleine* episode where the Proustian protagonist must identify the former moment in order to recover it, María Eugenia's mind progresses from a general past to a more specific one. We can also detect a similarity between the metaphorical language implied in the description of the bird's timid flight and Proust's typical comparisons. His narrator says of the memory process,

> je sens tressaillir en moi quelque chose qui se déplace, voudrait s'élever, quelque chose qu'on aurait désancré, à une grande profondeur; je ne sais ce que c'est, mais cela monte lentement, j'éprouve la résistance et j'entends la rumeur des distances traversées. (1:46)

> [I feel something tremble within me, which moves and tries to rise, something that is no longer attached but is at a great depth; I do not know what it is, but it is mounting slowly, I observe the resistence involved and I hear the clamor of the distances traversed.]

And, finally, as in the case of Proustian memory, María Eugenia has the impression of being transported to the past and even across the Atlantic Ocean. Seeing herself as a small child, she writes:

sentada yo sobre la hierba, bajo los guayabos colgados de frutas, con mis manos libres, independientes y completamente mías, jugaba con tierra durante horas y horas acompañada por mi amiga María del Carmen, la hijita negra de la cocinera. (165)

[sitting on the grass, beneath the guava trees loaded with fruit, with my hands free, independent and completely mine, I played with dirt for hours and hours in the company of my friend María del Carmen, the little black daughter of the cook.]

Within the context of the Spanish American literature of the period, this passage is indeed remarkable. Not only does it constitute the best proof of the intertextual relation between Teresa de la Parra and Marcel Proust, but also it can be considered the first fully developed example of Proustian memory in all of Spanish American narrative. Its subtlety and completeness are very surprising because, when Teresa created this memory experience, she had access only to Proust's early volumes. She could not read his final explanation of involuntary memory until it appeared in *Le temps retrouvé* in 1927. It is also worth noting that, in spite of her European education and elevated social status, Teresa de la Parra used Proustian memory to recapture an essentially Spanish American experience. Her character recalled the smells and earthiness of Venezuela and the pleasure of playing with a child from another ethnic group and social class. Thus, this Venezuelan writer demonstrated how the inspiration of a French novelist could assist her in searching for what was authentically Spanish American.

As for Luis Alberto Sánchez's accusation that the Spanish American followers of Proust slowed down the *tempo* of their novels but were not truly meticulous, I would have to conclude that this assessment does not apply to *Ifigenia*. Most certainly, Teresa de la Parra did emphasize details, but not merely for their own sake. They were of value only in so far as they served the general structure of her work, which was precisely Proust's case. I must concede that her structure was more traditional than his because it still conformed to the concept of plot; yet she, like the French novelist, was able to develop her work slowly and meticulously without forgetting the architectural design of her novel. Although the memory experiences might have been more fully integrated into the text so that they would not appear to be a digression from the present of the narration, they nonetheless show how the modernist consciousness of the protagonist added to the unity of the text.

In contrast, a writer from Sánchez's own country, Peru, created a few years later an example of just the opposite, a work whose use of detail considerably weakened the general structure. I am referring to *La casa de cartón* [The Cardboard House] (1928) by Martín Adán. Written by a former student, whose actual name was Rafael de la Fuente Benavides, this text was very familiar to Luis Alberto Sánchez and perhaps affected his understanding of the influence of Proust in Spanish America.[9] In the prologue which he wrote for *La casa de cartón,* Sánchez emphasized the young author's attention to detail derived from the *Recherche:* "From Proust he assimilated a certain unhurried delight in his describing" (1984, 7).

La casa de cartón is, in fact, filled with minute and fleeting details. Each page is a careful description of an incident from the narrator's life in and around the beach resort of Barranco. At times, particularly when he alludes to odors, the text does bring to mind Marcel Proust and the art of sensation, which was part of his contribution to modernism. We read for example, in the early pages of the smells that the narrator associates with the pious women of the town: "Beatas que huelen a sol y sereno, a humedad de tohallas [*sic*] olvidadas detrás de la bañera, a elíxires, a colirios, a diablo, a esponja, a ese olor hueco y seco de la piedra pómez usada, entintada, enjabonada . . ." [Devout women that smell like the sun and night dew, like the dampness of towels left behind the bathtub, like exilirs, like eye-drops, like the devil, like a sponge, like that hollow and dry scent of used, stained and already lathered pumice . . .] (1984, 18). In a similar manner, the narrator of *Du côté de chez Swann* describes at one point the numerous odors found in Tante Léonie's rooms, some of which were due to her religious practice. Such rooms "nous enchantent des mille odeurs qu'y dégagent les vertus, la sagesse, les habitudes, toute une vie secrète, invisible, surabondante et morale. . ." [enchant us due to the countless odours emanating from virtues, wisdom, good habits, an entire secret, invisible, extremely rich and moral life. . .] (1:49).

In his descriptions, Martín Adan at times also recalls the *Recherche* because of his constant use of comparison, but an extensive passage where Proust and his work are specifically discussed suggests that even more importantly the Peruvian author wholly accepted Ortega's *puntillista* interpretation of the French novel and considered it to be only fragmentary in spite of its obvious structural elements. This passage which is located precisely at midpoint in the text begins with an intricate play on words which assumes an understanding of *Du côté de chez Swann* and *A l'ombre des jeunes filles en fleurs.* The narrator and his friend Lucho have called a particular *malecón* [street along the shore] "bulevar Proust," which is clarified by the remark, "no es un bulevar por los dos lados, sino por uno solamente—al otro, sicológica inmensidad del mar. . ." [it is not a boulevard along its two sides, but only along one—on the other, the psychological immensity of the sea. . .] (52). Obviously the narrator is toying with the concept of *lado* [side] because the *malecó* only has one, but there were two *lados* [*côtés,* sides] in "Combray." The *bulevar* and the sea allude to the two parts of Proust's second volume: the first, which often describes the streets of Paris, and the second, which takes place at the beach resort of Balbec. We note that the latter corresponds precisely to Barranco in Peru and the allusion to psychology and the sea draw attention to the depth of Proust's analysis. This idea plus the roles performed by imagination and emotion in the protagonist's love for Swann's daughter Gilberte are developed in the following phrase: "la acera de la calle en que está la casa de la familia Swann, la puerta sentida en cada una de sus moléculas, el cálculo infinitesimal de sus posiblidades de emoción, etcétera" [the sidewalk of the street on which is located the house of the Swann family, the door felt in each of its molecules, the infinitesimal calculus of its possibilities of emotion, etc.]. It is not that the narrator of *La casa de cartón* has a great deal of interest in psychology; for him analysis is merely a game, as he suggests later in the passage by saying, "juguemos al psicoanálisis" [let's play psychoanalysis] (54). It seems rather that Martín Adán was fascinated by the attention that Proust paid to the myriad of details associated with Swann's house and door. I might even hypothesize that the title of the Peruvian novel is directly related with this type of *puntillismo* because the concept of "house," which is scarcely mentioned elsewhere, appears to stand for (in a metonymic sense) the entire beach resort. This location is presented in the text as isolated "molecules", but it is never shown as a whole.[10]

THE PROUSTIAN APPRENTICESHIP OF A GENERATION: THE CONTEMPORÁNEOS REWRITE *A l'ombre des jeunes filles en fleurs*

During the second half of the 1920s and the early 1930s, as more Spanish Americans read *A la recherche du temps perdu,* at least a dozen authors were influenced by it because they incorporated elements from it into their own writing. In countries like Argentina, Chile or even Colombia can be found isolated cases (e.g., Roberto Mariani, José Santos González Vera, Luis López de Mesa).[11] I will return briefly to some of these writers later when I consider the treatment of Proust's favorite subjects. I prefer to focus my attention here upon a particular generation which collectively became attached to Proust and wrote a series of novels that are intertextually related to the *Recherche.* This is the Mexican generation known as the Contemporáneos, which, as we saw in chapter 1, demonstrated their admiration for Proust by devoting to him in 1928 an issue of their literary magazine *Contemporáneos.*

In general but very lucid terms, Guillermo Sheridan described the connection between three novels and Proust, as well as among themselves. He pointed out how the reading of *A l'ombre des jeunes filles en fleurs* greatly affected *Margarita de niebla* [Margarita of Mist] (1927) by Jaime Torres Bodet, *Dama de corazones* [Lady of Hearts] (1928) by Xavier Villaurrutia and *Novela como nube* [A Novel like a Cloud] (1928) by Gilberto Owen:

> In spite of notable differences, the three novels deal with exactly the same basic plot situation: a (young) man because of a fortuitous cause (a trip, an accident) comes into contact with a pair (of female friends, of sisters) and he must determine with which of the two he will remain (as husband, as lover) knowing that he will always question the justness of his choice. It is obvious that this cannot be due to a mere chance, but rather to the reading of the volume by Proust. (1985, 308)[12]

As evidence of this specific link with the French novelist, I would like to quote from the last part of *A l'ombre des jeunes filles en fleurs* a passage where the protagonist finds himself in precisely the same circumstances. He perceives the distinct qualities of the girls that he met on the beach at Balbec, but he is unable to decide which individual member of the *petite bande* he loves the most. Albertine and Andrée become the primary contenders and the former is eventually selected, but the protagonist's doubts remain:

> Mon hésitation entre les diverses jeunes filles de la petite bande, lesquelles gardaient toutes un peu du charme collectif qui m'avait d'abord troublé, s'ajouta-t-elle aussi à ces causes pour me laisser plus tard, même au temps de mon grand . . . amour pour Albertine, une sorte de liberté intermittente, et bien brève, de ne l'aimer pas? (1: 846)

> [My indecisiveness with regard to the various young girls of the little band, all of whom retained a bit of the collective charm which had affected me at first, also contributed, didn't it, to the factors which left me later, even during the time of my great . . . love for Albertine, a kind of intermittent, and very brief, freedom of not loving her?]

In addition to this general situation, which inspired the three Mexican writers because, like the Proustian protagonist, they were perhaps not deeply affected by women and tended to be indecisive, one can observe the influence of the *Recherche* in other ways. In the prologue to his anthology of these three works (plus *Return Ticket* by Salvador Novo), *La novela lírica de los contemporáneos* (1988), Juan Coronado suggested additional links.[13] Although he did not limit himself to a Proustian relation, this is implied, along with more general modernist traits, when he spoke of a morbid eroticism largely disconnected from sexual desire, a psychic androgyny and a subjective dream-like quality found in these texts.[14] We recall that Albertine and her band were somewhat masculine because these female characters were based upon young men that Proust had known in life.

To consider still other possibilities I would like to examine individually two of these novels, *Dama de corazones* and *Margarita de niebla,* because both of their authors, Xavier Villaurrutia and Jaime Torres Bodet, carried their relation with Proust to subsequent and more important works. Although *Dama de corazones* was published second, I will study it first because of its earlier composition date (1925–26).

In his prologue to the *Obras* by Villaurrutia, Alí Chumacero described this brief lyric novel in the following terms: "A precursor of the mystery that would preside over a stage in his lyrical work, Villaurrutia conceived *Dama de corazones* from the avid retreat of a premature Marcel Proust. . ." (1953, xxvi). Clearly at certain points in this work we can observe Proust's influence. In one particular section the narrator attributes to Mme. Girard a type of spontaneous memory triggered by physical sensations, which obviously recalls the *Recherche.*[15] He then procedes to list numerous examples, but he does not develop any of them in detail:

> Inmóvil, viaja en el tiempo abandonándose a la memoria, sin itinerario, confiada en las asociaciones de ideas que le despiertan las cosas, los sonidos, los colores, las horas, los paisajes. Un crepúsculo amarillo la traslada junto a su esposo muerto. Las primeras notas de un andante de Beethoven le recuerdan aquella pasión secreta . . . por un falso pianista belga. . . . (1953, 576)

> [Motionless, she travels through time giving in to memory, with no itinerary, trusting in the association of ideas that are awakened in her by objects, sounds, colors, times of the day, landscapes. A golden sunset transports her to the side of her deceased husband. The first notes of an andante by Beethoven remind her of that secret passion . . . that she felt for a deceitful Belgian pianist . . .]

The most anticipatory of these Proustian passages for Villaurrutia's later work appears at the very beginning of *Dama de corazones.* The initial sentence, "Hace tiempo que estoy despierto" [I have been awake for a long time] (571), by similarity and contrast brings to mind the first line in Proust's vast novel, "Longtemps, je me suis couché de bonne heure" [For a long time I went to bed early] (1:3). Also in Villaurrutia's initial paragraphs, the images associated with the darkened bedroom and its furnishings are very similar to the ones found near the beginning of Proust's text. The Mexican wrote for example: "Me cargo en el lecho hundiéndome temeroso y gustoso en los cojines, en las mantas, como deben hacerlo los enterrados vivos a quienes la vida les hace tanto daño que, a pesar de todo, no quieren volver a ella" [I cover myself in the bed sinking down fearfully and with pleasure in the pillows, in the blankets, as must do persons buried alive, whose life hurts them so much that, in spite of all, they do not want to return to it]. The depiction of the various bedrooms in which the narrator of *Du côté de chez Swann* had slept could have affected the Mexican writer, but we read later in the first part about a particular one where the images of death herald more specifically those of Villaurrutia. Remembering the pain in his childhood of being sent to bed early, the narrator says, "Une fois dans ma chambre, il fallut boucher toutes les issues, fermer les volets, creuser mon propre tombeau, en défaisant mes couvertures, revêtir le suaire de ma chemise de nuit" [Once in my room it was necessary to plug all the openings, to close the shutters, to dig my own grave by turning down the covers, to don the shroud of my nightshirt] (1:28).

Within the context of Xavier Villaurrutia's later poetry, as typified by his most famous volume *Nostalgia de la muerte* [Nostalgia of Death] (1939–46), we can see how the vocabulary and imagery of a bedroom, which was already apparent in the initial pages of *Dama de corazones*, acquired a special meaning for the Mexican poet. The Proustian source for some of this imagery can be observed in specific poems, for example, in the first lines of "Nocturno de la alcoba" [Nocturne of a Bedroom]:

> La muerte toma siempre la forma de la alcoba que nos contiene.
> Es cóncava y oscura y tibia y silenciosa,
> se pliega en las cortinas en que anida la sombra,
> es dura en el espejo y tensa y congelada,
> profunda en las almohadas y, en las sábanas, blanca.
> (1953, 60)

> [Death always takes on the shape of the bedroom that envelops us.
> It is concave and dark and warm and silent,
> it folds itself in the curtains in which the shadow makes its nest,
> it is hard and taut and frozen in the mirror,
> deep in the pillows and in the sheets, white.]

Proust's description of the bedroom in the hotel at Balbec, as found in the early pages of "Combray," was apparently a partial model for Villaurrutia. The concave shape of the ceiling described by the Mexican poet corresponds precisely to the "chambre . . . élevée de plafond, creusée en forme de pyramide" [the bedroom . . . with a high ceiling, hollowed out in the shape of a pyramid . . .] (1:8), which made the Proustian protagonist extremely uncomfortable. But, of greater significance is the unusual image of the first line "La muerte toma siempre la forma de la

alcoba . . ." because it is derived from a phrase found in the same Proustian passage: "Ma pensée, s'efforçant . . . pour prendre exactement la
forme de la chambre . . ." [My thought, striving . . . so as to take on
precisely the shape of the room . . .].

In general, we can conclude that the lyric richness of Proust's text
helped Villaurrutia discover his own poetic world and find his personal
voice. This type of assimilation began while he was writing *Dama de
corazones* but would continue for many years.[16]

Jaime Torres Bodet, who led the homage in 1928 and would later write
a book about Proust, had initially found the social themes of the *Recherche* to be an obstacle. In his memoirs *Tiempo de arena,* he explains how
he was able to enter Proust's world:

> fui lentamente advirtiendo la finura del análisis psicológico, la riqueza sensi-
> ble y la fuerza poética; es decir: todas las cualidades de un escritor que no es
> sólo un gran novelista del siglo XX, sino un narrador egregio y, en Francia,
> después de Montaigne y Stendhal, el mejor buzo de ese océano del "yo". . . .
> (1961, 246)

> [I was slowly noticing the subtlety of the psychological analysis, the sensitive
> richness, the poetic force, that is to say: all of the qualities of a writer who is
> not only a great novelist of the 20th century, but also a distinguished narrator
> and, in France after Montaigne and Stendhal, the best diver in that ocean of
> the "self". . . .]

As a poet who had already published several volumes, Torres Bodet,
like Villaurrutia, was able to determine the lyric value of the *Recherche.* In
particular, he was impressed by the Proustian comparison or metaphor
and by the sources of Proust's imagery. For this reason we find throughout his first novel, *Margarita de niebla,* the frequent use of the preposition
of comparison "como" [like], which corresponds to Proust's repetition
of the word "comme," and references to some of the same areas of
human experience as in the *Recherche:* psychology, medicine and art. A
typical example is the following: "Como esos medicamentos que
curan—o matan—según la oportunidad o la inoportunidad con que se
prescriben, la amistad de Margarita me entristece, próxima y me alienta,
lejana" [Like those medicines that cure—or kill—in accordance with
the appropriateness or inappropriateness with which they are pre-
scribed, Margarita's friendship saddens me when she is close and inspires me far away] (1985, 1:47). In *Albertine disparue,* we find a similar
comparison involving medicine to analyze love and to illustrate its vari-
able conditions. Referring to Albertine's departure, the narrator tells
what he felt:

Mais dans cette chaleur . . . ce que je trouvais (comme dans un remède que le remplacement d'une des parties composantes par une autre suffit pour rendre, d'un euphorique et d'un excitatif qu'il était, un déprimant) ce n'était plus le désir des femmes mais l'angoisse du départ d'Albertine. (3:482)

[But in that heat . . . what I found (as in a remedy in which the substitution of one of the ingredients for another is sufficient to change the original stimulant or tonic into a depressant) was no longer the desire for other women but instead my anguish for Albertine's departure.]

Unlike several other writers of this time who employed in a fragmentary way Proustian comparisons or psychological observations, Jaime Torres Bodet was always careful to build a context.[17] He placed the comparison cited above in an analytical chapter, where his narrator Carlos tries to explain his awkward relationship with Margarita Millers. Carlos is quite Proustian throughout and even suggests, like the narrator of *A l'ombre des jeunes filles en fleurs* with regard to Albertine, that Margarita at times seemed to be a different person.

To a large extent, *Margarita de niebla* was written in the shadow of Marcel Proust. Besides the hesitation between the German girl and her Mexican friend Paloma and his frequent comparisons and psychological observations, which were influenced by Proust, we also find the impressionist description of piano music and even one long passage where Carlos, like the narrator of *La prisonnière*, watches his girlfriend sleep. At one point Carlos combines several of these Proustian elements:

Margarita duerme con un sueño apacible, largo. En él, como en ciertos *andantes* de Beethoven—especialmente como en el *himno pastoral* que precede la tormenta de la *Sexta sinfonía*—nada hace prever la posibilidad de una catástrofe. Lo escucho transcurrir al lado de mi insomnio con el oído maravillado de que en una debilidad tan evidente quepa una confianza tan pura. (1: 89)

[Margarita enjoys a long, peaceful sleep. In it, as in certain *andantes* by Beethoven—especially the *pastoral hymn* which precedes the storm in the *Sixth Symphony*—nothing causes one to foresee the possibility of a catastrophe. I listen to her sleep transpire alongside my insomnia with my ear marveling that in so obvious a vulnerability may so pure a trust find room.]

Even though all of these Proustian echoes fit quite well together and contribute to the modernist nature of this text, their sheer concentration makes *Margarita de niebla* a very rhetorical work because it often lacks spontaneity and deep personal feeling.[18] At times, one almost has the impression that the influence of Proust was so strong that the Mexican author was stifled by it. Also, the reader is oppressed by the painstakingly slow development and may wonder why this man who felt so little desire for Margarita's presence wished to continue seeing her.

Among the Spanish American writers of this early period, Jaime Torres Bodet was the most Proustian in sensibility. Not only did he, like the French novelist, join the poetical and analytical realms and display a vast knowledge of literature and art, but also he felt the social pressure to feign an interest in women that he apparently did not feel in a profound way.

In his subsequent series of brief novels, one can trace Torres Bodet's struggle with the narrative form and his attempt to balance a close relation with Proust and a search for originality. To some extent his second novel *La educación sentimental* (1929) offers a type of allegory and indirect confession of his situation as a novelist. Just as the narrator at first greatly admires his intelligent friend Alejandro and for a time accepts his strong influence but later feels stifled by it, Torres Bodet must have realized his need to develop a sense of independence in order to exist as a novelist in his own right. Fortunately in this novel itself, we can discover the Mexican writer's progress. The style is more natural and the materials used, being autobiographical, are more authentic. As for the influence of the *Recherche,* it is less obvious but in one way more profound. Torres Bodet discovered through Proust's example the importance of reaching deeply into his own life and innermost being in order to create his literary work.

Torres Bodet's narrative relation with Proust culminated in his last novel *Sombras* [Shadows] (1937). Because of its fine use of Proustian memory, I will delay my discussion of it until chapter 8, where I will focus my attention upon this aspect of the Proustian connection. Let me provisionally conclude by saying that, like Xavier Villaurrutia, Jaime Torres Bodet was not immediately able to take advantage of all that Marcel Proust had to offer. Because of the originality of the *Recherche* and their own need to develop a creatively healthy relationship with it, these Mexican writers would have to read and work with it for more than 10 years.

A Narrative Discussion on Proust in the Sur Group

In Argentina during the 1920s there existed a movement to renew the national literature following the example of recent European writers, most of whom were modernists. To help define their position one young critic from the vanguard literary magazine *Martín Fierro,* Horacio Linares (Alberto Prebisch), voiced his opposition to the realist author Manuel Gálvez (26 June 1925). Curiously, because of Gálvez's interest in Proust, the *Recherche* became involved in a debate which lasted two months. Being accused of reproaching the young writers for their cult of European literature, Gálvez replied in *Martín Fierro* that they would never succeed in writing like Stendhal or Proust, but added that he himself was one of the first Argentines to discover the latter's work:

> When the young people of the new generation did not know even the names of the foreign masters whom they admire today and consider to be their masters, I had already read them and had even written about them. Such is the case of Proust. I have not waited for Proust to become fashionable in order to admire him. (5 August 1925) [19]

In spite of their differences in opinion both parties eventually agreed that Marcel Proust was an excellent writer and an appropriate model. Speaking for the Florida group from already a modernist perspective based upon individual subjectivity, Horacio Linares explained why the *Recherche* was of great interest to his entire generation:

> Beneath the appearance of a frivolous and conventional society life, Proust reveals to us an unsuspected psychological world. External life does not exist for him, except in so far as it helps him reveal a more intimate and general life. Reaching into the most hidden subjectivity of his characters, Proust universalizes them, he confers upon them a general, profoundly human interest. (28 August 1925)

Unfortunately the writers of the Argentine vanguard, who concentrated their attention on poetry, did not produce narrative works that clearly reflect this Proustian interest. Such fruits did not appear until the 1930s.[20] Gathering around her some of the writers from the Florida group (such as Jorge Luis Borges and his younger friend Eduardo Mallea), Victoria Ocampo helped to advance the cause of Argentine narrative and, as we saw in chapter 1, the discussion of Marcel Proust.

Ocampo's stated intention of creating in Argentina a literature of high quality (or as she said, "on the level of Henry James") is well-known. But her own desire to become a writer and how her frustrated literary vocation is perhaps directly related to Proust also should be examined. I have found suggestions of this connection in her essays, in her *Autobiografía* and in her responses to my questionnaire. When I requested an explanation for the anguish that she felt upon reading Proust's work, she said: "When *Du côté de chez Swann* fell into my hands it was a great discovery, but the childhood of Proust caused me so much pain that I did not advance in my reading. The child Proust was I myself." This remark may, of course, have more than one feasible interpretation. Like the protagonist of "Combray," young Victoria was perhaps deeply affected by nature and the world around her. These elements elicited an emotional or artistic response, and she too wished to become a writer. Because of her gender and the restrictions that her family and social class placed upon her, she soon realized the opposition that her choice of a writing career would provoke. But I also suspect that the pain of which she spoke had another source, one derived from her gender but in another way. The secrecy which she attached to her own life and the fact that she did not want her autobiography to be published until after her death seem to be clues in this regard. Is it possible that the scene in "Combray," where the protagonist happened to spy upon the ambiguous gestures and actions of the daughter of Vinteuil and her perverse female friend struck a personal chord in Victoria? I will not further speculate on this matter. I only wish to cite what Ocampo stated at the beginning of the fourth volume of her autobiography. In this text, which bears the suggestive title *Viraje* [Turning Away], she spoke, in particular, of what might have been her literary career:

> si hubiera aprovechado al máximo mis dones naturales, también hubiera logrado éxito en el campo de la literatura. A estas horas, quizás habría publicado un libro significativo, si no perfecto. Me he desperdigado. . . . En parte para no dejar este país al que me ligaban diferentes amores (padres, amante, amigos). Porque el amor fue mi vocación primera, antes que el teatro y que las letras. (1982, 10)

> [if I had taken maximum advantage of my natural gifts, I also might have achieved success in the field of literature. By now perhaps I would have published a significant, if not perfect book. I have scattered my energy. . . . In part in order not to leave this country to which I was bound by different loves (parents, lover, friends). Because love was my first vocation, before theatre and letters.]

Here we can detect a genuinely Proustian sense. Like Swann, Ocampo preferred love to writing in part because she did not have the courage to reach deeply into herself. Perhaps she did not wish to expose for her readers the recesses of her being, as Proust had done. In his analysis of Swann, who greatly admired literature and art but never succeeded in creating either, Proust was also describing the nature of other persons including Victoria Ocampo. He called them "célibataires de l'art" [the unmarried of art] and said of them,

> Ils sont plus exaltés à propos des oeuvres d'art que les véritables artistes, car leur exaltation n'étant pas pour eux l'objet d'un dur labeur d' approfondissement, elle se répand au dehors, échauffe leurs conversations, empourpre leur visage. . . . (3:892)

[They become more excited by the works of art than do actual artists, because their excitement, not being the product of an intense effort to reach deeply within themselves, bursts outward, it overly heats their conversations, it makes them red in the face. . . .]

Such an attitude toward literature, music and art, however, did not produce merely negative results. Unable to fulfill her own literary vocation, Victoria derived pleasure from the works of other persons and for this reason became a great patroness of the arts.[21] Through the magazine, *Sur* and its publishing firm Ocampo made available numerous texts written in Argentina or other Spanish American countries, as well as translations of European works. Some of the South American authors, such as Jorge Luis Borges or Eduardo Mallea, were already firmly established, while others were new, most notably the Chilean, María Luisa Bombal. Her friend, Pablo Neruda, with whom she arrived in Buenos Aires in 1933, most likely assisted her, but the obvious quality of her work and the relative openness of *Sur* were essential to the early diffusion of it. Thus, Ocampo published the novels *La última niebla* [The Last Mist] in 1935 and *La amortajada* [The Shrouded Woman] in 1938, and the magazine *Sur* included in its pages for 1939 the stories "Las islas nuevas" [The New Islands] and "El árbol" [The Tree].

Orlando Gómez-Gil has suggested a relation between Bombal and the *Recherche:* "Marcel Proust influences her a great deal, both in technique and in the preeminence of sensorial and intelectual elements" (1968, 688). Having traveled to Paris with her family in 1922 (coincidentally, at the time of Proust's death), María Luisa most likely began to read the *Recherche* while she was in high school or at the Sorbonne, where she wrote her thesis on Prosper Mérimée.

In *La última niebla* Proust's presence is most evident in the passages where the female protagonist-narrator watches first Regina and then her own lover sleep. These bring to mind a famous portion of *La prisonnière* where Proust's main character contemplates Albertine in slumber. Of her lover, Bombal's narrator remarks:

Lo abrazo fuertemente y con todos mis sentidos escucho. Escucho nacer, volar y recaer su soplo, escucho el estallido que el corazón repite incansablemente en el centro del pecho. . . . Entre mis brazos, toda una vida física, con su fragilidad y misterio, bulle y se precipita. Me pongo a temblar. (1988, 20)

[I strongly embrace him and with all my senses I listen to his breath as it emerges, flies and falls back, I listen to the explosion that his heart repeats without tiring in the center of his chest. . . . In my arms, an entire physical life, with its fragility and mystery, seethes and rushes forth. I begin to tremble.]

The Proustian passage is much longer, but the following excerpt contains the same type of auditory, visual and tactile elements:

> J'écoutais cette murmurante émanation mystérieuse, douce comme un zéphir marin, féerique comme un clair de lune, qu'était son sommeil. Tant qu'il persistait je pouvais rêver sur elle et pourtant la regarder, et quand ce sommeil devenait plus profond, la toucher, l'embrasser. (3:70)

> [I listened to that mysterious, murmuring emanation, gentle like a marine zephyr, fairy-like as a moonbeam, which was her sleep. As long as it lasted, I could dream about her and at the same time watch her, and when her sleep became deeper, touch her, kiss her.]

In general, the importance attributed to physical senstions and the consciousness of the narrator are quite similar in *La última niebla* and in the *Recherche* and make these works fine examples of modernism. Furthermore, memory plays a significant role in both novels, even though it functions in a distinct manner. In this regard, we can observe Bombal's independence and originality. Instead of being affected by involuntary memory, like Proust's characters, Bombal's heroine semiconsciously fabricates an amorous encounter and memory. Just the same, it does not seem by chance that her recollection of the experience depends upon a material object, a hat. Likewise Proustian memory normally required a physical stimulus derived from an object in order to begin.

Bombal's short story "El árbol" is even more closely bound to Proust, but this text also demonstrates her ability to work creatively with her source. In "El árbol," as near the end of "Un amour de Swann," the protagonist listens to music, recalls the past and comes to a greater understanding of a love relationship. In spite of the similar pattern associated with the human consciousness, we must examine the details in order to determine what the two texts have in common and how they are distinct.

First of all, the circumstances of listening to music are not identical. Swann happens to hear musical selections by Liszt, Chopin and Vinteuil while he is at a soirée of Mme. de Saint-Euverte. In contrast, Brígida is at a recital where pieces probably by Mozart, Beethoven and Chopin are performed. Also, we should note that because of Swann's vast culture he is already familiar with the music that he hears, while Brígida is not.

Let me point out that Proust described each musical selection using his typical impressionist manner. For example, to indicate the daring agility of the pianist in his performance of Liszt, Proust compared him to a trapeze artist. In regard to the one composer cited in both texts, Chopin, his work is portrayed in the *Recherche* in general terms through references to the musical education of one of the listeners, Mme. de Cambremer:

> Elle avait appris dans sa jeunesse à caresser les phrases, au long col sinueux et démesuré, de Chopin, si libres, si flexibles, si tactiles, qui commencent par chercher et essayer leur place en dehors . . . et qui ne se jouent dans cet écart de fantaisie que pour revenir plus délibérément. . . . (1:331)

> [She had learned during her youth to cherish the long, sinuous and exaggerated phrases of Chopin, which were so free, so flexible, so tactile, which begin by seeking and exploring their way outside . . . and which are played on that edge of fantasy only to return more deliberately. . . .]

In describing Chopin, Bombal also employed at times an impressionist style but was more concise when she wrote, "Puñados de perlas que llueven a chorros sobre un techo de plata. Chopin" [Handfulls of pearls that pour down upon a silver roof. Chopin] (1988, 52). In spite of this difference, we can find a similarity between this image and one used by Proust. To refer to Chopin's incisive endings, he said, "comme sur un cristal qui résonnerait jusqu'à faire crier—vous frapper au coeur" [as on a piece of fine glassware which would resonate to the point of making you scream—to strike you in the heart] (1: 331).

Listening casually to the pieces by Liszt and Chopin, Swann is unaffected, but when he recognizes the sonata by Vinteuil, he is overwhelmed by his past. The *petite phrase* from it, which he had often heard in the company of Odette during the early stages of their love affair, seems to usher her into the room and he begins to view again all that he had experienced with her:

> il retrouva tout ce qui de ce bonheur perdu avait fixé à jamais la spécifique et volatile essence; il revit tout, les pétales neigeux et frisés du chrysanthème qu'elle lui avait jeté dans sa voiture, qu'il avait gardé contre ses lèvres. . . . (1:345)

> [he recovered all that had established forever the specific and volatile essence of that lost happiness; he saw everything again: the snow-like and curled petals of the chrysanthemum which she had tossed to him into his carriage, which he held against his lips. . . .]

In Bombal's text Brígida also recovers the time that she spent with her husband, Luis, but the connection between music and memory is considerably different. Not having heard the three musical pieces before, she does not recognize them, nor do they automatically remind her of the past. It is rather the musical impression itself that each one causes and the emotional state that is induced that allow her to see again her previous life. For example, the first selection seems to lead Brígida by the hand to her past:

> Y Mozart la lleva, en efecto. La lleva por un puente suspendido sobre un agua cristalina que corre en un lecho de arena rosada. Ella está vestida de blanco con un quitasol de encaje, complicado y fino como una telaraña. . . . (46)

> [And Mozart leads her, in effect. He takes her across a bridge suspended above crystalline water which flows over a bed of pink sand. She is dressed in white with a lace parasol, which is intricate and fine like a spider's web. . . .]

But, even here we can suspect Bombal's Proustian source. He too had evoked the scene of a woman surrounded by water. Just the same the Chilean writer appreciably modified the scene by attributing it to the listener rather than to the music, as Proust had done:

> et comme dans un pays de montagne, derrière l'immobilité apparente et vertigineuse d'une cascade, on aperçoit deux cents pieds plus bas, la forme minuscule d'une promeneuse—la petite phrase venait d'apparaître, lointaine, gracieuse, protégée par le long déferlement du rideau transparent, incessant et sonore. (1: 264)

> [and as in a mountainous region, behind the apparent yet breath-taking immobility of a waterfall, one catches a glimpse two hundred feet below of the minute shape of woman out for a walk—the little phrase had just appeared, distant, graceful, protected by the long, unfurling of its transparent, constant and sonorous curtain.]

In a genuine sense, Bombal was inspired by Proust and though she used the same elements as the French author—music, memory, and impressionism—she created something that was quite new by transferring to the impressions themselves the role of stimulus.

In spite of this difference, listening to music has an analogous effect upon Swann and Brígida. As the music brings to mind the past and allows the two characters to see how an unfortunate experience with love developed, they acquire a greater understanding of that feeling. They realize why they had suffered: Swann because of jealousy and Brígida because she had married an older man without love. It is only then that they both can begin to heal. The *petite phrase* appears to speak to Swann about Odette and shows him the futility of his continuous pain. Likewise, the music by Chopin reminds Brígida how in the midst of suffering she discovered resignation and pleasure in minute sensations.

In short, María Luis Bombal learned from Proust's work how music, impressionism, and memory could be used to good literary advantage. Then, after employing her own imagination and intelligence to redefine these elements and their interconnection, she created her own text, which is quite Proustian and yet original. In other words, she was inspired by Proust. Again, we can see how the French author's subtlety and sensitivity helped a woman writer. Bombal's evident success with the subject of music and the example of Proust must have encouraged other members of the Sur group, such as José Bianco, and a few other authors (most notably Felisberto Hernández) to continue writing in this vein, as we shall see in chapter 5. Bombal's story may have even contributed to a renewed interest in the *Recherche,* which became evident about 1940.

As we saw in chapter 1, the Sur group constituted a veritable forum for the discussion of Proust. When the members gathered at Ocampo's house in San Isidro or elsewhere, they often talked about the *Recherche.* They did not all agree and even held opposing views concerning Proust. Jorge Luis Borges and to a lesser extent Eduardo Mallea often criticized the French novelist. Furthermore, their debate was extended to their narrative works, as I will demonstrate here by examining texts by Borges and Mallea, which contrast with the ones by Bombal.

The clearly distinct attitude toward Proust of Victoria Ocampo and Jorge Luis Borges can be easily documented. In her note "Borges," Ocampo labeled herself "a staunch reader of Tolstoy and Dostoievsky, of Proust and Virginia Woolf" and suggested that in spite of their widely divergent literary preferences, she could not deny the talent of Borges (1975, 75). On the other hand, Borges may have been referring at least in part to Victoria Ocampo when he said in *Discusión,* "there are writers of unquestionable value—Marcel Proust, D. H. Lawrence, Virgina Woolf—who tend to please women more than men" (1964, 22). Despite the obvious qualities and prestige of the *Recherche,* Borges held it in low esteem.[22] In fact, in his writing he rarely mentioned Proust except to criticize his work. For example, in his prologue to the novel by Adolfo Bioy Casares *La invención de Morel* (1940), Borges cited the *Recherche* as a prime example of the psychological novel and then heaped scorn upon its author: "There are pages, there are chapters of Marcel Proust that are unacceptable as products of imagination: to which, without realizing it, we resign ourselves as to the insipid and idle details of each day" (1953, 12).

This opposition to Proust apparently began very early. Even at the time of the Prix Goncourt, when Borges began to read the *Recherche,* he formulated a negative opinion of it.[23] Although he did not apparently mention Proust in his writings until after 1930, his early essay "La nadería de la personalidad" (1922, 1925) seems to be directed at least in part against *A l'ombre des jeunes filles en fleurs,* and "Sentirse en muerte" (1928) can be read as a response by Borges to the memory experiences found in *Le temps retrouvé.*[24] At one point in "Sentirse en muerte," which first appeared in *El idioma de los argentinos* (1928) and later in *Historia de la eternidad* (1936), the author even echoes Proust. Referring to a series of homogeneous elements that had not appreciably changed over time Borges wrote:

> Esa pura representación de hechos homogéneos—noche en serenidad, parecita límpida, olor provinciano de la madreselva, barro fundamental—no es meramente idéntica a la que hubo en esa esquina hace tantos años, es, sin parecidos ni repeticiones, la misma. (1953, 40)

> [That sheer representation of homogeneous elements—a serene night, a limpid little wall, the provincial fragrance of honeysuckle, essential dirt—is not merely identical to that which existed on that corner so many years ago, it is, without just similarities or repetitions, the same.]

Using almost the French equivalent of these words to describe two analogous sensations greatly separated by time, the narrator of *Le temps retrouvé* (which had appeared the year before) said, "Ce n'était d'ailleurs même pas seulement un écho, un double d'une sensation passée que venait de me faire éprouver le bruit de la conduite d'eau, mais cette sensation elle-même" [Furthermore, it was not just an echo, the duplicate of a past sensation that the noise in the water pipe had just caused me to feel, but rather that sensation itself] (3:874).

This similarity, as well as the fact that Borges, like Proust, used a personal experience in support of his own but different theory of time, suggests that the Argentine author had learned more from the French novelist than he was willing to admit. Along these same lines, I would also point out that, when Borges incorporated "Sentirse en muerte" into his essay "Historia de la eternidad," he introduced it by quoting from the study "Proust on Essences" but intentionally avoided mentioning the French novelist. He simply wrote, "leo en el español emersonizado Jorge Santayana . . .": "Vivir es perder tiempo: nada podemos recobrar o guardar sino bajo forma de eternidad" [I read in the emersonized Spaniard George Santayana . . . : To live is to lose time: we cannot recover or store anything except in the form of eternity] (1953, 34–35).[25]

Considering in general the lives and works of Marcel Proust and Jorge Luis Borges, it is apparent that they shared some of the same interests (philosophy, time, art, and the self) and possessed some of the same strengths (an excellent memory and fine sensibility) and weaknesses (a tendency toward insomnia and homosexuality).[26] On the other hand, their literary works are very different. Instead of creating a lengthy novel filled with a myriad of details, Borges wrote concise short stories using only a few carefully selected elements. The obvious contrast between their similar lives and dissimilar works suggests that Borges, who may have feared being too much like Proust (whose homosexuality was obvious), perhaps made a conscious decision to create a work that contrasted with Proust's.[27] This hypothesis could explain the attitude of Borges in his early essays, as well as his general reticence and apparent hostility toward the *Recherche*. In the case of one of his stories we can even detect an anxiety of influence. I am referring to "Funes el memorioso," which one may read as a parody of Proust and seems to confirm at least in part Harold Bloom's idea that an intentional misreading enables a second author to liberate himself from a stifling first author. "Funes el memorioso" was originally published in *La Nación* on 7 June 1942—three years after "El árbol" by Bombal—and was later included in *Ficciones* (1944). It can even be viewed as a response to Bombal's story involving memory.

Gene H. Bell-Villada suggested a vague relation between "Funes el memorioso" and Proust, but he made no attempt to explain it:

> The piece was written, according to Borges, as a means of staving off insomnia (a therapeutic trick that Borges claims did its work.) As Borges sees it, then the story is a fable about the need and the concomitant difficulty of being able to forget—a cleverly pointed inversion of Proust. (1981, 100)

The use of the word "inversion" here is astutely meaningful. It implies that behind the Argentine's story can be found a text by Proust or perhaps one about him which Borges chose to confront in a derisive manner. Until the present no one has discovered that text. This interpretation can help us understand the exaggeration and at times taunting tone because this story is in fact a parody. In this case Linda Hutcheon's definition is very pertinent. According to her, parody implies a repetition of elements, but with a critical ironic distance. Also parody emphasizes differences instead of similarities (1985, 32–38).

Although the numerous references to memory and the constant repetition of the verb form "recuerdo" can in themselves suggest a connection to the *Recherche,* these elements are not sufficient to spring the lock. The same is true for those details of the story that bring to mind aspects of Proust's life or work, such as the feasible parallel between the evening that the narrator spent with Funes and the famous noctural visits by Proust's friends and acquaintances to his cork-lined room. In both cases the visitors had to speak through smoke to the strange man in bed and listen to him discuss the past and memory. Paul Morand's famous poem "Ode à Marcel Proust", for which one Argentine version appeared in *Martín Fierro* in May 1924 and another in *Verbum* in 1931, illustrates this similarity. The earlier translation by Héctor Castillo begins: "Sombra nacida del humo de vuestras fumigaciones, / el rostro y la voz / con

sumidos por el uso de la noche . . ." [Shadow / born from the smoke of
your fumigations, / your face and your voice / consumed by the use of
the night . . .].[28]

The key, auspiciously, is suggested by the form of the short story itself.
Somewhat like other fictions by Borges that resemble book reviews or
literary studies, "Funes el memorioso" has the structure and content of a
personal testimonial written for a commemorative volume or homage.
The narrator explains, referring to Funes and addressing the editors of
the book: "Me parece muy feliz el proyecto de que todos aquellos que lo
trataron escriban sobre él; mi testimonio será acaso el más breve y sin
duda el más pobre, pero no el menos imparcial del volumen que edi-
tarán ustedes" [The project of having all those who dealt with him write
about him seems very appropriate to me; my testimonial will perhaps be
the briefest and certainly the poorest, but not the least impartial in the
volume that you will publish.] (1956, 107). With the aid of my study of
Proust in France and Spanish America, I realized that "Funes el memorioso" has a great deal in common with the famous *Hommage à Marcel
Proust,* which is precisely this type of commemorative volume and was
published by the *Nouvelle Revue Française* in January 1923. Another edition of it became available in 1927 and was widely known throughout
Spanish America.[29]

In both cases, persons who knew the man being honored recall the
circumstances of their meeting or of other times when they interacted.
Gaston Gallimard, the publisher of the first complete edition of the
Recherche, for example, tried to recapture, in the manner of Proust himself, the essence of the novelist through the initial impression caused by
him. Gallimard thus said in "Première rencontre" of the *Hommage à
Marcel Proust,*

> J'ignorais alors jusqu'à son nom. Mais je fus frappé de l'extrême tendresse de
> son regard, et aujourd'hui encore je le revois tel qu'il m'apparut avec ses
> vêtements noirs étriqués et mal boutonnés, sa longue cape doublée de ve-
> lours, son col droit empesé, son chapeau de paille défraîchi trop petit. . . .
> (1927, 56)

> [I did not know then even his name. But I was amazed by the extreme
> tenderness of his expression, and still today I see him again just as he ap-
> peared to me with his too tightly fitting and poorly buttoned black garments,
> his long cape lined with velvet, his starched straight collar, his worn, too small
> straw hat. . . .]

Likewise, in the story the narrator recalls the clothes that Funes was
wearing on the day of their first encounter, but we can detect a notable
difference which suggests the author's parodic intent. In spite of the

typical emphatic tone present, there is little to distinguish Funes from other ranch hands, only the threatening weather and the fact that Funes was walking on a higher plane:

> Había oscurecido de golpe; oí rápidos y casi secretos pasos en lo alto; alcé los ojos y vi un muchacho que corría por la estrecha y rota vereda como por una estrecha y rota pared. Recuerdo la bombacha, las alpargatas, recuerdo el cigarrillo en el duro rostro, contra el nubarrón ya sin límites. (108)

> [It had suddenly become dark; I heard swift and almost secret footsteps up above; I raised my eyes and I saw an adolescent who was running along the narrow and broken path as along a narrow and broken wall. I remember the baggy breeches, the rope-soled sandals, I remember the cigarette in his hard face, against the already limitless storm cloud.]

In themselves, these similar descriptions of a first encounter might seem to be coincidental. Most homages contain texts of this nature. However, another depiction of Funes, which the narrator repeats three times with slight variations, appears to deride a very unique text found in the *Hommage à Marcel Proust*. We read at the beginning of the story: "Lo recuerdo . . . con una oscura pasionaria en la mano, viéndola como nadie la ha visto, aunque la mirara desde el crepúsculo del día hasta el de la noche, toda la vida entera" [I remember him . . . with a dark passionflower in his hand, seeing it as no one has ever seen it, even though one might look at it from the twilight of the morning until that of night, for an entire life.] (107). Reynaldo Hahn, Proust's intimate friend born in Venezuela, described Marcel in a similar pose. In "Promenade" he explained how the young writer (whom he had just previously met) stopped during their walk in order to examine carefully a rosebush and continued staring at it for several minutes:

> Ayant fait le tour du château, je le retrouvai à la même place, regardant fixement les roses. La tête penchée, le visage grave, il clignait des yeux, les sourcils légèrement froncés comme par un effort d'attention passionnée. . . . (33)

> [Having walked around the château, I found him in the same spot, staring at the roses. With his head tilted and his face serious, he screwed up his eyes and slightly knit his brows as in an effort of passionate attention. . . .]

For a reader of the *Recherche* and other Proustian texts, such as "La contemplation artistique," it is evident that the French writer, like his protagonist, was making an intense effort to understand his impression. That is to say, he was searching deeply within himself for the spiritual equivalent of what he had felt upon first seeing the rosebush. In the case of Funes, no attempt is made to explain why he gazed so passionately (to use Hahn's word) at the passionflower. It is almost as if he were simply memorizing its infinite detail. This contrast may also suggest that where Proust discovered the mystery of human consciousness, which he had inherited from writers of the late nineteenth century (e.g., Maurice Barrès) and which became incorporated into modernism, Borges found only a mere illusion of profundity. Thus, we can interpret the Argentine's mocking of Funes as the beginning of a postmodern response.

In Proust's aesthetic system understanding his impressions was essential because he stored these in his memory and later used them to create his famous *métaphores*. A good example of this technique can be found in Proust's description of dried tilleul leaves, which correspond roughly to the passionflowers in the story:

> Les feuilles, ayant perdu ou changé leur aspect, avaient l'air des choses les plus disparates, d'une aile transparente de mouche, de l'envers blanc d'une étiquette, d'un pétale de rose, mais qui eussent été empilées, concassées ou tressées comme dans la confection d'un nid. (1:51)

> [The leaves, having lost or altered their appearance, seemed like the most dissimilar things: the transparent wing of a fly, the blank underside of a calling card, a rose petal, but which had been stacked up, crushed or woven together, as in the making of a nest.]

According to the narrator of the story, Funes also discovered, using his excellent memory, a similarity between diverse objects and experiences. The distance between the elements, however, is so great that his comparisons are simply absurd. Again, we note the critical distance typical of parody. The narrator says of Funes:

> Sabía las formas de las nubes australes del amanecer del treinta de abril de mil ochocientos ochenta y dos y podía compararlas en el recuerdo con las vetas de un libro en pasta española que sólo había mirado una vez y con las líneas de la espuma que un remo levantó en el Río Negro la víspera de la acción del Quebracho. (113)

> [He knew the shapes of the southern clouds of the dawn on April 30, 1882 and he could compare them in his memory with the streaks of a marbled-leather-bound book that he had only looked at once and with the lines of the foam that an oar stirred up in the Río Negro on the eve of the battle of Quebracho.]

Being aware of the Argentine's intention concerning the *Hommage à Marcel Proust,* we can more easily understand other aspects of "Funes el memorioso," which may be related to the life and work of Marcel Proust.

As some of these elements deal with the real world and not just literature, this text is at times satiric as well as parodic.[30] Being confined to his
cot after falling from a horse and being paralyzed, Funes leads an existence devoted to thought and memory which satirizes Proust's during
his last years, when he quite literally spent his days and nights in bed.
Indeed, unlike the French novelist, Funes does not write, but his obsession with the infinite details of his life resembles the image that Borges
had of the *Recherche,* if not Proust's text itself. Here we are reminded of
the Argentine's comments in his prologue to *La invención de Morel* (see
above).

Even the ambitions of Funes with regard to memory seem to be bound
to the *Recherche.* Somewhat like Proust, who built *La prisonnière* around
the events of a particular day, Funes tried to reconstruct in his own mind
all of the details of a twenty-four hour period. Not only did Borges
exaggerate this purpose by saying "cada reconstrucción había requerido
un día entero" [each reconstruction had required an entire day] (113),
he even placed into the character's mouth his own criticism of the result:
"mi memoria . . . es como vaciadero de basuras" [my memory . . . is like
a rubbish drain].

At times, Borges carried his satiric parody to the extreme, in part to
exercise his imagination, but perhaps also to "destroy" in a Bloomian
sense the father figure that he saw in Proust. Thus, we find an implicit
misreading (or Clinamen) of the *Recherche.* For example, the intention
of classifying all of the recollections of childhood is a distorted view of
Proust's detailed description of the life of the child protagonist in "Combray."[31] Likewise, when the narrator of the story speaks of the character's
incapacity to formulate general ideas, Borges is misrepresenting Proust,
who simply tried to be accurate in describing the nature of perception
and in showing the imprecision of names. The narrator says of Funes,

> No sólo le costaba comprender que el símbolo genérico perro abarcara tantos
> individuos dispares de diversos tamaños y diversa forma; le molestaba que el
> perro de las tres y catorce (visto de perfil) tuviera el mismo nombre que el
> perro de las tres y cuarto (visto de frente). (115)

> [Not only was it hard for him to understand that the generic symbol "dog"
> might encompass so many dissimilar individuals with diverse sizes and diverse
> shapes; it bothered him that a dog at three fourteen (viewed in profile)
> should have the same name as the dog at quarter past three (viewed from the
> front).]

As Professor Simone Garma of the Alliance Française of Buenos Aires
pointed out in a lecture perhaps inspired by Borges, the narrator of *A*

l'ombre des jeunes filles en fleurs suggests precisely the need of creating different names for himself and for Albertine:

> Para ser exacto debería dar un nombre distinto a cada uno de los 'yo' que en el curso de mi vida pensaron en Albertine; más todavía, debería dar un nombre distinto a cada una de estas Albertinas que aparecieron delante mío, nunca las mismas. (quoted by Garma, 1949, 62)[32]

> [In order to be precise I should give a different name to each of my selves which in the course of my life thought about Albertine; even more, I ought to give a different name to each of these Albertines that appeared before me, who were never the same.]

This interpretation of "Funes el memorioso," as a satiric parody of the *Hommage à Marcel Proust* and of the life and work of the French novelist, might seem to differ from the Argentine's explanation that this story is "una larga metáfora del insomnio" [a long metaphor of insomnia] (1956, 105), but these two ways of viewing the text do not involve a contradiction. Instead they complement each other very well. In retrospect, it is almost natural that Borges chose as the target of his self-exorcism of insomnia and memory the author of the *Recherche,* who was famous for both and for whom Borges had displayed his opposition for many years. In this way, the Argentine short-story writer could attack through parody his secret archrival and at the same time combat those facets of himself that he wished to suppress.

As Bell-Villada implied, Borges apparently was able to cure himself of his insomnia by writing this story. The case of his veiled relation with Proust is not so obvious. The mere fact that he kept his attack on the French novelist as a personal secret or inside joke for friends, like Bioy or Mallea, could induce us to believe that he was not totally cured. His explicit hostility toward Proust remained, but in his poetry he came to treat memory in an almost Proustian manner.[33] This silence may also be explained by his desire not to offend Victoria Ocampo, whose admiration and defense of Proust remained ardent. In any case, I can imagine Borges laughing at the *Recherche* and its supporters when he created his phenomenal (but intellectually limited) ranch hand, who, like Proust, was confined to his bed and recalled in great detail the past. Furthermore, even the character's paralysis must have seemed to Borges both comic and appropriate because José Ortega y Gasset, who had also participated in the *Hommage,* later criticized in *Ideas sobre la novela* the *Recherche* for being precisely "una novela paralítica" (1925, 126).

Although this parody of Proust and of memory did not respond directly to Bombal's interpretation of the link between music and memory, a novel by a third member of the Sur group did. In this way Eduardo

Mallea, who had oscillated in his attitude toward Proust, entered the narrative debate between Borges and Bombal.

Initially, Eduardo Mallea was not attracted to the *Recherche*. In one of his early articles, "Tentativa de novela moderna" (*La Nación,* 26 February 1928), he even suggested that Jean Giraudoux was a better novelist than Marcel Proust. Over the years and under the influence of the Sur group, his opinion of the *Recherche* became more favorable. At the end of his essay on Kafka, which was published in *Sur* in December 1937, Mallea asserted that Proust and Joyce, along with Kafka, had created the greatest poetical systems of their time. In *El sayal y la púrpura* (1941), where he expanded his essay on Kafka, Mallea further explained his ideas concerning the other modernists Proust and Joyce. He praised the author of *Le côté de Guermantes* not because of the aristocratic salons that he described but rather for the metaphysical lessons which he had been able to draw:

> Proust deepens his permanence in that society, he researches its absolute; without wishing to, he creates the need for a metaphysical system and carries his reason and sensibility to such a deep inquiry into the study of sensations, slow developments, pleasures that his work positively attains the universality and transcendence of a metaphysics. (1941, 73)

Again we can see how Proust's ability to generalize from his individual consciousness was attractive to writers like Mallea who had not yet begun to question the modernist perspective.

In *La bahía de silencio* (1940), which is from this period, Mallea demonstrated a somewhat favorable attitude toward Proust by creating the story of a literary vocation which resembles the one found in the *Recherche*. (I will return to this subject in chapter 8.) However, following the publication of "Funes el memorioso," Mallea took a decidedly negative stance toward memory and, in particular, the involuntary variety associated with Proust. This attitude is especially evident in Mallea's two part novel *Rodeada está de sueño* [She is Surrounded by Dreams], whose volumes were entitled *El alejamiento* [The Withdrawal] (1944) and *El retorno* [The Return] (1946).

According to Mario Benedetti this work is imbued with "una morosidad casi proustiana" [an almost Proustian sluggishness] (1951, 100). Indeed, *Rodeada está de sueño* develops very slowly and in some ways resembles the *Recherche*. Mallea's subtitle, "Memorias poemáticas de un desconocido" [Poetic Memoirs of an Unknown Person] could apply to Proust's own text, which is at times very poetic and whose narrator is largely nameless. Furthermore, Mallea's principal character, somewhat like Proust himself, has withdrawn from society in order to reflect upon his life and to write. As for the slow development of this novel, I observe that similar to Proust, Mallea avoided using plot to create his structure and relied primarily upon the repetition and interweaving of themes to provide unity. These notably are very similar in both cases: solitude, the relationship between people, writing, memory and imagination.

In particular, the subject of memory is treated in a very Proustian manner but is assigned a negative value. Describing one of his walks early in *El alejamiento,* the narrator says,

Al volver de la estación, uno de los primeros días de confinamiento en este sitio, oí el rumor bastante lejano de una vieja música familiar. Sentí como si esa resonancia me echara violentamente al fondo de mí mismo, allí donde todo es arduo y silencioso y duro de tener como la piedra; me sentí repentinamente enternecido y ablandado, desamparado, en mitad del camino. (1965, 2:125)

[Upon returning from the station, one of the first days of my confinement in this place, I heard the rather distant sound of an old familiar song. I felt as though that resonance had hurled me violently to the depths of my being, to a place where everything is arduous and silent and hard to endure like a stone; I felt suddenly vulnerable, weakened, helpless, out in the middle of the road.]

Here, we find a memory experience triggered by familiar music, somewhat like Swann's recollection of Odette at the soirée of Mme de Saint-Euverte. It, however, lacks the redeeming qualities of Swann's return to the past. The music is quite ordinary and Mallea's character is totally overcome by the painfulness of his memories. Just the same, he describes his emotions metaphorically in the manner of Proust: "Sentí como una cuerda quebrada en la caja interior—semejante a la sensación de aquel que ve de pronto reabierta la cicatriz de una herida. . ." [I felt as though a string were broken in my inner sound box—similar to the sensation of a person who suddenly discovers that the scab of his wound is reopened . . .]. Moreover, as in the *Recherche,* this memory experience entails an associative phase: "Mil imágenes vinieron a tirar de la cuerda rota en la caja interior" [A thousand images came forth from the broken string of the sound box]. On the other hand, unlike Proust's narrator, Mallea's does not give any hint as to what was remembered.

This passage from *El alejamiento* also has a clear parallel with "El árbol" by María Luisa Bombal because of the use of music and memory. Yet, unlike both Brígida and Swann, Mallea's character finds no consolation in recalling the past and makes no attempt to resign himself to his suffering. He only wishes for the pain to cease: "Experimenté, entonces, la necesidad de contrarrestar ese efecto a la vez dulce y brutal, tierno y desmoralizador" [I experienced, then, the need to resist the effect which was at the same time sweet and brutal, tender and demoralizing].

In the following sections of his journal, which forms the text of this two-part novel, the writer is often distracted by the past, which he would like to forget. In spite of his resistence to memory, at one point he concedes, "todo uno es recuerdo" [all of a person is memory] (2:130). This definition recalls the ideas of Proust's narrator for whom the unity of personality can be most easily perceived through memory. Significantly and despite his experience with the past, Mallea's narrator eventually rejects this definition of the self. Near the beginning of *El retorno*, he asks, "¿Acaso yo, el hombre, yo en tanto que hombre, soy el hombre vago ligado a esas memorias inmemorables? ¿U otra cosa? ¿Está el hombre, veamos, construido de pasado?" [As a man, am I perhaps the ill-defined man bound to those forgettable memories? Or something else? Let's see, is man constructed of the past?] (2:184).[34]

Henceforth Mallea's narrator renders increasingly evident his rejection of memory and of some of Proust's ideas about it. All of this constitutes a response to the *Recherche* and other modernist works like it that focused upon the protagonist's individual consciousness and past. In contrast with the narrator of *La prisonnière*, who concludes that one can never truly know other persons, the writer in *El retorno* asserts, somewhat like Rimbaud, "Yo también soy otros" [I am also other persons] (2:187). This affirmation becomes crucial for Mallea's novel because the protagonist discovers that he can escape from his own temporal and spatial limitations by imagining the lives and conflicts of other human beings.

In conclusion, *Rodeada está de sueño* is built around a dialogue with the *Recherche* and may be considered both a Proustian and an anti-Proustian novel. It was constructed in the manner of the *Recherche* through theme development and by using some of Proust's ideas on memory, personality, etc. These, however, are explicitly rejected. Involuntary memory is the protagonist's principal obstacle in *El alejamiento*, while imagination gains relevance in *El retorno* because it can serve as a substitute for memory and holds certain advantages over it. Imagination can increase a person's empathy for his fellow human beings and save him from being immersed in his personal past.

Within the context of the narrative works produced by the Sur group and their general thrust, we can also conclude that in this text Mallea approached Borges in his rejection of memory and opposed Bombal. I cannot claim that Sur, as a whole, became disenchanted with Proust or even that Mallea's new stance was definitive. Younger Argentine writers who joined the Sur group, such as Ernesto Sábato and Manuel Mujica Láinez, would follow Proust, each in his own way. In some of his later texts, such as *Simbad,* Mallea himself would eventually return to the

French author, at least in a general sense. As for the narrative dialogue on the *Recherche* itself, this exercise proved to be very fruitful. Not only did the writers of Sur consider more carefully Proust's novel and ideas and encourage their collaborators and readers to do the same, but also they created their own literary works, whose value was enriched by the dialogue.

SWANN'S WAY AND OTHER WAYS OF FOLLOWING PROUST

When Spanish Americans began to read *Du côté de chez Swann* and *A l'ombre des jeunes filles en fleurs* during the early 1920s, they could not predict where Proust's first person narrator would lead them. They saw in the initial volume the life of a young boy in a small provincial town of France. He and his parents did not reside in that town, but they spent their vacations there and often took two distinct walks. One led past the country home of Charles Swann, an upper middle class dilettante, and the other went through the area that had belonged to the aristocratic Guermantes family. The first of these walks seemed quite important because the title of the initial volume *Du côté de chez Swann* and that of its second section "Un amour de Swann" referred specifically to the dilettante, whom the protagonist admired and began to emulate. Likewise, the other walk appeared significant because the Guermantes family was cited in the title of the already announced third volume *Le côté de Guermantes*. This opposition, which suggested Proust's novelistic structure, was also matched by another: the difference between the general title *A la recherche du temps perdu* and the title of the anticipated last volume *Le temps retrouvé*. In this case, the meaning was even more elusive because it was not clear how time could be lost and then regained. Proust's readers in Spanish America, like those elsewhere, had to wait until the publication of the final volume in 1927 in order to understand the enigma.

Similarly, when Manuel Gálvez and Teresa de la Parra began to follow Proust in their writing, they did not comprehend all aspects of the *Recherche*. They perceived the importance of psychological analysis, art, love and memory, but they were not certain of Proust's ultimate intent. The *Recherche* was by no means a simple work, so that, even after reading *Le temps retrouvé* most writers, like other readers, still did not understand everything about it or realize how they could take advantage of Proust's text while they created their own.

As we have seen, the whole question of the "use" of Proust's example is an complex one. Gálvez, who found in the *Recherche* a rich source of raw materials, imitated certain aspects of it when he wrote *El cántico espiritual*, but he ignored others due to his realist preconceptions. In contrast,

Teresa de la Parra more thoroughly assimilated Proust's new, modernist manner and allowed it to inspire her. Likewise, in "El árbol" María Luisa Bombal employed Proust's themes and ideas as a point of departure for her own.

These two ways of relating to Proust's text have been called influence and inspiration. The first appears to be more conscious and deliberate. It implies admiration and the desire to resemble the model at least in part, but it does not necessarily involve digesting it fully. The second is more creative and unconscious, but it may lead to a superior blending of Proust's manner with one's own. Here, similarity is implicit, but is not always apparent on the surface level.

Although these two types of literary relations can explain the case of most of the Spanish American works of the 1920s and 1930s, after 1940 when writers began to question modernism we find the emergence of two other types that I have mentioned above. These imply a movement away from the passive modes of being influenced or inspired by and toward a more active mode. In *Rodeada está de sueño,* Eduardo Mallea treated the *Recherche* in such a way. He did not invoke Proust's ideas on memory or the self merely to follow them or to enrich his work, but so that he could respond to them as if in a dialogue. Similarly, but in a more extreme form, Jorge Luis Borges used in "Funes el memorioso" the *Hommage à Marcel Proust* and specific aspects of the French author's life and work so that he could play with these and discredit them.

These last two types of literary relations may be called dialogue and parody and involve a conscious action: to dialogue with a text or to parody one. The former generally is based upon differences as well as similarities, and to become manifest it requires a reader familiar enough with the previous text to understand the exchange in the subsequent one. This mode is for the most part logical and has ultimately a constructive purpose. The latter type presupposes a critical ironic distance and often the desire to belittle or to destroy. But, as Hutcheon has pointed out with regard to postmodern parody, it may be merely playful even though it emphasizes differences rather than similarities. In the case of parody a knowledgeable reader is also highly preferred so that the subtleties of the text can be appreciated.[35]

Considered together these four types of literary relations—influence, inspiration, dialogue and parody—constitute a spectrum that advances from admiration to questioning and then to levity and even scorn. Focusing upon the extremes we can observe a contrast between imitation in order to resemble and imitation for ironic purposes. Influence and inspiration do not require of the readers (but certainly of the scholar) a knowledge of the source, while dialogue and parody address the readers as an audience and take advantage of their familiarity with the previous text as they proceed through the subsequent one. Being what I call a "Proustian reader," I will continue to share in this study my knowledge of the *Recherche* with readers of Spanish American literature that are not necessarily Proustian.

Analogous to the greater diversification of literary relations, we can ascertain during the 1940s a more thorough understanding of Proust's themes and techniques, which was due in part to the elucidation of the *Recherche* by Proustian scholars. The treatment of high society, love, art, memory, and time became more sophisticated in the Spanish American novel during those years.

For Marcel Proust, his themes or subjects were of capital (to use his term) importance because he employed them in the construction of his novel. Following the manner of Richard Wagner, Proust treated them as leitmotivs. He introduced them early in his work, he developed them slowly, and he returned to them constantly as he interwove them into the fabric of his text. Some of these themes or subjects received special attention in particular volumes or parts of volumes and were often referred to specifically in Proust's titles, such as "Un amour de Swann," *Sodome et Gomorrhe* or *Albertine disparue*. In the name for our present section I have cited the English title of Proust's first volume, *Swann's Way*, because I find it very suggestive. It alludes to Charles Swann's personal manner of viewing reality. This character was interested in art and society, but he was willing to sacrifice both of these for the sake of love, and certain aspects of this emotion nearly destroyed him. According to Proust, Swann's way or approach to life proved to be mistaken. He later suggested that the Guermantes' way, that is, the search for social position, was likewise an erroneous course.

In order to examine Proust's subjects systematically and to show how individual Spanish American authors and works followed the diverse ways of viewing reality that are suggested in the *Recherche,* I will present in the remaining chapters the said themes or subjects one by one employing Proust's own titles to designate them. In this manner by focusing upon the pertinent volumes or parts, I can first explain each theme of the *Recherche* and then proceed to examine the corresponding Spanish American works. In general, I will follow a chronological order, but in some cases I will treat particular subthemes separately. This organization will allow us to observe development and to study the literary relations *among* Spanish American authors, as well as *between* each one and Proust.

As for the ordering of the chapters, I have chosen not to use that of Proust's volumes, which was merely based upon the chronological progression of the protagonist's life. It seems to me more logical to begin with the most superficial and easily extracted themes (high society, love and consciousness, and the appreciation of art), then move toward

Proust's more essential themes (time and memory), and end with a subject (the protagonist's literary vocation) which he employed to draw together all of his themes into a master narrative. In this manner, we can build our own cathedral-type structure (which is modeled on Proust's) and conclude with other structural elements found in the *Recherche*. This ordering has an additional advantage: it allows me to confront immediately the suggestion by some critics (mostly Marxist) that Proust was only interested in describing high society and was, therefore, an inappropriate model for Spanish American literature.

3

On High Society: *Le côté de Guermantes* in the New World

SOME OF THE PARISIANS AT THE BEGINNING OF THE TWENTIETH CENtury who knew of Marcel Proust through his articles in *Le Figaro* or by way of his first book *Les plaisirs et les jours* assumed that he was merely a social dilettante. He had spent his youth attending upper-class social events and seeking personal contacts that would provide him access to more exclusive aristocratic circles. Even in his dress and manner he seemed too concerned about refinement and elegance to be able to create a literary work of merit. For this reason, years after Proust had ceased to visit regularly the elite and had withdrawn from the world to write his novel, the more "serious" author André Gide was predisposed to dismiss the lengthy manuscript that Proust submitted in 1912. This situation fortunately changed the next year after *Du côté de chez Swann* was published at the author's expense, and Gide finally read the book. It was only then that the latter perceived the value of this work and recommended that Gallimard purchase its rights and publish the entire text of *A la recherche du temps perdu*.

In spite of Gide's discovery of an introspective Proust, who penetrated deeply into the mind of Tante Léonie, the cook Françoise and the clubman Swann, and who portrayed with great subtlety the mechanisms of memory and the creative process, the idea of a dilettante Proust did not vanish. It would plague the author of the *Recherche* for the remainder of his life and affect the acceptance of his work for years to come. Proust could not deny his interest in high society because this subject is treated throughout his vast novel, as his opponents frequently recalled.

In Proust's first volume *Du côté de chez Swann,* which deals principally with the childhood of his protagonist in the small town of Combray and Swann's love affair with Odette, the social themes are not of prime importance. Just the same, they are implicit in the analysis of Legrandin as a snob and in the social milieus known by Swann. This character in "Un amour de Swann" frequents the artistic-bourgeois salon of the Verdurins, and on one occasion he attends an upper-class soirée of Mme. de

Saint-Euverte. There Swann chats with his dear friend Oriane, who will later inherit the title of the Duchesse de Guermantes. This aristocratic woman, who is known for her exquisite manner and wit, becomes the focus of the narrator's attention in the third volume *Le côté de Guermantes*.

It is here that Marcel Proust came closest to the realist tradition represented by Honoré de Balzac and to the subject of high society. Not only did he treat more directly external reality in this volume than in the previous ones, but also he depicted an aristocratic milieu similar to those found in a few of the novels of *La comédie humaine*. Referring to *La duchesse de Langeais,* as well as the readers of Balzac and Proust, Ramon Fernandez wrote, "those who, in the salons of the Duchesse de Guermantes, find reminiscences of the Duchesse de Langeais, will not deny that the dissector of Swann is the most Balzacian of our great novelists" (1927, vii). But, Fernandez also pointed out a significant difference. He noted (as Malcolm Bradbury would likewise say years later in his explanation of Proust as a modernist) that the author of the *Recherche* did not use an omniscient narrator nor did he merely describe high society in a realist manner. Proust chose his character's subjectivity as the basis for his perspective and subordinated all of his observations to the story of his consciousness.

Le côté de Guermantes is, in fact, the most social and aristocratic of Proust's volumes because it encompasses, in addition to a detailed portrait of the Duchesse de Guermantes and the members of her family, a lengthy depiction of a few of their social gatherings. In these pages, one finds allusions to their beautiful homes and elegant dress and a representation of their refined conversations. But, more importantly, the narrator's attitude toward the world of the Guermantes affects the entire text. Although he tended to idolize these persons when he observed them from a distance, once he gained access to their intimate circle he discovered their weaknesses, which he exposed in the text through irony and satire. Not only did he show that the Duc de Guermantes lacked intelligence and sensibility, eventually he illustrated how frivolous and cruel the Duchesse de Guermantes could be.

Ultimately, from Marcel Proust's point of view, it was of slight importance that the Duchesse de Guermantes was a member of the aristocracy. He analyzed her thoughts and motives with the same depth as he did those of the cook Françoise, and his purpose was identical: he wished to understand more fully the human species. He finally concluded that Oriane and all other persons had essentially the same needs, desires and frailties. I would also add that he used knowledge of himself to help understand other people. Inevitably, his own social class became involved, but this was the case of other modernist writers who generalized from their own bourgeois, subjective point of view.[1] This limitation would eventually cause some critics and authors to question the validity of modernism, and in this way they opened the door to postmodernism.

In spite of Proust careful and profound analysis, some of his upper-class friends and acquaintances contributed themselves to the myth that the *Recherche* was primarily social in intent. Throughout the 1920s, they published numerous articles and books where they attempted to show a connection between actual persons that they knew and the upper-class characters of Proust's novel. This extraliterary type of commentary eventually exhausted itself, but it played into the hands of certain critics of the *Recherche* who were all to eager to classify Proust's novel as superficial and therefore negligible.

In Spanish America this polemic concerning the social intent of the *Recherche* spawned a critical and narrative debate over its possible relation with New World literature, which I will examine here. We will then see how a few writers, particularly of the Boom period, tried to reconcile Proust's work and Spanish American literature, and how others used the *Recherche* to defend French influences in general and the artistic freedom of all writers, but not everyone was convinced.

A Debate over the Appropriateness of Proust's Work as a Model for Spanish America

As we saw in chapter 1, several critics in the New World, such as Magdalena Petit, Marta Vergara, and Alone in Chile and Francisco Ayala in Argentina, felt compelled to defend Proust and his work on social grounds. They wished to show that he was neither a snob nor servile and that *Le côté de Guermantes* was more valuable for its psychological analysis than for its portrayal of high society.

Contrary to such efforts the Guatemalan writer Mario Monteforte Toledo in an article of 1949, "Marcel Proust, profundo superficial," tried to prove that the author of the *Recherche* was essentially superficial, and he labeled him "a great historian of the European capitalist society" (254).[2] The motivation for this belated attack becomes apparent at the end of the article where the author revealed his concern for the effects of the influence of the *Recherche*. He considered this literary relation especially pernicious and condemned it broad terms:

> For this reason I am surprised that it still influences many writers of Spanish America and that it influences them in the worst sense: by causing them to invent classes or persons that are not representative nor transcendent in our time and place.

These remarks allege that the social facet of Proust's novel had been very influential during the early period and had remained so until the late 1940s. Although one can detect in *El cántico espiritual* and *Ifigenia* characters from the upper classes (particularly in those chapters that take place in Paris), the social aspect of these novels was so minor that I scarcely mentioned it. In other works, such as *La vuelta de las horas* [The Reversal of Time] (1933), which is set in Paris, and *A batallas de amor . . . campo de pluma* [For Battles of Love . . . a Field of Feathers], which occurs near Buenos Aires, upper-class characters and themes play a larger role. But, even here, the authors generally used as a source more their own experience in high society than Proust's text, which had merely legitimized this subject and had shown how it might be treated.[3]

Only in one work of the late 1930s have I found Proust's clear and unequivocal presence with regard to the subject of high society, but this text is not fictional. In his memoirs, *Tiempos iluminados* [Illustrious Times] (1939), Enrique Larreta refers explicitly to Proust. He tells how, when he was a diplomat in France before World War I, he attended some of the same Parisian salons as had Proust. The Argentine notes that he never heard anyone speak at that time of this French author, because he had already withdrawn from society in order to work on his novel. But, in retrospect by reading the *Recherche* Larreta was able to recapture some of his own memories of the period:

> Para formarse idea cabal de lo que fue uno de esos salones literarios en el París de entonces, nada mejor que abrir un libro de Proust. Siempre que releo, yo mismo esas páginas prodigiosas, vuelvo a vivir los días no muy lejanos, por cierto, de aquella era completamente abolida, vuelvo a sentirme el rumor de las charlas. (1958, 559)

> [In order to form an accurate idea of what one of those literary salons of the Paris of that period was like, there is nothing better than to open up one of Proust's volumes. Whenever I myself reread those prodigious pages, I live again those certainly not so distant days of that completely obliterated time, I hear again the sound of its conversations.]

In the same text, Larreta talks about several of Proust's friends and acquaintances, that he himself had the opportunity to meet: Jacques Emile Blanche, the Comtesse Greffulhe and Gaston Calmette. He describes, in particular, Anna de Noailles, whom he considered to be a symbol of the elegant Paris that existed before the War. At one point Larreta even makes her resemble Proust's character the Duchesse de Guermantes by showing the curiosity of other persons about the feasibility of her appearance at a particular salon:

en la tertulia de Madame Bulteau me fue dado conocer a la Condesa de Noailles, el orgullo de aquel salón, su adorno mayor, su mayor atractivo, su ídolo. Muchos eran los que sólo acudían a esas reuniones por la esperanza de encontrarla, de escucharla. ¿Vendrá? ¿No vendrá?

[at Madame Bulteau's social gathering I had the opportunity to meet the Countess of Noailles, the pride of that salon, its principal adornment, its greatest attraction, its idol. Many people attended those gatherings merely in the hope of finding her, of listening to her. Will she come or won't she?]

From the years that immediately preceded Monteforte Toledo's article, I have discovered no Spanish American novels that specifically followed *Le côté de Guermantes*. For this reason, I find it difficult to imagine who were the "many writers of Spanish America" who continued to invent classes or persons that the Guatemalan might have considered to be atypical, false or inauthentic. In his own Central American environment, I know of only one writer related to Proust with whom he had actual contact: the Costa Rican, Yolanda Oreamuno. She received in Guatemala in 1948 (the year immediately after Monteforte Toledo) the Premio Centroamericano 15 de septiembre for her novel *La ruta de su evasión* [The Route of Their Escape].[4]

Obviously, this innovative, modernist work has many Proustian elements, but these are more closely tied to the psychological manner of the *Recherche*, as I will show in chapter 4. In terms of social strata, most of Oreamuno's characters belong to the urban lower middle class. There are, however, two exceptions: Elena and her father, Fernando Viales. These two characters were certainly unusual for any Spanish American novel during the late 1940s, but they find their justification within Oreamuno's text. Fernando was of French origin and was very wealthy. Dissatisfied with the submissiveness of Hispanic women in general and of his *criolla* wife in particular, he raised Elena as a free spirit and he encouraged her whims. Here, we can see one aspect of Oreamuno's critique of timid women, but also a facet of her own personality which struggled to be free. As for the two upper-class characters themselves, they have few traits that can be called Proustian. I would also point out that the absence of large social gatherings in *La ruta de su evasión* further distinguishes this novel from *Le côté de Guermantes*.

Apparently Mario Monteforte Toledo and other Marxist critics, who in general had a limited knowledge of the *Recherche*, assumed that all of Proust's influence was somehow contaminated by the upper classes and was, therefore, counterrevolutionary and detrimental to Spanish American literature and culture.[5] Another aspect of their critique can be observed in the book *Imperialismo y cultura (La política en la inteligencia argentina)* (1957) by Juan José Hernández Arregui. This Argentine sociology professor focused his attention upon Proust's distinction between art and life and concluded that the author of the *Recherche* was an extreme case of the type of artist who wished to live apart from society. In Hernández Arregui's view, such isolation implied Proust's bourgeois decadence, which could have an adverse effect on Argentine intellectuals, such as Ernesto Sábato, whose case is examined specifically.

This leftist interpretation of Proust and the alleged negative impact of his influence upon Spanish American literature inevitably led to a debate, which took place orally, as well as in written form. A manifestation of both can be seen through an article that Virgilio Piñera published in the Cuban newspaper *Revolución* on 5 February 1960 (scarcely a year after Fidel Castro's triumph). In "Después de la novela social" [After the Social Novel] and using the pseudonym "El Escriba" [The Scribe], Piñera recounted how at a public forum at the Casa de las Américas Miguel Angel Asturias asserted that the *novela social* was the only type of work appropriate for New World literature. When asked if the *Recherche* could be considered "social," the Guatemalan novelist answered categorically "no." Using his article as a response, Piñera defended Marcel Proust in order to show the limitations of socialist realism. He pointed out, for example, that Proust had carefully examined mankind and in particular the "agonizante sociedad francesa" [dying French society], which came to an end during World War I. For the Cuban author, the distinction made by Asturias between describing a decadent society and portraying a society in the process of liberation was of no real substance and simply involved splitting hairs. Thus he concluded: "Proust, like Balzac, like Dickens, like Stendhal, is also one who reflects his time, therefore, he is a commentator on the society of his time, and his novel is as social as *Hombres de maíz* [Men of Corn] or as *Los de abajo* [The Underdogs]".

In the Spanish American novel after 1960, we can find echoes of the leftist critique of Proust, as well as a defense of the *Recherche* and its possible influence or literary example. Both positions can be seen is *El buen salvaje* [The Noble Savage] (1964) by Eduardo Caballero Calderón. This Colombian author, who had perhaps been criticized for his upper-class perspective and for the strong influence of Proust in his first book *Caminos subterráneos* [Underground Paths] (1936), took a defensive stance.[6] The aspiring novelist in *El buen salvaje,* who is of a leftist persuasion, claims that no Spanish American can write successfully a social novel in the manner of Marcel Proust. He specifically asks himself, "¿Por qué fracasa en América todo intento de novela que se desarrolla en medios sociales elevados? ¿Por qué la novela de Proust resultaría profundamente cursi si se escribiera en la Argentina o en Colombia?" [Why does every novelistic attempt that transpires in elevated social circles fail in Spanish America? Why would Proust's novel prove to be extremely pretentious if it were written in Argentina or Colombia?] (1979, 198). This attitude might seem to be anti-Proustian, but Caballero Calderón cast doubt upon it himself by having his weak-willed and contradictory character attempt to write a novel about the upper classes where he even follows Proust in some ways. This proposed work *El rey Midas,* whose focal point is a wealthy man's funeral and the thoughts of his mourners, of course, reminds us of other writers including García Márquez, but when the fictional author considers different types of characters he thinks precisely in Proustian terms. Concerning a woman from the upper middle class that he had just met, he writes in his notebook:

> Se me plantearía con ella un problema que me preocupa desde hace tiempo. Ella es una señora burguesa, pero la absoluta inconsciencia de su estado social la priva de todo dinamismo sicológico. Es una Madame Verdurin que ignora a la Duquesa de Guermantes y está contenta de sí misma. (204)

> [I could explore with her a problem that has concerned me for a long time. She is a bourgeois woman, but the total unconsciousness of her social state deprives her of any psychological dynamism. She is a Mme. Verdurin who is unaware of the Duchesse de Guermantes and is satisfied with herself.]

During the 1950s (the period between Monteforte Toledo's article and Caballero Calderón's novel), works on high society paradoxically became more frequent, but I would not consider all of these texts failures or even extremely pretentious. The Argentine, Manuel Mujica Láinez, in fact, specialized in this type of literature. Following the example of his older friend and mentor Enrique Larreta, Mujica Láinez created his so-called "saga de la sociedad porteña" [saga of Buenos Aires high society]. These works were quite popular in Argentina and warranted the praise of Enrique Anderson Imbert, who said of Mujica Láinez in *Los ídolos* (1953), *La casa* (1954), and *Los viajeros* [The Travelers] (1955), "he has fictionalized, with a Proustian nostalgia, irony, and elegance, the search for a lost golden age, that of the upper crust, in an oligarchical Argentina" (1974, 2:292).

In these novels we find characters that bear a distinct resemblance to Proust's aristocrats. The elegant, but already elderly Duma is a fine example, as a reviewer of *Los ídolos* noted in *La Nación:* "Tía Duma . . . dazzles and captivates the narrator just as the Duchesse de Guermantes made Marcel Proust a slave of her prestige . . . " (1953). At times the influence of Proust upon the novels by Mujica Láinez is very striking. The description of Duma at the Opera in Buenos Aires clearly follows Proust's depiction of the Duchesse de Guermantes at the Opéra in Paris. Both authors transform the elegant woman into a type of bird because of the feathers that she is wearing. We read in *Le côté de Guermantes:* "la duchesse n'avait dans les cheveux qu'une simple aigrette qui dominant son nez busqué et ses yeux à fleur de tête, avait l'air de l'aigrette d'un oiseau" [the Duchess wore in her hair only a simple egret feather, which rising above her arched nose and prominent eyes, had the appearance of the plumed head of a bird] (1954, 2:53). Citing his mother, the narrator of *Los ídolos* remarks:

> Me había descrito la torera de brillantes de la tía de Gustavo y su tocado de plumas de ave del paraíso. . . . Por eso . . . la mujer anciana que se detenía para señalarme un pájaro o una nube desaparecía para dejar su sitio a aquella evocación espléndida, a aquel ser mitad ave y mitad joya que sonreía en el oro de un "avant-scène". . . . (1976, 110)

> [She had described to me the diamond fitted jacket of Gustavo's aunt and her headdress with bird of paradise feathers. . . . Thus . . . the aging woman who stopped to point out a bird or a cloud disappeared to leave in her place that splendid evocation, that half-bird and half-bejeweled creature that smiled in the gold of a proscenium. . . .]

However, in this case, as well as in general, Mujica Láinez did not merely imitate or reproduce what he found in Proust's text. He was careful to add an affective distance. Although the Argentine wished to draw a parallel between the Paris of the 1890s and Buenos Aires at the turn of the century, he chose to present the results of imagination rather than the description of a specific reality. For this reason, the narrator acknowledges the age of the woman standing before him and suggests the influence of his mother's idealized reminiscences and of his own admiration for Duma's nephew Gustavo.[7]

To some extent, Mujica Láinez wished to attribute to the wealthy family of Buenos Aires the same aristocratic manner found in *Le côté de Guermantes*. He came closest to this ideal in *La casa,* but even here he did not dare to make his rich *porteños* [residents of Buenos Aires] too much like Proust's nobles. He was well aware of their differences and preferred not to look too closely. The same is true of the social gatherings depicted in this novel. Although there are numerous references to them in the text, the Argentine author hesitated to show them directly and always found a way to create a distance. The reader may almost have the impression of being like the elderly Clara or the son's tutor, Krohg, who spied from upstairs upon the elegant hosts and their guests as they stolled from the dining room to the parlor. The only meal that is in fact described in detail was so intimate that two aged and rather ludicrous cousins were invited.

In order to portray the upper-class family from Buenos Aires, Mujica Láinez (like Proust in the early part of *Le côté de Guermantes*) was especially careful in his selection of a narrator, one that was generally favorable and credible, yet at the same time so naive that he could easily gloss over the flaws of the wealthy. The subjectivity of Proust's narrator, who was guided more by his feelings and impressions at a particular moment than by what other people might believe, seems to have provided the model, which Mujica Láinez freely adapted to his own needs and purposes. In *Los ídolos* the narrator's poorly understood homosexual feelings for Gustavo color all, including his view of the rich boy's family. In *La casa* the prospect of imminent demolition causes the mansion, which narrates the text, to show her glories of the past in their best conceivable light. The case of *Los viajeros* is somewhat different, but here the distancing is even more obvious. The narrator, Miguel, an orphan member of the poorest branch of the family, describes this motley group with considerable irony and humor.

Miguel's attitude and perspective are especially evident in his description of the principal social gathering found in *Los viajeros*. For example, using a Proust-like impressionism to depict the arrival of the wealthy members of the family, he says that because of their fancy cars and fur coats they resembled circus animals being brought in shiny cages. He then reminds the reader of the elegant description of Duma cited above and parodies this fragment by noting of her sister Ema: "era un frágil y rebelde animal mítico, mitad zorro y mitad cuervo" [she was a fragile and rebellious mythical animal, half fox and half crow] (1955, 188).

In some ways, Manuel Mujica Láinez and Marcel Proust were very similar in their modernist tastes, so we should not be surprised that their works so often resemble each other.[8] Just the same, the Argentine writer always tried to justify the similarity within the context of his novels. Like Swann, the narrator of *Los viajeros* compared persons to paintings, but in Miguel's case he had studied museum guidebooks for many years in preparation for the family's elusive trip to Europe. Thus, in spite of his lack of direct experience with the paintings themselves, Miguel could closely resemble the highly cultivated Swann. Of the aristocratic members of his *porteño* family at the social gathering, he writes:

> ellos reprodujeron para mí algo semejante a la tela oficial que presenta a la familia de Felipe V, de Louis-Michel Van Loo, en el Museo del Prado, por la distribución de los personajes y la suntuosidad borbónica de las actitudes . . . [se] formó ese cuadro con otros cuadros, pues cada uno de mis tíos me evocaba a un pintor distinto—Tío Fermín, al Greco; Tía Duma, a Largillière. . . . (198–199)

> [they reproduced for me something analogous to the official canvas that presents the family of Philip V, by Louis-Michel Van Loo, in the Prado Museum, due to the arrangement of the persons involved and the Bourbonic sumptuousness of their poses . . . only that this portrait was composed of

other portraits, since each of my uncles or aunts evoked for me a different painter—Uncle Fermín, El Greco, Aunt Duma, Largillière. . . .]

This use of art, of course, helped to spiritualize Mujica Láinez's upper-class characters, just like Proust's. Moreover, it demonstrates the Argentine's profound connection with the aestheticism typical of modernist literature. Let me also point out that, because he was an art critic for many years, this type of description was very natural for him.

In reality, Manuel Mujica Láinez, who had traveled with his family to France immediately after Proust's death and studied for two years at a Parisian *lycée,* would have preferred to emulate Marcel Proust even more. But, the nature of Argentine culture did not allow him to do this. Therefore, it was not until his novel about the Italian renaissance, *Bomarzo* (1962), that Mujica Láinez felt free enough to depict the type of refinement that he himself admired. We can observe, for example, how the social gatherings in this novel are presented with a purely aesthetic sense and without the distance or irony which typified the description of social events in his saga of the Argentine oligarchy.

Finally, I should mention that Mujica Láinez's interest in high society and in Proust remained with him until the end of his career. In his last novel *El escarabajo* (1982) he showed in the course of the extremely long life of his bejeweled scarab, which narrates the text, numerous scenes of aristocratic elegance. After passing from the Egyptians, Greeks and Romans to the troops of Charlemagne and a rewritten scene from *Bomarzo,* the scarab eventually reaches the hands of a few of Proust's acquaintances: the actress Sarah Bernhardt, the Comte Robert de Montesquiou, and the Argentine, Gabriel Iturri (as is well-known, these persons served as models for la Berma, Charlus, and Jupien in the *Recherche*). In this portion of *El escarabajo,* young Marcel Proust also appears, but he is snubbed by the Count, who considers him a mere social climber and predicts that he will never become a serious writer.

Obviously, the work of Manuel Mujica Láinez was not readily accepted by writers and critics from the political left. His favorable, albeit ironic portrait of high society seemed to be a modernist apology for it. Some of the reviewers of *Los ídolos* were quick to label this book: "superficial," "falso," "inauténtico," or "europeo." After the publication of *La casa,* David Viñas concluded that because most of its characters were already dead the same must be true of Mujica Láinez (1954). Since most of the disfavorable reviewers did not detect the Proustian connection, they did not attribute the Argentine's alleged inauthenticity to the influence of the French novelist. Mario Benedetti, who did notice the relation, did not blame Proust *per se.* Instead, he concluded that Mujica Láinez had not learned well the lessons of the *Recherche* and had failed to apply them

(1956). In spite of such negative assessments, time and his subsequent works have largely vindicated this Argentine, who may be considered one of the most Proustian writers for all of Spanish America and who has shown other novelists how it is possible to use the *Recherche* to good literary advantage.

ATTEMPTS AT RECONCILIATION: SPANISH AMERICANS IN PARIS AND PROUSTIANS IN SPANISH AMERICA

As José Donoso explains in his book *Historia personal del "Boom,"* about 1960, a new generation of Spanish American writers began to emerge. These young authors were dissatisfied with the regionalist literature of their respective countries because it remained tied to the realist-naturalist method of objective observation, a simple style and structure, and the use of merely national subjects. In search of a greater artistic freedom and a truly universal and profound literature, they looked to as models the leading and most innovative authors of Occidental narrative: James Joyce, Marcel Proust, Virginia Woolf, Franz Kafka, Thomas Mann, and William Faulkner. These figures were the ones that have been associated with the term "modernism" because they wanted to go beyond the positivism of the nineteenth century through a more subjective type of literature. It was their goal to penetrate into human consciousness, to show all humanity as one, to escape from the limitations of time and space, and to be free in their experimentation with literary forms.

In the search of the young Spanish American writers for universality, they crossed borders of various kinds and met persons of a like mind. Julio Cortázar, who had left Peronist Argentina for France during the 1950s suggested by his place of residence that a common spiritual capital for Spanish American writers could be Paris. He was eventually followed there by Mario Vargas Llosa, Carlos Fuentes, and Gabriel García Márquez, whose stays were of varying lengths. Because of the quality and success of their narrative works, these writers, along with José Donoso himself (who preferred to live close to the publishing houses of Spain) came to be known as the Boom generation. A few other important authors, such as Ernesto Sábato and Mario Benedetti, approached the manner and success of the big five, but they were not as cosmopolitan and were never universally accepted by the literary critics of Europe and the United States, who helped to create the Boom.

Politically speaking, at least at first, the Boom writers were liberal and supported the Revolution of Fidel Castro in Cuba. Unlike Mujica Láinez, for the most part they were critical of the oligarchies of their respective countries and supported a democratization of these, if not a radical transformation of them. Nonetheless, they admired the intellectual life that the middle and upper classes of France had been able to produce. This cultural environment was especially apparent in the work of Marcel Proust, who had captured through literature decades before the artistic and aristocratic salons of Paris. Such a world was a very tempting model for at least some of the Boom writers, who were also enticed by its elegance. But, they had to be careful how they presented a similar world in their works. Otherwise, like Mujica Láinez, they would be attacked by the critics from the left. To this end they employed at least two strategies which allowed them to create authentic or credible Spanish American characters in sophisticated, elegant social situations. The first of these approaches was to set at least part of the novelistic action in Paris and to have the Spanish American characters interact with wealthy and refined persons that lived there. The second was to use a Proust-like subjectivity for the Spanish American narrator and/or characters who remained in the New World. But, in either case such an installation into a Proustian view of reality often implied parody and other postmodern elements.

According to Julie Jones in her recent book *A Common Place: The Representation of Paris in Spanish American Fiction* (1998), the use of the French capital as a setting for New World texts was fashionable at the end of the nineteenth century when Spanish American *modernismo* was in vogue but lay dormant for several decades until the appearance of *Rayuela* [Hopscotch] in 1963. Nonetheless, some of the Proustian novels that I have mentioned—*El cántico espiritual, Ifigenia* and *La vuelta de las horas*—take place at least in part in Paris, but were not cited in the book by Jones. The same is true for *El buen salvaje,* which was published shortly after *Rayuela.* In portions of the Colombian text can be found a few scenes of high society life, as when the protagonist attends events at the embassy, but many others show the bohemian side of Paris, as is the case in Cortázar's famous novel.

Curiously in *Rayuela,* which was indeed the first Boom novel set in the French capital, we find almost exclusively this type of ambiance.[9] Just the same, I would not say that Proust is absent. On the contrary, in regard to social life, as well as art, time, memory, and writing (which we will examine later), the *Recherche* is present, at least by opposition. I will even dare to claim that the parties described in *Rayuela* parody the social events depicted in the *Recherche.* Not only are both disproportionately long (in comparison with the remainder of the narration) and appear to stop time for the portrayal of the social group, but also both involve conversation and listening to music. Significantly, some of the same topics are discussed: memory, love and literature. Even la Maga's recollection of Montevideo and description of her first sexual experiences resemble (because of their subject matter and audacity) the discussion by Charlus of pederasty in *La prisonnière* (Compare *Rayuela* 1986, 192–93 and the *Recherche*, 3:296–310).

Obviously, Cortázar was dealing with a different social class and his world view was very distinct from that of Proust. But, this difference itself forms the very basis for the parody and explains why the vulgarity of Babs contrasts so sharply with the refinement of the Duchesse de Guermantes.

Following the appearance of *Rayuela* and *El buen salvaje*, Alejo Carpentier wrote *El recurso del método* [Reasons of State] (1974), which is not only set largely in Paris, but is also much closer to Proust in terms of social class and ambiance. Although (according to his then recently published lecture on the *Recherche*) he did not believe that Proustian characters could be easily transposed to the New World, he incorporated into the Parisian sections of his novel real persons that Proust knew and characters from the *Recherche*.[10] Having written his novel within the context of communist Cuba, Carpentier wished to present both sides of the controversy surrounding the *Recherche*. The proponents of this work seemed to desire social status while its detractors pointed out the human cost that this personal ambition might entail. For this reason, the Cuban author juxtaposed within the life of a single character the refinement of Proust's world and the barbarism associated with Spanish American dictatorships and ruthless political repression.

On the Proustian side of the coin, it was not by chance that Carpentier drew attention to Reynaldo Hahn. As we saw in chapter 1, while living and working in Caracas, Carpentier devoted one of his early "Letra y solfa" articles to the close friendship between Proust and Hahn and another to their correspondence. In *El recurso del método*, the Primer Magistrado calls Hahn on the telephone:

> Acaso sería oportuno llamar a Reynaldo Hahn, su amable y ameno "paisano" de Puerto Cabello. El compositor acudió al teléfono, hablándole en su grato español de acento venezolano, singularizado . . . por unos giros de marcada inflexión rioplatense. (1974, 94)

> [Perhaps it would be timely to call Reynaldo Hahn, his friendly and pleasant "countryman" from Puerto Cabello. The composer came to the telephone, speaking to him in his pleasing Spanish with a Venezuelan accent, marked by . . . certain expressions of a pronounced River Plate inflexion.]

It is also worth mentioning that Carpentier took advantage of his vast knowledge of music to allude to a few of Hahn's compositions and to suggest that one of these was inspired by the Spanish American tropics:

antes de haber escrito sus sublimes coros para la *Esther* de Racine, había estrenado, años atrás, una finísima ópera llena de nostalgias del Trópico natal, ya que su acción transcurría en paisajes escénicos que en todo evocaban la costa venezolana, conocida en la niñez, aunque se tratara . . . de un "idilio polinesio". . . . (23–24)

[before having written his sublime choruses for *Esther* by Racine, he had premiered, years ago, a very fine opera full of nostalgia for his native tropics, since its action transpired in scenic landscapes that in everything evoked the Venezuelan coast, known in his childhood, even though its subject was . . . a "Polynesian idyll". . . .]

Carpentier's principal character wishes to be accepted by the social and artistic circles that Proust had described. The Primer Magistrado is familiar with the music by Vinteuil and owns paintings by Elstir. I note that these two artists existed only in the *Recherche* and exemplified the type of art that the young Proustian protagonist hoped to create. Also like the socially ambitious snobs in the French novel, Carpentier's character tries to climb the ladder of Parisian high society. Invitations by another of Proust's characters represent an important milestone: "se había abierto camino que . . . lo había conducido . . . por tres veces a las veladas musicales de Madame Verdurin" [he had made inroads that . . . had taken him . . . on three occasions to the musical evenings of Madame Verdurin] (96).

As a wealthy Spanish American and patron of the arts, the protagonist of *El recurso del método* would have been perfectly acceptable in some if not all of the upper-class salons of Proust's Paris. As I mentioned above, Reynaldo Hahn performed as a young pianist in many, and two Argentine writer-diplomats—Lucio V. Mansilla and Enrique Larreta—had been welcomed in a few of the best. Unfortunately, Carpentier's somewhat refined *rastaquouère* has his barbarous side. His wealth and social position depend upon his being dictator of a small Spanish American nation and in order to retain power he believes that he must be ruthless. In the second part of the novel the Primer Magistrado returns to his country where he commits major atrocities while crushing a rebellion. This cruel, unscrupulous method horrifies the French upper classes, and they close their doors to him. Several Proustian characters and acquaintances treat the dictator in a like manner:

Llamó por teléfono al Quai Conti de los gratos conciertos: la señora no estaba en casa. Llamó al violinista Morel, que lo felicitó por su regreso con el tono presuroso y evasivo de quien desea dar rápido término a una conversación. . . . Llamó a Brichot, el profesor de la Sorbona: "Estoy casi ciego"—le dijo—: *"pero me leen los periódicos"*. Y colgó. (93)

[He called by telephone to the Quai Conti, where he had heard the delightful concerts: Madame was not at home. He called the violinist Morel, who congratulated him for his return with the hasty and evasive tone of one who wishes to end quickly a conversation. . . . He called Brichot, the professor of the Sorbonne: "I am almost blind," he told him, "*but they read me the newspapers.*" And he hung up.]

Here, the intertextual relation between *El recurso del método* and the *Recherche* is very explicit. To understand this passage thoroughly, the reader must realize that the woman in question is Madame Verdurin, that the violinist (who was the *protégé* and lover of Charlus) performed during a particular period at the Verdurins', and that the professor had been a member of the *petit clan* [Verdurin clique] for many years.

Some critics have asserted that Carpentier's numerous allusions to the *Recherche* imply that the Cuban novelist wished to parody this French work in the Oedipal desire of destroying his father Proust. But, Carpentier did not misread or swerve away from the *Recherche* as Bloom's cited category, Clinamen, would require. *El recurso del método* may in fact be called a parody in a postmodern sense because its author toys with Proust's text, but this relation is not primarily critical or merely ludic.[11] The references to the *Recherche* do not show the emptiness of the European aristocratic world to a greater extent than Proust had already done. Their function is to demonstrate the absurd contradiction in the life of the Primer Magistrado: how could such a brute ever be refined? As Graziella Pogolotti suggested in her early review of *El recurso del método*, Carpentier was far more interested in showing the weaknesses of the dictator than in attacking Proust's work itself: "Please understand that the criticism displayed in this irony is not directed against that end-of-the-century culture, but rather to place in relief the incongruity with respect to reality that the Primer Magistrado bears" (1974, 127). Using the terms of Linda Hutcheon, Carpentier installed his character in the modernist world of Proust's novel in order to call into question in a postmodern way the character's participation in that world.[12]

To a large extent, the social structure and system which Carpentier very consciously borrowed from Proust's novel serves as a judge and jury for the dictator's cruel actions. It is precisely for this reason that the Parisians from the *Recherche* ostracize him. Even though Carpentier greatly admired Proust's work and praised the manner in which it had helped Spanish American writers like himself understand and depict their own reality in a more subtle and profound manner, he could not in any way condone political repression or a system that sacrificed the many so that a few could enjoy privilege. Specifically, in the case of the Primer Magistrado, his desire to become part of a Proust-like world was no excuse. Likewise the character's willingness to imitate blindly a European model and to forget the deep meaning of his own culture was unacceptable. In chapter 7, I will return to this question of authenticity in *El recurso del método* and show how it is involved in a dialogue on Proustian memory.

Among the writers of the Boom generation itself, one in particular was very interested in the Proustian subject of high society, José Donoso. Like Mujica Láinez, this Chilean placed his upper-class characters in the New World and used as a second strategy for reconciliation a Proust-like subjectivity in order to make such persons appear credible within their national context. We find, for example, in *El obsceno pájaro de la noche* [The Obscene Bird of the Night] (1970) that mere references to the European education and aristocratic class consciousness of Don Jerónimo de Azcoitía are not sufficient. In order to underscore Don Jerónimo's refinement and to elevate his exquisiteness to almost mystifying proportions, Donoso had to show them through the very subjective eyes of Humberto and his father, who was obsessed by the upper classes and idolized Don Jerónimo. At one point, the relation with Proust becomes distinctly intertextual when Humberto's words echo those of Proust's narrator:

> De pronto mi padre me dio un tirón de la mano. Yo seguí la dirección de esa mirada suya a la que uní la mía. Por la vereda avanzaba entre el gentío alegre de esa mañana un hombre alto, fornido pero gracioso, de cabello muy rubio, de mirada airosa encubierta por algo que yo interpreté como un elegante desdén, vestido *como jamás soñé que ningún hombre osara vestir:* todo era gris, muy claro, perla, paloma, humo, zapatos alargados, polainas de gamuza y unos guantes ni grises ni cáscara ni amarillos ni blancos, piel pura, suavísima, casi viva. (1972, 104, my emphasis)

> [Suddenly my father pulled me by the hand. I followed the direction of that gaze of his to which I joined mine. Along the pavement among the cheerful crowd of that morning there approached a tall, hefty but attractive man with very blond hair, with a graceful expression veiled by something that I interpreted as an elegant disdain, dressed *as I never dreamed any man might dare to dress:* everything was in gray, but very light, the color of pearls, doves, smoke, his elongated shoes, chamois gaiters and a pair of gloves that were neither gray nor eggshell, nor yellow nor white, pure hide, very soft, almost alive.]

Similarly, in *A l'ombre des jeunes filles en fleurs* the protagonist admired from a distance a young member of the Guermantes family, Robert de Saint-Loup, who was also more daring in his dress than any man that he had ever known:

je vis, grand, mince, le cou dégagé, la tête haute et fièrement portée, passer un jeune homme aux yeux pénétrants et dont la peau était aussi blonde et les cheveux aussi dorés que s'ils avaient absorbé tous les rayons du soleil. Vêtu d'une étoffe souple et blanchâtre *comme je n'aurais jamais cru qu'un homme eût osé en porter*. . . . (1: 728–729, my emphasis)

[I saw coming by, tall, slender, with his collar open, his head held proudly erect, a young man with piercing eyes and whose skin was as fair and his hair as golden as if they had imbibed all of the rays of the sun. Dressed in a pliant and whitish fabric *as I would have never believed that a man might dare to wear*. . . .]

Going beyond the obvious similarities due to color and exquisite taste, I would like to emphasize the same subjective thrust but varying degrees of it used by the two narrators. Although Proust's young protagonist was fascinated by the elegance and refinement of the upper classes and was affected by his own subjectivity, he was not as obsessed as Humberto, who had been contaminated by his father's groveling attitude. The reference to following "esa mirada" [that gaze] is indeed significant because it implies not only a personal perspective but also an increased level of deformation. As in the case of Mujica Láinez's narrators, this change in affective distance helps to justify within a Spanish American context all that Humberto says.

A particular term that has often been applied to Proust, "vision," is very pertinent here.[13] As Carpentier pointed out in his lecture, the French novelist taught Spanish Americans a new way of "seeing." We also recall that Proust described his novel as a type of lens and suggested how it might help its readers understand themselves better. He said in *Le temps retrouvé*, "mon livre n'étant qu'une sorte de ces verres grossissants comme ceux que tendait à un acheteur l'opticien de Combray; mon livre, grâce auquel je leur fournirais le moyen de lire en eux-mêmes" [my book being only a sort of magnifying glass like those which the optician in Combray handed to a customer, my book thanks to which I would provide them with the means of reading within themselves] (3:1033). The modernist implications of Proust's attitude are of course obvious. He used his subjectivity as the basis for his totalization.

In *Casa de campo* [Country House] (1978), José Donoso carried the idea of aristocratic vision still further and in doing so parodied *Le côté de Guermantes* and other portions of the *Recherche*. As in his previous works beginning with *Coronación* (1958) and *Este domingo* [This Sunday] (1966) and similar to Proust, Donoso portrayed in *Casa de campo* a world composed of only the wealthy and their servants. But, here the differences between these two social groups are more extreme and lead to caricature.

To a large extent, *Casa de campo* may be considered a historiographic metafiction as Linda Hutcheon has described this postmodern sub-genre. Her remarks concerning such works also apply in this case: "its theoretical self-awareness of history and fiction as human constructs is made the grounds for its rethinking and reworking of the forms and contents of the past" (1988, 5). Although Proust is not the only novelist that Donoso enshrined in order to undermine his work, he is certainly an important one. As the Chilean himself admitted, the attention that he paid to names in this work was Proustian in origin.[14] Just as the narrator of the third part of *Du coté de chez Swann*, "Nom de pays: le nom" [Place Names: The Name], tells how the names of Italian cities, such as Parme, affected his imagination when he was a child, Donoso chose the names of his aristocratic characters because of their romantically evocative power. But, even here we can detect his satiric intent because of the bizarre quality of many of the names: Higinio, Aglaée, and Clelia.

Donoso's parody of Proust is especially evident with regard to Celeste and her son Juvenal. The former, whose name ironically coincides with that of the French novelist's last housekeeper (whose book Donoso indubitably read) is so exquisite in her manner that she often brings to mind the Duchesse de Guermantes.[15] In this case, I cannot claim that she is more refined than Oriane, but Celeste's blindness puts into question the value and purpose of her exquisiteness, as well as the aristocratic subjectivity of all of the Ventura y Ventura. Even though, due to her excellent memory (which we can distantly associate with Proust) Celeste is able to move easily around the house and gardens during the family's vacation, she is totally helpless at the country house out of season.

In a similar manner Juvenal reflects all that is refined and decadent in a Proust-like world but carried to the extreme. In the chapter "La marquesa" [The Marchioness] Juvenal plays for his mother on the piano a piece by Liszt, somewhat like various characters in Proust's novel. Yet, being a twenty year old, his dependency upon his mother is even more surprising than that of the child protagonist of "Combray." Thus, we are amused when Juvenal demands a good-night kiss from his mother.

Besides using an obsessive narrator in *El obsceno pájaro de la noche* and a postmodern parody in *Casa de campo,* José Donoso created a Proustian fantasy in "El tiempo perdido" [Lost Time]. In spite of its general neglect by the critics, this *novelita* from *Cuatro para Delfina* (1982) offers Donoso's most complete narrative dialogue with Proust's text.[16] It inscribes numerous references to the characters, situations and ideas found in the *Recherche* and places a special emphasis on Proustian names.

Using a small group of devoted readers of Proust in Santiago, Donoso created the illusion of a *côté de Guermantes* in the New World. Being disgusted by what they consider the mediocrity of their native cultural environment, these persons consciously follow Proust's text as a canon or guide toward a more refined and aristocratic world: one in which real people are attributed names borrowed from the *Recherche*. In this way the Proustian readers, who have social as well as creative aspirations, hope to be treated as honored guests.[17]

Indubitably, from the first moment such efforts appear to be largely futile. Even though the readers of Proust chose persons from Santiago, who vaguely resembled the Duc and Duchesse de Guermantes, Madame Verdurin, Charlus, Odette, etc., the contrast between the Chileans who were assigned these names and Proust's actual characters is obvious to everyone except these devoted readers of the *Recherche* themselves. The so-called Duque or Basin is a typical example. Juanito Irisarri, indeed, comes from the local upper classes. He knows socially and politically influential people (such as the cultural *attaché* to the French Embassy), and he is married to a very elegant and refined woman. However, his custom of drinking in sordid night clubs and his propensity for getting into trouble with the police are so extreme that to attribute these to Basin's characteristic lack of sensibility is sheer blindess. Although we may suspect here a parody of Proust, there is even more of a satire of the Chileans themselves.

In the course of this dialogue with Proust, we as readers can observe how the carefully fabricated illusion disintegrates and how the narrator, who wanted to become a *petit Marcel* and desired to write his own Chilean version of *A la recherche du temps perdu,* is only able to complete the text that we are discussing: "El tiempo perdido." Part of his own disillusionment is like that of the Proustian protagonist himself. Similar to the latter, Héctor Muñoz de la Barra (as Donoso's narrator is really called) comes to know the Duquesa too well. This elegant woman, who is the only character that has a single name, Oriane, once invites Héctor home for lunch. Like an ordinary bourgeois woman, she then talks excessively about herself and seems even physically approachable. In passing, I should note that Donoso describes Oriane in a manner that apparently echoes Mujica Láinez, as well as Proust, for he compares her to a bird:

> levanté la vista, y con un vuelco del corazón reconcí el bello rostro de pájaro rubio de Oriane. . . . Levantó su mirada azul de *vitreaux* [*sic*] que cruzó con la mía . . . iluminando con su repentina sonrisa dorada su rostro maravilloso, y el mío, y el ámbito entero del gran almacén. (1982, 170)

> [I raised my line of sight, and with a tumbling of my heart I recognized the beautiful face of the blond, bird-like Oriane. . . . She raised her blue gaze of stained glass which crossed with mine . . . illuminating with her suddenly

golden smile her marvelous face, and mine, and the entire atmosphere of the department store.]

Another factor which contributes to Héctor's dismay is his utter failure in Paris. Sent there with a fellowship to write his thesis, "Influencia del Impresionismo en la visión novelística de Marcel Proust," he neither completes this study nor is he able to observe even from a distance anyone who resembles the Guermantes.

Upon returning to Santiago, Héctor realizes that his Proustian friends are no longer Proustian, but his greatest disillusionment occurs when he is invited to Basin's house. There he does not find the Oriane that he had so admired—she is now deceased—but, rather Basin's new wife, Madame Verdurin (Olga Fuad). This situation is clearly in dialogue with *Le temps retrouvé* where there is a similar marriage between an aristocrat and a member of the bourgeoisie, but in this case the Duque violates the Proustian canon because Madame Verdurin should have married Basin's brother, the Príncipe.

It is at this point and through the character of Madame Verdurin (Olga Fuad) that the essential meaning behind the text comes into focus. This upper middle-class woman, who had often hosted the Proustians in spite of their snide remarks about her, represents all that was most xenophobically limited in Chilean literature and art. Earlier in the text, she had expressed the opinion that reading the numerous volumes of *A la recherche du temps perdu* was "puro tiempo perdido" [a sheer waste of time]. Also she considered aesthetic European works associated with modernism, such as Proust's, a danger for Chilean authors. According to her, the refined manner of such works was not an appropriate model for the national writers and might corrupt "la autenticidad del estilo sencillo y del pensamiento de nuestros creadores" [the authenticity of the simple style and thought of our creators] (160).

This warning directed against Proust brings to mind the remarks by Mario Monteforte Toledo and Juan José Hernández Arregui, as well as the words of the protagonist of *El buen salvaje* and even those of the Chilean humorist Jenaro Prieto (which we saw in chapter 1). In this way Donoso's *novelita* also gave voice to those Spanish Americans who opposed Proust's influence or example.

As for his own personal opinion about the Proustian controversy, José Donoso was somewhat ambiguous in "El tiempo perdido." He allowed his most faithful Proustian to present both sides of the issue but then to fail in his illusion. Nonetheless, the very negative presentation of "la cosa nuestra" [our thing], which resembles certain remarks found in his *Historia personal del Boom* concerning the isolation and closed attitude of the Chilean generations that preceded his own, suggests that the author of "El tiempo perdido" sided more with the Proustians—no matter how foolish—than with their opponents.

As suggested above, in his *Historia personal del boom*, José Donoso explained how he and other members of his generation, such as Jorge Edwards, felt toward the narrow perspective of Chilean literature *c.* 1950. Critics and already established authors insisted that only a simple, realist approach to national subjects was appropriate. Both *criollistas* [regionalist authors] and the proponents of socialist realism criticized very severely young writers who treated subjects outside of the national borders or introduced elements that did not conform to the precepts of realism. Concerning the attitude of the socialist writers, Donoso added:

> the novel was supposed to be above all—besides unequivocally "ours" like the *criollistas* wanted—"important", "serious", an instrument that would be useful in a *direct* manner for social progress. Any attitude suggesting the unpleasant taste of something that could be branded "aesthetic", was an anathema. . . . Both the structure of the novel and its language had to be simple, flat, faded, sober and poor. (1984, 22)

In reaction to this point of view the young Chilean writers saw themselves as orphans and looked to modernist authors, like Proust and Joyce, along with those that had followed them, as preferable adoptive parents.

In this context the question of Proustian vision is especially meaningful. Like Manuel Mujica Láinez, José Donsoso saw his national environment as being all too common and did not want to reduce it further by merely showing it in a realist manner. The reference to *vitraux* [stained-glass windows] in the description of Oriane's eyes cited above, is very pertinent, as is Héctor's remark concerning his feelings for Oriane: "¡Pero no fue amor, sólo deslumbramiento, sentir su aliento como emblema de otros seres que existen de veras" [But it was not love, only being dazzled, feeling her breath like an emblem of other beings that actually exist] (208). Similar to his self-proclaimed Proustian narrator, José Donoso wished to show his world through a special type of glass, even though he realized that this implied a very subjective distortion. Proust, whose narrator described in detail stained-glass windows and showed how his own naive illusions had affected his vision of the Duchesse de Guermantes and her family, provided for Donoso a sample lens, which he was able to adjust to his own eyes and national situation. Over time Donoso had progressively deformed such a vision and began to parody Proust as well as himself. Thus, even though the Chilean started his career with a Proust-like vision (similar to that of the modernist Mujica Láinez), as he further distorted it through parody in *Casa de campo* and through a dialogical fantasy in "El tiempo perdido" he contributed to the development of postmodernism in Spanish America.

Near the end of his career Alejo Carpentier, who continued to defend Proust even while he served the Revolution of Fidel Castro, participated in this narrative discussion through his longest novel, *La consagración de la primavera* [The Rite of Spring] (1978). In this case, he did not use parody and indirectly showed through his faithfulness to Proust that he had never intended to destroy his parent. Mixing elements from his own past with fiction, he intertwined two stories about art and revolution, each of which is focused upon a single character and dialogues in specific ways with the first person narration of the French novelist.

In the one case, the Cuban Enrique recalls how, in spite of his upper-class family and training as an architect, he came to oppose the government of Gerardo Machado, fled from Cuba to Mexico, traveled to Europe and fought in the Spanish Civil War. Later, after returning to Cuba before the invasion of France by Adolf Hitler, he timidly supports the rebels against Fulgencio Batista, has to escape Havana to Caracas and returns after the triumph of Fidel Castro. Finally, he defends the Revolution by fighting against the Bay of Pigs invasion. The second case is that of the Russian dancer Vera, who recalls how she spent her life fleeing revolution across Europe and does not find peace even in Cuba after she arrives there with Enrique. I will return to the subject of art in chapter 5, but I will discuss here the question of social class and revolution.

It is not that Carpentier described either upper-class Cubans or French aristocrats in Proustian terms. In fact, it is almost as if he systematically avoided comparing Enrique's aunt with the Duchesse de Guermantes. Although she is a countess, her frivolity has none of the charm of Proust's famous duchess. She, in fact, more closely resembles the aristocratic characters of Tolstoy's novels. Symptomatically, Enrique's aunt has a natural aversion for the *Recherche*. Trying to appear more intellectual than the members of the Cuban bourgeoisie, she claims to have read Proust's early volumes, but she never proceeded beyond the *madeleine* episode. Of it she vulgarly remarks, "¡y cómo jode este hombre con la magdalena esa!" [and how this man pisses me off with that madeleine!] (1993, 56).

In contrast, the struggling protagonists Enrique and Vera have an obvious affinity for Proust. Upon returning to Havana, Enrique recalls with nostalgia (like Carpentier himself in the Spanish version of his lecture on Proust) the bookstore where he had discovered the *Recherche*: "andando un poco más me hallaba ante la librería del francés Morlhon, donde había trabado conocimiento, años atrás, con Swan, Saint-Loup, Albertina y Charlus. . ." [walking a little further I found myself in front of the bookstore of the Frenchman Morlhon, where I had become acquainted, years ago, with Swann, Saint-Loup, Albertine and Charlus. . ."] (206). Furthermore, both Enrique and Vera undergo memory experiences somewhat like those of the Proustian protagonist. Smells and tastes of la Habana Vieja remind Enrique of his childhood, while those of Paris evoke for Vera the time when she had lived and loved in that city. In this regard, I should point out that Carpentier avoided following all of the characteristics of Proustian memory. As we shall see in Chapter 8, he had already created in *Los pasos perdidos* [The Lost Steps] and *El recurso del método* memory experiences that were orthodox-ically Proustian. For this reason, neither the recollections of Havana nor those of Paris are presented in detail. I concede that in two segments Vera recovers her past in Russia, but in both cases Carpentier side-stepped the Proustian memory mechanism. For example, in the first instance, even though a traffic circle in southern France reminds Vera of a similar one in Russia, the past that she recalls is unrelated to the traffic circle itself.

Apparently, Alejo Carpentier wished to de-politicize Proust. His prin-cipal characters, who live both in Europe and Spanish America, are Proustian by nature and not merely because of their social class. Both Enrique and Vera, of course, were born and raised in bourgeois milieus, but their artistic temperaments allow them to transcend their social class and to ignore it. Throughout most of their lives, their political point of view was generally opposed: Enrique felt drawn toward revolution, while Vera constantly fled it. Nonetheless, due to circumstances related to their art, both welcome the triumph of Castro. In this way Carpentier's Proustians ultimately support the socialist revolution and demonstrate that one can be both Proustian and advocates for justice and radical political change. In this way Carpentier tried to reconcile Proust with a leftist perspective.

USING PROUST TO DEFEND THE INFLUENCE OF FRANCE AND THE CREATIVITY OF THE INDIVIDUAL

To some extent the viability of a Spanish American novel about high society in the manner of Proust is also bound to a larger question: What should be the role of French influences in Spanish American culture in general? This subject has been hotly debated, and some nationalistic leftists have claimed that all French and even European influences (with the paradoxical exception of Karl Marx) tend to be detrimental. Accord-ing to them, any attempt to follow the trends in European culture sepa-rates Spanish American intellectuals from their authentic roots and does not allow the national culture to develop in its own unique way.

On the other hand, many persons have defended the contributions of French culture by pointing out that since the decades that preceded the Revolution of 1789 numerous authors and artists from France have left a propitious legacy to Spanish America.[18] In general, the writers of the Boom generation, who followed the cosmopolitanism of the European modernists and often lived in Paris, implicitly ascribed to this view. We can observe their position especially well in the novel *Una familia lejana* [Distant Relations] (1980), which Carlos Fuentes developed within the context of the *Recherche*. Of the Proustian atmosphere found in this text Wendy Farris wrote:

> Meditations on the passage of time, the nostalgic mood in autumnal Paris, vistas of the city and its parks, friendships between the young and the old, and a number of long sentences that seem to postpone their endings, all recall *Remembrance of Things Past*. (1983, 179)

Along these same lines and tied to the strategy of setting part of the novel in Paris, I observe that the elderly French count, who tells his unusual story to the character Carlos Fuentes in an elegant Parisian restaurant (which is like Proust's favorite Ritz), is reminiscent of the aristocratic characters found in *Le côté de Guermantes*. Conde de Branly displays the same type of *mondanité* and wit. Also, like some of the representatives of the upper classes in the *Recherche*, his mansion is furnished with beautiful objects from the Empire period. Furthermore, his constant attempt to understand what is hidden behind words and gestures is very similar to that of the Proustian protagonist.

As for the French connection with Spanish America, the narrators of this novel make the point that it is longstanding and encompasses even family ties. The surname, Heredia, which is mentioned throughout the novel, not only binds the Mexican character, Hugo Heredia, and the French character Victor Heredia, it also alludes directly to a pre-Romantic Cuban poet who wrote in Spanish and a Parnassian poet who wrote in French but was also born in Cuba. The fact that both of these writers had the same name, José María de Heredia, encourages us to join together the first names of the French and Mexican Heredias, Victor and Hugo, and this combination designates one of France's most famous writers, Victor Hugo, who exerted a considerable influence on Spanish American literature during the nineteenth century.

Yet, more relevant than these nominal coincidences is the personal case of the Mexican character Hugo Heredia, which allows us to understand the defense by Fuentes of French-Spanish American cultural relations. Significantly, this Mexican archaeologist does not restrict his intellectual interests to the study of indigenous ruins. Hugo is also fascinated by France and has examined carefully the cultural implications of this attachment. Having taken courses at the Instituto Francés de América Latina in Mexico City and having married a woman of French origin, Hugo understands particularly well what he calls "ese extraño amor a Francia" [that strange love for France], which numerous Spanish Americans have felt. For him, French influence represents a bulwark against Spanish cultural domination and Anglo-Saxon economic-political hegemony. Also, according to Hugo, French reason serves as a corrective for the possible excesses of the New World temperament.

The decision by Fuentes to place his defense of French-Spanish American relations within a Proustian context can be observed in several ways throughout *Una familia lejana*. In chapter 4, I will discuss the Proustian elements involved in Branly's discovery of the strange friendship between the French and Mexican boys and the memory experience which convinces him not to intervene. For the present, I will merely point out that Hugo and Branly speak briefly about the *Recherche* near Cuernavaca, Mexico and that Proust's words concerning a painting by Gustave Moreau—"flores envenenadas entrelazadas con joyas preciosas" [poisonous flowers interlaced with precious jewels] (1980, 18)—set the stage for all that follows.

It is also worth mentioning that, for the Mexican novelist, the work by Proust has been closely associated with the very nature of literary relations. In a letter to Gloria Durán (1980, which has been quoted on occasion in reference to *Una familia lejana*), Fuentes says, "there is no literature without parents, no matter how much the mediocre critics in our countries demand such." He then cites as a bad example a statement, to which he himself lends no credence even though some United States scholars have attributed it to him, "he who reads Proust proustitutes himself." Thus, we can see why the author of *Una familia lejana* chose a Proustian context for his defense of the French connection because this novel is at least in part a response to "a sanctimonious literary chauvinist in México."[19] I would also add that this novel constitutes a defense of his cosmopolitanism and even that of the Boom generation. In *Myself and Others* Fuentes cites the same narrowminded Mexican critic and similar persons:

> A Marxist teacher once told me it was un-Mexican to read Kafka; a fascist critic said the same thing . . . and a rather sterile Mexican author gave a pompous lecture at the Bellas Artes warning that readers who read Proust would proustitute themselves (1990, 23).

The subject of high society and the acceptable role of French influences including Proust's can also be seen in *El amor en los tiempos del cólera*

[Love in the Time of Cholera] (1985) by Gabriel García Márquez.[20] One of the principal characters, Dr. Juvenal Urbino, is a member of the elite in a city along the Colombian coast. Near the end of the nineteenth century he travels to France to study medicine, but he also learns of the literature, music, and art of the time. When he returns to his old, proud city he brings with him his newly acquired knowledge and experience. There, Dr. Urbino promotes modernization in a scientific and cultural sense using his French model.

On numerous occasions, García Márquez's character and novel approach Marcel Proust and his world. In particular, Juvenal Urbino uses what he learned from the French novelist's father to reduce the effects of cholera. He simply applies the system of *cordones sanitarios* [quarantine lines] instituted by Adrien Proust (1986, 159). Furthermore, some of the technological firsts described in the Colombian novel are vaguely reminiscent of Proust. For example, similar to this French author, García Márquez depicted a person's impression of talking on the telephone.[21] Likewise, Juvenal Urbino's subscription to *Le Figaro* and his reading of the most recent works by Anatole France, Pierre Loti, and Paul Bourget can be seen as indirect allusions to Proust, who published numerous articles in that newspaper and who followed these same French authors, especially in his early texts.

In his treatment of social class, García Márquez also has a connection with Proust. Social ambition is the primary motivation for one of the characters in *El amor en los tiempos del cólera:* Lorenzo Daza. Like Legrandin and other snobs in the *Recherche,* the father of Fermina is willing to sacrifice everything including her happiness so that their family can advance socially. In this regard, I must concede that Fermina follows unwillingly her father's plan and her own personal qualities allow her to make the transition to upper-class life with relative ease, but her acceptance in that society means that Florentino Ariza must also become a social climber so that he can eventually be her equal. His ambition is motivated by love rather than by snobbery, but the joining of persons from distinct social classes by the end of the Colombian novel contributes to the unity of this text, somewhat like the marriage between the daughter of Swann and a nephew of the Guermantes near the conclusion of the *Recherche.* Similarly, the ultimate success of Florentino Ariza's love for the woman that had been married to Dr. Urbino for fifty years implies a vague linking, if not bonding, between certain popular elements of Colombian society and the most progressive facets of French culture. Thus, even though García Márquez has not been as closely associated with cosmopolitanism as Carlos Fuentes, he has an undeniable connection with Europe, like all of the Boom writers.

Approaching from a different angle the feasible relationship between the Proustian subject of high society, European influences and Spanish American literature, Ernesto Sábato confronted in dialogue form Marxist critics in his last novel *Abaddón, el exterminador* (1974). There, his fictional novelist, who is called Ernesto Sabato, has a lengthy discussion (particularly in the original, pre-military-coup version of this novel) with several young people concerning the type of literature represented by Marcel Proust and other introspective writers.[22]

In this fragmentary novel, which includes the depiction of a few upper-class social gatherings attended by Sabato, we find the old novelist debating with radicals in the early 1970s. These young men question the value of all non-political writing and assert that in a world of suffering even reading is suspect. From their point of view, it is preferable to pick up a rifle to fight oppression than to read any book. During the discussion, one of the young leftists quotes the Argentine sociologist that I mentioned above. Hernández Arregui claimed that writers from monoculture countries tend to develop an introspective literature in order to avoid discussing socio-political problems. To this Sabato retorts that *Huasipungo* [The Villagers] was written in Ecuador, thus implying that single crop countries have also produced novels devoid of subjectivity. He then adds, with obvious sarcasm, that following such a form of logic Henry James and Marcel Proust must have lived in monoculture countries because of their emphasis on introspection.[23] Finally, the character Sabato summarizes the typical leftist argument of that time and proceeds to refute it:

> la introspección significa hundirse en el yo, el yo solitario es un egoísta que no le importa el mundo, o un contrarrevolucionario que intenta hacernos creer que el problema está dentro del alma y no en la organización social, etc. Pasan por alto un pequeño detalle: el yo solitario no existe. El hombre existe en una sociedad, sufriendo, luchando y hasta escondiéndose en esa sociedad. Vivir es convivir. (1977, 195)

> [introspection means plunging into the self, the solitary I is an egotist who does not care about the world, or a counterrevolutionary who tries to make us believe that the problem lies within the soul and not in the social organization, etc. They overlook a small detail: the solitary self does not exist. Man exists in a society, suffering, struggling and even hiding in that society. To live is to live with others.]

Clearly for the speaker, the distinction between self and society (or what is solitary and what is social) is a false one because the two areas are inextricably bound together. The real author, Ernesto Sábato, was in part defending his own type of novel, in which he had portrayed introspective, solitary characters such as Castel, Martín or Fernando; but, he was also referring to Proust, who had withdrawn from the world to his cork-lined room in order to write his vast novel and who has been considered one of the outstanding examples of modernist subjectivity.[24] Thus, the character Sabato concludes:

> Desde ese punto de vista, la novela más subjetiva es social, y de una manera directa o tortuosa está dando un testimonio de la realidad entera. No hay novelas de introspección y novelas sociales, amigo; hay novelas grandes y novelas chiquitas. Hay buena literatura y mala literatura.

> [From that point of view, the most subjective novel is social, and in a direct or convoluted manner it is giving a testimonial of all of reality. There are not novels of introspection and social novels, friend; there are major novels and very minor novels. There is good literature and bad literature.]

Here, we find a critique of socialist realism, which has denied the importance of individual concerns and claimed that "social" matters (in a Marxist sense) override all that is subjective or individual.

Later, in a private conversation, Sabato makes explicit his reference to Proust and uses this French novelist to explain that the connection between art and society is not as simple and direct as some Marxist critics have suggested. It may be as complex as the relationship between dreams and day-time activity:

> *Porque* Proust era un señorito su literatura es la expresión podrida de una sociedad injusta, te afirman. Comprendes? Hay una relación, pero no tiene por qué ser directa. Puede ser inversa, antagónica, una rebelión. No un reflejo, ese famoso reflejo. Es un acto *creativo* con que el hombre enriquece la realidad. (1991, 193)

> [*Because* Proust was a rich kid his literature is the corrupt expression of an unjust society, they tell you. Do you understand? There is a relation, but it does not have to be direct. It can be inverse, antagonistic, a rebellion. It is not a reflex, that famous reflex. It is a *creative* act with which man enriches reality.]

Obviously, Sabato the character, like Sábato the author, is drawing attention here to the creative process and rejects as unfounded the conclusion by some Marxist critics that a work like Proust's is of little value because of the French novelist's social class (bourgeoisie), his choice of subject matter (the upper classes) or his narrative focus (introspection). Sabato's desire to generalize beyond Proust is also eminently clear. He is defending his own creative freedom, as well as that of all writers, from the New World or elsewhere. Thus, we can respond in the affirmative to the question concerning the legitimacy of Spanish Americans writing about high society in the manner of Proust. This is implied when Sabato points out that Karl Marx greatly admired Balzac and might have preferred the *Recherche* to the proletarian literature of Russia: "Entre esos productos y las obras de ese snob . . . que se moría por las duquesas, no cabe duda, el que subsistirá será ese señorito" [Between those products and the works of that snob . . . who was dying to meet duchesses, there is no doubt, the one who will endure will be that rich kid] (225).

Perhaps offended by the remark concerning *Huasipungo* and Sábato's critique of socialist realism, the Ecuadorian Jorge Enrique Adoum presented one of the most direct narrative responses from the political left in his novel *Entre Marx y una mujer desnuda* [Between Marx and a Naked Woman] (1976).[25] Here, we find at least five explicit and generally ironic references to Proust and several implicit ones to Ernesto Sábato. Although this Argentine writer is never specifically cited, he seems to be precisely the author that Adoum's narrator promised never to name (1983, 156) and who serves as the primary Spanish American target in the Ecuadorian text. Sábato's concept of the total novel complements the idea that "una novela que se escribiera con la economía de recursos imprescindible en el cuento, sería ilegible" [a novel that might be written with the economy of means indispensible to a short story would be illegible]. Also, given Hernández Arregui's attack on Sábato, who had abandoned the left during the 1930s, and the Argentine novelist's response in *Abaddón*, the phrase "su histórica infamia universal" seems to refer to Sábato, rather than Borges, who is actually mentioned elsewhere in the text.[26]

In many ways, *Entre Marx y una mujer desnuda* is a postmodern parody of *Abaddón, el exterminador* and other fragmentary novels of the period, as well as of the *Recherche* itself. Adoum, somewhat like Sábato, has assembled a wide variety of texts, but as his title suggests, these are so diverse that they appear to encompass everything from Karl Marx to pornography. We find, for example, in addition to the story of an extramarital affair and the depiction of various types of Ecuadorians, memories from the past, commentaries on writing and European literature, and references to leftist political ideas and activities. The use of newspaper articles, various sizes of print, and miscellaneous graphics, of course, bring to mind *El libro de Manuel* (1973) by Julio Cortázar. But, this novel, which reflects a more politically radical point of view than *Rayuela*, is clearly not the main target of Adoum's parody. His narrator seems to excuse Cortázar when he says, after referring to the unmentionable author, that "otro, cuyo nombre has citado ya muchas veces, decía que en el cuento hay que ganarle al lector por K.O., en tanto que en la novela se le gana por puntos" [another, whose name you have cited already many times, used to say that in a short story one must win over the reader with a knockout while in the novel one must win him over by points] (156).

Concerning our subject at hand, high society, it is best to single out a brief series of texts that begins on page 175. It focuses upon a conversation between four upper-class characters who meet on a particular Sunday for dinner. In this case, we do not find an elegant exchange like those that appear in *Le côté de Guermantes,* and there is no attempt to reproduce the atmosphere implied by the elegant surroundings. On the contrary, Adoum has reduced the episode to the mere words of the conversation itself, which flows continuously with only frequent dashes to indicate a change in speaker. In this regard, as well as with its extremely frivolous tone, Adoum obviously comes much closer to certain portions of *Abaddón, el exterminador* (such as the coctail party at Dr. Carranza's apartment, beginning on p. 74) than to Proust's text.

In the commentary, which alternates with portions of the conversation, Adoum's narrator makes his attitude toward the upper-class characters and his own intentions very explicit. He detests these persons and merely wishes to satirize them. For him they are scarcely more than "objects," and he plays with this concept as he cites the author of the *Recherche* and other modernist writers: "Alguien ha dicho que Proust se deja invadir por los objetos en vez de golpearse contra ellos como Joyce" [Someone has said that Proust allows himself to be imbued by the objects instead of bumping into them like Joyce] (178). To describe the bourgeois characters he also toys with Marxist terminology:

> La crisis de valores es una crisis del lenguaje y qué valores existen o subsisten en esa pequeña burguesía, más pequeña que burguesa, tan falta de tradición, es decir cultura, y tan falta de autenticidad que, aun cuando hayan poseído siempre el dinero, siempre piensan y actúan como nuevos ricos y se expresan, por lo mismo, con una caricatura de lenguaje que no es el de su clase y tampoco el del pueblo. (178)[27]

> [The crisis of values is a crisis of language and what values can exist or subsist in that petite bourgeoisie, more petty than bourgeois, so devoid of tradition, that is to say culture, so devoid of authenticity that even though they have always possessed the money, they always think and act like the nouveaux riches and express themselves, likewise, through a caricature of language that is not the one of their class nor that of the common people.]

The narrator of *Entre Marx y una mujer desnuda* approaches Monteforte Toledo and other Marxists when he calls these characters "tan mamarrachos e inauténticos que se consideran nobles" [such scarecrows and inauthentic people that they consider themselves to be nobles] (179), but I should point out that they do not seem to be invented or even unusual. On the contrary, they appear to be all too typical of the Ecuadorian upper classes and to represent an endemic problem for the country, at least from the narrator's point of view.[28]

Along with the satire of these characters, which at times reminds us of the manner of Jorge Icaza, we find a distinct parody of Sábato because of the form and tone of the conversation, as suggested above. In a post-modern manner, which has served the purposes of the left as well as the right, Adoum worked within such conventions in order to subvert them. Apparently he wished to contest the work of Sábato, the fragmentary novels of the Boom, and even liberal humanist culture itself.

As for the matter of introspection, Adoum's purpose is less evident. His narrator does in fact deride the idea that "el objeto de la novela es la conciencia" [the object of the novel is consciousness] (209), but he makes little attempt to show or even to parody the analysis of character motivation. In reality, he understands psychological analysis only in terms of Freud, whose ideas appeared many years after the traditional psychological novel which Proust and even Sábato had followed.

To this remark, however, I must add one qualification: the narrator does attempt to understand his own reasons for writing the text. But, here, the motivation is more closely allied to political thought than to human psychology. The fictional writer is nominally a leftist in terms of his political sympathies and party membership, but he retains so many vestiges of the *pequeño burgués* [lower middle class] mentality that he contributes little to bring about social or political change. His affair with the landowner's wife makes him more an accomplice to the system than a true revolutionary. For this reason, the allusions to his health problems and flatfeet to explain why he cannot be a man of action are mere excuses and in no way justify his writing. This activity is also questionable because most of his readers will be from the middle and upper classes. In a real sense Adoum has shifted the subject of the narrative dialogue away from the opposition between introspection and socialist realism to the purpose of reformist literature and the writing of a novel. But this matter, which is even more specifically Proustian, must be left until chapter 8.

The great changes of the mid-1970s which led the Spanish American novel from the Boom to the post-Boom period affected the way in which Proust's work would be treated. Although scholars in this area, like Donald L. Shaw, have scarcely mentioned the French novelist, the modifications that they discuss implied a retreat from all that was European, modernist and upper-class. At least for a while, some of the major novelists became more politically engaged, they wrote about the struggle of the lower classes, they shifted their interests from high to popular culture, from the written to the spoken word and from Europe to their own native lands. Furthermore, as José Agustín noted they changed their focus from internal to external reality:

> Joyce's *Ulysses* and Proust's *A la recherche du temps perdu* initiated a literary movement leading inward. . . . But now, almost at the end of the century, the pendulum has reached the subjective extreme, and any dogmatic attempt to keep it there disrupts this natural development, which now needs to turn back to external reality. . . . (quoted by Shaw, 1998, 47)

In a parallel manner, but with a broader, international scope and with a continued use of experimentation, postmodernism during these years consolidated its attack on modernism. We have already seen how since *Rayuela* some Spanish American authors (like their European and North American counterparts) began to question the basic tenets of modernism. In *Casa de campo,* José Donoso used parody and satire to suggest the apparent blindness of the overly subjective point of view of the upper classes and of specific literary works about them, including parts of the *Recherche.* Likewise, but in a more extreme political manner, Jorge Enrique Adoum in *Entre Marx y una mujer desnuda* lampooned the wealthy at the same time as he used the fragmentation of experimental novels to ridicule the totalizing intention of these texts themselves. Such a use of postmodern parody would continue throughout the 1980s and 1990s, but it served to criticize the political left as well as right.

As a member of the younger generation, Alfredo Bryce Echenique illustrates particularly well how some writers after the Boom viewed the *Recherche* and the question of social class in a new and different way.[29] Even before the publication of *Abaddón el exterminador,* this Peruvian demonstrated how an aristocratic subject did not necessarily imply atypical or inauthentic characters or even a politically conservative point of view. In his first novel *Un mundo para Julius* [A World for Julius] (1970) Bryce did not merely portray the life of a wealthy family in the elegant Lima suburb of San Isidro. He exposed through satire the injustice derived from the privileges of these persons and in particular their less than humane treatment of their servants. Contrary to what one might have expected given the tenor of Marxist criticism, the leftist military government in power at that time in Peru did not consider the aristocratic subject inappropriate or the novel's possible connection with Proust objectionable. On the contrary, the generals were eager to honor Bryce Echenique in spite of and even perhaps because of his upper-class origins.

As for the relation between the *Recherche* and *Un mundo para Julius,* this is more specific and subtle than some scholars have suggested.[30] Only a few passages (e.g., the night when Julius had difficulty sleeping because of his parents' party beneath his window) are verbally or situationally reminiscent of the *Recherche*. Even the treatment of time and memory are quite different in the two works. A more crucial link is the focal character. In spite of the fact that Bryce used a third person narrator, instead of one in the first person like Proust, he was careful to underscore the innocent and unprejudiced perspective of Julius through which are exposed the frivolity of the boy's mother and the selfishness of his stepfather and brothers. This child-like innocence closely resembles that of the protagonist of "Combray," who saw his provincial world with fresh, new eyes. Similarly, Bryce's subtle satire is often akin to Proust's and very distinct from what is often found in works of socialist realism.

In more explicit terms, Alfredo Bryce Echenique demonstrated his relation to Proust in his two-part novel *Cuadernos de navegación en un sillón Voltaire* [Notebooks about Navigating in a Voltaire Chair]. We find in the first of these volumes, *La vida exagerada de Martín Romaña* (1981), a surprising number of direct references to Proust, and Martín's mother openly expresses her admiration for the *Recherche*. In fact, this woman appears to be a fanatic and demands that her son write like Marcel Proust. She says in a letter,

> Martín, mientras no escribas *La búsqueda del tiempo perdido* peruana, o algo muy por el estilo . . . no estoy dispuesta a contarle a nadie de la familia, ni a ninguna de mis amigas, que te estás convirtiendo en escritor en París. (1985, 189)

> [Martín, until you write the Peruvian *Search for Lost Time*, or something very much like it . . . I will not be disposed to tell anyone in the family nor any of my friends that you are becoming a writer in Paris.]

The novelist from Peru has presented in lucid terms the intricate connection between social class, Proust and literary authenticity. Although from a wealthy family like Julius, the aspiring novelist Martín finds himself in a situation where he cannot write about the upper-class life that he knew from personal experience. Living in Paris during the mid- to-late 1960s, Martín is surrounded by young Latin Americans (including his girl friend Inés) who are involved in leftist political activity. In spite of his impoverished condition as a struggling writer and Spanish teacher, Martín is considered by all to be suspect because of his family origins. Pressured by Inés (who had abandoned God for Karl Marx) and their leftist friends, Martín agrees to write in the manner of socialist realism a novel about the unionization of Peruvian fishermen. This project eventually fails because Martín had no personal experience with unions or fishermen in his country. He attempts to adapt his observations concerning his poor immigrant neighbors in Paris, but such human details are insufficient. Due to the limitations of his actual background and experience, he cannot with authenticity write about persons so distinct from himself. Likewise, Martín is unable to convince Inés or her leftist comrades that he is essentially different from his upper-class family. For the Marxists, Martín will always be "un intelectual de medias tintas" [an uncommitted intellectual] and not even his participation in the street demonstrations of May 1968 can redeem him. Here, of course, Bryce was satirizing the Spanish American Marxists of the late 1960s and their view of literature. Furthermore, he was responding to their type of literary criticism and narrow view of authenticity.

Martín's social position proves to have dire consequences for his personal life as well as for his literary career. Near the end of *La vida exagerada de Martín Romaña,* Inés leaves the protagonist definitively because she wishes to become politically involved in Peru. Ironically, in the second volume, *El hombre que hablaba de Octavia de Cádiz* (1985), the fact that Martín's family is not aristocratic enough leads to exactly the same result: the abandonment of Martín by the woman that he loves. In this case, Octavia's patrician father, who is more concerned about her social status than her happiness, rejects violently Martín's proposal of marriage.

Underlying both of these socially motivated rejections, which contribute greatly to Martín's unhappiness and mental instability, we can detect a specifically Proustian theme, which is almost ubiquitous in the *Recherche:* snobbery. To this social ambition or prejudice Proust's narrator attributes a wide range of selfish human acts. It is also worth noting that in Bryce's second volume Martín has the opportunity to meet modern-day princes and nobles, and the atmosphere described brings to mind *Le côté de Guermantes.* Such is the case when the Peruvian artists visit Leopoldo's aristocratic home in Brussels and when Martín and Octavia stop at Solre, the country manor house of this same noble. Such settings, however, do not convey that high society proves to be the principal source of Martín's literary inspiration, which is instead suffering through love. But, Bryce also treated this subject in a somewhat Proustian manner, as we shall see in chapter 4. Likewise, I will return to *Cuadernos de navegación en un sillón Voltaire* in chapters 5 and 8 because of its development of the subject of art and of the story of a literary vocation.

In summary, *Le côté de Guermantes* has inspired numerous Spanish American writers in diverse ways, particularly since 1950. At times these works about the upper classes have been criticized by persons from the political left because of the allegedly inauthentic, atypical or overly European characters. In some cases, these attacks have come from the writers of such countries as Guatemala or Ecuador, where the discovery of

Proust was late and limited to a small number of readers and where the resistence to European influences has generally been strong. However, the admirers of the *Recherche* in Cuba, Colombia and Peru, as well as Chile and Argentina, have also felt the effects of such criticism. For this reason, some of Proust's followers have carried the modernist subjectivity of the narrator a step further so that their characters and texts would not appear false within their Spanish American context. Also, they have exaggerated this view of reality through postmodern parody. Others have set their novels at least partly in Europe and have included French characters in an attempt to reconcile the differences between the Old and New Worlds. Some of them have incorporated into their narrative works a discussion, debate or dialogue with their leftist critics, and the texts themselves have served as a response. Also Proust's novel has been used to justify French influences and to defend the individual creativity of the artist, but the Marxists themselves have not remained silent. In at least one case, there has been a narrative response from the left, where Proust and one of his followers were parodied also in a postmodern manner. This narrative debate has continued and even the concept of authenticity has been examined critically because a writer must first of all be authentic to himself. In this regard, we can see a parallel between Proust's relation with Spanish America and the influence of France in another way. Likethe ideas of Voltaire and Rousseau, those found in the *Recherche* have proved to be very liberating. In the chapter which follows, we will see how the same is also true concerning the subject of love.

4

On Love, Illness, and Consciousness: New World Variations on "Un amour de Swann," *La prisonnière,* and *Sodome et Gomorrhe*

LOVE AND SEXUALITY WERE OTHER SUBJECTS OF PROUST THAT CAP-
tured the attention of his readers and critics. Since time immemorial
such feelings have preoccupied numerous literary artists, and in France
since the seventeenth century love has been the primary focus of what
has been called the psychological novel. In the first of these works, *La
princesse de Clèves* (1674), Madame de Lafayette analyzed in considerable
detail this feeling and showed how it evolved over time. During the
nineteenth century the great master of this genre was Stendhal, who
carried in *Le rouge et le noir* [The Red and the Black] (1830) and his other
novels the analysis of love to its apparent limits. For the remainder of the
century, no one was able to surpass Stendhal even though writers like
Gustave Flaubert and Paul Bourget continued to depict various aspects
of love.

With the appearance of "Un amour de Swann," which constitutes the
second part of Proust's initial volume, Stendhal's primacy over the psychological novel was declared a thing of the past. As Jacques Rivière
pointed out in "Marcel Proust et la tradition classique," more than any of
his predecessors, the creator of Swann was able to dissect the most
powerful human emotion. Not only did Proust show how love was born,
grew and totally filled the existence of the lover, he also portrayed, like
no one before him, the most minute stages and details imaginable of
love and its concomitant elements of jealousy and possessiveness.

In addition to the plethora of details found in "Un amour de Swann,"
Proust demonstrated his unique treatment of love by studying an especially painful case of it. He began by selecting an unlikely couple and an
initially adverse feeling. The very refined gentleman Swann is not immediately attracted to the somewhat coarse woman Odette. The latter,
however, is very adept at seducing men; thus, in spite of Swann's considerable experience with love, he allows himself to be ensnared. Also

with the aid of music and art, he semiconsciously convinces himself that he actually loves Odette. This affair probably would have ended quickly like many others; but, due to an unusual series of circumstances Swann becomes jealous. This emotion, which is more intense than his love, then grows like a cancer and nearly destroys his life.

Some critics immediately concluded that Proustian love was abnormal and resembled an illness or infirmity. Given the lamentable condition of Proust's health, the clinical metaphors that he used to describe love, and the painfulness of Swann's experience, such an assessment was understandable. With the publication of his subsequent volumes, Proust unwittingly provided further evidence in support of this argument. In *La prisonnière* and *Albertine disparue* the protagonist relives to some extent Swann's experience with jealousy, but interlaced with this emotion there is a complicating factor: the suspicion that his mistress Albertine loves women. By itself, this complication would have been sufficient to label Proust an infirm, if not perverse writer. But already in the previous volume, *Sodome et Gomorrhe,* Proust had attributed to some of his other characters a homosexual love.

As has been generally suggested by the critics, the author of the *Recherche* wished to demonstrate that in its essence homosexual love is really quite similar to the heterosexual variety. The persons in love have basically the same feelings, only the object of their affection is dissimilar. Thus the Baron de Charlus in *Sodome et Gomorrhe* and the subsequent volumes often experiences love and jealousy in nearly the same manner as Swann, but his Odettes are of his own gender. To a large extent all of the amorous affairs in the *Recherche* follow the same pattern. The beloved is essentially the creation of the lover's imagination and only vaguely resembles the actual person involved. The selection of the beloved is the result of circumstance because it is the temperament of the lover and his disposition at a particular moment that allow the process to begin. Such a love is born from an unsatisfied desire for possession and dies once the need is fulfilled unless the imagination of the lover is further stimulated by something that the beloved says or does. Love for Proust almost inevitably leads to jealousy because this feeling more than any other is capable of prolonging the attachment and making the lover increasingly dependent upon the beloved. Finally, as the Argentine critic and writer Federico Peltzer pointed out in his essay "Marcel Proust y el amor creación," love has one very beneficial outcome. It induces in the lover an expansion of his being and the development of his most intimate mental faculties.

Not content to limit himself to love, as had his predecessors, Marcel Proust also analyzed other human feelings, plus pertinent gestures, thus expanding the realm of the psychological novel and at times the field of psychology itself. The French novelist's subjective treatment of time and memory are quite unique and will be examined in separate chapters, but his attention to other aspects of consciousness are also worthy of note. As Bradbury has observed, consciousness was an essential component of Proust's modernism:

> It is also an alertness, an analytic power, a sense of the vividness of being, a search for revelation. . . . This whole matter of the nature of consciousness and psychology was the great preoccupation of his age, and one of the marks of the "modern" vision of existence. (1990, 139)[1]

Proust carried his analysis in various directions. His narrator explains, for instance, the relation between individuals within the context of the home and friendship, between masters and servants, and the psychology of groups. In the case of the latter, his analysis of snobbery is especially acute, and he found manifestations of this phenomenon in numerous contexts and on all levels of society.

For Proust, gestures were extremely significant because they seemed to provide the key for understanding the thoughts of other people. Having realized that persons often use their words to mask their true feelings, the protagonist of *La prisonnière* concludes that what people say is less revealing than how they say it. This idea appears to form the basis of much of Proust's psychological analysis, which is often presented as a series of hypotheses. Among these, the one most closely bound to a specific gesture normally proves to be the most accurate.

Clearly, this method is not based upon experimentation and cannot be termed scientific. Although some critics have tried to establish a parallel between its results and the work of Sigmund Freud, such a relation is tenuous at best. Far more than the Austrian master (whose writings were only starting to be known in France at the time of the creation of the *Recherche*) Proust based his conclusions primarily upon introspection and intuition. Here, I should reiterate the essential subjectivity of Proust's work, which constituted one of his major contributions to modernism. His narrator is never absolutely certain of his conclusions, but in spite of their subjective nature he presents them as his particular view of the world. Also, his consciousness itself can be associated with modernism because it binds together all of the *Recherche* into a master narrative or, as Ramon Fernandez said years ago, this vast French novel is the story of a consciousness.

Finally, Proust sometimes used metaphors or comparisons to express keen psychological insights. He realized that such spiritual equivalents could help the reader understand a particular aspect of psychology, as well as of art, which we will consider later.

For the Spanish American examples, we will first see how, during the years that preceded the Boom, Proust's modernist ideas about consciousness and analysis were generally accepted. To demonstrate that the French author's treatment of homosexual love influenced the inception and helped to encourage the development of gay literature in the New World, I will devote a special section to this subject. Finally, we will consider how during the Boom there was a reaction against the psychological novel in the manner of Proust by writers who advocated an increasingly postmodern perspective.

LEARNING TO UNDERSTAND THE CONNECTION BETWEEN LOVE AND ILLNESS

As we saw in chapter 2, several Spanish American authors perceived at an early date the value of Proust's psychological analysis. Even before the New World critics began to discuss the *Recherche*, Manuel Gálvez and Teresa de la Parra had incorporated into their texts the analysis of gestures following Marcel Proust. For the subsequent years, I should cite Roberto Mariani, along with Jaime Torres Bodet. The Argentine, who was one of the leaders of the Boedo group and delivered a lecture on Proust, included in his narrative collection of 1926 *El amor agresivo* a story that is very Proustian in its method of analysis. The narrator of "Un viajero" says, for example, of facial expressions as they are affected by memory:

Las escenas y las emociones retornan, algo desdibujadas, y amontonadas unas sobre otras, pujando cada una por dominar y desalojar por fin a las otras, lo que explica la escasa duración de una sonrisa o de un gesto malhumorado. (1968, 13)

[The scenes and emotions return, somewhat blurred, one piled upon another, with each struggling to dominate and finally to dislodge the others, which explains the brief duration of a smile or of an ill-tempered gesture.]

Furthermore, the protagonist recovers an incident from his past because the regional pronunciation of a particular word, *bullicio* [noise], stimulates his memory. In his later works Mariani continued to apply the psychological lessons that he had learned from Proust. We find, for example, in his novel *Regreso a Dios* [Return to God] (1943) that the mental state of the character Aguilar closely resembles that of the protagonist of *Albertine disparue*. Neither man is able to forget the woman whose love he had lost. Minute, everyday details constantly remind him of her and renew his suffering.[2]

Another Argentine who had written about the *Recherche*, José Bianco,
applied some of Proust's ideas on psychology in his novel *Las ratas* [The
Rats] (1943). In several analyses, Bianco followed the example of the
French author quite closely. To describe the way in which his mother
justified the banning of an aluminum stewpot from the kitchen because
of his half-brother Julio's scientific theories, the narrator remarks: "Mi
madre hablaba con ese fervor que ponen las personas cuando explican
asuntos que apenas comprenden. Entusiasmada, arrebatada, suplía la
indigencia de su vocabulario con una abundante gesticulación" [My
mother spoke with that passion that people add when they explain
subjects that they scarcely understand. Excited, carried away, she made
up for the indigence of her vocabulary with copious gestures] (1973,
44). The narrator of "Un amour de Swann" employs the same type of
comparison and analysis to illustrate Odette's difficulty in explaining
what she meant by the phrase "de l'époque" [period] furniture:

> elle lui reparla de son amie et ajouta, sur le ton hésitant et de l'air entendu
> dont on cite quelqu'un avec qui on a dîné la veille et dont on n'avait jamais
> entendu le nom, mais que vos amphitryons avaient l'air de considérer comme
> quelqu'un de si célèbre qu'on espère que l'interlocuteur saura bien de qui
> vous voulez parler: "Elle a une salle à manger . . . du . . . dix-huitième!" (1954,
> 1: 244)

> [she spoke to him again about her friend and added, with a faltering tone and
> air of understanding used when mentioning someone with whom one dined
> the preceding evening and whose name one had never heard, but whom
> yours hosts appeared to consider to be someone so famous that one hopes
> that the listener will certainly know of whom you wish to speak: "She has a
> dining-room set . . . from . . . the eighteenth century!"]

Moreover, I must note that José Bianco went beyond the occasional use
of this Proust-like analysis, which had become relatively common in
Spanish America during the 1930s. The Argentine constructed *Las ratas*
in such a way that the reader must function almost like the protagonist
in *La prisonnière*. Confronted by certain perplexing words and gestures
of the very subjective and essentially modernist narrator, the reader must
discover what is hidden beneath the surface of appearances. Otherwise
the narrator's guilt for the murder of Julio and the implicit confession of
this crime will not be understood.

From the opposite bank of the Río de la Plata, the famous novelist
Carlos Reyles attempted Proust's psychological manner in his last work *A
batallas de amor . . . campo de pluma* (1939). After also writing a study on
Proust, Reyles portrayed a psychological crisis and moments of suffering
derived from love and desire. The principal male character, a frivolous,

middle-aged *niño bien* [rich kid], experiences serious doubts about his personality and the wholeness of his being when he is faced with financial ruin and a weakened health condition. Here, we can find numerous echoes from the *Recherche* dealing with memory, insomnia and love, as well as even a direct reference to the French author (1939, 148). To some of Proust's ideas Reyles added his own interpretation. For example, "la memoria del cuerpo" [the memory of the body] has a far more lubricious sense here.

In particular, the subject of jealousy and a suspicion of lesbianism can be found in this novel. It was in this regard that another Uruguayan writer, Mario Benedetti, saw Proust's influence in the scene where the main character Pepe spies upon the ambiguous caresses exchanged by his former and future wives:

> The cited passage from *A batallas de amor* has its probable model in a page from "Combray" where Marcel sees by chance through an open window, the apparently innocent games played by the daughter of Vinteuil and a female friend. (1951, 61)

In his essay "Marcel Proust y el sentido de la culpa" (1951) Benedetti discussed in detail the subject of love in the *Recherche*. He conveyed that Proust's treatment of this emotion was perhaps related to his homosexuality or to a type of insufficiency (sexual or otherwise). In this regard Benedetti also tried to define Proust's influence on the literature of the period:

> It is interesting to observe that a good deal of his transmissible influence— principally that which refers to the much discussed theory of love-infirmity— rests precisely upon the assumption that Proust declares to be insufficient normal, consummated love, when strictly speaking it is considerably more probable that it implies the dearth of his personal love, which furthermore is not consummated. (1951, 12)

These words would seem to imply that Benedetti scorned what he called "amor-enfermedad." He even regretted that this tendency had affected some writers who had never read the *Recherche*. Nonetheless, in his own first novel *Quien de nosotros* [Who of Us] (1953), one of the main characters, Miguel, suffers precisely from a type of love infirmity. He himself refers to his "incapacidad para celar a Alicia" [incapacity to be jealous of Alicia], and he strongly encourages his wife to meet with her former boyfriend. It appears as if Miguel's relationship with Alicia depends at least in part upon this man Lucas. Before their marriage and while Alicia was living elsewhere Miguel thought that his question "¿Qué dirá Alicia de esto?" [What can Alicia think about this?] was a proof of his love for her. However when he analyzed more deeply his thoughts and feelings, the result was shocking: "Pero toda probabilidad quedó disipada el día en que me sorprendí preguntándome qué opinaría Lucas sobre algo, pues evidentemente yo no estaba enamorado de Lucas" [But all probability was dispelled on the day in which I caught myself wondering what Lucas might think about something, since obviously I was not in love with Lucas] (1974, 39).

In the first part of *Quien de nosotros* and to a lesser degree in the other two sections of this novel, we can see how Benedetti vaguely suggested the motivation of his characters. Broadly speaking the Uruguayan novelist was following Proust's intention of reaching into the human consciousness, but his approach was neither psychological nor specifically Proustian. It did not imply an examination of gestures or an inquiry into possible underlying causes, such as jealousy or homosexuality, as one often finds in the *Recherche*. For this reason, in spite of his experimentation with new literary forms, Benedetti's first novel is largely a sketch in ambiguity.

During these years, in the Southern Cone one of the best examples of the analysis of love in the manner of Proust is *El túnel* (1949) by the Argentine Ernesto Sábato. Here the love infirmity is precisely the one found in "Un amour de Swann" and *La prisonnière*, jealousy. Furthermore, the protagonist's manner of interpreting reality closely resembles that of Proust's two main characters. It is not only very subjective, but also in a modernist manner Juan Pablo Castel generalizes from very few facts.

First, like the protagonist of *La prisonnière*, who sees life as a palimpsest which conceals beneath the surface of appearances a deeper, unsuspected reality, Castel systematically rejects simple or obvious reasons. In his confessions, which constitute the novel, he explains: "Yo me pregunto *por qué la realidad ha de ser simple*. Mi experiencia me ha enseñado que, por el contrario, casi nunca lo es y cuando hay algo que parece extraordinariamente claro . . . casi siempre hay debajo móviles más complejos" [I ask myself *why reality must be simple*. My experience has taught me that, on the contrary, it almost never is and when there is something which seems extraordinarily clear . . . almost always beneath the surface there are more complex motives] (1966, 80).

Furthermore, similar to the Proustian protagonist, Castel often attributes greater significance to gestures and inadvertent remarks than to conscious statements. Referring to the woman that he loved, María, he confesses: "Mis interrogatorios, cada día más frecuentes y retorcidos, eran a propósito de sus silencios, sus miradas, sus palabras perdidas, algún viaje a la estancia, sus amores" [My interrogations, being each day more frequent and devious, were related to her moments of silence, her glances, her inadvertent remarks, a certain trip to the ranch, her loves] (93). In *La prisonnière,* we find precisely the same type of interrogations, which nearly always result from Albertine's words, silence or glances because these reawaken the protagonist's suspicions. According to him, in spite of her statements to the contrary, they reveal that Albertine had enjoyed sexual relations with women and that she intends to leave in search of similar adventures:

> L'intention de me quitter, si elle existait chez Albertine, ne se manifestait que d'une façon obscure, par *certains regards tristes, certaines impatiences,* des phrases qui ne voulaient nullement dire cela, mais si on raisonnait . . . ne pouvaient s'expliquer que par la présence en elle d'un sentiment qu'elle cachait et qui pouvait la conduire à faire des plans pour une autre vie sans moi. (3:345, my emphasis)

> [The intention to leave me, if it existed in Albertine, only revealed itself in an obscure manner, by *certain forlorn glances, certain impatient gestures,* phrases that belied it, but if one analyzed them . . . they could only be explained by the presence in her of a feeling that she concealed and which could lead her to make plans for another life without me.]

Finally, one of the decisive incidents in *El túnel*—the one that leads to the murder of María—occurs when Castel discovers a similarity between María's facial expression and one that a particular prostitute had assumed. Castel's categorical conclusion from this single gesture that María is a prostitute is very much like the assumption by Proust's main character that Albertine is a lesbian because she used in his presence the obscene phrase "me faire casser" [to rupture me]. Both protagonists base their deductions on an almost identical form of analogy. Castel writes, "María y la prostituta han tenido una expresión semejante, la prostituta simulaba placer, María, pues, simulaba placer; María es una prostituta" [María and the prostitute have had a similar expression, the prostitute simulated pleasure, María, thus, simulated pleasure; María is a prostitute] (137). We read in *La prisonnière:*

> Double horreur! car même la dernière des grues, et qui consent à cela, ou le désire, n'emploie pas avec l'homme qui s'y prête cette affreuse expression. Elle se sentirait par trop avilie. Avec une femme seulement, si elle les aime, elle dit cela pour s'excuser. . . . (3:340)

> [Twofold horror! for even the lowest category of wenches, and those that agree to do such a thing or desire it, do not employ with the man that requests it that ghastly expression. She would feel excessively degraded. Only with a woman, if she likes them, does she say that to excuse herself. . . .]

142   MARCEL PROUST AND SPANISH AMERICA

Given this similar method of thought, as well as assumptions, but with a contrasting result—the murder of a person in Castel's case—we can observe how close the Proustian protagonist comes to a pathological manner of thinking and how easily Sábato was able to lead his character over the brink. In other words, we can see how Proust's association between love and illness, which has been considered modernist, leads directly to a pre-Boom novel like *El túnel* where we also find an instance of extreme subjectivity that brings criminal results and thus casts doubt upon that form of thought.

In the years that preceded the Boom itself one can see how a Proust-like analysis was carried beyond the Río de la Plata, where it had been widespread. One of the best examples from another geographical area, Central America, can be found in *La ruta de su evasión* (1949) by the Costa Rican Yolanda Oreamuno. Far more candid than most New World writers, this woman from San José openly declared her connection with the *Recherche:* "I make a confession of faith in Proust, of a limitless admiration, of similarity and of influence. I make it with a full measure of joy and honor. And, if I know someone intimately, if I read someone with passion, it is he" (letter reprinted by Urbano 1968). Throughout her one published novel, (the other two or three have been lost), it is possible to find numerous echoes from the *Recherche*. Many of these are in fact derived from the psychological facet of Proust, but not in the same manner as in the cases that we have just examined.[3] As Oreamuno suggested herself, the *Recherche* served as her point of departure or source of inspiration rather than of influence:

> Marcel Proust is my best fairy tale. The magic of Proust comes to fruition in me because he is the only author capable of inciting my emotion, ideas— ideas that are genuinely mine, not Proustian. With writers as contagious as Galdós, Mallea, Huxley, D. H. Lawrence, Malraux, I may fall into the sin of producing ideas that are like those of Galdós, Mallea. . . . With Proust only ideas are born to me. (1961, 335)

In reality, Proust affected Oreamuno on a more profound plane. From the *Recherche* she learned the value of personal suffering and how to use it in the creation of her own literary work. Concerning suffering, Proust himself was quite explicit. He began *Albertine disparue* by asserting that one can learn more from personal anguish than from reading scientific treatises on this subject: "'Mademoiselle Albertine est partie!' Comme la souffrance va plus loin en psychologie que la psychologie!" ["Mademoiselle Albertine has left!" How much deeper does anguish penetrate into psychology than psychology itself!](3:419). In her case Yolanda said of Proust, "With him I have learned how to suffer. . . . I

have learned how to taste the intensity of pain even in its deepest folds"
(quoted by García Carrillo 1971). By delving into her personal consciousness through introspection, as well in other ways, Oreamuno was
showing her profound modernism of the Proustian variety.

Suffering is a constant theme and presence in *La ruta de su evasión* and
is generally associated with love. Being a woman, Yolanda wrote of other
women and of their difficult, but nearly inevitable relationships with
men. The latter, convinced of their innate superiority, wield their power
to control the former. The women, for the most part unsure of themselves, submit and suffer. Analyzing the members of a particular family,
which includes don Vasco; his wife, Teresa; their sons, Roberto and
Gabriel; and the women involved with these young men, Oreamuno
explored in depth the question of gender relations in Spanish America.
In this regard, Proust often served as her inspiration.

Early in the Costa Rican novel, the narrator shows the importance of
gestures through an analysis of don Vasco's peculiar type of greeting,
which was at least partly derived from an analysis found in the *Recherche*:

> Para saludar don Vasco se doblaba materialmente en dos, acusando gruesas
> arrugas en el impecable chaleco, haciendo ondular el opulento vientre. Ex-
> tendía una mano que presionaba violenta y seca. Ese apretón no significaba
> nada especial, sólo parecía valorar la tensión muscular de la otra mano.
> (1984, 39)

> [In order to greet a person don Vasco bent over physically in two, creating
> thick wrinkles in his impeccable waistcoat, causing his enormous belly to
> ripple. He stretched out a hand that squeezed in a brusk but dry manner. That
> handshake did not mean anything in particular, it only seemed to assess the
> muscular tension of the other person's hand.]

The narrator of *Du côté de chez Swann* describes in a like manner Legrandin's exaggerated form of bowing:

> il fit un profond salut avec un renversement secondaire en arrière, qui
> ramena brusquement son dos au delà de la position de départ. . . . Ce re-
> dressement rapide fit refluer en une sorte d'onde fougueuse et musclée la
> croupe de Legrandin que je ne supposais pas si charnue. . . . (1:124–25)

> [he made a deep bow with an accessory movement backwards, which abruptly
> brought his shoulders behind their starting point. . . . This quick straighten-
> ing up caused a kind of impetuous muscular wave to flow over Legrandin's
> behind, which I did not imagine to be so plump. . . .]

During the narration of Teresa's life with her overbearing husband,
gestures assume a particular significance because they reveal to her and

other characters don Vasco's desire to control and manipulate them. Here Proust's presence is more distant, but his inspiration is still evident. In one specific episode the glint in don Vasco's eyes exposes his feelings, just as Legrandin's passionate gaze revealed his snobbery (see chapter 2). Through it, Teresa discovers her husband's evil intention. Don Vasco wished to trick their guest Esteban into petting the family's dog in the hope that Yoka would attack him. Likewise, after Teresa's intervention, where she risked showing her own tender feelings for Esteban, she has to suffer don Vasco's angry glare, which reveals his disappointment. Throughout the entire passage, the reader can follow Oreamuno's subtle analysis of gestures learned from Proust as each of the characters tries to understand what is happening by watching each other's eyes. One fine example is Esteban's interior monologue near the end:

> Ahora él vuelve, un resplandor amarillo en el extremo donde sus ojos son más amarillos. Un punto casi indefinible, pero horriblemente peligroso. Ha visto la mirada que yo dirijo a Teresa y la respuesta silenciosa que recibo. ¿Qué pensará de esa mirada? (108)

> [Now he turns, a yellow gleam in the corner where his eyes are more yellow. An almost indefinable dot, but a horribly dangerous one. He has seen the gaze that I direct toward Teresa and the silent response that I receive. I wonder what he may think about that look?]

In various situations involving these characters, as well as others, we can see how Proust inspired Oreamuno's imagination. Teresa's agony, which lasts throughout the novel, and the process of giving birth and the subsequent death of Roberto's neglected wife Cristina suggest how Oreamuno, like Proust himself, used her personal experience with suffering in the creation of her text.

One other example is very instructive. It shows Yolanda Oreamuno's direct relation with Marcel Proust, as well as her original development of the situation described. The young woman Aurora, who is living with the second son Gabriel near the end of the novel and who suffers from his neglect and abuse, is only able to forget her anguish when she watches him sleep. She confesses this fact to him in the following way: "eres mío cuando duermes. Entonces me perteneces por completo. Yo te miro dormir, oigo tu respiración y siento que eres mío" [you are mine when you sleep. Then you belong to me completely. I watch you sleep, I hear your breathing and I feel that you are mine] (317). Clearly, like Torres Bodet in *Margarita de niebla* and María Luisa Bombal in *La última niebla*, Oreamuno was inspired by the famous passage from *La prisonnière* where the protagonist finds calm in the midst of his doubts and anguish when he watches Albertine in slumber: "Il me semblait à ces moments-là que je venais de la posséder plus complètement, comme une chose inconsciente et sans résistance de la muette nature" [It seemed to me at those moments that I had possessed her more completely, like an unconscious and unresisting thing of mute nature] (3:73).

Going beyond the obvious similarities, I wish to emphasize that for Oreamuno this situation constituted a point of departure rather than the beginning a similar type of development. Through it the Costa Rican writer was able to explain Aurora's feelings for Gabriel, his reaction to these and his subsequent decision to satisfy her desires by taking an overdose of aspirin. Gabriel realizes that he has treated Aurora cruelly, but in spite of his sensitive nature he does not believe that he can change the pattern of female abuse, which was instilled by his father. Barring this, he can only give to Aurora his meaningless life and thus liberate her by always sleeping for her.

Efforts to Understand Homosexual Love

The mention of Albertine, whose principal model in real life was a man called Alfred Agostinelli, leads us to another facet of gender associated with Proust, homosexuality. Even though the critics of Europe began quite early to examine this aspect of Proust's work, and many novelists there soon followed it in their texts, the Spanish Americans were reticent on this subject for many years.

Indeed in the androgynous novelettes by the Mexican *Contemporáneos* one can detect a link. Also, a few works, such as *Vigilia* [Wakefulness] (1934) by Enrique Anderson Imbert, provided more than a hint of this subject. Here, the protagonist Beltrán feels a greater attraction for his male friends than for women. He is disgusted when he goes to a house of prostitution, and even though he has a girlfriend his feelings for her are almost exclusively platonic. He persists in this relationship more due to imitation of and camadaderie for his friends than because of physical love or desire. The description of his movements as "mariposeando" [fluttering] tells us a great deal about him.

At times Beltrán's emotional, enthusiastic nature even seems modeled on that of the young Proustian protagonist. At the beginning of *Vigilia* when he is walking through the rain with his friends, Beltrán becomes very excited:

Ya no pudo más de felicidad, y Beltrán escapó del tibio y móvil recinto que componían los paraguas, para sentir en la cara y en sus manos la caricia violenta de la lluvia, para patear un tacho, y golpear las puertas, y confiarle al mundo, en gritos de gozo, esas confusas sensaciones que lo exaltaban. (1934, 12–13)

[He could no longer restrain his happiness, and Beltrán escaped from the warm and movable enclosure which the umbrella provided, in order to feel on his face and on his hands the rude caress of the rain, in order to kick a trash can and to pound on doors and to confess to the world in shrieks of pleasure, those jumbled sensations that excited him.]

In a nearly identical manner the young hero of "Combray" expresses non-verbally the excitement that he derived from reading a book and from walking in the rain:

Les murs des maisons, la haie de Tansonville, les arbres du bois de Roussain-ville, les buissons auxquels s'adosse Montjouvain, recevaient des coups de parapluie ou de canne, entendaient des cris joyeux, qui n' étaient, les uns et les autres, que des idées confuses qui m'exaltaient. . . . (1:154)

[The walls of the houses, the hedge of Tansonville, the trees of Roussainville woods, the bushes adjacent to Montjouvain received blows from my umbrella or walking stick, heard my shouts of glee, all of which were only poorly understood ideas that excited me. . . .]

Although David William Foster has unearthed a few early Spanish American literary texts involving homosexuality, almost none of these fall within the period that we discussed in chapter 2.[4] From 1920 until 1950, homosexuality remained an unmentionable subject. Thus, as late as 1949, Mario Benedetti, who had pointed out the suggestion of lesbianism in A batallas de amor, was able to assert about Spanish America: "until now its principal novelists have not imported, save with few exceptions, the various species of literary pederasts, of which the European market shows itself to be so fond" (1951, 70). This situation, however, began to change during the 1950s, in part due to the influence of Sodome et Gomorrhe and Proust's other volumes. One Argentine writer, Manuel Mujica Láinez, who followed Proust in the areas of high society, time, memory and writing and shared a similar modernist perspective, then dared to treat homosexuality but with Proust's assistance.

Initially, Mujica Láinez approached the subject in such a timid and subtle way that many of his readers and critics apparently did not understand that he was doing so.[5] Each of the sections of Los ídolos—"Lucio Sansilvestre," "Duma," and "Fabricia"—seems to deal with a different person, but in all three cases the narrator's beloved former classmate, Gustavo, is the hidden agenda. Although his explicit subject in the first two sections is the life of a poet and that of an elderly aunt, the narrator consistently pays more attention to Gustavo and to his own feelings toward him. He says, for example, of the hint of a smile on Gustavo's face and of a story told by Duma, "Es curioso que recuerde ese detalle y en cambio no sepa nada de lo que aconteció con Gabriele d'Annunzio" [It is curious that I remember that detail and in contrast know nothing about what happened to Gabriele d'Annunzio] (1976, 126). Here, we find not only a case of self-delusion but also of homoeroticism. The narrator's love for Gustavo becomes increasingly evident in spite of his silence concerning its physical implications.

Proust's influence with regard to homosexuality can be observed especially well in section 3. Here, we find a Proust-like substitution on the level of plot when the narrator momentarily falls in love with Fabricia. Not only is this young woman's name based upon a masculine name, Fabricio, as in the case of Albertine, but also her imagined intimacy with Gustavo allows the narrator a socially acceptable means of expressing his affection for his deceased friend. By kissing Fabricia he satisfies his earlier desire to embrace Gustavo in nearly the same way as the protagonist of *La prisonnière* kisses Albertine (or the novelist, Alfred) at night in order to reproduce years past childhood the evening ritual that he had enjoyed with his mother.

In his third novel about the decadent upper-class family, *Los viajeros*, Mujica Láinez made the subject of homosexuality more explicit, and he used what he had learned from Proust's psychological analysis to a far greater extent.[6] In this regard Guillermo de Torre wrote, "Let us register . . . the perspicacity and slow development of the meticulous psychological analyses that bring to mind at times—but with originality and not mere imitation—the art of Marcel Proust" (1955, 34).

In general, *Los viajeros* conforms to the patterns of the traditional psychological novel. The narrator, Miguel, explains how he fell in love with Berenice and how their intimate relationship developed over time. Specifically, he is analytical when he describes his feelings and when he considers the motivation of the people around him, but the tragic death of Berenice also causes him to sentimentalize this woman to some degree.

In the analysis of the members of his extended family, at one point, Miguel comes very close to Proust. Referring to Gustavo and other relatives described in *Los ídolos* and his uncle Baltasar in *Los viajeros* itself, he concludes that they were obsessed by semi-artistic endeavors because of their lack of true creative ability:

esa actitud representaba una defensa disimulada contra el horror inconfeso de la propia incapacidad creadora, de la debilidad del espíritu, un afán desesperado por asirse a una tabla de salvación espectacular, garantizada por el tiempo y por el prestigio. . . . (1955, 115)

[that attitude represented a covert defense against the unconfessed fear of their own creative inability, of a weakness of the mind, a desperate urge to take hold of a spectacular life preserver, one that had proved the test of time and of prestige.]

As we saw in our discussion of Victoria Ocampo, the incapacity to delve deeply enough into one's self caused a similar reaction in some of Proust's characters, whom he called in *Le temps retrouvé* "célibataires de l'art" (3:892).

More closely associated with our subject at hand is Miguel's analysis of his uncle Baltasar, whose semi-artistic activity was translating into Spanish the complete poetical works of Victor Hugo. From the very beginning of *Los viajeros* this, the nominal head of the impoverished branch of the family seems excentric and reminiscent of Proust's character the Baron de Charlus. Both men are contradictory in similar ways. They are violent and tender, proud and timid. They claim to despise all that is effeminate in other males but are obviously concerned about their own refinement and elegance. Furthermore, both have unusual relationships with women. For instance, Baltasar often locked himself in his greenhouse study with a naked prostitute, but he never touched her.

In particular, the initial episode of *Los viajeros* (15–19) brings to mind a passage from *Le côté de Guermantes* where Charlus inflicted unjust verbal abuse upon the Proustian protagonist because of an allegedly defamatory comment (2:555). In the Argentine novel we find a similar example of injustice. To punish the adolescents Miguel and his friend Simón for arriving home late from fishing, Baltasar forces them to look at the naked woman. It is symptomatic that the narrators in both texts underscore the impression of power that the shouting man caused. Even Baltasar's emotional collapse, which is precipitated by the arrival of Simón's father, is similar to the abrupt changes from lion to lamb that are characteristic of the Baron.

In attempting to understand his enigmatic uncle, Miguel employs a method of analysis which closely resembles that of Proust's protagonist. He learns to attribute slight importance to Baltasar's own verbal explanation of his behavior and much more to his gestures and general attitude. Miguel thus speculates upon the probable reasons for his uncle's actions and searches for an underlying cause. His long lists of conjectures resemble those found in the *Recherche*. Miguel considers, for example, as the possible reasons for Baltasar's destroying his own nearly complete version of Hugo's poetry: his pride, fear of the public, insanity, timidity or the realization of his mediocrity. Miguel ultimately concludes that the essential cause for the destruction of the work of many years, as well as for most of Baltasar's other apparently senseless acts, is a hidden trait in his character. Notably Baltasar suffers from the same weakness as the Baron de Charlus. Due to their natures, both male characters are inclined to love other men. For this reason, it is suggested that Baltasar destroyed his translation in a fit of anger against his nephew because Miguel translated poetry better than he but did not correspond to his homosexual feelings.

In spite of the obvious similarities between Baltasar and Charlus, both of whom undergo a process of decay over time, I must emphasize Mujica Láinez's ability to adapt this type of character to an Argentine environment and to his own type of novel. Unlike Charlus, Baltasar merely wishes to appropriate European culture, similar to the other members of his family, but can never embody it, and he is too timid to express his homosexuality in any overt way.

As for the novel itself, Miguel's speculative approach to reality leads the text in a slightly different direction than what we find in Proust's work. Near the end of *Los viajeros* the reader may have the impression that this psychological novel comes very close to detective fiction. In the aftermath of a series of petroleum explosions, finding the corpses of Berenice and Simón along side that of Baltasar in the unlikely location of the greenhouse study causes Miguel to suspect an act of malice. He is able to confirm this hypothesis when he finds the key to the locked greenhouse door in his uncle's pocket. The narrator can then deduce that Baltasar, who felt abandoned and betrayed by him, had lured the two persons that the nephew loved most to a place where they would surely die. Here again, we can perceive the same underlying cause: Baltasar's homosexual love for Miguel, which is related to *Sodome et Gommorhe*. However, because the French author's speculation and analysis almost never dealt with crime *per se*, we can see how Mujica Láinez adapted these elements for his own purposes.

In his subsequent works *Invitados en "El Paraíso"* [Guests at Paradise Estate] and *Bomarzo*, Mujica Láinez used even more freely and openly the subject of homosexuality. The artist in the first of these novels is implicitly gay, and the Italian duke in the second is bisexual. On the surface, it might appear that the Argentine's liberated attitude implies also moving away from Proust. In *Bomarzo*, in particular, we find fewer verbal and situational echoes from the *Recherche* concerning homosexuality, as well as other subjects. Likewise the narrator seems more interested in justifying himself than in analyzing his or anyone else's motives. Nonetheless, on a more profound level—that of novelistic intentions— Mujica Láinez seemed more Proustian than ever. In fact, he did precisely what the French author himself might have enjoyed doing but lacked sufficient courage. The Argentine chose as his focal character one that was not heterosexual. For this reason the similarities between the Duque de Bomarzo and the Baron de Charlus are especially meaningful. By attributing to his principal character, who speaks in the first person, the same type of interest in genealogy, social position, refinement and art, plus a similar propensity toward vice, Mujica Láinez moved to center stage his Charlus-like character. This clearly implies an attempt to justify the type of person that Proust himself felt compelled by his audience to condemn. In this way the Argentine novelist both suggested his source of inspiration and moved a step beyond his literary model.[7]

A few other Spanish American writers during these years began to treat the subject of homosexuality in a Proustian manner, but often for dissimilar purposes. Such was the case of Mario Benedetti in his novel *La tregua* [The Truce] (1960), where gay characters are introduced in nearly the same way as in the *Recherche*. In this regard the Uruguayan's comments in his essay on Proust about the presentation of Charlus anticipate certain facets of his own work:

> Instead of defining first of all his peculiar nature so that the reader can watch carefully his future actions, Proust presents him in a brief passage of action and mimicry in order that the reader may subsequently speculate upon the type of characer to whom such nervous gestures, such gratutious movements and so much restlessness could correspond. Proust registers symptoms, not characteristics. (1951, 30)

In *La tregua,* one can easily see how this lesson was applied. Early in the diary which forms the text the narrator Santomé makes the following remark concerning his son and two friends:

> Jaime pasó por la vereda de enfrente. Iba con otros dos, que tenían algo desagradable en el porte y en el vestir, no me acuerdo bien, porque me fijé especialmente en Jaime. No sé qué les iría diciendo a los otros, pero éstos se reían con grandes aspavientos. (1974, 41)

> [Jaime came along the sidewalk across the street. He was walking with two others, who had an unpleasant manner in their appearance and dress, I do not remember well, because I paid special attention to Jaime. I do not know what he could be saying to the others, but they were laughing in a very exaggerated fashion.]

Much later when Santomé learns that his son is gay, he suddenly under stands his own confused impressions. Such was precisely the case when the Proustian protagonist made a similar discovery about Charlus. San tomé draws a conclusion and then remarks, "Así que esos amigos . . . Era un mazazo. Sin embargo, me di cuenta de que en el fondo de mí mismo ya existía una sospecha" [So those friends . . . It was a heavy blow. How ever, I realized that in the back of my mind a suspicion already existed] (119–20).[8]

Although very different from *Bomarzo,* José Lezama Lima's *Paradiso* (1968) is also a large, ambitious novel related by similarity and contrast to *Sodome et Gomorrhe.* In broad terms the Cuban novel deals with the same three aspects of the subject of homosexuality as do the French and Argentine volumes. It attempts to show the nature of homosexual love, it depicts various types of gays, and it portrays a particular society in which gays have had to live. Lezama Lima, of course, assigned his own interpretation to each of these areas. He contrasted, for example, homosexuality with heterosexuality and androgyny. Also in his text, family and society often play different roles, as when the father of Fronesis tries to separate this young man from Foción.

In some instances, homosexuality is treated in a Proust-like manner in *Paradiso,* especially when it first appears. The introduction of the gay character Foción is very much like that of the Baron de Charlus in *A l'ombre des jeunes filles en fleurs* (which, as we saw, Benedetti described above). Foción's unusual gestures and tone of voice suggest to José Cemí that his new acquaintance somehow differs from most of the people that he knows. Likewise, when Cemí happens to hear Foción talk to a young man in the next aisle at a bookstore we are reminded of the encounter between Charlus and Jupien at the beginning of *Sodome et Gomorrhe.* This Proustian procedure involving words and gestures, however, does not continue.

Unlike Marcel Proust, José Lezama Lima had little interest in psychological analysis. Similar to the other writers of the 1960s, the Cuban author rarely attempted to explain the workings of the human mind. He treated the subject of homosexuality in other ways. In particular, he described specific sexual acts, but in such a poetic way that he did not offend most of his readers. Furthermore, Lezama's highly intellectualized characters discuss homosexuality just as they do literature and philosophy. For them this subject offers a similar opportunity to display their erudition, subtle ideas and ability to convince. André Gide's dialogue in defense of homosexuality, *Corydon,* has often been cited as a model for their oral discussion in chapter 9, but because of its expository nature this passage also corresponds roughly to Proust's essay on the same subject, which appears in the first section of *Sodome et Gomorrhe.*

Beginning in the late 1960s, the treatment of homosexuality became increasingly more frequent and daring in Spanish American narrative. The cultural rebellion of that time and the postmodern tendency to explore the value of marginalized groups, such as gays, contributed to the increased use of this subject. I certainly cannot claim that all or even most of these works were directly related to Proust. The Spanish American authors drew from their own experience or knowledge of the gay world, as well as upon other literary sources from Oscar Wilde and André Gide to Jean Genet and William Burroughs. Even in the case of José Donoso, who followed various aspects of the *Recherche* in several works, his gay novel *El lugar sin límites* [Hell Has No Limits] (1967) is clearly distinct from *Sodome et Gomorrhe*. I acknowledge that both texts show the self-destructive tendencies of the principal gay character and his progressive decay, but these traits can be found in numerous gay works, some of which preceded the *Recherche*. Such a negative trajectory and tragic outcome made these novels more acceptable to the general reading public. Just the same from the 1970s until the present there have appeared several Spanish American novels whose treatment of homosexuality is unmistakably related to Proust.

One interesting but somewhat complex example is *Una familia lejana* by Carlos Fuentes. We already saw in chapter 3 how the famous Mexican author placed this novel about French-Spanish American cultural relations in a Proustian context by using the Guermantes-like character Conde de Branly. Fuentes also tightly wove into his text other Proustian themes: homosexuality, memory and exclusion.

In *Una familia lejana,* a very intimate relationship between the French boy André and the young Mexican Víctor develops quickly. Although this friendship entails several traits that are distant from Proust, Branly begins to discover its homosexual nature in a very Proustian way: through the boys' words heard by chance. Furthermore, Branly, who considers intervening in what he imagines to be a dangerous type of intimacy for the boys, chooses not to do so for reasons closely associated with the *Recherche* and its treatment of memory and personal relationships.[9]

Early in the novel, Branly undergoes a Proustian memory experience in part triggered by young Víctor Heredia. On the edge of a ravine near Cuernavaca, this boy whistles along with a song that is heard in the distance. Immediately, Branly begins to recall two similar incidents that had taken place in Paris: one from his recent past and the other from his childhood. The narrator summarizes:

Mi amigo miró al niño y recordó que pocos meses antes había pasado una tarde sentado en el Parc Monceau, viendo a los niños jugar. No supo si al verlos recordaba a los niños que jugaron aquí mismo con él cuando él era niño, o si sólo miraba de nuevo a los niños de antes, pero ahora, para siempre, sin él. (1980, 20)

[My friend looked at the boy and recalled that only a few months before he had spent an afternoon sitting in the Parc Monceau, watching the boys play. He could not determine if upon seeing them he remembered the boys that

played right there with him when he was a child, or if he only watched again
the boys from before, but now, forever, without him.]

Branly's memory experience remains for a long time incomplete. He
feels a profound sense of loss, but he cannot ascertain why. Like the
Proustian protagonist, Branly must identify the actual moment that he
remembered in order to recover the past. His approach, however, proves
to be somewhat different from that of Proust's character. Branly succeeds with the aid of Víctor's presence, his own reflections, and dreams.

Symptomatically, the incident recalled is directly tied to our present
subject. It is not that this episode involved homosexuality *per se*, but the
attraction between two pre-teen males is central to it. Branly remembers
the time when an ungainly boy, who lived next to the park, finally came
out to play but was shunned by the other boys. For a brief moment,
young Branly felt the urge to be cordial and even to embrace the boy, but
fearing what the others might think, he refused to accept the boy's
outstretched hand.

For the old count, this incident is significant and even decisive because it meant the rejection of a relationship which could have been of
personal value. Moreover, for a reader of the *Recherche* this portion of
Una familia lejana takes on a greater meaning because Fuentes appears to
be dialoguing with a passage from the third part of *Du côté de chez Swann*.
Here, we find a description of the the activities of the child protagonist,
who regularly goes to the Champs-Elysées for exercise and recreation.
When he sees for the first time the girl Gilberte and her friends having
fun, he feels painfully excluded. Of her fortunate playmate who shouts,
"Adieu, Gilberte," the narrator comments:

> elle revoyait ou du moins, possédait en sa mémoire, de leur intimité quoti-
> dienne, des visites qu'elles se faisaient l'une chez l'autre, de tout cet inconnu
> encore plus inaccessible et plus douloureux pour moi d'être au contraire si
> familier et si maniable pour cette fille heureuse. . . . (1:394)

> [she saw again or at least held in her memory, from their daily intimacy, visits
> that they had made to each other's house; all of those unknown things were
> even more inaccessible and painful for me since they were on the contrary so
> familiar and tractable for that fortunate girl. . . .]

Here, we find the theme of exclusion, which the narrator later develops
in numerous ways and contexts, but particularly with regard to Proust's
characteristic subject of snobbery. Fortunately, for the young protagonist, Gilberte does not withhold her friendship very long. A few days
later, when she needs another child to participate in one of her games,
she invites him to play. In contrast, the author of *Una familia lejana* froze

the situation described above so that he could use it in his novel. The implicit dialogue heightens the reader's emotion because it suggests what might have been. Unlike the Proustian protagonist, who would come to love Gilberte, Branly as a child did not experience the joys of a particular friendship. Upon remembering this incident, the old count feels great remorse which convinces him that he should not try to sever the relationship between the boys in the present, even though it may involve homosexuality.

Specifically, in regard to the unusual friendship between André and Víctor, I must concede that its link with Proust is tenuous at best. Carlos Fuentes developed it in ways totally disconnected from the *Recherche*. In the car Branly does confirm his suspicion concerning its homosexual nature, somewhat like the Proustian protagonist when he finds Charlus in a compromising situation, but the fantastic and symbolic aspects of this bond carry it so far beyond common reality or reason that neither Branly nor the reader can understand it fully. In this case we can observe the gothic side of Fuentes and a similarity between *Una familia lejana* and *Aura*. Such a distancing from Proust, nonetheless, does not seriously undercut the essential relation between the French and Mexican works. It is merely an example of the numerous plays of proximity and distance typical of this novel.

It is also feasible to detect a Proustian relation in another Mexican novel of these years—one that is truly gay—*En jirones* [In Shreds] (1985) by Luis Zapata. As José Joaquín Blanco subtly suggested in his "Presentación" but never stated, the gay love story depicted has a direct connection with "Un amour de Swann" and other parts of the *Recherche*. However, it is not that the beloved of the narrator Sebastián, who is first called O. and then A., simply represents a modern version of Odette or Albertine. Nor can we say that Sebastián is often jealous like Swann or displays a prison-guard mentality like the protagonist of *La prisonnière*. Even Blanco's suggestion that A. was not of the narrator's type does not help us clarify this literary relation. Obviously, from the very first Sebastián finds the man that he describes in his diary-notebook physically attractive, unlike the case of Swann with Odette. Granted, the two males are indisputably distinct. Sebastián has accepted his homosexuality and is looking for a partner to share his life. In contrast, because of his Roman Catholic upbringing and pressure from his bourgeois family, A. can never admit his sexual nature. Such differences, however, do not ultimately block their physical relationship. Quite soon, A. does overcome his post-coital disgust and moves in with Sebastián.

The narrator's feelings are often dissimilar to those of Swann or the Proustian protagonist. Learning from Mario (Vanessa) about A.'s anything but innocent past of course angers Sebastián, but his love for A. is so strong that he quickly forgives his friend's deceitfulness. Unlike the protagonist of *La prisonnière*, Zapata's narrator never interrogates his partner. In fact, he systematically avoids putting A. in the uncomfortable position of Albertine.

In spite of the differences between the *Recherche* and *En jirones* a profound but elusive connection remains. Specifically, Proustian notions appear at frequent intervals. Like Swann and the protagonist of *La prisonnière*, Sebastián becomes obsessed with the idea of possession. He wants A. entirely for himself: "quiero que A. me pertenezca por completo, que sea como un esclavo, que satisfaga mis mayores necesidades y cumpla hasta mis menores caprichos" [I want A. to belong to me completely, for him to be like a slave, to satisfy my greatest needs and to comply with my slightest whims] (1994, 69). This desire to possess the other, which was the underlying cause for Swann's jealousy and the Proustian protagonist's interrogations, has a more physical goal for the narrator in part 1 of *En jirones:* anal intercourse, which is consistently denied.

One might point out that physical possession was of slight importance in Proust's fictional world. Swann is not totally satisfied when he is able to *faire catleya* with [to deflower] Odette, and he certainly would not have said in the manner of Sebastián when he finished "por fin me pertenece" [finally he belongs to me] (118). Nonetheless, when Vanessa claims that A. enjoyed playing the passive role, the narrator of *En jirones* finds himself in precisely the same situation as another Proustian lover: Saint-Loup in his affair with Rachel. Various men regularly enjoyed the love object which cost him so much. To a large extent, particularly early in the affair, A. uses the same strategy as Odette or Rachel. He frequently lies and withholds his favors so that he can better ensnare and retain Sebastián. A. even confesses the nature of his ploy by saying, "para que te enamores de mí" [so that you may fall in love with me] (35), but Sebastián pays no attention, in part because he enjoys the game and its surprises.

Another Proustian idea that underlies this Mexican novel is that the lover can never truly know the beloved. Even after living together for an extended period of time, neither the protagonist of *La prisonnière* nor the narrator of *En jirones* is able to discover the real thoughts or motives of the other person. Both lovers constantly speculate and try to understand the beloved's facial expressions and actions, but they never fully know what the other person is thinking or what will happen next. Sebastián sees A. exit a church, just as Proust's protagonist notices Albertine's malaise, but both lovers are shocked when their beloved leaves—A. to get married and Albertine to escape.

The most striking parallel between the French and Mexican works can be observed in part 2 of *En jirones*, where the obsessed lover must confront the absence of the beloved. Having focused all of his attention and interest upon A., when the latter is no longer present, Sebastián is totally lost. Significantly Zapata's character, like the protagonist of *Albertine disparue,* discovers that forgetting is extremely difficult. He is perhaps less affected by the evocative power of objects, but his dreams constantly remind him of A.

Most of the second part of *En jirones* (which bears the same title as the novel itself and is central to it) has nearly the same tone and atmosphere as *Albertine disparue.* Sebastián remains in his room, thinks only about his sensations and feelings and exists only on a conscious level. His intro-spective analysis is in specific ways very Proustian. Similar to the narrator of the *Recherche,* he eventually concludes that his image of A. has little in common with the man A. himself. Yet, unlike the Proustian protagonist, Zapata's narrator is trapped in his cycle of pain and makes only slight progress toward forgetfulness and recovery.

Finally and most importantly, Luis Zapata creates a complete reversal of *Albertine disparue* when A. returns. Strengthened by his family's money and the permanent excuse that he must spend time with his wife, A. seizes total control over the still depressed and insecure Sebastián. The latter, who has finished his work and wishes to return to the capital, cannot do so. He is not pleased with the idea of sharing A., and at one point, like Swann and the Proustian protagonist, he suffers from the thought of A.'s having sex with his wife and other persons. Sebastián's former goal of totally possessing A. comes to nothing, even though A. is now willing to play the passive role on occasion. In contrast, A., who still refuses to accept the idea that he is in any way homosexual, wants to possess Sebastián totally. He says, "no quiero que pienses en otra cosa que no sea yo" [I do not want you to think about anything besides me] (194). When the narrator insists upon leaving, A. beats him. In a literal sense, Sebastián becomes A.'s prisoner and his life is reduced to having sex with A. He concludes, "No puedo hacer nada; no soy dueño de mi tiempo. A. es el único poseedor de mis horas, el que dispone a su antojo de mi utilización" [I cannot do anything; I am not the owner of my time. A. is the only possessor of my hours, the one who can use me at his own whim] (204).

This reversal, in conjunction with the Proustian ideas and analyses scattered along the way, suggests that Luis Zapata wrote *En jirones* as a long and detailed response to Proust. Although it cannot be termed a parody because it is so very serious, it is indeed postmodern because of its exploration of a marginal perspective and its rewriting of a modernist text. Perhaps remembering that the author of *La prisonnière* and *Albertine disparue* had used in these volumes his homosexual experiences with Agostinelli but whitewashed them by transforming this man into a woman, the Mexican novelist decided to show the dangers of sexual dishonesty and of obsessive love. Marcel Proust tried to sequester Agostinelli and use him as he wished (even as a literary subject) but, as in the case of one of Sebastián's nightmares, the pursuer could easily become the pursued.

The Cuban novelist, Reinaldo Arenas, who learned of Proust through José Lezama Lima and Virgilio Piñera, also treated the subject of homosexuality in a Proustian manner. In the fourth volume of his *Pentagonía*, *El color del verano* [The Color of Summer] (1991), similar to Proust in his own fourth volume *Sodome et Gomorrhe*, Arenas focused his attention upon this subject more than in any of his previous works. Like Proust and Lezama Lima (but in his own way), Arenas explored the nature of homosexual love, he depicted various types of gays and he portrayed a society in which gays had to live. In this regard, I should emphasize an important difference between Reinaldo Arenas and José Lezama Lima. Unlike his mentor, who tried to deny his connection with Proust, Arenas openly confessed his. He stated in his last interview before committing suicide that *El color del verano* "is somewhat like *Sodoma y Gomorra* by Proust, but with a touch of imagination, of irony and with the desolation that is always found in my books" (1991, 62). Furthermore, throughout *El color del verano* we are constantly reminded of its relation with Proust. Not only is the French novelist cited to illustrate the second category of *locura* [gayness], *belleza* [beauty], and is discussed briefly by the character Lezama in a lecture, but also one of the gay characters uses as an alternate name Delfín Proust.[10] As a result, the surname of the French novelist is mentioned several dozen times. Let me also interject that the subject of writing is treated in a Proustian manner in this novel, as we shall see in chapter 8.

One major difference, which Arenas himself emphasized in the interview, is the sexual preference of the narrator: "Proust is is not presented in the novel as a homosexual character, but as a seducer of women . . ." (62). By contrast, the Cuban's protagonist-narrator, who is designated by three names—Gabriel, Reinaldo and the Tétrica Mofeta [the Gloomy Skunk]—is clearly gay, even though he tries to hide this fact from his mother. This dissimilarity has a profound effect upon both texts. In the early volumes of the *Recherche*, the narrator mentions in passing the enigmatic gestures and manner of the Baron de Charlus, but he offers no explanation because at that stage in his life he did not understand them. As suggested above, at the beginning of *Sodome et Gomorrhe* we find a case of anagnorisis. The protagonist witnesses by chance an encounter between the Baron and another male, Jupien, and from their gestures he realizes that they are both homosexuals. This discovery allows him to understand their previous words and gestures, as well as future ones. It also sparks his curiosity, and he follows them. Listening through a thin wall, he realizes that they are engaged in some sort of physical activity, but he is unable to determine what. The noise suggests an act of violence by one against the other, but the sighs of both indicate pleasure.

In sharp contrast, the overtly gay narrator of *El color del verano* understands from the very first all things gay, and he describes in visual and erotic terms numerous homosexual acts. The first instance in the Cuban novel is most relevant for our purposes because it appears to have been constructed in response to Proust's description involving sound cited above. Several middle-aged gays, who were just evicted from a beach by a plainclothes policeman, watch the Tétrica Mofeta approach and seduce the same officer. Aware of the meaning behind the gestures, the pleasure that is derived and the danger that is implied, these gays first become aroused and then jealous. To a large extent, unlike the Proustian protagonist, they are participants in the episode.

By comparing these two same-sex passages, we can discover the fundamental difference between the French author's emphasis on the psychological aspects of homosexuality and the Cuban's focus upon the physical ones. Whereas Proust wished to illustrate the psychological nature of all forms of love, including that practiced by homosexuals, Arenas even limited the physical range to sex between men. The lesbian world, which Proust called "Gomorrhe," is thus generally ignored. As a result the Cuban novel is composed of long descriptive passages, while the French text has many expository ones.

As for the second area of exploration in both novels—the classification of various types of gays—there are also pertinent differences. Using images taken from botany and entomology, Proust tried to appear as scientific as feasible, and again he emphasized human psychology.[11] Thus, at the beginning of *Sodome et Gomorrhe,* the narrator discusses the solitary invert, those males that are attracted to masculine women and those males that are excited by men that love women. He pays little attention to sexual roles. In contrast, this aspect is of primary importance to Arenas, at least at first. He devoted sections of his book to *las locas* and to *los bugarrones* [buggers], where these passive and active homosexual types are divided into sub-categories. Furthermore, Arenas was far less serious in his treatment than his French counterpart and was therefore more humorous. In a postmodern way, he creates rational categories, somewhat like Proust's, so that he can subvert them. *Locura* is defined twice in contradictory terms, but in each case it seems to encompass most men. Similarly, the group *bugarrones* appears to exclude no males other than *pájaros* [queers]. In short, Arenas wished to suggest that all Cuban males have been or could be involved in same-sex activities, including the dictator Fifo, who obviously represents Fidel Castro.

In the third area—the depiction of gays in society—Proust showed in particular how an aristocratic and well-connected invert, like the Baron de Charlus, was able to function in elite circles and could even be considered a highly esteemed member. Over time, after using his prestige to assist his young male friends, the Baron's true nature becomes evident to more people and his position in society falls. This decline continues in the volumes after *Sodome et Gomorrhe*. In *La prisonnière*, he is expelled from a social gathering, and he is later abandoned by his protégé Morel. In *Le temps retrouvé* he reaches the depths of society when he is beaten with chains by a male prostitute.

Conspicuously, *El color del verano* begins with more humble ambiances with the depiction of gays at the beach, in public restrooms and on trains. Given that the protagonist is an aspiring writer, it is only natural in this novel that we also find gay intellectuals like Lezama and Piñera. On this level, the novel by Arenas resembles the works by both Proust and Lezama Lima. Yet the author of *El color del verano* did not stop here. In spite of the apparent contradiction between communism and high society, Arenas made Fifo's enormous celebration for the fiftieth (which is really the fortieth) anniversary of his regime seem like one of the elegant soirées found in *Le côté de Guermantes* or *Sodome et Gomorrhe*. Here once again we can detect a parodic relation with Proust, especially because along side the famous international guests appear several gays, including the Tétrica Mofeta. Like the French author, Arenas thus illustrated the social trajectory of his gay characters, but the order is reversed. Finally, I note that in this carnivalesque scene, around which the entire book revolves and where the guests participate in unmentionable activities, Arenas not only lampooned the communist regime for its cruelty and contradictions, but also he presented on another level his principal thesis: that all men (and perhaps women) are somehow gay. Even here we can find a distant echo of Proust, who suggested that homosexuality was far more common than most people would admit.

GOING BEYOND THE PSYCHOLOGICAL NOVEL DURING AND SINCE THE BOOM

Within the larger context of the non-gay world we can see for the period following 1960 how the Proustian subjects of love, illness and consciousness began to receive a different kind of treatment in Spanish American narrative. Psychological analysis in the manner of Proust was called into question, and some writers criticized it openly in their works. Nonetheless love, illness and the human mind remained important subjects for these Spanish American authors, who at times sought an ironic or parodic postmodern relation with Proust.

A few novelists during the 1960s continued to follow Proust's modernist example in the area of analysis. Such was the case of the Uruguayan Carlos Martínez Moreno in his novel *La otra mitad* [The Other Half] (1966). Here, the narrator Mario Possenti, being shocked by the death of his mistress Cora, whose body was found next to her husband's, evokes the past and tries to understand how she could have died without leaving a word of warning. In his quest Possenti, who teaches literature courses, tries several approaches, some of which are associated with Proust. I readily admit that others are not. For example, in the first chapter when the professor poses as a journalist in order to interview the cleaning woman who found the bodies, his unconscious model seems to be that of detective fiction.

La otra mitad most closely follows the psychological manner of Proust in those parts where the narrator seeks to interpret specific gestures and the impression that these caused within him. Referring to the quirky movements of Cora's arms when he first met her at a bookshop, Possenti writes: "Prefiero limitar este capítulo a describir la impresión inicial que suscitó en mí, a restaurar esa impresión que ha quedado debajo de otras que el tiempo y la intimidad escribieron, como en un palimpsesto" [I prefer to limit this chapter to describing the initial impression that she provoked in me, to restoring that impression that has remained beneath others which time and intimacy wrote, as upon a palimpsest] (1966, 27). I recall here, as before with *El túnel,* that Proust's narrator attributed a great significance to impressions because they offered him the hope of penetrating beneath the surface of appearances and of discovering a hidden truth. He also spoke about palimpsests.

Unfortunately for Possenti, this approach does not help him solve the mystery of Cora's death any more than others that he attempts, such as comparing Cora's life and death with those of the Uruguayan poet Delmira Agustini. The professor can never be certain if the husband killed Cora because of jealousy or another motive and then committed suicide, or if the two of them decided jointly to end their lives. Possenti's doubts are of the same type as those of the Proustian protagonist and other characters of a similarly inquisitive but skeptical nature (e.g., Castel, Sebastián). For this reason, the final pages of *La otra mitad* seem to reflect Proust's shadow. Here, we find a similar desolation as in portions of *Albertine disparue* and the causes are nearly identical. In both instances, the pain of the solitary lover is acute, his need to forget the lost woman struggles with his fear of doing so, and his intellectual pursuit of truth brings no result or consolation.

Although several of the major writers of the Boom itself developed a relation with Proust in the areas of time, memory, writing and high society, none of them, with the exception of Ernesto Sábato (if we include him as a Boom writer) followed the psychological manner of the *Recherche*.[12] This was due in part to the apparent rejection of psychological analysis by the writers of the *nouveau roman* in France, who were eager to move beyond this aspect of modernism. In her book *L'ère du soupçon* (1956), Nathalie Sarraute wrote disparagingly of the psychological novel in general and of Proust in particular:

> The word "psychology" is one of those that no author today can hear to be said on his account without lowering his eyes and blushing. It is associated with something that is a bit ridiculous, old-fashioned, overly intellectual, narrow-minded if not pretentiously foolish. (1956, 83)

Somewhat like Borges before him, Julio Cortázar was especially critical of the psychological novel but appears to echo Sarraute when his character Morelli writes in chapter 62 of *Rayuela*, "Psicología, palabra con aire de vieja" [Psychology, a word that is like an old woman] (1986, 522). By this, I do not wish to imply that Cortázar was merely following a French fashion or that he modeled his texts on the *nouveau roman*.[13] His opposition to the psychological novel typical of modernism was clearly fundamental and even helped him to define the nature of his literary work. In this regard we can note that Cortázar often associated the psychological novel with Proust, and in *Rayuela* he questioned specific aspects of the *Recherche* almost as if he were engaged in a debate about it.

Already in *Los premios* (1960), Cortázar cast doubt upon Proust's analysis of jealousy. There, we read of Raúl's feelings for Paula: "Entonces los celos del pasado, que en los personajes de Pirandello o de Proust le habían parecido una mezcla de convención y de impotencia para realizar de verdad el presente, podrían empezar a morder en la manzana" [Thus jealousy of the past, which in the characters of Pirandello or of Proust had seemed to him a mixture of convention and impotence in order to fulfill truly the present, could begin to bite into the apple] (1960, 301). Similarly, in *Rayuela*, Oliveira chuckles to himself about Proust when he learns of la Maga's friendship with Emmanuèle: "Pero sí era eso, porque la Maga no le había confiado más que una parte de su trato con la clocharde, y una elemental generalización lo llevaba, etc. Celos retrospectivos, véase Proust, sutil tortura and so on" [But it certainly was that, because la Maga had not confided in him more than a part of her dealings with the woman hobo, a basic generalization got him started, etc. Retrospective jealousy, consult Proust, a subtle torture and so on] (1985, 360).

It is not that Cortázar was opposed to the treatment of strong feelings like jealousy. This emotion deeply affects his characters and causes them to become suspicious and to interrogate each other, somewhat like the characters of *La prisonnière* or *El túnel*. Once la Maga questions Oliveira about his relationship with Pola, and on another occasion he confronts la Maga because he suspects that she has become sexually involved with Ossip. Here we can detect a mild parody of Proust and Sábato, but the feelings are apparently real because Oliveira does become angry and leaves. Eventually—but, in a gender reversal—he, like Albertine, tries to end the relationship.

As in the case of Nathalie Sarraute (according to Ernesto Sábato), human emotions play an important role in *Rayuela* and Cortázar's other works.[14] They create reactions in his characters which the reader must notice in order to understand what is happening. Yet even more than Sarraute, Cortázar wished to avoid dealing directly with the human consciousness. His "interacción," as defined in chapter 62 of *Rayuela,* might appear to correspond to Sarraute's "sous-conversation" [subliminal conversation], but Cortázar chose to remain totally silent concerning mental processes.[15]

The Argentine's opposition to the psychological novel and to analysis in the manner of Proust was intimately bound to his rejection of what he called "la novela rollo" [the reel-like novel] and even "el lector-hembra" [the biddy-reader]. The author of *Rayuela* was highly critical of the continuous tracing of emotion, which had been typical of the psychological novel and which Proust and his modernist followers carried to an extreme. Emblematically in chapter 94, where Cortázar's fictional novelist Morelli discusses with another person the importance of establishing elements, these are defined specifically in opposition to Proust.[16] The interlocutor asserts, "Fijar el carbono vale menos que fijar la historia de los Guermantes" [establishing carbon is worth less than establishing the history of the Guermantes] (598). In his response Morelli is more personal than categorical. He states that, at least for his type of writing, it is better to perfect the elements or individual fragments than to produce the type of narrative found in Proust's third volume *Le côté de Guermantes.* Although the word "historia" is very ambiguous and might even seem unfair to Proust (who was never concerned about exterior events or plot), Cortázar's idea is clarified in chapter 109, where we also find subtle allusions to Proust: "Al final queda un álbum de fotos, de instantes fijos; jamás *el devenir realizándose ante nosotros,* el paso del ayer al hoy, *la primera aguja del olvido en el recuerdo*" [In the end a photo album of fixed moments remains, never *the process of becoming taking place before us,* the movement from yesterday to today, *the first needle prick of forgetfulness in memory*] (646, my emphasis). Here, the Argentine is referring most specifically to *Albertine disparue,* whose narrator focuses his attention on the process of becoming and in particular on the various stages of forgetfulness. He shows how time affects the abandoned and grieving lover and how forgetfulness begins to occur and then proceeds. Concerning the first occasion when he was distracted from thinking about Albertine and her departure, he says,

> Dès que je m'en aperçus, je sentis en moi une terreur panique. Ce calme que je venais de goûter, c'était *la première apparition* de cette grande force intermittente, qui allait lutter en moi contre la douleur, contre l'amour, et finirait par en avoir raison. (3:447, my emphasis)

> [As soon as I realized it, I felt within me a panic terror. That calm which I had just enjoyed was the *first appearance* of that great intermittent force, which was going to struggle within me against my pain, against my love, and would finally prevail over everything.]

Likewise, in the next portion of chapter 109 we find another remark that seems at least in part directed against Proust. Continuing to use the image of photographs to show his opposition to "la novela rollo" and to explain his preference for novelistic fragments, Morelli postulates:

> dar coherencia a la serie de fotos para que pasaran a ser cine (como hubiera gustado tan enormemente al lector que él llamaba el lector-hembra) significaba rellenar con literatura, presunciones, hipótesis e invenciones los hiatos entre una y otra foto.

> [giving coherence to a series of photos so that they might become a movie (as the type of reader that he had called biddy-reader would have enjoyed enormously) meant filling in with literature, presumptions, hypotheses and inventions the gaps between one photo and another.]

Here, we can see how Cortázar's persistent questioning of Proust's psychological manner reaches the level of stern criticism and even disparagement. For a reader of the *Recherche* the word "hipótesis" alludes directly to Proust's analytical method and the flanking terms "presunciones" and "invenciones" deride that methodology itself. Moreover the phrase "rellenar con literatura" [fill in with literature] constitutes an insult. In his efforts to show the nature of time and process of becoming, Proust attributed words and actions to his characters which seemed to contradict their personality as depicted earlier in the novel. Then, with great subtlety and often relying upon hypotheses and information that his narrator could more easily invent than know, Proust explained how these same characters had changed over time.[17]

As for the concept of "lector-hembra," which is mentioned above and which has been interpreted by the critics in various ways, it may at least partially allude to the passive type of reader that the *Recherche* seems to require. Only a person willing to submit to Proust's intricate style, lengthy analyses and digressions can ever hope to enter fully his world. The reference to "hembra," along with the frequent mention in *Rayuela* of "tías tomando té con gallegas Bagley" [aunts drinking tea with Bagley biscuits] perhaps even echoes the remark by Borges that Proust was more an author for women than for men.[18]

In short, in order to explain and justify the fragmentary nature of his novel *Rayuela*, which involved human emotions but avoided analysis and refused to trace the development of feelings, Julio Cortázar used the *Recherche* as a primary point of reference and as a literary example to be shunned. Although the Argentine's ideas can be understood without realizing that he was engaged in a debate or conversation about Proust in the course of *Rayuela*, "hearing" and comprehending such remarks enriches our understanding of this work. I would also add that Cortázar's rejection of the psychological novel brought with it an important first step away from the modernist idea of consciousness and toward a postmodern understanding of the human mind. Through his use of fragmentation Cortázar was challenging Proust's attempt to totalize from a very subjective perspective.

With the publication of *Rayuela* in 1963, the abandonment of the psychological novel became largely the order of the day in Spanish America. Even though many writers of the Boom generation continued to refer at least indirectly to human consciousness they temporarily refrained from psychological analysis in the manner of Proust. In some cases, Cortázar's type of fragmentation apparently helped them resist the temptation to analyze (e.g., *El obsceno pájaro de la noche*). Tracing the process of becoming did not disappear, but this procedure took on a non-psychological focus, as we shall see in the chapter on time.

To demonstrate the shift that occurred during the 1960s with regard to the treatment of consciousness. I would like to examine a short story by Gabriel García Márquez. Its title "El mar del tiempo perdido" [The Sea of Lost Time] (1961) suggests a possible connection with *A la recherche du temps perdu*, but to my knowledge no one has succeeded in explaining it. This story is important because, as Mario Vargas Llosa pointed out, it constituted a major step for García Márquez in his transition from realism to magical realism.

Given Martín Adán's remarks on Proust and the "sicológica inmensidad del mar" (see chapter 2), as well as the description of a deep-sea diver in Eduardo Zalamea Borda's novel *4 años a bordo de mí mismo* [4 Years Aboard Myself], one might suspect that "El mar del tiempo perdido" involves a connection between the sea and the human mind in the manner of Proust.[19] However, nowhere in the story, even near the end where Tobías and Mr. Herbert descend to the bottom of the sea, do we find an actual example of psychological analysis. Clearly García Márquez chose to treat consciousness in another way.

The most obvious point of contact between the two texts is the town along the coast rather than the sea itself. Proust loved the shores of Normandy and set the second part of *A l'ombre des jeunes filles en fleurs* and most of *Sodome et Gomorrhe* at or near the fictional town of Balbec. This fashionable French resort might appear to have little in common with the desolate town on the Colombian coast in García Márquez's story, but a specific fragment from *Sodome et Gomorrhe* suggests a relation worth considering. When the protagonist discusses flowers with Mme. de Cambremer, she compares the smell of roses at her home Féterne with those at la Raspelière near Balbec:

> "C'est vrai que nous avons beaucoup de roses . . . notre roseraie est presque un peu trop près de la maison d'habitation, il y a des jours où cela me fait mal à la tête. C'est plus agréable de la terrasse de la Raspelière où le vent apporte l'odeur des roses, mais déjà moins entêtante." (2:813)

> ["It is true that we have many roses . . . our rose garden is almost a bit too close to our dwelling place, there are days when it gives me a headache. It is more pleasant on the terrace of la Raspelière where the wind brings the fragrance of roses, but not so headily."]

This attention to the scent of roses and its effect upon a person is quite typical of Proust, who found flowers beautiful but often suffered because of hay fever, like his protagonist. We also recall the importance attributed to smells by many Spanish Americans who followed Proust, such as Martín Adán.

Symptomatically, in "El mar del tiempo perdido" we also find a person who is strongly affected by odors and in particular the fragrance of roses, Tobías. Of him, we read early in the story: "En sus largos insomnios había aprendido a distinguir todo cambio de aire. De modo que cuando sintió un olor de rosas no tuvo que abrir la puerta para saber que era un olor del mar" [During his long hours of insomnia he had learned to distinguish every sort of change in the air. Thus, when he smelled the fragrance of roses he did not have to open the door to know that it was an odor from the sea] (1972, 23). Here, in addition to a Proust-like sensitivity to the smell of flowers, we find several elements that are even more Proustian and suggest a direct intertexual relation. The initial lines of Proust's fifth volume *La prisonnière* are remarkably similar:

Dès le matin, la tête encore tournée contre le mur et avant d'avoir vu . . . de quelle nuance était la raie du jour, je savais déjà le temps qu'il faisait. Les premiers bruits de la rue me l'avaient appris, selon qu'ils me parvenaient amortis et déviés par l'humidité ou vibrants comme des flèches dans l'aire résonnante et vide d'un matin spacieux, glacial et pur. . . . (3:9)

[Since dawn, with my head still turned toward the wall and before having seen . . . what shade were the beams of the sun, I already knew what the weather was like. The first noises from the street had informed me, depending on whether they reached my ears muffled and distorted by the humidity or quivering like arrows in the resonating and moistureless air of a spacious, frosty and clear morning. . . .]

The Proustian protagonist, like Tobías, sensitized by insomnia and lying awake early in the morning, is so acute in his sensory perception that he does not need to employ his eyes in order to determine what is the atmospheric condition outside. The mere quality of a sound is sufficient to tell him if the air is humid or dry. This conclusion based upon a single sensory perception closely ties these two fragments and their authors. I should, however, point out that, even though both characters could be mistaken in their judgement, the intentions of Proust and García Márquez are somewhat different. Whereas the French author wished to prove how sensitive his protagonist was, the Colombian writer hoped to show how tenuous and even suspect were his character's form of logic and conclusions. Tobías had almost no experience with roses and only a slight reason to associate them with the sea (flowers were tossed into the water with corpses brought from elsewhere). Thus, we may surmise that the Colombian author was parodying the French novelist.

In the text by García Márquez we do not find an example of psychological analysis in the manner of Proust, but rather an extreme form of subjectivity based upon individual perception, which is similar to Proust's and has been considered characteristic of modernist writers. As we saw above with regard to the French author's primary area of inquiry—the functioning of the human mind—specific impressions are very important for the protagonist's understanding of the world around him, and these examples of intuitive thought are often derived from a single detail. In our discussion of *El túnel* and Proust, we observed how Albertine's use of a particular phrase convinced the protagonist of *La prisonnière* that she was a lesbian even though she claimed that she was not. Also I should add that the character's conclusions remain suspicious because neither he nor the reader ever has any definitive proof.

The conclusion by Tobías that the scent of roses came from the sea is even more audacious. He believes that he smelled roses on that particular morning, but he made no effort to verify his hypothesis. Other per sons in the town may have perceived the fragrance, but only Petra is sure, and she does not believe that Tobías could have smelled the roses also. From her point of view, the odor was a sign from God and had nothing to do with the sea. Furthermore, the wife of Tobías categorically denies that the smell of roses even existed, and she rejects as absurd the notion that any pleasant odor can originate in the sea. Apparently, Clotilde believes that her husband is somewhat unbalanced and that he easily jumps to conclusions.

Both the protagonist of *La prisonnière* and Tobías live with women that are essentially distinct from themselves. The two females are less sensitive to stimuli from the world around them, they are generally more practical and forcefully deny the conclusions that their partners have drawn. Just the same, the men persist in their beliefs and as a result they radically transform the world in which they live. Because of his conclusion, the Proustian protagonist tries to keep Albertine in the apartment so that she can be protected from herself, but his suspicions and jealousy cause him to interrogate her to such a extent that even if she had not wished to leave him she ultimately decides to do so. Likewise, the conclusions by Tobías change his world. He convinces most of the people in the town of the nature and origin of the fragrance. In this case, García Márquez carried the results of a single peception much farther than Proust, well beyond the limits of the real world. It seems as if the highly questionable conclusions of Tobías have taken control.[20] People begin to arrive at the town surprisingly quickly, a large cloud with the scent of roses appears and remains for several weeks. In spite of this difference in degree, the fact that the desolate town becomes a seaside resort, somewhat like Balbec, seems to confirm the Proustian connection.[21]

I most certainly concede the importance of exaggeration, which is undeniable and which, as Vargas Llosa pointed out, plays a key role in García Márquez's transition to magical realism. I would add that through exaggeration García Márquez was parodying the subjectivity that was typical of Proust, and was thus closer to postmodernism than modernism, as some critics have suggested.[22]

Furthermore, we can see the importance of humor, which according to the Peruvian writer helped to make the fantastic more human and acceptable. In "El mar del tiempo perdido" humor is also applied to Proust and in particular to involuntary memory. Like Swann, the inhabitants and visitors to the town listen to music and recall the past. They, however, do not hear the sublime music of Vinteuil, but rather Catarino's old records. Also, what they remember is almost negligible: the taste of food after an illness or something that they intended to do but never did. Perhaps the most comic remark concerning memory is that Jacob and Máximo Gómez are too old for any records to remind them of the past. In this same humoristic vein, the priest who regularly eats bread dipped in *café con leche* [coffee with milk] can be seen as a mini-parody of the Proustian protagonist who tasted morsels of *madeleines* soaked in tea. Besides the obvious material link, there is a very interesting spiritual one between the miracle of the priest's levitation and the marvelous effects of involuntary memory. The point of contact may appear minute, but is in fact decisive. Similar to the Proustian protagonist, the priest is the only person who knows that the experience occurred.

Here, we find another example of subjectivity based upon individual perception, which constitutes the crux of the Proustian relation and suggests the point of departure for García Márquez. Beginning with a single sensation or impression and a character who totally believes in it and who systematically ignores what other persons may say or what common sense may dictate, García Márquez was able to transform a desolate town along the Colombian coast into a type of Balbec. Apparently, it was only necessary for Tobías to have faith in his impression and to convince other people of its validity for the transformation to begin. In this light even the descent to the bottom of the sea without diving equipment has meaning. Given that Mr. Herbert is convinced that persons besides the dead and scientists can travel to the depths, Tobías merely needs to follow him.

In this way, a subjective perspective, which was an essential modernist tenet of Proust's work and frequently the basis for his psychological analysis, has become for García Márquez a means of going beyond common reality in his texts, and, thus, realism in his writing. As the author of "El mar del tiempo perdido" parodied a Proust-like subjectivity, he freed his own imagination from the constraints of verifiable data and could formulate his own sense of magical realism.

Indeed, for Spanish America this type of literature has had various sources. But, in 1955, when Angel Flores attempted to distinguish magical realism from what he called "photographic realism" he named as one of its primary literary precursors Marcel Proust, along with Franz Kafka (1955, 188). Unfortunately, Flores did not explain what he meant and devoted his attention to the creator of "Metamorphosis." Just the same he must have assumed that the reader would understand how Proust's essential subjectivity and magical sense of memory helped to liberate French and Occidental fiction from the realist-naturalist manner of Gustave Flaubert and Emile Zola. This seems to be likewise the case of Gabriel García Márquez in *Cien años de soledad,* as well as "El mar del tiempo perdido." Although José Arcadio Buendía's subjective view of the world is not as closely bound to sensation as the perspective of Tobías or the Proustian protagonist, it is nonetheless of fundamental importance for it allows the reader to enter the magical yet realist world of *Cien años de soledad*. Thus, even here we can suspect a Proustian connection, albeit more distant than the one related to time, which we will examine in chapter 6.

There were, of course, during these years other attempts to approach consciousness in ways that were Proustian in their purpose without involving psychological analysis. In *El libro* (1970) Juan García Ponce constantly toyed with the opposition found in the *Recherche* between interiority and exteriority, which his epigraph from *Lecture de Proust* by Gaeton Picon set forth as a challenge.[23] García Ponce, who had studied Proust on several occasions, adroitly chose as his subject matter a university literature class on modern European narrative from Mann to Musil and the relationship between the professor Eduardo and his attractive female student Marcela. This highly erotic (and on occasion quite scandalous) novel at times approaches the author of *A l'ombre des jeunes filles en fleurs* especially through the comparisons used to describe what is external or internal, as well as through the multifaceted nature of Marcela. As the title implies their relationship is like a book of fiction that exists in its reading but has little connection with reality. Although both characters talk about love and suggest that they have "entered" each other in more than a physical way, neither is willing to change his or her bourgeois form of life, and the affair ends with the completion of the academic term. Eduardo may actually believe that Marcela found more in their love-making than a substitute for written work, but that was the ultimate effect. This type of self-deception perhaps seems more extreme than the conclusions of the Proustian protagonist concerning Albertine and her possible lesbianism, yet both deal with human feelings and the confusing nature of love.

Following the avoidance of psychological analysis in the 1970s, the resurgence of the subject of love during the 1980s brought with it an occasional analysis. One of the best examples of this phenomenon can be found in *El amor en los tiempos del cólera*. Here García Márquez depicted numerous cases of love at the end of the nineteenth century and the beginning of the twentieth. As the city along the Colombian coast was greatly affected by the French culture of the time, it is only natural that French love literature often associated with Paul Bourget should play an important role.[24] But, also we find additional elements from the psychological novel, and some are directly tied to Marcel Proust. Especially in the early stages of the innocent and unfortunate love affair between Florentino Ariza and Fermina Daza, there is a clear tracing of emotion. The female character, for example, sees how her feelings move from curiosity and pleasure because of the young man's attentions to anxiety and despair while she waits for the situation to progress. Obviously, García Márquez did not treat love as jealousy in the same manner as the author of "Un amour de Swann," but he did follow the French novelist in one very specific way. He often compared Florentino's love to a type of disease, just as Proust had done in Swann's case. On more than one occasion the narrator of *El amor en los tiempos del cólera* says that Florentino seemed to have the symptoms of cholera (1986, 89). This comparison is highly significant because, as we saw above, this disease is associated with Proust's father, who became famous for the method that he devised for halting the spread of it.

I cannot claim that the Colombian work should be considered a psychological novel, even in Proust's modernist way. García Márquez moved quickly beyond the emotions of his characters to portray diverse elements surrounding their love and went as far afield as the search for lost treasure ships. Just the same the tracing of the characters' feelings serves as a point of departure for the story of their love, which would last for more than a half century. Here we can detect another subject that entails a connection between the Colombian and French novels, time, but we will have to leave that matter until chapter 6.

During the years after the Boom one Spanish American writer in particular revisited all three of the Proustian subjects that we have been discussing: love, illness and consciousness.[25] In his two-volume novel *Cuadernos de navegación en un sillón Voltaire,* Alfredo Bryce Echenique presented his own type of love infirmity and parodied psychological analysis in the manner of Proust.

Early in *La vida exagerada de Martín Romaña* the narrator makes explicit his relation with the *Recherche* by suggesting that his text could be "un loco marcel-prousteo, sin asma" [a crazy Proustian discourse, without asthma] (1985, 18). The word "loco" is especially revealing because Martín's infirmity is not jealousy or asthma (like that of Proust's characters), but rather a type of mental illness. This disease has several causes, one of which is associated with love and another with the *Recherche.* Martín's self-esteem is seriously affected when he realizes that his wife's love for him is dying. As I will show in chapter 8, his difficulty in fulfilling his literary vocation is also a factor and his mother's insistence that he write like Marcel Proust is a major complication.

In general, the actual description of Martín's mental state near the end of *La vida exagerada de Martín Romaña* resembles more closely the manner of Freud and modern psychoanalysis than that of the French novelist. However, at times in this volume and the next, *El hombre que hablaba de Octavia de Cádiz,* the narrator parodies Proust's type of analysis. Similar to the postmodern writers, Bryce installs his narrator into a Proustian framework and then proceeds to undercut it. This is especially evident in two instances when, like the hero of *Albertine disparue,* Martín receives a message from the woman that he loves. In the first case immediately before the events of May 1968, Martín finds next to the radio a farewell note from Inés, and in the second a telegram arrives from Octavia, who is recovering from an accident.

Quite naturally, the message from Inés echoes the one left by Albertine and other departing women. Inés says, "Me es imposible seguir viviendo contigo" [It is impossible for me to continue living with you] (1985, 258) just as Albertine wrote, "Entre nous, la vie est devenue impossible" [Between us, life has become impossible] (3:421). Both women state their reasons for leaving, which are categorical and would appear to offer no hope to the men left behind. Just the same, like the Proustian protagonist, Martín succeeds in discovering another message beneath the surface. Notably, both men deny the validity of the woman's arguments. The protagonist of *Albertine disparue* pays no attention to the woman's complaints and imagines that her letter and departure are a ploy to extract money, gifts or more freedom. Martín tries to analyze politically the ideas of Inés and concludes that they are stereotypical and absurd. His belief that she really loves him and will return because she closes the note with *chau* instead of *adiós,* demonstrates more his persistent hope than her conscious purpose. Such attention to a single word ties Martín's mode of analysis to Proust's, but the fact that the distinction between *chau* and *adiós* has become so banal suggests that Bryce is mocking the author of *Albertine disparue.*

The case of the telegram in *El hombre que hablaba de Octavia de Cádiz* is even more distinctly parodic. Martín begins his analysis by saying, "deseé tener en casa un aparato de rayos X para verle el corazón al telegrama" [I wished to have at home an x-ray machine in order to see the heart of the telegram] (1988, 155). Given the hyperbolic images that the critics have often used to describe the depth of Proust's analysis, the reference to x-rays seems aimed at him. Martín's remarks concerning the analysis of handwriting in spite of the fact that telegrams are printed with uniform characters appears even more specifically related to Proust. Near the end of *Albertine disparue* a telegram supposedly from Albertine leads the protagonist to believe that she is still alive when in fact the telegrapher simply misread Gilberte's ornate signature (3:656).

Throughout this portion of Bryce's text we can notice the Peruvian's typical humor but also his wish to deride the search of the Proustian protagonist for significant details and the emotion that he displayed when he found them (recall the case of "Double horreur!" cited with regard to *El túnel*). The attention paid to spelling in the following passage implies also the critical distance characteristic of parody:

Volví al telegrama, desesperado, y descubrí para mi desesperación una falta de octografía [sic], como le llamaba yo . . . a las faltas de ortografía que cometía Octavia: DIVERTIDISSIMAS con doble ese. Se lo atribuí a la anestesia, para calmarme un poco, pero los superlativos en castellano, mi querida Octavia, se escriben con una sola ese. Tu esposo era italiano. Empezabas a olvidarte de mi idioma. . . . (157)

[I returned to the telegram, in despair, and I discovered to my desperation a mistake in octography, as I called the orthographical mistakes that Octavia made: DIVERTIDISSIMAS [very enjoyable] with double s. I attributed it to the anesthetic, in order to calm me down a bit, but the superlatives in Spanish, my dear Octavia, are written with a single s. Your husband was Italian. You were beginning to forget my language. . . .]

This parody of the *Recherche,* as well as several others found in *Cuadernos de navegación en un sillón Voltaire,* leads me to suspect that, somewhat like Borges, Bryce Echenique wished to do battle with his literary father Proust. His struggle with the French novelist might appear to conform with Bloom's idea concerning the anxiety of influence, but I believe that the question is more complex. Martín's frustrated literary vocation and its effects upon his mental condition suggest other facts, which we will examine in chapter 8.

In conclusion, from José Bianco and Ernesto Sábato to Julio Cortázar and Alfredo Bryce Echenique, we can see how a Proustian analysis of love and human motivation was first admired and used as a model but later rejected and parodied. In all of these cases as well as others, such as that of Yolanda Oreamuno, Manuel Mujica Láinez, Carlos Fuentes and Gabriel García Márquez, each author borrowed from Proust what was most applicable to his or her own work. In their modifications we can observe a progressive movement away from the subjective perspective that was used by Proust and other modernists and toward a more critical or ludic postmodern stance. Most of the Spanish American writers treated an atypical aspect of love, such as jealousy, and they did not limit themselves to the heterosexual variety. In fact, by following or reacting to Proust's example, authors like Luis Zapata and Reinaldo Arenas were able to create openly gay novels. Frequently Proust's idea concerning the deceptiveness of appearances and his belief that gestures can help one to discover truth were used by these authors in one way or another and may even be considered a narrative technique. At times, this relation conformed more to what we have called influence, inspiration, dialogue or parody, but in nearly all cases the connection has proved to be very fruitful and helped to create interesting and at times profound narrative works.

5

On Art, Artists, and Their Admirers: "A l'ombre des artistes en fleurs" in Spanish America

Early in *Du côté de chez Swann* the child protagonist discovers the world of art and the individuality of the artist. He realizes that behind each novel, painting or musical composition one can intuit the mind of the person that created it. Comparing works, he suspects that all outstanding creators are unique. He is fascinated by specific artists, and he tries to learn more about them and their other creations. In particular, he begins to examine the contrast between their life and their work when he notices that the local piano teacher Vinteuil, whom Swann disdained, had actually composed the musical scores that this dilettante greatly admired. The protagonist also becomes very interested in the novelist Bergotte, the painter Elstir and the actress la Berma. Along with these four artists we should add a fifth one, who was in reality the first that he knew, the cook Françoise. She prepares for the family culinary dishes that are so fine that the narrator compares them to the work of great artists in spite of the fact that Françoise has obvious personal flaws.

By focusing his attention on this gallery of artists, Marcel Proust was linking his work to the literary aestheticism of the late nineteenth century. Just as Charles Baudelaire had considered the great painters of the past to be "Les Phares" or the beacons of the future, the author of the *Recherche* presented his artists as models to be followed. Like other modernists that continued the tradition which was championed by Baudelaire with his articles on *la vie moderne* and which was exemplified by J. K. Huysmans' novel *A rebours* [Against the Grain] (1884), Proust treated art as one of the great aspirations of man and almost as a religion.[1]

Even more than Proust's first volume, his second one *A l' ombre des jeunes filles en fleurs,* presents the main character's thoughts and feelings about his favorite artists. In the same way that he develops emotionally through his experiences with the young women Gilberte, Albertine and Andrée, he grows culturally and aesthetically in the shade or protection of the successful artists that he admires. For this reason the title of Proust's second volume might have been, as I implied in the subtitle of this chapter, "A l'ombre des artistes en fleurs" [In the Shadow of Artists in Flower].

In particular, *A l'ombre des jeunes filles en fleurs* calls into question the very nature of the relationship that exists between the actual person that creates art and the artist as seen through his or her work. After reading for many years the novels by Bergotte and imagining what this man must be like, the young protagonist has the opportunity to meet him. This encounter proves to be disappointing because Bergotte does not seem to possess the spiritual qualities that were so evident in his work. The case of Elstir, which is treated in the second part of the volume, is distinct but equally instructive. The reader is surprised to find that the apparently frivolous young painter of the Verdurins' salon in "Un amour de Swann" has become the accomplished artist Elstir. His originality is of great interest to the protagonist, who meets him near Balbec.

The narrator describes at length some of Elstir's impressionist paintings because they will eventually assist him in the creation of his own literary art. By observing Elstir's seascapes, the protagonist learns, for example, that external reality should be only a stimulus and not a model. Elstir did not merely reproduce the characteristics of the sea; instead he translated his impressions of them. The metaphorical nature of Elstir's paintings can be observed through the way in which he used images of the land to render aspects of the sea and vice versa. In one passage the narrator describes how a boat in the sea appears to drive up a steep embankment out of the water: "on pensait à quelque chaussée de pierres ou à un champ de neige, sur lequel on était effrayé de voir un navire s'élever en pente raide et à sec comme une voiture qui s'ébroue en sortant d'un gué. . ." [one thought about a stone roadway or of a field of snow, where one was alarmed to see a ship drive up its steep and dry slope, like a carriage that shakes when coming out of a ford. . .] (1954, 1:838).

Using Elstir's ideas on painting, along with his own discoveries concerning the effect of nature upon himself, the Proustian protagonist is eventually able to establish the bases of his personal art and, in his view, of all true art. The term impressionism has been used to describe this manner, which is Proust's own. However, it must be distinguished from that of Manet, Monet, and Renoir. Proustian impressionism is based upon spontaneous, deeply felt sensations or impressions, which appear at first to be a mystery and can only be elucidated through intense effort. Benjamin Crémieux explained: "The impressionism of Proust thus does not consist of recording in a gradual manner fleeting impressions, it consists of overcoming the natural indolence of the mind and not surrendering until one has revealed the portion of nourishing profound reality contained in the impression" (1924, 83).

According to the narrator of *Le temps retrouvé,* the impression is fundamental and even a means of discovering truth because it allows the observer to penetrate beneath the surface of reality and thus discover what is hidden by appearances:

> Seule l'impression, si chétive qu'en semble la matière, si insaisissable la trace, est un critérium de vérité, et à cause de cela mérite seule d'être appréhendée par l'esprit, car elle est seule capable, s'il sait en dégager cette vérité, de l'amener à une plus grande perfection et de lui donner une pure joie. (3:880)

> [Only the impression, no matter how slight its material may seem to be, no matter how difficult it is to capture its traces, is a criterion of truth, and for that reason it alone deserves to be apprehended by the mind, for only the impression is capable, if one knows how to extract this truth, of leading the mind to a greater perfection and of giving it a pure joy.]

Here, we can see very clearly how the modernist idea of consciousness, which Proust embodied, implied aesthetic as well as psychological phenomena. As Bradbury said of consciousness for the modernists, "it was not only a means of exploring the inner being and perception of their characters, but of opening out the actual form and structure of fiction. . . " (1990, 139).

In another portion of *Le temps retrouvé,* the narrator explains specifically his concept of metaphor, which is essential to his style and is directly related to his impressionism. For him, the principal task of the artist is to translate through comparison or metaphor the impressions that objects or stimuli cause within him. Also the impressions themselves are generally the source of his comparisons because they provide the spiritual equivalents of what he wishes to describe. He begins his definition of metaphor by discounting other forms of description, and then he says of the writer:

> On peut faire se succéder indéfiniment dans une description les objets qui figuraient dans le lieu décrit, la vérité ne commencera qu'au moment où l'écrivain prendra deux objets différents, posera leur rapport . . . et les enfermera dans les anneaux nécessaires d'un beau style. . . . (3:889)

> [In a description one can list indefinitely the objects present in the place described, but the truth will only begin to appear when the writer chooses two different objects, shows their relation . . . and encloses them in the necessary links of a beautiful style. . . .]

He finally suggests that what the two items have in common allows the writer to use one to explain the other because the point in which they coincide is their shared essence: "en rapprochant une qualité commune à deux sensations, il dégagera leur essence commune en les réunissant l'une et l'autre pour les soustraire aux contingences du temps, dans une métaphore" [by discerning a quality common to two sensations, he will extract their common essence by joining one to the other in order to free them from the contingencies of time, in a metaphor]. Here, we also note that Proust added a temporal dimension to his comparisons or analogies, which is also on occasion spatial or at least bound to a particular field of human endeavor or nature. In the words of Gérard Genette, Proust's comparisons are *diégétiques* (1972, 47–48). That is to say, they are taken from the world of the narration and implicitly join two moments from his protagonist's life and even two locations where he had spent time. For this reason, Proust rarely used metaphors that were disconnected from the subjects that his protagonist knew intimately.[2]

In the volumes that precede *Le temps retrouvé*, the narrator develops other subjects related to art and in particular music. Even more than Swann, the protagonist of *La prisonnière* comes to understand the musical vision of Vinteuil when he listens again to the sonata that Swann loved and when he has the opportunity to hear the master's septet. In this way, he discovers the personal suffering and uniqueness of each artist and how an admirer can approach most directly an artist through his work rather than through his life.

The passages concerning music reflect especially well the impressionist manner of Marcel Proust because they are highly metaphorical, but they also serve another very important function. They suggest that the French author's manner of constructing his novel was patterned on a technique devised by the nineteenth-century German composer Richard Wagner.[3] As in the development of *Tristan und Isolde* through the use of leitmotivs, Proust built his vast novel by repeating and interweaving his personal themes (which are precisely the subjects of most of our chapters: high society, love, art, time and memory). For this reason when the narrator portrays Wagner's manner in *La prisonnière*, he is indirectly describing the construction of the *Recherche* itself:

> ces thèmes insistants et fugaces qui visitent un acte ne s'éloignent que pour revenir, et parfois lointains, assoupis, presque détachés, sont à d'autres moments . . . si viscéraux qu'on dirait la reprise moins d'un motif que d'une névralgie. (3:159)

> [these insistent, fleeting themes that are present in one act, only withdraw in order to return, and although at times distant, dormant, nearly detached,

they are at other moments . . . so visceral that one might call them less the
reprise of a musical motif than the reappearance of a neuralgia.]

This manner of creating his novel allowed Proust the option of avoid-
ing a tightly knit plot. He could join the diverse aspects of his work by
binding them to his personal themes. In itself, this application of
Wagner's technique is quite modernist, but the way in which Proust drew
together all of his themes is even more so. When the protagonist eventually discovers the means of writing his novel, *A la recherche du temps
perdu* becomes the story of a literary vocation, and all of the themes are
subordinated to this one great subject and become part of Proust's
master narrative. As Bradbury says, "In the end, this book, like so many
other of the great modern novels, is a book about its own coming to
existence, and the portrait of an artist" (141). Because of the truly essential nature of this aspect and the fact that it depends upon other themes,
most notably memory, I have decided to devote a special chapter to it
and to place it last. In the present one, I will restrict the discussion to the
preliminary stage where the main character is still an admirer of art or
where he happens to create in one of the arts that is not literary.
     For the Spanish American examples, I will first discuss Proust's influ-
ence during the pre-Boom period on novels involving music and the
arts, many of which contain impressionist descriptions and treat the lives
of specific artists. Secondly, we will see how during the years of the Boom
there was a reaction and narrative response to this modernist type of
novel associated with *Recherche,* plus a few novels that developed the
Proustian subject of art in postmodern ways. Thirdly, I will examine a
series of narrative texts in which we find among the secondary characters
an already successful writer who serves as a model for the young
protagonist.

MUSIC AND ART IN THE NOVEL: IMPRESSIONIST DESCRIPTIONS AND THE LIFE OF AN ARTIST

In Spanish America, there have been several novels directly related to
Proust and hence modernism in their treatment of music and art. Musical compositions or performances and plastic works have been
described in a manner very reminiscent of the *Recherche.* In many of
these texts we find creators or performers, as well as admirers of art. The
latter often think about the nature of beauty and dream of becoming
artists.
     Already during the early period of the Proustian connection with
Spanish America, a few works of this type were published, such as *El*

cántico espiritual by Manuel Gálvez. The protagonist, Mauricio Sandoval, develops first as a painter and then becomes a sculptor when he interacts with other artists and begins to look more deeply into himself. In chapter 2, we also saw a few examples of a Proust-like impressionism based upon comparison in *Ifigenia* and *Margarita de niebla*. Further, we examined in particular the case of "El árbol," where Brígida's impressions of music actually stimulated her memory.

Somewhat like Bombal but closer to Proust, José Bianco described piano music in *Las ratas:*

> Las manos de Cecilia trazaban curvas en el aire, retrocedían, se detenían en un acorde. De pronto, obedeciendo a una caprichosa inspiración, se alejaban hacia la derecha y arrancaban arabescos de sonidos sobrecargados de notas, altos, nítidos, burlones, persistentes, como si el teclado no hubiera de terminar jamás. (1973, 73)

> [Cecilia's hands traced curves in the air, they retreated, they stopped on a chord. Suddenly obeying a whimsical inspiration, they moved away to the right and wrenched arabesques of sound overly laden with notes that were high, clear, teasing, persistent, as if the keyboard were never to end.]

Although Bianco further developed in his novel the theme of music by treating a subject that Proust never considered—the study of the piano—the above cited passage is remarkably similar to Proust in its impressionist manner.[4] Likewise, in "Un amour de Swann" the narrator says of the *petite phrase* and its effect upon Swann:

> D'un rythme lent elle le dirigeait ici d'abord, puis là, puis ailleurs. . . . Et tout d'un coup, au point où elle était arrivée et d'où il se préparait à la suivre . . . brusquement elle changeait de direction et d'un mouvement nouveau, plus rapide, menu, mélancolique, incessant et doux, elle l'entraînait avec elle vers des perspectives inconnues. (1:210)

> [With a slow tempo it directed him first this way, then that, then elsewhere. . . . And suddenly at the point where it had arrived and from which he was getting ready to follow it . . . it abruptly changed direction and with a new, swifter, delicate, melancholy, unceasing and gentle movement, it led him off toward unknown prospects.]

During the years immediately after 1940, the Spanish American who was perhaps most clearly influenced by the aesthetic facet of Proust's work was the Uruguayan Felisberto Hernández. Francisco Lasarte has already discovered in the narrative structure of *Por los tiempos de Clemente Colling* [Through the Times of Clemente Colling] (1942), *El caballo perdido* [The Lost Horse] (1943), and *Tierras de la memoria* [Lands Remembered] a direct link with the *Recherche*.[5] Referring to this decisive intermediate stage in Felisberto's work, Lasarte said,

> In it we have the use of a binocular technique, in the manner of Proust, which combines the narration of events that occurred in the immediate past with the recollection of experiences from a more distant temporal plane. (1981, 27)

This relation with Proust is even more evident when one considers that Felisberto used the movement of a streetcar in *Por los tiempos de Clemente Colling* and that of a train in *Tierras de la memoria* to join together the various elements of his narration. Proust had already employed a similar technique in portions of *A l'ombre des jeunes filles en fleurs* and *Sodome et Gomorrhe,* where the protagonist rides on a train to or near Balbec and thinks about diverse subjects, including the past.

Also related to Proust's vast novel are other elements that are even more important, especially in the case of *Tierras de la memoria*. In this unfinished work, which was written during the 1940s but published in 1966 after Hernández's death, we find a young man who becomes a pianist because he was inspired by a great artist of the piano. Notably, the spectacular performance at the beginning of the novel, which greatly affected the protagonist-narrator, is described in an impressionist manner very similar to Proust's:

> veía sembrar notas picadas y sentía su consecuencia sonora: una escala como un camino con cerco de postes pasado a toda velocidad; las manos retardaban el movimiento y se detenían contra una nota agradablemente extraña; el camino recomenzaba y tomaba otra direción. . . . (1983, 3:10)

> [he saw staccato notes being scattered and he felt its sonorous effect: a scale that was like a road with fence posts passed at top speed; his hands slowed down the movement and stopped on a pleasantly strange note; the road began again and headed in another direction. . . .]

This passage holds much in common with the ones by Bianco and Proust cited above, but it emphasizes in particular those elements shared by the flow of music and movement along a road or path.

In many other portions of *Tierras de la memoria* Felisberto Hernández, like Marcel Proust, used one sensation to translate another. Some of these passages are very interesting and beautiful. Talking about his own piano playing, the narrator remarks:

> Después toqué mi nocturno: al principio tenía acordes grandes, de sonidos graves, que yo hacía con las manos abiertas y con la lentitud de un espiritista al ponerlas sobre la mesa y mientras espera que lleguen los espíritus, y aquellos

acordes provocaban un silencio espectante; el ambiente se cubría de gruesos nubarrones sonoros y yo tenía la emoción del dibujante que aprieta el lápiz y pone mucho negro. (3:26)

[Afterwards I played my nocturne: at first it had large chords, with grave sounds, which I made with my fingers spread and with the slowness of a medium when he puts his hands on the table and while he waits for the spirits to arrive, and those chords induced an expectant silence; the atmosphere was covered with thick, sonorous storm clouds and I felt like a sketch artist who bears down on his pencil and leaves behind a lot of black.]

Here we can see not only how, similar to Proust, the Uruguayan used one art to explain another, but also how he drew an analogy from popular spiritualism. Likewise in "Un amour de Swann" to describe the intimate relationship between a particular violinist and the *petite phrase,* the narrator speaks of what may occur at a séance:

Merveilleux oiseau! le violiniste semblait vouloir le charmer, l'apprivoiser, le capter. Déjà il avait passé dans son âme, déjà la petite phrase évoquée agitait comme celui d'un médium le corps vraiment possédé du violiniste. (1:352)

[Such a marvelous bird! the violinist apparently wanted to charm, to tame, to capture it. Already it had entered his soul, already the little phrase, having been evoked, shook like the body of a medium that of the violinist which seemed truly possessed.]

I should, of course, mention that Hernández did not limit his impressionism to the depiction of music but treated it as a general descriptive technique. At times he applied it to other subjects, for example, the extraction of a tooth (3:44–45). Furthermore, other points of contact with the *Recherche* are evident, particularly with regard to memory, which functions in a somewhat Proustian mannner. Just the same, Felisberto came closest to the French novelist in the musical passages, where he even linked psychological analysis to his impressionism. In doing so, he inadvertently showed that he too was a modernist like Proust because he joined the psychological and aesthetic facets of consciousness. At one point, the narrator compares his body to a locomotive in order to illustrate its excitement and seeming will of its own in the presence of female listeners and performers:

Apenas veía un piano se ponía como una locomotora que empieza a juntar presión. Si había muchachas se quedaba inmóvil, pero le echaba más carbón a la caldera. Y si las muchachas tocaban primero, él parecía que iba a estallar; cuando le pedían que tocara yo ya no lo podía sujetar, ni siquiera para el cumplimiento de hacerse rogar un poco; él ya veía desprenderse de sí los nubarrones del "nocturno" y ya estaba en marcha. (3:33)

[With the mere sight of a piano, it became like a locomotive that starts to build up pressure. If there were girls present, it remained stationary, but it threw more coal into the boiler. And if the girls played first, it seemed as if it were going to explode; when they requested that it play, I could no longer restrain it, not even for the satisfaction of being asked more than once; it could see already the storm clouds of the nocturne billowing forth and it was now in motion.]

This passage is quite brilliant and somewhat dissimilar in temperament from Proust's manner. However, the locomotive itself is appropriate and *diégétique* because, as I suggested above, the narrator of *Tierras de la memoria* is riding on a train.[6]

In her book, *Carpentier's Proustian Fiction: The Influence of Marcel Proust on Alejo Carpentier* (1994), Sally Harvey amply demonstrated the importance of metaphor in the works by Proust and Carpentier and showed how these writers consistently selected one of the elements for their analogies from the world of art, music or theatre. In this way, they both continued the aesthetic tradition of modernism. I do not wish to dispute or repeat what Harvey already said very well. I would add, however, that in Carpentier's novel of the 1950s, *Los pasos perdidos,* the prinipal character is a composer, and he is inspired to write a musical score. This composition unfortunately is lost, and the protagonist has little hope of recovering it. For the most part, I will delay my discussion of this novel until chapter 7, where I will show how memory is portrayed in it. I wish to cite here only one example of the impressionist style of both authors in order to illustrate their relation in this regard.

Upon recovering memories from the past when he finally listens to the Ninth Symphony by Beethoven, Carpentier's principal character sees at one point the image of his father while he was playing a type of horn:

Cada vez que la sonoridad metálica de un corno apoyaba un acorde, creía ver a mi padre . . . adelantando el perfil para leer la música abierta ante sus ojos, con esa peculiar actitud del cornista que parece ignorar, cuando toca, que sus labios se adhieren a la embocadura de la gran voluta de cobre que da un empaque de capitel corintio a toda su persona. (1969, 92)

[Each time that the metalic sonority of a horn struck a chord, I thought that I was seeing my father . . . leaning forward his profile in order to read the musical score open before his eyes, with that peculiar pose of a horn player who does not seem to realize, when he plays, that his lips adhering to the mouthpiece of the great brass spiral give his entire person the appearance of a Corinthian capital.]

In this case, Carpentier followed Proust's manner by using an art based metaphor to describe the father's physical appearance, but the next sentence is even more reminiscent of the *Recherche:* "Con ese mimetismo singular que suele hacer flacos y enjutos a los oboístas, jocundos y mofletudos a los trombones, mi padre había terminado por tener una voz de sonoridad cobriza, que vibraba nasalmente . . . " [With that strange form of imitation that tends to make oboists thin and skinny, trombonists, jovial and chubby, my father ended up having a voice with a brass-like sonority, which vibrated nasally . . .]. By attributing to the musicians a characteristic of their instruments, Carpentier obstensibly reversed what Proust had done in one particular case. The narrator of "Un amour de Swann" suggests that violins emitted a human-like sound:

Il y a dans le violon . . . des accents qui lui sont si communs avec certaines voix de contralto, qu'on a l'illusion qu'une chanteuse s'est ajoutée au concert. On lève les yeux, on ne voit que les étuis, précieux comme des boîtes chinoises, mais, par moments on est encore trompé par l'appel décevant de la sirène. . . . (1:347)

[There are in the violin . . . accents that are so similar to certain contralto voices that one has the illusion that a female vocalist has been added to the ensemble. One raises one's eyes, and one only sees wooden cases, which are as precious as Chinese boxes, but, for an instant, one is tricked by the siren's deceptive call. . . .]

In another novel of the 1950s, *Los viajeros,* Manuel Mujica Láinez included, along with impressionist descriptions of music, other elements associated with the arts which obviously echo the *Recherche* and modernism. We find, for example, that the pianist Angioletti shares various traits with Vinteuil. He lives in an isolated manner in a small, provincial town and serves as an artistic model for the young protagonist Miguel, who wishes to become a writer. Even the pianist's motivation for living in the village recalls Proust because it is due to jealousy and the fear of losing his beautiful wife that he remains there.

The impressionist descriptions overtly follow the Proustian pattern and at times coincidentally resemble fragments by Felisberto Hernández or José Bianco. Mujica Láinez depicted piano music by the effect that it caused upon the listener or observer and did so through analogy:

Angioletti se sentaba al piano y era como si se lanzara en una barca audaz, desplegadas las velas, al mar revuelto y nocturno de Federico Chopin. ¡Con

qué destreza manejaba su navío negro! ¡Cómo se alzaba sobre el oleaje impe-
tuoso, en las crestas sonoras, y se dejaba caer en los abismos! (1955, 146)

[Angioletti would sit down at the piano and it was as if he were casting off in a
daring boat, with its sails unfurled into the rough nocturnal sea of Frederic
Chopin. With what skill he handled his black vessel! How he rose above the
impetuous waves on the sonorous crests, and then allowed himself to fall into
the abyss!]

I note in this case that the comparison with a boat is especially appropriate because the family in *Los viajeros* thinks constantly about traveling to
Europe and even their house is said to resemble an ocean liner.

In other portions of this Argentine novel, the narrator portrays in an
impressionist manner aspects of the world that are not directly associated with music or the plastic arts. Here, the author demonstrated his
fine sensibility, as well as his use of this Proustian technique. Not only did
he frequently describe by comparing, but he was also careful to choose
the basis for his analogies from the world of the narration. One of the
best examples is the depiction of the family's burial crypt, which is
likened to an elegant dining room because during their lifetime these
persons enjoyed offering sumptuous dinner parties:

El sepulcro-capilla . . . hacía pensar en un gran comedor, en un escenario de
banquetes de fin de siglo, porque las tumbas de mis bisabuelos, ubicadas la
una frente a la otra, adosadas a la pared, coronadas de sendos vasos de
guirnaldas y ejecutadas con toda suerte de mármoles multicolores . . . pare-
cían dos majestuosas alacenas más o menos Luis XIV. . . .(182–83)

[The mausoleum-chapel . . . reminded one of a great dining room, of the
setting for end of the nineteeth century banquets, because the tombs of my
great-grandparents, located one facing the other, with their backs to the wall,
each one crowned with vases of garlands and made with all types of multicolored marble . . . resembled two majestic cupboards approximately in the
style of Louis XIV. . . .]

In this instance, Mujica Láinez's description subtly echoes Proust, who
in *A l'ombre des jeunes filles en fleurs* compared a glass enclosed dining
room by the sea to an aquarium:

celle-ci devenait comme une immense et merveilleux aquarium devant la
paroi de verre duquel . . . les pêcheurs et aussi les familles de petits bourgeois,
invisibles dans l'ombre, s'écrasaient au vitrage pour apercevoir . . . la vie
luxueuse de ces gens, aussi extraordinaire pour les pauvres que celle de
poissons et de mollusques étranges. . . . (1:681)

[this became like an immense and marvelous aquarium, adjacent to whose glass wall . . . the fishermen and also lower middle-class families, being invisible in the shadows, crowded themselves against the glass to observe . . . the luxurious life of these people, which was as extraordinary for the poor as that of strange fish and mollusks. . . .]

The aesthetic style of *Los viajeros,* as well as its numerous references to the various arts, are ultimately tied to the literary vocation of the narrator, which I shall discuss in chapter 8. Similarly Mujica Láinez's subsequent novel, *Invitados en "El Paraíso"* (1957), deals specifically with the life of an already successful artist, Silvano. Here, many aspects of this painter's life and work are discussed and at times these distantly bring to mind portions of the *Recherche.* This similarity is especially evident in the passage devoted to Silvano's death, which echoes the final agony of the novelist Bergotte. I should note, however, that by this time the Argentine writer had begun to assert his literary independence through a greater use of his own imagination.

In this moving sequence, the narrator draws attention to its Proustian source of inspiration. In Silvano's room there is on display a letter that had been written by the French author. Moreover, upon waking the painter undergoes a brief involuntary memory experience. The fragrance of magnolias and the chirping of birds seem to transport the old, dying painter back to the time and place of his childhood: "Al cuarto día, de madrugada, Silvano tuvo la impresión de que había retrocedido en el tiempo, y de que, como cuando era muchacho, estaba en Quilmes, en la quinta de su abuela" [On the fourth day, early in the morning, Silvano had the impression of having moved backwards in time and that, as when he was a boy, he was in Quilmes, at the country home of his grandmother] (1969, 266).

This initial sensation, combined with the painter's agonic state, leads to a moment of catharsis. Examining his final painting, which stands next to the bed, Silvano discovers the lost garden of his childhood: an earthly paradise that he had created through art. He even has the sensation of being able to enter his painting and of discovering that he had so completely portrayed reality that he had depicted the other side of things and had given life to the human figures. With these sublime ideas Silvano dies.

Although differing in its development, this passage had as its point of departure the description of the death of Bergotte. In *La prisonnière* this fictional novelist directs his last thoughts to a painting by Jan Vermeer and questions a particular aspect of his own work. Bergotte realizes that his writing should have been less dry and more like the "petit pan de mur jaune" [little patch of yellow wall] found in *View of Delft.* Perhaps, most importantly, both Proust and Mujica Láinez used the description of the artist's death to exalt the sublimeness and transcendence of art. The French novelist suggested that an afterlife was indeed conceivable for Bergotte because his books like angels would protect him. Analogously, the author of *Invitados en "El Paraíso"* asserted that in art was found the true paradise. In both cases, art offered the creative artist the hope of life beyond death.[7]

This reverent and almost religious attitude toward art characterized Mujica Láinez's work especially during the late 1950s and constitutes one of his many points of contact with Proust. It also gives testimony to the Argentine's profound modernism, which kept alive a nineteenth century faith in the transcendence of art. As we saw in chapter 3, the narrator of *Los viajeros* compared persons to paintings in the manner of Swann because he wished to add dignity to his depiction of them. The aesthetic strain in Mujica Láinez's work culminated in *Bomarzo,* whose protagonist is fascinated by the arts of the Italian renaissance. Not content merely to reproduce such Proust-like comparisons with paintings, the author carried this procedure a step further. Throughout *Bomarzo,* the narrator relates his previous existence as if it were a series of paintings or frescoes, which he brings to life for the reader. As we shall see in chapter 8, the narrator also tells the story of his artistic vocation, which combines in an original way sculpture and writing.

I concede that music does not play as large a role in *Bomarzo* as it did in *Los viajeros* nor as it would years later in *El gran teatro* (1979), which was built around a performance of *Parsifal.* Nonetheless, the reader can detect in *Bomarzo* an almost Wagnerian sense of construction through the use of leitmotivs (albeit following the example of the *Recherche*). The events described follow in a generally chronological order, but they are so numerous and detailed that many of them have little importance for the work as a whole. Far more relevant are the themes which the events illustrate. Notably these subjects serve the same type of function as they do in the *Recherche,* and most of them are very similar: memory, art, immortality, jealousy, snobbery and pederasty. In each case, Mujica Láinez has reinterpreted these subjects and placed them in a different context, the Italian renaissance, but the link with Proust remains evident. Also, like the French novelist, the Argentine writer carefully drew together his themes at the end. Not only does the narrator of *Bomarzo* explain how jealousy is related to snobbery and immortality to art, but even a minor theme, renaissance crimes, becomes intertwined for Pier Francesco is poisoned near the end.

UPDATED INTERPRETATIONS OF ART AND THE ARTIST:
Rayuela and Its Followers

Soon after 1960, literary aestheticism, which reached its culmination with Proust and other modernists, came under attack in Spanish America and was rejected by some new writers, most notably Julio Cortázar. José Lezama Lima was quick to point out the radically distinct attitude toward art and the artist of the author of *Rayuela,* and he spoke in particular of the Argentine's reaction against the so-called Wagnerian novel:

> The great novel, prior to the type of novel that Cortázar writes, was of Wagnerian origin, since Joyce, Proust, Thomas Mann and Hesse, were men of a Wagnerian formation. Their devotion for myths, for music . . . gives their novels a truly Wagnerian origin. (1968, 10)

Obviously, the Cuban poet-novelist was speaking in very broad terms and was alluding at least in part to the interweaving of themes or motifs, which writers like Proust patterned on the manner of Richard Wagner. However, Cortázar's critical attitude toward aestheticism and his often irreverent depiction of classical music were also encompassed by his anti-Wagnerian stance.[8] Furthermore, this Argentine seems to have been reacting against the type of modernist novel that his fellow countryman Manuel Mujica Láinez continued to write.

The best example of Cortázar's position can be found in the pages devoted to Berthe Trépat's recital. Here, the author of *Rayuela* portrayed a mediocre pianist in the classical tradition. Admittedly, he chose to satirize avant-garde first performance concerts, but he also wished to ridicule the pianist's still modernist devotion to art. His narrator remarks: "Oliveira se sabía incapaz de imaginar más allá de la atmósfera general, de la derrotada e inútil sobrevivencia de esas actividades artísticas para grupos igualmente derrotados e inútiles" [Oliveira knew that he was incapable to imagining anything beyond the general atmosphere, of the failed and useless survival of artistic activities for groups that are likewise failed and useless.] (1986, 249).

For the most part, Cortázar did not describe in an impressionist manner Trépat's performance. He merely followed the techniques of contemporary musical criticism when he wrote, for example, "Mezcla de Liszt y Rachmaninov, la *Pavana* repetía incansable dos o tres temas para perderse luego en infinitas variaciones, trozos de bravura (bastante mal tocados, con agujeros y zurcidos por todas partes) . . . " [A mixture of Liszt and Rachmaninoff, the *Pavane* repeated tirelessly two or three themes, which then became lost in numerous variations, bits of bravura

(rather poorly played, with holes and stitches everywhere) . . .] (247).
But, it is worth noting that in at least one passage Cortázar approached
Proust, Hernández and Mujica Láinez. His depiction of Trépat's growing nervousness is undeniably metaphorical: "parecía que se le para-
lizaban las manos, seguía adelante sacudiendo los antebrazos y sacando
los codos con un aire de gallina que se acomoda en el nido . . . " [it
seemed that her hands were growing stiff, she moved forward shaking
her forearms and sticking out her elbows much like a hen settling down
in her nest . . .] (250).

Symptomatically in Cortázar's description of a type of music that he
admired more, jazz, he came remarkably close to Proust's impressionist
manner. His phrase "los juegos de Dizzy Gillespie sin red en el trapecio
más alto" [the tricks of Dizzy Gillespie without a net on the highest
trapeze] (177) echoes a specific fragment from "Un amour de Swann."
In this case, Proust related the impression of watching a pianist play a
virtuoso intermezzo by Liszt:

> Mme. de Franquetôt [regardait] anxieusement, les yeux éperdus comme si
> les touches sur lesquelles il courait avec agilité avaient été une suite de tra-
> pèzes d'où il pouvait tomber d'un hauteur de quatre-vingts mètres. . . .
> (1:328)

> [Mme. de Franquetôt [watched] anxiously, with bewildered eyes as if the keys
> over which he sped with agility had been a series of trapezes from which he
> might fall eighty meters to the ground. . . .]

Such a reminiscence is very suggestive because the act of listening to
music at times serves an analogous role in the *Recherche* and *Rayuela*. In
both novels the principal characters are inspired by the music that they
hear, and they begin to speculate upon precisely the same metaphysical
questions. Oliveira, like the protagonist of *La prisonnière*, considers the
nature of time, reality and art. The two of them doubt the significance of
their daily lives and perceive through music the feasible existence of a
more profound reality. To suggest the depth which is apparent in the
music, both narrators allude to the immortality of the soul and to a
religious or mystical experience.[9] We read in Proust's text:

> Enfin le motif joyeux resta triomphant, ce n'était plus un appel presque
> inquiet lancé derrière un ciel vide, c'était une joie ineffable qui semblait venir
> du Paradis. . . . Je savais que cette nuance nouvelle de la joie, cet appel vers
> une joie supra-terrestre, je ne l'oublierais jamais. (3:260–61)

> [Finally the joyful motif became triumphant, it was no longer an almost
> anxious appeal hurled toward an empty sky, it was an ineffable joy that

seemed to come from Paradise. . . . I knew that this new gradation of joy, this appeal for a supraterrestrial joy, would never be forgotten by me.]

Likewise in *Rayuela* we find:

Una mano de humo lo llevaba de la mano, lo iniciaba en un descenso, si era un descenso, le mostraba un centro, si era un centro, le ponía en el estómago . . . algo que otra ilusión infinitamente hermosa y desesperada había llamado en algún momento inmortalidad. (180)

[A hand of smoke led him by the hand, initiated him into a downward movement, if it were downward, showed him a center, if it were a center, put into his stomach . . . something that another infinitely beautiful and desperate illusion had at some moment called immortality.]

We can see how Cortázar was dialoguing with Proust's text. Aware of the fact that the French novelist early in the twentieth century had used classical music to create an almost mystical experience, the Argentine writing *c.* 1960 attempted to achieve the same result, but through jazz. In a real sense, Cortázar was responding to the French author while at the same time updating the Proustian musical experience.

I, of course, must concede some obvious differences between the effect of listening to music in the *Recherche* and in *Rayuela*. Whereas Vinteuil's sonata and septet themselves inspire lucid thoughts and give the Proustian protagonist the sensation of transcending his immediate circumstances, Dizzy Gillespie's playing and Bessie Smith's singing mainly intensify the atmosphere created by the presence of Oliveira's friends and the consumption of vodka. For this reason, the thoughts of Cortázar's character never attain the sublimeness and abstract quality of the ideas of the Proustian protagonist. In fact, Oliveira has the greatest hope of reaching his type of epiphany when he is the most inebriated and the least lucid.

Indubitably, Cortázar's world view was essentially distinct from Proust's. It is decidedly anti-modernist and implies a giant step toward what we have come to know as postmodernism. Unlike the French novelist, who saw in art a conceivable means of salvation, the Argentine author, similar to his main character, found only a relative value in music and the arts. These merely offered the hope of transcending the self and suggested a means of reaching the "other." This is, of course, the principal objective of Horacio Oliveira's quest and an important interest of his favorite novelist Morelli. The desire for trancendence remains as a last vestige of modernism, but the use of jazz as a stimulus already suggests an interest in popular culture, which would be typical of the post-Boom, as well as of postmodernism.

I will return shortly to the question of Morelli's presence in *Rayuela* after we conclude our discussion on music and the arts. Here, I would like to make just two points concerning this fictional writer. First of all, he appears to be one of the few even modestly successful artists in *Rayuela*, a novel where failed artists abound: Berthe Trépat, Babs, Ronald, la Maga and Oliveira. Secondly, Morelli's description of his hypothetical funeral monument heaps apparent scorn on his own life and work, if not on those of all artists. When compared with the depiction of Bergotte's death in *La prisonnière* and that of Silvano in *Invitados en "El Paraíso,"* this passage attests to the enormous distance that separated Cortázar's attitude toward art and the views that were held by Proust and Mujica Láinez. The parodic tone of Cortázar's text causes me to suspect that the contrast was intentional. Morelli wrote while he was in the hospital:

> Tengo amigos que no dejarán de hacerme una estatua en la que me representarán tirado boca abajo en el acto de asomarme a un charco con ranitas auténticas. Echando una moneda en una ranura se me verá escupir en el agua. . . . (638)

> [I have friends who will not fail to make a statue of me in which they will portray me face down in the act of leaning over a puddle with actual little frogs. By tossing a coin in the slot, one will see me spit into the water. . . .]

I can even argue that Morelli's monument is a parody of the painting described in Mujica Láinez's novel, "Los bañistas" [The Bathers]. In this work, we do not find frogs, but rather young males in bathing suits relaxing in the garden. The reference to water in this case is implicitly metonymic, but also the water games of Silvano's models both before and after their posing, as well as their long limbs could have suggested to Cortázar his frogs.

The new, no longer modernist but rather emerging postmodern attitude toward art and the artist can be observed in Spanish America in the years that follow. José Lezama Lima, for instance, began to treat metaphor in the novel in a revisionist manner. In *Paradiso* we can detect a Proustian connection but also a sense of rebellion. Although Luz Aurora Pimentel was primarily interested in defining concepts and providing examples and did not discuss literary relations in the preface to her book *Metaphoric Narration: Paranarrative Dimensions in A la recherche du temps perdu* (1990), this Proustian critic of Mexican origin suggested more than a shared interest in metaphor on the part of Marcel Proust and José Lezama Lima.[10] The similarity between the ideas and intentions of these two writers would preclude a simple coincidence, especially because we know that the Cuban poet carefully read the *Recherche* and mentioned his ideas on it in his diaries, letters, and well-documented personal conversations.[11]

I cannot merely accept the remarks by Jaime Valdivieso, who claimed that Lezama's "concept of image as a bridge between the self and reality, as well as the constant use of simile are derived from Proust to a large extent" (1980, 123). José Lezama Lima consciously sought to distance himself from Proust. For this reason, we do not find in *Paradiso* the same type of lengthy impressionist descriptions of music or of other subjects, which were typical of the modernists Felisberto Hernández and Manuel Mujica Láinez. Moreover, as Pimentel indicated, there is often an "extreme arbitrariness of the association" found in Lezama's comparisons (1990, 142), and this runs contrary to a Proustian sense of *diégèse*. The Cuban poet obviously preferred to be original than to appear in any way Proustian.

On the other hand, I would contend that Proust's use of comparison in the *Recherche* served as a challenge and point of departure for Lezama, who wished to attribute an equal importance to metaphorical language in his novel. Significantly in the first chapter of *Paradiso*, Lezama used so many comparisons that he felt compelled to say of one of his characters, "La señora Augusta . . . no podía prescindir de los símiles. . ." [Madame Augusta . . . could not do without similes] (1973, 15). Yet, even in these comparisons, Lezama was generally more concise and less overtly aesthetic than Proust had been. For example, concerning the sentries stationed outside the house, he simply wrote: "El del frente de la casa, con voz tan decisiva que atravesó toda la casa como un cuchillo. El de atrás, como un eco, apagándose como si hubiese estado durmiendo . . . " [the one in the front of the house, with a voice so decisive that it passed through the entire house like a knife. The one in back, like an echo, being muffled as if he had been sleeping . . .] (13).

Lezama Lima signaled a change in the poetic prose related to Proust. Although at times he used explicit comparisons, somewhat like the French novelist, the Cuban author relied more heavily upon actual metaphors themselves, which gave his text a greater density. Furthermore, Lezama's comparisons often serve more for adornment than to translate deeply felt impressions in the manner of Proust. Nonetheless, as Pimentel asserted, Lezama often used his metaphors to launch mini-narratives, which generally take on a symbolic value in his novel as a whole.

During the years immediately following the publication of *Rayuela* and while the Boom was in its prime, the treatment of music and the arts necessarily became different. The novels by Mujica Láinez would always retain some of their aestheticism but echoes from the *Recherche* faded, particularly in these areas. The same can be said of Carpentier's novels even though *El recurso del método* contained direct references to both Vinteuil and Elstir. It is fascinating to note that in this work the one description of music is extremely comical and suggests that the Cuban novelist was parodying himself as well as Proust. When the Primer Magistrado attends a performance of *Pelléas et Mélisandre* by Debussy, he is totally disoriented by his impressions: "Esos músicos . . . no acababan de hacer nada. Probaban sus lengüetas, sacaban la saliva de las trompas dando una media vuelta al instrumento, hacían vibrar una cuerda, barrían el arpa con la punta de los dedos, sin llegar a concertarse en una segura melodía" [Those musicians . . . had not succeeded in doing anything. They tested their reeds, they expelled the saliva from their horns giving a half turn to their instruments, they made a string vibrate, they swept across their harps with the tips of their fingers, without being able to produce together a well-defined melody] (1974, 38). In the works of the principal Boom writers themselves, the subject of music and the arts had a reduced importance. I find it quite revealing that in *Casa de campo,* even though the Guermantes-like character Celeste listens to her Proustian son Juvenal play Liszt on the piano, the music is not described. For this reason, we can conclude that even though the *Recherche* remained present in regard to art, its impact moved in a new direction.

During the years since the Boom, we can still feel the effects of Cortázar's rebellion against the modernist conception of art, albeit not his iconoclastic tone. Two Spanish American authors in particular have presented through their works a revisionist attitude toward art even as they linked their texts to Proust's. Although the first novel still reflects a modernist admiration for art, it is distinctly political in its intention like many of the texts of the post-Boom and some of those associated with postmodernism. The second novel more clearly follows the latter movement by mixing elitist and popular culture and treating both from a particular distance, as we shall see.

In *La consagración de la primavera,* where Carpentier interwove the themes of social class and memory (as we saw in chapter 3) he joined the subject of art to revolution as he drew together his two principal characters and this novel as a whole. In the same way as the Cuban Enrique wishes to be an innovative architect, the Russian Vera hopes to create beauty through dance, but both of them are thwarted for many years because of their economic and political circumstances. Enrique's case is notably simpler, and he is more quickly defeated. His leftist sympathies and desire to experiment with new forms (somewhat like his French mentor Le Corbusier) run contrary to what is feasible for him in the Havana of the 1950s. In order to survive financially, he concludes that he has no choice except to design sumptuous but aesthetically mediocre mansions for wealthy Cubans, many of whom are friends of his aunt.

Vera's struggle is longer and more complex and connects the beginning of the novel with its end, as well as her childhood and her future. While she is still in Bakú, along the shores of the Caspian Sea, two dance sequences from the opera *Eugen Onégin* convince her to become a dancer. Her artistic vocation, which develops over time and seems to have been patterned on that of the Proustian protagonist, receives new impetus when Vera has the opportunity to watch Anna Pavlova perform in London and to meet this great Russian dancer. However, this experience proves to be a mixed blessing because Vera discovers in Pavlova the rare gift of apparently defying gravity, which she herself can never match. Thus by the time of her flight from Europe with Enrique, Vera comes to the conclusion that she will never be a great dancer.

This personal limitation, nonetheless, does not deter her will to create. Vera first establishes a dance school for young girls in El Vedado, but unlike Enrique, she does not resign herself to serving a merely upper-class clientele. Having watched the prodigous leaps of the traditional, black male dancers, she conceives of a performance of Stravinsky's *Rite of Spring* in which these men can play a major role. In her opinion, such production will be a great work of art because up until that time no troupe anywhere in the world had succeeded in realizing the full potential of Stravinsky's innovative ballet concerning ancient rites.

Without knowing it, Vera's conception is politically revolutionary for its time, as well as artistically original. Not only does she wish to place on the high-art stage black dancers, but also her prima ballerina, who is white, is to be paired with a black male. In the Cuba of the 1950s this idea puts at risk Vera's financial solvency because her bourgeois clientele will certainly ostracize her. It is for this reason that she creates a second dance school where she trains largely at her own expense young black dancers. Taking advantage of their innate ability and rich dance traditions, Vera comes close to producing her version of *The Rite of Spring*, but just as the trained performers are preparing to travel to Paris (where Vera has obtained financial support) Batista's henchmen attack the dance school and kill several of the dancers.

The fulfillment of Vera's artistic creation, like the vocation of the Proustian protagonist, must wait for propitious circumstances. These do not depend upon her own sensibility or need to discover the nature of her art; these stages were fulfilled earlier in the novel. In his reinterpretation of the story of an artistic vocation, Carpentier was audacious and rendered Proust's structural model political. It is only after the triumph of Castro and at the end of the novel that Vera can consider again mounting her production of *The Rite of Spring*, but in the new,

racially inclusive society, her revolutionary concept should meet no opposition and will most likely be applauded by all.[12]

The broader interpretation of art, which first became apparent in
Spanish American literature with the description of jazz in *Rayuela* and
was increasingly accepted as the post-Boom and postmodern periods
advanced, reached a new level in *Como agua para chocolate* (1989). However, in spite of the numerous elements from popular culture which
Laura Esquivel incorporated into her novel (e.g., recipes, popular expressions, a *folletín* format), she did not disdain the assistance of a modernist and high-culture author like Marcel Proust. In several ways her
artists of the kitchen are direct descendants of the cook Françoise, who,
as we saw above, is the fifth artist of the French novel.[13]

Early in the *Recherche,* the young protagonist begins to discover in the
cook Françoise many of the qualities of an artist. Later, in the first pages
of *A l'ombre des jeunes filles en fleurs,* the narrator tells how Françoise
prepared an excellent dish, *boeuf à la gelée* [cold spiced beef], when the
diplomat M. de Norpois was invited to dinner. In order to describe the
cook's very demanding criteria for the selection of the cuts of meat, the
narrator compares her to Michelangelo, who spent months searching
for the ideal blocks of marble for some of his masterpieces. Following
the meal the diplomat expresses his admiration for Françoise's culinary
skill by complimenting the protagonist's mother:

"Vous avez un chef de tout premier ordre, Madame. . . . Et ce n'est pas peu de
chose. Moi qui ai eu à l' étranger à tenir un certain train de maison, je sais
combien il est souvent difficile de trouver un parfait maître queux. Ce sont de
véritables agapes auxquelles vous nous avez conviés là." (1:458)

["You have a first-rate cook, Madame. . . . And that is no small matter. Residing abroad, I have needed to maintain a certain standard of living; thus I
know how difficult it is to find a perfect head chef. This was certainly a great
feast that you invited us to attend!"]

The hero of the *Recherche* becomes increasing aware of the genius of
other artists, but even in *Le temps retrouvé* he remembers Françoise's fine
meat dish, which he cites as a partial model for the novel that he intends
to write. Thus he asks himself the following question: "ne ferais-je pas
mon livre de la façon que Françoise faisait ce boeuf mode, apprécié par
M. de Norpois, et dont tant de morceaux de viande ajoutés et choisis
enrichissaient la gelée?" [would I not create my book in the manner in
which Françoise made that stewed beef with carrots, which was highly
esteemed by M. de Norpois, and for which so many cuts of meat added
and carefully selected enriched the jelly?] (3:1035).

In her novel, Laura Esquivel likewise elevated the cooks Nacha and Tita to the level of true artists. She featured in her text their recipes and explained in detail how they prepared succulent dishes, which were enjoyed by all. Granted that Esquivel did not compare these cooks to Michelangelo, but she removed all hint of irony that Proust's comparisons often implied. Furthermore her narrator does point out similarities between these women and representatives from the most respected fields of art. For example, referring to Tita's efforts to improve her cooking skills and to invent new recipes in order to impress Pedro, the narrator remarks: "Y así como un poeta juega con las palabras, así ella jugaba a su antojo con los ingredientes y con las cantidades, obteniendo resultados fenomenales" [And just as a poet plays with words so she toyed as she pleased with the ingredients and the quantities, obtaining phenomenal results] (1990, 76).

In other ways associated with the arts, Esquivel's novel is quite similar to the *Recherche* and many of the works that we have been examining. Tita develops her skills under her mentor's guidance, and by modeling herself on Nacha she too becomes an artist of the kitchen. Furthermore, like the Proustian protagonist, Tita decides to write a book. This is in fact a cookbook consisting of new recipes and autobiographical notes instead of a novel, but this text later serves as the basis for the book that is written by Tita's grandniece: *Como agua para chocolate*. In a real sense Esquivel combined the roles of Proust's protagonist and cook, and, thus, moved the latter from the wings to center stage. In this shift, we can see the Mexican writer's originality, as well as her source: Marcel Proust.

For additional evidence of this relation one can discover several passages where it becomes specifically intertextual. In one instance it is possible to observe how Esquivel used in a creative manner Françoise's dark side. The author of *Como agua para chocolate* did not attribute to Tita the same type of cruelty with defenseless creatures which was characteristic of Proust's cook, but she did not discard this trait either. Instead she transferred it to another character. I will explain after first citing a well-known fragment of "Combray" where the narrator says of the cook,

elle était en train . . . de tuer un poulet qui, par sa résistance désésperée et bien naturelle, mais accompagnée par Françoise hors d'elle, tandis qu'elle cherchait à lui fendre le cou sous l'oreille, des cris de "sale bête! sale bête!", mettait la sainte douceur et l'onction de notre servante un peu moins en lumière. . . . (1:121–22)

[she was involved . . . in killing a chicken, which because of its desperate and understandable resistance, along with Françoise's loss of composure, as she sought to split its neck beneath the ear while shouting, "filthy brute! filthy brute!,'" put the saintly gentleness and unction of our servant into a somewhat worse light. . . .]

In Esquivel's novel we find a similar but contrasting scene, which is evidently related to Proust's, although it is not immediately clear in what way. It demonstrates Tita's difficulty in killing quail for dinner, while at the same time suggesting her mother's skill in this same task. Of Tita and the quail, the narrrator remarks:

> Tomando una gran respiración, agarró a la primera y le retorció el pescuezo como había visto a Nacha hacerlo tantas veces, pero con tan poca fuerza que la pobre codorniz no murió, sino que se fue quejando lastimeramente por toda la cocina. . . . En ese momento pensó en lo bueno que sería tener la fuerza de Mamá Elena. Ella mataba así, de tajo, sin piedad. (54)

> [Taking a deep breath, she grabbed the first one and rung its neck as she had seen Nacha do so many times, but with so little force that the poor quail did not die, but wandered pitifully groaning all over the kitchen. . . . At that moment she thought how good it would be to have Mamá Elena's strength. She killed like that, with one chop and no pity.]

Here we might suspect a case of influence or inspiration.[14] As she developed her ideas for *Como agua para chocolate,* the author apparently used certain elements from *A la recherche du temps perdu.* Proust's cook not only served as a partial model for Nacha and Tita, but also Françoise's cruelty helped to enrich the creation of Mamá Elena, who also possessed some cooking skills but allowed her evil side to predominate. The references to Elena's ability to cut up watermelon and to shuck walnuts suggests how Esquivel further developed this aspect of the mother's cold precision.

Another point of contact between Proust and Esquivel associated with art is the type of description by analogy that we find consistently throughout both works. In at least one brief case, Esquivel employed a comparison from the world of art that even verbally echoes Proust. Referring to Tita at the wedding of her sister Rosaura and Pedro, the narrator says, "Como una gran actriz representó su papel dignamente . . . " [Like a great actrice, she played her role in a worthy manner . . .] (42). This type of explicit comparison using *como,* as well as the allusion to theatre, brings to mind numerous Proustian passages, including the following one from *Du côté de chez Swann:*

> Parfois dans le ciel de l'après-midi passait la lune blanche, *comme* une nuée, furtive, sans éclat, *comme* une actrice dont ce n'est pas l'heure de jouer et qui, de la salle, en toilette de ville, regarde un moment ses camarades, s'effaçant, ne voulant pas qu'on fasse attention à elle. (1:146, my emphasis)

[Sometimes in the afternoon sky the white moon passed by *like* a stealthy, lusterless cloud, *like* an actress whose time to appear has not yet arrived, and who in the auditorium, still in street clothes, watches for a moment her fellow actors, in a withdrawn manner, not wanting to call attention to herself.]

For the most part, the Mexican novelist used such analogies to describe either love or food, often treating one as the equivalent of the other and calling upon heat to fuse them. In a well-known example, the narrator of *Como agua para chocolate* describes the intensity of Pedro and Tita's love in this impressionist manner. Concerning the young girl's reaction to Pedro's passionate gaze, we read:

> En ese momento comprendió perfectamente lo que debe sentir la masa de un buñuelo al entrar en contacto con el aceite hirviendo. Era tan real la sensación de calor que invadía todo su cuerpo que ante el temor de que, como a un buñuelo, le empezaran a brotar burbujas por todo el cuerpo . . . Tita no pudo sostenerle esa mirada. . . . (21–22)

> [At that moment she understood perfectly what fritter dough must feel upon coming into contact with boiling oil. The sensation of heat that invaded her entire body was so real that, faced with the fear that, as in the case of the fritter, bubbles might begin to appear all over her body . . . Tita could not bear that gaze of his. . . .]

In this brilliant passage, where the heat of Pedro's gaze is said to fry Tita's body like a fritter, we can also observe an intertextual relation with Proust. The narrator of "Combray" says that an open fire seemed to cook like a turnover the odors in Tante Léonie's room:

> le feu cuisant comme une pâte les appétissantes odeurs dont l'air de la chambre était tout grumeleux . . . il les feuilletait, les dorait, les godait, les boursouflait, en faisant un invisible et palpable gâteau provincial, un immense "chausson". . . . (1:50).

> [cooking like dough the appetizing smells of which the air of the room was all curdled. . . . the fire puffed them up, it browned them, it made folds in them, it swelled them, creating an invisible yet palpable provincial pastry, an immense "turnover". . . .]

We can see how Proust also used heat and metaphorical language associated with cooking to describe a particular aspect of Combray: the aunt's room. As Victor E. Graham pointed out in his book *The Imagery of Proust*, cooking, like music, art and many other fields of human endeavor as well as nature, was an important source for Proust's comparisons.[15] Another example is a passage from *La prisonnière* where after living with the protagonist for several months, Albertine imitates his metaphorical style

She says of one of the many varieties and shapes of ice cream served at the Hotel Ritz, "Ils font aussi des obélisques de framboise qui se dresseront de place en place dans le désert brûlant de ma soif et dont je ferai fondre le granit rose au fond de ma gorge qu'ils désaltéreront mieux que des oasis. . ." [They also make raspberry obelisks, which will be erected from place to place in the burning desert of my thirst and whose pink granite I will cause to melt in the depths of my throat, which they will quench better than any oasis. . .] (3:130).

Observed in isolation Esquivel's impressionist descriptions closely resemble Proust's. She, like him, used one element from the world of her narration to translate another. Her range might appear to be more restricted than his since nearly all of her analogies are derived from food or the kitchen. However, this fact should not be viewed as a limitation or weakness because Esquivel expanded the use of culinary analogies in an entirely new direction and went beyond the level of influence and inspiration. Although her intention was not especially ironic and she did not generally parody the *Recherche* in the same way as she did her popular sources, she was evidently dialoguing with Proust by using the culinary comparisons in a very creative and sophisticated manner akin to the reworking mode of postmodernism.[16] The author of *Como agua para chocolate* did not leave her analogies on the level of image, but rather she assumed that they stated an actual truth, which she then incorporated into the narrative structure of her novel. In the terminology of Luz Aurora Pimentel, Esquivel lexicalized or attributed a literal meaning to her metaphors. The repetition of what we call in English a simile—love and passion are like heat—lends credence to the notion that the sexual excitement of Gertrudis can burn down the outdoor shower and that the effects of the consummation of Pedro and Tita's love can be viewed by someone else as if they were a fireworks display. For this reason, at the end of the novel we, the readers, can accept as believable the proposition that Tita's passion and ingesting of matches can cause a great conflagration which destroys all of the ranch with the exception of Tita's book.

The results of this extension of metaphorical language to narrative structure are of course related to magical realism. Although Esquivel's exaggeration of the subjective impression which is implied in the analogies seems more serious and sincere than García Márquez's treatment of subjectivity in "El mar del tiempo perdido," the point of departure is likewise Proust and the magical results are equally effective. Indubitably, she had other sources, but Proust's role seems undeniable. I will even dare to assert that the Mexican novelist carried her dialogue with the French author to the title of her work *Como agua para chocolate,* where we find an example of the same type of analogy.

The phrase itself "como agua para chocolate" alludes to a specific situation in the novel where Tita is especially irritable. She feels like boiling water that is ready for the mixing of chocolate. Some scholars have mentioned that this phrase is a popular Mexican expression, or they have interpreted it as an allusion to Tita's extreme displeasure at not being able to marry the man that she loves. Such remarks are certainly pertinent, but they do not exclude other contingencies that may coincide with the same general intent. I would point out that we find here a perfect example of a Proust-like comparison. Esquivel used one element from her *diégèse* to explain metaphorically another. The situation presented is the spiritual equivalent of the feeling that she wished to transmit. In this regard, I will concede that the said simile, or explicit comparison with *como,* is part of everyday language and resembles many of the other similes found in the novel ("fresca como una lechuga" [fresh like lettuce] or "enojo como la levadura" [anger like yeast]). Just the same I wish to emphasize how frequently these explicit comparisons appear in the *Recherche.* Besides the numerous examples cited throughout this chapter, I will conclude with an extreme case where Proust's narrator summarizes how he planned to write his novel:

> car cet écrivain . . . devait préparer son livre, minutieusement . . . l'accepter *comme* une règle, le construire *comme* une église, le suivre *comme* un régime, le vaincre *comme* un obstacle, le conquérir *comme* une amitié, le suralimenter *comme* un enfant, le créer *comme* un monde. . . . (3:1032, my emphasis)

> [for this writer . . . ought to prepare his book meticulously . . . accept it *like a* discipline, construct it *like* a church, follow it *like* a diet, overcome it *like* an obstacle, win it *like* a friendship, overfeed it *like* a child, create it *like a* world. . . .]

MATURE WRITERS IN THE NOVEL

Just as many Spanish American authors who followed Proust's example depicted the creators of music and art in their novels, they also portrayed in some of their texts established poets, novelists and other writers. These persons who employ the written word in order to create are in some ways similar to those who use sound, form, color, movement and even taste in their works of art. However, their ideas, style, and medium are often so closely bound by similarity or contrast to the work in which they appear as characters that these artists warrant a separate discussion, particularly because Bergotte was a novelist like Proust.

The presence of a writer in a narrative text can also be observed in simpler ways. The mere naming of a literary figure can be significant and an oral discussion concerning a writer and his work can have a profound effect upon the text in which it appears.[17] Although literary name-dropping and the discussion of literature in the novel started before Proust's time, the author of the *Recherche* employed both techniques frequently in order to draw attention to his dialogue with other writers. The Proustian narrator refers on numerous occasions to his favorite authors (Racine, Mme. de Sévigné, Saint-Simon) and several characters, including the protagonist and the Baron de Charlus, discuss such novelists as Dostoevski, Hardy, and Balzac.

Curiously, one of the first Spanish American writers to use extensively in his texts the names and works of literary figures was Jorge Luis Borges, who, as we saw in chapter 2, presumably had rejected the manner of Proust. This seeming paradox might be explained by the Argentine's interest in literature and vast erudition, which would merely coincide with those of the French novelist. However another of the stories by Borges suggests again a hidden relation between the Argentine and his rival.

In "El jardín de los senderos que se bifurcan" [The Garden of Diverging Paths] the characters Stephen Albert and Yu Tsun discuss the bizarre novel by Ts'ui Pên. Similar to the case of Funes, the life and work of this Chinese writer bear a considerable resemblance to those of Marcel Proust. Like the author of the *Recherche*, Ts'ui Pên abandoned the pleasures and banquets of the world in order to write a novel, and he left at the time of his death an enormous, incomplete manuscript.

Indubitably, there are apparent differences between the texts by Proust and by Ts'ui Pên, but most of these can be attributed to the Argentine writer's imagination and tendency to exaggerate. As Anderson Imbert pointed out in "El taller de Marcel Proust," the *Recherche* contained several obvious contradictions and alternate developments.[18] These were due primarily to the fact that the ailing French novelist often inserted new pages into his notebooks, he sometimes forgot what he had written before, and he never had the opportunity to revise his final volumes. For these reasons, at least three of his characters (Bergotte, la Berma, and Mme de Villeparisis) die and later appear alive in the text, the same actions are assigned to more than one character, and the same subject is discussed from differing perspectives. Although more frequent in number, similar contradictions led the readers of Ts'ui Pên to conclude that his novel was totally chaotic. Here, we may detect another example of the Argentine's secret humor used at Proust's expense. Indirectly, Borges was calling the *Recherche* chaotic, but he probably enjoyed "improving" upon it by transforming it into a labyrinth. Symptomatically, like some scholars who invoked Proust's correspondence to explain his true intentions, Albert found the key to the Chinese writer's manuscript in a letter. This text suggested that Ts'ui Pên had created alternate developments of specific events in order to illustrate how time can appear to be divergent, convergent or parallel.

The implicit dialogue found in this story is apparently confirmed by the use of the word that designates time itself, which is intentionally opposed.[19] Whereas Proust emphasized the importance of his theme of time by citing it in the first and as the last word in his multivolume novel (*longtemps, temps*) and by alluding to it constantly, for precisely the same purpose Ts'ui Pên suppressed it entirely. It is for this reason that I suspect that the references by Borges to the novel as being "un género subalterno" [a minor genre] or "despreciable" [negligible] may be aimed at least in part at the *Recherche,* and thus he attacked this work once again. Just the same, the following remark seems to indicate a mild admiration for Proust, who wove into his text numerous philosophical digressions, like Ts'ui Pên and Borges himself:

> Ts'ui Pên fue un novelista genial, pero también fue un hombre de letras que sin duda no se consideró un mero novelista. El testimonio de sus contemporáneos proclama—y harto lo confirma su vida—sus aficiones metafísicas, místicas. La controversia filosófica usurpa buena parte de su novela. (1956, 98)

> [Ts'ui Pên was a brilliant novelist, but also he was a man of letters who most certainly did not consider himself a mere novelist. The testimony of his contemporaries proclaims—and his life fully confirms —his metaphysical, mystical interests. Philosophical controversy takes up a good portion of his novel.]

If such is the case, this judgement appears to be the most favorable one that Borges ever made of Proust and his work, but it is tainted by irony and has remained concealed from most readers.

In many narrative works from Spanish America, especially during the years that preceded the Boom, throughout this period and after, we find scenes or episodes where the characters discuss well-known writers or literary subjects. One example can be found in *El túnel* by Ernesto Sábato, where Hunter, Mimí, and Castel talk about the detective novel as a genre. Likewise, in *Sobre héroes y tumbas* Bruno speaks to Martín about Argentine writers, such as Jorge Luis Borges, and assorted authors from other countries. Featured among these is Marcel Proust, of whom Bruno says the following in order to prove that absolute originality does not exist:

> Hay un fragmento de *El molino del Floss* en que una mujer se prueba un sombrero frente a un espejo: es Proust. Quiero decir el germen de Proust.

Todo lo demás es desarrollo. Un desarrollo genial, casi canceroso, pero un desarrollo al fin. (1966, 175)

[There is a passage in *The Mill on the Floss* where a woman tries on a hat in front of a mirror: it is Proust. I mean the seed of Proust. Everything else is development. A brilliant, almost cancerous development, but development after all.]

Of all of the Spanish American works from these years, probably the one in which such intellectual discussions play the largest role is *Paradiso* by José Lezama Lima. In this case Fronesis, Foción, and Cemí discuss literature, philosophy, and other subjects and mention the names, ideas, and works of numerous writers, including Proust. In this regard I must acknowledge that many other European writers besides Proust (but generally after him) have incorporated discussions on literature into their narrative texts. André Gide in *Les faux-monnayeurs* [The Counterfeiters] and Aldoux Huxley in *Point Counter Point* are obvious examples.[20] As in these modernist works, many Spanish American novels since 1950 include as an important secondary character a mature or successful writer. Specifically like the *Recherche,* the protagonist often discovers the writer's work, he reads it with obvious relish, and he eventually has the opportunity to meet the writer. This encounter is often disappointing because of the contrast between the author and his work, but each case is somewhat different.

An example of this general pattern can be found in a novel by Mujica Láinez, *Los ídolos*. Its first part significantly bears the name of the writer Lucio Sansilvestre. In this case, the narrator's best friend Gustavo receives as a gift the sole poetical work by Sansilvestre, and the two high school youths read together "Los ídolos." Because of his passion for this volume of poetry, Gustavo devotes his life to studying it, and when the two friends happen to meet years later in England, they attempt to interview Sansilvestre. In addition to the elements derived from *A l'ombre des jeunes filles en fleurs,* I should acknowledge that Mujica Láinez borrowed a few traits from the American author Henry James ("The Aspern Papers") as well as from detective fiction. Concerning Sansilvestre there is an obvious enigma. Following the publication of "Los ídolos," Sansilvestre abandoned his South American country and moved to Great Britain, where he lived in total isolation with his English wife. This mystery continues even after the young men are able to circumvent the spouse, who tries to prevent the encounter, because Lucio Sansilvestre refuses to discuss "Los ídolos."

The Proustian question concerning the relation between an author and his work is given a new twist in the novel by Mujica Láinez. Not only are Gustavo and the narrator disappointed when they meet the author, but also the former, who is very familiar with the volume of poetry, comes to the startling conclusion that perhaps Lucio Sansilvestre did not write it at all. This idea, which Gustavo expresses in a letter to the narrator, is based in part upon the indisputable contrast between the poems in the famous volume and later ones by Sansilvestre, which Gustavo has the chance to examine. Furthermore, the strangely tender manner in which Sansilvestre treated Gustavo because of his resemblance to a deceased friend, Juan Romano, contributed to the young critic's suspicions. The homosexual overtones and the doubt that remains at the end because Gustavo dies in an automobile accident with Sansilvestre are somewhat Proustian, albeit distantly so.

The Spanish American author, who developed in the largest number of ways the presence of a mature writer in the novel, was Julio Cortázar. Despite his opposition to the Wagnerian novel, he appropriated this essentially modernist subject and used it for his own purposes. In *Rayuela,* Horacio Oliveira and his friends from the Club de la Serpiente become interested in Morelli's work. Oliveira sees this writer by chance in the street when he is hit by an automobile, and he then visits the man at the hospital. There the writer gives Oliveira a key to his apartment so that certain personal matters can be resolved. Such access allows the members of the Club to read Morelli's notebooks and to discuss them. Oliveira, in particular, finds the ideas very interesting, and since he considers becoming a writer, he thinks seriously about employing some of them in his own work. Obviously, Cortázar believed that these ideas were of value because he included in his "capítulos prescindibles" [dispensable chapters] some of Morelli's notes, explanations of them and commentaries about them.

Most certainly, there are appreciable differences between the treatment of Morelli in *Rayuela* and the way Bergotte is depicted in the *Recherche.* The initial encounter between the protagonist and the writer, for example, appears distinct in nature. On the one hand, the young hero of *A l'ombre des jeunes filles en fleurs* is formally introduced to Bergotte at Swann's house and then has great difficulty in understanding how the little man with a snail-like nose and a goatee beard could have written the beautiful novels attributed to him. On the other, Oliveira first sees the writer as the victim of an accident, but he does not realize that the old man is his favorite novelist until he talks to him at the hospital.

In spite of such differences Oliveira's dialogue with Morelli corresponds roughly to the dinner party at Swann's house because both aspiring writers have the opportunity to hear their idols speak. Again we can observe several contrasts, but these were perhaps in part intentional and may suggest a type of response. While Cortázar presented almost exclusively dialogue, Proust included in his text lengthy analyses and few actually spoken words. Just the same, certain comments in *Rayuela*, such as "Se trataba de encontrar un lenguaje que no fuera literario" [It was a question of finding a language that was not literary] (735), demonstrate the author's desire to show similarities and differences between Morelli's spoken and written words. This was in fact the principal intention of Proust's protagonist: "Les paroles méconnaissables sorties du masque que j'avais sous les yeux, c'était bien à l'écrivain que j'admirais qu'il fallait les rapporter . . . " [The unrecognisable words that emerged from the mask I had before my eyes needed to be ascribed to the writer that I admired. . .] (1:552).

In the hospital scene there are other suggestions of a possible dialogue between Cortázar and Proust in this regard. The reference to *Le Figaro,* where the Proustian protagonist eventually publishes some of his first literary articles, does not appear to have been made by chance, but the mention is quite humorous. Morelli says of the notice concerning his accident, "Salió en el *Figaro*. Debajo de un telegrama sobre el abominable hombre de nieves" [It came out in *Le Figaro*. Beneath a telegram about the abominable snowman] (734). More importantly, when Morelli alludes to his approaching death and states one of his final regrets concerning his work, one is reminded of Bergotte's thoughts when he is about to die. Morelli says, "Me hubiera gustado entender mejor a Mallarmé, un sentido de la ausencia y del silencio era mucho más que un recurso extremo, un *impasse* metafísico" [I would have liked to understand Mallarmé better, his sense of absence and silence was much more than an extreme technique, a metaphysical impasse] (736). Likewise, Bergotte is sorry that he did not write in the way that Vermeer had painted: "C'est ainsi que j'aurais dû écrire. Mes derniers livres sont trop secs, il aurait fallu passer plusieurs couches de couleur, rendre ma phrase en elle-même précieuse. . ." [It is thus that I should have written. My last books are too dry, it would have been necessary to set down several layers of color, to render my phrasing itself precious . . .] (3:187).

As I suggested above in the section on updated interpretations of art, Morelli's and in turn Cortázar's attitude toward life, death, and art are essentially distinct from those of Proust's character and of the French novelist himself. Morelli's description of his funeral monument, which I cited, illustrates the radical contrast. Cortázar's opposition to Proust's conception is reinforced by the manner in which he indicated to the reader Morelli's actual demise. Instead of eulogizing his fictional novelist or suggesting his survival through his literary work, as Proust had done, Cortázar made of his chapter 85 a mere footnote, whose meaning is only implicit:

Las vidas que terminan como los artículos literarios de periódicos y revistas, tan fastuosos en primera plana y rematando en una cola desvaída, allá por la página treinta y dos, entre avisos de remate y tubos de dentrífico. (572)

[Those lives that end like the literary articles in newspapers and magazines, so splendid on the front page and being finished off in a washed-out train, back there on page thirty-two, among the ads for auctions and toothpaste.]

Here, of course, we find an echo of the reference to *Le Figaro* and the location of the notice of Morelli's accident. In both cases we can perceive a sharp contrast with *La prisonnière:*

On l'enterra, mais toute la nuit funèbre, aux vitrines éclairées, ses livres, disposés trois par trois, veillaient comme des anges aux ailes éployées et semblaient, pour celui qui n'était plus, le symbole de sa résurrection. (3:188)

[They buried him, but throughout the night of mourning, in the illuminated shop windows, his books, displayed three by three, kept vigil like angels with out-spread wings and seemed, for him who was no more, the symbol of his resurrection.]

Cortázar's irreverent, anti-modernist attitude toward the death of Morelli, however, does not imply that this novelist's ideas were negligible. Those found in his notebooks apparently interest Oliveira and his friends more than any work that Morelli had actually published. The members of the Club discuss these ideas at length. Their conversation, of course, reminds us of the discussion of literary works in the *Recherche*, *El túnel,* and other novels. A few subtle allusions are made to Proust in this section of *Rayuela,* in particular, on the level of language. The references to the concepts of "mundo" [world] and "ciudad" [city] to indicate Morelli's personal vision echo passages from Proust's text, such as the following one from *La prisonnière:* "Chaque artiste semble ainsi comme le citoyen d'une patrie inconnnue, oubliée de lui-même, différente de celle d'où viendra . . . un autre grand artiste" [Each artist thus seems to be the citizen of an unknown country, which he himself has forgotten, and which is different from the place of origin of . . . another great artist] (3:257). Even the allusions to salvation and escape from time, which are developed elsewhere in *Rayuela,* appear to be related to Proust, as we shall see in chapter 7.

The ideas themselves, as they were extracted from the notebooks and incorporated into the "capítulos prescindibles," often develop more fully the opposition by Morelli and Cortázar to Proust. We already examined in chapter 4 the case of the psychological novel and Proust's connection to it, but there are other examples, such as the actual form of the

two works. On the surface Morelli and Cortázar's emphasis on presenting fragments instead of a continuous narration seems diametrically
opposed to Proust's manner. Even visually the printed text of *Rayuela*
contrasts starkly with that of the *Recherche*. Some of the "capítulos prescindibles" are composed of just a few lines on an essentially blank page,
while Proust's extremely long paragraphs fill the entire space and even
indentations for paragraphing are rare.

Despite such appearances, I wish to point out that there are some
significant points of contact which confirm a relation, albeit that of
opposition. Both Proust and Cortázar incorporated into their texts numerous extranovelistic elements: ideas, theories, pastiches, etc. Neither
author limited himself to the mere presentation of events. Proust
developed his work very slowly. Each incident and many specific details
serve as a pretext for an explanation or analysis. For this reason the
Recherche is filled with digressions in which the narrator discusses memory, art, love, the difficulty of knowing the "other" and novelistic theory.
Furthermore, he relates at length the lives of secondary characters. In
contrast, Cortázar traced in chapters 1 to 56 a bare sequence of events
and rarely offered a commentary or analysis. The ideas suggested are
only those of the characters. Entire pages are composed merely of
dialogue. Nevertheless, Cortázar also employed a complex system of
intercalation, which are his "capítulos prescindibles." These also constitute digressions from the general plot. In these chapters we find some
of the same subjects as in the *Recherche:* art, love, memory, the "other,"
and novelistic theory. Cortázar's narrator, also like Proust's, relates parallel actions, such as Oliveira's affair with Pola, and develops secondary
characters, for example, Ossip. In short, Cortázar created his own type of
digression, which differs from Proust's by form, as well as by specific
content, but which does in fact imply a response with a contrasting, anti-
modernist if not postmodernist point of view.

Following the example of Cortázar, who had chosen a Proustian, modernist subject and had greatly expanded upon it, other Spanish Americans have included in their works a mature novelist as a character. The
authors of these texts have often suggested a relation with Proust, but in
each case they have attempted to be different from the French novelist
and from Cortázar.

Ernesto Sábato, for example, placed in *Abaddón el exterminador* a nearly
identical double of himself, Ernesto Sabato. At one point in the text this
character suggests the reasons for his inclusion in the novel: "Hablo de la
posibilidad extrema que sea el escritor de la novela el que esté dentro.
Pero no como un observador, como un cronista, como un testigo" [I am
speaking of the extreme possibility that it may be the writer of the novel
who appears within it. But, not as an observer, as a chronicler, as a

witness] (1991, 238). When his interlocutor asks what he means, Sabato responds, "Como un personaje más, en la misma calidad que los otros, que sin embargo salen de su propia alma. Como un sujeto enloquecido que conviviera con sus propios desdoblamientos." [As just another character, in the same capacity as the others, who nonetheless emerge from his own soul. Like a deranged individual who lives alongside his own doubles]. The actual novelist, Sábato, in effect depicted a version or caricature of himself in the novel and even at his worst moments, for example, when his namesake fumbles with objects or when he has difficulty coping with store clerks. In this way, the reader can see the awareness that Sábato had of himself as a public person and how defensive he often appeared when faced with criticism from his readers.

The relation between Proust and Sábato in regard to the life and work of a novelist can be noted on several levels, which are often underscored through subtle textual allusions. The character Sabato considers his life at times even parallel to that of Marcel Proust. When he finds that he is criticized for attending upper-class social gatherings, he remembers the French author, who was accused of being a snob and of "dying" to meet duchesses. It is thus almost frightfully coincidental for Sabato when he wanders into Carranza's library during one of these social events and notices by chance Proust's second volume *A la sombra de las muchachas en flor.* For this reason, he exclaims, "cómo era posible?" [how could this be possible?] (43). Although not everyone may understand this allusion, it is crystal clear for a Proustian reader. In *Le temps retrouvé,* while waiting in the library of the Prince de Guermantes, the protagonist sees a novel by George Sand that he had read as a child, and its title causes him to remember the past.

In another section of *Abaddón,* the dialogue with Proust is especially evident because the narrator describes the encounter between a young aspiring writer and the mature novelist. This fragment is intertextually related to the portion of *A l'ombre des jeunes filles en fleurs* involving the meeting of Bergotte, but the Argentine reversed the situation by using as his focal character the old writer. Here, we do not find the young man (whose name significantly is Marcelo), confused by the differences between Sabato the man and Sabato the novelist. No. It is the mature writer who feels extremely frustrated. He encourages the young man to express his ideas and to develop his interests and talent, but ultimately he discovers that he has merely embarrassed Marcelo, who is apparently ashamed of his literary propensities. The reader might even suspect that the young man does not possess all of the qualities and potential that Sabato attributes to him, but when Marcelo is left alone in the café, he takes out his notebook and begins to write.

Abaddón el exterminador also shows the mature novelist in other situations associated with Proust's work. In the chapter on high society, we already saw how Sabato discusses socialist realism with young leftists and how he suggests in another conversation that Proust was a better novelist than any of the representatives of the Soviet school. The efforts to write of the already twice successful Sabato and those of his frustrated double Bruno are also treated in a Proustian manner, but I will leave this subject until chapter 8 because it is more closely allied to the literary vocation of a writer than the mere life of a mature author.[21]

Mario Vargas Llosa also depicted in one of his novels, *La tía Julia y el escribidor* [Aunt Julia and the Scriptwriter] (1977), the figure of an author, Pedro Camacho. In this case the character who writes is not admirable because of the excellence of his work. As the reader can observe from Camacho's texts, which alternate with those of the first person narrator, the man from Bolivia who became famous for his radio dramas displays few literary attributes. His composition techniques are too obvious and he frequently shows poor taste and judgement. Over time, his verbal and narrative facility begins to disintegrate.

For the young, aspiring writer, Mario (who speaks in the first person and who holds much in common with young Mario Vargas Llosa), Camacho, as a man and as a writer, can only serve as a partial model. Obviously aware of the script hack's weaknesses, Mario rejects his manner as unliterary. Just the same, living in a country and during a time in which most of the so-called *literatos* [men of letters] supported themselves economically through nonliterary means, Mario cannot help but admire Camacho, who lives entirely from his writing. Referring to his own literary vocation and his strong desire to become a full-time writer, Mario says, "Lo más cercano a ese escritor a tiempo completo, obsesionado y apasionado con su vocación . . . era el radionovelista boliviano: por eso me fascinaba tanto" [The closest thing to that full-time writer obsessed and passionate in his vocation . . . was the Bolivian radio novelist: for this reason he fascinated me so much] (1984, 236).

In *La tía Julia y el escribidor* the presence of Proust is less evident than in the other cases that I have discussed. Far more interested in the realism of Flaubert than in the modernist aestheticism and psychological analysis of Proust, Mario Vargas Llosa chose few details overtly bound to the *Recherche*. However, a Proustian connection is apparent, albeit weak or through an intermediate source of inspiration, such as Cortázar or Sábato.[22] Not only did the Peruvian author construct his novel around the already successful writer and the young man who would like to write, but also he cited Proust's name in a strategic manner. Precisely in the context referred to above and at midpoint in *La tía Julia* the author mentioned Proust and other modernist writers in order to contrast Camacho's ignorance of world literature with the broad knowledge of the part-time *literatos* of Peru. Mario thus asks himself:

> ¿Por qué esos personajes que se servían de la literatura como adorno o pretexto iban a ser más escritores que Pedro Camacho, quien *sólo* vivía para escribir? ¿Porque ellos habían leído (o, al menos, sabían que deberían haber leído) a Proust, a Faulkner, a Joyce, y Pedro Camacho era poco más que un analfabeto? (236)

> [Why were those figures who used literature as an adornment or pretext to be considered more legitimately writers than Pedro Camacho, who *only* lived in order to write? Was it only because they had read (or, at least, knew that they should have read) Proust, Faulkner, Joyce, and Pedro Camacho was scarcely more than an illiterate?]

The more recent Peruvian author Alfredo Bryce Echenique also portrayed in his two-part work, *Cuadernos de navegación en un sillón Voltaire,* successful writers along with his aspiring novelist Martín Romaña. The latter meets two already published Peruvian authors, Julio Ramón Ribeyro and Alfredo Bryce Echenique, when the three of them visit their mutual friend Mauricio in the hospital.[23] Ribeyro, who has by now achieved a certain degree of literary success and maturity and is very likeable, encourages Martín and constitutes a positive role model for him. In contrast, the character Bryce Echenique (who shares specific traits with the real author) has only published up to that time one volume of short stories, but he subsequently becomes Martín's principal rival.

As one reads through *La vida exagerada de Martín Romaña* and *El hombre que hablaba de Octavia de Cádiz,* one can follow Bryce's successful career and see how it markedly contrasts with Martín's failed literary vocation. Not only is Bryce able to complete and publish his books with little apparent difficulty, but he is also luckier than Martín in several ways. Even though Bryce remains in his Parisian apartment and writes throughout the month of May 1968, the publication of one of his books in Cuba exonerates him from all political responsibility. As we saw above, Martín is ostracized by the Latin American Marxists because his participation in the street demonstrations is not considered radical enough. Over time, Martín comes to resent and to be jealous of Bryce Echenique's success, which the latter often flaunts. Martín even feels persecuted by Bryce, who tells jokes at his expense and spreads false rumors about him. Emblematically, one of these involves Proust. Referring to the ways in which he financed his many trips in *El hombre que hablaba de Octavia de Cádiz,* Martín expresses his anger concerning Bryce's remarks:

"Y falsa de toda falsedad la respuesta de Bryce Echenique según la cual
mi madre se arruinó costeándole viajes a esa especie de Proust oral que
era su hijo . . . " [And entirely and in every way false the reply of Bryce
Echenique, according to which my mother went broke paying for the
trips of that sort of oral Proust who was her son . . .] (1985, 291).

In all of these details we can detect the humor of the real author of the
two-part novel, which is turned back upon himself whenever he refers to
either Martín Romaña or the character Alfredo Bryce Echenique because both of them show different aspects of his own person. Yet, more
important for our purposes is the manner in which the literary rivalry is
connected to Proust's novel. Indeed, the subject of rivalry is not
developed in the *Recherche* to the extent that it is in *Cuadernos de navegación,* but it is present. Bloch does compete with the Proustian protagonist in several ways, but he is no more successful in his life or work than
the latter. Also Swann, who had been the model for Proust's young hero,
at times seems to be a rival that must be defeated.

To some extent, the competition between Martín and Bryce represents an extreme case of the rivalry that exists between every aspiring
writer and every already successful author, including the one implicit in
the relationship between the Proustian protagonist and Bergotte. Before they have published a major work, both Martín and Proust's hero
find themselves beneath a shadow from which they must escape. They
are aided and protected by the shade of good role models, such as
Ribeyro or Bergotte, whose path they can initially follow. However, they
must also develop their own talents and free themselves from their
literary masters in order to become true writers. To remain under the
mentor's shadow implies literary obscurity if not death.

Martín is especially aware of this danger and his literary name dropping is even more extreme than in the case of *Rayuela.* The plethora of
references to the writers that preceded him, such as Hemingway and
Baroja, as well as numerous others from Jorge Manrique to García Márquez, not only demonstrates his knowledge of literature, but also the
large number of rivals with whom he must contend. In this regard,
Marcel Proust, whose name Martín mentions obsessively more than forty
times, remains particularly ominous for him. As we saw in the chapter on
high society, the admiration of Martín's mother for Proust of course
contributes to this obsession. The character Alfredo Bryce Echenique,
even though he is just starting to become known when Martín meets
him, symbolizes the first great obstacle that must be overcome: the
completion and publication of the first book. Martín's inability to move
beyond this stage becomes increasingly painful with the publication of
each of Bryce's subsequent books. We shall return to the question of
Martín's literary vocation in chapter 8, where we will see how he must vie

not only with Alfredo Bryce Echenique but most especially with Marcel Proust, whose work he confronts in a postmodern manner.

Finally, in order to prove that this vein of Proustian inspiration has not yet exhausted itself, I will discuss briefly the case of *El color del verano* by Reinaldo Arenas. In this instance, we can find both positive and negative models for the aspiring novelist Reinaldo, and nearly all of them closely resemble real writers that Arenas actually knew. On the one hand, José Lezama Lima delivers a lecture on phallic imagery and Virgilio Piñera reads his ephemeral poems. On the other hand, Alejo Sholejov provides for Fifo's international guests a guided tour of la Habana Vieja. It seems ironic that this Alejo, who is unmistakably a caricature of one of Cuba's outstanding Proustians, Alejo Carpentier, is presented in such a disfavorable light by the Proustian that Arenas is in this novel. But political, as well as personal differences, seem to have been decisive factors. Also parody and humor are essential elements of *El color del verano,* whose author derides the manner of some of the most important Cuban writers since Gertrudis Gómez de Avellaneda. In this regard Arenas follows to some extent Guillermo Cabrera Infante, who parodied seven Cuban writers in *Tres tristes tigres* [Three Sad Tigers], but we should also remember Proust's pastiches of French authors, one of which appears in *Le temps retrouvé.*[24]

In point of fact, Reinaldo Arenas has taken our present subject derived from Proust and other modernists—the mature writer in the novel—much farther than any of his predecessors, including Bryce. In the postmodern farce that introduces *El color del verano,* we find a large cast of both major and minor Cuban authors. Some of them appear under their own names, while the names of others have been deformed for satirical purposes. Significantly in the list of characters and in the play itself we find Delfín Proust but no explanation for his inclusion along with so many Cuban writers. But as we saw in the section on homosexual love, Arenas also parodied Proust, whose namesake here describes himself as "un pájaro cursi y a la vez serio" [a pretentious and at the same time serious queer] (45).

Reviewing this chapter, we can observe a chronological progression with regard to our subject and approach and even an allegorical sense of our version of Proust's title "A l'ombre des artistes en fleurs". During the pre-Boom period the modernist subject of art was most apparent in the impressionist descriptions of music, which were clearly influenced by Proust, whose shadow remained strong for the authors of these texts. Over time the inspiration rather than influence of the French novelist helped to expand the subject of art and can be seen in the work of authors like Mujica Láinez. He, for example, began to elude that shadow when his reworking of Proustian situations in *Los ídolos* and *Los viajeros* was replaced by his using Proust's text as a point of departure in *Invitados en "El Paraíso"* and *Bomarzo*. With *Rayuela* we find a rejection of the shadow because, instead of merely following Proust, Cortázar both reacted and responded to the French work. Since that time each of the new writers has tried to converse with Proust implicitly but did not rely upon the protection of his shade. Moving in the direction of the post-Boom and postmodernism, Carpentier made his artists unintentionally political while Esquivel gave her artist of the kitchen a place of prominence. In a distinct manner, Sábato inserted himself into his novel as an aging writer, Bryce divided his literary person into two parts which had to compete with each other and Arenas parodied nearly all of his possible Cuban models but most especially Marcel Proust.

6

On Lost Time and the Search for it: Spiritual Equivalents of "Combray" and *Albertine disparue*

A LESS EASILY UNDERSTOOD, BUT MORE PROFOUNDLY PROUSTIAN theme than high society, love or even the appreciation of art is time. In spite of the fact that Proust's general title *A la recherche du temps perdu* and the initial pages of his first volume refer directly to the subject of time, it took his readers and critics many years to understand the full meaning and significance of time in the work itself. Such a slowness to comprehend is indeed understandable. Even though all of the readers of the *Recherche* knew the definition of time in a chronological sense and how this form of objective time differed from subjective time, the actual meaning of *temps perdu* [lost time] was not obvious from Proust's title. The numerous word plays on it during the 1920s, some of which suggested the idea of "wasted time," serve to illustrate this confusion.[1] Only with the publication of *Le temps retrouvé* in 1927 could Proust's readers find in this volume his complete explanation.

The subject of time is an ancient one, and Proust followed many of its traditions, one of which had been especially evident during the fifteenth century in both France and Spain: time as transitoriness and disappearance. In French literature, the best example was François Villon's "Ballade des dames du temps jadis," [Ballad of the Ladies from Times Gone By] where the once famous women of the past are said to have left no more trace than the snows of bygone years. Similarly in Spain Jorge Manrique wrote in his "Coplas por la muerte de su padre" [Ballad for the Death of His Father] that the most elegant and powerful men of the court of Juan II had disappeared like the morning dew. In an analogous manner, Proust often portrayed time as change, decay and disappearance. Like some of his predecessors, he referred to the recent past and how it was affected by time. In this regard, he chose as one of his primary arenas the elegant aristocratic salons of Paris, which correspond roughly to the court of Juan II in Manrique's poem or to the famous women of Villon.[2] In particular, beginning in *Le côté de Guermantes* and continuing in *Sodome et Gomorrhe,* he demonstrated how the composition of elite social salons was influenced by important historical events, such as the Dreyfus Affair (1894–1906) and the Great War (1914–18). During the trial and attempts to exonerate the Jewish officer Alfred Dreyfus, Jews were often excluded from some of the salons while persons of German descent were included. Later, the war with Germany reversed this situation. To represent the changeability of this refined world, as well as the mutable realms of fashion and politics, Proust used frequently the image of a kaleidoscope, whose colors and shapes are constantly in flux and whose combinations are often surprising. Although he focused his attention upon the period of his own life, he often cited examples from the historical past, for instance the seventeenth century when two of his favorite writers were active: the Duc de Saint Simon and Mme. de Sévigné.

Parallel to this portrait of high society across time, Proust showed the evolution of his numerous characters and in particular the Baron de Charlus. This aging nobleman, who enjoyed great prestige in the early volumes of the *Recherche,* undergoes a steady decline in the second half. As we saw in the section on homosexuality of chapter 4, this aspect of his character is largely responsible, but also the aging process itself plays a major role. Thus the Baron changes both physically and morally, and he often appears in the text to be a different person. In the description of this process of decay, Proust was following specific writers in the realist tradition, but he also showed his own originality in several ways, most notably through the surprising quality of the changes.

Besides using high society and individual characters to illustrate the effects of time, Proust also called upon the tradition of the psychological novel, which since the seventeenth century had traced the development of love over time. As we saw in chapter 4, "Un amour de Swann" conforms quite well to this genre. It shows how Swann's love for Odette begins, develops, and eventually ends. *La prisonnière* also represents to some extent this genre, even though the protagonist's love for Albertine seems quite static because the routine of these two characters is depicted through the events of a single day. In contrast, the next volume *Albertine disparue* carries the evolutionary aspects of the psychological novel to a heightened level. There time is presented as becoming through the progressive forgetfulness of the protagonist for Albertine. At this point, Proust approached the ideas of his famous relative Henri Bergson, who spoke of *le devenir* [becoming] and *la durée* [duration] to explain how reality changed over time. Also we can note the subjectivity of time and how it is related to a modernist sense of consciousness, somewhat like that of Virginia Woolf.[3] In another context, Proust also echoed the philosopher Bergson (whose ideas greatly affected all of modernist literature) when he compared the subjective nature of time to the different velocities of an automobile: "Il y a des jours montueux et malaisés qu'on met un temps infini à gravir et des jours en pente qui se laissent descendre à fond de train en chantant" [There are some uphill and uneasy days in which one invests an infinite amount of time to climb and some downhill days that allow one to descend at top speed singing as one goes] (1954, 1:391).

In an even more original way, Proust developed the theme of time throughout his seven volumes as his protagonist grows up, matures and ages. In this case we can see the debt of the French author to the novel of apprenticeship and the nineteenth-century realist tradition, as well as the nonfictional genres of biography and autobiography. However, far more than his predecessors, Proust drew attention to time itself by presenting his own ideas about it and by returning frequently to this subject. In *A l'ombre des jeunes filles en fleur,* for example, the narrator explains how he began to forget the past and felt as if he had become a different person. When he ceased to love Swann's daughter Gilberte, he could no longer understand why he had performed specific acts derived from that love (e.g., sell objects of personal value in order to buy flowers for Gilberte's mother). It is in this context that Proust's narrator begins to use extensively the concept of *temps perdu* in order to refer to an entire period of time that apparently becomes lost when one forgets the way things were. In this forgetfulness there is a type of death, which continues throughout a person's life and precedes his ultimate demise. In assessing this facet of the second volume of the *Recherche,* Paul Souday highly praised Proust's originality: "One has rarely translated with greater force and bitterness the sense of change and incessant mobility which makes of life an uninterrupted succession of fragmentary deaths" (1927, 28).

In each of the successive volumes, the protagonist undergoes new experiences linked to high society, love, and art, but he continually loses them through forgetfulness. Also, the happiest period of his life, childhood, appears to be irrevocably lost because he cannot remember it in detail. As suggested above, he in fact changes so completely that he begins to doubt the unity of his personality. The only apparent evidence that he is the same person as the boy in Combray are certain intimate experiences derived from memory. For years he is not able to understand how on occasion he seems to return to the past, but these experiences give him such joy that he would indeed like to discover how and why they occur. I am alluding here to Proust's concept of involuntary memory and the actual key to *A la recherche du temps perdu.* For it is through this type of recollection that Proust's hero discovers in *Le temps retrouvé* in what way he can search for a lost time and recover it, and how he can have the impression of escaping from time.

In Proust's seventh and last volume, the treatment of time reaches its climax. Not only does the narrator explain here the mechanism of involuntary memory, but he also portrays in visual terms the physical effects of time upon the persons that he knows and upon himself. While he is at the *matinée* of the Prince de Guermantes, he sees how his friends and acquaintances have grown old. Their hair has turned gray and some of them are totally unrecognizable. Through these individuals he also becomes aware of his own advanced age. Thus, we can see how time has had a chronological, objective effect upon him, as well as a subjective one. Similarly he notices how the aristocratic society itself has changed over time. In order to assure his financial position, the Prince de Guermantes decided to marry the bourgeois woman Madame Verdurin. In this context, after discovering how to fulfill his literary vocation, the protagonist finds himself in a race against chronological time in order to complete his literary work before his death.

Proust's emphasis on time greatly contributed to the choice of this subject as one of the most important ones of the twentieth century.[4] Although it may be considered a modernist subject, other writers developed it further, and many postmodern authors have installed themselves in the past to rewrite it. Thus, Hutcheon has cited as one of the characteristics of postmodernism "the presence of the past" (1988, 4).

For our study of Spanish American narrative, we will examine the various facets of time separately and in two cases according to what has been lost. Because the Proustian protagonist near the end of his life sees his childhood as a lost paradise and Albertine as a lost woman, we will consider those Spanish American texts related to these aspects of "Combray" and *Albertine disparue*. Even though memory is often implied in the recovery of such entities, I will treat in this chapter only those cases where memory is in part conscious or related to familiar objects instead of abstract physical sensations. I will delay until chapter 7 the discussion of those texts involving what we have come to know as Proustian involuntary memory. Later in the present chapter, I will study time as change and time as a destructive force, as well as the specific case of Gabriel García Márquez, whose work may be considered a culmination of the Proustian themes of time in Spanish America.

CHILDHOOD AS A LOST PARADISE

Although Proust's narrator knew through conscious memory that his early years did not transpire in a perfect world—some of his relatives were quite cruel and he himself suffered every night when he was sent to bed—the Combray that he recovered through unconscious memory was permeated with a poetic sense that made it appear idyllic. Furthermore, all that he knew from that world felt so essential and grounded in his original system of beliefs that details from later periods seemed to be less real. As a result when Proust's narrator evoked his childhood, he often did so with great nostalgia, and this attitude toward the past has often been considered characteristic of his type of modernism.

Quite naturally in Spanish America, the concept of lost time was first associated with childhood. Soon after the publication of *Le temps retrouvé*, there began to appear throughout the New World a series of books based upon the particular author's recollections of childhood. Some of these were related in one way or another with "Combray."[5]

Raúl Silva Castro saw this to be the case of *Alhué* (1928) by José Santos González Vera: "Like Proust, the author has cast in this book his net to the depths of lost time. He lingers in childhood, the warm, tender age in which the senses begin to live and memory to store images" (1960, 315). Indeed, as González Vera claimed in his personal memoirs, *Cuando era muchacho* (1951, 297–98), he read *Por el camino de Swann* very early, supposedly in the same period as Mariano Latorre's *Zurzulita* (1920). Yet, the relation with Proust in *Alhué* can only be deemed vague. The narrator describes the small town and several of the persons that lived there, but he says almost nothing about himself, his nature or his aspirations. He merely formulates at the beginning a project of self-exploration, which is somewhat Proustian, but he never brings it to fruition:

> Si alguna vez mi pensamiento se curva hacia el recuerdo y trato de verme en mi primera edad, sólo consigo desenmarañar tres o cuatro hechos significativos, pero insuficientes para establecer el sentido de mi carácter. (1961, 21)

> [If my thoughts ever turn toward memory and I try to see myself during my first years, I only succeed in disentangling three or four significant events, but these are insufficient to establish the sense of my character.]

A more successful and at the same time more Proustian work was Teresa de la Parra's *Memorias de Mamá Blanca* (1929). Here, not only does the principal narrator recall her childhood on the Venezuelan *hacienda* of Piedra Azul, but she is also able to provide a portrait in depth of herself Blanca Nieves, her sister Violeta, her mother and father, their cousin Juancho, the governess Evelyn, and the handyman Vicente Cochocho. These portraits, which she masterfully weaves into her narrative, demonstrate fully her child-like innocence devoid of prejudice and her psychological perspicacity, both of which resemble the manner of Proust's narrator.

To describe this general relation Anderson Imbert wrote, "Proust was one of her masters in the art of depicting the undulating succession of memories" (1974, 2:99). Employing to a large extent her own recollections and imagination, Teresa de la Parra captured diverse facets of Venezuelan life as the young daughter of a landowner might have perceived them. Her description of the *trapiche* [sugar-cane mill] is so vivid that it appears almost as if she had set in motion this now defunct water-driven machine used to crush sugar cane and to extract its sweet liquid.[6]

Furthermore, this Venezuelan author, who had written *Ifigenia* a few years before, on occasion appears to dialogue specifically with Proust concerning the subjects of time and memory. For example, when Mamá Blanca refers to the origin of her white hair, she implicitly responds to the comments of the narrator of *Le temps retrouvé* concerning his gray-haired friends and acquaintances:

Como al pasar los años, indiferentes, no se llevaron entre sus dedos raudales de belleza, de amor, ni de honores, no detesto los años pasados en mí, ni aquéllos que aún no han pasado en los otros. El tiempo, al besarme los cabellos, me coronó con mi propio nombre, sin nunca llegar a clavarme en el alma sus dientes de amargura. (1991, 382)

[Since with the passing of years, which seemed indifferent, torrents of beauty, love or honors did not slip through the fingers of Time, I do not detest the years that took place within me, nor those that have not yet occurred in others. Time, upon kissing my hair, crowned me with my own name and its teeth of bitterness never succeeded in piercing my soul.]

Teresa even attributed to these fictional memoirs a sense of *temps perdu*, albeit for more material reasons than Proust. Whereas his protagonist lost Combray because he could no longer remember it distinctly, Blanca Nieves and her family actually lost possession of Piedra Azul when it had to be sold for lack of money. It is quite revealing that, as in the French work, we find in the Venezuelan text an allusion to John Milton's title *Paradise Lost*. Just as the narrator of *Le temps retrouvé* says, "les vrais paradis sont les paradis qu'on a perdus" [the true paradises are the paradises that have been lost] (3:870), Blanca writes near the end of her text, "La época lejana de Piedra Azul, . . . Edad de Oro en Paraíso Perdido, se cristalizaba allá, en el fondo del pasado" [The distant years of Piedra Azul . . . a Golden Age in Paradise Lost, became crystallized there in the depths of the past] (399). This nostalgic perspective is very much like that of Proust.

The idea of childhood as an earthly paradise, which entails a period of innocence, maternal protection, and essential things, was developed in many of the childhood memoirs of the 1930s and since. A characteristic example is *Cuadernos de infancia* (1937) by Norah Lange. Here even though this Argentine writer was describing actual events from her childhood, her manner of evoking the past was often quite Proustian. She began her text, for example, by alluding to the landscape that could be viewed only imperfectly through the steamed up windows of a train car: "Entrecortado y dichoso, apenas detenido en una noche, el primer viaje que hicimos desde Buenos Aires a Mendoza, surge en mi memoria, como si recuperase un paisaje a través de una ventanilla empañada" [Interrupted yet happy, scarcely detained on a single night, the first trip that we made from Buenos Aires to Mendoza, rises in my memory as though I were recovering a landscape through a steamed-up train window] (1973, 9). Proust, who set portions of *A l'ombre des jeunes filles en fleur* and *Sodome et Gomorrhe* in train cars, at times referred to windows in his evocation of the past (e.g., 2:784–85). Also, he employed the image of fog over the sea to suggest how time obliterates memories and makes the past appear indefinite (3:593–94).

Years later, during the period of the Boom, several Spanish American writers were also quite reminiscent of Proust in the manner in which they described childhood. Curiously this was even the case of Cortázar in chapter 123 of *Rayuela,* where his narrator speaks of "la casa de la infancia" [the house of childhood] and of the way in which a child perceives reality:

> la sala y el jardín en un presente nítido, con colores como se los ve a los diez años, rojos tan rojos, azules de mamparas de vidrios coloreados, verde de hojas, verde de fragancia, olor y color una sola presencia a la altura de la nariz y los ojos y la boca. (1986, 669)

> [the living room and the garden in a sharp present, with colors as one sees them at age ten, reds so red, blues of colored-glass partitions, the green of leaves, green with a fragrance, smell and color a single presence at the height of one's nose, eyes and mouth.]

This description could almost apply to the house of Tante Léonie in "Combray" and brings to mind the way in which Proust's narrator evokes it. Indirectly it suggests a closer relationship between Proust and Cortázar with regard to memory than in other areas. Concerning a child's perception of color and referring to a particular shade of pink displayed by some of the hawthorne bushes, the narrator of "Combray" says,

Et justement ces fleurs avaient choisi une de ces teintes de chose mangeable . . . qui . . . sont celles qui semblent belles avec le plus d'évidence aux yeux des enfants, et à cause de cela, gardent toujours pour eux quelque chose de plus vif et de plus naturel que les autres teintes. . . . (1:139–40)

[And precisely these flowers had chosen one of the shades of an edible thing . . . which . . . are those that seem most obviously beautiful to the eyes of children, and for that reason, they retain always for them something that is more alive and natural than other shades. . . .]

Among the Spanish American authors of this period, probably the one that comes closest to Proust in language and ideas concerning the memories of childhood is Ernesto Sábato. Near the end of *Abaddón el exterminador,* Bruno's returning to the town of his early years, Capitán Olmos, echoes in specific ways passages from "Combray" and other parts of the *Recherche.* The description of approaching the town by train is very similar in both texts. We read in *Abaddón el exterminador:*

Ahora el tren empezaba el descenso y describía la curva hacia el oeste, después de dejar atrás el monte de Santa Ana, y entonces se vería pronto la torre de la iglesia y poco después la mole del molino: los elevadores del molino Bassán, su propia casa, la infancia. (1991, 440)

[Now the train began its descent and followed the curve toward the west, after leaving behind Santa Ana hill, and then soon one would see the tower of the church and a bit later the massive structure of the mill: the elevators of the Bassan mill, his own house, his childhood.]

Likewise Proust began section II of "Combray" with the following words:

Combray, de loin, à dix lieues à la ronde, vu du chemin de fer quand nous y arrivions la dernière semaine avant Pâques, ce n'était qu'une église résumant la ville . . . et, quand on approchait, tenant serrés autour de sa haute mante sombre . . . les dos laineux et gris des maisons. . . . (1:48)

[Combray, from a distance of ten leagues all around, as it was seen from the train when we arrived there during the last week before Easter, was only a church which summarized the town . . . and, when one approached, it held tightly around its high, dark cloak . . . the fleecy, gray backs of its houses. . . .]

In such a Combray-like context, Bruno thinks of the relationship between the present and the past, as well as the contrast between the years that he spent outside of Capitán Olmos and the time of his childhood there. In effect, Sábato's text is in dialogue with Proust's and perhaps that of other writers, including Cortázar.[7] The narrator says of Bruno,

> Y cuando por fin llegó a Capitán Olmos, idéntica a sí mismo, sintió como si durante esa multitud de años hubiese vivido bajo una especie de ilusión. . . . Y aquella sensación lo inducía a pensar que lo único verdaderamente real era su infancia, si lo real es lo que permanece idéntico a sí mismo: un trozo de eternidad. (440–41)

> [And when he finally arrived at Capitán Olmos, which was identical to itself, he felt as though during those numerous years he had lived with a type of illusion. . . . And that feeling caused him to think that the only true reality was his childhood, if what is real is what remains identical to itself: a slice of eternity.]

In this case, Sábato coincides with Proust and Cortázar, both of whom considered childhood to be more essential and real than the later stages of life. The narrator of "Combray," for example, even suggests the falseness or unreality of flowers that he had not known as a child: "les fleurs qu'on me montre aujourd'hui pour la première fois ne me semblent pas de vraies fleurs" [the flowers that one shows me today for the first time do not seem to me to be real flowers] (1:184). Similarly, the narrator of *Rayuela* emphasizes in the chapter mentioned above "la solidez y la permanencia de la sala" [the solidity and permanence of the living room] (670). It is emblematic that Sábato used a Proust-like metaphor about forgetting dreams immediately upon waking to illustrate how Bruno's life outside of Capitán Olmos suddenly lost its sense of importance and reality. Those years seemed to vanish, "como al despertar pierden fuerza y vida los sueños, convirtiéndose en inciertos fragmentos de una fantasmagoría, a cada segundo más irreales" [as when waking up our dreams lose force and life, turning into doubtful pieces of a phantom world, which each second seem more unreal]. Proust's narrator on the very first page of the *Recherche* says of an idea found in a dream, "Cette croyance survivait pendant quelques secondes à mon réveil. . . . Puis elle commençait à me devenir inintelligible, comme après la métempsycose . . . " [This belief survived for a few seconds after my waking up. . . . Then it started to become unintelligible for me, as after a transmigration of souls . . .] (1:3).

  The actual significance of Sábato's dialogue with Proust and his successors is not immediately clear, but we soon realize that, similar to the Proustian protagonist near the end of his life, Bruno is undergoing a profound crisis. He begins to view as meaningless most of the activities of his life. Admittedly, the town itself does not disillusion him in exactly the same way as Combray affects the Proustian protagonist when he visits it one last time. For Bruno, everything is both similar and different from the way that he remembers it. Nonetheless, the general situation is nearly identical. In spite of years of effort neither character has been able to realize his dream of writing a novel. In Bruno's case, the agony and death of his father, which occur at that time, contribute to his growing despair because he starts to see death as inevitable. I will return to this question later in the section on time as a destructive force, but also and most especially in chapter 8, where I will examine in detail Bruno's literary vocation.

José Lezama Lima also treated childhood as a type of paradise in his novel, which is called precisely *Paradiso*. In this respect Julio Ramón Ribeyro detected a relation with Proust, as well as with Dante. In "Notas sobre *Paradiso*," the Peruvian explained how, in spite of Lezama's then political stance, he seemed to yearn for his middle-class way of life, as well as for childhood itself. Even Lezama's negative remarks echoed the French author: "he yearns for that world, but criticizing it at the same time, just a Proust yearned for the world of the Guermantes which he attacked with so much sarcasm" (1970, 179).

Other critics, particularly from the United States (e.g., Peter Moscoso-Gongora and Michael Wood) and shortly after Harold Bloom had published *The Anxiety of Influence* (1973), cited mere coincidences and spoke almost of the Cuban author's imitation of Proust. Lezama became infuriated and wrote to his sister Eloísa about Wood's review:

And the eternal, idiotic comparisons with Proust, with Joyce, with Mann, demonstrate the negative and closed-minded intention with which he has read the work. I am already weary of those ridiculous simplifications. Because there is asthma, a grandmother and a mother Proust must be present, as if I could not be as asthmatic as Marcel. (1979, 263)

As suggested in the previous chapters, I must agree with Ribeyro that there exists a literary relation between Lezama Lima and Proust. But, I also believe that some of the critics were mistaken in their definition of it. Lezama was not influenced by Proust in the same way as Torres Bodet or Mujica Láinez during their early years. The Cuban author's case should be considered one of inspiration, like that of María Luisa Bombal or Yolanda Oreamuno. He often used Proust's text as a point of departure for his personal ideas and manner of development. For this reason, Lezama's treatment of asthma is more explicit than Proust's and the life of his mother and father is projected retrospectively to their personal past. Significantly *Paradiso* was written in the third person instead of the first because it is not the protagonist José Cemí, but rather the author himself who wished to recover his past through writing. In this process, the Cuban author's method of reconstruction was primarily conscious. But, at times, as in Proust's case, it appears to have been involuntary, at least in its inspiration. Thus, we read, for example, at one point how Oppiano Licario "pudo reconstruir la historia de la vajilla apoyándose en la desaforada excepción de un asalto" [he succeeded in reconstructing the story of the set of dishes relying upon the outrageous exception of being assailed] (1973, 465). This experience is in itself quite similar to Proustian memory for a sensation in the present brings to mind an identical one from the past. In this way, Oppiano suddenly finds himself transported from Havana to Paris:

> El primer salón más pequeño hacía que los clientes al abandonar sus asientos causaran la impresión de una turba de asaltantes. Esta última sensación atenaceó y aterrorizó a Licario con tal violencia que le produjo un trastrueque de vivencias. Regresaba de la Sorbonne, cuando se encontró con incesantes grupos de jóvenes. . . . (463)

> [The first and smaller waiting room made the clients, when they left their seats, give the impression of a mob of assailants. This last sensation adversely affected and terrified Licario with such violence that it produced in him an inversion of life experiences. He was returning from the Sorbonne, when he met one group of young people after another. . . .]

Since the publication of *Paradiso* several other Spanish American writers have attempted to recapture the memories of childhood through writing and have often used Proust's "Combray" as a point of reference, as well as inspiration. This is true even in the case of those authors that distanced themselves from Proust's modernism and began to treat the *Recherche* in a postmodern way.

As suggested in the chapter on high society, Alfredo Bryce Echenique recreated the world of a pampered young boy from San Isidro. Although in specific passages from *Un mundo para Julius* we can find a sense of *temps perdu* in the manner of Proust or Teresa de la Parra, these moments symptomatically are not related to the affluence of the family or even the tenderness of the boy's mother. In this regard, Bryce's work contrasts with Proust's and even more so with that of Manuel Mujica Láinez. It is worth noting that in *La casa* this Argentine writer recreated through a Proust-like nostalgia the elegant life of a wealthy *porteño* family.[8] In the case of Julius, his happiest moments are those that he spends with the servants and his sister Cinthia before her death. In effect, Bryce's novel comes closest to a Proustian sense of *temps perdu* when Julius begins to eat with his family in the formal dining room and no longer receives in his own eating area the loving attention of the servants: "Algo se había terminado en su vida. Algo caducaba, también, porque no todo en los textos escolares era como Nilda o Vilma o los mayordomos le habían contado" [Something had ended in his life. Something was expiring, also, because not everything in the school texts was like Nilda or Vilma or the butlers had told him] (1992, 114).

Thus, we can construe *Un mundo para Julius* as a response to Proust with regard to two subjects: time and high society. Clearly Bryce was more interested in showing the moral weaknesses of upper-class society in Peru and the possible seeds of its decay than in justifying its splendor or any value that might be missed in the future. For this reason at the end of the novel only the servants are nostalgic for their intimate past with the young boy. Likewise, it is quite revealing that Susan is more concerned that she put on the wrong perfume before going out than because of her youngest son's depression. In this way, the mother of Julius resembles the Duchesse de Guermantes at her worst. Similarly, at the end of *Le côté de Guermantes*, the Duchess does not have time to listen to her friend Swann talk about his deteriorating health, but she is able to return home to put on shoes of a more appropriate color.

In their discussion of the early texts by another author that came after the Boom, Reinaldo Arenas, Rafael Ocasio and Fiona Doloughan suggested that Proust's child protagonist had served as a model. This source is indeed apparent in the Cuban writer's initial stories. "La punta del arco iris" [The End of the Rainbow] is built around a Proust-like enthusiasm for rain. Similarly in "La puesta del sol" [Sunset] the boy's discovery of the beauty of nature and of the value of solitude are reminiscent of "Combray." Nonetheless, the connection between Arenas and Proust is by no means as simple and direct in *Celestino, antes del alba* [Celestino, before Dawn] (1967) as these scholars have purported. This relation must be defined with greater precision. I concede that childhood and writing are important themes in the first novel by Arenas, but the world of the protagonist's family is more like a purgatory or hell than a paradise. Moreover, writing is discouraged by the adults who consider it as shameful as the boys' homosexual tendencies.

At least to some extent the Cuban writer's portrait of a destitute family before the Revolution, of its struggle to survive, and of its mutually inflicted abuse constitutes an extreme caricature of the portrait of the relatives that spent their vacations together at Tante Léonie's house in "Combray." Some of these persons were not morally admirable and even mistreated each other. The great-uncle enjoyed pulling the protagonist's curls when he was small. Likewise, the great-aunt perversely offered liquor to the grandfather precisely because she knew of his doctor's prohibition. Then she tormented his wife by calling out: "Bathilde! viens donc empêcher ton mari de boire du cognac!" ["Bathilde! so come and stop your husband from drinking brandy!"] (1:11). These examples of cruelty are mild in comparison with all of the domestic abuse that Arenas describes, but that is precisely the point. If *Celestino, antes del alba* is related to Proust, it must be considered a postmodern parody.

Like the Proustian protagonist, the narrator of Arenas applies his imagination to the world around him, but this environment is so desolate that he can only create by exaggerating the misery that he sees. For this reason, the grandfather, who forces everyone to work in the corn field, is portrayed as a slave driver. The boy's approach allows him to develop his creativity by describing a fanciful world in the midst of extreme poverty.

As for writing, the narrator in the Cuban work, like the boy in the French novel, must undergo an apprenticeship, but because of his deprived living conditions this process is necessarily more distorted. Having no literary model to follow, the Cuban boy invents a cousin, Celestino, and realizing the opposition of his family to literature, he imagines that whenever Celestino writes a poem on a tree their grandfather cuts the tree down. In spite of his family's hostile attitude toward creation the narrator intuitively understands that he can preserve his imaginary world through memory and eventually recreate it through writing. Consequently, in spite of its differences with "Combray," *Celestino, antes del alba* achieves some of the same results. The protagonist-narrator discovers the value of his sensibility and personal view of the world, he learns how to use the diverse elements of that world in order to create specific situations and he realizes that writing can give meaning to his life, no matter how impoverished or unpleasant it may be. In short, through his fertile imagination Reinaldo Arenas depicted his own type of "Combray," but one that resembles the negative of a photograph instead of a print of it. In this creative act, we can note a certain playfulness with Proust's text, as well as a bitter satire of the Cuban family and of the life of poor people who regularly mistreat each other.

The Guatemalan professor and writer Mario Alberto Carrera also portrayed a case of unhappy childhood in *Diario de un tiempo escindido* [Diary of a Severed Time] (1988). The young protagonist at approximately age seven is neglected by his father, beaten by his mother and receives only negative feedback from his Catholic schoolteachers. Although one can easily find bleak works of this type, Carrera distinguished his by placing it in a Proustian context. Not only does the forty-two-year-old narrator, like Proust's, begin to think about his life and his past while lying awake early in the morning, but also in the first section of the text he refers specifically to the French novelist and his concept of time: "Me alivia un poco hundirme en el pensar pesimista de Schopenhauer y su tiempo circular, y me enerva el tiempo de Proust, el tiempo de sus padres, verdugos que amó . . . " [It comforts me a little to immerse myself in the pessimistic thought of Schopenhauer and his circular time, and Proustian time gets on my nerves, the time of his parents, tormentors that he loved . . .] (1988, 27). This brief statement, in fact, proves to be crucial because *Diario de un tiempo escindido* appears to have been written as a narrative response to *A la recherche du temps perdu,* and in particular to "Combray."

The dialogue between Proust and Carrera (who had written about the *Recherche* in a series of articles that were collected in a book on literary, philosophical and psychological figures) is particularly evident in the chapter entitled "Magdalena, té y Rossebuck." Here, the narrator does not develop in the text either of the first two items of the title which obviously refer to Marcel Proust, but he expresses overtly his disagreement with those persons and writers who regularly yearn for the happy days of childhood. For him that period never existed. As a boy, he knew only personal suffering, and he never felt later in life nostalgia for his early years. Likewise, involuntary memory has little meaning for him because his essential past was never lost and remains excruciatingly present.

In broad terms, Carrera opposed his concept of time to Proust's. Although in the text he never denied change or the process of becoming, he emphasized those aspects of the protagonist's consciousness which remained the same over time: his fear, doubt, loneliness, and liberal ideas. Moreover, the Guatemalan writer took advantage of the similarities in temperament between the boy and his father in order to suggest that the differences between a seven-year-old and a man in his forties are more the result of circumstance than of essence. Therefore time appears to be cyclical rather than progressive as the boy nearly becomes his father.

To emphasize his contrasting concept of time Mario Alberto Carrera even avoided using the past tenses that are characteristic of Proust's text (e.g., the imperfect). All of the four sections of his novel, which are called *tiempos* [periods], are written in the present tense. With the exception of the third, which is composed of a series of letters, each *tiempo* reflects the point of view of the same protagonist-narrator but at a different age: forty-two, seven, and twelve. This technique is experimental, but it is quite effective. It forces the reader to discover the similarities and differences between the protagonist-narrator at distinct stages in his life because these points of contact are not explained the way they are in Proust's text. Also, even though *Diario de un tiempo escindido* depicts temporal periods and places (the 1980s in Guatemala and the 1950s in El Salvador and California) that are very distinct from those found in the *Recherche* (from 1870 to 1920 in France), the contrasting tenses and the

ideas on time and the self constantly remind the reader of the dialogue
with Proust and render the differences in themselves more significant.
In spite of the fact that Carrera's narrator is dealing with a personal past
instead of a historical one, the self-consciousness of this text makes it
approach the postmodern genre of historiographic metafiction as
Hutcheon defined it. Most notably, *Diario de un tiempo escindido* confronts
and contests Proust's nostalgia and recovery of the past.

During the same years of the late 1980s, we find a resurgence of
childhood memoirs, and these non-fictional texts are at times related to
Proust. Such is the case in *La luna no era de queso* [The Moon Was Not
Made of Cheese] (1988) by José Luis González. Not only does this Puerto Rican writer who was born in Santo Domingo allude to the process of
memory and to the difficulty of recalling specific details from the past,
but he also mentions Proust and suggests that the smell of burning
charcoal used in baking certain Dominican pastries had the same effect
upon him as the madeleines for Proust (1988, 74). Furthermore, besides
the discussion of food and the description of the cook, which bring to
mind the exquisite dishes of Françoise and she herself, the frequent
references to literature and González's vocation as a writer seem at least
in part inspired by the *Recherche*. The same can be said, although to a
lesser extent, of the importance that he attributes to names and words.

A subsequent example of such childhood memoirs linked to Proust is
Los buscadores de oro [The Gold Prospectors] (1993) by Augusto Monterroso. When this Guatemalan author speaks, for example, of his intense
effort to remember particular details from the past, he appears to be
questioning Proust's ideas on memory. Likewise, when he recalls other
incidents with slight effort and no assistence from involuntary memory,
he seems to be refuting Proust.[9]

In the last book published before his death, *Conjeturas sobre la memoria
de mi tribu* [Conjectures on the Memory of My Clan] (1996), José Donoso
also participated in this resurgence of Proust-inspired memoirs, but he
introduced the element of fiction by speculating upon his family's past.
Symptomatically, this Chilean writer, who had followed in various ways
the *Recherche*, used its author in both the non-fictional and fictional
portions of *Conjeturas sobre la memoria de mi tribu*. Not only does he often
mention Proust when he talks about his own life and literary work.[10]
Also, the first of his conjectures treats one of Proust's acquaintances,
Laure Hayman, who had served as the primary model for Odette. Intentionally searching for a personal connection with Proust's world,
Donoso speculates on the possibility that his nanny as a child had played
with Laure. This feasible encounter makes the Chilean writer feel closer
to the world of the French novelist especially because of actual biographical facts and a photograph of Hayman (perhaps by Paul Nadar, who had

portrayed Proust and many of his friends).[11] From this Proustian point of departure, Donoso expands his focus to encompass family pictures and anecdotes. The final result is a deep personal bond with the entire nineteenth century and with his family's life in Chile during that time.

THE LOSS OF A BELOVED AND ATTEMPTS AT RECOVERY

Most certainly, the loss of a spouse, child, close friend, or lover is a universal human experience. But, Marcel Proust depicted the effects of losing a loved one especially well in his sixth volume *Albertine disparue,* where he associates such a loss with his concept of *temps perdu.* The protagonist-narrator shows his feelings toward Albertine's departure and death, how he continues to be reminded of her by material objects and similar situations and how he begins to forget her. Only later is he able to recover her through memory and writing.

One of the first Spanish American novels specifically related to *Albertine disparue* was *Proserpina rescatada* [Proserpina Recaptured] (1931) by Jaime Torres Bodet. As the title suggests, we find in this Mexican work a perspective that is both opposed and connected to Proust's sixth volume. The protagonist recovers the woman that he loved through memory. This conception was inspired by Proust because the process begins involuntarily when the man hears the sound of Proserpina's voice over the telephone. He is then able to reconstruct through association all that he knew about his former mistress and of their life together. It is also worth noting that Proserpina resembles Albertine in more than just the sound of her name. She has a very elusive personality, and the male protagonist can never be certain of her feelings and motives.

Around 1950, this type of novel inspired by *Albertine disparue* became relatively common. In *La ruta de su evasión,* for instance, Oreamuno's character Teresa searches in the past for the happiness that she had known with the compassionate man Esteban. This man was not Teresa's husband or lover, and he did not die in the text, but he did disappear and was the only man that Teresa ever loved. He treated her with gentleness and respect and defended her against her abusive husband. Also and most importantly, he sacrificed his own freedom and welfare for Teresa and her children. Knowing that the authorities planned to arrest don Vasco for a serious crime, Esteban went to the house at the appointed time and assumed the role of the husband. In this way he saved Teresa from destitution.

As she lies in bed during a protracted terminal illess, Teresa evokes the moments that she had shared with Esteban. Her remembering is in part intentional, but the narrator's use of the term "voluntario" suggests a connection with Proust, who denied the efficacy of conscious recollection. The narrator of *Du côté de chez Swann* says of the past, "C'est peine perdue que nous cherchions à l'évoquer, tous les efforts de notre intelligence sont inutiles. Il est caché hors de son domaine et de sa portée . . . " [It is a waste of time for us to seek to evoke it: all of the efforts of our intellect are useless. The past is hidden beyond its realm and reach . . .] (1:44). Similarly Oreamuno's narrator remarks concerning Teresa:

> Quiere reintegrarse al pasado en forma voluntaria. . . . Hace un nuevo esfuerzo y agarrada a la tenue evocación que hizo la palabra "marzo", emprende la reconstrucción de su pasado. Las imágenes . . . comienzan a perfilarse en su memoria, pero no tienen el contagioso realismo de las visiones anteriores. (1984, 148–49)

> [She wishes to reinsert herself in the past in a voluntary manner. . . . She make a new effort and clutching onto the tenuous evocation that the word "March" induced, she undertakes the reconstruction of her past. The images . . . begin to take shape in her memory, but they do not have the contagious realism of her former visions.]

In *La ruta de su evasión* we do not find a pure example of the type of memory experience that we will discuss in chapter 7. Teresa's suffering and agony help her to recover the past to a greater extent than any particular sensation in the present. Teresa herself concludes: "En verdad el recuerdo en la vida no tiene la misma vitalidad que el recuerdo en la muerte" [Truly memory in life does not have the same vitality as memory in death] (149). In spite of this difference, Oreamuno displayed a Proust-like ambition for her character's recollection of the past. For this reason not only do we find a similar completeness, vividness, and material quality but also echoes of Proust's resurrections through memory. Describing a particular evening when Esteban was present for dinner, Oreamuno's narrator writes, "El recuerdo de aquella tarde había vuelto a Teresa tan real, que ni los ruidos fáciles de caer en el olvido por vulgares y frecuentes querían irse de sus oídos más sensibles por la enfermedad" [The recollection of that afternoon had returned to Teresa with such vividness, that not even those sounds which easily fall into oblivion because of their ordinary and frequent nature wished to leave her ears that were more sensitive due to the illness] (77). As in two of the memory experiences depicted in *Le temps retrouvé*, special attention is paid to the sound of eating utensils and the touch of a napkin, but in this case the sensations are recovered and do not serve as stimuli.[12] The narrator writes: "Volvía el chocar del vaso con la taza, el chirrido de los cuchillos en el fondo del plato al cortar la carne, el roce de las servilletas con la boca, el movimiento del cucharón que por inercia golpea la sopera" [The clink of a glass with a cup returned, likewise the screech of knives on the surface of a plate when one cuts meat, the touch of a napkin against the mouth, the movement of a ladle which by inertia strikes a soup tureen] (77).

In another Spanish American novel of these years, *Los ídolos* by Manuel Mujica Láinez, we find a similar Proust-like intention allied to forms of memory that are only partially Proustian. This suggests the author's desire to imitate an aspect of the *Recherche* while adapting it for specific purposes.[13] A comparable nostalgia is created, but the means are somewhat different.

As in the case of *Albertine disparue, Los ídolos* portrays the loss of a beloved person. But, in the Argentine novel one male laments the death of another male, which is only implicit in Proust's work. The narrator describes the circumstances of his friend's death in England, and he evokes other moments directly or indirectly associated with Gustavo. The evocation of the latter is primarily conscious as the narrator writes about his deceased friend. Yet, in the narration itself the writer refers to the various ways in which he recovered his memories of Gustavo, and these mechanisms are at least in part Proustian.

Having met his friend by chance in Stratford-on-Avon, Gustavo's physical presence allowed the narrator to recover the high school years that they had enjoyed together in South America:

> La luz le dio de lleno sobre la cara, sobre la piel lisa, sobre el pelo negro. Casi no había cambiado, y sentí una gran alegría porque era como si en ese instante reconquistara mi adolescencia perdida, a través de ese muchacho. . . . (1976, 24)

> [The light fell fully on his face, on his smooth skin, on his black hair. He had scarcely changed, and I felt a great joy because it was as if in that instant I recovered my lost adolescence through that boy. . .]

This form of memory stimulated by a person's presence is quite common in literature, as well as in life. However, Mujica Láinez attributed to it a sense of mystery following the example of Proust, whose narrator says of Albertine when she happened to visit him in Paris, "Elle semblait une magicienne me présentant un miroir du temps. En cela elle était pareille à tous ceux que nous revoyons rarement, mais qui jadis vécurent plus intimement avec nous" [She seemed to be a magician providing me with a mirror of time. In this, she resembled all those people whom we seldom see now, but who formerly lived more intimately with us] (2:351).

Another somewhat common variety of memory is triggered by familiar objects. Proust's narrator acknowledges the importance of this type in *Le temps retrouvé,* but he qualifies it by saying of a book that he had known during his childhood, "une chose que nous avons regardée autrefois, si nous la revoyons, nous rapporte, avec le regard que nous y avons posé, toutes les images qui le remplissaient alors" [an object that we have contemplated in the past, if we see it again, returns to us, along with the gaze that we laid upon it, all of the images that filled it then] (3:885). Significantly the narrator emphasizes here the sensations caused by objects rather than the objects themselves because in general sensations are the stimuli for his type of involuntary memory, which he carefully distinguishes from the conventional manner of recalling the past:

> C'est que les choses—un livre sous sa couverture rouge comme les autres—, sitôt qu'elles sont perçues par nous, deviennent en nous quelque chose d' immatériel, de même nature que toutes nos préoccupations ou nos sensations de ce temps-là, et se mêlent indissolublement à elles. (3:885)

> [It is that things—a book beneath its red cover like anything else—as soon as they are perceived by us, become within us an immaterial substance, of the same nature as all of our concerns or our sensations from that time, and they are indissolubly mingled with them.]

In contrast, the narrator of *Los ídolos* is less abstract and suggests that a magical quality can be found in special objects. In some sense he has reduced involuntary memory to more ordinary proportions. Just the same, the Proustian source is evident because the object in question is also a book which even has a red cover like the one in *Le temps retrouvé.* When the narrator sees it in Gustavo's hotel room, it gives him the impression of returning to the past:

> Entre la confusión de frascos y cepillos reconocí el libro de tapas rojas de la tía Duma y el retrato de Sansilvestre que le había regalado yo, y esos testigos de nuestra pasada intimidad obraron en seguida sobre mí, recreando el clima de la biblioteca de nuestros encuentros juveniles, suprimiendo años de distancia. . . . (25)

> [Among the confusion of bottles and brushes I recognized the book with red covers from Tía Duma and the picture of Sansilvestre that I had given him and those witnesses of our former intimacy immediately affected me, recreating the atmosphere of the library of the encounters of our youth, suppressing years of distance. . . .]

This brief memory experience is later followed by a more fully developed one at the climax of the third part of *Los ídolos.* In this case years after Gustavo's death, the narrator finds the same book and portrait when he enters an attic belonging to Gustavo's relatives. Clearly

Mujica Láinez wished to create a magical atmosphere similiar to the one found in the Proustian memory experiences even though he relied more upon objects than the sensations that they caused. For this reason, not only did he cite *1001 Nights*, like the narrator of *Le temps retrouvé*, in order to show the marvelousness of the moment, but also his character is so overcome by the past that he forgets the present:

> Era como si de repente hubiera entrado en una cueva de Alí Babá en la que en vez de esparcidas riquezas, de alhajas, de tesoros, me esperaban los recuerdos, tan deslumbrantes en su profusión como las maravillas del relato. Vuelto súbitamente a la época de mi vida en que fui más feliz, . . . me olvidé de Fabricia. (241)

> [It was as if I had suddenly entered the cave of Ali Baba in which instead of precious objects scattered about, jewels and treasures, remembrances awaited me, so dazzling were they in their profusion as the marvels in the story. Suddenly carried back to the time in my life when I was happiest . . . I forgot about Fabricia.]

Similarly, Proust had written:

> aussitôt, comme le personnage des *Mille et une nuits* qui sans le savoir accomplissait précisément le rite qui faisait apparaître . . . un docile génie prêt à le transporter au loin, une nouvelle vision d'azur passa devant mes yeux . . . l'impression fut si forte que le moment que je vivais me sembla être le moment actuel. . . . (3:868)

> [immediately, like the character from *One Thousand and One Nights* who without realizing it accomplished precisely the rite that made appear . . . a docile genie who was ready to transport him far away, a new vision of azure passed before my eyes . . . the impression was so strong that the moment that I was experiencing seemed to me to be the present one. . . .]

In short, Mujica Láinez wished to create the same emotional quality and sense of recovering the past as Proust had done, but he chose simpler means. The Argentine was obviously influenced by the French novelist, but in his adaptation he displayed a certain degree of independence. Likewise, when his narrator evokes Gustavo through writing, he is generally more explicit: "Mientras copio su frase . . . vuelvo a ver, con una claridad tan intensa que los menores detalles se recortan en mi mente, la cara de Gustavo" [While I copy his sentence . . . I see again with a clarity so intense that the smallest details of Gustavo's face stand out in my mind] (11). Proust's narrator rarely mentions the act of writing while he is recalling the past, but when he is in a nostalgic mood, he does make exclamations, like the following concerning the church in Combray:

"Que je l'aimais, que je revois bien notre Eglise!" [How much I loved it, and how well I see again our church!] (1:59).

Another work, which appeared a few years later, was inspired even more directly by *Albertine disparue: La tregua* (1960) by Mario Benedetti. In this Uruguayan novel, we find the search for a lost woman, a sense of recovering her, and then of losing her definitively.

Twenty years before the first entry in his diary, which constitutes the text of this novel, the fictional author Martín Santomé had lost his beloved wife, Isabel. A visit from a former acquaintance, Mario Vignale, causes Santomé to realize how incompletely he remembered Isabel's face and other things about her. Not content to rely upon upon photographs or to search for her features in the faces of their children, Santomé makes a conscious effort to recall Isabel, but soon he becomes very frustrated. His difficulty in remembering her face is similar to specific portions of the *Recherche* where this aspect of memory is treated in diverse ways. At times, the young protagonist is bothered when he forgets the features of Gilberte. On at least one occasion the protagonist recognizes a face, but he does not remember the person's name (2:650).

In Benedetti's novel one can observe how he depicted a search for the past derived from Proust, but curiously the Uruguayan author called upon the physical aspects of handwriting and word usage to bring this quest to a conclusion. Given that Santomé was an office clerk for many years, the focus on personal script is especially appropriate. But, the handwriting itself may have been suggested by Proust, whose protagonist-narrator frequently notices minute details, such as how a person writes, and who uses as the focus of an episode in *Albertine disparue* the confusion between the signatures of Albertine and Gilberte.

In *La tregua*, we find a memory experience which occurs when Santomé reads a letter that Isabel wrote in 1935. He recognizes her handwriting and begins to recover the past: "Me sentí un poco extraño al enfrentarme a aquellos caracteres delgados, de largas y perfiladas colas, en los que era posible reconocer una persona y también una época" [I felt a bit strange when faced with those slender characters with long, shapely tails, in which it was possible to recognize a person and also a period] (1974, 133). After transcribing the letter, he explains how he succeeded in recovering his wife's face:

Es curioso que con la relectura de esta carta haya vuelto a encontrar el rostro de Isabel, ese rostro que, a pesar de todos mis olvidos, estaba en mi memoria. Y lo hallé a partir de esos "tú", de esos "puedes", de esos "tienes", porque Isabel nunca hablaba de "vos". . . . Leí esos "tú" y en seguida pude reconstruir la boca que los decía. Y en Isabel la boca era lo más importante de su rostro. (136)

[It is curious that with the re-reading of this letter I have found again Isabel's face, that face, which in spite of all my forgetfulness, remained in my memory. And I found it starting with those "you", those "you can", those "you have", because Isabel never spoke with the local "you all". . . . I read those "you" and suddenly I succeeded in reconstructing the mouth that used to say them. And in the case of Isabel the mouth was the most important feature of her face.]

Here, we can see in particular a memory process that is related to Proust and his ideas, but which is also different from the typical cases of involuntary memory. The stimuli—the written letters and words—are physical and are encountered by chance. Also the process is associative. The grammatical forms and their personal usage are linked in Santomé's mind to the physical articulation of them, and the position of the mouth in the formation the word *tú* serves as a point of departure for the reconstruction of the entire face. Here, I should emphasize Benedetti's originality. Not only did he take into account the contrast between *vos* and *tú*, which is typical of his native Uruguay, but also, unlike Proust, he was able to employ handwriting and word usage as stimuli for memory.[14] Furthermore, the results of the memory experience are somewhat different. The recovery of Isabel's face gives Santomé a sense of peace and satisfaction, rather than euphoria. It allows him to become reconciled with his past and to live more fully in the present with the young woman that he loves, Laura Avellaneda. In short, because of the many differences we can conclude that Benedetti was inspired by Proust, rather than merely influenced by him.

The same can be said concerning the ending of *La tregua*. Santomé's love for the two women is as distinct as the women themselves, yet his sensations and emotions at age forty-nine help him to recover what he felt during his twenties. For the first time in years Santomé enjoys life, but when Avellaneda also dies, he has the impression of losing both women at the same time: "Mientras estuvo Avellaneda, comprendí mejor la época de Isabel, comprendí mejor a Isabel misma. Pero ahora ella no está e *Isabel ha desaparecido* detrás de un espeso, de un oscuro telón de abatimiento" [While Avellaneda was present, I understood better the time of Isabel, I understood better Isabel herself. But now she is not around and *Isabel has disappeared* behind a thick, dark curtain of depression] (177, my emphasis). In this passage, the similarities and differences between Benedetti's novel and *Albertine disparue* are especially evident. The narrator draws an explicit parallel between *La tregua* and Proust's sixth volume, whose Argentine edition was called *Albertina ha desaparecido* [Albertine Has Disappeared].[15] Obviously, the painful sense of loss and despair are similar, but Santomé's experience is much more abrupt. He lost Isabel the second and definitive time very quickly, unlike the Proustian protagonist. Moreover Santomé's grief is double instead of single.

During the period of the Boom, the most complete search for a lost woman can be found in *Rayuela,* and even here, in spite of Cortázar's general opposition to Proust, a relation with *Albertine disparue* is manifest. Although Horacio Oliveira wishes to reject a Proust-like nostalgia, he eventually must acknowledge its power over him.

Indubitably, the question that initiates the novel, "¿Encontraría a la Maga?" [Would I find la Maga?], has several feasible interpretations or meanings. First of all, it alludes to the personal version of hide-and-seek that Oliveira played with la Maga in the labyrinth of the streets of Paris. Also, it may refer to the possible resolution of the interpersonal conflict between the two characters. Third, as Oliveira writes the first chapter, he attempts to recapture the essence of la Maga by evoking the time that they spent together in Paris. In chapter 8 I will show how this type of evocation through writing is related to the *Recherche.* But, in another Proustian fashion closely tied to memory, Cortázar's main character also searches for la Maga.[16]

In the same initial chapter of *Rayuela,* the first person narrator suggests a parallel between his girlfriend and Albertine when he tells how he toyed with Proustian memory while sitting on a pile of trash next to la Maga: "Convencido de que el recuerdo lo guarda todo y no solamente a las Albertinas y a las grandes efemérides del corazón y los riñones, me obstinaba en reconstruir el contenido de mi mesa de trabajo en Floresta . . . y acababa temblando . . . " [Convinced that memory retains everything and not just the Albertines and the great feats of the heart and kidneys, I adamantly tried to reconstruct the contents of my worktable in Floresta . . . and I ended up trembling . . .] (1986, 126). The references to Proust are indisputable. Besides the name of the protagonist's beloved, we find an allusion to the "intermittences du coeur" [intermittences of the heart], which is rendered humorous by the addition "y los riñones" [and the kidneys].[17] Furthermore, in this passage we can detect Oliveira's opposition to Proust's memory theories. Not only does he ridicule the marvels of involuntary memory associated with the senses and the body, but also he tries to prove that through intense effort one can recover the most insignificant details from the past. From a Proustian perspective, this idea is tantamount to heresy.

Concerning the phrase "las Albertinas" and its possible connection with la Maga, the reader must be careful to understand its exact meaning, otherwise the significance of this passage may be lost. In some portions of the *Recherche,* the narrator speaks of more than one Albertine to suggest the diverse facets of her personality, how she changed over time, or how his perspective toward her also became different. However, this interpretation of the phrase "las Albertinas" does not seem to be pertinent because la Maga is rarely if ever portrayed as a multiple being. On the other hand, one specific passage from *Albertine disparue* has an obvious parallel with the treatment of la Maga in *Rayuela* because it suggests how a woman can be recovered through memory. This fragment appears after the protagonist has already suffered because of Albertine's departure and death and when he finally begins to experience more pleasure than pain upon recalling his lost beloved. It is then that he truly misses Albertine and has the impression of seeing her everywhere through other women:

> Toutes me semblaient des Albertine, l'image que je portais en moi me la faisant retrouver partout, et même, au détour d'une allée, l'une qui remontait dans une automobile me la rappela tellement, était si exactement de la même corpulence, que je me demandai un instant si ce n'était pas elle que je venais de voir. . . . (3:561–62)

> [They all seemed to me to be Albertines, the image that I bore within myself caused me to encounter her again everywhere, and even, at the bend in a lane, a girl who was getting into an automobile reminded me so much of her, was so precisely of the same build, that I wondered for an instant whether it was not she whom I had just seen. . . .]

Already in the first chapter of *Rayuela,* Oliveira depicts the same situation of confusing other women with his beloved: "Oh Maga, en cada mujer parecida a vos se agolpaba como un silencio ensordecedor, una pausa filosa y cristalina que acababa por derrumbarse tristemente, como un paraguas mojado que se cierra" [Oh Maga, in each woman resembling you there crowded around like a deafening silence, a sharp and crystalline pause which finally collapsed unfortunately, like a wet umbrella that is closed] (120).[18]

Later in the novel Oliveira does, in fact, lose la Maga when their personal conflict reaches a breaking point, and he, in contrast with the Proustian protagonist and more like his mistress, leaves the apartment. As in *Albertine disparue,* there is the suggestion that the female later dies. At this point Oliveira realizes that he loved la Maga more than any other woman, and he begins to yearn for her. When his boat stops in Montevideo (her place of birth), like the protagonist of *Albertine disparue,* he has the impression of seeing her and similarly realizes the confusion:

> La Maga salió de detrás de un ventilador, llevando en una mano algo que arrastraba por el suelo, y casi en seguida le dio la espalda y caminó hacia una de las escotillas. Oliveira no hizo nada por seguirla, sabía de sobra que sería una de las pitucas. . . . (447)

[La Maga came out from behind a ventilator, carrying in one hand something that she dragged along the floor, and almost immediately she turned her back and walked toward one of the hatchways. Oliveira made no attempt to follow her, he knew all too well that she was probably just one of the posh women. . . .]

In addition to the nearly identical situation, Oliveira's interpretation of it resembles that of Proust's narrator, who speaks of the image that he carried within himself which caused him to see Albertine everywhere. Only Oliveira's negative reaction is distinct: "Haber creído ver a la Maga era menos amargo que la certidumbre de que un deseo incontrolable la había arrancado del fondo de eso que definían como subconciencia y proyectado contra la silueta de cualquiera de las mujeres de a bordo" [Having believed that he saw la Maga was less bitter than the certainty that an uncontrollable desire had extracted her from the depths of what people defined as the subconscious and projected her against the profile of just any of the women on board] (448). On a conscious, intellectual level Oliveira wishes to reject this type of memory experience and nostalgia, almost as Morelli repudiated the psychological novel. The effects of involuntary memory, however, are undeniable. When Oliveira arrives at the port of Buenos Aires, the wife of his friend Traveler, Talita, induces in Cortázar's protagonist a similar experience:

> volvió a sentir que ciertas remotas semejanzas condensaban bruscamente un falso parecido total, como si su memoria aparentemente tan bien compartimentada se arrancara de golpe un ectoplasma capaz de habitar y completar otro cuerpo y otra cara. . . . (448)

> [he felt again that certain remote similarities abruptly condensed into a deceptive total resemblance, as if his apparently so well compartmentalized memory drew forth suddenly a bit of ectoplasm that was capable of inhabiting and filling another body and another face. . . .]

In spite of his ideas on the French novelist and his particular kind of memory, Oliveira comes to see as nearly inevitable the appearance of other Magas, like Proust's Albertines. Fortunately he also realizes that experiences of this type can assist him in his search for the "other." I will return to this subject in chapter 7, where I will discuss another manifestation of involuntary memory depicted in *Rayuela,* one that brings more satisfactory results. I will also explain the dialogue which is implied. Here, I only wish to point out that this experience is preceded by one of the type that we have been discussing. On the night in question, Oliveira sees once again la Maga through another woman who is playing hopscotch in the courtyard of the asylum. Only later does he realize that this female is Talita: "Desde lo alto veía el pelo de la Maga, la curva de los hombros y cómo levantaba a medias los brazos para mantener el equilibrio, mientras con pequeños saltos entraba en la primera casilla . . . " [From above he saw la Maga's hair, the curves of her shoulders and how she half raised her arms to keep her balance, as she entered with little hops into the first square . . .] (474).

Since *Rayuela* the loss of and/or search for a beloved man or woman has embodied several different forms in Spanish American narrative. We already examined the case of *La otra mitad* in connection with the psychological novel. In the section on homosexual love of the same chapter, I also discussed *En jirones,* where the loss of A. is related to *Albertine disparue,* and its second part can be seen as a reversal of Proust's sixth volume. Later in the present chapter, I will study the case of *El amor en los tiempos del cólera.*

In Bryce Echenique's two part novel, *Cuadernos de navegación en un sillón Voltaire,* the subject of loss is often treated in a parodic, postmodern manner. Martín Romaña loses and then yearns for two women: his wife Inés and his girl friend Octavia. The second case, in particular, entails several comic echoes from *Albertine disparue.* The narrator of *El hombre que hablaba de Octavia de Cádiz* cites specifically the various appearances and disappearances of Octavia. In order to cope with his loss, on more than one occasion he mentions his conscious attempts to forget his girl friend: "decidí emprender el interminable camino del olvido de Octavia. Operativo O-O. Olvido de Octavia. El día que, en vez de decir O-O, dijera cero-cero, habría olvidado a Octavia . . . " [I decided to undertake the endless path toward the oblivion of Octavia. Operation O-O. Oblivion of Octavia. The day in which, instead of saying O-O, I might say zero-zero, I would be oblivious of Octavia . . .] (216). Martín's purpose clearly runs contrary to the attitude of the protagonist of *Albertine disparue,* who is terrified by the idea of forgetting his beloved, even though the absence of memory would lessen his pain. We can also note how Bryce's narrator plays with the concepts of voluntary and involuntary memory. Along these same lines, in order to remember Octavia or an incident involving her, he often sniffs benzene. Because of personal circumstances he associated this odor with her, but its pungent scent reminds a Proustian reader of the smell of varnish mentioned in *Du côté de chez Swann.*

TIME AS CHANGE AND AS A DESTRUCTIVE FORCE

Time is an essential component of every novel or narrative work. Thus in Spanish America, as well as elsewhere, characters have regularly grown older and situations have changed over time in picaresque, romantic, and realist novels. However, since the publication of Proust's novel and due to his example, New World writers, like Teresa de la Parra, began to pay closer attention to the process of change. As we saw above, her narrator actually discussed time as a subject in *Las memorias de Mamá Blanca*.[19]

In a few Spanish American novels and stories of the 1930s and 1940s, Proust's influence or inspiration with regard to time is quite noticeable. The narrator of *La última niebla*, for instance, not only shows how the passage of time affected her consciousness and the creation and destruction of her illusion, but also time becomes almost visible in a Proustian manner near the end. Bombal's protagonist has difficulty in recognizing her husband, she realizes how much he has aged, and she begins to see through him the effects of time upon herself:

> Entreveo la cara roja y marchita de un extraño. Luego me aparto violentamente, porque reconozco a mi marido. Hace tiempo que lo miraba sin verlo. ¡Qué viejo lo encuentro, de pronto! ¿Es posible que sea yo la compañera de este hombre maduro? (1988, 42)

> [I catch a glimpse of the red and withered face of a stranger. Then I draw back violently, because I recognize my husband. For a long time I have looked at him without seeing him. How old I find him to be, unexpectedly! Is it possible that I may be the mate of this older man?]

This realization is nearly identical to what we find in the so-called *bal costumé* [masked ball] scene in Proust's last volume. There the protagonist has the impression that his friends and acquaintances have disguised themselves as old people, while in fact due to the ravages of time they have become like strangers.

Although similarly interested in the subject of time, Jorge Luis Borges made a conscious effort to distinguish his work from Proust's but often inadvertently revealed his familiarity with the *Recherche*. As we saw in chapter 2, in spite of the fact that Borges denied the process of change in "Sentirse en muerte," he, like the author of *Le temps retrouvé*, offered as sole proof of his concept of time an isolated, personal experience. One of his stories from *Ficciones*, "El milagro secreto," can also be seen as an example of this tendency. Here Borges emphasized the mere chronological advancing of time and ignored the process of aging. Nonetheless, the secret miracle itself may have been inspired by Proust. It constitutes an escape from time, and, as in the case of the involuntary memory experiences, the year conceded to Hladík is known only by the man affected. Even his standing in the courtyard waiting to be shot is remarkably similar to the pose of the protagonist of *Le temps retrouvé* when he first arrived at the courtyard of the Prince de Guermantes and then repeatedly stepped upon the uneven paving stones that had triggered his memory.

In a few of his stories since "Funes el memorioso," Borges treated time itself in a more Proustian way, but his relation with the French novelist remained ambiguous. The author of "La espera" [Waiting], for example, who had derided the interest of Funes in "los avances de la corrupción, de las caries, de la fatiga" [the progress of corruption, tooth decay, fatigue] (1956, 116) allowed his protagonist to observe the effects of time: "los manchados plátanos" [already darkened bananas], "los judíos . . . desplazando a los italianos" [Jews . . . supplanting Italians] (1957, 137). In the latter example, we may even suspect an echo of the Jewish guests' replacing the ones of German descent in the World War I salons of *Le temps retrouvé*. Just the same, the protagonist of "La espera" attempts to deny the mutable circumstances of his existence, including those that cause his own death.

An emphasis on time and its effects became more evident during the 1950s, particularly in the work of those writers connected to Proust in other ways. Mujica Láinez built the second novel of his saga, *La casa,* around the life of an elegant mansion on the Calle Florida and portrayed in it several aspects of time. The mansion narrator tells of her construction, period of splendor, and long process of decay. Her time of greatest elegance is very reminiscent of *Le côté de Guermantes* and suggests that the period that Proust had described—the end of the nineteenth century and the beginning of the twentieth—was a Proust-like time in Argentina, at least for the upper classes. In this portion of the text, we find a few details that appear to have been extracted from Proust's novel almost as if it were a historical source. For example, the *cocotte* [tart] Mlle Aimée de Monvel speaks French with an affected English accent, just like Odette.

For the final period, time as decay is examined with particular care by the mansion, who analyzes her remaining inhabitants in order to explain how their moral decadence caused her physical decline. In this regard, we can observe several parallels with Proust, but the mansion's race against time to finish telling her story before the work crews totally demolish her is even more closely related to the *Recherche*. Emblematically, analogous to the narrator of *Le temps retrouvé*, the mansion narrates at night and likens herself to Scheherazade (compare the *Recherche* 3:1043 and *La casa* 1954, 146).

In another but also Proustian manner, the narrator of *Los viajeros* presents the physical and moral decay of his uncle Baltasar. In some ways, this mutable portrait over time parallels that of the Baron de Charlus, but in one segment of the text the sudden realization of the effects of time seems to have been modeled on Proust's treatment of another character: the protagonist's grandmother. In both instances, a brief absence allows the character to see more distinctly how much the said relative has aged. For this reason the protagonist of *Le côté de Guermantes* views his grandmother with more objective eyes:

> pour la première fois et seulement pour un instant, car elle disparut bien vite, j'aperçus sur le canapé, sous la lampe, rouge, lourde et vulgaire, malade, rêvassant, promenant au-dessus d'un livre des yeux un peu fous, une vieille femme accablée que je ne connaissais pas. (2:141)

> [for the first time and only for an instant, since she vanished very quickly, I noticed on the sofa, beneath the lamp, red-faced, heavy and ordinary, ill, day-dreaming, casting her slightly crazed eyes over a book, an old, worn-out woman whom I did not know.]

Similarly, but in more general terms, the narrator of *Los viajeros* remarks concerning his uncle:

> Indudablemente, esa mudanza había comenzado a producirse antes, y yo había advertido en el andar de los dos o tres años últimos, sus rasgos salientes, pero la perspectiva de ese mes de separación me ayudó a valorar el rigor de la obra del tiempo y de las desilusiones. (1955, 185)

> [Indubitably, that change had begun to occur before, and I had noticed in the course of the last two or three years, his increasingly prominent features, but the perspective of that month of separation helped me to assess the harshness of the work of time and of disillusionment.]

Clearly, several Spanish American writers tried to go beyond Proust in order to develop the subject of time in new and different ways, but even in these cases they often revealed their connection with the *Recherche*. In *La tregua,* Mario Benedetti took advantage of the traditional diary form to show the process of change over time. Without knowing what the future would bring, his narrator tells how Avellaneda first began to work in his office, how he discovered her personal qualities and how his affection for her grew. He also refers constantly to the evolution of numerous facets of reality: his handwriting, his feelings toward Isabel since her death, and even Escayola's sense of humor. In these commentaries on time, Santomé is somewhat Proustian, but his remarks concerning the physical metamorphosis of Escayola are obviously more so:

> Nunca he sentido con tanto rigor el paso del tiempo como hoy, cuando me enfrenté a Escayola después de casi treinta años de no verlo, de no saber nada de él. El adolescente alto, nervioso, bromista, se ha convertido en un mon-

struo panzón, con impresionante cogote, unos labios carnosos y blandos, una calva con manchas que parecen de café chorreado. . . . (79)

[Never have I felt with such precision the passage of time as today, when I came face to face with Escayola after nearly thirty years of not seeing him or knowing anything about him. The tall, nervous, jocular adolescent has turned into a potbellied monster, whose nape has become prominent, his lips, fleshy and flabby; he has a bald patch with blotches which seem to be of dripped coffee. . . .]

It was precisely because of such extreme physical changes in M. d'Argencourt that the narrator of *Le temps retrouvé* concludes: "il me semblait que l'être humain pouvait subir des métamorphoses aussi complètes que celles de certains insectes" [it seemed to me that the human being could undergo as complete metamorphoses as as those of certain insects] (3:922–23)

Among the Spanish American writers of the pre-Boom and Boom periods, the one that has been most consistently associated with both the subject of time and the *Recherche* is Alejo Carpentier. Although I certainly will not deny the presence of Proust in *La guerra del tiempo* [The War of Time] and *Los pasos perdidos* because of the importance of memory, I would like to emphasize the Cuban writer's originality in his treatment of time in these texts. I concede that the French novelist used specifically the duration of the Italian song "Il sole mio" near the end of *Albertine disparue*, but Carpentier's idea of developing "El acoso" [The Persecution] around a performance of Beethoven's Third Symphony was very original. Likewise, in spite of the fact that Proust considered time a fourth dimension and often associated time and space, he never suggested, in the manner of the author of *Los pasos perdidos,* that by moving away from the centers of modern urban life one is traveling back in time.[20] These cases are clearly of Proustian inspiration, rather than of mere influence.

The Cuban novelist moved closer to the Proustian idea of time as change and time as a destructive force in *El siglo de las luces* [The Century of Enlightenment] (1962). Particularly in those sections which portray the French Revolution in Europe, political change is so constant and volatile that it destroys itself. The liberal gains of the early years are later undone as the Revolution degenerates over time. Esteban becomes especially aware of the futility of change when he is sent to the Basque region:

A medida que pasaba el tiempo, advertía Esteban que el alejamiento de París poblaba su espíritu de confusiones, acabando por no entender los procesos de una política en constante mutación, contradictoria, paroxítica, devoradora de sí misma. . . . (1983, 110)

[As time passed, Esteban realized that his withdrawal from Paris filled his spirit with confusion and he ceased to understand the process of a political system in constant flux, one that was contradictory, hysterical and devoured itself. . . .]

Although Carpentier's subject matter is far more political than Proust's, we can detect the same kaleidescopic effect, as when the ostracized *dreyfusards* [defenders of Dreyfus] became popular. I should also mention that the political changes affect Víctor Hugue to such an extent that, like several of Proust's characters, he seems to become another person. It is difficult for the reader to imagine how the man who had freed the slaves in Guadeloupe in 1794 could so cynically and cruelly reinstate slavery in French Guiana in 1802.

This type of rapid change over time, where a character becomes physically or spiritually unrecognizable, may even be considered a Proustian narrative technique because it has been so frequently used in novels related to the *Recherche*. As if to prove this connection, Carpentier refers very specifically near the end of *El recurso del método* to some of the characters that he borrowed from Proust's novel. While discussing the changes that occurred after the Great War, the narrator tells how time affected the artists Elstir and Vinteuil:

> Me enteré . . . que la pintura de Elstir había descendido mucho en la estimación del público. . . . Amargado por el descenso de sus valores, se había retirado rabiosamente en su estudio de Balbec. . . . En la música ocurría algo parecido: nadie tocaba ya las obras de Vinteuil—y menos su *Sonata*. . . .
> (1974, 306)

> [I found out . . . that the painting of Elstir had declined greatly in the estimation of the public. . . . Embittered by its decrease in value, he had withdrawn angrily to his studio in Balbec. . . . A similar thing was happening in music: no one played any longer the works of Vinteuil—and least of all his *Sonata*. . . .]

Once again, we can see Carpentier's dialogue with Proust and how the Cuban author showed that the effects of time could relegate to oblivion even the artists that Proust's character greatly admired. In this case, I suspect more a confirmation of the French author's ideas than a derision of his work, as has been suggested by at least one critic.[21]

Concerning specifically the idea of time as a destructive force, Ernesto Sábato developed this subject more completely than any other Spanish American writer to my knowledge. The very title of Sábato's third novel *Abaddón el exterminador* suggests that time and death will eventually destroy all things. The final words of this text assert the same idea: "todo un día será pasado y olvidado y borrado: hasta los formidables muros y el

gran foso que rodeaba a la inexpugnable fortaleza" [One day everything
will be finished and forgotten and erased: even the formidable walls and
the great moat that surrounded the impregnable fortress] (1991, 463).

Admittedly, Sábato's thesis is even more extreme than what the
French author contended about the destructive force of time. Proust's
narrator focuses upon the personal level instead of the universal one
when he speaks of his need to write (3:930). Nonetheless, it is significant
that in *Le temps retrouvé* forgetfulness and death are seen to be the ultimate effects of time. Not only does one constantly lose one's former
selves through oblivion, but also upon dying all that one knows and has
experienced disappears. During the final pages of Proust's last volume,
the protagonist-narrator lives with the idea of death and its consequences for his life. He even considers what will happen to his memories
of Albertine: the woman that he had loved and began to forget after her
death:

> Car après la mort le Temps se retire du corps, et les souvenirs, si indifférents,
> si pâlis, sont effacés de celle qui n'est plus et le seront bientôt de celui qu'ils
> torturent encore, mais en qui ils finiront par périr quand le désir d'un corps
> vivant ne les entretiendra plus. (3:1047)

> [For after death Time withdraws from the body, and one's memories, so
> indifferent, grown so dim, are erased from her who is no longer and they will
> be soon likewise from him whom they still torment, but in whom they will
> eventually perish when the desire of a living body can no longer sustain
> them.]

As we shall see in chapter 8, the author of *Abaddón el exterminador* makes
clear his Proustian connection because, as in the second half of *Le temps
retrouvé*, he suggests that only writing can offer any hope against oblivion
for even memory disappears upon one's death.[22]

The relation between the works by Sábato and by Proust can also be
observed in another way associated with time, and this helps to confirm
their dialogue. At one point in *Abaddón el exterminador*, time is treated not
only in terms of memory but also space. After returning late one night to
the house that had belonged to the Olmos and remembering what had
transpired there, Bruno expresses a wish:

> Ah, si fuera posible volver a ciertas épocas de la vida como se podía volver a los
> lugares en que transcurrieron. . . . Los mismos sitios en que treinta años
> antes había escuchado su voz grave recitar un poema de Machado. (457)

> [Oh, if it were possible to return to certain periods in life as one can return to
> the places in which they had transpired. . . . The same locations in which

thirty years before he had listened to her grave voice recite a poem by Machado.]

In a similar manner, Proust ended *Du côté de chez Swann,* but he implied that the spatialization of time was a fact rather than a wish and even that some places had almost ceased to be a reality except in memory:

> Les lieux que nous avons connus n'appartiennent pas qu'au monde de l'espace où nous les situons pour plus de facilité. Ils n'étaient qu'une mince tranche au milieu d'impressions contiguës qui formaient notre vie d'alors; le souvenir d'une certain image n'est que le regret d'un certain instant; et les maisons, les routes, les avenues, sont fugitives, hélas! comme les années. (1:427).[23]

[The places that we have known do not belong only to the world of space where we situate them for greater convenience. They are only a thin slice surrounded by the contiguous impressions that constituted our life at that time; the memory of a certain image is only the longing for a certain instant; and thus houses, by-ways, avenues are fleeting, alas! just like years.]

A CULMINATION OF THE THEMES OF TIME IN THE WORK OF GABRIEL GARCÍA MÁRQUEZ

More than any other of the principal Boom writers, Gabriel García Márquez developed in his novels diverse facets of the subject of time, and he has often used as his primary literary context the work of Marcel Proust. In his article "*A la recherche du temps perdu* in *Cien años de soledad,*" John P. McGowan asserted that time was the principal point of contact between the two works mentioned in his title, but he found more differences than similarities, and he was not able to account for the former in any systematic way. As in the case of "El mar del tiempo perdido," which I examined in chapter 4, the nature of this relation is very elusive, but it can be defined with greater precision.

To a large extent the terms of influence and even inspiration are not adequate to describe the relation between the *Recherche* and *Cien años de soledad.* As in the case of Proust's work, which deals with the life of his protagonist, the novel by García Márquez traces the passage of time over an extended period: one hundred years. In both cases, chronological time advances without stopping and all persons and things change. We can observe a vague similarity both in the focus upon an outstanding family—the Guermantes and the Buendías—to show the process of change and in the progressive decay of that family. For this reason the economic decline of the Prince de Guermantes and the moral decadence of the Baron de Charlus foreshadow the downward spiral of the Buendía family. But, this similarity is so general that we could hardly attribute it to influence, at least of the direct variety. These same characteristics can be found in many works including *La casa* by Mujica Láinez, where the house also decays. A more direct influence of the *Recherche* can be seen in the numerous characters that change to such an extent over time that they become unrecognizable (e.g., José Arcadio, the son of the founder, 1996, 187–89).[24] But among the plethora of details found in *Cien años de soledad* this point of contact seems minor.

Using the concepts associated with dialogue, we can discover how the Colombian novel is actually a response to the French work because *Cien años de soledad* adds to the conversation several major points with regard to time. It demonstrates, for instance, that a chronological sequence of events does not necessarily lead in a single direction. It can encompass reversals, and time may be cyclical. Ursula appears to summarize the nature of time in the Colombian novel when she says, "Es como si el tiempo diera vueltas en redondo, y hubiéramos vuelto al principio" [It is as if time ran about in circles, and we had returned to the beginning] (307). Even though change is constant and all persons and things necessarily grow older, their most essential characteristics can hide beneath the surface and eventually reassert themselves. Thus, the ultimate effect of change is a return to the beginning and no change at all.[25]

Cien años de soledad offers many examples of this concept of time. The founder of the family, José Arcadio Buendía, oscillates between two roles: he is either an enterprising town leader or a solitary, obsessive alchemist. His son Aureliano makes golden fish both before and after the civil wars. The founder's great-grandsons, José Arcadio Segundo and Aureliano Segundo, reflect their condition as identical twins during their childhood and at the time of their deaths, but they appear to be opposites during most of their lives. Even the cataclysmic destruction of Macondo at the end of the novel demonstrates how the results of human endeavor can be voided by nature. All of these cases seem to respond to Proust's work where time advances constantly and can be reversed only through involuntary memory.

This dialogue concerning time can also be noted in other ways. Like the narrator of the *Recherche*, that of *Cien años de soledad* often alludes to distinct moments in time as he both recalls events from the past and anticipates those of the future. In "Discours du récit" [Narrative Discourse] (1972) Gérard Genette used the terms *analepse* and *prolepse* to designate such alterations in the chronological order of events found in Proust's novel, and he concluded that these modifications were an essential characteristic of it. For the most part, the author of the *Recherche* merely suggested in passing what had happened before or what would occur later in his narration, but to emphasize his interest in time he occasionally created syntactic labyrinths of it. The narrator of *Sodome et Gomorrhe,* for example, mentions in rapid succession and within the same sentence the numerous incidents that had taken place in his hotel room at Balbec:

> Je restai seul dans la chambre, cette même chambre trop haute de plafond où j'avais été si malheureux à la première arrivée, où j'avais pensé avec tant de tendresse à Mlle de Stermaria, guetté le passage d'Albertine et de ses amies . . . où je l'avais possédée avec tant d'indifférence . . . où j'avais connu la bonté de ma grand-mère, puis appris qu'elle était morte. . . . (2:1125–26)

> [I remained alone in the room, that same room with a too high ceiling where I had been so distressed on my first arrival, where I had thought with such tenderness about Mlle de Stermaria, watched for the appearance of Albertine and her friends . . . where I had possessed her with such indifference . . . where I had discovered the goodness of my grandmother, then realized that she was dead. . . .]

In a nearly identical manner and also within the confines of a single sentence, García Márquez used near the end of his text a rocking chair to produce the same summarizing effect.[26] The narrator says of the last Aureliano:

> Se derrumbó en el mecedor, el mismo en que se sentó Rebeca en los tiempos originales de la casa para dictar lecciones de bordado, y en el que Amaranta jugaba damas chinas con el coronel Gerineldo Márquez, y en el que Amaranta Ursula cosía la ropita del niño. . . . (556)

> [He flung himself down into the rocking chair, the same one in which Rebeca sat during the earliest period of the house to teach embroidery lessons, and in which Amaranta played Chinese checkers with Colonel Gerineldo Márquez, and in which Amaranta Ursula sewed the tiny clothes for the child. . . .]

Emblematically, *Cien años de soledad* begins with a similar temporal labyrinth, but one in which the future is implied, as well as the past: "Muchos años después, frente al pelotón de fusilamiento, el coronel Aureliano Buendía había de recordar aquella tarde remota en que su padre lo llevó a conocer el hielo" [Many years later, facing the firing squad, Colonel Aureliano Buendía would remember that distant afternoon when his father took him to experience ice] (79). In the novel by García Márquez, as in the one by Proust, such passages serve an important narrative function and can be considered a technique: they help to unify the text by binding together characters, themes and events. Furthermore, because they allude to distinct moments in time, they suggest that through memory such moments can be joined in the mind of the characters, the narrator and the readers. In this regard, the Colombian novelist added to the conversation by treating the future in the same way as the past.

Given the connection between time and memory in the *Recherche,* it is not surprising that memory also constitutes an important subject of García Márquez's dialogue with Proust. The characters in the Colombian novel frequently recall the past and feel nostalgia for it. At times music serves as a stimulus, just as it does for Swann. In at least one instance I can cite an involuntary memory experience, somewhat like those that we will discuss in chapter 7. When Fernanda puts on her queen's dress for the first time in many years, she smells once again the shoe polish worn by the officer who had come to make her queen (496– 97). This odor in turn allows her to recall the past, and she reacts emotionally. Her memory experience and tears, as well as the reference to footgear, even seem to echo a passage from Proust's text. In *Sodome et Gomorrhe,* the protagonist is overwhelmed by the remembrance of his grandmother when he reaches down to unfasten his boots (2:755–56).

In spite of such an example, we ultimately must conclude that memory does not offer salvation for García Márquez's characters in the same way as it does for the Proustian protagonist. Fernanda is not able to escape from time or to perceive it in a pure state, and her memory experience is quickly erased by time. As the book dealer from Barcelona suggests and implicitly responds to Proust: "la memoria no tenía caminos de regreso" [memory did not have any roads of return] (541). This conclusion, however, does not signify that García Márquez was indifferent to the idea of escaping from time. In fact, his creation of the fantastic room of Melquíades can be interpreted as a response to or equivalent of Proustian memory. Being skeptical about the nearly miraculous effects that the French author had attributed to memory in life, García Márquez made time and even space magical. In this way, associated with Proust, he added to *Cien años de soledad* one of the most essential aspects of its magical realism. Also he offered a somewhat postmodern reworking of Proust's treatment of time and memory.

Consequently, within the confined space of the room made for Melquíades, time does not appear to advance at least for many years. For most persons, although not all, that area of the house is not affected by dust or decay, and time exists in a pristine, unchanging state. Even a few persons, such as Aureliano Buendía, are able to see and converse with Melquíades due to hereditary memory and the magical powers of the founder's dear friend. Such a miraculous spanning of time allows Melquíades to assist the last Aureliano in his efforts to decipher the manuscript. In short, García Márquez created in his own manner what Proust called, referring to the memory experiences, "un peu de temps à l'état pur" [a bit of time in a pure state] (3:872).

Likewise, the manuscript by Melquíades greatly condensed time by summarizing events in written form and in some ways resembles the *Recherche,* as well as *Cien años de soledad.* But also here García Márquez called upon the power of magic. Not content merely to affirm with Proust that "l'oeuvre d'art était le seul moyen de retrouver le Temps Perdu" [the work of art was the only means of recapturing Lost Time] (3:899), the Nobel Laureate from Colombia claimed that a single moment of time in the manuscript could contain an entire century: "Melquíades no había ordenado los hechos en el tiempo convencional de los hombres, sino que concentró un siglo de episodios cotidianos, de modo que todos coexistieran en un instante" [Melquíades had not ordered the events in the conventional time of men, but instead he concentrated a century of daily episodes in such a way that they coexisted in an instant] (557). This magical concept of time has only a slight link to reality, and the very fact that the last Aureliano requires time in order to read the manuscript's pages is a proof of its fiction. Just the same we can see how Proust remained García Márquez's primary literary context and co-participant in the conversation.[27] Not only does the narrator of *Le temps retrouvé* refer to genies like those found in *1001 Nights* in order to portray the marvelousness of one of his memory experiences and says how these gave him the impression of seeing time in a pure state, but also he claims: "Une minute affranchie de l'ordre du temps a récrée en nous pour la sentir, l'homme affranchie de l'ordre du temps" [One minute emancipated from the order of time re-created in us, so that we might experience it, man emancipated from the order of time] (3:873). In a like manner, we can see how the complex sentences of Proust and García Márquez which allude to different moments in time are an attempt to represent syntactically a single instant which contains all of time.

Among the subsequent novels by García Márquez, *El amor en los tiempos del cólera* is without doubt the one most closely related to Proust. This work, in fact, develops so many different facets of the Proustian subject of time that it can be considered both a summary and culmination of nearly all of the aspects that we have examined in this chapter.

First of all, like Mujica Láinez in his saga of *porteño* society, García Márquez chose as his principal time period the end of the nineteenth century and the beginning of the twentieth. Because of Proust's outstanding depiction of the elegance and refinement of those years we might consider this, the so-called *Belle Epoque,* a Proustian time.[28] As we saw in the chapter on high society, García Márquez followed Proust in his portrayal of the Colombian upper classes of this period, and in particular of Dr. Juvenal Urbino, who had been a student of Proust's father. As suggested above, the very title of the Colombian novel, *El amor en los tiempos del cólera*, alludes to this Proustian connection because the father of the French novelist is specifically called "el epidemiólogo más destacado de su tiempo y creador de los cordones sanitarios" [the most distinguished epidemiologist of his time and the creator of the quarantine line] (1986, 159).

In this novel, we find the story of a love that first blooms and grows, but which does not reach fruition because of the girl's father and his social ambitions. We have seen how the tracing of the initial stages of this love and its painfulness akin to disease were related to the psychological novel and Proust's work itself. Also we can construe in the loss of that love and in Florentino Ariza's desire to recover it a Proustian intention. He, somewhat like the protagonist of *Albertine disparue*, wishes to return to the past: to a time in his youth when he was loved by the woman that he adores.

However, most importantly, García Márquez followed Proust in the treatment of time itself. He showed how the life and love of Florentino Ariza, Fermina Daza and Dr. Juvenal Urbino, advanced through evolutionary stages. The narrator explains how all three of these characters change, mature and grow old. In this process that lasts more than fifty years, we find some of the same Proustian elements associated with time as in *Cien años de soledad*. Just as Proust presented the events of a particular day in *La prisonnière* and those of a lifetime in the course of the *Recherche,* and García Márquez depicted those of one hundred years in his earlier novel, the later one traced the events of a half century.[29] Indeed, the narrator of *El amor en los tiempos del cólera* is less psychological than that of the *Recherche,* although he does on occasion return to this manner, as when he analyzes Fermina Daza's feelings toward Dr. Urbino's family and ancestral home. The Colombian novel comes closest to the French work when the narrator refers to change over time and tells how one character has difficulty in recognizing another. Significantly, when confronted by Florentino after her husband's death, Fermina finds it hard to recognize the man that she had loved a half century before:

No le resultaba fácil imaginarse a Florentino Ariza como era entonces, y mucho menos concebir que aquel muchacho taciturno, tan desvalido bajo la lluvia, fuera el mismo carcamal apolillado que se le había plantado enfrente sin ninguna consideración por su estado. . . . (385)

[It was not easy for her to imagine Florentino Ariza as he was then, and much less to conceive how that taciturn boy, so helpless in the rain, could be the same decrepit old fogy who had confronted her so resolutely with no consideration for her bereavement. . . .]

The parallel between this situation and the examples that I cited from *La última niebla* and *La tregua* should make the relation beween García Márquez and Proust very evident, but I wish to emphasize that the Colombian novelist developed this connection in far greater detail than any of his New World predecessors.

Throughout the course of his text, García Márquez depicted time as change and decay very much like Proust and often echoed the French novelist. Notably, Florentino discovers changes in Fermina before perceiving them in himself. After watching her briefly on several occasions while attending the same social events, one day he notices that she has been affected by time: "él había conocido la sevicia del tiempo no tanto en carne propia como en los cambios imperceptibles que notaba en Fermina Daza cada vez que la veía" [he had discovered the cruelty of time not so much in his own flesh as in the imperceptible changes that he had noticed in Fermina Daza each occasion that he saw her] (312). In a very similar manner, the protagonist of *Le temps retrouvé* discovers the changes in himself only after observing such in the other persons who are present at the *matinée* of the Prince de Guermantes: "je m'aperçus pour la première fois, d'après les métamorphoses qui s'étaient produites dans tous ces gens, du temps qui avait passé pour eux, ce qui me bouleversa par la révélation qu'il avait passé aussi pour moi" [I became aware for the first time, in accordance with the metamorphoses that had occurred in all of these people, of the time that had elapsed for them, which overwhelmed me by the revelation that it had also elapsed for me] (3:927).

It is especially important that one of the changes in Fermina entails her difficulty in walking. Referring to the episode where Florentino sees her leaving a movie theatre accompanied by her husband, the narrator remarks: "lo que más lo conmovió fue que el esposo tuvo que agarrarla por el brazo para indicarle el buen camino de la salida, y aun así calculó mal la altura y estuvo a punto de caerse en el escalón de la puerta" [what moved him most was the fact that her husband had to take hold of her arm to show her the right way out, and even so she miscalculated the height of the large step at the door and nearly fell down] (351). For Proust, old age was most apparent through the manner in which a person walked. In the very last paragraph of his seven volume novel, his narrator describes the old Duke's efforts to move about on his feet and uses what is now a famous comparison for old age and time. Years seem to add length to a person's legs in such a way that these resemble constantly growing stilts from which that person will eventually fall:

le duc de Guermantes . . . ne s'était avancé qu'en tremblant comme une feuille, sur le sommet peu praticable de quatre-vingt-trois années, comme si

les hommes étaient juchés sur de vivantes échasses, grandissant sans cesse . . .
finissant par leur rendre la marche difficile et périlleuse, et d'où tout d'un
coup ils tombaient. (3:1047–48)

[the Duc de Guermantes . . . walked forward only by trembling like a leaf,
upon the summit of his scarcely manageable eighty-three years, as if men were
perched upon living stilts, which grew unceasingly . . . and finally made walking for them difficult and dangerous, and from which suddenly they fell.]

Apparently remembering this image or perhaps the fear that the
Proustian protagonist had of falling on the stairs (3:1041), García Márquez incorporated such an accident into his novel and used it to create a
Proustian effect. Florentino undergoes a rapid aging process after he
himself falls downstairs. In this way, he becomes unrecognizable to the
two women that know him best. According to them, "No parecía posible
que fuera el mismo hombre. . ." [It did not seem possible that he was the
same man. . .] (431).

Although, here, it might appear that Gabriel García Márquez was
simply inspired by Marcel Proust in his treatment of time, as well as
social class, love and disease, another closely related subject, memory,
demonstrates that the Colombian author was in fact engaged in a
dialogue with the French novelist. All three principal characters frequently recall the past because of a physical stimulus, especially odors,
which play an important role in this novel. Their memory experiences,
however, are quite brief and rarely satisfying. As in *Cien años de soledad,* no
one in *El amor en los tiempos del cólera* truly recovers the past in a Proustian
sense. Each of the main characters is simply left with a feeling of
nostalgia, which ultimately leads to frustration.

On occasion, particularly with regard to Fermina Daza, the Colombian text approaches the French one. Like the protagonist in the last
volume of the *Recherche* who returns to the place of his childhood, Combray, Fermina tries to satisfy her nostalgia by going back to San Juan de la
Ciénaga, where she grew up and where she traveled as a young woman.
Both characters are disappointed because each location in the present
seems very different from their recollections of it. Proust's narrator says,
"Mais ce qui me frappa el plus, ce fut combien peu . . . je revivais mes
années d'autrefois . . . trouvais mince et laide la Vivonne" [But what
struck me the most was how little . . . I relived my years of the past . . . I
found narrow and ugly the Vivonne] (3:693). Likewise, we read in *El
amor en los tiempos del cólera:* "Fermina Daza estaba tan deprimida con lo
que vio y oyó desde que salió de su casa, que en el resto del viaje no se
complació en el recuerdo del viaje anterior, como tanto había añorado,
sino que evitaba el paso por los pueblos de sus nostalgias" [Fermina Daza

was so depressed by what she saw and heard since she left the house, that during the remainder of the trip she did not take pleasure in recalling the previous trip, as she had so yearned to do, but rather she avoided going through the towns linked to her nostalgia] (346).

Clearly, in some portions of his novel, García Márquez chose to give an alternate development to a Proustian situation. Similar to the protagonist of *Albertine disparue,* who is constantly reminded of his mistress by things associated with her following her departure and death, Fermina suffers greatly because of the presence of Dr. Urbino's belongings after his demise. Not content to live in the past, however, and unlike the Proustian protagonist, Fermina gives away many of her husband's things and burns the rest. Unfortunately for her, this ploy against memory proves to be largely futile. Only with time, as in the case of Proust's character, is Fermina able to forget her beloved and reconcile herself with the past.

The dialogue concerning memory reaches the level of debate when the attitude of Florentino and Fermina toward their adolescent love comes into conflict. Having kept his passion alive for more than fifty years by systematically remembering it, Florentino feels a strong bond between the two of them, which he tries to renew after Dr. Urbino's death. In this regard, we can note that involuntary memory has a more favorable effect upon Florentino, as when he notices Fermina's voice in the theatre (349–50) and when he hears the tolling of bells (374). In contrast, Fermina, who had learned to love her husband, forgot her feelings toward Florentino and was disappointed when she tried to recover her memories of San Juan de la Ciénaga, doubts the very existence of her previous love for Florentino. For her, any effort to resurrect the past is useless and childish. Thus she writes to Florentino, "¿Por qué te empeñas en hablar de lo que no existe?" [Why do you insist upon talking about something that does not exist?] (429). From her point of view, "La memoria del pasado no redimía el futuro . . . " [The memory of the past could not redeem the future . . .] (432). At this point García Márquez was making his most direct response to Proust, for whom the past, through involuntary memory and writing, provided the opportunity to justify the present and the future (see chapters 7 and 8). Being skeptical, like his female protagonist, the Colombian author created circumstances in which his two characters could fall in love again. This occurs over time and as Fermina discovers in Florentino present reasons to love him: his understanding of life and his courage to defend her in the press. Their love is consummated during their voyage along the Río Magdalena, where they can finally talk about the past and enjoy the present.

At least to some extent, the ending of *El amor en los tiempos del cólera* can also be read as an answer to Proust. Even though the characters in this

Colombian novel cannot escape from time in a Proustian sense (any more than those in *Cien años de soledad*) they create for themselves the illusion of existing outside of time. By pretending to be infected by cholera, raising a yellow flag on their river boat, and traveling back and forth along the Magdalena, they have in appearance returned to the time of cholera and eliminated the necessity of contact with the outside world. This situation frees Fermina Daza and Florentino Ariza from the social judgement of their acquaintances and supposedly will permit them to love each other continuously until they die. Such a solution to the novel is primarily literary because the actual needs of food, fuel and wages are never addressed, but for the Colombian master of magical realism, these concerns are of less importance than the satisfactory joining together in a somewhat Proustian manner his themes of social class, time, love, and disease. In this sense we can view his characters' escape from time as a spiritual equivalent of the Proustian memory experiences, which were also more literary than real and which intimately linked the themes of the *Recherche*. Furthermore, the self-conscious reworking of time and memory must be considered postmodern and due to its historical dimension *El amor en los tiempos del cólera* fits to a large extent Hutcheon's definition of historiographic metafiction.

Going beyond the ending of this work, which also implies, because of the defoliated forests along the riverbank, the destructive force of time, we can observe how fruitful the subject of time has proven to be for Spanish American literature and the role that Proust's work has played in the development of it. Indeed, I cannot claim that the French writer was the first to use in a literary manner the opposition between loss and recovery, be that of a woman or an idyllic past. Nor did he invent the idea of time as change or as a destructive force. Nonetheless, Marcel Proust can be credited with reintroducing and drawing together these elements, which many modernist and postmodern writers have used in various combinations. Spanish American modernists, like Manuel Mujica Láinez or Teresa de la Parra, remained quite close to Proust even though they always adapted his ideas to their own purposes. In contrast, others (who have moved in the direction of postmodernism) from Jorge Luis Borges and José Lezama Lima to Julio Cortázar and Mario Alberto Carrera, have demonstrated varying degrees of opposition to Proust. All of these writers, but in particular Alejo Carpentier, Reinaldo Arenas and Gabriel García Márquez, have been very creative in their use of time and its connection with Proust. We can also note concerning this subject, as well as others, the full range of literary relations from influence and inspiration to dialogue and parody.

7

On Involuntary Memory: From Applying the Lessons of *Le temps retrouvé* to Dialoguing with Them

OF ALL OF PROUST'S THEMES, HIS MOST ESSENTIAL ONE IS INVOLUNTARY memory. This subject more than any other reflects both his psychological perspicacity and his aesthetic intuition. It not only demonstrates his retrospective view of life but also his capacity to recover the gems of the past and to render them palpable for our present.

During the centuries that preceded the *Recherche*, memory played a valuable ancillary role in expository and narrative literature. Being considered one of the three mental faculties (along with understanding and will), memory was often a subject of discussion in a wide variety of prose texts.[1] Memory also provided in an implicit way the material for autobiographies and confessions, as well as those fictional genres that resembled these nonfictional ones, in particular the first person picaresque and the novel of apprenticeship. But, as José Ortega y Gasset noted, Proust took his first decisive step toward originality when he chose to shift his focus from recollections and memoirs to memory itself.[2] Consequently, his narrator not only recalls the past, somewhat in the manner of Jean-Jacques Rousseau, Lazarillo de Tormes, or Gil Blas de Santillane, but also he examines the mechanism involved in the process of recovering the past.

Indeed, Marcel Proust was not totally original in either his ideas on memory or in the specific type of it that he described. As his narrator confesses in *Le temps retrouvé*, Chateaubriand had already alluded to spontaneous memory and depicted it in his posthumous work *Mémoires d'outre-tombe* [Memoirs from beyond the Grave] (1848).[3] The following passage, cited from this work in the last volume of the *Recherche*, is remarkably similar to what critics now call Proustian memory:

"Hier au soir je me promenais seul . . . je fus tiré de mes réflexions par le gazouillement d'une grive perchée sur la plus haute branche d'un bouleau. A l'instant, ce son magique fit reparaître à mes yeux le domaine paternel; j'oubliai les catastrophes dont je venais d'être le témoin, et, transporté subitement dans le passé, je revis ces campagnes où j'entendis si souvent siffler la grive." (1954, 3:919)

["Yesterday evening I was walking alone . . . I was drawn from my reflections by the warbling of a thrush perched upon the highest branch of a birch tree. Instantaneously, this magical sound made my father's estate reappear before my eyes; I forgot the calamities that I had just witnessed, and being transported suddenly to the past, I saw again that rural area where I so often heard the thrush sing."]

Here, we can observe what in film studies has been termed a flashback, but already for Chateaubriand was very complex because it involved a mental or psychological process. A physical stimulus, the singing of a particular type of bird, perceived at one moment in his life gave the author the impression of returning to an earlier time and place where he had heard that sound frequently. The stimulus is poetic or aesthetically pleasing, and the experience is emotional and is said to be magical. Furthermore, recalling the past in this manner has a beneficial effect upon Chateaubriand because he forgets the reasons for his suffering in the present. I would also point out that this description is brief and serves primarily as a transition within Mémoires d'outre-tombe itself.

In Proust's seven volumes this type of memory experience is repeated on several occasions.[4] The episode of the madeleinc, which appears near the beginning of Du côté de chez Swann, is of course the most famous. In A l'ombre des jeunes filles en fleurs there is another occurrence when the protagonist waits for the cook Françoise in a public lavatory of the Champs Elysées, and a third can be found in Sodome et Gomorrhe when he stoops down to unfasten his boots. In these and one or two incomplete memory experiences, which fail to reach fruition because of the presence of another person, the protagonist discovers a connection with the past. He often feels great joy, but he is unable to understand the actual memory mechanism. It is not until he undergoes in rapid succession a series of five experiences in Le temps retrouvé that he can comprehend the true nature of the process.

Proust's ideas on memory, which are largely implicit in the early volumes, are explained in detail in the final one. Here, the narrator discounts the value of conscious or voluntary memory, which, according to him, can bring to mind only a fossilized view of the past. He compares this type of memory to looking at old photographs. From his intentional efforts to recall his visit to Venice, he concludes:

> J'essayais maintenant de tirer de ma mémoire d'autres "instantanés" . . . mais rien que ce mot me la rendait ennuyeuse comme une exposition de photographies, et je ne me sentais pas plus de goût, plus de talent, pour décrire maintenant ce que j'avais vu autrefois. . . . (3:865)

> [I now tried to draw from my memory other "snapshots" . . . but this very word rendered the idea as boring as a photograph exhibit, and I no longer felt that I had the desire or talent to describe now what I had seen in the past. . . .]

To demonstrate the stark contrast between this conventional type of memory and one that is spontaneous or involuntary, Proust's narrator describes how by stepping on a pair of uneven paving stones in the courtyard of the Prince de Guermantes he had the impression of being transported back to Venice itself.

By comparing the description of this memory experience with the passage from *Mémoires d'outre-tombe* quoted above, we can ascertain several important differences and similarities between the two French authors with regard to memory. On the one hand, Proust made the stimulus more abstract and purely physical, and he removed from it the inherent beauty and poetry associated with the singing of a bird.[5] Although it is still dependent upon sensory perception, he reduced the support of the link with the past from the habitual to the momentary because the time recalled was unique. On the other hand, the Proustian protagonist experiences a similar type of joy and of escape from the present moment. Also, he feels as if he were transported back to the past, but only after he has succeeded in identifying the exact moment that he is recalling. Referring to the sensation of blinding light that he felt when he stepped on the paving stones, the narrator speaks as if the impression were addressing him personally:

> "Saisis-moi au passage si tu en as la force, et tâche à résoudre l'énigme de bonheur que je te propose." Et presque tout de suite je la reconnus, c'était Venise, dont mes efforts pour la décrire et les prétendus instantanés pris par ma mémoire ne m'avaient jamais rien dit et que la sensation que j'avais ressentie jadis sur deux dalles inégales du baptistère de Saint-Marc m'avait rendue avec toutes les autres sensations jointes ce jour-là à cette sensation-là. . . . (3:867)

> ["Seize me as I pass by if you have the strength to do so, and try to solve the enigma of happiness that I offer you." And almost immediately I recognized the vision, it was Venice, concerning which my efforts to describe it and the so-called snapshots taken by my memory had never told me anything, but which

the sensation that I had previously felt when I stepped on two uneven flagstones in the baptistery of St. Mark's had returned to me with all of the other sensations joined that day to that sensation. . . .]

This passage contrasts even further the two types of memory. The protagonist's conscious efforts, which implied his intelligence and will, proved to be futile, but the sensation of stepping by chance on the uneven paving stones in the present brought to mind a similar sensation from the past. This identification bridged the gap between the two moments distant in time. Then through the process of association he was able to recover all that he had experienced on the day during his visit to Saint Mark's.

Gérard Genette explained particularly well the two stages that are involved in Proustian memory and showed how the first is related to metaphor and the second, to metonymy. Because the involuntary memory mechanism is triggered by the spontaneous identification of two like sensations separated by time and space, Proust called the beginning of the process "le miracle d'une analogie" (3:871). In doing so, he was suggesting that involuntary memory is for life what metaphor is for art because both entail the discovery of a single quality shared by two sensations. Genette asserted that the memory experience also involves metonymy since the other sensations and images that are recovered during the experience are associated with the initial one by temporal and spacial proximity or contiguity and not by similarity. He concluded:

this first explosion is always accompanied, necessarily and immediately by a type of chain reaction which proceeds, no longer by analogy, but rather by contiguity, and which is precisely the moment when the metonymical infectiousness . . . carries forth the relay of the metaphorical evocation. (1972, 56)

With each of the successive memory experiences described in *Le temps retrouvé* the protagonist comes to understand more fully the nature of involuntary memory and how it can affect his life. During one of these, for example, the superposition of past sensations upon present ones is so overwhelming that he doubts for an instant whether he is actually in the past or in the present. He, in fact, is not totally certain until he realizes that his joy does not correspond to a specific feeling from the past or the present. The joy results from what the narrator calls "un peu de temps à l'état pur" [a bit of time in a pure state]. Since the identifying sensation is found in both the present and the past, he can experience what the two moments hold in common, which is their essence and which appears to exist outside of time.

The revelations of involuntary memory affect the Proustian protagonist in several ways. They allow him to recover the past, which had been apparently lost because of the nature of time and forgetfulness. In this way, he is able to counteract the perpetual transformation of reality, which he had observed throughout his life. Time continues to advance until his death, yet he can enjoy temporal retrievals through involuntary memory. Furthermore because of such experiences he can convince himself of the unity of his personality. If he is able to recapture moments from his past, he must be essentially the same person.

As the reader can notice, many of these ideas are linked to the theme of time, which we discussed in chapter 6, and Proust's definition of metaphor, which we saw in chapter 5. The French author, who wished to join his principal themes into a vast structure like a gothic cathedral, used involuntary memory as the ribs of his vault. This type of construction, which is fundamental to the *Recherche*, will be more fully examined in our final chapter because it is intimately bound to the literary vocation of the protagonist. I will necessarily leave this subject until then, but I would like to point out the essential role of involuntary memory. The experiences described above constitute a quasi religious revelation or conversion which transforms the protagonist's life. Thus, with great conviction, he decides to devote the remainder of his existence to the perpetuation of these moments of exaltation by writing a novel that explains them and demonstrates the miracle of involuntary memory. In this way, not only does he tell the story of his life, but also how he came to understand the memory experiences and to fulfill his literary vocation.

For modernism involuntary memory would prove to be Marcel Proust's most valuable contribution. Building upon the treatment of memory by Baudelaire, who is also cited in *Le temps retrouvé* along with Chateaubriand and Nerval, and following other late nineteenth century writers, such as Pierre Loti in *Le roman d'un enfant*, Proust greatly enhanced the role of spontaneous memory in the novel and demonstrated how it could be the focus of consciousness and connect widely diverse moments in a person's life. Other modernists, from Virginia Woolf to William Faulkner, would be quick to assimilate this aspect of the *Recherche*. Numerous other writers would likewise follow it, but eventually postmodernists would question the exclusivity of its mechanism and totalizing value, and a few writers would parody it.

In Spanish America, the use of Proustian memory developed in three principal stages, which I will describe here. First, after several realist authors learned how to portray such emotional experiences, modernists began to weave them more skillfully into the fabric of their texts. Second, some writers began to experiment with involuntary memory and to associate it with other subjects, most notably bourgeois sensibility. Third, the most daring of these writers carried their experimentation even further and created extended dialogues with Proust's ideas on memory, which they at times questioned.

LEARNING HOW TO INTEGRATE PROUSTIAN MEMORY INTO A NARRATIVE STRUCTURE

In the short stories and novels of Spanish America one can find the description of a large number of involuntary memory experiences in the manner of the *Recherche* because this aspect of Proust's novel has had a greater impact than any other. A few of these examples appeared as early as the 1920s and 1930s. Often, these experiences with memory were quite brief and served more as an adornment within a realist text than as a means to create a new type of novel of the modernist variety. In a few cases, such as *Ifigenia,* the experiences were more fully developed, but even in this text by Teresa de la Parra they were not totally integrated into the novel as a whole. It is never made clear how María Eugenia's recovery of the past affects her present.

One typical example from the initial period is *El chileno en Madrid* (1928) by Joaquín Edwards Bello. In this still largely traditional, plot-driven novel, the Chilean author, who discussed Proust in some of his articles of those years, presented a series of brief memory experiences. When the protagonist Pedro Wallace returns to Madrid in search of his former mistress and their son, sensations and circumstances in the present bring to mind incidents from the past. In some cases, the stimulus involves one of the senses and thus reminds us in particular of the *Recherche.* We read, for example: "El olor de los pimientos era otro motivo de recuerdos para Pedro; así como el freír de un huevo de repente y las chispitas que le quemaban las manos le recordaba a Dolores, de pie, frente a la angosta ventana de la cocina, mientras el niño jugaba . . . " [The smell of peppers was another another reason for Pedro to remember; likewise the frying of an egg unexpectedly and the spattering that burned his hands reminded him of Dolores, standing opposite the narrow kitchen window while the boy was playing . . .] (1928, 191). I note, however, that these episodes involving spontaneous memory merely show Wallace's nostalgia and remorse for having abandoned the woman and child. They do not deeply affect the structure of the text, which had been precisely the case in Proust's novel. Through thematic development instead of plot, he carefully prepared for and constructed his memory experiences and then used these to bind together all of his text.

In another case, *La vuelta de las horas* (1933) by the Argentine Juan P. Ramos, it is apparent that the author understood in the abstract Proust's memory theories, but he did not succeed novelistically in applying these well. Ramos, who had presented a lecture on Proust in 1926, made his character Julio Melves actually cite the ideas of the French author in a letter to a friend:

> Basta ver un objeto, para que renazca una imágen o un episodio. . . . Sentimos el placer o la emoción dolorosa que vincularon el objeto con tal acontecimiento olvidado. Revivimos la vida y el tiempo perdido, para emplear una idea grata a tu adorado Proust. (1933, 40)

> [It is enough to see an object for an image or an episode to be reborn. . . . We feel the pleasure or painful emotion that linked the object to such a forgotten event. We relive life and lost time, to employ an idea dear to your beloved Proust.]

In spite of the references to the French author's memory theories, which the character discusses with Ramón Férnandez (who curiously has the same name as an early Proustian critic of Mexican origin), when Melves mentions the object in question we realize that it has nothing to do with the past. It is merely the statue in a store window that attracted the character's attention and that of two women passing by. Indeed, as the title suggests, the protagonist of *La vuelta de las horas* has the impression of returning to the past, but the reason is more closely bound to nineteenth century writers like Maupassant than to Proust. Upon realizing that the older of the two women is his former mistress and that the younger is their daughter, of whose existence he did not know, Melves becomes obsessed with the past and wishes to reconcile himself with it. Thus, I must conclude that in spite of his attempt at dialogue, Ramos used Proust's words cited above in merely a literal sense—the object is no more than an object—and thus he adulterated the meaning of Proustian memory.

In *A batallas de amor . . . campo de pluma* Carlos Reyles created a longer, more fully developed memory experience. Here, the mechanism functions in a somewhat Proustian manner, although the search for the past is in part consciously induced. While shamelessly rummaging through the underwear of his former wife, the protagonist recovers through her personal scent memories of the past: "Y cien seductoras imágenes de Pichona en pijama, de Pichona en camisa, de Pichona desnuda le pasan a la carrera por la mente" [And a hundred seductive images of Pichona in pyjamas, of Pichona in a shirt, of Pichona nude run quickly through his mind] (1939, 65). In the text itself, the narrator describes the circumstances in which Pepe met Pichona at the home of the sculptor Zonza Briano. At one point the protagonist does in fact perceive the scent which constitutes the link between the present and the past. But the author did not restrict his attention to Pepe's recollections or even to his point of view. Reyles employed here the same omniscient narrator typical of realism as elsewhere in the novel and used the memory experience merely as a technique to shift the time frame of the action to an earlier period in the lives of the characters.

Probably the best Spanish American example from these years of an involuntary recovery of the past can be found in *Sombras* [Shadows] (1937) by Jaime Torres Bodet. In a modernist manner this Mexican writer carefully created a character, context, and narrator for his memory experience, developed this incident in detail, and made it the center-piece for his entire text, which is unified more by themes than by plot.[6] The principal character Doña Eulalia is a middle-aged woman who lives alone in her ancestral mansion. In general, she thinks about the past more than the present, but her need to consider the fate of the illegitimate son of a rebellious nephew causes her to remember her life in greater detail. Within this retrospective and associative mode it is almost natural that Doña Eulalia recalls a particular memory experience which had affected her deeply.

This embedded episode begins when she happens to enter for the first time in years the church where she was married. There, a pair of sensory perceptions—the smell of incense and termite-eaten wood and the sound of the church door closing behind her—confuse her sense of time and space:

> Entró en la nave. Por un minuto, perdió conciencia del tiempo, fe en el espacio. ¿Dónde estaba? . . . Respiró con fuerza, varias veces, hasta que en la celdilla más escondida de sus pulmones penetrara ese aroma encerrado . . . que constituía para su olfato, la memoria del templo. (1985, 2:198)

> [She entered the nave. For an instant, she lost consciousness of the time, faith in the location. Where was she? . . . . She breathed vigorously, several times, until the hidden most cell of her lungs was saturated with that musty odor . . . which constituted for her sense of smell, the recollection of the temple.]

This situation is very similar to portions of the *Recherche* where the protagonist feels as though he has returned to the past. Doña Eulalia even imagines that she is younger: "¿Cómo puede el perfume de un templo aniquilar en una persona, de pronto, veintidós largos años de ausencia?" How can the scent of a temple obliterate in a person, suddenly, twenty-two long years of absence?] (199).

Nonetheless, Doña Eulalia's experience of going back in time is not exclusively Proustian and suggests how Torres Bodet used his imagination to add other elements. His character does recall the wedding march from *Lohengrin* and the faces of some of the people that attended the marriage ceremony, but she also recovers the image of her mother from years before. The various moments of the past are blended together and even the present becomes involved to some degree. The old sexton, who enters while Doña Eulalia is seated on a bench, looks the same as he did two decades before. It is apparent how much Torres Bodet had progressed since *Margarita de niebla* because he allowed Proust to inspire him rather than merely to influence him. For this reason, the narrator simply presents the sensations and feelings of the character and avoids commenting on them. This is, of course, more appropriate for the female protagonist, who does not intellectualize her experiences and is affected primarily by emotion. Likewise the setting in the church may have been suggested by Proust, who described the church in Combray and compared his novel to a cathedral, but Torres Bodet showed a certain independence by using this location which Proust might have rejected for being too closely bound to habit. Within the context of the entire novel, this highly emotional experience associated with Doña Eulalia's past and family helps the reader understand the woman's final decision to accept into her home the orphan son of her nephew. Even though she still feels hostility toward the latter and would have preferred a life of solitude to one of responsibility, she realizes all that she owes to her family and accepts her duty. Thus we can see how the theme of memory is joined to the other themes of this novel.

Another example of Proustian memory during this period can be found in *Las cenizas* [Ashes] (1942) by María Flora Yáñez. This Chilean author (who would later write at least two articles on Proust and was a relative of José Donoso) used quite adeptly a memory experience at the beginning of her text as a starting point for all that follows. After Irene recaptures an essential incident from her childhood, she begins to reflect upon her life in general and becomes aware of its emptiness. In contrast, with little structural justification another Chilean Magdalena Petit attributed a memory experience to a secondary character in her historical novel *Don Diego Portales* (1937). The emotion involved adds sense of poetry to the fragment, but the experience is disconnected from the novel as a whole.

During the early 1950s, Alejo Carpentier, who then wrote several brief articles on Proust in his column for *El Nacional,* began to use the theme of memory extensively in his novels, along with his principal subject time. In *Los pasos perdidos*, for example, we find the lengthy description of a memory experience. This passage, however, is more closely related to the recovery of the past through music found in "Un amour de Swann" than the memory experiences of the protagonist, which appear elsewhere in the *Recherche*.

The use of music to stimulate memory, which we saw in *Rodeada está d sueño* and "El árbol" in chapter 2, is in some sense less specifically Proustian. Several nineteenth century authors used music to evoke the past. Such was the case in George Sand's rustic novel *Les maîtres sonneurs* [The Master Ringers] (1853) and in the poem "La serenata de Schubert" by Manuel Gutiérrez Nájera. Nonetheless, Carpentier intentionally suggested his specific connection and possible wish to dialogue with the *Recherche* by placing his memory experience in a Proustian context. He made it occur in the presence of a blazing fire and aromatic herbs.[7] Both of these elements bring to mind the description of Tante Léonie's rooms, which immediately follows the *madeleine* episode in "Combray." After mentioning the numerous odors apparent in one of the rooms and how they were affected by a fire (see our discussion with regard to *Como agua para chocolate* in chapter 5), the narrator describes in profuse detail the dried leaves of the herb *tilleul*, which are used to make tisane. This passage begins: "Le dessèchement des tiges les avaient incurvées en un capricieux treillage dans les entrelacs duquel s'ouvraient les fleurs pâles . . . " [The drying of the stems had twisted them into a whimsical latticework in the interlacing of which pale flowers opened . . .] (1:51). In a similar manner Carpentier wrote of the wild herbs near the fireplace: "La joven se me acercó y, sacando hojas secas, musgos y retamas, para estrujarlas en la palma de su mano, empezó a alabar sus propiedades, identificándolas por el perfume" [The young woman approached me and, extracting dried leaves, mosses and broom stems, to crush them in the palm of her hand, she began to extol their characteristics, identifying them by their scent] (1969, 90).

I should also point out that Carpentier's introduction is linked to a more essentially Proustian memory experience which is embedded in the longer one stimulated by music. It in fact has a sensorial stimulus, the scent of hemp, and variations on this experience appear elsewhere in the novel (e.g., 47–48). The narrator remarks:

> Ese olor cuyo recuerdo regresa del pasado, a veces, con tal realidad que me deja todo estremecido. Ese olor que vuelvo a encontrar esta noche, junto al armario de las yerbas silvestres, cuando el *Adagio* concluye sobre cuatro acordes *pianissimo*. . . . (99–100)

> [That smell whose recollection returns from the past, at times, with such a sense of reality that it leaves me all trembling. That smell that I find again this evening, next to the cupboard of wild herbs, when the *Adagio* concludes *pianissimo* on four chords. . . .]

Studying the experience set in motion by the music, we can observe how it reflects many elements related to Proust and is well integrated into the novel as a whole. We find, for example near the beginning of *Los pasos perdidos,* that the protagonist's refusal to listen to the music by Beethoven is very similar to Swann's reaction to the sonata by Vinteuil. When he unexpectedly hears the *petite phrase* at the soirée of Mme. de Sainte-Euverte, Swann initially thinks: "N'écoutons pas!" [Let's not listen] (1:345).

As is well known, in section 9 (chapter 3) of *Los pasos perdidos* the protagonist ultimately listens to Beethoven's Ninth Symphony. The rural, Spanish America setting and the fact that the orchestra is not present contribute to his decision. With the radio transmission he is free to hear echoes from within his mind instead of just the musical notes. This symphony, which is very familiar to him, evokes his personal past, as does the sonata by Vinteuil for Swann. Carpentier's character first notices:

> Al cabo de tanto tiempo sin querer saber de su existencia, la oda me era devuelta con el caudal de recuerdos que en vano trataba de apartar del *crescendo* que ahora se iniciaba, vacilante aún y como inseguro del camino. (91–92)

> [After so much time of not wanting to know of its existence, the ode was returned to me with an exuberance of memories that I in vain tried to separate from the *crescendo* that now began, still hesitant and apparently unsure of its path.]

As mentioned in chapter 5, Carpentier's narrator recovers the image of his father through the sound of a horn and an associative process related to Proust's type of impressionism. Similarly because of the music, Swann feels as though Odette had entered the room. It is then that images from the past gush forth, and Swann recovers in great detail the stages of his love for Odette. For instance: "il sentit l'odeur du fer du coiffeur par lequel il se faisait relever sa 'brosse' . . . les pluies d'orage qui tombaient si souvent ce printemps-là, le retour glacial dans sa victoria. . ." [he perceived the smell of the barber's heating iron by which his 'crew cut' was made to stand up . . . the stormy rains that fell so often that spring, the freezing rides back in his victoria . . .] (1:345–46).

Perhaps to show that he doubted that a single musical phrase could could evoke all of the past in the manner of Proust, Carpentier used the various parts of the musical composition. With each successive movement of the Ninth Symphony, his character recalls a different stage in his life when he had heard it before. The coda reminds him of his father's singing it in their home in the Antilles and what his father said in the United States about European workers who often listened to the Ninth. Similarly the adagio evokes the time when his mother played it on the piano, and the chaotic beginning of the final movement brings to mind the end of the Second World War.

Another apparent difference can be seen in the consolation that Swann derives from the music. With each repetition of the *petite phrase* Proust's character comes to a fuller understanding of his love for Odette and of the meaning behind his suffering. By the end of the sonata he experiences "la grâce d'une résignation presque gaie" [the grace of an almost cheerful resignation] (1:348), which is a modernist form of redemption through art. In contrast, Carpentier's character does not attain the same degree of peace and resignation. Having grown up under the shadow of his father, he came to believe in the existence of intelligent, cultivated workers, who offered the hope of a more civilized world. This illusion was dashed when he found in Germany before the War mindless political activity and mass demonstrations. Even the Ninth Symphony became associated with his bitter realization when he heard Germans, who had created the concentration camps, sing the idealized words of Schiller's "Ode to Joy." In this circumstance all reference to human brotherhood seemed meaningless, and as a result Carpentier's character turned his back on the Symphony and that entire portion of his life.

Fortunately, as in Swann's case (and that of Brígida in "El árbol"), listening to music and the recovery of the past allow the protagonist of *Los pasos perdidos* to confront directly the causes of his anguish and to begin the healing process. This greater understanding of his past and of himself is by no means gratuitous. The recovery of his moments of happiness with the girl María del Carmen facilitates his union with the young woman who had described some of the herbs to him, Rosario. Indirectly, his reconciliation with Beethoven's most ambitious symphony, which included the participation of singers, opened the way for the creation of his own *treno* [choral piece]. I, of course, must acknowledge that the idyllic return to the past of Carpentier's character and his progress along the road toward authenticity come to naught when he leaves the village in the jungle and can no longer return to it. But, such a loss, like the others found in *Los pasos perdidos,* is even more regrettable because of its contrast with the joy experienced through the miracle of involuntary memory in *Le temps retrouvé.*[8]

PROUSTIAN MEMORY AND BOURGEOIS SENSUALITY 1955–1970

In the years that immediately preceded the Boom and at the beginning of this period of generally successful experimentation, Proust's ideas on involuntary memory were often used in conjunction with the new techniques employed. Just as Marcel Proust took advantage of spontaneous and associative memory to avoid a simple chronological order and a traditional plot-based structure and in this way created his own architectural design, numerous Spanish American writers attempted to do the same, particularly from the mid 1950s until the 1970s. Initially, they embraced Proust's modernist perspective, but as the years passed many of these same novelists became more experimental and began to question Proust's ideas and example. For this period, the number of Proust-like memory experiences was so large that I cannot discuss all of them here. In some cases, Proustian memory appears to have been used almost exclusively as a narrative technique to join different moments in time and diverse portions of the text. In such instances, the episodes involving memory often do not have a strong internal justification, nor are they intimately related to the specific personality of the characters. This seems to be true in one of the stories by René Marqués. In "El juramento" [The Oath] (*Otro día nuestro* [Another Day of Ours], 1955), the protagonist's present in the courtroom and his past on his first day of classes in Arecibo are in fact linked by the coldness of the floor and the sound of the judge's gavel. But, the Puerto Rican's political intention becomes excessively obvious when he has his character—originally from the site of the proclamation of freedom, Lares—recall how he was mistreated when he was unable to pledge allegiance to the United States flag.[9]

For the sake of brevity and quality of example, I have chosen to exclude those texts where Proustian memory is used only as a technique and has little to do with character development or other facets of the text. Furthermore, in this section I will restrict the discussion to an important subject of the period that was associated with a particular social class: the alleged immersion of the bourgeoisie in their sensuality and personal past.

Manuel Mujica Láinez, who had used familiar objects to evoke the past in *Los ídolos* (see chapter 6), created a more specifically Proustian memory experience in his fourth novel of those years *Invitados en "El Paraíso."* This episode is carefully integrated into the text and shows how this Argentine writer experimented with the functioning of memory.[10]

Upon meeting his hostess Tití, the painter Silvano has the impression that he has seen her face before, but he does not remember where or when. Likewise the mistress of the country estate vaguely recognizes Silvano. Throughout the novel both characters, who are now elderly and have changed considerably in appearance since their youth, try to recall the circumstances of their first encounter. Slowly but surely the author provides the elements that will eventually serve as the key. Once these are all present Silvano undergoes a memory experience, which is quite similar to those found in the *Recherche*. The mechanism differs only in the number of stimuli required: two instead of one. They are the figure of Othello and a traditional French song. In this memory experience we can even find the two stages consistently used by Proust, as Genette explained. The first is based upon an analogy whereby sensations in the present bring to mind identical ones from the past:

> La imagen de Otelo . . . trajo a su memoria, desgastada por los excesos y los años, la figura de la oleografía del Moro de Venecia que dio la clave. El canto de Kurt hizo lo demás. Fue como si, de dos polos, brotara la chispa. (1969, 227)

> [The image of Othello . . . brought to his memory, frayed by his excesses and the years, the figure from the cheap reproduction of the Moor of Venice, which offered the key. Kurt's song did the rest. It was as if a spark emerged from the two poles.]

Once this link with the former moment is established, Silvano is able to recover through the process of association those feelings and sensations that were contiguous in time and space:

> Al recobrarla, Silvano recobró el cuarto entero de la calle Maipú: la cama de hierro, el ropero, el baúl, y el fonógrafo. . . . Afuera, en el patio, entre las plantas, tres o cuatro mujeres con batones transparentes . . . se hacían aire con pantallas . . . más allá, en el zaguán iluminado, los vidrios de la puerta tenían visillos rosas. Y encima estaba el cielo de Buenos Aires, las estrellas. . . . (227–28)

> [Upon recovering it, Silvano recovered the entire room on Maipú Street: the wrought-iron bed, the wardrobe, the trunk and the gramophone. . . . Outside, in the courtyard, among the plants, three or four women with translucent dressing gowns . . . were moving air with their fans . . . farther along, in the lighted entryway, the glass of the door had pink lace curtains. And above was the sky of Buenos Aires, the stars. . . .]

In point of fact, Silvano's discovery is quite different from what the Proustian protagonist generally learned through involuntary memory and lacks the redemptive value of this phenomenon. The painter realizes that he had met Tití when she was a prostitute in Buenos Aires. Nonetheless, the results of the memory process are very similar.[11] Just as Silvano sees again the house and the city, the Proustian protagonist recovers all of Combray:

> Et dès que j'eus reconnu le goût du morceau de madeleine trempé dans le tilleul que me donnait ma tante . . . aussitôt la vieille maison grise sur la rue, où était sa chambre, vint comme un décor de théâtre s'appliquer au petit pavillon, donnant sur le jardin . . . et avec la maison, la ville. . . . (1:47)

[And as soon as I recognized the taste of the morsel of madeleine soaked in the lime-blossom tea that my aunt used to give me . . . immediately the old gray house on the street where her room faced appeared like the scenery of a play to attach itself to the little wing that opened onto the garden . . . and with the house, the town. . . .]

Within the larger context of the Argentine novel, Silvano's discovery plays an essential role. The painter, who fears losing his male secretary to a marriage that Tití wishes to arrange attempts to use his knowledge of the woman's past to force her to desist. But when Silvano tries to threaten her, his emotion is so intense that he suffers a stroke, which leads to his death. This interweaving of Proustian memory into a somewhat traditional plot structure illustrates how Mujica Láinez was inspired by the French author and suggests how he was moving toward a more innovative type of work, one where memory would play an even larger role. I am alluding to *Bomarzo,* whose discussion I will delay until the final section of this chapter because it entails a fully developed dialogue with the *Recherche.*

As for the Proustian memory mechanism itself, other Spanish American authors followed during the 1960s Mujica Láinez's lead. Not only did they experiment to some extent with Proust's ideas and techniques concerning involuntary memory, but also their characters were from the same social class as Silvano, and these persons recovered incidents from their past that were remarkably similar to the one experienced by Mujica Láinez's protagonist. For this reason we can detect an implicit, albeit brief dialogue with Proust's ideas on memory, as well as the possible influence of the Argentine novelist.

El peso de la noche [The Heaviness of the Night] (1965) by the Chilean Jorge Edwards is representative of the period and involves the retrospective point of view of the two principal male characters, who constantly think about their past. Edwards, who had written about Proust a few years earlier, used involuntary memory to intensify the emotions implied and to demonstrate the presence of the past. Both male protagonists— the high school student Francisco and his middle-aged uncle Joaquín— recover some of the most essential moments of their lives when they allow their past to invade their present. Francisco's lack of interest in classroom activities and Joaquín's drinking facilitate the process, but it is important to note that memory in this novel functions in an associative manner and is often spontaneously induced.

In particular, Francisco's memory experience at the beginning of *El peso de la noche,* which sets the tone for the entire work, is very reminiscent of Proust, even though Edwards has introduced specific modifications to the memory process. Here, the stimulus is primarily situational and does not involve one of the five senses as in the *Recherche*. Francisco hears a classmate tell how he forced a female servant to have sexual relations with him. In spite of this difference, the process of memory advances in a Proustian manner and physical sensations play another type of role. First of all, Francisco is affected by vague recollections which have a strong sensorial content, but he cannot immediately identify what he is remembering:

> El relato lo había dejado inquieto, con un asomo de angustia que no se delineaba. Imágenes confusas de la primavera del año anterior: duraznos recién florecidos, hojas nuevas de los plátanos orientales, olor agudo que emanaba de su cuerpo y se confundía con el olor cálido de la vegetación, de la tierra húmeda. . . . (1967, 13)

> [The story had left him uneasy, with a hint of anxiety that did not become clear. Jumbled images from the spring of the previous year: peach trees that had recently bloomed, new leaves on oriental banana trees, a penetrating odor that emanated from his body and became mixed with the warm fragrance of vegetation and moist earth. . . .]

As in the case of the madeleine episode where the Proustian protagonist first experiences a "tourbillon des couleurs remuées" [whirlwind of stirred-up colors] (1:46) and then is able to move beyond it, Francisco eventually perceives a distinct image from the past. This image, however, is not recovered through intense effort, as in the case of Proust's hero. It is merely the result of the associative process itself. Just the same Edwards used an impressionist description and metaphorical language to illustrate the mechanism, as did Proust:

> Las imágenes se iban hilvanando. Una rueca que se había desatascado sola, por efecto de un golpe involuntario, y se había puesto a hilar. . . . Los escombros rápidamente acumulados, arrojados ahí por la memoria, empezaban a despejarse.

> [The images strung themselves together. A spinning wheel that had become unblocked on its own as a result of an involuntary bump and had started to spin. . . . The quickly accumulated debris, tossed there by memory started to become clear.]

From this point Francisco's mind moves quickly to the image from the past itself:

> Veía una pieza con rajaduras en el papel de la pared, un paisaje del norte de Canadá recortado de una revista. . . . En la esquina del espejo, un ramo reseco de Domingo de Ramos. La música que atravesaba el tabique, desde la sala del lado se repetía una y otra vez. . . .

[He saw the room with shreds of paper peeling off the wall, a landscape from the north of Canada clipped from a magazine. . . . In the corner of the mirror a dried palm branch from Palm Sunday. The music that came through the partition, from the adjacent sitting room, was played again and again. . . .]

The third person narrator eventually depicts in detail the scene that Francisco remembered: the afternoon when he first had sexual relations with a prostitute. Curiously, the setting resembles the house of prostitution described in *Invitados en "El Paraíso"* and could suggest a connection, even though Edwards used his episode in a very different way than Mujica Láinez.

For the Chilean novelist, Francisco's recollection of the encounter with the prostitute and the incident itself portray the young man's initiation into the type of decadence represented by his uncle. The situation of both characters implies vice and a propensity to focus upon the past instead of the present or future. With the help of his family Joaquín had been able to survive with little effort and in spite of his worsening alcoholism. During his solitary drinking sessions, which are portrayed in detail, Joaquín recalls obsessively the past and his personal failures. With the death of Sra. Cristina (his mother and Franciso's grandmother) Joaquín realizes that he must take responsibility for his life, but at the funeral dinner he begins to drink again. In this context, spontaneous and associative memory appears to be vaguely connected with the upper middle class, but it is no longer treated in a nostalgic way and implies a critique of the bourgeoisie.[12] Francisco is more intelligent and sensitive than many of his school mates, but unless he can focus his attention upon a worthwhile activity, such as art or an intellectual career, he seems destined to follow the path of his uncle.

A similar situation and comparable use of involuntary memory can be found in one of the most famous Chilean novels of this period, whose relation with Proust has been frequently suggested: *Este domingo* (1966) by José Donoso. Here the aging upper middle class don Alvaro recovers an essential episode from his youth when he smells a plate of *empanadas* [pasties] that the former servant Violeta had prepared for the family. Georges R. McMurray has written of this connection, speaking of Alvaro:

> His recollection of the incident in question brings to mind the famous initial episode of Proust's *Remembrance of Things Past*, in which the taste of *madeleine* (sponge cake) dipped in tea reminds the narrator of a similar taste he experienced many years previously. . . . (1979, 73)

Moving beyond this clear parallel with regard to the sensorial stimulus and the evocative result, there are several things to be said about the intertextual relation between Donoso and Proust. Also, we should take into account the feasible contribution of Donoso's friend and contemporary Jorge Edwards. Similar to Edwards, but apparently one year later, the author of *Este domingo* both experimented and dialogued with the French novelist's treatment of memory.

Indeed, as McMurray suggested, Donoso did not discuss in a theoretical manner his ideas on memory, as Proust had done in *Du côté de chez Swann* and *Le temps retrouvé*. From a brief description of the aroma itself, which fills don Alvaro's car, and after a break in the text, the Chilean author moved immediately to an evocation of the past. I should emphasize that his procedure is different from the one employed by Edwards and Mujica Láinez. These contemporary writers, like many others, stated overtly that the character had begun to remember, and they described metaphorically the nature of the process. Donoso's technique of halting the narration and beginning again at a new point is masterfully conducted. Even though the author changes from a third person to a first person narrator and shifts from the present to the past, the smell of the *empanadas* and the day of the week associated with them, Sunday, make this transition relatively easy to follow. It is worth noting that such breaks were becoming widely accepted during the 1960s as part of the experimentation of the Spanish American Boom. But, also due to other reasons associated with Proust, José Donoso did not overly startle the reader of that time. By then, involuntary memory experiences were quite common and required no explanation. Furthermore like the French novelist himself, Donoso took advantage of the similarity between waking and remembering in order to transport both don Alvaro and the reader back to the past. As in the case of the beginning pages of *Du côté de chez Swann,* where the narrator refers to the experience of waking up and not knowing where he is or how old he is, Alvaro regains consciousness slowly and finds himself on a Sunday morning in the bedroom where he slept as an adolescent.

In this lengthy passage, which is clearly related to Proust because of the aroma of the pastry and the past, we find numerous other echoes from the early pages of the *Recherche*. Curiously the most significant involve nocturnal emissions and appear to have been inspired by the following portion of Proust's text:

Quelquefois, comme Eve naquit d'une côte d'Adam, une femme naissait pendant mon sommeil d'une fausse position de ma cuisse. Formée du plaisir que j'étais sur le point de goûter, je m'imaginais que c'était elle qui me l'offrait. (1:4)

[At times, just as Eve was born from one of Adam's ribs, a woman would be born during my sleep from the awkward position of my thigh. Conceived from the pleasure that I was about to enjoy, I imagined that it was she who offered it to me.]

Donoso, of course, further developed the subject of masturbation, which Proust had merely suggested. The Chilean novelist also used this subject to illustrate the fears and weaknesses of Alvaro, which would never totally be overcome in spite of his sexual initiation by Violeta. In this regard, we can suspect a link with *El peso de la noche,* where sexual contact between young masters and female servants is implied and where a Proust-like immersion in the past is associated with the bourgeoisie. Donoso was clearly less political in his orientation than Edwards and was primarily interested in character development. But, as we noted in the chapter on high society, Donoso regularly acknowledged a connection between Proust and the upper classes.

Examining specifically the function of don Alvaro's memory experience in *Este domingo,* we can observe how the use of the first person narrator, which was characteristic of Proust, offers the reader a totally different view of the character. His fear and indecisiveness are easily attributed to his young age and do not appear to be ridiculous or effeminate as in the case of the aging don Alvaro. Also, the subject of weekly rituals takes on a new significance when we see how important the Sunday *empanadas* were for young Alvarito and his social development. In short, the involuntary memory experience is very well integrated into Donoso's text and conveys a somewhat lengthy dialogue with the *Recherche,* which a Proustian reader can easily follow.

In this regard I wish to make one final point. Even though, unlike Edwards, Donoso later abandons the Proust-like retrospective stance, his focus on Sundays and Sunday rituals may be considered Proustian and carries the dialogue to the title, if not all of the text.[13] It does not seem by chance that Alvaro, like the Proustian protagonist, remembers precisely a Sunday morning when the smell of *empanadas,* like the taste of madeleine dipped in tea, provides a bridge to the past. A juxtaposition of the following two fragments should make this dialogue eminently clear:

Et tout d'un coup le souvenir m'est apparu. Ce goût c'était celui du petit morceau de madeleine que *le dimanche matin* à Combray . . . quand j'allais lui dire bonjour dans sa chambre, ma tante Léonie m'offrait après l'avoir trempé dans son infusion de thé ou de tilleul. (1:46–47, my emphasis)

[And in a flash the memory appeared to me. The taste was the one of the little morsel of madeleine that on *Sunday mornings* in Combray . . . when I went to her room to wish her a good day, my aunt Léonie offered me after having dipped it into her influsion of tea or lime-blossom.]

este domingo, este olor a domingo, a *domingo en la mañana* pero no muy temprano, cuando las sirvientas están atareadas en la casa . . . una limpiando el salón . . . otra canturreando en la cocina al destapar el horno para ver cómo están las empanadas. . . . (56–57)

[this Sunday, this aroma of Sunday, of *Sunday in the morning* but not very early, when the servants are busy with chores in the house . . . one cleaning the living room . . . another humming in the kitchen while opening the oven to see how the meat pies are doing. . . .]

To end my discussion of Proustian memory and bourgeois sensuality during the Boom period, I would like to consider one final example, which is not from Chile or Argentina where this type of relation was especially prevalent.[14] Its author was a woman from Costa Rica, Julieta Pinto, and the novel was entitled *La estación que sigue al verano* [The Season that Follows Summer] (1969).

In this text memory is likewise bound to the sentimental or sexual life of the characters, perhaps because both elements involve sensory perception and emotions, instead of human intellect or the practical facets of life. Here we can also detect the influence of another French writer, Michel Butor, but this relation complements rather than contradicts Proust's presence. The New Novelist from France, who had written about the *Recherche,* often experimented with Proust's ideas on time and memory, just like his Spanish American counterparts. It is, of course, likely that Butor's experimentation encouraged theirs.

The general subject of *La estación que sigue al verano* is quite similar to that of *La modification* [A Change of Heart] (1957), where Butor's protagonist attempts to decide during a train trip from Paris to Rome if he should once and for all leave his French wife in order to live with his Italian mistress. Pinto's four characters, like that of Butor, find themselves regularly confronted by the past when they consider the option of making an important change in their sentimental life. Also, we should note that the unfaithful husband in the Costa Rican novel holds much in common with the protagonist of the French work, but Pinto adds to the husband's point of view that of the man's wife, his mistress, and the latter's former spouse.

With regard to the treatment of memory, Julieta Pinto distinguished her text even more from that of Michel Butor, who generally used a situation in the present to evoke the past. In this regard, she is closer to Proust because for her, memory is almost always stimulated by a perception of the senses: a smell, a cold breeze, a word, etc. The most fully developed of these memory experiences, which appears near the beginning of the novel, is especially Proustian and sets the stage for all that follows. It is apparently triggered when one of the characters notices the slight movement of a bird. Also, the narrator suggests the mechanism involved:

> El aire y el tiempo se habían detenido. El pájaro inclinó la cabeza en actitud de escuchar. ¿Fue un movimiento de alas? ¿Fue la luz? El tiempo se lanzó hacia atrás, como en esos rollos de película que al devolverse nos muestran un comienzo que ya habíamos olvidado. (1969, 21)

> [The air and time had stopped. The bird tilted its head as if to listen. Was it a movement of its wings? Was it the light? Time hurled itself backwards, as with those rolls of film, which, upon rewinding, show us a beginning that we had already forgotten.]

FOUR EXTENDED NARRATIVE DIALOGUES ON SEARCHING FOR THE PAST AND FOR WHOLENESS

From the early 1960s until the near present, I have found several works in Spanish American narrative whose authors have tried to engage Proust's treatment of memory and text in a more active and extended manner. Not content merely to take advantage of or mildly experiment with Proust's ideas on involuntary memory and his example, these writers created their own interpretation of these ideas or sought to dispute them in a postmodern way. Furthermore, like Proust himself, these authors were often deeply concerned by the apparent differences that exist between a person's present and former selves and used memory to help reconcile these disparities. In their texts, to even a larger degree than in other cases, we often find a series of passages that are specifically related to Proust's text, and these prove to be extremely valuable. Not only do they serve to demonstrate the connection (as in most types of literary intertextuality), but also they constitute the actual exchanges in the prolonged conversation and can suggest the author's agreement or disagreement with Proust on one or more points.

One of the first and most audacious examples of this type of extended narrative dialogue can be found in *Rayuela* by Julio Cortázar. Here, somewhat like the Proustian protagonist who wished to join his present and former selves in order to achieve unity and wholeness, Horacio Oliveira semiconsciously searched for his past so that he could reach what he called "lo otro" [the other]. This search is not originally conscious, but arises in an involuntary way from Oliveira's subconscious. It makes itself known during the character's sleep and is closely bound to what the narrator calls in chapter 123 "el verdadero sueño" [the true dream]. He explains that this type of dream occurs when a person is partially awake and recalls a reality that is essentially his because he perceived it with the faith of a child. In this regard the narrator emphasizes "la casa de la infancia", which, as we saw in chapter 6, is treated in very Proustian terms.

Cortázar's dialogue with Proust's text is further developed by showing the effect of the dream upon Oliveira. This character becomes very confused about his present location when he gets out of bed and goes to the water closet. Like the protagonist at the beginning of *Du côté de chez Swann,* who, because of darkness and the imagined arrangement of the furniture, thinks that he is in one bedroom when he is actually in another, Oliveira believes that he is in his family's living room in Burzaco, Argentina instead of la Maga's room in Paris:

> Tal vez el verdadero sueño se le apareció en ese momento cuando se sintió despierto . . . a las cuatro de la mañana en un quinto piso de la rue du Sommerard y supo que la sala que daba al jardín en Burzaco era la realidad, lo supo como se saben unas pocas cosas indesmentibles. . . . (1986, 670)

> [Perhaps the true dream appeared to him at that moment when he felt that he was awake . . . at four in the morning on the fifth floor of the Rue du Sommerard and realized that the living room which faced the garden in Burzaco was his reality, he knew it as one knows a few undeniable things. . . .]

In itself, this circumstance derived from a dream and a half-wakened state may appear to be quite different from what Proust described at the beginning of his work. Mere light dispels the protagonist's illusion. Nonetheless, what Oliveira feels is very comparable to the Proustian involuntary memory experiences, where the past blocks out the sensations of the present. The narrator of *Le temps retrouvé* says of these moments,

> ces résurrections du passé, dans la seconde qu'elles durent, sont si totales qu'elles n'obligent pas seulement nos yeux à cesser de voir la chambre qui est près d'eux pour regarder la voie bordée d'arbres ou la marée montante; elles forcent nos narines à respirer l'air de lieux pourtant lointains. . . . (3:875)

> [these resurrections of the past, in the second that they last, are so totalizing that they not only compel our eyes to stop seeing the room that is close to them in order to look at the railway lined with trees or the rising tide; they even force our nostrils to breathe the air of places that are in fact far away. . . .]

Similarly, overpowered by a total memory experience which involves even his sense of smell, Oliveira actually believes that he is far away in the past:

supo sin ningún asombro ni escándalo que su vida de hombre despierto era un fantaseo al lado de la solidez y la permanencia de la sala . . . supo que el lugar era la sala de Burzaco con el olor de los jazmines del Cabo que entraba por las dos ventanas. (670)

[he realized without any surprise or shock that his life as a man awake was a mere fantasy when compared to the solidity and permanence of the living room . . . he realized that the real place was the living room in Burzaco with the fragrance of Cape jasmine entering through the two windows.]

Oliveira's case does not conform to Proust's explanation of involuntary memory because Cortázar wished show in his dialogue with the French novelist another type of stimulus. From his point of view, the past can be resurrected in a half-wakened state as well as through sensory perception. Although Proust had speculated on this possibility, and the good-night kiss episode, which was often recalled upon waking, may even be considered an example, the author of "Combray" rejected it because it was not as totalizing in its effects as his type of involuntary memory.[15] Just the same, the French author might have been somewhat sympathetic to Cortázar's addition because he appeared to anticipate it in the early pages of the *Recherche* where we read about a man who falls asleep in a nonhabitual setting:

Que s'il s'assoupit dans une position encore plus déplacée et divergente, par example après dîner assis dans un fauteuil, alors le bouleversement sera complet . . . le fauteuil magique le fera voyager à toute vitesse dans le temps et dans l'espace, et au moment d'ouvrir les paupières, il se croira couché quelques mois plus tôt dans une autre contrée. (1:5)

[Imagine that he dozes off in an even more abnormal or uncharacteristic position, for instance after dinner sitting in an armchair, then his confusion will be complete . . . the magical armchair will make him travel at top speed through time and space, and when he opens his eyelids, he will believe that he went to bed several months earlier in another region.]

On the other hand, it appears that Cortázar wished to confess his relation with Proust and to encourage the reader to follow this dialogue because he placed part of Oliveira's experience with the past precisely in a water closet. For a Proustian reader, this location is very significant because one of the memory episodes of the protagonist occurs in a water closet of the Champs Elysée. The narrator of *A l'ombre des jeunes filles en fleurs* begins this passage by saying:

Les murs humides et anciens de l'entrée où je restai à attendre Françoise dégageaient une fraîche odeur de renfermé qui, m'allégeant aussitôt des

soucis . . . me pénétra d'un plaisir non pas de la même espèce que les autres
. . . un plaisir consistant auquel je pouvais m'étayer. . . . (1:492)

[The old damp walls of the entryway, where I remained waiting for Françoise,
emitted a cool, musty smell, which, suddenly alleviating my worries . . . filled
me with a pleasure which was not of the same type as others . . . a solid
pleasure in which I could find support. . . .]

Between the two texts, we can note a greater contrast in the reaction of
the two protagonists than in the circumstances themselves of the incident involving memory. Unlike the Proustian protagonist, who derives
great pleasure from the resurrection of the past and would have preferred to continue it, Oliveira tries desperately to reject his own: "Hizo
un violento esfuerzo para salirse del aura, renunciar al lugar que lo
estaba engañando, lo bastante despierto como para dejar entrar la no-
ción de engaño, de sueño y vigilia . . . " [He made a violent effort to
escape from the aura, to reject the location that was deceiving him, since
he was enough awake to allow the notion of deception, sleep and
wakefulness to enter his mind . . .] (670). On a conscious level Oliveira
wishes to live in the present instead of the past, more like la Maga. But he
is fascinated by his search for "lo otro", and he finally realizes that his
memory experience in the water closet offers him the opportunity of
reaching his goal. At one point Oliveira explains to Ossip the impression
of ubiquity that dreams and memory give him and he calls himself "un
buzo de lavabos" [a wash-basin diver].[16] He even says "hasta ahora el
agujero más grande es el del lavabo" [up until now the largest hole is the
one in the wash basin] (330).

In our chapter on lost time, we saw how Oliveira unconsciously
searches for la Maga through women that resemble her. This nostalgic
type of involuntary memory associated with love becomes joined with the
variety that we are discussing in the asylum sequence in Buenos Aires.
After seeing Talita play hopscotch and momentarily imagining that this
woman is la Maga, Oliveira descends to the morgue with Talita.

This essential episode in the basement of the asylum has been interpreted in diverse ways and has been compared by some scholars with
surrealism. However, it clearly involves memory and conforms at least in
part to Proust's ideas on the involuntary recovery of the past. Although
these are not specifically stated, it is implicitly a sensation of coldness,
which contrasts with the sweltering heat of the asylum, that sets into
motion the memory process. Of Oliveira, the narrator writes: "mientras
cerraba la puerta de la *heladera* y se apoyaba sin saber por qué en el borde
de la mesa, un vómito de *recuerdo* empezó a ganarlo . . . " [while he was
closing the door of the *icebox* and was leaning without knowing why on

the edge of the table, a spewing forth of *memory* began to overcome him
. . .] (479, my emphasis). The sole mention of the stimulus without any
explanation should not surprise us any more than the case of the *empanadas* in *Este domingo,* which appeared a few years later. Also, the
similar temperature and/or humidity of the water closet in chapter 123
helps the reader to understand this memory experience, as does Morelli's remark in chapter 74 that "una accesión en la que culmina un
proceso de despojamiento enriquecedor" [a bout in which the process
of enriching divestment reaches fruition] can occur in a WC or anywhere else (548). Again, we should remember that "une fraîche odeur
de renfermé" [a cool, musty smell] in a water closet of the Champs
Elysées allowed the Proustian protagonist to recover a portion of his
past.

From the sensation of coldness, and wetness Oliveira feels as though
he were transported back to his past. Again the narrator does not explain, but the references to rain and pity and the fact that Oliveira speaks
in French seem to imply that he is remembering the time in which he led
Berthe Trépat home in the rain, although la Maga later becomes involved. As in the chapter on the true dream, Cortázar has introduced
other elements into the memory experience, most likely in response to
Proust for whom the past was recovered in a pure form. Notably,
Oliveira's recollection of Paris is affected by the presence and compassionate attitude of Talita:

> Estaba viendo con tanta claridad un boulevard bajo la lluvia, pero en vez de ir
> llevando a alguien del brazo, hablándole con lástima, era a él que lo llevaban
> . . . para que estuviera contento. . . . El pasado se invertía, cambiaba de
> signo. . . . (480)

> [He was seeing with great clarity a boulevard in the rain, but instead of
> leading someone by the arm, talking to her with pity, it was he who was being
> led . . . so that he might be content. . . . The past was inverted, it changed its
> sign. . . .]

In his dazed state, Oliveira kisses Talita as if she were someone else
most certainly la Maga. This type of substitution may also be related to
Proust, whose protagonist regularly kissed Albertine at night in *La prisonnière* in order to receive from her the type of peace and calm that his
mother provided in "Combray."[17] In any case, the kiss allows Oliveira to
join the past and the present and to advance toward "lo otro."[18]

This type of reconciliation of the past and present, of Paris and
Buenos Aires and of la Maga and Talita suggests how Cortázar used
Proustian memory in order to illustrate how one can advance from
common reality to "lo otro." The Argentine novelist, like his characte

Oliveira, did not accept all of Proust's ideas on memory and might have even preferred another means of reaching his goal. Nonetheless, Cortázar came to acknowledge the general validity of these ideas and chose to employ those aspects of Proustian memory that he found most appropriate. In his modifications we have seen the originality of *Rayuela*, as well as its dialogue with the *Recherche*. Although Cortázar's search for transcendence still ties him to modernism, his reinterpretation of memory demonstrates his wish to go beyond this movement.

Just one year before the appearance of *Rayuela* another ambitious Argentine novel was published, and it drew even more heavily upon Proustian memory to join together elements greatly separated by time and space. But, this novel, *Bomarzo*, was constructed in a very different manner. Its author Manuel Mujica Láinez, who had already written several novels related to the *Recherche*, used his ingenuity to create a novel that was highly original and profoundly Proustian at the same time.

Weary of his usual fare—the decadent upper classes of Buenos Aires—Mujica Láinez chose a subject distant from his own time and place of origin. He wrote about the sixteenth-century Italian duke who had created the garden of monstruous statues found at Bomarzo, a village and estate near Rome. On the surface, it might appear that this Argentine writer had decided to portray only *el lado de allá* [the side over there] and to neglect, at least in this work, *el lado de acá* [the side back here], but the situation in this lengthy novel is much more complex.

Bomarzo has the form of an autobiography, somewhat like the *Recherche*. Initially it seems as if a man from the renaissance is telling the story of his life: how he was born and how he became duke even though he was the second son rather than the first. Certain anomalies, however, alert the reader to the uniqueness of this case. Not only does the first person narrator refer to the sixteenth century, but also he talks about the twentieth as if he were still alive. His horoscope, which predicted a limitless existence, appears to have been accurate in spite of its seeming impossibility.

For the most part, Pier Francesco Orsini is all too human and ages like other mortals. Only his physical deformity (a humpback), his personal vices, his love for beauty, and his obsession with immortality define the uniqueness of his character. In his search for a life without end, he resorts to magic and sorcery, but none of his experiments appear to be successful. Only his artistic efforts which result in the creation of the monstruous statues offer him any real hope of prolonging his earthly life beyond its normal length. In the final chapter I will return to Pier Francesco's work of art, which is related to the *Recherche*, but *Bomarzo* is also very Proustian in its treatment of memory, and this in turn is tightly bound to the subject of immortality.

In Mujica Láinez's novel about the Italian renaissance can be found examples of involuntary memory similar to those which appear in the *Recherche* and *Invitados en "El Paraíso."* When Pier Francesco is in Bologna the sound of a dog's bark and the sight of a flower falling at his feet give him the impression of reliving an incident that had occurred in Florence a few years before:

> Una rosa cayó a mis pies, como cuando huía de Florencia, se me antojó que, por un prodigio, la máquina de Tiempo había andado hacia atrás y tornaba a proyectar gastadas imágenes, porque, gracias a la mágica virtud de esa flor y ese can . . . la muchedumbre tumultuosa . . . en vez de esperar la salida de Carlos Quinto de San Petronio acechaba la de los Médicis. . . . (1967, 258)

> [A rose fell at my feet, as when I was fleeing from Florence, and I fancied that, because of a miracle, the machine of Time had moved backwards and was projecting again worn-out images, because, thanks to the magical power of that flower and that dog . . . the tumultuous crowd . . . instead of waiting for the exit of Charles V from Saint Petronius was was lying in wait for the flight of the Medicis. . . .]

The inclusion of such involuntary memory experiences in these fictional memoirs constitutes an essential part of the author's carefully devised strategy and architectural design, which in many ways resemble Proust's manner of construction. As in the *Recherche,* the first person narrator of *Bomarzo* recalls numerous minute details from his distant past, but he does not explain the obvious contrast between his former and present selves, both of which are designated by the pronoun *yo.* Already in Proust's novel these two first persons appeared contradictory and cause the reader to ask, "how can a weak-willed person who has no faith in his own talent ever write the long, brilliant work that is being read?"[19] In the case of *Bomarzo* these differences are even more extreme. It is hardly conceivable that the sixteenth century Italian duke can ever become the twentieth century writer who mentions in passing Italian museums that he visited some years after World War II.

Throughout both of these novels, the narrators often play with these contrasts and distances while they intentionally delay their explanation of them until nearly the end of the text. Significantly the bridge between the former and present selves is essentially the same and thus confirms the implicit dialogue between these two works. As I already suggested, the involuntary memory experiences in *Le temps retrouvé* show the protagonist how to recover his past and how to write the story of his life. Similarly, but even later, on the final two pages of the Argentine novel the twentieth century narrator tells how he visited the garden at Bomarzo and realized not only that he had seen the statues before, but also that he had created them in a previous life. This surprising experience of *déjà vu* involves in a very real sense Proustian memory and entails both its spontaneous and associative phases. The narrator explains the nature of his endless life, which had only been suggested by Benedetto's horoscope:

> Yo he gozado del inescrutable privilegio, siglos más tarde—y con ello se cumplió, sutilmente, la promesa de Sandro Benedetto, porque quien recuerda no ha muerto— de recuperar la vida distante de Vicino Orsini, en mi memoria, cuando fui hace poco, hace tres años a Bomarzo . . . y el deslumbramiento me devolvió el tropel de imágenes y las emociones perdidas. (648–49)

> [I have enjoyed the inscrutable privilege, centuries later—and with it the promise of Sandro Benedetto was subtly fulfilled, because he who remembers has not died—to recover the distant life of Vicino Orsini, in my memory, when I went a short time ago, just three years ago to Bomarzo. . . and the dazzling experience returned to me a throng of lost images and feelings.]

In the subsequent passage the narrator also suggests how he was able to recover his entire life and to write his lengthy text by examining the individual statues and by using in a conscious manner associative memory. Within this context he also refers in a vague way to Buenos Aires:

> En una ciudad vasta y sonora, situada en el opuesto hemisferio, en una ciudad que no podía ser más diferente al villorio de Bomarzo, tanto que se diría que pertenece a *otro planeta*, rescaté mi historia, a medida que devanaba la áspera madeja viejísima y reivindicaba, día a día y detalle a detalle, mi vida pasada, la vida que continuaba viva en mí. (649, my emphasis)

> [In a vast and noisy city, located in the opposite hemisphere, in a city that could not be more different from the isolated village of Bomarzo, so much so that one would say that it belongs to *another planet*, I recaptured my story as I spun the very old, rough skein and I restored, day by day and detail by detail, my former life, the life that remained alive in me.]

In spite of the obvious similarites with regard to involuntary memory, we can ascertain the originality of Mujica Láinez in his interpretation of it. He has rendered Proustian memory fantastic, which seems quite appropriate given his imagination, which had assigned the role of narrator to the mansion in *La casa*, as well as that of his fellow countrymen Julio Cortázar, Jorge Luis Borges, and Adolfo Bioy Casares.

In this interpretation we can also detect a more specific dialogue with the *Recherche*. Proust himself spoke in his novel on several occasions of the feasibility of a previous life. In fact, on the very first page of *Du côté de chez Swann* we find a direct allusion. To describe how quickly upon waking one often forgets an idea found in a dream, the narrator says,

"Puis elle commençait à devenir inintelligible, comme après la *métempsycose* les pensées d'une existence antérieure . . . " [Then it started to become unintelligible for me, as after a *transmigration of souls* the thoughts of a former existence . . .] (1:3, my emphasis). But, in spite of this remark the Proustian protagonist recovers through involuntary memory only his own life and never that of another person or of a former existence. He admits that such may be conceivable and even suspects that certain unidentifiable reminiscences could have come from a former life, if not from a dream. Apparently, from these mere suggestions Mujica Láinez created much of *Bomarzo* because his narrator does in fact recover another man's past. In this light, a few statements found in the *Recherche* take on a totally different meaning. It is as if the French author had anticipated the Argentine's novel or Mujica Láinez responded in a monumental way to Proust's text. Such is indeed the case of a fragment from *Sodome et Gommorhe* where the narrator discusses the nature of forgetfulness and suggests that the recovery of another man's life may be possible:

> Si je puis avoir en moi et autour de moi tant de souvenirs dont je ne me souviens pas, cet oubli . . . peut porter sur une vie que j'ai vécue dans le corps d'un *autre homme, même sur une autre planète*. Un même oubli efface tout. (2:985, my emphasis)

> [If I can have in me and around me so many memories which I do not remember, such a forgetfulness . . . can extend as far as a life that I have lived in the body of *another man, even on another planet*. The same forgetfulness erases everything.]

Although it may be coincidental that Proust, just like Mujica Láinez in his last passage cited above, refers to a man from another planet to show the distance that can be spanned by memory, their dialogue seems undeniable. I would point out, however, that it involves elaboration rather than questioning and thus remains within the limits of modernism, unlike the two dialogues that follow.

Alejo Carpentier, who had used Proustian memory since *Los pasos perdidos*, developed the theme of memory systematically throughout *El recurso del método*. He wished to show the differences between the present and the past and the consequences of ignoring one's own cultural authenticity. In this general area, Carpentier engaged Proust and apparently several Spanish American Proustians in an extended narrative dialogue.

In chapter 3, we saw how the social and cultural ambitions of the protagonist of *El recurso del método* led him to commit atrocities in order to maintain his wealth and power, but these violent actions resulted in his rejection by Parisian high society. On another level, that of his consciousness, we can detect a similar dysfunction. His personal ambition runs contrary to his sensory perception, emotions, and relationship to Hispanic culture. Significantly, these feelings are most intimately bound to memory, which is treated in a very Proustian way.

When the Primer Magistrado travels to the New World to reestablish his power, certain smells and tastes cause him to recover the past and in turn weaken his defenses:

> Aflojado en mis iras por el reencuentro con lo mío, advertí, en el pálpito de una iluminación, que este aire era aire de mi aire; que una agua ofrecida a mi sed, tan agua como otras aguas, me traía, de repente, remembranzas de olvidados sabores, ligados a rostros idos, a cosas recogidas por la mirada, archivadas en mi mente. Respirar a lo hondo. Beber despacio. Vuelta atrás. (1974, 44–45)

> [Abated in my fury by reencountering what is mine, I noticed, with the hunch of an enlightenment, that this air was the air of my air, that the water offered for my thirst, brought me, suddenly, the recollection of forgotten tastes, linked to departed faces, to things gathered by a glance, stored in my mind. Breathe deeply. Drink slowly. Flash back.]

To his pragmatic sense such tender feelings induced by spontaneous memory constitute an inner opponent, which he feels the need to repress in order to retain his power. The Primer Magistrado is convinced that he must recover his aggressiveness: "Había que ser duro, implacable: lo exigían las Fuerzas implacables . . . " [I needed to be hard, relentless, the Relentless Forces demanded it . . .] (45). Only when he returns to Europe can he allow smells and tastes free reign and his personal tendency toward nostalgia to prevail. In this context, the Cuban novelist chose to join the theme of memory explicitly with Proust and perhaps one of his early Spanish American followers. Somewhat like the Colombian Luis López de Mesa's character in *La tragedia de Nilse,* the protagonist of *El recurso del método* recovers Paris through sensations associated with its traditions of food and in particular its fine pastry:[20]

> Todo hablaba en lenguaje de olores y sabores sobre y detrás del cinc de los bares: las brioches, en sus pequeñas canastas; las *magdalenas, estriadas como veneras de Compostela* en cuadrados pomos de cristal. . . . (92, my emphasis)

> [Everything spoke in the language of smells and tastes on and behind the zinc counters of the bars: the brioches, in their small baskets; the *madeleines fluted like the scallop shells from Compostela* in square glass containers. . . .]

Here, of course, the reference to the madeleines is overtly Proustian and serves as a knowing glance or wink to the readers of the *Recherche*. Emblematically, Carpentier even described the pastry in the same manner as the French novelist. Both texts refer to its shape which resembles the shells of Santiago de Compostela. The narrator of *Du côté de chez Swann* notes, "ces gâteaux courts et dodus . . . qui semblent avoir été moulés dans *la valve rainurée d'une coquille de Saint-Jacques*" [those squat, plump cakes . . . that seem to have been molded in the fluted valve of a scallop shell of Saint James] (1:45).

As we have seen, according to some interpretations of Proust's presence in *El recurso del método,* the numerous allusions to the *Recherche* reflect Carpentier's desire to parody it in an attempt to free himself from the French author's allegedly stifling influence. In the above cited passage, as in his centenary lecture on Proust, Carpentier demonstrated far more respect and admiration than irony and exaggeration. Thus, once again I question this Bloomian reading.

The treatment of involuntary memory in the Cuban novel culminates in a passage near the end which is very Proustian. Most certainly, this fragment has a critical intent but, as I suggested in chapter 3 and as Graziella Pogolotti implied, Carpentier's negative assessment is directed far more against inauthentic Spanish Americans than against Marcel Proust. In this case, it is not the dictator who is affected involuntarily by his past, but rather his pretentious daughter, who persists in her European social ambitions and snobbery even after her father has been defeated militarily and socially.

Ofelia's experience with memory can be considered one of the most complete to have been written in Spanish America because it dialogues with so many aspects of Proust's text and appears to allude to the works of several Spanish American Proustians. This experience even encompasses a previous mental state, whose imperviousness, contrary to appearances, makes the character especially vulnerable. In this way, Ofelia closely resembles the Proustian protagonist, who feels very depressed and discouraged before he tastes the *madeleine* dipped in tea: "Et bientôt, machinalement, accablé par la morne journée et la perspective d'un triste lendemain, je portai à mes lèvres une cuillerée du thé où j'avais laissé s'amollir un morceau de madeleine" [And soon, in a mechanical manner, being overwhelmed by the dismal day and the prospect of a sorrowful tomorrow, I raised to my lips a spoonful of the tea in which I had allowed to soften a morsel of madeleine] (1:45). In Ofelia's case, having been rudely awakened by the French cook, who complained bitterly about the dark-skinned woman who had left her kitchen in terrible disarray by preparing "des mangeailles de sauvage" [pigswill of savages], the daughter of the former dicatator is in no mood to accept anything served by Elmirita: "Ofelia estuvo por patear la improvisada mesa y acabar violentamente con el holgorio. Pero, ahora, un tamal de maíz, alzado en tenedor, se acercaba a sus ojos, descendiendo a su boca" [Ofelia favored kicking over the makeshift table and violently doing away with the revelry. But, now, a corn tamale, being raised on a fork, approached her eyes, as it descended to her mouth] (314). Suddenly, in a nearly identical manner, the taste of the pastry—both of which are very authentic to their region—has an almost miraculous effect upon the adversely inclined person. Proust's narrator says, "Mais à l'instant même où la gorgée mêlée des miettes du gâteau toucha mon palais, je tres-saillis, attentif à ce qui se passait d'extraordinaire en moi. Un plaisir délicieux m'avait envahi, isolé, sans la notion de sa cause" [But at that very instant when the mouthful mixed with cake crumbs touched my palate, I trembled, paying close attention to the extraordinary thing that was happening to me. A delightful pleasure had invaded and isolated me, but I had no sense of its cause] (1:45). Of Ofelia we read: "Cuando lo tuvo frente a la nariz, una emoción repentina, venida de adentro, de muy lejos, de un pálpito de entrañas, le ablandó las corvas, sentándola en una silla" [When she had it in front of her nose, a sudden emotion, coming from inside, from far away, from a presentiment of her entrails, softened the back of her knees, making her sit down on a chair].

The principal difference between Proust's text and Carpentier's is not the critical distance that is associated with parody, but rather the contrast between what is explained and what is implicit. Unlike the protagonist of *Du côté de chez Swann,* who tries to understand what is happening and makes an intense effort to identify the image within himself, Ofelia simply recovers a very rich moment from her past. In this regard, she more closely resembles don Alvaro in *Este domingo* or Oliveira in *Rayuela.* Also, due to her impression of being younger she is like Doña Eulalia in *Sombras:* "Mordió aquello y de súbito, su cuerpo se le aligeró de treinta años. Estaba, de calcetines blancos, recogidos los moños con papelillos de China, en el patio de los metates y del tamarindo" [She bit into that thing and unexpectedly, her body became lighter by thirty years. She was, with white socks, with her hair drawn up in Chinese curlpapers, in the courtyard of the grinding stones and the tamarind tree].

In response to the suggestion of a parodic intent I would also point out that Ofelia's recovery of the past is remarkably similar in content and tone to what the protagonist of *Los pasos perdidos* recaptured through the scent of hemp. We read in this earlier work, "Llamo a María del Carmen, que juega entre las arecas en tiestos, los rosales en cazuela, los semilleros de claveles, los girasoles del traspatio de su padre el jardinero" [I call María del Carmen, who is playing among the potted Areca palms, the rose bushes in pans, the carnation seedbeds, the sunflowers from the back patio of her father, the gardener] (1969, 99). Ofelia, like the protagonist in this previous novel, recalls a time when she had direct contact with very humble people and the physical environment and customs of Spanish America.

In both of these memory experiences, I find even specific parallels with the first major example of Proustian memory in Spanish America, the one that we saw in *Ifigenia*. The protagonist of Teresa de la Parra also recovers a similarly humble image, and surprisingly her childhood friend has the exact same name as the playmate in *Los pasos perdidos:* María del Carmen. Furthermore, in the Venezuelan novel (which Carpentier may have read while he was living in Caracas), María Eugenia recalls sitting on the grass with her black playmate under a particular kind of tree: "guayabos colgados de fruta" [guava trees laden with fruit] (1991, 165). In *El recurso del método* Ofelia sees herself in a nearly identical position and recovers precisely the smell of the fruit *guayabas:*

> Y bajaban hacia ella las pardas pulpas del árbol, metidas en sus crujientes estuches de pergamino canelo, trayéndole un agraz agridulce que le ponía bajo la lengua, olvidadas salivas. Y aquel devuelto olor de guayabas fermentadas—equívoco mosto de pera y frambuesa—. . . . (1974, 315)[21]

> [And the brown, pulpy fruit of the tree dangled before her, wrapped in its rustling pods of cinnamon-colored parchment, evoking for her a bitter-sweet grape juice which placed under her tongue forgotten salivas. And that recaptured fragrance of fermented guavas—an ambiguous must of pear and raspberry—. . . .]

In Carpentier's innumerable details, we find the effects of associative memory, which correspond to all of Combray as it was recaptured in Proust's work. From the taste of the *tamal de maíz*, which links Ofelia to a specific moment and location in her childhood, other sensorial perceptions are added to her experience because of their spatial and temporal contiguity. These sensations include the smells of a kitchen, the sight of a newborn calf and even the cries of a *pregonero* [peddler]. We recall that Carpentier spoke in his lecture of the use of such cries in the *Recherche,* and this detail also functions as a knowing glance to his Proustian readers.[22]

As for the humble source of Carpentier's details and their apparent contrast with the more refined world of the French provinces recaptured by the Proustian protagonist, this difference does not necessarily entail parody as has been suggested.[23] The Cuban author merely wished to demonstrate the lower-class origins of Ofelia and her father, which they had tried to ignore. For Carpentier, such a past, like the *tamal de maíz* itself, was authentic and worthy to be considered Spanish American. For this reason Ofelia remembers even a song that she knew when she was seven years old.

Following her memory experience Ofelia undergoes a perceptible, although not total change. Indeed, she does not become a writer like the Proustian protagonist, nor does she forget about her upper-class friends. At the end of the novel, like the Duc de Guermantes, who chooses to delay the announcement of a relative's death so that he can attend a social event, Ofelia does the same concerning her father's demise so that she can go to the Drags. Nonetheless, after recovering her past, she radically modifies her attitude toward Elmirita, the Hispanic food that this woman prepared, the party that is in progress and even Spanish American culture in general. Ofelia wants to taste all the dishes, she sits on her father's lap, and she sings and dances with Elmirita. In spite of their difference in age, educational level, social class and perhaps ethnic group, these two women become friends. They stroll around Paris together and take turns caring for the ailing ex-dictator. Ofelia's new moral assessment of Elmirita is very revealing because it specifically alludes to the world of Proust's novel. Referring to Mme Verdurin, who reached the pinnacle of French society in *Le temps retrouvé* when she married the Prince de Guermantes, Ofelia tells her father that Elmirita is "mucho más decente y más honrada que muchas de las amigas de la Madama esa, de las tenidas musicales, que ya no quiere verte desde que se ha metido a princesa" [much more decent and honorable than many of the friends of that lady who had the musical gatherings, but no longer wants to see you since she has become a princess] (317).

Ultimately, Carpentier joins the themes of memory and social ambition to his overriding subject of authenticity. I cannot claim that by the end of the novel Ofelia has warmly accepted the customs of Spanish America, in the manner of her defeated and dying father. But, somewhat like the protagonist of *Los pasos perdidos* after his memory experience, Ofelia has at least begun to realize that she should not sever her present from the past. In spite of her desire to be like upper-class Europeans, she will necessarly retain her humble but worthy Spanish American origins, as Proustian memory may illustrate again to her in the future. In this way, as in so many others, we can observe Carpentier's extended dialogue with Proust's text. Even though the Cuban author has demonstrated more respect than irony toward the *Recherche*, he has clearly installed *El recurso del método* in Proust's world and treated literature and history as constructs. Thus we can consider this novel (like *El siglo de las luces,* which Hutcheon cited herself) to be a historiographic metafiction.

A much more obvious example of parody directed against Proustian memory can be found in Bryce Echenique's short story "Magdalena peruana" [Peruvian Madeleine] (1986).[24] In this case, don Eduardo recovers the happiness of his past from the odor of his own flatulence. Having lived in Paris and Madrid for thirty-five years, this friend of the narrator's grandfather dines one day by chance in a new Peruvian restaurant. There, even more than the taste of the chicken prepared with *aji* [red pepper], the flatulence that it produced allows him to recover from the beginning of the century a lost friendship in Lima. His pleasure is so intense that he decides to eat the same dish every subsequent Thursday:

> con la esperanza de un nuevo pedo, *en busca del tiempo perdido* o del viento perdido, más bien, en su caso, con el más tierno deseo de un *tiempo recobrado* como único medio de volver a encontrarse con su viejo amigo don Felipe Alzamora. . . . (1989, 187, my emphasis)

> [with the hope of a new fart, *in search of lost time* or of lost wind, rather, in his case, with the most tender desire of *time regained* as the only means of meeting again his old friend don Felipe Alzamora . . . .]

This comical incident involving memory also explains don Eduardo's happiness at the end of his life when, as he dies in his garden, he is able both to reproduce the experience and to make a joke about his flatulence by calling it "una magdalena peruana."

Bryce's parodic intent is, of course, very explicit because there are direct references to Proust, whose work don Eduardo had read carefully. The Peruvian author has followed the well-known ideas on involuntary memory but with a humorous, critical distance. He did this by linking an unmentionable subject—farts —with the beautiful madeleine episode, thus deflating through ridicule a subject which has been treated with great respect and often tenderness. Similarly the narrator plays constantly with Proust's concepts and vocabulary within the same scabrous context. Besides the two translated titles highlighted above, I will cite one other example. In this case, Proust's idea of recovery is combined with the title of Margaret Mitchell's famous novel: "recuperó íntegro lo que el viento se llevó" [he recovered completely what was gone with the wind].

Since *El recurso del método*, the most important Spanish American dialogue on Proustian memory is the one found in *Como agua para chocolate*.[25] Víctor Zamudio-Taylor and Inma Guiu suggested this connection in general terms: "Involuntary memory in *Like Water for Chocolate*—modeled after Proust's *A la recherche du temps perdu* . . .—is brought about in the process of cooking and the visceral relationship the narrator has with gastronomy" (1994, 47). Indeed Proustian memory plays an important role in the development of several chapters in the text. As Kathleen M. Glenn pointed out, while Tita is preparing the wedding cake "the aroma of a newly-opened jar of jam transports Tita back to the afternoon when she made the preserves" (1994, 45). Similarly, the feel of sausage in her hands causes her to remember an incident involving Pedro (1990, 100–02). These scholars, however, did not explain how Laura Esquivel used the various categories of memory to suggest her disagreement as well as agreement with Proust.

For the most part, the Mexican novelist, like Carpentier, associated memories with smells and tastes, particularly as these are derived from food. Even though her sensorial range might appear to be more limited than Proust's—he dealt with all five senses—it must be noted that Esquivel displayed a very broad range concerning memory itself.

Early in *Como agua para chocolate*, the narrator shows Tita's pleasure upon evoking semiconsciously the past. While she waits between the various steps of sausage making, she freely allows odors to affect her memory:

> es muy agradable gozar del olor que despide, pues los olores tienen la característica de reproducir tiempos pasados junto con sonidos y olores nunca igualados en el presente. A Tita le gustaba hacer una gran inhalación y viajar junto con el humo y el olor tan peculiar que percibía hacia los recovecos de su memoria. (16)

> [it is very pleasant to savor the aroma that it exudes, since smells have the characteristic of reproducing times past along with sounds and smells never equaled in the present. Tita liked to inhale deeply and travel along with the very unique smoke and aroma that she perceived toward the recesses of her memory.]

This type of evocation might appear to be quite different from what has been called Proustian memory. But, in the volumes prior to *Le temps retrouvé* the protagonist experiments with such modes of recalling the past. Near the beginning of *La prisonnière*, for example, we find the same kind of semiconscious evocation in a fragment which may even be intertextually related to the one cited above:

> Françoise venait allumer le feu et pour le faire prendre y jetait quelques brindilles dont l'odeur, oubliée pendant tout l'été, décrivait autour de la cheminée un cercle magique dans lequel, m'apercevant moi-même en train de lire tantôt à Combray, tantôt à Doncières, j'étais aussi joyeux . . . que si j'avais été sur le point de partir en promenade. . . . (3:26)

> [Françoise would come to light the fire and to make it take off tossed upon it some twigs whose scent, having been forgotten during the entire summer, traced around the fireplace a magical circle within which, seeming to glimpse myself in the act of reading at times in Combray or in Doncières, I was as gleeful . . . as if I was about to take a walk. . . .]

Here, the parallels are manifest. In both cases, smells are eagerly used to stimulate memory. The past is evoked as if by magic. The person involved has the impression of traveling through time and space and derives great pleasure from the memory experience.[26]

However, more importantly, there appears in *Como agua para chocolate* one fully developed involuntary memory experience similar to those that we have discussed throughout this chapter. I am referring to the episode where Tita eats the *caldo de colita de res* [oxtail soup] that Chencha prepared and served to her at Dr. Brown's house. This memory experience could be compared to some of our Spanish American examples, but it is generally closer to those found in Proust's work.

In this episode, as in the *Recherche* and *El recurso del método,* the protagonist at first feels separated from the past, but more like Proust's character than Carpentier's, Tita has a sense of being blocked in what she most aspires to do. In the same way as the protagonist of *Du côté de chez Swann* is discouraged by his inability to write, Tita is so traumatized by the altercation with her mother that she cannot even remember how to cook. Furthermore, all three characters undergo a memory experience when they taste a particular type of food that they enjoyed in the past, but the spoonful of soup more closely resembles the spoonful of tea and *madeleine* than the *tamal de maíz.* Concerning the initial effects of the taste of the soup on Esquivel's character we read: "Cuando dio *el primer sorbo* Nacha llegó a su lado y le acarició la cabeza mientras comía, como lo hacía cuando de niña se enfermaba y la besó repetidamente la frente" [When she took the first sip, Nacha came to her side and caressed her hair while she ate, as she used to do when as a girl Tita became sick, and she kissed her forehead repeatedly] (131, my emphasis). Clearly, "el primer sorbo" is more like Proust's phrase "à l'instant même où la gorgée . . . toucha mon palais" than Carpentier's "Mordió aquello," but all three cause essentially the same result (see the other examples above). Indeed, one might suspect an important difference because of the sudden appearance of the deceased Nacha, but to some extent this old cook corresponds to Tante Léonie, who is recovered through the tea and *madeleine* because she had served these elements to the protagonist in "Combray." On the other hand, we note that Esquivel increases the magical sense of her text by treating Nacha as a type of fairy godmother.

Perhaps the most specifically Proustian aspect of Tita's memory experience can be seen through the manner in which Esquivel took advantage of the two stages of the memory mechanism. Not only does Tita pass through the analogical (or metaphorical) stage when the taste of the soup in the present links her to a moment of eating soup in the past, but also her subconscious proceeds to the associative (or metonymical) stage. As in *Invitados en "El Paraíso," El recurso del método,* and the *Recherche* itself, Tita feels as though she had recovered by association all of her "Combray":

> Ahí estaban, junto a Nacha, los juegos de su infancia en la cocina, las salidas al mercado, las tortillas recién cocidas, los huesitos de chabacano de colores, las tortas de navidad, su casa, el olor a leche hervida . . . . (131–32)

> [There they were, along side Nacha, the games of her childhood in the kitchen, the outings to the market, the recently prepared tortillas, the colored apricot pits, the Christmas rolls, her house, the smell of boiled milk. . . .]

In a true sense, Laura Esquivel has used Proustian involuntary memory as an important component of her magical realism. This use of Proust's text is of course justifiable because, as we saw in our discussion of García Márquez, Proust often referred to genies and other magical beings to show the effects of the miracle of memory. Likewise, when his protagonist is deeply moved by the presence of three trees near Balbec but cannot recall where he saw them before, he considers the possibility that he was under a type of spell: "Cependant ils venaient vers moi; peut-être apparition mythique, ronde de sorcières ou de nornes qui me proposait ses oracles" [In the meantime they were coming towards me; perhaps they were a mythical apparition, a dance of witches or of Norns who were offering me their oracles] (1:719). It is thus quite significant that after the oxtail soup episode Esquivel's narrator mentions the *zootropo* which Tita had received as a child and apparently recovered through involuntary memory. This visual toy corresponds directly to the magic lantern described in Proust's text and which some critics have viewed as a symbol of the mysterious elements found in the *Recherche.*[27]

Throughout *Como agua para chocolate,* the author plays with the idea that food can serve as a stimulus for memory. Nacha's recalling all of the wedding feasts of her past because of the taste of *turrón* [nougat] conforms in general terms to the mechanism of involuntary memory, although her death due to an excess of memory does not. Such exaggeration, as well as that implied in the first nostalgic and then visceral reaction by the wedding guests to the cake and icing adulterated by Tita's tears, suggests Esquivel's at times parodic intent with regard to involuntary memory.

As for a more conscious means of recalling the past associated with food, this aspect is developed as the text advances. Like the narrator of "Combray" who suggests that he carried his impressions home like fish or that the freshness of a rushing stream can be stored in a glass jar (1:168), Tita tries to pack in the suitcase for Gertrudis the memories of their first communion, including the tastes of *tamales* and of *atole* [maise-flour drink] (77). Later, we see how Gertrudis herself feels the desire of carrying into battle the smells and tastes of her maternal home. For this reason, she packs *torrejas de natas* [cream fritters] in her saddle bags (203).

In all of these details a Proustian reader can follow an implicit dialogue between Esquivel's text and the *Recherche*. I should emphasize, however, that Laura Esquivel, like Tita, was indeed capable of protesting against her forebear. For this reason the following remark by the narrator seems emblematic in its intention: "Tita sabía que dentro de las normas de la casa no estaba incluido el diálogo, pero aun así, por primera vez en su vida intentó protestar . . . " [Tita knew that within the norms of the house dialogue was not included, but even so, for the first time in her life he tried to protest . . .] (17).

Along with the allusions to both involuntary and semiconscious memory, we find several examples of conscious or voluntary memory. In specific circumstances, like Oliveira in the first chapter of *Rayuela*, Tita forces herself to recall the past. During the ceremony of Rosaura's marriage to Pedro, for example, Tita intentionally evokes moments from her childhood in order to escape from a present that she finds extremely distasteful:

> Se transportó al día en que a los 9 años se había ido de pinta con los niños del pueblo. . . . Se fueron a la orilla del río grande para ver quién era capaz de cruzarlo a nado, en el menor tiempo. Qué placer sintió ese día al ser ella la ganadora. (42)

> [She transported herself to the day in which at age 9 she had played hooky with the boys of the town. . . . They went to the bank of the big river to see who could swim across it in the shortest time. What pleasure she felt that day when she was the winner.]

Within a Proustian context this type of memory, like that of Oliveira's game, appears rebellious and suggests Esquivel's rejection of Proust's idea that the richness of the past cannot be recalled at will.[28] In *Como agua para chocolate*, the author never makes explicit her opposition to Proust, but it is very revealing that at the climax of her novel the protagonist uses precisely this type of memory, which is then called "artificial." I should also note that this method proves to be successful because Tita is able to reignite her emotions and join her beloved Pedro in death:

> Al masticar cada fósforo cerraba los ojos fuertemente e intentaba reproducir los recuerdos más emocionantes entre Pedro y ella. La primera mirada que recibió de él, el primer roce de sus manos, el primer ramo de rosas, el primer

beso. . . . Y logró lo que se proponía. Cuando el fósforo que masticaba hacía contacto con la luminosa imagen que evocaba, el cerillo se encendía. (243)

[As she chewed each match, she closed her eyes tightly and tried to reproduce the most exciting memories that she shared with Pedro. The first gaze that she received from him, the first touch of their hands, the first bouquet of roses, the first kiss. . . . And she succeeded in her purpose. When the match that she was chewing made contact with the brilliant image that she evoked, it burst into flames.]

This final experience plus the one stimulated by the taste of ox-tail soup serve to demonstrate that for Esquivel both voluntary and involuntary memory can allow a person to return to the past and to recover part of it.[29] Even though the use of will runs contrary to Proust's theories, I should point out that Tita's conscious recollection of the most important moments of her relationship with Pedro helps to unify the structure of *Como agua para chocolate* in the same way as Swann's spontaneously remembering the various stages of his love affair with Odette contributes to the unity of "Un amour de Swann." In both cases, the reader is reminded of what has occurred before and can survey the entire text as a whole. In a similar manner following Proust, García Márquez had joined different moments in time, as we saw in chapter 6.

In conclusion, as in the chapter on art, we can observe Esquivel's postmodernism. She installed her novel within a Proustian framework with which she toyed and dialogued and which on occasion she parodied and contested.

Moving beyond this work we can see how the creation of textual unity through memory suggests one of Proust's most significant contributions to the Spanish American novel. Indeed, by following the example of Proustian memory numerous writers were able to add to the poetic, emotional, and even magical quality of their texts. But, Proust's type of memory, which was not controlled by will or reason and arose from the subconscious spontaneously and associatively, also allowed the writers to connect diverse narrative elements. At first, it was quite difficult to apply systematically Proust's lessons concerning memory in texts that still reflected the realist tradition, but by the 1950s many Spanish American writers had learned how to choose a type of narrator and structure that could take full advantage of unconscious memory. In this way through Proust's modernism they succeeded in renovating the novel.

During the pre-Boom and Boom periods, many Spanish American writers experimented with involuntary memory. Most followed Proust in the use of a sensorial stimulus, but in *Invitados en "El Paraíso"* Mujica Láinez presupposed two stimuli and delayed the recognition of a face until both elements could appear simultaneously. Also, this Argentine novel suggested the associative, as well as the analogical, phase of the memory experience and described the process of the human mind in a metaphorical or impressionist manner. Since *Rayuela* and *Este domingo* there has been a tendency to suppress such descriptions or explanations and to shift the temporal plane immediately from the present to the past. Although the results of involuntary memory have not been disputed, a few writers from Spanish America have questioned in a postmodern way the exclusivity of its evocative power and have suggested that through dreams or voluntary memory one can also recover the past. For Oliveira in *Rayuela* conscious effort to recall a former time served as a mere game, but Tita in *Como agua para chocolate* was apparently successful in remembering the past voluntarily.

Following the experiments which implied first Proust's inspiration and then brief dialogues with portions of his text, there appeared longer and more elaborate dialogues. Novelists, like Carpentier who perceived the alienation of modern man or the inauthenticity of Spanish Americans trying to be Europeans, took advantage of involuntary memory to demonstrate the importance of the past and of authenticity. In differing ways, Cortázar in *Rayuela* and Mujica Láinez in *Bomarzo* used involuntary memory to link persons in the present with portions of their past that they had forgotten or never suspected. This type of invasion of the past into the present allowed both Argentine writers to create works that contained fantastic elements. Laura Esquivel carried this tendency a step further and used involuntary memory as an essential component of her magical realism.

On the level of creation, Proustian memory allowed Spanish American authors to construct their novels with greatly enhanced freedom. No longer were they so firmly bound to questions of chronological development. Authors from Torres Bodet to Donoso who were describing one segment of time could use involuntary memory to shift to a period of the past, which had essentially affected the present. Furthermore, an involuntary memory experience presented early in the text, as in *Cenizas* or *El peso de la noche*, could establish a retrospective mode for the entire work, while, on the other hand, the theme of memory could be developed slowly and culminate in an experience near the end, as in *Invitados en "El Paraíso"* or *El recurso del método*. In this regard, Proust had already provided examples of both through the madeleine episode, which introduces "Combray II," and through the five memory experiences in *Le temps retrouvé*, which are a culmination of all that preceded them.

In general, involuntary memory allowed Spanish American novelists the option of creating a new type of unity on both the level of character development and that of the text. The case of each author and work was, of course, different because diverse aspects of the *Recherche* came into play and some writers were more daring and original than others. *Como agua para chocolate* was no exception and even reflects both levels. Involuntary memory helped Tita recover her personality, as well as her past, and the various categories of memory, along with her principal subject food, assisted Esquivel in her creation of a unified text.

8

On Becoming a Writer: Following Proust's Way from "Combray" to *Le temps retrouvé*

Fᴏᴍ ᴛʜᴇ ɪɴɪᴛɪᴀʟ ꜱᴇɴᴛᴇɴᴄᴇ ᴏꜰ *Du côté de chez Swann,* "Longtemps je me suis couché de bonne heure" [For a long time I went to bed early] (1954, 1:3), the narrator begins to tell in the first person the story of his life. He does not explain who he is, who his parents were, where he lives, or even what his name is. He simply identifies himself by one of his former habits: going to bed early. Given that sleep is a universal necessity, all readers can understand this custom, but they will have to continue for several pages before starting to comprehend who is the "je" [I] that speaks. They will not find any name for the protagonist or narrator until volume five (*La prisonnière*), and because at the time of his death Proust was systematically eliminating all references to it I have decided to avoid employing such a name.[1]

Through the use of a first person narrator, Proust linked his vast work to both real and fictional autobiographies. This meant that he was distinguishing his text from the majority of novels written during the nineteenth century. Even though the *Recherche* retained certain aspects of French realist fiction from Balzac to Flaubert and even Zola, it abandoned the third person narrator, except in "Un amour de Swann." Proust's major predecessors in first person narrative were from an earlier period and can even be traced back to the Spanish picaresque or before. Thus, we find some rather surprising parallels between the *Recherche* and a work like *Guzmán de Alfarache* (1599–1604). Not only does the narrator in both cases refer to different moments of his past as he brings his life story up to the present, but he also speaks of his most recent time in such a way that it appears essentially distinct from all of his pasts. Due to a religious-like experience his attitude toward life has changed radically. The actual sources for the *Recherche* in this regard are probably less distant, but Proust's text is a novel of apprenticeship, like Mateo Alemán's and many others from the intervening centuries.[2] Like Guzmán, Gil Blas, and a host of characters, the Proustian protagonist learns from new experiences and tries to apply such lessons to his life.

Most certainly, Proust gave his first person narrative a new and original focus. In spite of the fact that he took advantage of the freedom offered by this genre and in this way incorporated a wide variety of experiences that are bound together through a first person narrator rather than through a unified plot, the French novelist was very careful to limit these episodes to those that were somehow related to his protagonist's literary vocation. This characteristic of the *Recherche* is largely implicit in the first half, but in *Le côté de Guermantes* the narrator refers specifically to it when he speaks of "la vocation invisible dont cet ouvrage est l'histoire" [the invisible vocation of which this work is the story] (2:397).

In reality, Marcel Proust created his own subgenre, the story of a literary vocation. Since the late nineteenth century, when modernism started to develop, the artist had become an important character in European fiction, and the lives of writers, as well as of painters and musicians, were often examined. Nonetheless, the *Recherche* was quite unique. *Portrait of an Artist as a Young Man* was another example of this tradition, but James Joyce depicted in it only the initial stages of a writer's life. Also he employed a third person narrator in this work, which appeared three years after *Du côté de chez Swann*. In fact, no one until Proust had conceived of the story of a literary vocation in such monumental terms nor had tied it so closely to a first person narrator. It is worth noting that Proust's idea of joining the novel of apprenticeship with the life of a writer was fundamental in his own literary development. It permitted him to use widely diverse materials, like those found in *Jean Santeuil*, but to forge them into a much more unified whole. Also, the first person narrator allowed him to join the "I" of the past with the "I" of the present and to show how he came to write the literary text that the reader has before him. As Bradbury suggested of Proust, his story of a consciousness becomes the story of a literary creation, and the fusion of the two result in the type of master narrative which we regularly associate with modernism.

This account naturally starts in "Combray." After reading novels and examining small reproductions of paintings, the young protagonist begins to discover that his interaction with the world around him is somewhat like the relationship between the artists that he admires and their world. He notes, however, specific differences and in particular his own inablity to describe in an exterior manner. Thus, he begins to doubt his own talent. Moreover, since each new creative work must have a specific subject and outstanding literary texts often possessed a deep philosophical meaning, he becomes discouraged. Toward the end of "Combray" the narrator explains:

puisque je voulais un jour être un écrivain, il était temps de savoir ce que je comptais écrire. Mais dès que je me le demandais, tâchant de trouver un sujet où je pusse faire tenir une signification philosophique infinie, mon esprit s'arrêtait de fonctionner. . . . (1:172–73)

[since I wished some day to be a writer, it was time to know what I intended to write about. But as soon as I asked myself this, trying to find a subject by which I could make this work have an infinite, philosophical significance, my mind would stop functioning. . . .]

In the pages that follow, the child protagonist becomes fascinated by three bell towers that appear to move as he himself rides across the plain in Dr. Percepied's vehicle. He is then inspired to write a short descriptive piece of considerable beauty, but he does not perceive the connection between the subject matter of the text—a personal experience—or its metaphorical style and a more extensive work that he might create in the future.

Throughout the subsequent volumes from *A l'ombre des jeunes filles en fleurs* until halfway through *Le temps retrouvé*, as he first grows up and then grows old, the protagonist retains his desire of becoming a writer, but he still has doubts concerning his ability. As we saw in chapter 5, he learns more about art and artists, but this knowledge in itself is not sufficient. Nor is his will strong enough to force himself to write. High society and love distract him, and his worsening health condition leads him to suspect that he will never complete any major literary text. It is only after the memory experiences in the second half of *Le temps retrouvé* that he realizes that the subject of his work should be his own life, that his ideas on time and memory can provide a deep philosophical meaning, and that involuntary memory can allow him to recapture his past, which he can then describe in beautiful, rich detail. Furthermore, through his experience in the world of nature, love, high society, and art, he is able to show not only his life but also that of other people. In this way, his own subjective consciousness allows him to produce a totalizing effect which gives us the impression that he has created a world. This world may be distinct from the one that we know, and its values may be only relative, but its vast proportions and sense of construction attest to its validity in a modernist manner.

Proust's story of a literary vocation constitutes a structural model that other writers have been able to follow, adapt and dialogue with. As a technique, it has allowed them to incorporate into their texts diverse materials and to create monumental novels where life, memory, society, and love or other similar subjects can be bound together through art and the story of a literary vocation. I will treat the Spanish American examples in this chapter in three segments: 1) largely modernist novels until the 1960s in which the vocation was generally successful, 2) novels that are set in Paris and whose protagonists created at least notebooks, and 3) postmodern novels since the 1960s in which the possibility of failure was especially ominous.

ACHIEVING SUCCESS IN WRITING (AND READING)

Among the principal aspects of the *Recherche*, one of the last to be fully assimilated by the Spanish American novel was the story of a literary vocation. Already in *El cántico espiritual* appeared an account of a sculptor's life and in *Ifigenia* the narrator wrote her long letter and diary with considerable artistic skill. But, neither work dealt specifically with a literary vocation, and it would be nearly three decades before Proust's architectural model reached fulfillment.

Admittedly, quite early a few writers began to move in this direction. We might even consider *Don Segundo Sombra* (1926) the initial example. In this case the novel of apprenticeship narrated in the first person merges with the story of a literary vocation when the narrator, who is familiar with gaucho life, decides to write about his experiences. For this reason in the final pages of this novel the young man, who has inherited great wealth, talks about his reading and explains how he has developed his literary skill.

Our critical problem here does not lie with the text, which offers considerable evidence of a possible relation with Proust, but rather with the feasibility that Güiraldes actually knew the *Recherche* in detail at the time of his creation of *Don Segundo Sombra*. Arturo Torres-Rioseco has already suggested a connection, but none of the Argentine writer's numerous scholars have corroborated it:

> Güiraldes does not attribute a great value to fiction instead he trusts in the song of remembrance. A Ulysses from a land of vast horizons, like Proust he sets forth "in search of lost time". All of the pampa is in his memory and he immerses himself in it. (1941, 82)

Indubitably, Güiraldes knew of Proust's work before the publication of his novel. He cited it in a book review in August 1925.[3] Probably the Argentine's close friend, the French writer Valéry Larbaud (who knew Proust personally and who had read *Du côté de chez Swann* as early as 1914) introduced Güiraldes to the *Recherche* when he was in France in 1919–20.[4] This was precisely the period of the Prix Goncourt, when Proust was widely discussed, and the time when Güiraldes wrote the first nine chapters of his novel.

In combination with the literary vocation, other aspects of *Don Segundo Sombra* add weight to my thesis. The Argentine's impressionist style largely conforms to the Proustian pattern that we discussed in chapter 5. Güiraldes constantly describes by comparing and invariably uses one element of his *diégèse*, the pampa, to say what another is like.[5] On a few occasions, the Argentine approaches in subtlety and temperament the French novelist. Both authors even describe the reflection of sunlight in puddles in a similar manner. We read in *Du côté de chez Swann:*

> Le toit de tuile faisait dans la mare, que le soleil rendait de nouveau réfléchissante, une marbure rose, à laquelle je n'avais encore jamais fait attention. En voyant sur l'eau et à la face du mur un pâle sourire répondre au sourire du ciel, je m'écriai dans mon enthousiasme. . . . (1:155)

> [The tiled roof created on the pond, which the sun caused again to reflect, a pink marbling which I had never noticed before. Upon seeing on the water and on the surface of the wall a pale smile respond to the smile of the sky, I cried out in excitement. . . .]

In *Don Segundo Sombra* we find:

> El cielo, aún zarco de crepúsculo, reflejábase en los charcos de forma irregular o en el agua guardada por las profundas huellas de alguna carreta, en cuyo surco tomaba aspecto de acero cuidadosamente recortado. (351–52)

> [The sky, with the still light blue of twilight, was reflected in the oddly shaped puddles or in the water found in the deep tracks of a cart, whose rut took on the appearance of a carefully cut strip of steel.]

In general, water is attributed a considerable importance in both novels, and their authors describe rain in an impressionist manner. Notably, Proust's narrator says that the drops are "comme des oiseaux migrateurs qui prennent leur vol tous ensemble" [like migratory birds that take to flight together] (1:150), while the Argentine claims that the drops run off the indifferent faces of the gauchos "como sobre el ñandubay de los postes" [like over the ñandubay wood of the posts] (388).

To unify his text Güiraldes understandably employed the theme of water, but also he utilized a type of memory that is very close to Proust's. The narrator in chapter 10 says,

> Mi vista cayó sobre el río, cuya corriente apenas perceptible hacía cerca mío un hoyuelo, como la risa en la mejilla tersa de un niño. Así evoqué un recuerdo que parecía perdido en la aburrida bruma de mi infancia. (390)

[My gaze fell upon the river, whose scarcely perceptible current created near me a dimple, like the laugh on the smooth cheek of a child. In this way I evoked a memory that seemed lost in the boring mist of my childhood.]

The memory mechanism in this case depends upon a visual stimulus and is very associative. The contour of the water recalls the shape of a child's laughing face, which in turn reminds the narrator of an experience from his childhood. The recaptured moment—when the orphaned child realized the futility of his existence—does not in itself give pleasure to the character. But, it does connect the first chapter with the tenth and later with the final one, where the character again looks at water and compares his present with the past. The final phrase "un recuerdo perdido en la aburrida bruma de mi infancia" also brings to mind the language and imagery of Proust, whose narrator, as we have seen, frequently speaks of a *temps perdu* and on occasion uses mist or fog to suggest the general indefiniteness of the past.

The use of memory, along with the story of a literary vocation, appears to demonstrate how Güiraldes took advantage of the lessons that he received from the then new writer Marcel Proust because these allowed him to bind together his almost too episodic novel of gaucho apprenticeship. Furthermore, the literary vocation served to justify an innovative style which we can more easily attribute to the literary scene in Paris than to the pampa in spite of its constant allusions to this vast plain. Perhaps in the future new biographical information can confirm the validity of this reading, but I will presently allow it to stand on its own textual merits.

In 1940, Eduardo Mallea constructed his ambitious novel *La bahía de silencio* [The Bay of Silence] around the story of a literary vocation. The narrator Martín Tregua tells how he wrote his early articles, his first novel *Las cuarenta noches de Juan Argentino* [The Forty Nights of Juan Argentino], and the book of memoirs which forms the text of *La bahía de silencio*. Proust is mentioned on one occasion and a few passages echo portions of the *Recherche*. For example, the aristocratic woman whom Martín sees in the streets of Buenos Aires and to whom he directs his memoirs resembles the Duchesse de Guermantes, whose path the protagonist of the third volume often crosses during his walks before he has a chance to meet her. Likewise, when Mallea's narrator talks about his difficulty in writing and the comments of his possible readers, his thoughts are very much like those of the Proustian protagonist on the occasion of the appearance of his first article in *Le Figaro*. Nonetheless, I must conclude that *La bahía de silencio* is closer to Proust in broad structural terms than in specific details. The more frequent mention of another modernist, James Joyce, and of his novel *Portrait of an Artist as a*

Young Man suggest that Mallea felt inspired by this work at least as much as by Proust's even though the narrator speaks in the first person and advances further in his career than Stephen Dedalus. As we saw in chapter 2 with regard to *Rodeada está de sueño,* even though Mallea was depicting the life of a writer, he disagreed with the French author on several major points and sought to distinguish his own work from Proust's. I would also note that for the Argentine his portrait of the city itself was more important than the consciousness and literary vocation of his character, who produced the text in a nonetheless modernist fashion.[6]

According to my research, the first fully developed example in Spanish America of the story of a literary vocation following Proust was *Los viajeros* (1955) by Manuel Mujica Láinez. Throughout this modernist text the narrator Miguel is careful to explain how he became a poet and prose writer. In particular, he mentions the persons and artists that influenced him and the stages of his early literary career. In the same way that Proust's young hero was affected by Swann's cultural refinement, Bergotte's novels, and Elstir's paintings, Miguel had his own personal sources: his beloved Berenice's inspiration, the cook Ursula's imagination, and the pianist Angioletti's advice and encouragement. Through the latter, Miguel discovered the work of Rimbaud, Rilke, and Bach. Furthermore, like the Proustian protagonist, who at times speaks of his early articles, Miguel mentions his first poems, "El clavicordio de mi abuela" [My Grandmother's Clavichord] and "La injusticia," and he alludes to the publication of his volume of poetry *El alba* [Dawn].

At several key points in *Los viajeros* the connection between Mujica Láinez and Proust with regard to the story of a literary vocation is particularly evident. Significantly, Miguel begins to compose a text based upon his impressions of the provincial town while he is riding on a train. The initial lines of this passage echo the reference to the sound of trains at night on the first page of "Combray" (1:3): "El movimiento de la estación me recordó . . . las noches de mi niñez. A veces, de chico, entre dormido y despierto, oía pasar los atontados trenes . . ." [The commotion of the station reminded me . . . of the nights of my childhood. At times, as a boy, neither asleep nor awake, I heard the dimwitted trains go by . . .] (1955, 228). However, more than this reminiscence itself, Miguel's writing in the train compartment is intertextually related to the famous passage from "Combray" where the protagonist composes his first literary piece on the steeples of Martinville while bouncing around in Dr. Percepied's vehicle. Both aspiring writers are very excited because of the impressions that they have just experienced, and they feel an urgent need to express them in words. They are hampered by the movement of the conveyance, but they are glad to be alone so that they can write. It is worth noting that Mujica Láinez's narrator uses an impressionist style like Proust's, and his description of seeing the family's house for the last time recalls the words with which the young hero of "Combray" depicted the final image of the steeples:

> Cuando dimos vuelta a la barranca . . . la silueta de la casa se perfiló como un barco parado un segundo en la cresta de una ola enorme y que al instante, no bien yo le diera la espalda, se precipitaría para siempre en el abismo. . . . (228–29)

> [When we went around the ravine . . . the silhouette of the house became distinct like a ship for an instant stationary on the crest of an enormous wave, and which an instant later, as soon as I might turn my back to it, would be hurled forever into the abyss. . . .]

In "Combray" after comparing the steeples to the three abandoned maidens of a legend, the narrator concludes:

> je les vis timidement chercher leur chemin, et après quelques gauches tré-buchements de leur nobles silhouttes, se serrer les uns contre les autres . . . ne plus faire sur le ciel encore rose qu'une seule forme noire, charmante et résignée, et s'effacer dans la nuit. (1:182)

> [I saw them timidly search for their way and after some awkward stumbling around of their noble silhouettes, huddle up one against the other . . . no longer forming upon the still rosy sky more than a single dark, charming and resigned shape, which was erased by the night.]

Even though it might appear that the Argentine passage is a rather obvious case of influence, I would point out that the author combined the situation found in *Du côté de chez Swann* with specific images of the sea from *A l'ombre des jeunes filles en fleurs*. Furthermore, Miguel's vocation as a prose writer develops naturally from his verse, unlike the case of the Proustian protagonist. In spite of the obstacles to his happiness that we saw in chapter 4, due to his poetry he apparently has become so well-known that his memoirs should have an audience waiting for them. Thus, without difficulty, he will be able to publish his first book of prose, which coincides with *Los viajeros*.

In a similar but more complex and original way, Manuel Mujica Láinez constructed one of his most ambitious works, *Bomarzo*, using the artistic vocation of his protagonist, as well as involuntary memory, as we saw in chapter 7. Following the same technique as in the *Recherche* and *Los viajeros*, the narrator explains how he, then Pier Francesco Orsini, came to create the Sacro Bosque de los Monstruos [Sacred Forest of Monsters] found at Bomarzo. He shows how his artistic talents developed from his personal inclinations and thirst for beauty, both of which counterbalanced his physical deformity. He tells how his interest in monumental structures and allegory began and grew, and how he learned from the native artisans of the suitability for carving of the local volcanic rock.

The relation between Mujica Láinez and Proust appears in this case to be more distant. There are fewer verbal and situational echoes from the *Recherche* in *Bomarzo,* and the vocation in the latter work seems to be that of a plastic artist rather than a literary one. Nonetheless, the subject matter that Pier Francesco chooses for his creative work and the way that he conceives of it following a highly emotional experience, somewhat like the one found in *Le temps retrouvé,* connect Mujica Láinez's work directly with Proust's. In effect, Pier Francesco makes precisely the same discovery as the Proustian protagonist. He realizes that he must create a work of art whose subject matter will be his life. In this case, he will not write a book using paper in the manner of the hero of the *Recherche,* but instead a book of stone, which is to represent allegorically the principal events of his existence. Like the Proustian novel itself, this work of art offers him the hope of immortality and a justification for his life. Discussing the monstruous statues, the narrator of *Bomarzo* explains:

> Mi pobre existencia se redimiría así, y yo la redimiría a ella, mudado en un ejemplo de gloria. Hasta los acontecimientos más pequeños cobrarían la trascendencia de testimonios inmortales. . . . El amor, el arte, la guerra, la amistad, las esperanzas y desesperanzas . . . todo brotaría de esas rocas. . . . Rodeadas por ellas no podría morir, no moriría. Habría escrito un libro de piedra y yo sería la materia de ese libro impar. (1967, 542)

> [My forlorn existence would thus be redeemed, and I would redeem it, being transformed into an example of glory. Even the smallest incidents would take on the transcendence of immortal evidence. . . . Love, art war, friendship, hope and despair . . . all would spring forth from those rocks. . . . Surrounded by them I could not die, I would not die. I would have written a book of stone and I would be the subject of of that exceptional book.]

Allow me to emphasize Mujica Láinez's implicit dialogue with Proust in this regard and the relative facility with which Pier Francesco created his book of stone. Examining in detail the experience which inspired it, we find several clear, albeit somewhat distant echoes from the *Recherche.* Beginning with a description of the rocky landscape around Bomarzo, the narrator says, "Cada roca representaba para mí y para mis recuerdos un personaje encantado. El personaje permanecía prisionero bajo la costra. Había que liberarlo y ganar su amistad" [Each rock represented for me and my memories an enchanted character. This person remained a prisoner beneath the crust. It was necessary to liberate him and to win his friendship] (536). In the passage which precedes the madeleine episode of Proust's novel, we find a similar idea:

> Je trouve très raisonnable la croyance celtique que les âmes de ceux que nous avons perdus sont captives dans quelque être inférieur . . . perdus en effet pour nous jusqu'au jour . . . où nous nous trouvons passer près de l'arbre, entrer en possession de l'objet qui est leur prison. (1:44)

> [I find very reasonable the Celtic belief in which the souls of those whom we have lost are held captive in some inferior being. . . . They are thus lost for us until the day . . . when we happen to pass close to the tree or to obtain possession of the object which is their prison.]

Like Proust's narrator, Mujica Láinez's character perceives in objects a soul which is held captive, but which can be released by creating an intimate bond with them.

Moreover, at one point in the the episode time emblematically stops or at least appears to do so. This sensation, however, is not the result of memory as in *Le temps retrouvé,* but rather the presence of a snake. Just the same, the effect is analogous. Speaking of the two young men with him, the narrator of *Bomarzo* asserts, "Al advertir el riesgo, también ellos quedaron inmóviles. Los cuatro—los muchachos, la sierpe y el duque— seguimos así, quietos, trémulos, unos segundos, como si el día se hubiera detenido en torno. . ." [Upon noticing the danger, they also became motionless. The four of us—the boys, the serpent and the duke—we continued in that way, still, tremulous, a few seconds, as if the day had stopped around us . . .] (538). Concerning the memory experience and its mechanism, Proust's narrator in a like manner remarks, "ce subterfuge avait permis à mon être d'obtenir, d'isoler, d'immobiliser— la durée d'un éclair—ce qu'il n'appréhende jamais: un peu de temps à l'état pur" [this subterfuge had allowed my being to procure, to isolate, to immobilize—for the duration of a flash of lightning—what normally it never apprehends: a bit of time in the pure state] (3:872). Armed with such an experience and the awareness of how one can use one's life to create a book, Pier Francesco merely needs to bring his work of art to completion in order to satisfy his artistic vocation. In this way, he is also like the Proustian protagonist for whom the actual writing of the text was the easiest part of his task.[7]

As we shall see, over the years there have appeared in Spanish America numerous variants on the story of a literary vocation. Although writing relatively early in this period, García Márquez must be credited with one of the most audacious texts, and this one can even be termed postmodern. In *Cien años de soledad,* he turned the various elements upside down and thus created a surprising dialogue with Proust. Instead of making his writer Melquíades compose the story of his past, García Márquez chose to have this magician write about the future lives of the family of his friend José Arcadio Buendía. The writing itself is quite easy. Using his magical powers, Melquíades simply summarizes in his native Sanskrit the daily existence of the individual family members for the next one hundred years. It takes Melquíades a certain amount of time to compose the manuscript, but with his total knowledge it is no more difficult to write about the future than the past.

The difficulty does not lie in the writing, but rather in the reading of the manuscript. First of all it is necessary to wait for the appearance of the appropriate person. Due to their tendency toward solitude, several members of the family could have been the reader, as well as perhaps a writer. Both Aureliano Segundo and José Arcadio Segundo attempt to read the manuscript, but they do not succeed largely because the time has not arrived yet for the reading. Meme's illegitimate son Aurelio Babilonia is the person chosen by fate, but the reading is not simple for him either. Following the inverse process of what we have been examining, this, the last of the Aurelianos must undergo an apprenticeship in reading instead of writing. He has to discover that the manuscript is written in Sanskrit and then learn this ancient language. He continues to study the manuscript for many years, but it is not until he sees his son being devoured by ants that he realizes that the subject of the text is his family's history. The epigraph provides the key: "El primero de la estirpe está amarrado en un árbol y al último se lo están comiendo las hormigas" [The first of the lineage is tied to a tree and ants are now eating the last] (1996, 556).

Many years ago, Emir Rodríguez Monegal suggested this interpretation of *Cien años de soledad* but only in broad terms:

> If on the strictly Proustian plane man vanquishes time through the work of art, escapes from the destructive force of time by creation, recovers lost time through a process of immortalization which is writing, on the plane in which Melquíades (and thus, García Márquez) posits himself, the book is the world because the book is the word and the word is the creation. (1974, 2:294–95)

In support of this interpretation of García Márquez's novel as the story of a vocation in reading, I would like to emphasize the Proustian context for *Cien años de soledad* that we saw with regard to the subject of time in chapter 6. Furthermore, I wish recall that for the French author, reality was a kind of palimpsest or manuscript which needed to be deciphered. Only by penetrating beneath the surface level of what Albertine or other persons say can the Proustian protagonist discover what they actually think or feel. By playing with such elements derived from the *Recherche*,

García Márquez was creating his own postmodern rewriting of it. For this reason, as well as others that Hutcheon mentioned herself, *Cien años de soledad* may be considered to be a historiographic metafiction.

Notebooks Written in Paris

Before moving on to the more recent cases that strongly suggest a possible failure in the literary vocation, let us consider a series of Spanish American novels whose main characters produce at least preliminary sketches, rough drafts or isolated chapters. Such fragments by the aspiring writers may in themselves convey the idea of a connection with Proust because upon his death he left a large number of notebooks. Some of these were used to piece together the final volumes of the *Recherche,* while others, with the patient reordering of scholars, were transformed into Proust's posthumous works *Jean Santeuil* and *Contre Sainte-Beuve.* In several cases, the Spanish American authors themselves have suggested their relation with the French writer by citing him or his work repeatedly and by setting their novel in the city where he wrote: Paris.

The first of these works and the one that launched the story of a literary vocation beyond the shores of Argentina was *Rayuela.* As I suggested in the chapter on art, artists, and their admirers, Morelli and his notebooks greatly affected Horacio Oliveira. Also, Morelli's relative success in contrast with the failure of Berthe Trépat, la Maga and others provides an appropriate context for the aspiring writer Oliveira.

Scattered throughout *Rayuela* we find more than a dozen chapters that Oliveira appears to have written using the first person: 1, 2, 7, 8, 21, 67, 78, 80, 83, 84, 98, 132, 138, and 144.[8] Although quite diverse, most of these deal with a single subject, la Maga, and many are in one way or another associated with Proust. Focusing his attention on chapter 1, where we saw an explicit reference to Proustian memory and Albertine, Davi Arrigucci Jr. made the following remark in his book *O escorpião encalacrado* [The Tricked Scorpion]: "It is sufficient to think . . . of the autobiographical account that makes to some extent Horacio Oliveira into a Proustian narrator in search, through narrative recollection, of his beloved, lost in the flow of time" (1973, 292). Especially in the initial chapter, Oliveira evokes from an indefinite present several incidents that occurred when he and la Maga were lovers. Other chapters suggest that Oliveira generally wrote while they were living together or shortly thereafter. Chapter 7 deals with their then present lovemaking, while in chapter 98 Oliveira watches la Maga perform a series of simple acts, which he attempts to understand.

Some, although not all, of the texts about la Maga imply a parallel between her and Albertine, who lived with the Proustian protagonist and was later evoked by him. For example, chapter 98 shows that la Maga is an unknowable "other," somewhat like Albertine. The narrator of *La prisonnière* describes his relationship with his mistress in the following way:

> Ainsi nous présentions-nous l'un à l'autre une apparence qui était bien différente de la réalité. Et sans doute il en est toujours ainsi quand *deux êtres sont face à face,* puisque chacun d'eux ignore une partie de ce qui est dans *l'autre,* même ce qu'il sait, ne peut en partie le comprendre. . . . (3:344, my emphasis)

> [Thus we presented to each other an appearance which was very different from reality. And indubitably it is always so when *two beings are face to face,* since each one of them is unaware of something that is in *the other,* and even what he knows, he cannot entirely understand . . . .]

I concede that Cortázar's main character is more interested in observing la Maga's nonrational form of thought than in discovering her actual feelings or ideas in the manner of Proust's protagonist with regard to Albertine. Just the same a fragment from chapter 98 distinctly echoes a passage from *La prisonnière* that I cited in chapter 4 in connection with the psychological method of the Proustian protagonist and of Castel in *El túnel:*

> La Maga no sabrá nunca cómo su dedo apuntaba hacia la fina raya que triza el espejo, hasta qué punto *ciertos* silencios, *ciertas* atenciones absurdas, *ciertas* carreras de ciempiés deslumbrado eran el santo y seña para mi bien plantado estar en mí mismo, que no era estar en ninguna parte. (1986, 609, my emphasis)

> [La Maga will never know how her finger was pointing to the fine scratch that shatters the mirror, to what extent *certain* moments of silence, *certain* absurd concerns, a *certain* racing around like a confused centipede were the password for my well-established being within myself, which was to be nowhere.]

The repetition of the forms of *cierto,* like that of *certain* seems to imply that Cortázar used Proust's text as a point of departure for his own or that he wished to dialogue here with the *Recherche.* Oliveira's subsequent reference to *signos* could suggest the same because, as Gilles Deleuze demonstrated in his study *Proust et les signes,* signs play a fundamental role in the *Recherche.*

In other chapters written by Oliveira, but unrelated to la Maga, there also appear Proustian echoes. Some were intentional, while perhaps others were not. The description of waking up in the second section of chapter 67 recalls several Proustian passages where the first indications of dawn can be seen through the light above or below the bedroom curtains.[9] Oliveira's rejection of the regularity of the natural world may result from his resistence to Proust (or to the evocative power of dreams, which we saw in our discussion of involuntary memory):

Me desperté y vi la luz del amanecer en las mirillas de la persiana. Salía de tan adentro de la noche que tuve como un vómito de mí mismo, el espanto de asomar a un nuevo día con la misma presentación, su indiferencia mecánica de cada día: conciencia, sensación de luz, abrir los ojos, persiana, el alba. (532)

[I awoke and saw the light of dawn between the slats of the blinds. I emerged from such a deep part of the night that I seemed to be spewing myself up, as if in the fright of facing a new day with the same order of events, the mechanical indifference of each day: consciousness, a sensation of light, opening my eyes, the blinds, the dawn.]

For Oliveira and for Cortázar's third person narrator, the *Recherche* was at the very least a common point of reference and a source of inspiration.[10] But, Oliveira's literary vocation itself involves a dialogue with the *Recherche.* This character's desire expressed in chapter 2 to write "una novela transcendente" corresponds directly to the search of Proust's young hero for "un sujet philosophique pour une grande oeuvre littéraire," but the Argentine's sense of conviction is much weaker perhaps because of his questioning of modernism. Another parallel is Oliveira's struggle with the material of his life and with his need to understand it. Like the Proustian protagonist who has to confront the death of his grandmother and of Albertine before he can write about these loved ones, Oliveira sees the death of la Maga's son Rocamadour as a major stumbling block. Apparently for this reason, the first person narrator who began *Rayuela* cannot proceed beyond chapter 2: "No quiero escribir sobre Rocamadour, por lo menos hoy, necesitaría tanto acercarme mejor a mí mismo, dejar caer todo eso que me separa del centro" [I do not want to write about Rocamadour, at least today, I would need so much to hone in on myself better, to drop everything that separates me from my center] (138).[11]

For the remainder of *Rayuela,* Oliveira wrote only brief, miscellaneous texts. Most of these were composed in Paris, but two were written soon after his arrival in Buenos Aires (78 and 80). Generally speaking, these chapters are more like journal entries than texts that could be incorporated, at least directly, into his proposed novel. Ultimately Cortázar's character becomes more interested in life than in writing, especially after he moves into an apartment adjacent to the one occupied by Traveler and Talita. As suggested in the chapter on involuntary memory, the wife of Oliveira's friend offers him a greater hope of reaching the "other" than writing a novel does. Thus he abandons his literary vocation in failure. In such a reaction, which suggests his inability to totalize his life through writing, we can also intuit an important step toward postmodernism.

Writing *El buen salvaje* shortly after the publication of *Rayuela,* Eduardo Caballero Calderón developed more fully his main character's literary vocation, relied more heavily upon notebooks, and made his relation with Proust more explicit. The protagonist of this work has gone to Paris to write a novel, he records his ideas and some of his rough drafts in a series of fourteen notebooks, and he mentions Marcel Proust a dozen times.

The aspiring writer in this Colombian novel uses Proust as a point of departure and explicitly ties the French novelist to his own notebooks. He says that he needs to record his ideas because he lacks the microscopic memory of Proust. Indeed, I cannot claim that this young South American greatly admired the *Recherche.* As we saw in the chapter on high society, he did not believe that its social manner could serve as a model for the Spanish American novel. Furthermore he disliked Proust's use of the first person narrator and considered the French author's sensibility to be monstruous. He even went so far as to attack Proust personally by calling him effeminate.

In this rather extreme position, we can suspect a major rift between Caballero Calderón and his fictional writer. The real Colombian author, who had frequently displayed an interest in Proust and translated one of his minor works, obviously held another view. His own remarks on the French writer found in *Memorias infantiles* (1964) radically contrast with those of the protagonist of *El buen salvaje,* even though both books were apparently composed in the same Parisian apartment, which was located almost next door to where Proust's parents died.[12]

Throughout *El buen salvaje* we can observe numerous contrasts between the would-be writer from South America and the Proustian protagonist. Having a very different life style from the latter, who withdraws from the world because of Albertine and in order to write his novel, the former spends most of his time drinking in the Latin Quarter and transcribing his thoughts. Unlike the Proustian protagonist, Caballero Calderón's character has numerous ideas and can develop a plot and text quickly, but he is unable to complete any of his many novelistic projects. Most of these are far removed from his own personal experience and at times fail because of his unresolved inner conflicts. Such was certainly the case of his novel about high society, which we discussed in chapter 3. Not only was he too unfamiliar with that world, but also he doubted the validity of the subject for a Spanish American novel.

In spite of the differences between the principal characters of *El buen salvaje* and the *Recherche,* they are bound together by their literary vocation and their lack of success. Both want desperately to become writers in order to justify their lives, but neither finds within himself the willpower and discipline to bring a work to completion. At the end of *El buen salvaje,* as at midpoint in *Le temps retrouvé,* the protagonist sees failure as inevitable. The South American character can no longer employ tricks and lies to remain in Paris, and he is forced to return to his country without finishing any of his texts.

From this apparent case of failure, Eduardo Caballero Calderón was astutely able to give his story of a literary vocation an ingenious and for its time a surprisingly postmodern twist. He used as his own text the fourteen notebooks that his character had discarded. In this way not only did the actual Colombian author succeed in completing a literary project (if not vocation) where his character had failed. Also he wrote a Spanish American novel taking advantage of a specific aspect of the *Recherche*—the story of a literary vocation—even though his character suggested that it was impossible to create a Proustian novel about any Spanish American subject. Here, we can perceive a subtle response to the leftist critics of the *Recherche,* as well as an affirmation of the validity of Proust's work as a model for Spanish American literature.

In the two-part novel by Alfredo Bryce Echenique *Cuadernos de navegación en un sillón Voltaire,* we also find the story of a literary vocation set in Paris and even a direct reference to notebooks in the title.[13] According to the narrator, he was inspired by Ernest Hemingway's novels about France and Spain and traveled from his native Lima to Paris in order to write a novel like those of the North American author. In this confession, I suspect an element of self-deception, if not the desire to mislead the reader. Within a particular one-hundred-page span of *La vida exagerada de Martín Romaña* (1985, 157–256) Proust's presence far outshines that of Hemingway for the narrator repeats Proust's name obsessively forty-one times.

In his literary and cultural formation at the Alliance Française of Lima, Martín Romaña was surrounded by persons (mostly women) who claimed that, like Charles de Gaulle, Marcel Proust represented the essence of French spirituality. Furthermore, Martín's mother, who staunchly supported this view, greatly admired the *Recherche* and its author. When she visits her son in Paris, she insists that he and his fiancée Inés go with her to Illiers: the town that Proust called Combray and described in *Du côté de chez Swann.* There the mother's enthusiasm overflows and in spite of the difficulty implied, she recites entire passages from Proust's text. To the caretaker of Tante Léonie's house, she asserts:

> En el Perú, entre la gente que yo conozco, se idolatra a Proust, monsieur. Claro, hay mucha gente que no sabe ni siquiera leer en el Perú, pero entre nosotros le llamamos Marcel a secas. Pobre Marcel, si supiera cuanto se le quiere en el Perú. (200)

> [In Peru, among the people that I know, one idolizes Proust, sir. Of course, there are many people that do not even know how to read in Peru, but in our circle we simply call him Marcel. Poor Marcel, if only he knew how much he is loved in Peru.]

As I conveyed in chapter 3, Martín's mother truly wants him to write in the manner of Marcel Proust, while his fiancée and their leftist friends insist that he compose a novel about the unionization of Peruvian fishermen. Pulled from both sides, Martín develops a very conflictive attitude toward the French writer. For this reason, he describes the visit to Illiers in Freudian terms where the successful writer Proust is seen as a good son if not father figure. Alluding to his mother, he says, "A la mierda con Freud, me dije, y decidí acompañarla edipísimo . . . a la burguesa y podrida casa de Marcel Proust, que era más o menos el hijo escritor que yo no le había dado a mi madre" [To hell with Freud, I told myself, and I decided to accompany her in a manner very much like Oedipus . . . to the rotten, bourgeois house of Marcel Proust, who was more or less the writer-son that I had not given to my mother] (195).

Martín eventually finishes, during May 1968, his novel about Peruvian fisherman, but he never attempts to publish it because it involves so little of himself. At this point in his life, Martín begins to doubt his literary talent and suspects that he will never be able to fulfill his literary vocation. Yet, in his nascent despair he realizes that some of his personal experiences may be of literary interest and that Proust can offer him a model. Of the street demonstrations in which he participated, he later writes:

> que venga un Proust sin tanta marquesa y sin tanto asma para recuperar todo este tiempo perdido que empezó con gente corriendo a gritos y slogans por las calles y conmigo perdiéndome todo el tiempo entre esa gente, confundidísimo. . . . (236)

> [may there appear a Proust without so many women of nobility and without so much asthma in order to recapture all of this lost time which began with people running through the streets hurling shouts and slogans and with me constantly getting lost among those people as I felt very confused. . . .]

During the remainder of *La vida exagerada de Martín Romaña* and throughout all of *El hombre que hablaba de Octavia de Cádiz,* the reader can see how Martín comes to write these two notebooks about his life in spite of considerable obstacles, most notably serious psychological problems due in part to his abandonment by the two women that he loves. Paradoxically these obstacles help him fulfill his literary vocation. Martín first becomes aware that even his daily existence may be of literary interest when his Catalonian psychoanalyst asks him to write an account of his life. Such a narrative text flows very easily for him, and he writes 117 pages instead of the ten requested. Later, Martín continues this type of evocation when he tells his student Octavia of his life with Inés. Similarly, after being abandoned by the girl, Martín starts to talk to other persons about her. By this time, he does not care who is his audience when he speaks in bars and elsewhere. For this reason, he develops the reputation of being an excentric, as the title of the second volume implies.

In *El hombre que hablaba de Octavia de Cádiz,* Proust's name is conspicuously absent due to the contrast with the first volume and because so many situations involving love, high society, the past, memory, and writing bring to mind the *Recherche.* Thus the virtually sole overt reference—"Proust oral"—is so very significant. After traveling around the world composing books for tourists and talking to anyone that will listen, Bryce's character finally reaches the very same conclusion as Proust's protagonist: he must write about his life in order to save it from oblivion. Like the narrator of *Le temps retrouvé* who sees death as his enemy and fears dying before finishing the story of his life, Martín summarizes his idea: "antes moría porque sólo hablaba y ahora no muero porque sí escribo" [before I was dying because I merely spoke, and I am no longer dying because I actually write] (1988, 161).

In spite of the obvious differences between Proust's carefully knit structure, which he compared to a church, and Bryce's freer and even more associative type of development, the two texts combined tell essentially the story of a literary vocation.[14] Indeed, both notebooks, which ultimately become novels, are more oral in style and tone because nearly all of Martín's text was spoken before it was written, but the act of writing itself and of reaching the end of the text are proof of the success of such a literary vocation. In effect, Bryce chose Proust's modernist subject and revisited it in a postmodern way through orality, popular elements and a subjectivity that does not try to totalize its experience beyond a very marginalized, personal level.

In this regard, I must also emphasize Bryce's parodic intent. Throughout the two volumes, he frequently parodies the *Recherche* and satirizes Spanish American Proustians like his mother. Among the numerous references to the act of writing included in the second volume, we find, for example, the following: "la única razón por la cual me encantaría ser un escritor conocido es por salir en los periódicos que compran mis vecinos" [the only reason for which I would love to be a famous writer is to appear in the newspapers that my neighbors buy] (193). Here, the Peruvian author chose to deride a passage from *Albertine disparue* where the protagonist speculates on what his friends and acquaintances might think about one of his articles that appeared in *Le Figaro* (3:567–72).[15]

This parody is especially evident in the final pages of *El hombre que hablaba de Octavia de Cádiz* and even casts doubt upon the success of Martín's literary vocation. Bryce's character dies before finishing his epilogue, but somehow from *outre tombe* [beyond the grave] he is able to present in written form his impressions of heaven. This situation is indubitably related to the fear of death of the narrator of *Le temps retrouvé* mentioned above. Likewise, Bryce's final pages are intertextually bound to the passage from *La prisonnière* where the narrator describes the final suffering and death of Bergotte, and which Proust apparently reworked during his own last days. Somewhat like Cortázar in the case of Morelli's funeral monument, the Peruvian writer avoided any possible solemnity dealing with art, but he made clear the fictional writer's salvation. Martín is accepted into heaven simply because of his sentimental personality. Perhaps the most significant detail is the nature of Bryce's heaven, which holds a terrible irony for Proust's world as well as his own. In this heaven, neither time nor social distinctions exist.

Going beyond the textual level of Bryce's two-part work, which we have considered in the areas of high society, human consciousness, the recovery of a lost woman, novelists in the novel, and now the story of a literary vocation, we see that one question remains, that of the author's motivation. Why did Alfredo Bryce Echenique choose to build so many aspects of *Cuadernos de navegación en un sillón Voltaire* around Proust's work, and why did he parody it so frequently? Here, we do not find a classic example of the anxiety of influence. Unlike Martín and more analogous to the character Alfredo Bryce Echenique, the real Peruvian author wrote with relative facility and considerable success. Although clearly involving Proust, this connection in his first novel *Un mundo para Julius* remained subtle and was not overwhelming. It never constituted a stumbling block for the author's creativity, as in the case of Torres Bodet in his early novels. If anxiety existed for Bryce, I suspect that it was motivated more by a fear of the critics and their claim of Proust's influence than the actual influence itself. Perhaps for this reason the Peruvian novelist so often toys with his readers, particularly those that are familiar with the *Recherche*. Bryce is apparently saying, "This is more Proustian than anything that you found in *Un mundo para Julius*. I dare you to call it merely influence." Ultimately, this playing with Proust and the reader constitutes a lengthy postmodern dialogue which generated an enormous text, one that nearly rivals Proust's own in terms of length.[16]

Although the narrator of the sixth novel by Zoé Valdés, *Café Nostalgia* (1997), never states that she wants to become a writer nor explains how or why she created the text that we read, the six chapters of this book are implicitly a series of notebooks written in Paris and are constantly associated with Proust.[17]

In her case, Marcela Roch does, in fact, refer specifically to an artistic vocation, which she discovers almost by chance. She takes a series of photographs, presents them in a contest and then wins a scholarship to study in the United States. Upon returning to Paris, she becomes a very successful photographer, but feeling unworthy she abandons her career. Unlike the protagonists of *El buen salvaje* and *Cuadernos de navegación en un sillón Voltaire*, Marcela did not choose to reside in Paris for artistic reasons. She is there because she cannot live in her own city Havana. Her childhood and teenage years in communist Cuba allowed her friendship and moments of happiness, but soon after her parents left the island from the port of Mariel, she decided to accept an offer of marriage from an elderly French aristocrat. This act greatly facilitated her departure, but once in France she renounced his wealth and assistance because she knew that she could never love him.

Marcela's connection with Proust can be observed in several ways. From the very first page of *Café Nostalgia*, it is evident that she is deeply affected by smells and other sensations which cause her to remember the past. Yet, more importantly, she refers nearly twenty times to Marcel Proust and his work.[18] She had read the *Recherche* twice in Havana and she immerses herself in it a third time while living in Paris. On this subject, she is very explicit. In the first instance she used an old, well-worn copy that had belonged to Virgilio Piñera and still contained his notes. The second time she read it in Spanish (apparently in the Alianza edition) from the volumes that a friend had stolen for her. Her third reading is in French in the popular Flammarion edition, which was published in 1986.

Instead of having a vocation in writing, Marcela seems to have been called to reread Proust. As she confesses, the *Recherche* allows her to go beyond a simple recollection of her past in Cuba. It encourages her to examine more carefully the meaning underlying events and persons and even to imagine the future. This interpretation of the value of rereading the *Recherche* is entirely justified and is apparently derived from Proust's ideas on rereading books that were known during childhood. The narrator of *Le temps retrouvé* says of the words and names found in a book by George Sand, "Tel nom lu dans un livre autrefois, contient entre ses syllabes le vent rapide et le soleil brillant qu'il faisait quand nous le lisions" [Such a name read in a book in the past contains among its syllables the swift wind and dazzling sunshine that were present while we read it] (3:885). Likewise, Marcela says of Proust's works, "releerlas me retrotraen a mi inocencia inexplorada" [rereading them takes me back to my unexplored innocence] (1997, 65).

In point of fact Marcela's experiences in Havana, Paris and New York are radically distinct from the life of the Proustian protagonist. The parties that she attends and the people that she meets (with the exception of the elderly French aristocrat) have little in common with what we find in "Combray" or *Le côté de Guermantes*. This difference is especially evident with regard to the tragic death of the man Jorge, in spite of the fact that his murder seems to have been motivated by jealousy. Just the same, the narrator of *Café Nostalgia* regularly attributes a Proustian interpretation to persons and events. It is symptomatic, for instance, that she claims to have more in common with Swann than with Gilberte, Odette, or Albertine. Like the hero of "Un amour de Swann," Marcela seems condemned to suffer in love and to fail in her artistic vocation. Analogously, when her beloved Samuel leaves for New York, she draws an explicit parallel: "Una vez Samuel desaparecido, cual la Albertina de Proust, tomé mi vieja Canon y decidí matar el ocio retratando la ciudad" [Once Samuel had disappeared like the Albertine of Proust, I took my old Canon and decided to kill my free time by taking pictures of the city] (303).

Even in the case of Samuel, the connection with Proust is not immediately obvious. Marcela never feels jealous of her boyfriend, nor does she ever interrogate him. Instead of keeping him as a prisoner, when she confesses her presumed inadvertent role in his father's death, Marcela makes it very difficult for their relationship to continue. Fortunately, through his own investigations, Samuel is able to discover the truth and to free Marcela from the guilt that burdened her for so many years. In this way Samuel "recovers" himself for Marcela and opens the door to success in love and, perhaps, in photography.

In this respect, as well as in the narrator's writing of *Café Nostalgia,* the reader is confronted by great ambiguity. The penultimate sequence, in which the two principal characters appear to devour each other for lack of meat, casts serious doubt upon the final result. If we accept the cannibalistic scene as literal, the fictional narrator could not have completed the text even in her own mind. The eating scene, in fact, is more closely tied to works by Laura Esquivel and Virgilio Piñera than to the *Recherche* because the first author described the pleasures of food and the second depicted the eating of human flesh. Just the same, somewhat like Alfredo Bryce Echenique (and as we shall see, Reinaldo Arenas),

Valdés was playing with the Proustian goal of completing a literary text before death. Knowledge of this intertextual dialogue can help us understand what is happening. Also we can observe at this point how very dialogical *Café Nostalgia* is. Its author seems to be constantly dialoguing with Proust or one Spanish American author or another. Here we can detect yet another aspect of postmodernism, but carried to the extreme: the revisiting and playing with canonical works.

In a larger sense, Zoé Valdés has chosen to use Proust and Spanish American notebook-novels written in Paris as a recognizable context for her work about the plight of Cubans in exile. These persons may enjoy living in the French capital (or elsewhere) and even visit the *quartiers* frequented by Proust, Cortázar, other writers, and their charcters. It is not by chance that Marcela and Samuel play their own game in the Latin Quarter, which involves a dialogue between them. Her question below is followed by his response: "Aquel señor de paraguas negro, ¿quién podría ser? Swann. No, no estamos en los Campos Elíseos, piensa un poco Samuel. No acierto, no percibo. Henry Miller. ¡Qué va, demasiado elegante! James Joyce" [That man with a black umbrella, who could he be? Swann. No, we are not in the Champs Elysées, think a bit, Samuel. I can't guess. I don't see. Henry Miller. Come now, he is too elegant! James Joyce" (274–75). But, living in such a refined or cosmopolitan environment and being successful do not necessarily provide happiness. All Cuban exiles must somehow become reconciled with their yearning for their native island and with their recollections of it. In this task rereading Proust allows Marcela to insert her personal and national experience into a universal context. Also, her Cuban friends, even though they are scattered around the world, can be of assistance for they, like Marcela and Samuel, can join together to recapture their past. Indeed, few of these persons will be as consciously Proustian as Marcela, but in their Café Nostalgia they may be involuntarily so.

NARRATIVE CONFRONTATIONS WITH FAILURE

Since *Rayuela*, several Spanish American novels set in the New World have been constructed using the story of a literary vocation or of a novel to be written and have treated the *Recherche* as a primary field of reference, but as in Cortázar's text, the completion of the novel or the success of the vocation has not been guaranteed. On the contrary, the authors of these works have toyed in various ways with failure perhaps because struggle is more interesting than easy success and postmodernism has emphasized the difficulty of the kind of totalization which success might imply. Thus, some aspiring writers, like the protagonist of *El buen salvaje*, have been unable to finish any novel, while others, like Martín Romaña, complete their work in a strange or unsuspected manner.[19]

Such circumstances associated with a possible failure make perfect sense within a Proustian context. Before the end of the nineteenth century, Marcel Proust himself abandoned the lengthy manuscript which we know today as *Jean Santeuil*. In the *Recherche* itself, Charles Swann represents a man of considerable talent who never fulfilled his literary vocation, and the Proustian protagonist does not find the means of writing his text until the second half of *Le temps retrouvé*.

José Bianco, who had written articles on the *Recherche* since the 1930s and would receive in 1973 a literary prize for an essay on Proust, published in 1972 the story of a literary vocation that ended in failure. Even more than Bianco's second novel *Las ratas*, his third one, *La pérdida del reino* [The Loss of One's Kingdom], has an implicit intertextual relation with Proust's work.

The ultimate failure is evident from the very beginning. The first person narrator, who resembles Bianco himself, tells how he originally met Rufino Velázquez in 1942 and then spoke to him nearly a decade later shortly before his death. The narrator, who works for a publishing firm, explains how on the first occasion Velázquez requested information concerning the future publication of a volume of literary criticism, and on the second the two of them discussed novelistic theory with a mutual friend after having dinner together. Realizing his own deteriorating physical condition and that the narrator had helped the friend complete a biography, Velázquez leaves to the narrator an unfinished manuscript and other materials for a novel about his life. The narrator is then faced with the task of recreating the life of a man who wanted to write a novel but was unable to finish it.

The novelistic theory presented after dinner proves to be essential for an understanding of the text and is remarkably similar to my own ideas concerning the relation between literary works. In particular, Velázquez speaks of a possible dialogue between writers: "Un buen escritor enriquece las ideas ajenas, les da prolongaciones inesperadas, de algún modo las refuta. Ya no son las mismas. Por momentos hasta reniegan de su origen" [A good writer enriches the ideas of others, he gives them an unexpected continuation, in some way he refutes them. They are no longer the same. At times, they even disown their origin] (1972, 33). In this same conversation the narrator specifically cites Proust's remarks concerning those elements that are merely implied in a literary text:

En una novela lograda la realidad se halla siempre presente, hasta cuando el escritor prescinde de ella. Proust ha dicho que la ausencia de toda descripción de un medio externo, es ya la descripción de un estado interno. Podemos afirmar que cuando el escritor no dice, o no atina a decirnos cómo son las cosas, las cosas nos están diciendo cómo es él. (34–35)

[In a successful novel reality is always found to be present, even when the writer dispenses with it. Proust has said that the absence of any description of an external milieu is already the description of an internal state. We can assert that when the writer does not say anything, or does not succeed in telling us what things are like, the things are saying to us what he is like.]

With the aid of these three elements—the feasibility of dialogue, Proust as a point of reference, and attention to the implicit—the reader of *La pérdida del reino* can follow throughout this work a continual dialogue with the *Recherche*.

In general terms, the story of Rufino Velázquez's life proceeds through the same stages as the life of the Proustian protagonist, but there are, of course, numerous individual differences, which in the dialogue prove to be as important as the similiarites. Rufo (as his parents and friends call him) has a strong bond with his mother but feels distant from his father, somewhat like the young Proustian protagonist. At first Rufo is more innocent because of his Jesuit high school education, but eventually he loses his faith. The portrait of Bianco's young hero comes closest to the *Recherche* in the passages about reading, but the Argentine author developed more fully the association between reading and masturbation. For the most part, sex plays a more explicit role in *La pérdida del reino* than in "Combray" or *A l'ombre des jeunes filles en fleurs*. Young Rufo fantasizes about the women that he sees on the streetcar, but he also feels attracted to a slightly older male classmate, Nestor Sagasta.[20]

Like the protagonist of "Combray," Rufo is deeply affected by nature and loves his family's small estate in the province of Córdoba. Also, after finishing high school, he passes through a period of intense social activity. Rufo dines, drinks, and enjoys the company of several wealthy young people, who live near Buenos Aires. In this context Nestor reappears and accepts Rufo's friendship once he realizes that it is only vaguely tainted by ambiguous feelings.

In a real sense, Bianco's protagonist later has his own Albertine. Clearly Rufo's relationship with his mistress Inés is not one of possessiveness or jealousy, but it does entail certain sexual ambiguities. The fact that Inés is the daughter of the man that killed Rufo's father and a former mistress of Nestor oddly increases the protagonist's love for her. The two of them enjoy many years of happiness together, but she ends the relationship by marrying another man, who can provide her with greater financial security.

Rufo's literary vocation develops slowly from his love for reading. Like the Proustian protagonist and Bianco himself, he publishes several articles on French writers. Changing his profession from law to teaching literature in high school allows Rufo to think more seriously about writing. Substituting on one occasion for a French teacher even gives him the opportunity to lecture on memory in literature and Marcel Proust.

Concerning memory, I should point out an important difference between Proust and Bianco which distinguishes their protagonists. As Rufo explains in his lecture, he recalls his past spontaneously through the association of analogous situations rather than because of physical sensations. This phenomenon reflects the theories advocated by the great twentieth-century French philosopher Henri Bergson. Also, the affective impact is not as overwhelming as Proust suggested for his protagonist. Indeed Rufo frequently remembers previous events. But, as when Nestor reappears, the results of memory are not as intense, and Rufo never imagines that he is reliving the past.

The principal facets of Rufo's life—his friendship for Nestor, his love for a woman associated with Nestor, high society, and his literary vocation—all converge when he travels to Paris and lives in the world that Proust had known years before. There he meets several famous people and attends elite social gatherings somewhat reminiscent of *Le côté de Guermantes*. It is precisely in this context that we find a reference to Proust's friend Robert de Montesquiou (343). Fearing that Rufo will steal again his mistress, Nestor hesitates introducing Laura to him. This woman, who feels the need to have several men close to her, eventually accepts Rufo in lovemaking along with her husband and Nestor. In this sexually ambiguous environment, jealousy never reaches the level known by Swann or the Proustian protagonist but is often present. Laura's love for Rufo proves to be essentially spiritual, and more than anyone else she encourages him to write a novel, to which he devotes the last two years of his life.

Rufo's failure is in part due to his premature death. He is never able to progress beyond the rough draft of a few chapters and mere sketches of the others, but time is not the only factor. Rufo planned his structure in only the broadest of terms and commenced writing before he knew how the parts would fit together. Furthermore, even though he understood in the abstract that a writer must approach his characters and work from a critical distance, Rufo never succeeded in developing this ability. As Nestor had suggested concerning his friend's literary articles, Rufo did not employ enough mistrust of his subject or sufficient malice to penetrate beneath the surface.

At this point Bianco approached one of the ideas that he first expressed in his article "El sentido del mal en la obra de Proust" and then

repeated in "El ángel de las tinieblas." The Argentine was, thus, suggesting that, unlike Proust who had stretched his personal limits by experi-
menting with extreme emotions, Rufo was too timid in examining his
subject and as a result was superficial. Fortunately Bianco's first person
narrator, who reworked and completed the story of Rufo's life, was able
to supply the psychological penetration and novelistic skill that Rufo
lacked.[21] To a large extent, the narrator executed well the ideal of narrative dialogue that Rufo had expressed in theory. For this reason, *La
pérdida del reino* can be considered a subtle spiritual equivalent of *A la
recherche du temps perdu* but without the second half of *Le temps retrouvé*.
Although its coordinates are still quite modernist, in his rewriting of
Proust we can see how Bianco was veering away from this movement.

In a less traditional and more contradictory postmodern way, José
Donoso treated the Proustian subject of a novel to be written in *El obsceno
pájaro de la noche* (1970). The principal narrator, Humberto Peñaloza,
alludes to his desire of becoming a writer and to his intention of creating
a text about Jerónimo de Azcoitía's refuge for his deformed son, Boy.
Significantly there are references to a notebook that he purchased for
writing and to instances when he met with other aspiring authors. While
living at la Rinconada, Humberto attempts to write on several occasions,
but his stomach ailments, duties, and activities represent major obstacles, somewhat like those of the Proustian protagonist. He plans his text
and seems to know how to begin it, but according to Emperatriz, Humberto never wrote anything. This statement is contradicted by the fact
that the first paragraph appears in Donoso's novel, and the character
thinks seriously about revising it.

This fundamental contradiction is accompanied by numerous others,
which cannot be resolved in a logical manner because of chronological
anomalies. These perplex the reader even though numerous postmodern novels are contradictory, as Hutcheon has pointed out. Humberto
supposedly wrote a book during his youth, which was published through
the assistence of Don Jéronimo, who subscribed in advance to one hundred copies of it. The subject of the book is not evident, but its style is
said to be refined and decadent. Its suggested contents are highly unlikely, if not impossible: the life of Boy, which necessarily commenced
after Humberto became Jerónimo's secretary.

The passage where Boy reads in a copy of the text his parent's name as
well as his own is, of course, related to the end of *Cien años de soledad*
where Aureliano Babilonia finds in the manuscript the story of his life.
Yet *El obsceno pájaro de la noche* also dialogues with other texts beginning
with the *Recherche* where the subject of writing a novel is fundamental
and the absence of writing implies oblivion (e.g., *Bomarzo*). Donoso was
ostensibly playing with these concepts, as well as with time itself.

Rather than attempting to explain logically the contradictions concerning the novel to be written, the narrator of *El obsceno pájaro de la noche* suggests that these are inherent to the work as a whole. Such can be found throughout the text on all levels and are attributable to Peta Ponce. Referring to his difficulty in writing, Humberto remarks:

> todo vivo en mi cabeza, el prisma de la Peta Ponce refractando y confundiéndolo todo y creando planos simultáneos y contradictorios, todo sin jamás alcanzar el papel porque siempre oigo las voces y las risas envolviéndome y amarrándome. . . . (1972, 263)

> [all teeming in my head, with the prism of Peta Ponce refracting and confusing everything and creating simultaneous and contradictory planes, everything but never reaching the paper because I always hear voices and laughter wrapping me up and binding me. . . .]

This passage is of utmost importance for an understanding of the Chilean novel, but it also implies that Humberto's proposed text is more than a mere chronicle of la Rinconada and may even be *El obsceno pájaro de la noche* itself. The narrator also says in the same paragraph:

> Mi obra entera va a estallar dentro de mi cuerpo, cada fragmento de mi anatomía cobrará vida propia, ajena a la mía, no existirá Humberto, no existirán más que estos monstruos, el tirano que me encerró en la Rinconada para que lo invente, el color miel de Inés, la muerte de la Brígida, el embarazo histérico de Iris Mateluna . . . el padre de Humberto Peñaloza señalando a don Jerónimo. . . . (263)

> [My entire work is going to explode within my body, each portion of my anatomy will acquire its own life, distinct from mine, Humberto will not exist, only these monsters will exist, the tyrant that locked me up in the Rinconada so that I might invent him, the honey color of Inés, the death of Brígida, the hysterical pregnancy of Iris Mateluna . . . the father of Humberto Peñaloza pointing out don Jéronimo. . . .]

The possibility that *El obsceno pájaro de la noche* is Humberto's text also entails several indisputable contradictions. How, for example, could Humberto write about his own disappearance or death at the end? El Mudito (Humberto) is sewed inside innumerable burlap bags, is dumped onto a fire and apparently falls into the river. Nonetheless, this contradiction is no more extreme than the others. In support of this thesis we find the suggestion that El Mudito wrote while he was living in la Casa de Ejercicios Espirituales de la Encarnación de la Chimba and that he kept a manuscript under his bed. This could be the text of the novel, even though he asserts that it will never be published.

Furthermore, there exists another feasible explanation. Perhaps the text that we read was never actually written in the course of the novel in spite of the fact that Humberto is the narrator. In this case, *El obsceno pájaro de la noche* existed only in the character's imagination. Similar to the Proustian protagonist, he formulated it in his mind, but unlike the narrator of *Le temps retrouvé* near the end of his task, Humberto was never able to transfer his thoughts to paper. Only the real author, José Donoso, performed this function. According to this interpretation, we have the story of an aspiring writer that failed but an actual author that succeeded. Given Donoso's own lengthy struggle to complete this difficult novel, such an idea is very attractive and implies a carefully constructed dialogue with Proust. Furthermore, it proves that fiction is merely that, and a writer can freely create his text even if it is built upon logical contradictions.

In another ambitious and complex Spanish American work of the 1970s, the author also intertwined the story of a literary vocation with other Proustian themes and left the question of success or failure very much in doubt. For this reason at the end the reader is not certain who, if anyone besides the author himself, wrote the text. I am referring to Ernesto Sábato's third novel, *Abaddón el exterminador.*

As we saw in chapter 5, the character Ernesto Sabato appears in this fragmentary work. Although, like the real author himself, this double has already completed two successful novels, he struggles in his attempt to write a third one. Similar to Proust's young hero, he is unable to decide upon an appropriate subject. Likewise, it is very difficult for him to begin to write, so he looks for excuses to delay the task until the next day. Sabato's literary paralysis is further complicated by presumably evil forces, which, as in Humberto Peñaloza's case, seem to keep him from writing. In spite of these obstacles, a few scholars have concluded that the character Sabato actually completed *Abaddón el exterminador.* They, however, have not provided an adequate explanation of how he did it.[22] Since the text is entirely mute on this subject I suspect that he did not, especially because, for reasons associated with Marcel Proust, another character may have.

In this Argentine novel, the story of a literary vocation and of a novel to be written are separate but interconnected themes, and both are treated in specifically Proustian terms. It is not at all by chance that the young man that wishes to become a writer is called Marcelo and physically resembles the French novelist.[23] He has a swarthy complexion, black hair, and large, dark, moist eyes. He appears to offer great potential as a writer, but he never has the opportunity to fulfill his literary vocation. The mere fact that his roommate is a young leftist suspected of subversive political activity places Marcelo's life in danger. For this reason, he is abducted, tortured, and eventually dies. Clearly, the author of *Abaddón el exterminador* wished to criticize such a system that destroyed its greatest artistic potential for the future.

Using the political circumstances of the early to mid-1970s in Argentina, Ernesto Sábato focused his attention on the apparent conflict that may exist between creativity, memory, and death. During their lifetime, potential artists often experience great beauty and can make fascinating discoveries which they store in their memory, but if they fail to complete a work of art all that they know will disappear upon their death. This eventuality was, of course, the greatest fear of the protagonist of *Le temps retrouvé*, who found himself in a race against time to finish the story of his life. In *Abaddón el exterminador* the third aspiring writer, Bruno Bassán, thinks in precisely these terms and considers writing in order to preserve the memory of the innocent victims of the Dirty War like Marcelo, as well as that of other persons, including Sabato himself. For this reason he conceives early in the text a work that closely resembles *Abaddón el exterminador:*

> Una novela sobre esa búsqueda del absoluto, esa locura de adolescentes pero también de hombres que no quieren o no pueden dejar de serlo; seres que en medio del barro y el estiércol lanzan gritos de desesperación o mueren arrojando bombas en algún rincón del universo. Una historia sobre chicos como Marcelo y Nacho y sobre un artista que en recónditos reductos de su espíritu siente agitarse esas criaturas. . . . (1991, 15)

> [A novel about that search for the absolute, that madness of adolescents but also of men who do not want to or cannot cease to be such; beings surrounded by mud and excrement utter cries of despair or die throwing bombs in some corner of the universe. A story about boys like Marcelo and Nacho and about an artist who feels those creatures flail about in the most hidden recesses of his spirit. . . .]

Having functioned as a double for the writer, Ernesto Sábato, in *Sobre héroes y tumbas* and performing a similar role in relation to the character Sabato in *Abaddón el exterminador,* Bruno represents a Swann-like figure. Similar to this intelligent and refined character from Proust's novel, Bruno shows great potential but does not appear to have the personal discipline to complete a literary text. Addressing Sabato near the end of *Abaddón el exterminador,* Bruno says, "Oh, hermano mío, pensó con palabras altisonantes, para púdicamente ironizar ante sí mismo su tristeza, que al menos intentaste lo que yo nunca tuve fuerza para hacer, lo que en mí nunca pasó de abúlico proyecto. . ." [Oh, brother of mine, he thought with high-sounding words in order to ridicule timidly in his own mind his sadness, at least you tried what I never had the strength to do, what in my case never advanced beyond a project that I did not have the will to complete. . .] (462).

Such words might suggest that, like the character Sabato, Bruno failed to write about Marcelo and other persons and that no one except the real author Ernesto Sábato wrote *Abaddón el exterminador.* However, other passages offer at least the hope that this Swann figure was able to overcome his weakness of will and actually began to write after the events of the novel had transpired. In this regard Sabato's tombstone seen by Bruno in a dream near the end of the text perhaps provided an incentive particularly because earlier in the novel Bruno had thought to himself: "si su amigo muriera, si él, Bruno, pudiese escribir esa historia" [if his friend died, if he, Bruno, could write that story] (16).

In this respect, Sábato's dialogue with Proust can be especially helpful to the reader. As we saw in the chapter on time, Bruno's growing despair, which resulted from visiting the place of his childhood and from observing his father's death and the effects of time, was treated in a Proustian manner and could suggest a Proustian solution: writing. Furthermore, in a few segments, such as "Bruno quería irse" [Bruno wanted to leave] (169–70), we symptomatically see Bruno taking on the role of a novelist. He is present only as an observer and tries to analyze the persons in the café almost as if they were characters in a novel. Within this context the explicit reference to Proust's ideas on analysis is very pertinent because it suggests the path that Sábato's Swann may take. Noticing the similar bone structure of Marcelo's face and that of his father, Bruno is reminded of one of the gentlemen in El Greco's painting "El entierro del conde de Orgaz" [The Burial of the Count of Orgaz], and he thinks of both Aristotle and Proust:

Una vez más comprendía qué poco significaban los huesos y la carne de un rostro. Eran sutilezas las que producían las diferencias, a veces abismales. Pero es que las cosas se diferencian en lo que se parecen, había descubierto ya Aristóteles, la parte proustiana de aquel genio multánime (170).

[Once again he understood what little significance had the bones and flesh of a face. It was the subtle details that created real and at times enormous differences. But it is because things differentiate themselves in ways that they resemble each other, as Aristotle had already discovered, and this was the Proustian part of that multifaceted genius.]

In conclusion, having advanced further than the character Sabato in the creation of a novel resembling *Abaddón el exterminador* and using Proust's conception of life and art in combination with his own experience and culture, Bruno quite likely fulfilled his literary vocation through the writing of this novel. Some readers may still have doubts about this conclusion, but our knowledge of the *Recherche* and understanding of the postmodern reworking of a text can help us to see its justification.

As I suggested in the chapter on high society, Jorge Enrique Adoum wrote *Entre Marx y una mujer desnuda* at least in part as a response to *Abaddón el exterminador* and the *Recherche*. This connection seems particularly evident with regard to the subject of a novel to be written. I concede that there are obvious political differences between the fictional writer in Adoum's text and Sabato and Bruno in *Abaddón,* but these can be attributed to Ecuadorian author's postmodern parodic intent. He wished to call into question the value of reformist literature of the type that Ernesto Sábato has generally written. Thus the excuses of Adoum's character for not embracing the revolution more fully can be seen as a critique of the Argentine's rejection of violence from the political left as well as from the right.

The fictional author in *Entre Marx y una mujer desnuda* is in some ways very similar to the would-be writers in *Abaddón el exterminador.* Like the character Sabato, he says "yo no soy un novelista sino un personaje más" [I am not a novelist but just another character] (1983, 209), and analogously he does not have a clear idea of his future work and struggles with the blank page. Furthermore, he has a problematic double which casts doubt upon the authorship of the text. At times Adoum's fictional writer quotes Galo Gálvez as if he were a distinct person and the two of them on occasion appear in the same episode as friends (e.g. at school, at the hospital). Yet in other cases they seem to be the same person because both of them are involved in a love affair with the landowner's wife. The intention of the real author becomes most evident when the narrator says, "tú escribes un libro sobre un escritor que piensa escribir un libro sobre un escritor—por fortuna este último escribe algo sobre sí mismo no sobre otro colega . . . " [you are writing a book about a writer who intends to write a book about a writer—fortunately the latter writes something about himself and not about another colleague. . .] (26) Clearly, the real author is playing with point of view so that the writer in the text can be *yo, tú,* or *él.* Likewise, Adoum toys with his characters in such a way that the narrator begins a few fragments that another character finishes. The author of *El escritor y sus fantasmas* gave his created beings considerable freedom but not to this extent. Such strategies involving obvious contradictions and exaggerations are typical of the postmodern left, who employed all means or techniques available to subvert liberal humanist culture.

Adoum's connection with Proust in this respect is made explicit on several occasions. Aware of the association between the *Recherche* and the writing of a novel within a novel, the Ecuadorian decided to give his work a Proustian sense. He even attributed the fragmentary nature of both his narrator and of his text to the French novelist. Referring to Proust's idea of the discontinuity of the self, Adoum's narrator states, "El propio Proust . . . afirmaba que no hay continuidad alguna entre el yo que sufre, que ama, que vive y el yo creador . . . " [Proust himself . . . asserted that there is no continuity between the I that suffers, that loves, that lives and I the creator . . .] (47).[24] In this first mention of Proust in the text, the fictional writer also shows how close his assessment of the French author is to that of Monteforte Toledo because he adds: "nos dejó el recuento más morbominucioso de sus recuerdos y experiencias de hipertestigo de la decadencia de la aristocracia . . . " [he left us the most infirmly meticulous inventory of his memories and experiences as a hypersensitive witness of the decadence of the aristocracy . . .] (46).

Also, like the Guatemalan writer, the narrator refers most specifically to Proust's early, immature works rather than to the *Recherche* itself, but in this case he uses, as his primary source of information, George D. Painter's biography instead of the actual texts by the French novelist. To justify his own fragmentation, Adoum's narrator cites without pertinent references an obscure remark by Painter on the weak structure of a book that Proust never published, *Contre Sainte-Beuve:* "Painter reprocha a los primeros (¿sólo los primeros?) libros de Proust: 'los capítulos suelen comenzar en la nada y terminan antes de haber llegado a la meta' . . . " [Painter finds fault with the first (only the first?) books by Proust: "the chapters tend to begin in a void and end before having reached their goal" . . .] (78). This statement was obviously quoted out of context because Painter had prefaced his remark by saying, "Like *Jean Santeuil, Contre Sainte-Beuve* is a marvellous failure. Both are works of art at a stage only half-way advanced from chaos, since the finger of the creator has imposed only here and there the imperfect beginnings of order" (1959, 2:142).

Somewhat like Ortega y Gasset in *Ideas sobre la novela,* who tried to judge the structure of the *Recherche* before the appearance of *Le temps retrouvé* and concluded que "le falta el esqueleto" [the skeleton is missing] (1925, 116), Adoum's narrator incorrectly believes that Proust's work has no spinal column. Using this misunderstanding, he concludes that it is legitimate to convert *voluntarily* into a technique what Painter had said of Proust's posthumous work. From the narrator's point of view, such fragmentation is especially appropriate for his own country Ecuador:

esa novela *voluntariamente invertebrada,* acaso es la que realmente corresponde a una sociedad como la nuestra, no amalgamada, hecha de superposiciones y asimetrías de ideas, costumbres, culturas, razas, llena no sólo de fisuras sino de vacíos. (118, my emphasis).

[that *voluntarily spineless* novel, perhaps is the one that really corresponds to a society like ours, which has not metallurgically combined, which is made up of the superposing of elements, an asymmetry of ideas, customs, cultures, races, and full not only of fissures but also of empty spaces.]

In this postmodern game, it is often difficult to know where the actual writer Jorge Enrique Adoum in fact stands. To what degree is he mocking the leftist intellectual who sees slight value in writing but continues to write and to what extent does he inadvertently show that he suffers from the same defect? We find little evidence that Adoum knew the *Recherche* firsthand any more than his writer. Likewise, in this fragmentary work, he did not seek even the degree of unity achieved by Cortázar or Sábato let alone the totalizing effect of Proust. In addition to parody we find considerable anti-intellectual sentiment. The final reference to the French novelist suggests the role that mere pretext plays in the unsystematic thinking of the leftist, *pequeño burgués* writer. Quoting a truly unidentifiable and insignificant statement by Proust, he says,

> Proust hablaba de "un baúl lleno de material situado en medio camino, que me impide pensar". Tú, en cambio, vas a hurgar en tu baúl—tu cuaderno de notas, tus recortes de revistas y periódicos—a ver qué puede salir de allí. (251)

[Proust spoke of "a trunk full of half-way-finished material, that keeps me from thinking". In contrast, you are going to rummage through your trunk—your notebook of observations, your magazine and newspaper clippings—to see what can come out of there.]

This remark serves merely as a pretext to add another series of miscellaneous fragments. Eventually Adoum's writer returns to the longest connected narrative in his text—the story of the landowner, his wife, and the fictional writer—but, even here, nothing is resolved. The author dreams of killing the husband, but when he wakes up he is not certain of anything.[25] In this manner the writer reaches the end of his "texto con personajes" [text with characters]. However, it is debatable whether he has actually completed a novel or not. More than anything else, the real author has parodied novels about the writing of a novel. From the point of view of postmodern leftists this achievement is sufficient, but for some readers it may not be.

Two rather brief narrative texts of the 1970s and 1980s were written by authors who had frequently followed Marcel Proust and had already composed works related to the story of a literary vocation. But, like their contemporaries, they decided to treat this modernist subject with greater distance and irony. Although *Cecil* (1972) by Manuel Mujica Láinez and *El jardín de al lado* [The Garden Next Door] (1981) by José Donoso are quite distinct, both illustrate how the particular author was able to use the story of a literary vocation in an ingenious way and to manipulate the role of the narrator and point of view.

In *Cecil*, we find the author of *Bomarzo* now installed in "El Paraíso," his country home in the province of Córdoba, and we watch him try to write another novel. Each of his attempts proves to be fruitless, even though the notes for his projected work on Heliogabalus, which appear in the text, are extensive. *Cecil* would seem to be the story of a failed literary ambition (if not vocation) had not the real author been able to perform a literary trick reminiscent of Virginia Woolf. Mujica Láinez, who had previously used as his point of view that of a book and a mansion, assigned in this case the role of principal narrator to his beloved dog, Cecil. In this way, the Argentine's whippet, taking full advantage of his "special" relationship with the author, tells of the latter's search for a subject and experience with failure. For this reason Luis Antonio de Villena claimed that this story of a novel within a novel is directly related to Marcel Proust (1976, 30).

Likewise, but without textual samples, José Donoso presented in *El jardín de al lado* the unimaginative attempts by an aging Chilean writer, Julio Méndez, to improve a novel that had been rejected for publication. As in most of these works, the reader can verify the Proustian connection through the presence of echoes from the *Recherche* in other areas besides the subject of writing.[26] We are reminded of Proust's text, for example, at the beginning of chapter 2 when Julio wakes up and in the descriptions of the garden of his childhood. However, more like Mujica Láinez, who on the last page of *Cecil* suggested that the writer had assumed the dog's point of view, Donoso changed the meaning of the text by switching near the end the fictional author. In this manner, it becomes the wife Gloria who was able to succeed where her husband had failed. More creative than he, she used his unsuccessful efforts as the subject matter of her novel. In retrospect, Julio's words written in the first person illustrate more than his frustration and profound machismo. They also demonstrate Gloria's literary talent because she was able to recreate these elements through her imagination.

Following his battle against AIDS and suicide in 1990, Reinaldo Arenas allowed his novel *El color del verano* to appear. Here, we find another type of struggle to complete a novel. In the text we learn of the intentions of the principal character Gabriel/Reinaldo/la Tétrica Mofeta to write a work that is to be called *El color del verano*. For him neither finding a subject nor writing about it constitute obstacles. He feels compelled to recreate those aspects of his life which have affected him most deeply, that is everything associated with his homosexuality. At first his only doubts concern his mother; he fears her adverse reaction to the subject.

Gabriel's motivation for writing closely resembles that of the Proustian protagonist. He sees his life and that of the gays that he has known as something worth preserving. As we noted before, Arenas attributed value to the gay margins in a postmodern way. Personally, he can remember his world, but if he does not write about it, his Cuba will be lost for future gay readers.[27] To underscore his relation with Proust, Arenas even incorporated into the chapter on Gabriel's visit with his mother a Proustian memory experience. Upon hearing the word *begonia*, Gabriel has the impression of being transported back to his childhood (1990, 104). Also, it is worth mentioning that, like the Proustian protagonist, Gabriel eventually sees the writing of his novel as the primary justification for his life.[28]

For the main character of Arenas the problem does not consist of the actual writing of the novel, which progresses easily. Gabriel finds it much more difficult to preserve the manuscript so that it can be completed and sent to a publisher. In the Cuba ruled by Fifo apparently no one, except Gabriel, wants *El color del verano* to appear in print. The gays who are described do not wish to have their private lives exposed. Gabriel's mother and aunt do not want him and in turn them to be associated with such a subject. Moreover, and most importantly, Fifo's regime is overtly antigay even though the dictator himself at times engages in same-sex activities. As a result the manuscript of the novel is repeatedly stolen, confiscated, and destroyed. Gabriel cannot leave it anywhere for an instant and finds himself having to rewrite it again and again. In his prologue, which appears halfway through the text of *El color del verano,* the real author explains that for similar reasons he had to write some of the chapters several times and eventually knew them by heart. Not surprisingly, his manuscript about homosexual activity in communist Cuba was considered subversive. Thus, Arenas could not finish this book until he was living in New York, where he could speak out openly against Fidel Castro.

At the end of the novel when the manuscript is nearly complete Gabriel places it in a series of bottles, which he hopes will somehow reach a publisher across the sea. Even this effort proves to be futile because the bottles are devoured by Fifo's trained sharks. At the moment, when the Tétrica Mofeta is being eaten by the Tiburón Sangriento [Bloody Shark], he comes to an important discovery about his life and literary work: "comprendió no sólo que perdía la vida, sino que antes de

perderla tenía que recomenzar la historia de su novela" [he understood
that not only was he losing his life, but before he lost it he had to begin
again the story in his novel] (441).

This ending, of course, puts into question the authorship of the novel
by the principal character. As in *El obsceno pájaro de la noche* and *El hombre
que hablaba de Octavia de Cádiz,* the fictional author dies before his responsibility of supplying the manuscript is fulfilled. Here, as in the other
cases, we can observe a relation with Proust, whose narrator like himself
feared dying before finishing the text. But, also we can see how the
Cuban author revisits this situation using postmodern irony and humor.
Furthermore, Reinaldo Arenas found his own way to be original and to
dialogue with Proust's text concerning time and structure. Whereas the
protagonist in *Le temps retrouvé* by starting to write implicitly reminds his
readers of the beginning pages of *Du côté de chez Swann* so that they can
recall the entire trajectory of the story of a literary vocation, Arenas used
his ending to suggest his own structure. While the Tétrica Mofeta is
being consumed and realizes that he must begin his novel again, he
finds himself in a whirlpool that is destroying the island, which has
broken loose from its base. This nearly final image of the book alludes
specifically to its structure, which Arenas called in the prologue
"ciclónica." At its center is Fifo's celebration from which all of the elements depart, but the whirlpool itself justifies the chronological anomalies and contradictions, which are also postmodern. Clearly unlike
Proust, for whom time advanced implacably and could be detained only
through involuntary memory, and more like García Márquez, Arenas
conceived of time as being cyclical.[29] Cuban history, which is discussed at
the very end of the book, repeats itself and is apparently condemned to
an unending cycle of political disagreement and repression.

Fortunately, our own subject does not reflect such futility. The story of
a literary vocation in Spanish America has undergone a brilliant development. Although the use of it began somewhat later than the other
Proustian subjects that we have discussed, this one passed quickly
through the stages of influence and inspiration with Manuel Mujica
Láinez and reached with Julio Cortázar the level of dialogue. Since
Rayuela and *Cien años de soledad,* writing and reading have been frequent
subjects of conversation in the Spanish American novel and these topics
have been generally infused with a Proustian subtext which can be understood by an audience familiar with the *Recherche.* In a few cases, such
as *La pérdida del reino* by José Bianco, Proust's work served almost as a
guide through the labyrinth of an aspiring writer's life, while in others,
for example, *Abaddón el exterminador,* the Proustian coordinates of the
protagonist and Swann have been freely manipulated. This subject and

the treatment of it in the *Recherche* have also been the target for several postmodern parodies, one of which was politically motivated, *Entre Marx y una mujer desnuda.*

Even more than any of the other aspects of the *Recherche* that we have studied, the story of a literary vocation has been treated as the subject of a narrative dialogue *among* the Spanish American writers, as well as *between* each one of them and Proust. The novelists from the various countries have ostensibly read each other's works and have successively added their own ideas to the conversation. Although clearly drawing upon the texts of previous Argentine writers and developing Oliveira's literary vocation in a somewhat limited way, Julio Cortázar brought continental attention to this subject which has not exhausted itself yet. Perhaps, as Eduardo Caballero Calderón and Alfredo Bryce Echenique conveyed through their works, the story of a literary vocation in the manner of Proust was politically more acceptable and did not draw as much fire from leftist critics, who considered the subjects of high society, human consciousness, art, and memory as being suspect of bourgeois values. Nonetheless, Adoum cast doubt upon even the story of a novel within a novel.

This narrative dialogue has been very creative and fruitful. As the Spanish American writers depicted the beginning and intermediate stages of the literary process and vocation, they were able to take advantage of their own experience and to confess their own struggles with writing. Also, they have used their fertile imaginations to show how success was achieved, how failure was combatted, and how the result was often ambiguous. The chronological progression from success to failure and ambiguous results is quite interesting for what it says about the Spanish American novel.

Ambiguity has proven itself to be the most inspiring to postmodern authors who have avoided what is simple and direct. This narrative subject derived from Proust allowed the writers of the Boom and subsequent generations to experiment with a subject that they knew well. Moreover, the possible ambiguity of the outcome allowed them to solicit the participation of the reader. As I have suggested, familiarity with the *Recherche* can help one understand such difficult texts as *El obsceno pájaro de la noche* and *Abaddón el exterminador.* Likewise, Bryce's parodies and to some extent those by Arenas and Adoum cannot be fully appreciated without at least a general knowledge of Proust's work.

Final Remarks: From Attention to Detail to the Creation of Vast Syntactic and Narrative Structures for a New Poetic Vision

IN HIS FAMOUS ESSAY ON MARCEL PROUST, WHOSE SPANISH VERSION first appeared in Buenos Aires, José Ortega y Gasset emphasized the importance of the minute details found in *A la recherche du temps perdu* and concluded that the structure of reality in this work was microscopic. Anticipating this inaccurate interpretation of his novel, Proust asserted in *Le temps retrouvé* that he had used in the creation of it a telescope instead of a microscope. He conceded that the things which he described were small, but "elles étaient situées à une grande distance et . . . étaient chacune un monde" [they were located at a great distance and . . . each one of them was a world] (1954, 3:1041). In the same context, the French author explained the narrative structure of his work by comparing it to a vast church. He also suggested that, like faithful believers, his readers would discover little by little its truths, sense of harmony, and "grand plan d'ensemble" [great master plan]. Although other French writers from Rabelais to Balzac had used minute details to create a large, complex whole, none had been more meticulous than Proust in the construction of their vast literary work. In spite of his use of fragmentation, like other modernists, he sought to create a totalizing effect.

In Spanish America, as throughout the world, Proust's readers, critics, and scholars, the writers that have in some way followed the *Recherche*, and the scholars that have studied this connection have all needed to consider the actual relationship between Proust's minute details and his monumental structure. Some, like Ortega, have paid too much attention to the details themselves and have failed to understand completely Proust's novel or the intentions of those Spanish American authors related to it. In the course of this study, I have alluded at times to this question, particularly in regard to specific literary relations and what some scholars have said about them. I mentioned, for example, the remark by Luis Alberto Sánchez, who seemed to believe that most of Proust's early Spanish American followers included details for their own sake and merely slowed down the tempo of their works or fractured the narrative structure. Although I admit that this type of influence has existed, I have avoided emphasizing it. The mere inclusion of Proust-like details or isolated echoes from the *Recherche* has not been a justification for my study of them. I have always tried to focus upon the structural value of such elements or how they are tied to the development of Proustian themes or subjects.

In the last six chapters, I have examined these themes and other aspects of the *Recherche* in conjunction with the numerous Spanish American works related with them. Such a thematic discussion has facilitated our analysis, but before ending this study I wish to reassemble the parts of the puzzle just as Proust joined the elements of his novel like the ribs of a gothic vault. Already in the chapters on involuntary memory and on the story of a literary vocation, I have suggested how Proust and some Spanish American writers, during the modernist and postmodern periods, have joined together diverse portions of their texts. In the first case, like the Proustian protagonist, some New World characters were able to recover through memory a forgotten segment of their past, which helped them understand themselves or reconcile their past and present. Furthermore, this type of memory experience has often served another structural function because the reader along with the character sees in summary form major events that had been previously depicted. In the second case, similar to the hero of the *Recherche,* many Spanish American characters have attempted to write a novel. All of their efforts to recapture the drama of literary composition, combined with their attempt to describe other aspects of their personal lives, constitute the primary material of the novel which the reader has come to know.

In addition to these means of creating unity, I wish to highlight a third technique employed by Proust, which some Spanish American authors have followed. As suggested above, the French novelist avoided the use of plot in the creation of his text. Instead, he developed separately and in combination his themes of memory, art, high society, etc. He alluded to these subjects frequently, and in his digressions he often examined new facets of his themes. Although many of these commentaries are quite long and seem to wander from the events being described, they are ultimately very important. In *Le temps retrouvé,* the narrator draws together his thematic threads as he shows how one theme or element is associated with another. A typical example is the daughter of Gilberte Swann and Robert de Saint-Loup. This young woman's very person symbolizes the bringing together of the two apparently irreconcilable *côtés* found near Combray, for her mother and father are the direct descendants of Charles Swann and of the Guermantes family. Likewise, the themes of art, writing, memory, and even high society and human consciousness are all joined through the memory experiences in the last volume. These occur at an elite social gathering, entail a psychological mechanism involving memory and ultimately result in the protagonist's using his knowledge about life and art to write his monumental work. At various points in this study, I have alluded to the case of particular Spanish American writers who have similarly diminished the importance of plot and developed their texts through the interweaving of themes in the manner of Proust. Such was the case of Torres Bodet in *Sombras,* of Mallea in *Rodeada está de sueño* and of Carpentier in *La consagración de la primavera.* I was even more specific in my discussion of *Bomarzo* by Mujica Láinez. There I explained how this technique, which was learned from Proust, can be traced back to the manner in which Richard Wagner intertwined his leitmotivs.

Gabriel García Márquez employed a similar procedure in *Cien años de soledad,* but made it more convoluted in a postmodern way. In addition to the themes of time and memory, which are most closely associated with the *Recherche,* other less famous Proustian subjects, such as reading, writing, sleep, and insomnia are discussed. The Colombian author combined all of these with his principal theme, solitude, and various personal motifs (e.g., the gypsies, the tail of a pig, ice, the banana company, the civil wars). Similar to Proust and Mujica Láinez, García Márquez regularly returned in his text to these elements and wove them into whatever subject he was treating. This Proustian technique was valuable and even essential to the novel as a whole. It permitted the Colombian author not only to show over the course of one hundred years some of the shared traits of the diverse members of the Buendía family, but also it gave a greater sense of unity to what might otherwise have appeared to be a series of anecdotes and widely diverse material.

Several other Spanish American texts also reflect a connection with Proust because of the way in which they treat thematic development. This characteristic is most observable at the beginning and at the end of these works. In the first and last chapters of novels as dissimilar as *Rayuela* and *Como agua para chocolate,* one can notice, as in the *Recherche,* how all of the principal themes are presented in the initial pages and then, after having been enriched in the course of the text, the same themes make their final appearance in the last chapter. We find, for example, near the end of Esquivel's first novel not only Tita's artificial memory experience, but also a marriage, a strange reaction to the food by the guests, a dance by Gertrudis and another intervention by Nacha. The author's desire to bind together the principal elements of her text is apparent in details as minute as the allusion to the moment when Tita felt like a solitary *chile en nogada* [chile in walnut sauce] left on a plate.

In contrast, Reinaldo Arenas treated motifs in a parodic and ultimately anti-Proustian manner in *Celestino antes del alba.* As with the

French author in his recurring description of a bedroom, the narrator of the Cuban novel returns frequently to the same situations, which he alters only slightly. For example, the mother is at the top of the well or at the bottom. The narrator or Celestino accompanies her or does not. These repetitions give an apparent sense of unity to the text, but as the three endings suggest, Arenas was more interested in playing with a Proust-like thematic development than in creating any true sense of structure or closure. For this reason, the novel proves to be whimsically fragmentary.

On the level of syntax, we can also observe the impact of Proust's architectural intent, that is, his desire to join diverse details into a complex whole. An analysis of his proverbially lengthy sentences reveals that there are at least three types which are related to facets of his work that we have discussed. The first is closely connected to his use of comparison and impressionist style, the second, to his speculation with regard to motive and psychological analysis, and the third, to his treatment of time. Similar syntactical complexities can be found in specific works by Manuel Mujica Láinez and Alejo Carpentier, and to a lesser extent José Donoso, Gabriel García Márquez and Adolfo Bryce Echenique. Indubitably, in the work of these authors we can find other sources for their baroque style, but their desire to emulate or parody Proust was at times definitely a factor.

In the case of Mujica Láinez we have already seen examples of a Proust-like syntax in passages from *Los viajeros* where the Argentine author was inspired both by the impressionism and by the psychological speculation of the French novelist. Certain passages from *Bomarzo* demonstrate that, like Proust, Mujica Láinez wished to join in a single sentence diverse moments of time. In Chapter 6, I cited comparable sentences from *Cien años de soledad,* as well as *Sodome et Gomorrhe.* All three cases illustrate that time is composed of distinct moments that can be joined through memory or in a written text. Also, the juxtaposition of such moments can unify the entire work. In one case the narrator of *Bomarzo* cites as his focal point a ring that he had received from Benvenuto Cellini, and he, thus, spans four hundred years between his present and past as he anticipates what will be described later in the text:

> Entre las infinitas cosas que he perdido desde entonces incluyendo el horóscopo de Sandro Benedetto; las cartas del alquimista Dastyn al cardenal Napoleón Orsini, que representaron tan eminente papel en mi destino; el cuadro de Lotto; mis hornos, fuelles, alambiques . . . a pocas añoro tanto como a esa sortija de oro y de acero que hacía girar en mi meñique. . . . (1967, 72)

> [Among the infinite number of things that I have lost since then including the horoscope of Sandro Benedetto; the letters from the alchemist Dastyn to

Cardinal Napoleon Orsini, which played such an eminent role in my destiny; the painting by Lotto; my kilns, bellows, stills . . . I long for few of them as much as for that gold and iron ring which I used to turn about on my little finger. . . .]

As for Alejo Carpentier, who in fact called Proust's style eminently baroque, he apparently vied with this French author in his search for new forms of syntactic complexity. For this reason, when he spoke about Proust's style in his lecture "Lo barroco y lo real maravilloso," Carpentier seemed to be describing his own:

> various "between parentheses" are inserted, which are like numerous pro-liferating cells, sentences placed within the sentence, which have their own life and at times bond with other "between parentheses", which are still other proliferating elements. (1984, 116)

Of the numerous examples that could be cited, the most pertinent one appears near the end of Ofelia's memory experience in *El recurso del método*. Here, the Cuban author, like Proust, chose widely diverse elements to show all that was recovered from the past:

> Y la vaca Flor de Mayo, recién parida, que llamaba a su ternero para que que aligerara las ubres, y el pregonero de las melcochas, allá, en la calle, y la campana de la ermita, metida entre nísperos y capulíes; y este maíz aquí— tengo siete años, y cada mañana, me miro ya en el espejo . . . —, entrándome por los poros. (1974, 315)

> [And Mayflower the cow, having recently given birth, called to her calf so that it might alleviate her udders, and the molasses peddler out there in the street, and the bell of the hermitage in the midst of medlars and capulí trees; and the corn here—I am seven years old, and each morning, I examine myself in the mirror . . . —entering through my pores.]

Thirdly, along with Proust's vast narrative and syntactic structural models, which have greatly affected the Spanish American novel, I must reiterate the importance of the French author's poetic vision, which also inspired many writers. Carpentier, of course, alluded to this aspect in his lecture "Marcel Proust et l'Amérique latine" because he considered it fundamental. But, it is also worth mentioning that Julio Cortázar suggested a similar idea years earlier in his essay "Situación de la novela." There he mentioned the author of the *Recherche* specifically in order to explain how poetry had invaded the twentieth century novel:

> The century opens with the impact of the philosophy of Bergson, and its instantaneous application in the work of Marcel Proust proves to what extent the novel was waiting for and needed the dimensions of pure intuition, the step forward which might be consistent with that intention. (1950, 232)

MARCEL PROUST AND SPANISH AMERICA

Throughout this study, I have alluded to various facets of Proust's lyricism, which he inherited from the precursors of modernism and came to embody. It is immediately apparent in his poetic imagery taken from life and art, in his constant references to sensory perception, and in the pervasive use of metaphor or comparison found throughout the *Recherche*. The Spanish American modernists Teresa de la Parra, Xavier Villaurrutia, and Jaime Torres Bodet were quick to follow Proust in this regard, but Felisberto Hernández, Manuel Mujica Láinez, and even the postmodern Laura Esquivel have continued in this vein. Proustian lyricism also entails a very subjective view of reality which is derived from intuition and strong emotion and is often bound to the past. A lost time when recovered through affective memory may be somewhat idealized and is generally portrayed in terms of nostalgia. In this respect, we have found numerous examples from *Las memorias de Mamá Blanca* to portions of *Los ídolos, Rayuela,* and *El recurso del método.*

I would also add that the tender, sensitive side of Proust opened doors to a type of literature that more robust writers like Balzac or Zola could have never suggested. Thus, aspiring women authors, such as Teresa de la Parra or Yolanda Oreamuno, who did not want to write like such males but wished to go beyond the typically feminine models of their time saw in Proust an excellent alternative. Even today Laura Esquivel and Zoé Valdés continue to take advantage of this facet of Proust. Similarly, the French writer's treatment of the tender feelings between men, coupled with his willingness to examine such a subject, has encouraged many bisexual and gay writers from Manuel Mujica Láinez and José Lezama Lima to Luis Zapata and Reinaldo Arenas.

Referring more specifically to a Proustian vision, I have pointed out how the French novelist affected other Spanish American writers. José Donoso's characters in "El tiempo perdido", *El obsceno pájaro de la noche,* and *Casa de campo* were fascinated by the upper-class way of life because of their subjective and somewhat distorted view of the world. In this way, Donoso was able to enhance a national reality which seemed to him almost too ordinary while at the same time deflect criticism from the left by acknowledging the distortion. In a distinct, but still comparable manner, the acute sensory perception of Tobías in "El mar del tiempo perdido" had a profound effect upon the other characters in this story by García Márquez. Thus, by using a Proust-like point of departure, the Colombian author was able to transform a desolate coastal town into a fanciful resort. In short, Proust's personal vision showed these Boom writers a direction which they could follow in their own way. The same can be said for Bryce Echenique and Arenas although they undercut through humor the totalizing effect of such a view of the world.

In a genuine sense, Proust's own radical subjectivity helped many Spanish American writers distinguish their work from the realist or naturalist modes of the past. Carpentier was most certainly correct in his lecture when he claimed that the author of the *Recherche* showed him and the novelists of his and succeeding generations how to escape from the influence of Zola. But, after examining several of his novels, we can also see how Carpentier learned from Proust more than just how to present a more profound view of life and to use liturgical and magical elements to transform common reality. By employing involuntary memory, the Cuban author was able to create some of his most marvelous and least realist passages.

I have even claimed that the *Recherche* was an important source for magical realism, as well as for *lo real maravilloso*. The magical elements already implicit in the experiences of involuntary memory and made explicit by Proust's references to genies and mythical beings inspired Manuel Mujica Láinez to add a fantastic dimension to involuntary memory in *Bomarzo,* where a man in the twentieth century recovered a previous life during the sixteenth century. Analogously, but in his own way, because he could not believe in the miracle of involuntary memory, García Márquez decided to create in *Cien años de soledad* his own equivalent of it: the room of Melquíades. More recently, Laura Esquivel blended Proustian memory with magical realism from other sources to prepare her own delicious postmodern variety of it. Thus we can see how in his first study of magical realism Angel Flores was essentially correct and even prophetic when he cited Proust along with Kafka as a European precursor of this type of Spanish American fiction.

Without doubt, as Carpentier said in 1971, Marcel Proust helped to foment a revolution in the Spanish American novel, one that incited writers from many countries to penetrate far deeper than Zola's shallow mines. In the course of this study we have seen how diverse Proust's impact has been with respect to various subjects and techniques, but I should not forget to mention how the relation itself has been of several types and has evolved over time. Some of the Spanish American writers from the modernist period, who greatly admired the *Recherche,* wholly accepted certain aspects of it and allowed these to influence them profoundly, at least in their initial works (e.g., Jaime Torres Bodet and Manuel Mujica Láinez). Over time such writers generally began to seek a more active type of relation. Others (e.g. María Luisa Bombal and José Lezama Lima), even though they perceived the value of Proust's novel, were from the very first mistrustful of it and used it more as a source of inspiration or as a point of departure than as a model. Having more confidence and perhaps pride in their own creativity, they always sought to mix deeply felt personal elements with what they had learned from Proust.

By the period known as the Boom, this dual relation between Proust and individual Spanish American writers was expanded to include an audience that could perceive not only the general connection but also the various elements of it as a dialogue or conversation. Julio Cortázar, who confronted the *Recherche* in several ways throughout *Rayuela,* illustrated how this could be accomplished and opened the way for the postmodern response. Other writers followed suit, but each in his or her own manner. Although less confrontational, José Bianco explicitly presented *La pérdida del reino* as a dialogue with Proust. To alert their readers to this type of conversation, several Spanish American novelists cited the French author frequently and, on one occasion in particular, both Alejo Carpentier and José Donoso made numerous references to Proust's characters and to the situations found in his novel. Furthermore, we have considered several examples of parody, which have also relied upon the reader's familiarity with the *Recherche.* Jorge Luis Borges created the first text of this type, but during the postmodern years such parodies have become especially frequent with the works by Jorge Enrique Adoum, Alfredo Bryce Echenique, and Reinaldo Arenas. In this regard, we can observe how an anticommunist such as Arenas and a Marxist like Adoum responded to each other at the same time as they both parodied the bourgeois writer Proust.

In short, *A la recherche du temps perdu* has had a profound effect upon the literature and culture of that part of the world where Proust's closest friend, Reynaldo Hahn, was born. This transatlantic connection began eight decades ago in the conversation of excited readers, in the discussion of Proust in newspapers and literary magazines, and in the treatment of Proustian themes and techniques in Spanish American short stories and novels. It has continued throughout these years and has not exhausted itself yet. Given the recent appearance of works such as *Como agua para chocolate, El color del verano,* and *Café Nostalgia,* I predict that Marcel Proust and his vast novel will continue to be a subject of oral, critical and narrative dialogue for many years to come. Thus, as we begin the twenty-first century, Proust, one of the greatest writers of the twentieth, will not fail to make his presence known on both sides of the Atlantic.

Notes

POINT OF DEPARTURE

1. Although María Elena Echenagucia was born off the Venezuelan coast in Dutch Curaçao, her father was a Basque and she was raised in Caracas. Upon marrying her, Carlos Hahn, who was in fact a Jew from Hamburg, adopted her Christian faith and was for the most part assimilated into Venezuelan society. The Hahns had twelve children in Caracas and did not leave until the political situation became unstable in 1878. They then settled in Paris, where Reynaldo received an excellent musical education and even studied with Jules Massenet.

2. Similarly, Alejo Carpentier, who visited Reynaldo in Paris during the 1930s, wrote in "Un venezolano amigo de Proust" *(El Nacional,* 16 August 1951) that Hahn spoke Spanish "with a distinct native-born accent," suggested that he hoped to return someday to Caracas and devoted his last operatic efforts to a version of Fernández de Moratín's *El sí de las niñas* [The Girls' Consent] (1975, 45–46).

3. As Berl suggests, in spite of their differing places of birth, first language, and nationality, Proust and Hahn had a great deal in common. Marcel by his mother and Reynaldo by his father were half Jewish. Both were interested in being accepted into high society and wished to have artistic careers. Their tender, wealthy families supported their friendship and largely refused to acknowledge its homosexual nature, which was of course also a very strong bond.

4. Jeanine Huas traced carefully the development of the intimacy between Proust and Hahn in her book *L'homosexualité au temps de Proust* (1992, 103–8).

5. Hahn's work was also affected by his friend. Following the death of one of Proust's favorite writers, John Ruskin, Hahn composed a musical piece entitled "Muses pleurant la mort de Ruskin" [Muses Weeping for the Death of Ruskin], which he dedicated to Proust.

6. In his biography *Proust* Ghislain de Diesbach, for instance, described in detail how Marcel interrogated Reynaldo about his previous loves and how the latter eventually rebelled. Referring more specifically to the novel, Diesbach said of Hahn, "Shortly afterwards, the latter, casting off his yoke, demonstrates his independence by refusing one evening, upon leaving a social event, to return home with Proust; this episode will appear transposed in 'Un amour de Swann' . . ." (1991, 210).

7. A few of Reynaldo's relatives still live in Venezuela. One of them, Martin E. Hahn, informed me by e-mail in 1997 that he had completed another play about the composer's life.

8. All translations are mine.

341

9. Picón-Salas said of Coll, "Because of the subtley of the analysis and at the same time the meticulousness with which he was able to view the external world, if he had written novels, they would have had a certain kinship with those of Proust" (1961, 146). After pointing out the contrast between Díaz Rodríguez and Venezuelan naturalism, Uslar Pietri wrote of *Sangre patricia,* "it opens the way to considerations of technique and to the problems of form so that someone will be able hear when Proust arrives" (1948, 263).

10. See "Un document probable sur le premier état de la pensée de Proust: 'Mystères' par Fernand Gregh" [A Probable Document on the First State of Proust's Thought: "Mysteries" by Fernand Gregh] by René de Messières. This idea has been contested, but I have new reasons to believe that Messières was correct.

11. Again Hahn, whose musical scores appeared in *Les plaisirs et les jours,* may have served as a link. During these years he was becoming famous in Paris, and Venezuelans soon discovered who he was. In June 1898 portions of an article by Pierre Loti on Reynaldo's first opera appeared in *El Cojo Ilustrado* [The Illustrated Lame Man]. of Caracas.

12. Because of the not yet mature nature of Proust's early texts and the fact that he was still unknown, it is difficult to prove a relation between him and Díaz Rodriguez or Coll. I have nonetheless attempted to do so in a separate publication and have shown other aspects of this connection.

13. I use the term Boom much in the same way as did José Donoso in his *Historia personal del Boom* (1971). This period began about 1960 and continued well into the 1970s. It encompassed the narrative work of a group of writers from various countries who set aside their regional and national models (e.g., Rómulo Gallegos) and chose to link their works to those of the masters of modernist narrative, most notably James Joyce, Marcel Proust, Virginia Woolf, and William Faulkner.

14. Furthermore, even though Proust has been considered one of the outstanding examples of high modernism, certain aspects of his work already anticipated the reaction against this phenomenon. As Margaret E. Gray explained in *Postmodern Proust,* the narrator of *La prisonnière* carries his hypothesizing to such an extreme that his efforts to understand reality at times seem futile. At such points he then contradicts his conclusions by stating a universal law which he could certainly not prove. In short, although he may not be parodying himself, he does cast doubt upon his own methodology.

15. A parallel and very impressive relation has existed for Brazil, but due to the dimensions of my study I have decided to focus my attention upon the Spanish-speaking areas of the New World. For this reason, I use the term Spanish American instead of Latin American.

16. In his recent biography *Marcel Proust,* William C. Carter claims that Proust and Hahn met on 22 May 1894 and that Leon Delafosse performed that evening at Madeleine Lemaire's (2000, 165). Other biographers, however, have not claimed to know the date of their meeting that spring and suggest that Reynaldo may have played.

17. Theatre and poetry will be mentioned only in passing because both Proust and a majority of his followers have written primarily narrative works.

18. As in a court of law, the words of the persons directly involved in a particular case are the best proof of the facts. Without their actual statements the lawyers' paraphrase or interpretation holds little weight. I realize that this procedure runs contrary to some literary scholarship, but I believe that in a study of intertextuality the text itself should not be ignored.

19. In his book *The Modern Latin-American Novel*, Raymond Leslie Williams acknowledged the contribution of Marcel Proust to the introduction of modernism in Spanish America, but he reduced it to the structuring of time "around a series of associations with an object" (1998, 4). Also, as I will show, I do not agree with his thesis that the Boom was primarily modernist and that the period after the Boom was postmodern. The transition began during the Boom itself.

CHAPTER 1: RECEPTION AND CRITICAL APPRECIATION

1. As Nathalie Mauriac and Etienne Wolff pointed out in their edition of *Albertine disparue* (1987), just before his death, Proust decided to eliminate a considerable portion of his sixth volume. Nonetheless, the new Pléiade edition chose for editorial purposes to ignore this decision. Because this controversy has not yet been resolved and because Spanish American writers have known the complete version (but not the variants found in the new editions), I have chosen to cite the earlier, 1954, Pléiade edition.

2. For a succinct, recent examination of French criticism of all periods, see "Proust recuperado por las vanguardias" [Proust Recovered by the Vanguard] by Antoine Compagnon, which was translated by Blas Matamoro and was published in *Cuadernos hispanoamericanos* [Spanish American Notebooks] 562 (1997).

3. I have performed research for nine months in Argentina (1976–77, 1986), two and a half months in Mexico (1977, 1993, 2000), two months in Chile (1977, 1986), five weeks in Uruguay (1977, 1986) and Venezuela (1986, 1996), one month each in Costa Rica, Colombia, Ecuador and Peru (1985), three weeks in Puerto Rico (1987, 1998), two weeks in Cuba (1998) and Guatemala (1997, 1999) and one week in the Dominican Republic (1987) and Nicaragua (1997). I have also worked in Madrid for a total of two and a half months (1984, 1988, 1995) to study the parallel case of Spain.

4. Various Spanish Americans have attempted to cite the first article on Proust to appear in the New World. Manuel Gálvez said that it was by Alfonso Reyes, Raúl Silva Castro attributed this honor to Enrique Gómez Carrillo, and Gervasio Guillot Muñoz claimed it for his brother. As we shall see, the articles to which they were referring appeared later. The one by Miomandre was indeed very early. It precedes by four months any of the texts that Pierre-Quint listed for the United States and by nearly seven months the first article published in *The New York Times* (13 August 1920).

5. In his literary memoirs *En el mundo de los seres ficticios* [In the World of Fictitious Beings], Gálvez later suggested the date of the arrival of Proust's early volumes to Argentina and his discovery of them: "The two years that came after *Nacha* and that same year 1919 were for me an almost absolute immersion in the psychological novel. From *Les liaisons dangereuses* [Dangerous Liaisons] to Proust, whose books had just arrived, I did not fail to read anything" (1961, 265).

6. This assertion about Chile seems to have been accurate and can be found in "Centenario de Proust" by Alone (*El Mercurio*, 4 July 1971).

7. In "Marcel Proust et Amérique Latine" Carpentier claimed that the early volumes of the *Recherche* "entered first of all through the gates of Havana, and of Buenos Aires" (1972, 1322). Even though he was referring to imported books instead of critical articles, the date that he states in the Spanish version of his lecture, 1924, is at least four years after the one suggested by Manuel Gálvez in note 5.

8. The index of the literary supplement of *El Diario de la Marina* for the very important years 1927–30 lists no article specifically about Proust. Carpentier's own first reference to the *Recherche* was on 4 November 1928 in an article about cinematography (*Carteles* [Posters]). See *Crónicas* (1976, 2:354).

9. At least Alfonso Reyes, however, mentioned Proust much earlier. In "*By-Products* de la Paz" (*El Heraldo de México*, 1919) he suggested that with the end of the Great War the *Nouvelle Revue Française* could treat, among other subjects "the literature of analysis, in the manner of Marcel Proust" (1960, 3:392).

10. In *Memorias infantiles (1916–1924)* [Memoirs of Childhood], Eduardo Caballero Calderón suggested that he learned of Proust about 1924 through a Swiss teacher, and soon after he began to read the *Recherche* (1964, 164).

11. Gómez Carrillo's critical assessment of Proust is also evident in his final book *La nueva literatura francesa*. In his essay on Paul Morand, he spoke of "the sleep-inducing and long-winded prose of Proust" and lamented the influence of the *Recherche* upon young French writers (1927, 70).

12. Curiously this magazine, whose title could suggest the soirées of Proust's novel, was inaugurated on his birthday, 10 July, and its initial article began with a quotation from *A l'ombre des jeunes filles en fleurs*.

13. Guido Guerra wrote nine brief notes for *La Nación* and Dedalus, two. Likewise the section "Bibliófilo" of *El Mercurio* contained five notes on Proust.

14. In his *Correspondencia*, Vicuña Luco also made about 1927 a very interesting remark on the development of Proustian cliques [capillas proustianas] in Santiago: "We the admirers of Proust are in the process of forming, without intending to do so an ecumenical religion: religion in the strict sense of the term, which is 'bonding with each other'. Everywhere an admiration for Proust induces affection, initiates friendships, creates spontaneously groups that do not grow tired of discussing him" (1946, 130).

15. Estuardo Núñez suggested that he and his friends began to read in Peru about 1925 Proust and other new European writers. See "Martín Adán y su creación poética" (1951, 127).

16. In his second article Reyes, who happened to live for a short time in the building where Proust died, reported that the *concierge* had spoken to him about the French novelist and his guests. Reyes mentioned, in particular, the critic of Mexican origin, Ramon Fernandez, and a secretary of the novelist who liked painting and supposedly went to Mexico a year before Proust's death. The latter was most likely the young man from Switzerland, Henri Rochat, but according to Céleste Albaret, Proust recommended him for a position at the Banque de Paris et des Pays-Bas in Buenos Aires, where he evidently traveled instead. See *Monsieur Proust* (1977, 188–89).

17. Even during the 1930s the social aspect of Proust's novel received only slight attention in Spanish America. Ventura García Calderón, who had been in communication with the French novelist, called him in "La literatura de lujo" [The Literature of Luxury] (*La Prensa* of Buenos Aires, 14 October 1934) "the first and perhaps last explorer of the so-called 'high society'," but he devoted only part of this article to Proust.

18. Apparently, Ocampo read Proust's prologue to his translation of Ruskin's *Sesame and Lilies* before she composed in French her article on this book, "En marge de Ruskin" [On the Fringe of Ruskin] (*La Nación*, 18 April 1920). As she later stated in "Palabras francesas" [French Words] of *Sur* 3 (1931), she was very impressed by the remarks of the translator, "un desconocido Marcel Proust" [an unknown writer Marcel Proust]. He even appears to have influenced her ideas on the British author

because Proust illustrated precisely her complaint against Ruskin: Proust revealed to her what she did not know about herself, namely how readings in childhood had affected her.

19. According to Enrico Santí, Paz had to shorten his text for this leftist newspaper, but the complete version of it can now be found in *Primeras letras* under the title "Distancia y cercanía de Marcel Proust" [Distance and Proximity of Marcel Proust].

20. Another example of the shifting attitude toward Proust at this time was the reassessment of his sexual nature and its link to the creative process. Spanish Americans demonstrated their interest in this subject by publishing in two magazines Robert Vigneron's controversial study "Genesis of 'Swann'," (*Letras de México*, 15 May 1942 and *Atenea*, October 1945). Here, Vigneron claimed that Proust's interest in a German scandal involving homosexuality inspired his return to the novelistic form.

21. Spanish reviews of its two parts were reprinted in the New World. The first by Benjamín Jarnés appeared in *La Nación* of Buenos Aires on 10 September 1931 and the second by Juan José Domenchina can be found in both *El Repertorio Americano* of San José (10 November 1934) and *El Tiempo* of Bogotá (31 December 1934).

22. To my question concerning this apparent oversight, Victoria Ocampo responded, "This fact can be explained because I did not have enough money for such an extensive work, which I would have, of course, desired to publish".

23. In contrast, the assessments in Argentina were generally favorable. The reviewer for *La Prensa* described *La prisionera* as being a "blemishless version" (10 December 1945) and spoke of the translator's "habitual neatness" in *Albertina ha desaparecido* (17 March 1946).

24. The Argentine literary magazine *Realidad* praised this edition by saying, "the novelistic work by Marcel Proust . . . acquires in Buenos Aires a complete version and a respectable edition, so that it can reach the general public to the degree that this type of literature may be capable of winning it over" (January–February 1947:128).

25. Two years earlier Eduardo Caballero Calderón had translated and published in Colombia a portion of *Chroniques* and had used as his title *Los salones y la vida de París*.

26. During these years Alone underwent a personal crisis related to Proust. Bothered by specific remarks made by Daniel de la Vega (*Las Ultimas Noticias* [The Latest News], 2 September 1948), he retorted angrily in "Defensa de Marcel Proust" (*El Imparcial*, 12 September 1948). The biography by André Maurois, *A la recherche de Marcel Proust* also disappointed him to such a degree that after his review of it (*El Mercurio*, 21 August 1949), he ceased to write about the *Recherche* for more than fifteen years even though this work was becoming very fashionable again.

27. In "Sobre la vida y la obra de Marcel Proust," which was dated September 1951, Jorge Fidel Durón claimed that this study of the French novelist was the first to appear in Honduras.

28. Although published separately, the study by Eneida Sansone, *La creación artística en Marcel Proust* (Montevideo, 1950), can be considered only a booklet because of its brevity and limited purpose.

29. Alejo Carpentier's position as Vice President of the Consejo Nacional de Cultura [National Council of Culture] and Executive Director of the Editorial Nacional de Cuba most likely facilitated this publication.

30. For information on the lectures see "Un siglo a la sombra de Proust" [A Century in Proust's Shadow] (*El Mercurio*, 18 July 1971) and Antonio Magaña-Esquivel's "Otro inventor de realidad" (*Hispanoamericano*, 28 October 1974).

31. The Spanish version published in Cuba added at this point several reservations which did not appear in the original lecture.These referred, in particular, to Proust's concept of paragraph, to his limited use of dialogue and to the connection between immediate reality and universality.

32. In a lecture that he delivered in Caracas in 1975, "Lo barroco y lo real maravilloso", Carpentier further suggested that true examples of "lo real maravilloso" can be found only in Latin America. However, for the more general but related phenomenon of the baroque, he cited Proust's work as a prime case (1984, 116).

33. Valdivieso recently published in *El espejo y la palabra* [The Mirror and the Word] (1997) a new version of his essay, which he called "Proust en nuestra América." But his ideas here are essentially the same as before. He has only added a few new quotations to substantiate his claim.

34. Even though both editions were allegedly published in their respective countries, the printed texts of the prologue by the Cuban critic Graziella Pogolotti and of Proust's work are identical and even have the same typographical errors.

35. New translations of the beginning of the *Recherche* have also appeared in Spain: *Por la parte de Swann* (1999) by Carlos Manzano and *Por la Parte de Swann* and *A la sombra de las muchachas en flor* (2000) by Mauro Armiño.

36. There have also been numerous theses and dissertations. In the bibliography I have listed six from Chile, one each from Cuba, Argentina, and Colombia. There were certainly others, but I have not been able to obtain information about them.

37. There have also been a few introductory booklets for students of literature. The Instituto Cubano del Libro published *Marcel Proust* in 1971 and created similar pamphlets on James Joyce and Alejo Carpentier. Likewise, Fascículo 20 of the *Historia universal de la literatura* (Bogotá, 1982) is devoted to Proust. *Apunte autodidáctico: Marcel Proust "En busca del tiempo perdido"* by Ana Victoria Mondada (México, 1989) is even more overtly pedagogical.

38. It is interesting to note that following his death *La Gaceta* recognized the attachment of Edmundo Valadés to Proust in a series of articles (November 1995).

39. Esteban Tollinchi became interested in Proust about the time of the Centennial and then published several articles and reviews linked to his work. Before these, however, little had appeared in Puerto Rico about the *Recherche*. I have only found two reviews of Proustian studies by Nilita Vientós Gastón (August 1950 and February 1960) and a few articles in *La Torre*.

40. Besides Alejo Carpentier and Magdalena Petit, few Spanish American Proustians have received the attention that they deserve. Curiously the Brazilians have been more warmly welcomed in France ever since Tristão de Athayde's study of Proust in *Revue de l'Amérique latine* (Paris, 1931). *Le Bulletin Marcel Proust* published in 1975 Ione de Andrade's angry response to Carpentier's suggestion that Proust was first known in Cuba. "Note sur les critiques brésiliens de Marcel Proust" does, in fact, recognize Brazil's contribution to the reading and study of Proust, but similar space has not been provided for a discussion of Spanish America.

41. Again, a comparison with Brazil is instructive. The Proustians themselves in this other Latin American country have studied much more carefully the importance of Proust's presence. See, for example, "Brasileiros nos caminhos de Proust" by José Nava (1960), "Proust et le Brésil" by Ione de Andrade (1972) or "A crítica literária Brasileira nos caminhos de Proust" by Ignacio Antonio Neis (1988–89).

42. Only one entire book has until now been devoted to this area and it dealt with a single author: *Carpentier's Proustian Fiction: The Influence of Marcel Proust on Alejo Carpentier* by Sally Harvey (London, 1994). There has also appeared recently a book

that is partially about Proust and a specific Spanish American writer: *Paraíso, meta-morfosis y memoria: La influencia de Proust y Kafka en la obra de Mujica Láinez* by Diana García Simón (Frankfort, 1998).

CHAPTER 2: THE EARLY STAGES

1. This definition of dialogue accounts for intertextualities that are non-literary as well as literary, and even those that are coincidental. In the present study I will, however, restrict our subject to those relations that imply the reading of a literary text and in some cases a critical one.

2. Harold Bloom's concept of "Tessera" (completion and antithesis) corresponds roughly to Bakhtin's "response," but it is much more difficult to understand or use.

3. In *Para leer a Marcel Proust* [For Reading Marcel Proust] Javier del Prado says, "*Pleasures and Days*, being at the same time a thematic archaeology, already sketches the narrative matrices in which we find some of the basic elements of the posterior work" (1990, 85).

4. In this instance, Painter quoted Proust's later essay "A propos du style de Flaubert" [On the Style of Flaubert]: "For writers intoxicated with Flaubert, I cannot recommend too highly the purgative, exorcizing virtue of parody; we must make an intentional pastiche in order to not spend the rest of our lives in writing involuntary pastiches" (1959, 2:99–100).

5. The narrator's remarks in *Le temps retrouvé* concerning the treatment of memory by Chateaubriand, Nerval and Baudelaire suggest how Proust wished both to follow and to distinguish himself from these precursors.

6. Because Bradbury studied in detail the relation between Proust's work and modernism in his book *The Modern World. Ten Great Writers*, I have selected him as my primary authority in this area.

7. As I suggested in the Point of Departure, it is in fact possible that the Venezuelans Manuel Díaz Rodríguez and Pedro-Emilio Coll were influenced twenty years earlier by Proust's first book *Les plaisirs et les jours*.

8. A few literary historians have been more accurate in assessing and defining this general relation. Rudolf Grossman, for example, wrote: "All of the great names in contemporary French literature find resonance in the New World. In the novel, Proust seems to take the lead, through the insistence with which he transposes to the present sensorial impressions linked to the past, he induces the Latin Americans to meditate more deeply upon their own genesis" (1972, 494).

9. Sánchez would later find in *La casa verde* [The Green House] "that unhealthy attention to detail acquired in Proust" (1968, 561), even though Vargas Llosa's connection with the *Recherche* in this regard is not particularly evident.

10. It is also worth noting that the protagonist-narrator is quite similar in the *Recherche* and *La casa de cartón*. He is not identified by name, but he designates himself by the first person, which links his past when he was a witness or participant, and his present, when he is the narrative speaker. Martín Adán's "yo" does not explicitly change over time like Proust's "je," but implicitly he becomes a writer who describes specific moments of his past. In the next few years, this Proustian type of narrator would become very common in Spanish America.

11. Critical references to this influence began to appear shortly thereafter. For example, in "Directrices de la novela y el cuento argentinos" [Directives of the Argentine Novel and Short Story] (*Nosotros* 295), E. Suárez Calimano wrote,

"Proust's way has tempted some new writers; we name *La pequeña Gyaros* [That Small Greek Island] by José Bianco (son) and *Europa* by Max Dickmann" (1933, 370).

12. In *Los Contemporáneos ayer,* Guillermo Sheridan also suggests the influence of André Gide on several of the Contemporaénos (including Salvador Novo) and how these writers progressed from the late stages of Spanish American *modernismo* to Occidental modernism. One can also find in this text an explanation of why these young writers, even though they may have learned of Proust relatively early, did not begin to write about him until somewhat late. First of all, they were primarily poets, but also they were distracted by various factors, including the cultural agenda proposed by José Vasconcelos.

13. Salvador Oropesa called "El joven" [The Young Man] (1928) by Salvador Novo "a Proustian exercise" (Foster 1994, 292). I agree that this prose text begins with echoes from the *Recherche* related to a bedroom and sounds of the morning, such as the cries of venders, and it is developed associatively as the young man wanders through the streets of Mexico City, somewhat like the protagonist of *Le côté de Guermantes* during his strolls through Paris. However, the slight attention paid to memory and imagination, as well as the very impersonal point of view (with the exception of the gay sites mentioned), distinguishes "El joven" from the manner of Proust.

14. Admittedly, other French writers of that period, such as Paul Morand or Jean Giraudoux, shared some of these same characteristics and helped to create in Mexico what Pedro Salinas called for Spain "la novela lírica." Just the same when Simone Bosveuil examined the parallel case of Spain, she attributed much of the lyricism of the time to Proust's influence. See "Proust y la novela española de los años 30: Ensayo de interpretación" (1978).

15. Curiously Mariano Azuela, who participated in the Proust homage of *Contemporáneos* in November 1928, began his experimental novel *El desquite* [Retaliation] (1925) with a flashback experience. Although the pungent odor of the woman's perfume, the immediate return to the past, and the male character's riding on a train, like the protagonist of *A l'ombre des jeunes filles en fleurs,* may have been inspired by Proust, there are few elements in the remainder of the text that seem in any way related to the French author.

16. Had it not been for the link between Villaurrutia's early prose and subsequent poetry, I would not have discussed the latter. Because of the need to limit my subject at least by genre, I have decided not to examine poetry or drama. This is somewhat regrettable because Pablo Neruda called Proust "el realista más poético" and suggested that the *Recherche* was a secret source for his imagery. See *Confieso que he vivido* [I Confess that I Have Lived] (1979, 137–39) or the anecdotes about Neruda that were told by Valdivieso in *Bajo el signo de Orfeo* (1980, 120–21).

17. Max Dickmann, for example, used a Proust-like observation in his story "Clocliot" (*Europa*): "De los seres que conocemos, que amamos, que odiamos, llevamos una sola imagen y es la que se superpondrá en nuestro espíritu a todas las sucesivas imágenes que de esos seres tendremos en la vida" [Of the beings that we know, that we love, that we hate, we carry a single image, and it is the one that will be superimposed in our mind upon all of the succeeding images that we will have of those beings in our life] (1930, 181). However, this remark applied to the destitute Parisian woman when she suddenly appears dressed very elegantly is ironic or humorous and not at all psychological. Clocliot has simply switched clothes with a wealthy American tourist.

18. In *The Postmodern Novel in Latin America* (1995, 8) Raymond Leslie Williams cites Martín Adán and Jaime Torres Bodet as two of the first modernists in Spanish

America, but I would contend that most of the early followers of Proust, beginning with Teresa de la Parra in *Ifigenia,* became modernists precisely by emulating the French author's emphasis upon the poetic and psychological facets of consciousness.

19. For Gálvez's interpretation of this polemic about him and the new generation, see *En el mundo de los seres ficticios* (1961, 254–60).

20. A possible exception is the novel by Ricardo Güiraldes *Don Segundo Sombra,* which I will discuss in Chapter 8. Also I will refer briefly to one of the Boedo writers, Roberto Mariani, in Chapter 4.

21. To some extent her sponsorship of the magazine *Sur* and of the publishing firm of the same name was an extension of her role as a reader, which she associated directly with Proust in the article that she wrote about him at the time of the Centennial. See "Proust" in *Testimonios: Novena serie 1971–1974* (1975, 106–11).

22. In *Le cosmopolitisme de Jorge Luis Borges,* Michel Berveiller noted in particular that Borges did not accord to Proust the position that he deserved in French and universal letters (1973, 228–29).

23. When I interviewed him in Buenos Aires on 10 November 1976, Borges said that he had begun to read Proust in Geneva (that is, either before he left Switzerland in 1918 or during a brief visit in 1920). From our discussion I was able to determine that he was quite familiar with the *Recherche* and in particular *A l'ombre des jeunes filles en fleurs* and *Le temps retrouvé.*

24. As these two texts are neither critical nor narrative, I have decided to discuss them in subsequent papers or articles. Until then one can see the pages that I have devoted to them in my dissertation "The Presence of Proust in Argentine Narrative" (University of Wisconsin, 1983, 158–69).

25. Julio Irazusta's translation of this same fragment from "Proust on Essences," which appeared in *Sur* in November 1936, makes the omission by Borges very evident: "life as it flows is lost time, and from it one can never recover or possess anything except in the form of eternity, *which is also as Proust tells us a form of art*" ("Una opinión de Santayana sobre el testimonio filosófico de Proust," 123, my emphasis).

26. Recent studies by persons such as Daniel Balderstron have exposed the fact that Borges, understood far more about homosexuality than he was willing to admit. See "The 'Fecal Dialectic': Homosexual Panic and the Origin of Writing in Borges" (1995).

27. From my discussion with Borges first in Madison, Wisconsin (April 1976) and then in Buenos Aires several months later, it became obvious to me that Proust's treatment of homosexuality in the *Recherche* both disturbed and secretly fascinated Borges. When I first asked him about Proust and his work, he responded abruptly and almost agressively, "I do not like the petty world of Proust, it is made of marchionesses and homosexuals."

28. It is interesting to note that a cousin of Borges, Alvaro Melián Lafinur, also composed a poem about the French novelist, "Elegía a Marcel Proust" (*La Nación,* 24 July 1927).

29. Alone cited it and listed its contents in his "Bibliografía crítica" of *Las mejores páginas de Marcel Proust* (1968, 40–41).

30. The distinction by Linda Hutcheon that parody has a literary target and satire, a social or moral one is quite instructive because it allows us to separate the elements of literary origin from those found in the world. Through it we can also see more clearly the differences between those types of parody that make a value judgement and those that do not.

31. It does not seem by chance that Silvia Molloy in *Signs of Borges* chose "Funes el memorioso" to compare Borges and Proust with regard to style. Although her purpose is very different from mine, she indirectly showed how much Borges exaggerated Proust's attention to detail. According to her, unlike Funes, Proust always "forgot" some elements in order to provide space (1994, 115–19).

32. Near the beginning of this lecture, which was presented 10 June 1949 at the Instituto Popular de Conferencias and can be read in this organization's *Anales* (35:57–68), Garma refers to an Argentine poet with whom she had discussed some of her ideas and who had called a portion of Proust's work "las páginas del tiempo que se obstina" [the pages about time as it persists]. The title of the lecture "Marcel Proust y la personalidad" and some of the ideas presented amply suggest that this poet was Borges because of the echoes from his early essay "La nadería de la personalidad." The French professor said, for example, of Proust, "He poses the problem of death, destruction, nothingness, and he discovers the nothingness of personality [la nada de la personalidad], since personality becomes for him an illusion" (1949, 62).

33. In his prologue to *El otro, el mismo*, Borges referred specifically to an important subject found in *A l'ombre des jeunes filles en fleurs*, which he eventually made central to his own poetical work: "la contradicción del tiempo que pasa y de la identidad que perdura" [the contradiction of time that passes and of identity that endures] (1972, 113). I note that this phrase is remarkably similar to the words that the Argentine poet mentioned by Garma used to describe Proust's text: "las páginas del tiempo que se obstina". Thus I can assert that in at least his poetry Borges made his peace with Proust and was able to accept the French novelist's inspiration.

34. In his rejection of memory, Mallea's character resembles to some extent Roquentin in *La nausée* [Nausea] (1938). Sartre's protagonist also examines involuntary memory and finds it devoid of meaning for his life.

35. Linda Hutcheon suggested that if a reader does not understand a particular allusion he will naturalize it (i.e., adapt it to the work as a whole), but in a parody "such naturalization would eliminate a significant part of both the form and content of the text" (1985, 34).

CHAPTER 3: ON HIGH SOCIETY

1. Despite the fact that Baudelaire spoke of the art of *la vie moderne* as a rebellion against bourgeois life and the modernist writers would always emphasize the spiritual over the material, Proust, like Woolf and similar writers, was able to devote his life to literature because of his financial position. Within the limits of his subjectivity he attempted to be impartial if not objective, but undeniably his social class colored his perspective and conclusions.

2. Although Marxists in the Soviet Union and Europe had previously interpreted Proust's work in this way (see the article by Marta Vergara or my discussion of it in chapter 1), to my knowledge, no Spanish American before Monteforte Toledo had presented in article form this type of judgement. The writers of Boedo, such as Roberto Mariani, had found value in the *Recherche* and José Carlos Mariátegui had considered Proust merely a dilettante. Leftist newspapers during the 1930s, such as *La Vanguardia* in Argentina and *El Popular* in Mexico, had been willing to publish articles on Proust by Enrique Anderson Imbert and Octavio Paz (albeit in the latter case with certain changes). Only in a translated text by John Strachey, "Literatura y Capitalismo" (*SECH* of Chile, July 1936) have I found a more critical point of view.

Yet, even here, Proust's work was merely used to prove the general decadence of capitalism and was in no way condemned.

3. Let me add that in these two works the presence of the *Recherche* is more apparent in other ways. Juan P. Ramos used Proust's ideas on memory in *La vuelta de las horas*, as we shall see in chapter 7, and in *A batallas de amor* Carlos Reyles followed Proust's psychological manner and treatment of memory, which we will examine in chapters 4 and 7.

4. According to Eugenio García Carrillo in "Marcel Proust en Costa Rica" (*La República*, 17 July 1971), Oreamuno did in fact know Monteforte Toledo, but they were not on friendly terms. The reference by García Carrillo to the Guatemalan's article on Proust suggests that their disagreement was political, but it could have also been personal.

5. Nonetheless it appears that Monteforte Toledo later studied more carefully the *Recherche* and tried to incorporate some aspects of it into *Una manera de morir* [A Way of Dying] (1955). This novel, unlike the Guatemalan's other works, portrays the interior life and conflicts of his principal characters and includes several flashbacks which approach Proust in their intention if not mechanism. It seems almost as if Monteforte Toledo wished to show the profound consciousness of his Marxist protagonist, but when he tried to depict Peralta's wealthy fiancée, she seemed more false than the bourgeois characters of most novels.

6. Caballero Calderón admitted to the influence of Proust in his prologue to *Caminos subterráneos:* "Proust me enseñó entonces a viajar dentro de mi propio espíritu. . . . Me adentré en el mundo proustiano con un fervor de navegante, porque los bosques de Méséglise y los jardines donde jugaron las niñas en flor tienen gran semejanza con los bosques y los jardines de mi infancia" [Proust taught me to travel within my own spirit. . . . I penetrated into the Proustian world with the passion of a navigator because the forests of Méséglise and the gardens where the girls in bloom played bear a marked resemblance to the forests and gardens of my childhood] (1936, 12). Although this early work was largely unsuccessful, it does show how the *Recherche* was a starting point for the career of this important Colombian writer.

7. Such modifications are indeed worth noting because Mujica Láinez did not merely borrow what he found in Proust's text. Such might appear to be the case according to the recent study by Diana García Simón, *Paraíso, metamorfosis y memoria: La influencia de Proust y Kafka en la obra de Mujica Láinez* (1998). Although admirable, because of the number of textual similarities that the author discovered between the work of Proust and that of Mujica Láinez, this study does not go beyond the situational reminiscences themselves and almost gives the impression that the Argentine created only by inlaying his work with the gems of the French text. I will not dispute the fact that Mujica Láinez used this type of *taracea* when he began to follow Proust, but his relation evolved over time from influence to inspiration, as we shall see.

8. In the case of Mujica Láinez, one can even see how his modernism is closely related to the Spanish American "modernismo" of the late nineteenth century. Some of his favorite authors were from that period, and he enjoyed depicting those years. Besides Enrique Larreta, he admired, for example, Lucio V. Mansilla, who had a personal connection with Proust. While living in Paris, this Argentine writer-diplomat had met Marcel through Robert de Montesquiou and is mentioned in one of their letters included in Proust's *Correspondance* (1970–1993, 6:350–51).

9. In *Writing Paris: Urban Topographies of Desire in Contemporary Latin American Fiction* (1999), Marcy E. Schwartz focused upon Cortázar's short stories set in the French capital. For her these texts still reflect the modernism that had originated with Charles Baudelaire, as well as the underbelly of Paris which he depicted in *Les fleurs*

du mal. As in the case of Jones, Schwartz significantly begins her detailed study with Cortázar, whose view of Paris and of contemporary literature had a profound impact on his Spanish American contemporaries and successors.

10. Carpenter said in his lecture on Proust and Spanish America, "his charcters did not accept any possible transposition to our world, being, as they were, too intimately bound to certain irreplaceable and immovable contexts. . ." (1972, 1323).

11. Sally Harvey implied this reduction when she wrote, "The key to the presence of these characters in Carpentier's novel lies not so much in the importance of their role in the narrative, but in Carpentier's ludic use of them. . ." (1994, 158).

12. As Hutcheon's book *A Poetics of Postmodernism: History, Theory, Fiction* (1988) focuses upon the literary aspects of postmodernism, and her ideas on parody in *A Theory of Parody: The Teachings of Twentieth Century Art Forms* (1985) are especially pertinent, I will use her as my primary authority in this area.

13. Milton Hindus called his study of the *Recherche* precisely *The Proustian Vision.*

14. When I asked José Donoso during a public symposium in Madison,Wisconsin in the Spring of 1975 about the relation between his work and Proust's, he spoke twenty minutes to the audience about the importance of names in the *Recherche* and in *Casa de campo,* which he was writing at that time. He also referred to his intention of parodying Proust's novel in this regard.

15. He alluded to *Monsieur Proust* in *Conjeturas sobre la memoria de mi tribu* (1996, 137).

16. Few critics have spoken in detail about "El tiempo perdido" perhaps because one must know Proust well in order to understand it. Ricardo González Vigil in his review of *Cuatro para Delfina* (*El Comercio,* Lima, 18 March) has provided the most accurate assessment: "Taking as a referential key the masterpiece by Proust, . . . it offers a very acute, bitter and ironic diagnosis of the cultural indigence of Spanish America, the castrating dependency upon what is European and the abandonment of principles by our generations" (1983, 16). I, however, do not agree with the suggestion that Donoso was against all aspects of the European connection.

17. The premise for this text is especially pertinent for Santiago, where during the late 1920s (two decades before the events described in the text) there existed a Proustian fervor, which was initiated and led by Alone, as we saw in chapter 1.

18. See, for instance, *Afinidades: Francia y América del Sur,* where Roberto F. Giusti, Eduardo Zalamea Borda, Benjamín Carrión, and other notable South Americans speak of the presence of France in Argentina, Colombia, Ecuador, etc.

19. For the complete text of the letter, see Gloria Durán's book *The Archetypes of Carlos Fuentes: From Witch to Androgyne* (1980, 204–5).

20. As Gene H. Bell-Villada pointed out in *García Márquez: The Man and His Work* (1990, 61), the former president of Colombia, Alfonso López Michelson, spoke of the kinship between *El amor en los tiempos del cólera* and Proust at the presentation of this novel in Bogotá. It is also interesting to note that García Márquez expressed his admiration for the *Recherche* in "El fantasma del Premio Nobel [2]" where he lamented the fact that some great writers like Proust had not received the Nobel Prize for Literature. See *Notas de prensa 1980–1984* (1995, 21–22).

21. The description in *El amor en los tiempos del cólera* (428) is of course much briefer, but its author, like Proust (2: 132–36), used new inventions to depict specific moments in time and to illustrate how time advances.

22. Although Sábato did not suppress this section in his later version (as he did in a few other cases), he omitted the initial, most controversial part. Perhaps the extreme violence of the Argentine military following the 1976 coup or the strong reaction by leftists to this portion of his text caused him to modify it. As certain aspects seem to have elicited the subsequent response by the Ecuadorian writer

Jorge Enrique Adoum, I have decided to cite here the original, but for other portions of *Abaddón*, I will quote from the 1991 edition.

23. Let me point out that this reference to Proust is very pertinent. The real novelist Sábato, who had been severely criticized in *Imperialismo y cultura* (1957, 255–75), was certainly aware that Hernández Arregui had considered the *Recherche* an extreme case of introspective literature, as I mentioned above.

24. Although Sábato's defense of Proust is somewhat different from that of Virgilio Piñera cited above, both rejected the idea of a *novela social* that excluded the *Recherche*.

25. To my knowledge, before *Entre Marx y una mujer desnuda*, only Mario Benedetti combined in a single novel from the left elements from the *Recherche* and a call to revolution. The past and social class are important themes in *Gracias por el fuego* (1965). The protagonist Ramón Budiño wishes to recover his past, his integrity, and that of his parents but not through involuntary memory itself. He imagines that by killing his corrupt and brutal father he can, as the text says, "recuperar el tiempo perdido" [recover lost time]. This idea, of course, implies a reinterpretation of the Proustian phrase, but it is closely allied to the guilt complex that Benedetti saw in the protagonist of *Du côté de chez Swann*.

26. Three other allusions to Sábato are found in close proximity on page 209: "yo no soy novelista, sino un personaje más" [I am not a novelist, but rather another chracter] (which I will discuss in chapter 8), the reference to characters that escape from their author's control, and the mention of a priest named Castelo and the virgin María, who bring to mind the principal characters of *El túnel*.

27. Let me point out that in a Spanish American context the term *burgués* generally refers to someone from the upper middle class, as in the title of Silvina Bullrich's novel *Los burgueses*. For the Marxists, *pequeño burgués* usually means a person from the lower middle class, but Adoum is playing with the idea of small and suggests that the *burgueses* in his country are few in number and ignorant from a cultural point of view.

28. The use of the word *inauténtico* by the Marxists appears to be contradictory or at least inconsistent. Are the characters inauthentic to the novel, to their national culture or to themselves?

29. Neither Donald L. Shaw nor Raymond L. Williams have claimed Alfredo Bryce Echenique for their side of the post-Boom versus postmodern debate, but the Peruvian novelist seems to fall more in the latter camp. According to Marcy E. Schwartz, Bryce is really a postcolonial writer because of his critical position toward his European or Occidental legacies. Although I agree with most of what she says about the relation between Proust and Bryce (*Writing Paris* 1999, 94), I would not attribute all of it to postcolonialism. Bryce comes very close to postmodernism through his rewriting and parody of the modernist Proust. Also his critical view of Marxist activism in *Cuadernos de navegación en un sillón Voltaire* would seem closer to postmodernism, which can be directed against the left as well as the right, than to postcolonialism, whose very name would seem to imply an anti-imperialist stance.

30. The *Diccionario de escritores hispanoamericanos* by Aaron Alboukrek and Esther Herrera, for example, has presented this relation as nearly pervasive: "Among the authors that have influenced his writing, one points to Marcel Proust because of the setting, the situations and the psychological traits of the characters" (1991, 46).

Chapter 4: On Love, Illness and Consciousness

1. Proust's approach to consciousness was, indeed, different from that of other modernists, such as Virginia Woolf. For example, in *Mrs. Dalloway* (1925) the third

person narrator enters selectively the consciousness of the various characters to show what they are thinking at a particular moment. Only the narrator has access to such information, and each character sees the consciousness of other persons as a mystery.

2. Enrique Anderson Imbert alluded to this relation when he wrote, "Roberto Mariani . . . was more complex: one of his complexities, his devotion for Proust" (1974, 2:136–37). The same can be said to some extent of Roberto Arlt whose two-part novel *Los siete locos* and *Los lanzallamas* reflects a Proust-like concern for consciousness. Not only did Arlt analyze his principal character by way of comparison, but also he considered the mechanisms of memory and the nature of time. Furthermore on occasion, he used physical sensations to stimulate Erdosain's visions of the future if not the past.

3. Rima de Vallbona described this relation but only in broad terms: "In general the literary production of Yolanda Oreamuno follows the Proustian vein of subtle psychological penetration and skillful depiction of the obscure depths of the subconscious" (1972, 41).

4. In *Gay and Lesbian Themes in Latin American Writing* Foster discussed in particular the 1914 play by the Argentine José González Castillo *Los invertidos* and the 1924 novel by the Chilean Augusto D'Halmar *La pasión y muerte del cura Deusto*, both of which are largely homophobic. *Latin American Writers on Gay and Lesbian Themes* also suggests that works of this type were unusual for Spanish America until 1950, even though they were already becoming somewhat common in Brazil.

5. The early reviewers of *Los ídolos*, for example, spoke of falseness, decadence or even mystery, but no one even pointed out the importance of Gustavo or the nature of the narrator's feelings for him.

6. With regard to some of the characters in the second novel *La casa*, Diana García Simón explained how their sexual ambiguity was modeled on that of some of Proust's characters (1998, 157–59).

7. It is in this context that the definition of *Bomarzo* that Mujica Láinez provided to me in a letter (1 March 1977) has greatest meaning: "it is a mixture of Proust and Alexandre Dumas, *père*."

8. I should acknowledge the fact that this aspect of *La tregua* is of secondary importance to the plot and that it has clearly homophobic overtones. Nonetheless, it shows how one Spanish American critic of the *Recherche* took advantage this model in his own work.

9. I would like to indicate that Julie Jones treated other aspects of Proustian memory in *Una familia lejana* in her book *A Common Place* (1998, 68).

10. In spite of Lezama Lima's denials concerning his relation with Proust, Arenas knew from personal experience how often Lezama talked about the author of the *Recherche* and in particular his concern for the subject of homosexuality. It is interesting to note that in his lecture in *El color del verano* the character Lezama associates Mary Magdalene, Proust's *madeleines* and the male member of Jesus Christ with no apparent contradiction (276).

11. J. E. Rivers has shown how Proust used the scientific theories on homosexuality of his time, most notably that of Karl Heinrich Ulrichs, who hypothesized the presence of a woman's soul in a man's body. See "The Myth and Science of Homosexuality in *A la recherche du temps perdu*" (1979).

12. In his second novel, *Sobre héroes y tumbas* (1961), Sábato at times approached Proust's psychological manner, especially through the use of analogy to explain a specific feeling or motive. A typical example is the comparison of Martín with a tightrope walker (1966, 22), which echoes Proust's trapeze artist (1:328) even

though the circumstances are linked to psychology instead of art. Furthermore Martín employs at times a Proust-like analysis of gestures in order to try to understand Alejandra and other persons (e.g., 183–87).

13. Although Cortázar's rebellion was in some ways similar to that of the writers of this French movement, his experimentation would never be as extreme or formalistic.

14. In a lengthy section from *El escritor y sus fantasmas*, Sábato pointed out the contradiction between Sarraute's stern criticism of the psychological novel and Proust and her own narrative practice, which dealt almost exclusively with the human mind and emotions. In this way he demonstrated that Sarraute was more a disciple of Marcel Proust and Virginia Woolf than one of their actual detractors. See "El extraño caso de Nathalie Sarraute" (1979, 49–55).

15. Like most Spanish American writers, Cortázar felt little attraction for such *nouveau roman* theories, which tended to intellectualize and dehumanize fiction. Even in *62: Modelo para armar* (1968) his characters remained individual and fully human. They were not reduced to being *simples supports* for his experimentation, as in the case of Sarraute's characters.

16. The discussion begins with a phrase that has been associated with Alain Robbe-Grillet, "fixer les vertiges" [capture vertigos], but Morelli immediately shifts the conversation to a subject that interests him more: "fijar elementos".

17. To elucidate this characteristic of the *Recherche*, Emir Rodríguez Monegal wrote in his article "Relecturas: Marcel Proust": "Each presentation of a character is a cross section in Time, it shows a moment in Time. . . . In each of these cross sections the Baron de Charlus is given entirely, is studied as a new being, is created and recreated before the reader so that the work of Time may be known" (1952, 14).

18. In "Una víctima de Proust" Jenaro Prieto illustrates quite well the reaction of at least some males to the protagonist-narrator of *A l'ombre des jeunes filles en fleurs* on his first night in the hotel at Balbec: "All of this, so it seems, denotes an exquisite sensibility; but the reader, being a normal and healthy man, feels the horrendous urge to get up along with the grandmother and lay a couple of punches on that little sissy so that once and for all he may lose his fear of clothes closets" (1973, 77).

19. This largely forgotten Colombian novel appears to have a direct relation with Proust. Antonio Curzio Altamar was correct in asserting that, like the author of the *Recherche*, Zalamea Borda discovered "deep chasms in a grain of sand" (1975, 243). This Proust-like *puntillismo* is especially apparent in Zalamea Borda's description of the deep-sea diver (1985, 112–13), which makes literal the image of Proust as an analyst who plunged to the depths of the human mind. He himself had suggested this image in *Le temps retrouvé* when he spoke of "un plongeur qui sonde" [a diver who probes the abyss] (3:879).

20. Vargas Llosa claimed that the smell became fantastic and said, "it no longer depends upon the subjectivity of the characters, it is autonomous" (1971, 466), but I contend that the original perception of the fragrance by Tobías is fundamental and its subjective nature is the point of departure for all that follows.

21. Mr. Herbert's vision of the future city with glass buildings and ballrooms resembles Balbec even more. See the description of the glass-enclosed restaurant by the sea in *A l'ombre des jeunes filles en fleurs* (1:681) or as I quote it in the section on Mujica Láinez in chapter 5.

22. In *The Postmodernist Novel in Latin America*, Raymond Leslie Williams argues that García Márquez privileged individual consciousness in *La hojarasca* [Leaf Storm] and was thus merely continuing the modernist strategies of William Faulkner (1995, 8). Nonetheless in "El mar del tiempo perdido" the Colombian author moved

beyond this stage and modernism itself, and thus he began to participate in postmodernism.

23. The author of *El libro* ends his quote from *Lecture de Proust* with these significant words: "What is sought is an external reality that can be converted into an internal one, one outside of the mind which would be the greatest possession of the mind, its light."

24. In *Physiologie de l'amour moderne* (1891) and other texts, Paul Bourget studied various types of love and perhaps inspired Florentino Ariza's numerous affairs.

25. In still more recent years Marco Tulio Aguilera Garramuño has treated the subject of love in his various works. At the beginning of *Buenabestia* (*El libro de la vida* I), this Colombian writer living in Mexico even states his intentions in Proustian terms (1994, 7). However, these appear to be related more to the vast dimensions of the multi-volume work than to a Proust-like vision or analysis. For the most part, Aguilera Garramuño remains closer to Henry Miller than to Proust even though the subject of writing appears frequently.

CHAPTER 5: ON ART, ARTISTS, AND THEIR ADMIRERS

1. I admit that Baudelaire was not the first French writer to exalt the creative artist or to claim that beauty and art had the right to exist for their own sake, but Malcolm Bradbury and other theorists of modernism have traced the idea of modernism back to Baudelaire (1990, 13).

2. I should point out that Proust employed the term *métaphore* to refer to comparisons that are explicit, as well as those that are implicit. Unlike English rhetoricians, he was indifferent as to whether the equivalent of "like" or "as" (*comme*) was included in the analogy. This was in part due to the fact that the word "simile" has no equivalent in French other than *comparaison*. Although I cannot claim that Proust was the first writer to describe by comparing, he most amply demonstrated the value of this technique and provided a justification for it. Perhaps for this reason other modernists, such as Virginia Woolf, increased their use of comparison as they moved closer to Proust. See, for example, the differences between *The Voyage Out* (1915) and *Mrs. Dalloway* (1925).

3. Emile Bedriomo summarized the principal critical remarks concerning this relation and expanded upon them in *Proust, Wagner et la coïncidence des arts* (1994).

4. It is worth noting that almost the same description appeared in one of Bianco's early short stories, "Rosalba," which can be found in his first book *La pequeña Gyaros* (1932, 88–89).

5. In his recent book *The Lust of Seeing* (1997) Frank Graziano pointed out various scattered points of contact between Proust and Hernández, such as the manner in which the Uruguayan evokes the past or eroticizes hopes.

6. I concede that Hernández's originality is more evident in other texts of that time, especially *El caballo perdido*, where his own peculiar form of imagination carried him farther away from Proust's example. In this case, we can see the Proustian subjects of piano playing and memory as a point of departure rather than as a model.

7. The spirituality of Proust's work has been studied in great detail, particularly by Barbara J. Bucknall in *The Religion of Art in Proust* (1969).

8. We can note, however, that Cortázar saw the work of James Joyce in a more favorable light because already *Ulysees* contained parodies of classical literature.

9. Barbara J. Bucknall studied with particular care the spiritual aspects of listening to music in the *Recherche*. See the fourth chapter of *The Religion of Art in Proust*.

10. Pimentel at first intended to write a book about Proust and Lezama Lima, but then shifted her focus to the *Recherche* itself and relegated her comments on Lezama to her prologue.

11. In "Lectura de Proust" (1990), for example, Antonio José Ponte referred in detail to Lezama's frequent oral commentaries on the French novelist.

12. Similarly, Enrique's creative aspirations reach fulfillment to a certain degree because the new government gives him the opportunity to restore some of the artistic treasures of Cuba's past.

13. Víctor Zamudio-Taylor and Inma Guiu (1994) suggested a relation between *Como agua para chocolate* and the *Recherche* but in the area of memory rather than art, as we shall see in chapter 7.

14. José Donoso appears to have followed the same Proustian passage in *Coronación* where he wrote of one of the family's cooks, "Rosario puso el pollo en el mármol de la mesa, y asestándole un golpe formidable con el cuchillo, separó la cabeza del cuerpo. Luego hizo una incisión entre los tutos, y metiendo la mano por el hueco extrajo un puñado de vísceras que dejaron un rastro sanguinolento en la mesa" [Rosario placed the chicken on the marble of the table, and dealing it a tremendous blow with the knife, separated its head from its body. She then made an incision between the wings and putting her hand through the hole, she extracted a fistful of innards which left a bloody trail on the table] (1968, 36).

15. For the images dealing with food and cooking, see in particular pp. 50–52 and 214–16 of Graham's book (1966).

16. In "Postmodern Parody and Culinary-Narrative Art in Laura Esquivel's *Como agua para chocolate*" (1994), Katheleen M. Glenn explained Esquivel's parodic relation with popular literature and culture but mentioned Proust only in passing.

17. At the very least, the mention of an author's name or work indicates knowledge and a possible comparison or contrast. Even though the use of *A l'ombre des jeunes filles en fleurs* as the title of chapter 17 of *El asalto* (1990) seems arbitrary (like the other borrowed chapter titles in this book), it demonstrates that Reinaldo Arenas was familiar with the *Recherche*. Also it suggests the enormous difference that existed between the Paris and Balbec that Proust had depicted and the checking station at the national prision that the Cuban author wished to describe.

18. As we saw in chapter 1, Anderson Imbert used these flaws to discover the secrets of Proust's narrative art.

19. Although Borges may be satiric of Proust's life and parodic of certain aspects of the *Recherche*, all of this appears within the conversation of the characters and between himself and the Proustian reader. Thus, I cannot claim that the story itself is a parody of a Proustian text.

20. In his case the not so modernist Lezama carried the practice of literary name dropping to an extreme. Cortázar used this practice frequently in *Rayuela* but reduced it in his later works. Jorge Enrique Adoum parodied it in *Entre Marx y una mujer desnuda*, as well as the Proust-like treatment of the novelist in the novel, as we shall see in Chapter 8.

21. It is interesting to note that Sábato also wrote a pastiche of Proust, "Tatarescu es invitado a comer en casa de Marcel", which can be found in *Genio y figura de Ernesto Sábato* (1971). This brief text is in fact "a la manera de Proust" as it claims, rather than a parody, because it simply illustrates the way in which the French novelist analyzed the patterns of thought of the cook Françoise.

22. Vargas Llosa on occasion has shown some interest in the *Recherche*, but this has never been strong. He published in *Marcha* (20 August 1965) "Proust en fotos," and he briefly discussed Proust's essay on Flaubert in *La orgía perpetua* (257–58).

23. Here, we may suspect an echo from *Rayuela,* which appears to have internationalized the subject of the novelist in the novel.

24. I must concede that there have been more parodies of Proust in Spanish America than pastiches of his manner. The one by Ernesto Sábato cited above is one of the few examples that I have found.

CHAPTER 6: ON LOST TIME AND THE SEARCH FOR IT

1. Referring to the title and length of the *Recherche,* Jenaro Prieto wrote in Chile, "It gives the impression not of trying to search for lost time, but rather of writing to waste time and to make others waste theirs" (1973, 75).

2. Certainly, other literary periods, such as that of Ronsard and the Pléiade, could be cited to illustrate the treatment of time. But, the similarity between the French and Spanish fifteenth century poets and their anticipation of this aspect of Proust seemed to me especially pertinent.

3. In *Mrs. Dalloway* the striking of Big Ben shows the chronological passage of time, but the sound itself often affects the individual characters in a subjective way, as when it causes Peter Walsh to see one of his clearest recollections of Clarissa (1925, 74–75). Here, Woolf came very close to Proustian memory but did not allow Peter to identify the moment. Also she did not present this past in detail the way that she did in other cases.

4. Scholars, from Hans Meyerhoff (*Time in Literature*) to Paul Ricoeur (*Temps et récit*), have emphasized the importance of time in modern literature and have demonstrated Proust's outstanding role in the development of this subject.

5. I concede that other writers, especially those who merely evoked in a general manner incidents from childhood had a closer connection with *La novela de un novelista* [The Novel of a Novelist] (1921) by the Spaniard Armando Palacio Valdés or such French works as *Le livre de mon ami* [My Friend's Book] (1885) by Anatole France or *Le roman d'un enfant* (1890) by Pierre Loti.

6. Louis Antoine Lemaitre has suggested that Teresa underwent a Proust-like memory experience in 1928 when she visited a sugar mill in Cuba and perceived the odor of raw sugar (1987, 134). Perhaps this experience inspired her description of the *trapiche* and other parts of *Las memorias de Mamá Blanca,* but not this work itself, which was begun earlier.

7. Another fragment from this same passage apparently echoes the beginning of *Cuadernos de infancia* and the *Recherche.* Bruno sees his past "como a través de un vidrio sucio, turbia e imprecisamente" [as through a dirty glass in a blurred and imprecise manner].

8. Here, Mujica Láinez treated his upper-class world as if it were a lost paradise. While the house is being demolished, she laments the disappearance of her former splendor.

9. Curiously, although written during the 1940s and only posthumously published recently (1998), *La estatua de sal* largely conforms to this pattern for Salvador Novo refers repeatedly to the process of memory. Of course, this private "diary," where the author traces, among other things, the origins of his homosexuality and describes his own promiscuity, differs considerably from other memoirs. But, this characteristic brings this work even closer to the author of *Sodome et Gomorrhe.* As Novo suggests in one of the rather scandalous sonnets published along with *La estatua de sal,* he intended in the work to unveil "Un Proust que vive en México!" [A Proust that lives in Mexico!] (1998, 124).

10. Donoso tells, for example, how, when he first sallied forth in search of a narrative subject, he did not encounter the marvels of the Chilean landscape or people, but rather he immersed himself in the world of Marcel Proust. He found more enticing the social ambiguity of *Le côté de Guermantes* than rural life in southern Chile (1996, 100).

11. *Le monde de Proust: Photographies de Paul Nadar* is composed of eighty-five such portraits. I also observe that Donoso's supposition about Laure Hayman even seems likely. In his note concerning her in *Marcel Proust: Selected Letters 1880–1903*, Philip Kolb said that she was born "at the Hacienda la Mariposa, in the Andes" (1984, 40). This location appears to coincide with the *fundo* Mariposas, which belonged to Donoso's family, as he explained.

12. In Proust's text the sound of a spoon striking a plate and the roughness of a napkin cause the protagonist to remember first a recent and then a distant moment from the past (3:868–69).

13. Although theatre by nature is quite distinct from narrative, one scholar has detected in a Cuban play of these years, *El chino* (1947), a Proust-like intention or ambition. According to Julio Matas, Carlos Felipe's principal character Palma is in search of a lost personal time: the evening when she experienced happiness with the sailor José. She, however, does not merely try to evoke the past through memory; she goes to considerable expense to reenact it through theatre. See "Pirandello, Proust and *El chino* by Carlos Felipe" (1983).

14. Perhaps Roberto Mariani, whose *Cuentos de la oficina* affected *La tregua* in several ways, may have inspired Benedetti for the use of the regional dialect. In his story from *El amor agresivo* "Un viajero" the Argentine pronunciation of the word *bullicio* causes the protagonist to recover the past.

15. Here, we can find the suggestion that some Spanish American authors, including perhaps Benedetti, knew Proust's work through versions in Spanish rather than by way of the original French. It is also worth noting that near the beginning of Cortázar's novel *Los premios* (1960, 19) Medrano's former girl friend, Bettina, spent her free time reading Menasché translation of the *Recherche*.

16. Julie Jones, among others, has examined the relation between la Maga and André Breton's Nadja (*A Common Place* 1998, 28–31). Although this connection is certainly valid for most of the circumstances related to Paris, when Oliveira's memory of la Maga begins to replace this character, her link with Albertine becomes more evident.

17. Proust named one of the sections of *Sodome et Gomorrhe* "Les intermittences du coeur" and used this term to designate the type of memory experience that his protagonist undergoes there when he reaches down to untie his boots. The narrator explains that a person's body seems to contain all of the moments of his past, but he only has access to them through physical sensations in the present (2:756–57).

18. A previous Argentine writer, Juan P. Ramos, had followed Proust briefly in a similar way. In *La vuelta de las horas* the principal character Julio Melves searches frantically through the streets of Paris for his former mistress and their daughter. He imagines seeing them several times but discovers that he is mistaken: "La misma apostura, los mismos tapados que descendieron en Viroflay. Sólo cuando llegaron a diez pasos de distancia vi que no eran ellas" [The same type of elegance, the same overcoats that got off in Viroflay. Only when they came within ten paces did I see that they were not the same women] (1933, 110–11).

19. Roberto Arlt, who compressed the action of *Los siete locos* into three days and used recollections of the past to provide background information about his characters, at one point, like Proust, has his narrator discuss the two forms of time: objective

and subjective. Of the Astrólogo we read, "La proximidad del crimen a cometer aceleraba en el espacio de tiempo normal otro tiempo particular. . . . Uno natural a todos los estados de la vida normal, otro fugacísimo y pesado en los latidos de su corazón . . . " [The proximity of the crime to be committed accelerated within the lapse of normal time another special time. . . . The one characteristic of all the states of normal life, the other very fleeting and heavy upon the beating of his heart. . .] (1978, 159).

20. Proust alluded to the possibility of traveling through time as through space but only in an imaginary sense. To describe his grandmother's vintage gifts and her affection for old things, the narrator of "Combray" says that they "exercent sur l'esprit une heureuse influence en lui donnant la nostalgie d'impossibles voyages dans le temps" [exert a favorable influence upon the mind by giving it a hankering for impossible voyages through time] (1:41).

21. See Harvey 1994, 158. Proust specifically made the point that not all art would survive. For this reason we find in Le temps retrouvé a critique of various types of mistaken or ephemeral literature.

22. It is interesting to note that in Sobre héroes y tumbas Bruno and Martín try to preserve Alejandra's life through their joint recollection of her. The above cited passage concerning the memories of Albertine may have inspired this idea. But also like Proust's principal character, Bruno realizes in Abaddón that all of his memories will disappear if he does not give them written form.

23. Curiously, Borges expressed this same idea in his poem "Adrogué," where he only slightly modified Proust's assertion that time is the fourth dimension by claiming this distinction for memory: "En ella sólo están ahora / Los patios y jardines" [Only in it are found now / the courtyards and gardens] (Obra poética 1972, 195).

24. There are also variants on this situation. Coronel Aureliano changes greatly during the civil wars (1996, 271), but when he returns home, it is he that cannot recognize Amaranta (280). Aureliano Amador, the last of the Coronel's seventeen sons, arrives at the house looking like a beggar, who paradoxically shows great dignity, and since no one recognizes him, he must identify himself (509).

25. "El mar del tiempo perdido" already displayed this trait because after the fragrance of roses disappeared the town returned to its former state.

26. Mujica Láinez employed Duma's portrait in a like manner in Los ídolos (1976, 191). Although less synthetic, the French author Michel Butor was more systematic in L'emploi du temps, where we find a constant juxtaposition of different moments in time. The narrator visits the same places and compares in his text what he experienced on each occasion.

27. McGowan examined the similarites and contrasts between the pure moment of time in García Márquez's novel and Proust's, but he limited the discussion to literature and metaphor and did not consider how such a moment may be directly related to involuntary memory itself.

28. Roger Shattuck named this period the "Banquet Years" in his book which bears this title (1968). Although he does not examine in this study the Recherche the way he does in other works, Shattuck followed Proust quite closely in his depiction of the time itself.

29. Similarly in "El mar del tiempo perdido," whose Proustian connection we examined in chapter 4, García Márquez used one year as his framing time unit.

Chapter 7: On Involuntary Memory

1. One example are the sections from the *Natural History* by Pliny the Elder that are discussed by Funes in the story by Jorge Luis Borges, but there were numerous other texts on memory.

2. In "Tiempo, distancia y forma en el arte de Proust," Ortega said "the remembrance of things is Proust's subject. For the first time here formally memory moves from being the material with which one describes something else to being the thing itself that is described" (1963, 2:703).

3. The narrator also talks about *Sylvie* by Gérard de Nerval and two poems by Charles Baudelaire "Parfum exotique" and "La chevelure" (3:919–20).

4. In *Proust* (1957, 23) Samuel Beckett cited eight memory experiences along with three "dark impressions," for a total of eleven incidents of exaltation in the *Recherche*.

5. Proust emphasized elsewhere its relation to a physical object. In "Combray" the narrator says of the past, "Il est caché hors de son domaine et de sa portée, en quelque objet matériel (en la sensation que nous donnerait cet objet matériel), que nous ne soupçonnons pas" [The past is hidden beyond its realm and reach, in some material object (in the sensation which that material object may give us), which we do not even suspect] (1:44).

6. In her book *Jaime Torres Bodet*, Sonja Karsen noted this Proustian relation, but she did not show how important this episode is (1971, 81–82).

7. Klaus Müller-Bergh suggested this idea in general terms when he wrote, "In reality it is the warm atmosphere of the inn and the intense aroma emanating from the cupboard filled with herbs that lends a unique Proustian light to these evocations . . . " (1972, 151).

8. Proustian memory plays a less important, yet perceptible role in "El acoso" (*Guerra del tiempo*). The ticket seller is reminded of his past by odors and other sensations. His memory of a love affair incites him to leave the concert hall and to visit a prostitute, which indirectly affects the outcome of the text.

9. Furthermore involuntary memory has been used at times merely to poeticize a common reality, as the writer in the third part of *Quien de nosotros* suggests. Lucas says in one of the notes to his short story, "creo que la recordaba, Alicia significaba un pormenor demasiado típico de aquellos años, como para olvidarla. . . . Pero, literariamente, es de más efecto recordarlo todo cuando ella aparezca, como si únicamente su imagen pudiera despertar mis recuerdos. Lo literario es siempre un poco *lo poético* y hay no sé qué cosa lírica en esa relación memoria-imagen" [I believe that I remembered her. Alicia signified a too typical part of those years to forget her. . . . But, literarily it creates a greater effect to remember everything when she appears, as if only her image could awaken my memories. What is literary is always to some extent *what is poetic* and there is an indescribable lyricism in that relation between memory and image] (1974, 78).

10. This Argentine's experimentation with Proustian memory appears to have began as early as his short story "La escalinata de mármol" (*Misteriosa Buenos Aires*, 1951). Here, on his deathbed in Buenos Aires the protagonist is able to recapture his early childhood through the process of association, and he thus realizes that he is the lost son of Louis XVI of France.

11. In her study of the influence of Proust and Kafka on the work of Mujica Láinez (*Paraíso, metamorfosis y memoria*), Diana García Simón observed a parallel between Silvano's finally recognizing Tití and the realization by the protagonist of *Le côté de Guermantes* that the woman who had caused Saint-Loup to suffer greatly was in reality *Rachel quand du Seigneur*, a prostitute that he had met before (1998, 160). Although

memory, of course, is involved in both cases and Proust's text may have in fact inspired Mujica Láinez, the Argentine showed his originality by creating a fully developed memory experience from the simple act of recognizing a person that had been met previously.

12. Indubitably persons from the working class are likewise affected by spontaneous memory, but the authors that wrote about such characters during those years, (e.g., Manuel Rojas and Carlos Droguett), were generally hesitant to describe their emotions fully or to analyze the memory process with great subtlety. Thus the memory experiences found in novels like *Mejor que el vino* (1958) or *El compadre* (1967) appear more distant from the *Recherche* and perhaps had an intermediate source.The novel by Rojas does contain specific Proustian echoes which could suggest a relation, but the case of Droguett's novel is less evident.

13. Weekly family rituals, particularly those of Saturday and Sunday, are described in detail in "Combray." In fact, approximately half of the second section of this part depicts a typical Sunday.

14. Again, let me emphasize that there were Spanish American novels of other types that were related to Proustian memory. Some even included brief dialogues with the *Recherche* that were quite original. Such appears to be the case of *La región más transparente*. See Helene I. F. De Aguilar's article "Secret Sharers: Memory in Proust and Fuentes" (1985). Also *Recuerdos del porvenir* by Elena Garro has a definite but elusive Proustian connection.

15. Referring to what is known as "le drame du coucher" [the drama of going to bed], the narrator says, "C'est ainsi que, pendant longtemps, quand, réveillé la nuit, je me ressouvenais de Combray, je n'en revis jamais que cette sorte de pan lumineux, découpé au milieu d'indistinctes ténèbres . . . à la base assez large, le petit salon, la salle à manger . . . " [Thus for a long time afterwards, when, woken at night, I recalled Combray, I never saw again any of it except this sort of luminous panel, cut out in the midst of an indistinct darkness, with its rather large base, to include the little parlor, the dining-room. . .] (1:43).

16. As we have seen several times, the concept of "buzo" [deep-sea diver] has often been associated with Proust (e.g. Eduardo Zalamea Borda's novel *4 años a bordo de mi mismo*) and a Proustian connection may be implied here.

17. Steven Boldy offered another Proustian interpretation of Oliveira's kiss, which in spite of its complicated symbolism appears also to be valid. Alluding to the binary oppositions found in both the *Recherche* and *Rayuela* and significantly represented by the same concept, "side" (*côté*, *lado*), Boldy spoke of the neutralization of the opposition through a kiss and a child of dissimilar parents (the nephew of the Guermantes and the daughter of Swann): "There is perhaps a certain Proustian element in the recovery of la Maga by Oliveira on kissing Talita.The syncretism of the two women unites Paris and Buenos Aires, 'This Side' and 'That Side', for Oliveira as does Mlle. de Saint Loup the *côtés* of Guermantes and 'chez Swann' in *Le temps retrouvé*" (1980, 65).

18. It is also feasible to consider a link between this episode in *Rayuela* and the climax of *Los ídolos*. Just as Mujica Láinez's narrator satisfies the desire that he had felt to embrace Gustavo in the outdoor cellar when he kisses Fabricia in the attic, Oliveira reconnects himself with la Maga by kissing Talita in the morgue basement of the asylum.

19. Louis Martin-Chauffier studied carefully the difference between the protagonist and narrator in "Proust et le double 'je' de quatre personnes" [Proust and the Dual "I" of Four Persons]. He said, for example, "Marcel the hero is expected to represent the void of a life that has not yet taken on meaning and the confusion of a

man who, anxious to find the reason for his stay on earth, constantly choses the wrong object. . . . The one who matters is the narrator, the one who discovers the secret of his sensations and, upon this discovery, he puts into order not his life but his art . . . " (1943, 60).

20. Near the end of this Colombian novel of 1928, the cry of a fruit vender allows the main character to recover his memories of Paris: "Al día siguiente de llegar me desperté al grito ritmado de 'Voilà les cerises, voilà les fraises: qu'elles sont bonnes!' Y para mí hubo más de la ciudad en este canto que en los cuatro kilómetros de calles que había recorrido para llegar a mi hotel la tarde anterior" [On the day after arriving, I woke up to the rhythmical cry of 'Here are my cherries, here are my strawberries: how good they are!' And for me there was more of the city in this chant than in the four kilometers of streets that I crossed to reach my hotel the preceding evening] (1977, 137). The street cries are reminiscent of the early pages of *La prisonnière*, but they also anticipate several passages in the work of Alejo Carpentier.

21. It was, of course, years later when García Márquez said that for him the smell of spoiled guava summarized the Spanish American tropics. See *El olor de la guayaba* (1982, 32). It is also interesting to note that, like María Eugenia, Ofelia has the impression of being transported across the Atlantic Ocean to the place of her childhood.

22. Carpentier further expanded upon this detail in another portion of his novel. In the episode where the Primer Magistrado stops in Havana and where the principal narrator momentarily speaks in the first person, we find in the listing of early morning sounds: "entrada de los pregoneros de la torreja, el aguacate y el tamal cantados a garganta de chantre gregoriano" [the arrival of the peddlers of slices of dried bread with sugar, avocados and tamales chanted with the voice of a Gregorian precentor] (1974, 43). In this case the reference to the religious origins of the cries reminds us that Carpentier had learned from Proust how to make this association. See chapter 1.

23. See "Alejo Carpentier à la recherche du temps perdu" (1980, 144) by Wendy Farris.

24. Although María Celia Darré saw a pastiche of Proust in "La Mayor" ("Proust a través de un cuento de Juan José Saer" [Proust through a Story by Juan José Saer]), this Argentine short story appears to be really a parody of the *Recherche* because of the critical distance with regard to Proust's ideas and style. Genette's distinction, as cited by Hutcheon, is pertinent: "parody is transformational in its relationship to other texts; pastiche is imitative" (1985, 38).

25. Another more recent dialogue on memory involving Proust can be found in *Pretérito perfecto* (1983) by the Argentine Hugo Foguet. Along with other recollections from the past, Clara Matilde remembers certain aspects of Proust's world, and in particular visiting the tomb of Gabriel Iturri, who was actually from Tucumán, Argentina like her and became the secretary and lover of Proust's aristocratic friend Robert de Montesquiou. As Gustavo Geirola points our in his article on Foguet in *Latin American Writers on Gay and Lesbian Themes*, the numerous references to Proust in *Pretérito perfecto* suggests Foguet's "Proustian attempt to reconstruct time" (1994, 158). But, I would add that the historian character Furcade tries to induce Proust-like memory experiences consciously by mentioning to Clara Matilde certain names and by serving her particular types of wine and snacks. Also this Proustian connection spreads to other parts of this work, including the writing of a novel and the use of Albertine-like characters.

26. Perhaps the remarks concerning food and memory by José Luis González in *La luna no era de queso* suggested to Esquivel the connection with Proust. Although a

364   MARCEL PROUST AND SPANISH AMERICA

Puerto Rican of half Dominican descent, he lived in Mexico for many years, and in this book of memoirs (published shortly before *Como agua para chocolate*) not only did he describe in affectionate terms the black cook that he had known in Santo Domingo (as I suggested in chapter 6) but also he explained how the smell of burning charcoal used in Dominican cooking affected him like Proust's *madeleines* (1988, 72–74).

27. In *The Magic Lantern*, Howard Moss wrote, for instance, "The affinity between the lantern slides and the stained glass window is one of the finer shades on Proust's palette, for it is through the 'lenses' of windows that Marcel is to observe certain secrets of life, each one illuminating a mysterious past he did not understand, or projecting a significant image into the future" (1962, 57).

28. Other Spanish American writers have expressed doubt concerning Proust's memory theories, although at times for other reasons. In *Tres tristes tigres*, Guillermo Cabrera Infante opposed his concept of "la memoria violenta" to that of involuntary memory (1983, 306).

29. In Esquivel's second novel, *La ley del amor* (1995), the association between music and memory is perhaps related to both Proust and Mujica Láinez. When the characters listen to beautiful selections from Puccini's operas, they recall the past somewhat like Swann, but the moments remembered are from a previous existence, as in the case of the narrator of *Bomarzo*. Clearly Esquivel has a profound interest in the mechanisms of memory and attributes to them a magical or fantastic sense.

CHAPTER 8: ON BECOMING A WRITER

1. In "Le 'je' proustien" Michihiko Suzuki studied in detail this matter and concluded that Proust wished his protagonist-narrator to appear anonymous in order to emphasize the distance between the "I" and the "other," that is, to present "an I that does not know other people" (1959, 80). Also, he did not want the reader to assume that the Marcel of the text was he himself, Marcel Proust. For this reason I refer to his character as the protagonist or narrator of the *Recherche* depending upon his age and function.

2. Goethe's *Wilhelm Meister* has been suggested as a possible model, but even Saint Augustine's *Confessions* has been proposed.

3. In his review of *Literaturas europeas de vanguardia*, Güiraldes criticized Guillermo de Torre's perspective because it led him to neglect writers like Proust and Joyce. See *Obras completas* 1962, 644.

4. Larbaud recommended that other foreign readers of French literature, such as a particular English woman, examine Proust. See the entry for 14 October 1919 in Larbaud's journal, *Oeuvres complètes 1954*, vol. 9: 428.

5. Already in *Raucho* (1917) can be found quite a few comparisons, but these often have little connection to the world of the narration. Thus, Proust seems to have helped the Argentine see the value of restricting himself to the *diégèse*.

6. In a minor Argentine work of these years, which is even called *La novela de una vocación*, Juan P. Ramos attributed a Proustian sense to the subject of a literary vocation by speaking in his introductory remarks about Proust and a particular memory experience that occurred when he found the letters which form the text of this work: "I suddenly revived . . . with the magic wand of hallucination . . . the life of two individuals to whom I owe spiritually the best part of what I still am . . . " (1946, 15).

7. I note, however, that Mujica Láinez's actual writing of his novel, like that of Proust, must have been laborious. In order to create the rich and diverse world of the Italian renaissance depicted in *Bomarzo* from the statues and the scant information available concerning the duke's life, the Argentine author had to work intensely.

8. It is difficult to make a complete list because in a few chapters like 93 some portions were written by Oliveira and others by the third person narrator, who comments on the character's remarks. Also, 73 and 87 are so universal in subject and tone that they are apparently the product of the principal narrator instead of Oliveira even though the first person is used.

9. The first portion of this chapter where Oliveira experiences anguish when he reaches down to tie his shoes is quite likely related to the passage in *Sodome et Gomorrhe*, where the protagonist is overwhelmed by the remembrance of his grand-mother when he bends over to untie his boots. Compare *Rayuela*, 532 and the *Recherche* 2: 755–56.

10. In his critical edition of *Rayuela*, Andrés Amorós cites, for instance as a Proustian echo, a metaphor concerning Japanese flowers (1986, 593).

11. Curiously Oliveira also echoes here the narrator of *La casa*, who would have preferred not to analyze Benjamín, the member of the upper-class family that was most responsible for its decline: "Ay, yo me niego a pensar en él ahora . . . . No quiero pensar en Benjamín, en la sordidez de Benjamín, el mediocre. . . . Sé que tendré que pensar en él . . . pero que no sea ahora . . . " [Oh, I refuse to think about Benjamín, about the squalor of Benjamín, the mediocre one. . . . I know that I will have to think about him, but may it not be now . . .] (1954, 94–95). Again it seems that Cortázar's relation to Proust is in some ways bound to the connection that he had with his more traditional fellow countryman Mujica Láinez.

12. Caballero Calderón spoke of that appartment and period of his life in the personal homage that he wrote at the time of the Proust Centennial. See "En torno y en el contorno de Marcel Proust" (1971).

13. Let me suggest that the title itself alludes to the beginning of French-Spanish American literary relations because the *limeño* Pablo de Olavide traveled to France to visit Voltaire. Also, Xavier de Maistre's title *Voyage autour de ma chambre* [Voyage around My Room] (1794) seems to be involved.

14. In "Alfredo Bryce Echenique o la reconquista del tiempo" (1985, 217), Luis Eyzaguirre saw this difference as being fundamental. I do not agree because it confirms by contrast the relation instead of denying it.

15. We saw earlier how both Mallea and Cortázar alluded to this passage concerning *Le Figaro*.

16. Also Adolfo Bryce Echenique in his two-volume set, like Reinaldo Arenas in his five volume series, *la Pentagonía*, seems to follow Proust, who had included seven volumes in the *Recherche*.

17. To a certain extent the same can be said of *Una familia lejana*. In this case, however, the character Carlos Fuentes primarily repeats what he heard from Count Branly and merely adds another layer of distance from the strange events.

18. Even her given name, like that of the young writer in *Abaddón el exterminador*, suggests a relation with Marcel Proust. I would also add that the name Martín, which shares the same first syllable, has been frequent in the novels that we have examined (e.g., *La bahía de silencio*, *Cuadernos de navegación en un sillón Voltaire*).

19. The close association between Proust and the story of a literary vocation can be observed in numerous ways. In addition to the texts examined in this chapter, the story by Augusto Monterroso "Leopoldo (sus trabajos)" [Leopoldo (His Works)] seems to confirm it. Although the Guatemalan author wished to satirize here those

Spanish Americans who all too easily believe that they have been "called" to write, the specific references in the text to both Proust and the *Recherche* (1994, 60, 69) serve to substantiate the relation.

20. In this respect portions of *La pérdida del reino* bring to mind the homoeroticism of *Los ídolos*.

21. Although Bianco's narrator appears timid in his presentation of Rufo's bisexual nature, he alludes to it constantly and in a very subtle manner.

22. Nivia Montenegro merely assumed that Sabato's ability to complete a text in the past will eventually lead him to success in the future (1978, 44).

23. It is interesting to note that in *Entre la vie et la mort* (1968) Nathalie Sarraute also modeled certain aspects of her fictional writer on Marcel Proust. By using only the subject pronoun *il* to designate him, she made her character more universal and anonymous than any of Sábato's aspiring authors, but several of her tropisms of a writer bring to mind situations from the *Recherche:* the character's vulnerablity in hotels at the seashore and his incapacity to describe in an exterior manner.

24. Proust first made this distinction in his essays on Sainte-Beuve, who had assumed that one can know a writer's work through his personal life. Also, as we have seen, Proust showed how his protagonist seemed to become a different person over time.

25. In the description of waking up, we can perceive a hint of Proust, as well as in the narrator's remarks concerning aging and his desire to finish the text before dying.

26. I willingly concede that not all stories of a literary vocation in Spanish America have a direct connection with Proust. In *Eva Luna* the narrator does tell how she became a writer, but here we find so few other points of contact with the *Recherche* that I cannot affirm that there is a direct relation between Isabel Allende and Proust. Instead she followed the picaresque tradition and apparently another Spanish American writer more closely allied with Proust. It seems to me significant that Eva's desire to become a writer appeared quite late in the text even though her storytelling ability was evident much earlier. Just the same, Allende's use of the phrase "recuperar el tiempo perdido" [to recover lost time] in the same passage where we find the suggestion that Eva could become a writer (1988, 207) led me to speculate on the feasibility of such a relation.

27. Curiously the narrator constantly addresses his readers as if they were all gay.

28. Even the subject of homosexuality, which we examined more fully in Chapter 4, is apparently linked to writing and Proust albeit through the author of the *Recherche* instead of the protagonist. According to the critic Robert Vigneron, Proust's personal interest in a German scandal involving homosexuality began the process that led to the writing of his great novel. Other critics have denied that the connection was so direct, but they have conceded that what Proust wrote after the Eulenburg affair in 1907 was incorporated into *Sodome et Gomorrhe.*

29. The whirlpool is, of course, linked to the end of *Cien años de soledad* and García Márquez's concept of time. Likewise the chronological contradictions in the Cuban novel can be compared to those found in *El obsceno pájaro de la noche.*

A Bibliography of Marcel Proust in Spanish America

I. Texts by Marcel Proust in Translation

A. Editions of Narrative and Expository Volumes

A1 *A la sombra de las muchachas en flor.* Trans. Pedro Salinas. Santiago: Zig-Zag, 1937.

A2 *A la sombra de las muchachas en flor.* Trans. Pedro Salinas. Buenos Aires: Santiago Rueda, 1944, 1980, 1995 (C. S. Ediciones), 1999 (Pluma y Papel).

A3 *A la sombra de las muchachas en flor.* Trans. Pedro Salinas. México: Libros de México, 1944.

A4 *Albertina ha desaparecido.* Trans. Marcelo Menasché. Buenos Aires: Santiago Rueda, 1946, 1980, 1995 (C. S. Ediciones), 1999 (Pluma y Papel).

A5 *Un amor de Swann.* Revised trans. Virgilio Piñera. La Habana: Editorial Nacional de Cuba, 1964.

A6 *El caso Lemoine.* Trans. Marcelo Menasché. Buenos Aires: Santiago Rueda, 1946.

A7 *El caso Lemoine (Parodias y Miscelánea I).* Trans. Antonio López Crespo. Buenos Aires: López Crespo Editor, 1976.

A8 *Crítica literaria.* Buenos Aires: NEED.

A9 *Crónicas.* Trans. Marcelo Menasché. Buenos Aires: Santiago Rueda, 1947.

A10 *Crónicas.* Trans. Eduardo Caballero Calderón. Bogotá: Instituto Colombiano de Cultura, 1972.

A11 *Crónicas.* Trans. Rubén Falbo. Buenos Aires: NEED, 1997.

A12 *Del lado de Swann.* Trans. Estela Canto. Buenos Aires: Editorial Losada, S. A., 2000.

A13 *En busca del tiempo perdido.* Trans. Pedro Salinas, José María Quiroga Pla, and Marcelo Menasché. Buenos Aires: Santiago Rueda, 1947.

A14 *En busca del tiempo perdido: Por el camino de Swann.* 2 vols. Trans. Ana Bergholtz Mujica. Guayaquil: Cromograf, S. A., 1974–75.

A15 *Final de los celos.* Trans. María Luz Huidobro. Santiago: Universitaria, 1990.

A16 *Flaubert y Baudelaire.* Trans. Juan Maurell. Buenos Aires: Galerna, Montevideo: Arca, 1978.

367

A17   *El indiferente.* Trans. Jorge Barón Biza. Buenos Aires: Rosenberg-Rita Editores, 1987.

A18   *El mundo de los Guermantes.* Trans. Pedro Salinas and José María Quiroga Pla. Buenos Aires: Santiago Rueda, 1945, 1980, 1995 (C. S. Ediciones), 1999 (Pluma y Papel).

A19   *Países y meditaciones.* Trans. Rubén Falbo. Buenos Aires: NEED, 1998.

A20   *Los placeres y los días.* Trans. Marcelo Menasché. Buenos Aires: Santiago Rueda, 1947.

A21   *Los placeres y los días.* Trans. Marcelo Menasché. Buenos Aires: C. S. Ediciones, 1996.

A22   *Los placeres y los días.* Trans. Pilar Ortiz Lovillo. México: Verdehalago, 1999.

A23   *Por el camino de Swann.* Trans. Pedro Salinas. Buenos Aires: Santiago Rueda, 1944, 1980, 1990, 1995 (C. S. Ediciones), 1999 (Pluma y Papel).

A24   *Por el camino de Swann.* Trans. Pedro Salinas. México: Promexa, 1979.

A25   *Por el camino de Swann.* 2 vols. Trans. Pedro Salinas. Bogotá: La Oveja Negra, 1982.

A26   *Por el camino de Swann.* 2 vols. Trans. Pedro Salinas. México: Editorial Origen-OMGSA, S. A., 1983.

A27   *Por el camino de Swann.* 2 vols. Trans. Pedro Salinas. Buenos Aires: Hyspamérica Ediciones, Orbis, S. A., 1983.

A28   *Por el camino de Swann.* La Habana: Editorial Arte y Literatura, 1987.

A29   *Por el camino de Swann.* Managua: Editorial Nueva Nicaragua, 1987.

A30   *Por el camino de Swann.* Trans. Pedro Salinas. Buenos Aires: Alianza Editorial, 1992.

A31   *La prisionera.* Trans. Marcelo Menasché. Buenos Aires: Santiago Rueda, 1945, 1980, 1995 (C. S. Ediciones), 1999 (Pluma y Papel).

A32   *Un relato.* Montevideo: Cele, 1978.

A33   *Los salones y la vida de París.* Trans. Eduardo Caballero Calderón. Bogotá: Librería Suramérica, 1945.

A34   *Sodoma y Gomorra.* Trans. Marcelo Menasché. Buenos Aires: Santiago Rueda, 1945, 1980, 1995 (C. S. Ediciones), 1999 (Pluma y Papel).

A35   *El tiempo recobrado.* Trans. Marcelo Menasché. Buenos Aires: Santiago Rueda, 1946, 1980, 1995 (C. S. Ediciones), 1999 (Pluma y Papel).

A36   *El tiempo recobrado.* Quito: Libresa, 1994.

A37   *La vida de Jean Santeuil.* Trans. Marcelo Menasché. Buenos Aires: Santiago Rueda, 1954.

A38   *La vida en París.* Buenos Aires: NEED.

B. Proust's Correspondence and Anthologies of His Work

B1   *Cartas a André Gide: Con tres cartas y dos artículos de André Gide.* Trans. Víctor Goldstein. Buenos Aires: Libros Perfil, 1999.

B2   *Correspondencia con su madre.* Trans. Magdalena Vicuña. Santiago: Zig-Zag, 1956.

B3   *Correspondencia* (with Madame Straus). México: Universidad Autónoma Metropolitana, 1985.

B4 En *busca de sí mismo*. Selection by Betty Ferber. México: SepSetentas, 1972.

B5 *Marcel Proust*. La Habana: Instituto Cubano del Libro, 1971.

B6 *Las mejores páginas de Marcel Proust*. Selection by Alone. Santiago: Nascimento, 1933, and Zig-Zag, 1968.

B7 *La memoria involuntaria*. Selection and prologue by Luis Antonio de Villena. Trans. Antonio Murillo. Buenos Aires: L. C. y Ecología Editora Argentina, 1988.

B8 *La muerte de las catedrales: A propósito de Marcel Proust y su obra*. Santafé de Bogotá: Norma, 1993.

B9 *Las palabras de Proust* (ring book). Selection by Edmundo Valadés. México: Editorial Extemporáneos, S. A., 1972.

B10 *Por el camino de Swann*. Selection by Mercedes Rein. Montevideo: La Casa del Estudiante, 1979, 1986.

C. Selections from Proust's Work, Poems, and Other Brief Texts

C1 "El Affaire Lemoine por Gustave Flaubert." Trans. Marco Antonio Campos and Bernardo Ruiz. *El Heraldo de México*, "El Heraldo Cultural" 523 (16 Nov. 1975): 7.

C2 "Aforismos Proustianos." Presented by Edmundo Valadés. *Novedades*, "México en la Cultura," 3d ser., 1163 (11 July 1971) 1, 3, 7.

C3 "A la sombra de las niñas floridas: Las jóvenes, Las flores, Las sirenas." *Revista de Revistas* (México) 514 (7 Mar. 1920): 19. Rpt. in *Orto* (Manzanillo, Cuba) 9.20 (18 July 1920): 4–5.

C4 "Albert Cuyp" and "Chopin." *Educación* (San Juan) 33 (June 1971): 117.

C5 "Un beso en cámara lenta." Trans. and presentation by Luz Aurora Pimentel. *Universidad de México* 550 (Nov. 1996): 7.

C6 "Los campanarios de Martinville." *El País* (Montevideo) 21 June 1928: 12.

C7 "Una carta de Marcel Proust." Trans. C. R. *Marcha* (Montevideo) 427 (7 May 1948): 15.

C8 "Cartas a la señora C." Presentation by Wilberto Cantón. *Excelsior* (México) 10 Oct. 1971, "Diorama de la Cultura": 8–10.

C9 "Chopin." *Excelsior* (México) 28 Feb. 1971, "Diorama de la Cultura": 6.

C10 "Comentarios sobre Dostoievsky y su obra". *¡Siempre!*, "La Cultura en México" 518 (12 Jan. 1972): 7–8.

C11 "De la estética de Proust: La falsedad del arte que pretende ser realista." Trans. Carlos Augusto León. *El Nacional* (Caracas) 11 July 1971, "El Papel Literario": 3.

C12 "Dos fragmentos de Marcel Proust: Los campanarios de Martinville. Los tres árboles." *Marcha* (Montevideo) 494 (9 Sept. 1949): 15.

C13 "El eclipse." Trans. and presentation by Javier García Méndez. *Plural* (México) 264 (Sept. 1993): 41–42.

C14 "El elogio de la lectura." *El País* (Montevideo) 14 Feb. 1938: 8.

C15 "Extractos de la correspondencia de Marcel Proust." Presented by Emilio Adolfo Wesphalen. *Las Moradas* (Lima) 2.4 (Apr. 1948): 10–16.

C16 "Fragmentos: La magdalena. Los campanarios de Martinville." In *Un amor de Swann*, 199–206. La Habana: Editorial Nacional de Cuba: 1964.

C17   "Gide/Proust: Correspondencia." *La Gaceta* (México), new ser., 77 (May 1977): 12–14.

C18   "El hotel de las cuatro torrecillas." Trans. C. de la Colina. *Nuevo Amanecer Cultural* (Managua) 396 (30 Jan. 1988): 6.

C19   "La iglesia de aldea." *El Tiempo* (Bogotá) 29 Mar. 1953, "Suplemento Literario": 1.

C20   "Las intermitencias del corazón." Trans. Emir Rodríguez Monegal. *Marcha* (Montevideo) 311 (7 Dec. 1945): 14–15.

C21   "La irrealidad del pasado." *La Nación* (Buenos Aires) 20 Jan. 1924, sec. 3: 8.

C22   "Maestro epistolar." Presentation by Edmundo Valadés. *Novedades,* "México en la Cultura" 1164 (18 July 1971): 3, 6–7.

C23   "Marcel Proust." *Marcha* (Montevideo) 1.4 (14 July 1939).

C24   "Marcel Proust a la condesa de Noailles." Trans. Ernesto Volkening. *Eco* (Bogotá) 135 (July 1971): 239–43.

C25   "El marqués de Guercy o la herencia de madame de Villeparisis." Trans. and presentation by Alberto Ruy Sánchez. *Uno más uno* (México), "Sábado" 271 (15 Jan. 1983): 1, 3.

C26   "Mirándola dormir." *El Comercio* (Lima), 13 June 1971 "Dominical": 26.

C27   "La música en la obra de Proust." Trans. and presentation by Carlos Malagarriga. *Nosotros* (Buenos Aires) 258–59 (Nov./Dec. 1930): 189–212.

C28   "Notas de lectura." *Letras de México* 3.2 (15 Feb. 1941): 4.

C29   "Pauline." Trans. Jaime Moreno Villarreal. *Biblioteca de México* 27 (Sept./Oct. 1993): 6–9.

C30   "Un pequeño pastel. Principio de Memoria Involuntaria." In *La técnica del fluir de la conciencia en la novela moderna.* Ed. Ervin R. Steinberg. Trans. Elisa Moreno C., 73–81. México: Noema Editores, S. A, 1979.

C31   "Un poema inédito de Proust." Presentation by León Roche. *La Nación* (Santiago) 11 Nov. 1928: 4.

C32   "Por el camino de Swann." *El Universal Ilustrado* (México) 444 (12 Nov. 1925): 55–56.

C33   "Por el camino de Swann." In *La literatura en sus fuentes,* by Francisco Montes de Oca, 564–67. México: Editorial Porrúa, S. A., 1979.

C34   "Por el camino de Swann. Combray I." In *Compilación de textos de literatura europea.* Ed. Jorge Avila Storer, Adelina Eugenia and Alcalá Gallegos, 554–70. Aguascalientes, Mex.: Universidad Autónoma de Aguascalientes, 1994.

C35   "La Princesa Matilde." *El Sol de México,* "En la Cultura" 202 (13 Aug. 1978): 8.

C36   "Proust, crítico literario a sus horas explora las novelas de Balzac, Chateaubriand, Tolstoi, Dostoievski, Georges Eliot . . . " Trans. Alvaro Mutis. *Novedades,* "Mexico en la Cultura" 622 (13 Feb. 1961): 10, 16.

C37   "Retratos de pintores (Cuyp, Watteau, Van Dyck)." Trans. José Lezama Lima. *Nadie parecía* (La Habana) 7 (Mar./ Apr. 1943): 12.

C38   "La sensibilidad de un mundo agonizante." *¡Siempre!,* "La Cultura en México" 110 (25 Mar. 1964): xxiii.

C39   "Sentimientos filiales de un parricida." Trans. Abraham Valenzuela. *Atenea* (Concepción) 2.10 (31 Dec. 1925): 515–26.

C40 "Sobre el gusto." Trans. M. D. M (Manuel Díaz Martínez?). *Mensajes* (La Habana) 1.24 (29 Oct. 1970): 8–9.

C41 "Sobre la lectura." Trans. Manuel Arranz. *La Gaceta* (México): 288 (Dec. 1994): 15.

C42 "La sonata de Vinteuil." Presented by Enrique Anderson Imbert. *La Vanguardia* (Buenos Aires) 22 Oct. 1933: 7.

C43 "El sueño de Albertina." *Novedades,* "México en la Cultura" 1163 (11 July 1971): 4.

C44 "Violante o la mundanidad." In *Narrativa francesa clásica y moderna.* Ed. Enrique Congrains Martín. Bogotá: Editorial Forja, 1986.

LITERARY CRITICISM OF PROUST'S WORK WRITTEN OR PUBLISHED IN SPANISH AMERICA

D. Books, Theses, Pamphlets, Essays, and Chapters or Extended Discussion in Books

D1 Albérès, René-Marie (René Marill). "El novelista-artista: Proust memorialista." In *Historia de la novela moderna.* Trans. Fernando Alegría, 144–49. México: Unión Tipográfica Editorial Hispanoamericana, 1966.

D2 Alone (Hernán Díaz Arrieta). "Ensayo sobre Marcel Proust" and "Bibliografía crítica." In *Las mejores páginas de Marcel Proust,* 7–60. Santiago: Editorial Nascimento, 1933. Rpt. in Zig-Zag edition, 9–47, 1968.

D3 ———. "De la introducción a 'Las mejores páginas' de Marcel Proust." In *Leer y escribir (Antología de Alone),* 170–76. Santiago: Zig-Zag, 1962.

D4 ———. "Epílogo" to *Las mejores páginas de Marcel Proust,* 319–28. Santiago: Zig-Zag: 1968.

D5 ———. "Univers de Proust," "El extraño caso de Painter y Proust," "El misterio de la creación literaria," "Segundo Tomo del 'Proust' de Painter," "Al margen del 'Proust' de Painter II tomo," "'Marcel Proust et Henry James, une confrontation,'" "Marcel Proust y Henry James," "Marcel Proust y Henry James confrontados," "Jean Santeuil," "Marcel Proust y Marcel Plantevignes," and "Marcel Proust du coté de la médecine." In *Crónica literaria: Literatura francesa,* 85–135. Santiago: Editorial Andrés Bello, 1971.

D6 Alvarez, María Edmee. "La novela psicológica: Marcel Proust." In *La literatura universal a través de autores selectos,* 312–14. México: Editorial Porrúa, S. A., 1976.

D7 Anderson Imbert, Enrique. "El taller de Proust." In *Los grandes libros de Occidente y otros ensayos,* 225–41. México: Andrea, 1957. Rpt. with additions as "El taller de Marcel Proust." In *Los domingos del profesor,* 226–33. Buenos Aires: Gure, 1972.

D8 ———. "Marcel Proust" and "Retrospectiva de la creación literaria." In *La flecha en el aire,* 68–69, 209–10. Buenos Aires: Gure, 1972.

D9 Arias Trujillo, Bernardo. "Evocación fugaz de Marcel Proust." In *Diccionario de emociones,* 129–37. Manizales, Colom.: Casa Editorial y Talleres Gráficos Arturo Zapata, 1938.

D10   Ayala, Francisco. "Proust en la inactualidad." In *Histrionismo y representación*, 133–45. Buenos Aires: Sudamericana, 1944.

D11   Azuela, Mariano. "Marcel Proust" (published lecture) and "Por el camino de Proust." In *Obras completas*. Vol. 3, 934–70, 1267. México: Fondo de Cultura Económica, 1960.

D12   Balza, José. *Proust*. Caracas: Universidad Central de Venezuela, 1969.

D13   ———. "Proust en noviembre." In *Transfigurable*, 181–88. Caracas: Universidad Central de Venezuela, 1983.

D14   ———. "Mnémonica: Paralelismos (Proust)." In *Ese mar narrativo: Ensayos sobre el cuerpo novelesco*, 133–73. México: Fondo de Cultura Económica, 1987.

D15   Barthes, Roland. "Proust y los nombres." In *El grado cero de la escritura, seguido de Nuevos ensayos críticos*, 171–90. Buenos Aires: Siglo XXI Argentina Editores, 1973.

D16   Beckett, Samuel. "Proust." Trans. Raquel Benolea. In *Eh Joe y otros escritos*, 47–103. Caracas: Monte Avila Editores, C. A., 1969.

D17   Bemol, Maurice. *Orientaciones actuales de la literatura francesa*. Trans. María Luisa Colombino. Buenos Aires: Troquel, 1960.

D18   Benda, Julien. *El triunfo de la literatura pura o la Francia bizantina*. Trans. Segundo V. Tri, 172–78, 181–85, 187–89. Buenos Aires: Argos, 1948.

D19   Benedetti, Mario. "Búsquedas." In *Peripecia y novela*, 41–46. Montevideo: Talleres Gráficos "Prometeo", 1948.

D20   ———. "Marcel Proust." In *Marcel Proust y otros ensayos*, 9–34. Montevideo: Número, 1951. Rpt. as "Marcel Proust y el sentido de la culpa," in *Sobre artes y oficios*, 54–83. Montevideo: Alfa, 1968 and in *El ejercicio del crítico*, 49–70. México: Editorial Nueva Imagen, 1981.

D21   Benjamin, Walter. "Para una imagen de Proust." In *Sobre el programa de la filosofía futura y otros ensayos*. Trans. Roberto J. Vernengo, 239–51. Caracas: Monte Avila, 1961, 1970.

D22   ———. "Para una imagen de Proust" (fragment). In *Capítulo universal. Literatura contemporánea* no. 21, 18. Buenos Aires: Centro Editor de América Latina, S. A., 1970.

D23   Beutler, Maurice. *Proust*. Colección Hombres de la Historia. Buenos Aires: Centro Editor de América Latina, 1970.

D24   Bianco, José. "Proust y su madre," "Centenario de Proust" and "El ángel de las tinieblas." In *Ficción y realidad (1946–1976)*, 19–39, 41–52, 59–109. Caracas: Monte Avila, Editores, C. A., 1977.

D25   ———. "Proust y su madre," "Centenario de Proust" and "Marcel Proust a los sesenta años de su muerte." In *Homenaje a Proust seguido de otros artículos*, 11–55. México: Universidad Nacional Autónoma de México, 1984.

D26   ———. "El ángel de las tinieblas." In *Páginas de José Bianco seleccionados por el autor*, 111–43. Buenos Aires: Editorial Celtia, 1984.

D27   Blanchot, Maurice. "La experiencia de Proust." In *El libro que vendrá*. Trans. Pierre de Place, 17–31. Caracas: Monte Avila, 1969.

D28   Boisdeffre, Pierre de et al. *Proust*. Trans. Patricio Canto. Buenos Aires: Editorial Jorge Alvarez, S. A., 1969.

D29 Botero Jiménez, Nodier. "Marcel Proust y la desmitificación de la profundidad afectiva." In *El mito en la novela del siglo XX: Joyce, Proust, Kafka, Hesse, Camus y Beckett,* 115–51. Bogotá: Ediciones Avance, 1985.

D30 ———. "Proust" and "La novela sicológica de Proust". In *Crítica de la novela moderna: Teoría narrativa, estética y esquemas didácticos.* 147–50, 162–67. Armenia, Colom.: Editorial Quingráficas, 1985.

D31 Bullrich, Silvina. "La Francia desconocida." In *El mundo que yo vi,* 31–34. Buenos Aires: Editorial Merlín, 1969.

D32 ———. "De Flaubert a Proust." In *La aventura interior,* 103–08. Buenos Aires: Emecé Editores, 1977.

D33 Cabrera Alvarez, Carlos. "El tiempo vivido: Marcel Proust" and "La paradoja de Marcel Proust." In *Tiempo y literatura,* 21–25, 97–102. Buenos Aires: Instituto Amigos del Libro Argentino, 1971.

D34 Campos, Julieta. *Función de la novela,* 39–42, 75–76. México: Editorial Joaquín Mortíz, 1973.

D35 Carpentier, Alejo. "Novedades acerca de Proust" and "Genio y voluntad." In *Letra y solfa,* 65–68. Caracas: Síntesis Dosmil, 1975.

D36 ———. "Novedades acerca de Proust." In *El Adjetivo y sus arrugas,* 36–38. Buenos Aires: Editorial Galerna, 1980.

D37 ———. "Un acontecimiento literario," "Ha muerto una heroína de novela," "Novedades acerca de Proust," "Un nuevo inédito de Proust," "Genio y voluntad," and "Un memorable entre los *Memorables".* In *Letra y solfa: Literatura. Autores,* 29–30, 51–53, 100–01, 151–52, 189–90, 266–67. La Habana: Editorial Letras Cubanas, 1997.

D38 Carrera, Mario Alberto. "Marcel Proust." In *Freud, Marcuse, Fromm, Reiche, Proust, Wilde, Ortega y Gasset, Nietzsche, Beckett y otros,* 2–11. Guatemala: Editorial RIN, 1981.

D39 Carrión, Benjamín. "Marcel Proust y la busca del tiempo perdido." In *En busca del tiempo perdido: Por el camino de Swann.* Vol. 1, 5–13. Guayaquil: Editorial Ariel, Ltd., 1974. Rpt. in *Plan del Ecuador,* 153–62. Quito: Casa de la Cultural Ecuatoriana, 1977. Rpt. in *El libro de los prólogos,* 317–29. Quito: Imagso, Cía, Ltd., 1979.

D40 Ciocchini, Héctor E. "Goncourt, Proust, Genet, metafísica de lo invisible." In *Temas de crítica y estilo,* 70–97. Bahía Blanca, Arg.: Homenaje al 150 Aniversario de la Revolución de Mayo: 1960.

D41 Coyné, André. *Note sur l'aventure humaine.* Lima: Imprenta Torres Aguirre, S. A. 1956.

D42 ———. *Nota sobre la aventura humana. El ejemplo de Proust.* Lima: Editorial San Marcos, 1957.

D43 ———. *Proust el admirable.* San Luis Potosí, Méx.: Instituto Potosino de Bellas Artes, 1962.

D44 Curtius, Ernst. *Marcel Proust y Paul Valery.* Buenos Aires: Losada, 1941.

D45 Dajes, Jorge. "Entre Swann y Guermantes: Marcel Proust y el mundo judío" (published lecture). In *Cuatro grandes escritores y el mundo judío: Joyce, Kafka, Proust, Mann.* Ricardo González Vigil, et al., 17–38. Lima: Industrial Gráfica, S. A. 1983.

D46 Delgado, Honorio F. "Marcel Proust y la penumbra anímica." In *De la cultura y sus artífices,* 281–93. Madrid: Aguilar, 1961.

D47   Destéfano, José Rafael. "Marcel Proust." In *Ocho ensayos*, 89–104. Buenos Aires: El Ateneo, 1943. Rpt. in *Baudelaire y otras rutas de la nueva literatura*, 141–56. Buenos Aires: El Ateneo, 1945.

D48   Díaz Ruiz, Ignacio. *Siglo XX: Sociedad, pensamiento y literatura: La novela y el cuento*, 47–49. México: Editorial EDICOL, S. A. 1976.

D49   Dickmann, Max. "Estudio preliminar." In *Marcel Proust: Juventud-Obra-Tiempo*, by Leon Pierre Quint, 7–28. Buenos Aires: Santiago Rueda, 1944.

D50   ———. "Cronología de la vida y las obras de Marcel Proust." In *En busca del tiempo perdido*, by Marcel Proust. Buenos Aires: Santiago Rueda, 1947.

D51   Durant, Will and Ariel. "Marcel Proust." In *Interpretaciones de la vida*. Buenos Aires: Editorial Sudamericana, 1973.

D52   "En busca de Marcel Proust." In *Un relato*, by Marcel Proust, 5–24. Montevideo: Cele: 1978.

D53   Estrada, Genaro. "Por el camino de Proust." In *Obras: Poesía/narrativa/crítica*, 350–52. México: Fondo de Cultura Económica, 1983.

D54   Ferber, Betty. "Una métafora de la felicidad." Trans. Jorge Arturo Ojeda. In *En busca de sí mismo*, 9–26. México: SepSetentas: 1972.

D55   Fernández, Sergio. "Una vejez largamente ensayada: el Barón de Charlus." In *El estiércol de Melibea y otros ensayos*, 399–402. México: Universidad Nacional Autónoma de México, 1991.

D56   Frank, Joseph. "La forma espacial en la novela moderna." In *Aspectos de la novela moderna*. Trans. Gustavo Goyen Larrosa, 6–12. Montevideo: Fundación de Cultura Universitaria, 1973.

D57   Franulic, Lenka. "Marcel Proust." In *Cien autores contemporáneos*, 761–72. Santiago: Empresa Ercilla, S. A., 1952.

D58   Frattoni, Oreste. "Para el nombre de Albertine (En Proust)." In *La forma en Góngora y otros ensayos*, 73–79. Rosario, Arg.: Universidad Nacional del Litoral, 1961.

D59   Frejaville, Eva. *Marcel Proust desde el Trópico* (published lecture). La Habana: La Verónica, 1942.

D60   ———. "Marcel Proust y la novela francesa actual." Thesis. Universidad de la Habana?, 1951.

D61   Galimberti, Ana. *La atmósfera estética de "A la recherche du temps perdu"* (published lecture). Tandil, Arg.: Universidad Nacional del Centro de la Provincia de Buenos Aires: 1982.

D62   ———. *Marcel Proust: estudio de antecedentes, materiales estéticos y estilo en "La Recherche."* Mendoza, Arg.: Universidad Nacional de Cuyo, 1992.

D63   Gallegos Valdés, Luis. "Marcel Proust reencontrado." In *Tiro al blanco*, 181–87. San Salvador: Ministerio de Cultura, 1952.

D64   Gálvez, Manuel. "La literatura y el conocimiento: A propósito de Marcel Proust." In *El espíritu de aristocracia y otros ensayos*, 145–66. Buenos Aires: Agencia general de librería y publicaciones, 1924. Rpt. as "Novela y conocimiento" in *El novelista y las novelas*, 54–62. Buenos Aires: Emecé Editores, S. A. 1959.

D65   Gannon, Patricio. "La Exposición Proust." In *Esqueletos divinos*, 125–29. Buenos Aires: Losada, 1971.

D66   García Calderón, Ventura. "La literatura de lujo y literatura proletaria." In *Arte de marear*, 131–53. Paris: Garnier Hermanos, 1936.

D67   García Ponce, Juan. "En torno a Marcel Proust." In *Entrada en materia*, 77–82.
      México: Universidad Autónoma de México: 1968.

D68   ———. "El lugar de Proust." In *Apariciones (Antología de ensayos)*, 343–51.
      México: Fondo de Cultura Económica, 1987.

D69   ———. "Marcel Proust: Imposibilidad del amor, posibilidad de novela." In
      Imágenes y visiones, 89–104. México Editorial Vuelta, S. A., 1988.

D70   Garrido, Felipe? "Advertencia." In *En busca de sí mismo*, 5–8. México: SepSe-
      tentas, 1972.

D71   Genette, Gérard. "Proust palimpsesto." In *Figuras*. Trans. Nora Rosenfeld
      and María Cristina Mata, 45–75. Córdoba, Arg.: Ed. Nagel Kop, 1970.

D72   Girard, René. "Los mundos proustianos." In *Mentira romántica y verdad nove-
      lesca*. Trans. Guillermo Sucre, 141–65. Caracas: Ediciones de la Biblioteca
      de la Universidad Central, 1963.

D73   Gómez, Eduardo. "Marcel Proust o la relación paradojal e irónica con el
      inconsciente." In *Ensayos de crítica interpretativa: T. Mann, M. Proust, F.
      Kafka*, 11–16. Bogotá: Ediciones Tercer Mundo, 1987.

D74   Gómez Brown, Juan Carlos. *Tres maestros de la novela francesa: Balzac, Bourget,
      Proust*. Montevideo: Biblioteca "Confraternité universelle balzacienne",
      Rpt. in *Camus en su Calígula literario y otros ensayos*, 5–35. Montevideo:
      Barreiro y Ramos, S. A., 1970.

D75   González González, Luis. "Contribution à l'étude de la langue de Françoise
      dans l'oeuvre de Proust: Aspects Phonétiques et Sémantiques". Thesis
      [*memoria*], Universidad de Chile, Facultad de Filosofía y Educación, 1958.

D76   Houston, John Porter. "Proust, Gourmont y la herencia simbolista." In *La
      moderna crítica literaria francesa: De Proust y Valery al estructuralismo*. Ed. John
      K. Simon. Trans. Coral Bracho, 57–77. México: Fondo de Cultura Eco-
      nómica, 1984.

D77   Inostroza R., Julio César. "La proposition subordonée chez Proust d'après
      Du côté de chez Swann, A l'ombre des jeunes filles en fleurs, et *Le côté de Guer-
      mantes*." Thesis [*memoria*] Universidad de Concepción (Chile), Escuela de
      Educación, 1961.

D78   "Introducción," to *Marcel Proust*, 3–5. La Habana: Instituto Cubano del Li-
      bro, 1971.

D79   Irazusta, Julio. "Proust." In *Actores y espectadores*, 153–66. Buenos Aires: Sur,
      1937.

D80   King, Shirley. *Comiendo con Marcel Proust: Recetas de la Belle Epoque*. Trans. Sara
      Luisa de Carril. Buenos Aires: Emece, 1982.

D81   Kolb, Philip. "Prefacio" to *Correspondencia de Marcel Proust con su madre*, 7–13.
      Santiago: Zig-Zag, 1956.

D82   Laguna López, Carlos. "Marcelo se redime." In *Notas de literatura contem-
      poránea*, 103–17. México: Compañía Editorial Continental, S. A., 1980.

D83   Levin, Harry. "Balzac y Proust." In *Interpretaciones críticas*. Trans. Edgar
      Rodríguez Leal, 101–16. Caracas: Ediciones de la Biblioteca de la Univer-
      sidad Central de Venezuela, 1967.

D84   Loayza, Luis. "Vagamente dos peruanos." In *El Sol de Lima*, 75–82. Lima:
      Mosca Azul Editores, 1974.

D85   Luna, Andrés de. *Proust y el cine: El proyecto imposible*. México: Imprenta de
      Juan Pablos, 1994.

D86 Mallea, Eduardo. *El sayal y la púrpura,* 72–75. Buenos Aires: Losada, 1941.

D87 "Marcel Proust." In *Los salones y la vida de Paris,* 5–9. Bogotá: Editorial A. B. C., 1945.

D88 "Marcel Proust." *Enciclopedia de la literatura.* Vol. 5. Ed. Benjamín Jarnés, 246–48. México: Editora Central, S. A.

D89 *Marcel Proust en Venecia.* Polanco, Uru.: Fundación Cultural Televisa, 1997.

D90 Martínez Estrada, Ezequiel. *Panorama de las literaturas,* 358–59. Buenos Aires: Editorial Claridad, 1946.

D91 Matamoro, Blas. *Por el camino de Proust.* Barcelona: Editorial Anthropos, 1988.

D92 Maurell, Juan. "Prólogo" to *Flaubert y Baudelaire,* by Marcel Proust, 5–17. Buenos Aires: Editorial Galerna, Montevideo: Arca, 1978.

D93 Mauriac, Claude. *Proust por él mismo.* Trans. Aurelio Garzón del Camino. México: Compañía General de Ediciones, S. A., 1958.

D94 Mauriac, François. *Escritos íntimos.* Trans. José Bianco. Buenos Aires: Criterio, 1955.

D95 Maurois, André. *Cinco rostros del amor.* Buenos Aires: Espasa-Calpe, 1942, Austral, 1951.

D96 ———. "Marcel Proust." In *Estudios literarios.* Trans. Guido Parpagnoli. Buenos Aires: Librería Hachette, S. A., 1942.

D97 ———. "Marcel Proust." In *Estudios literarios.* Trans. Nazario J. Domínguez, 67–99. México: Editorial América, 1946.

D98 ———. *En busca de Marcel Proust.* Buenos Aires: Espasa Calpe Argentina, S. A. (Austral), 1958.

D99 May, Derwent. *Proust.* Trans. Jorge Ferreiro. México: Fondo de Cultura Económica, 1986.

D100 Meneses, Guillermo. "El tiempo perdido y desmenuzado." In *Espejos y disfraces: 4 textos sobre arte y literatura,* 29–49. Caracas: Editorial Arte, 1967.

D101 Mondada C., Ana Victoria. *Apunte autodidáctico: Marcel Proust "En busca del tiempo perdido."* México: Fernández Editores, 1989.

D102 Monterroso, Augusto. "Proust." In *La letra e (Fragmentos de un diario),* 153. México: Ediciones ERA, S. A. de C. V., 1987.

D103 Montescaut, Jean Jacques. *Eco u origen: hacia una sistematización de la relación proustiana con el mundo* (project for promotion). Mérida, Vene.: Universidad de los Andes, 1978.

D104 Morán, Julio César. "La música como develadora del sentido del arte en Marcel Proust." Thesis, Universidad Nacional de La Plata, 1996.

D105 Morand, Paul. "No ha dejado nunca de ser un esteta." In *Enciclopedia de Educación: Suplemento de arte,* 333–34. Montevideo: Imprenta Nacional: 1932.

D106 Moreno, Artemio. "Semblanza de Marcel Proust." In *El Sentimiento en la vida y en el arte,* 197–210. Buenos Aires: Samay Huasi, 1929.

D107 Moro, César. "El sueño de la cena de Guermantes" and "Imagen de Proust." In *La tortuga ecuestre y otros textos,* 121–28, 139–58. Caracas: Monte Avila Editores, C. A. 1976.

D108 Mujica Láinez, Manuel. "Recuerdos de Proust." In *Placeres y fatigas de los viajes.* Vol. 2, 179–81. Buenos Aires: Editorial Sudamericana, 1984.

D109   Mutis, Alvaro. "La compañía de Proust." In *Poesía y prosa*, 389–90. Bogotá: Instituto Colombiano de Cultura, 1981.

D110   Nabokov, Vladimir. "Marcel Proust: Por el camino de Swann." In *Lecciones de literatura*. Trans. Francisco Torres Oliver, 305–59. Buenos Aires: Emece, 1984.

D111   Nieto de Arias, Gloria. *A la recherche des peintures du temps perdu/En busca de las pinturas del tiempo perdido*. . . . Bogotá: Editorial Veritas, 1993.

D112   O'Brien, Justin. "Proust confirmado por la neurocirugía." In *La técnica del fluir de la conciencia en la novela moderna*. Ed. Erwin R. Steinberg. Trans. Elsa Moreno C., 124–28. México: Noema Editores, S. A, 1982.

D113   Ocampo, Victoria. "Proust." In *Testimonios: Novena serie 1971/1974*, 106–11. Buenos Aires: Sur, 1975.

D114   Ortega y Gasset, José. "Ideas sobre la novela." In *Meditaciones del Quijote. La deshumanización del arte*, Buenos Aires: Espasa-Calpe Argentina, S. A., 1942.

D115   Ortiz de Montellano, Bernardo. "Por el camino de Proust." In *Obras en prosa*, 200–01. México: Universidad Nacional Autónoma de México, 1988.

D116   Palacios, María Fernanda. "Proust y la palabra insomne" and "Presentes sucesiones de difunto." In *Sabor y saber de la lengua*, 51–67, 69–75. Caracas: Monte Avila Editores, C. A., 1986.

D117   Paz, Octavio. "Distancia y cercanía de Marcel Proust." In *Primeras letras (1931–1943)*, 118–28. Barcelona: Editorial Seix Barral, S. A., 1988.

D118   Peltzer, Federico. "Marcel Proust y el amor creación." In *El amor creación en la novela*, 163–68. Buenos Aires: Editorial Columba, 1971.

D119   Peña, Carlos Héctor de la. *La novela moderna*, 83–90, 117–20. México: Editorial Jus, 1944.

D120   Pérez, Carlos D. "Proust o el gusto autobiográfico." In *La situación autobiográfica*. Ed. Juan Orbe, 79–86. Buenos Aires: Ediciones Corregidor, 1995.

D121   Petit (Marfan), Magdalena. "Marcel Proust y la literatura," "La psicología en las obras de Proust y Dostoiewsky" and "Proust y Azorín." In *Ensayos y cuentos*, 11–39. Santiago: "La Nación," 1966.

D122   Pierre-Quint, León. *Marcel Proust (Juventud-Obra-Tiempo)*. Trans. José Mora Guarnido. Buenos Aires: Santiago Rueda, Editor, 1944.

D123   ———. "El estilo de Proust." In *Un amor de Swann*, by Marcel Proust, 193–98. La Habana: Editorial Nacional de Cuba, 1964.

D124   Piñera, Virgilio. "Al lector," and "Realidad y ficción en las obras de Proust." In *Un amor de Swann*, vii-xvi, 207–08. La Habana: Editorial Nacional de Cuba, 1964.

D125   Pla, Roger. "Proust y el tiempo al estado puro." In *Proposiciones (Novela nueva y narrativa argentina)*, 47–54. Rosario, Arg.: Editorial Biblioteca, 1969.

D126   Pogolotti, Graziella. "Prólogo" to *Por el camino de Swann*, by Marcel Proust, 7–17. La Habana: Editorial Arte y Literatura, 1987. Rpt. in *Por el camino de Swann*, 7–17. Managua: Editorial Nueva Nicaragua, 1987.

D127   Ponce, Aníbal. "La sensación olfativa en Marcel Proust." In *Estudios de psicología*. Vol. 18, 265–70. Buenos Aires: El Ateneo, 1941. Rpt. in *Obras completas*. Vol. 2, 257–60. Buenos Aires: Editorial Cartago, 1974.

D128   "Presentación" of *Por el camino de Swann*, by Marcel Proust, ix-xiii. México: Promexa, 1979.

D129   Pujol, Carlos. *El tiempo de Proust.* Historia Universal de la literatura no. 20. Bogotá: Editorial Oveja Negra, 1982.

D130   Rangel Guerra, Alfonso. *Imagen de la novela,* 70–73. Monterrey, México: Universidad de Nuevo León, 1964.

D131   Rein, Mercedes. *Información general sobre la literatura del siglo XX,* 48–53. Montevideo: Ediciones de la Casa del Estudiante.

D132   ———. "Marcel Proust." In *Por el camino de Swann,* by Marcel Proust. Montevideo: La Casa del Estudiante, 1979.

D133   Repilado, Ricardo. "El lenguaje y la caracterización en Proust." In *Cosecha de dos parcelas,* 11–38. La Habana: Editorial Letras Cubanas, 1985.

D134   Requeni, Antonio. "En Illiers, cuyo nombre es Combray." In *Los viajes y los días,* 33–38. Buenos Aires: Santiago Rueda, Editor, 1970.

D135   Rest, Jaime. "Marcel Proust." In *Capítulo universal: Literatura contemporánea* no. 21, 19–24. Buenos Aires: Centro Editor de América Latina, S. A., 1970.

D136   Restrepo, María Cristina. *El olvido en la obra de Marcel Proust.* Medellín, Colom.: Universidad Pontificia Bolivariana, 1986.

D137   Revel, Jean-François. *Sobre Proust.* Trans. Jesús Morán. México: Fondo de Cultura Económica, 1988.

D138   Reyes, Alfonso. "Vermeer y la novela de Proust," "La última morada de Proust," and "Proust y los gusanos de cuatro dimensiones." In *Grata compañía,* 68–80. México: Tezontle, 1948. Rpt. in *Obras completas.* Vol. 12, 60–70. México: Fondo de Cultura Económica, 1960.

D139   Reyes, Salvador. "Por el camino de Proust." In *Peregrinajes literarios en Francia,* 63–70. Santiago: Editorial Andrés Bello, 1968.

D140   Reyles, Carlos. "Marcel Proust y su mundo fantasmagórico y realísimo, surgido de la memoria del olvido." In *Incitaciones: ensayos breves,* 109–25. Santiago: Ercilla, 1936. Rpt. in *Ensayos.* Vol. 3, 122–40. Montevideo: Biblioteca Artigas, 1965.

D141   Ribeyro, Julio Ramón. "Del espejo de Stendhal al espejo de Proust." In *La caza sutil,* 127–31. Lima: Editorial Milla Batres, 1976. Rpt. in *Antología personal,* 139–43. México: Fondo de Cultura Económica, 1994.

D142   Rivas González, Marta. "Marcel Proust: Face à l'Affaire Dreyfus." Thesis [*memoria*], Universidad Católica de Chile, Facultad de Filosofía y Ciencias de la Educación, 1967.

D143   Rivas, Marta. *Un mito proustiano.* Santiago: Editorial Universitaria, S. A., 1968.

D144   Rojas Osorio, Eliana. "Marcel Proust observateur." Thesis [*memoria*], Universidad Católica de Chile, Facultad de Filosofía y Ciencias de la Educación, 1966.

D145   Sánchez, Luis Alberto. "Marcel Proust." In *Panorama de la literatura actual,* 89–97. Santiago: Ercilla, 1934.

D146   Sansone, Eneida. *La creación artística en Marcel Proust.* Montevideo: Facultad de Humanidades y Ciencias, 1950.

D147   Santayana, George. "Proust y las esencias." In *Diálogos en el limbo.* Trans. Raimundo Lida, 61–65. Buenos Aires: Losada, 1941.

D148   Scarpa, Roque Esteban. "Proust y Plinio." In *El libro en la mano,* 81–85. Santiago: Editorial Universitaria, S. A. 1954.

D149 Schiefele, Hannes. "Importancia de Freud para la consideración del arte (Marcel Proust, James Joyce, Thomas Mann)." In *El psicoanálisis viviente.* Fritz Riemann et al. Trans. Irene Garfeldt-Klever de Leal, 167–92. Buenos Aires: Compañía general fabril editora, 1961.

D150 Serrahima, Mauricio. "Marcel Proust: Prólogo," to *Compilación de textos de literatura europea.* Ed. Jorge Avila Storer, Adelina Eugenia, Alcalá Gallegos, 547–54. Aguascalientes, Mex.: Universidad Autónoma de Aguascalientes, 1994.

D151 Serrano Poncela, Segundo. "El gran experimento: Marcel Proust." In *Literatura occidental,* 654–58. Caracas: Ediciones de la Biblioteca de la Universidad Central de Venezuela, 1971.

D152 Siré, Agustín. "Marcel Proust." Thesis [*memoria*], Universidad de Chile, 1944.

D153 Slochower, Harry. "Marcel Proust: La redención estética." In *Ideología y literatura (Entre las dos guerras mundiales).* México: Ediciones Era.

D154 Soto, Luis Emilio. "Benjamim Crémieux y algunos problemas de la crítica." In *Crítica y estimación,* 39–56. Buenos Aires: Ediciones Sur, 1938.

D155 Téllez, Hernando. "Las cartas de Proust." In *Textos no recogidos en libro.* Vol. 1, 150–52. Bogotá: Instituto Colombiano de Cultura, 1979.

D156 Thibaudet, Albert. "Novela y tiempo: Marcel Proust." In *Historia de la literatura francesa (Desde 1789 hasta nuestros días),* 471–74. Buenos Aires: Ed. Losada, S. A., 1939.

D157 Tollinchi, Esteban. *La conciencia proustiana.* Río Piedras, P. R.: Editorial Universitaria, 1978.

D158 Torre Reyes, Carlos de la. "Marcel Proust y su tiempo." In *Nuevas crónicas de Parsifal,* 277–80. Quito: Casa de la Cultura Ecuatoriana, 1976.

D159 Torres Bodet, Jaime. *Tiempo y memoria en la obra de Proust.* México: Porrúa, S. A. 1967.

D160 ———. "Marcel Proust: Resurrección." In *Obras escogidas,* 1105–19. México: Fondo de Cultura Económica, 1983.

D161 Torri, Julio. "Marcel Proust: La epopeya de los celos y el snobismo." In *Tres libros,* 129–32, México: Fondo de Cultura Económica, 1964. Rpt. in *De fusilamientos y otras narraciones,* 129–32, México: Lecturas Mexicanas, 1984.

D162 Untermeyer, Louis. "Marcel Proust." In *Forjadores del mundo moderno.* Trans. Julio Juelmo, et al. Vol. 2: 913–23. México: Biografías Gandesa, 1957.

D163 Valadés, Edmundo. *Por caminos de Proust.* Coyoacán, Méx.: Editorial Samo, S. A. 1974 and Miguel Angel Porrúa, 1983.

D164 ———. "Montesquiou y Proust." In *Excerpta,* 83–90. México: Editorial Katún, S. A., 1984.

D165 Valazzi Mackenzie, Ivy. "Tres grandes novelistas del siglo XX (Marcel Proust, James Joyce, Thomas Mann)." Thesis [*memoria*], Universidad de Chile, Facultad de Filosofía y Educación, 1949.

D166 Varderi, Alejandro. "Los dos caminos de Marcel," "Algunos triángulos de amor no correspondido en la obra de Marcel Proust." In *Anotaciones sobre el amor y el deseo,* 15–21, 23–26. Caracas: Academia de la Historia, 1986.

D167 Vargas Llosa, Mario. *La orgía perpetua: Flaubert y "Madame Bovary",* 257–58. Barcelona: Editorial Seix Barral, S. A., 1986.

D168 Vicuña Luco, Osvaldo. "Cartas acerca de Marcel Proust." In *Correspondencia: Crítica literaria, apuntes íntimos, artículos y divagaciones*, 132–42. Santiago: Imprenta Universitaria, 1946.

D169 Vientós Gastón, Nilita. "Cuatro libros sobre Marcel Proust." In *Indice cultural*. Vol. 1 (1948–56), 93–96. Río Piedras, P. R.: Ediciones de la Universidad de Puerto Rico, 1962.

D170 ———. "Cinco libros sobre Marcel Proust." In *Indice cultural*. Vol. 3 (1959–60), 95–96. Río Piedras, P. R.: Editorial Universitaria, 1971.

D171 Villena, Luis Antonio de. "Introducción," to *La memoria involuntaria*, 7–31. Buenos Aires: L. C. y Ecológica Editora Argentina, 1988.

D172 Volkening, Ernesto. "Marcel Proust (10 de julio de 1871)." In *Ensayos II: Atardecer europeo*, 187–97. Bogotá: Biblioteca Colombiana de Cultura, 1976.

D173 Winograd Yontef, Sara Miriam. "Para qué leer a Marcel Proust? Análisis de la función de la literatura a través de *En busca del tiempo perdido*." Thesis, Universidad de los Andes (Bogotá), 1977.

E. Articles, Reviews, and Notes on Proust Published in Spanish American Periodicals

E1 Acevedo Escobedo, Antonio. "Por el camino de Proust." Rev. of *Marcel Proust*, by Georges D. Painter. *El Nacional* (México) 12 Feb. 1968: 4.

E2 Achury-Valenzuela, Darío. "A la memoria de Marcel Proust." *Cultura Universitaria* (Caracas) 22 (Nov./Dec. 1950): 37–48.

E3 Adolph, José B. "Proust o la totalidad." *La Prensa* (Lima) 21 Oct. 1979: 23.

E4 Aguilera Garramuño, Marco Tulio. "Notas de lectura sobre: *En busca del tiempo perdido* (I): *Por el camino de Swann*." *Excelsior* (México), "El Búho" 397 (18 Apr. 1993): 1, 6.

E5 ———. "*A la sombra de las muchachas en flor* (II)." *Excelsior* (México), "El Búho" 399 (2 May 1993): 8.

E6 ———. "*En busca del tiempo perdido* (III): *El mundo de los Guermantes*." *Excelsior* (México), "El Búho" 403 (30 May 1993): 6.

E7 ———. "Notas de lectura de *En busca del tiempo perdido* (IV): La búsqueda de valores en el mundo de Guermantes." *Excelsior* (México), "El Búho" 407 (27 June 1993): 7.

E8 ———. "*Sodoma y Gomorra*: Notas sobre *En busca del tiempo perdido*." *Excelsior* (México), "El Búho" 410 (18 July 1993): 5.

E9 ———. "Notas sobre *En busca del tiempo perdido:* El verdadero placer: Sodoma y Gomorra." *Excelsior* (México), "El Búho" 412 (1 Aug. 1993): 2.

E10 ———. "Notas sobre *En busca del tiempo perdido:* La dualidad: *Sodoma y Gomorra*." *Excelsior* (México), "El Búho" 415 (22 Aug. 1993).

E11 ———. "La sociedad de los sodomitas según Proust." *Plural* (México) 263 (Aug. 1993): 71.

E12 ———. "El perseguidor de fantasmas: *Sodoma y Gomorra*." *Excelsior* (México), "El Búho" 420 (26 Sept. 1993): 2.

E13 ———. "Las ideas fijas y el sueño: *Sodoma y Gomorra*." *Excelsior* (México), "El Búho" 430 (5 Dec. 1993): 2.

E14 ———. "*Sodoma y Gomorra:* La hora de afrontar la vida." *Excelsior* (México), "El Búho" 435 (9 Jan. 1994): 2.

E15 ———. "Albertina ha desaparecido o la imposibilidad de la comunicación." *Plural* (México) 276 (Sept. 1994): 28–33.

E16 ———. "La función del amor en la literatura." *Plural* (México) 179 (Dec. 1994): 71–72.

E17 Alamán, Alfonso. "Marcel Proust." *Novedades,* "México en la Cultura" 288 (26 Sept. 1954): 3; 289 (3 Oct. 1954): 3; 290 (10 Oct. 1954): 3.

E18 ———. "Algo sobre Marcel Proust." *Excelsior* (México) 6 Aug. 1958, sec. A: 6, 8.

E19 Rev. of *Albertina ha desaparecido,* by Marcel Proust. *La Prensa* (Buenos Aires) 17 Mar. 1946: 17.

E20 "Albertine." "En torno a Marcel Proust." *Pluma* (Bogotá) 1.6 (Dec. 1975): 64–66.

E21 "Albertine-Albert o la extraña realidad de un famoso personaje proustiano." *Realidad* (Buenos Aires) 6 (Nov./ Dec. 1947): 453.

E22 Alcaraz, José Antonio. "Proust y Joyce: Ambos laberintos." *Excelsior* (México) 3 Oct. 1965, "Diorama de la Cultura": 5–6.

E23 ———. "En busca del Proust perdido." *El Heraldo de México,* "El Heraldo Cultural" 106 (19 Nov. 1967): 7.

E24 ———. "La Petite Phrase—Música de Proust" (lecture-performance). *El Heraldo de México,* "El Heraldo Cultural" 368 (26 Nov. 1972): 1–2; 369 (3 Dec. 1972): 2.

E25 Alone (Hernán Díaz Arrieta, see also Pedro Selva). "Marcel Proust." *La Nación* (Santiago) 17 June 1923: 4.

E26 ———. "Marcel Proust, juzgado por Bernard Fay." *La Nación* (Santiago) 27 July 1924: 6.

E27 ———. Rev. of *Les plaisirs et les jours,* by Marcel Proust. *La Nación* (Santiago) 16 Nov. 1924: 4.

E28 ———. "Un prodígio literario." *Atenea* (Concepción) 1.8 (Nov. 1924): 183–91.

E29 ———. "Algunas anécdotas sobre Marcel Proust." *La Nación* (Santiago) 20 Mar. 1927: 6.

E30 ———. "La situación de Proust—Notas para un estudio." *La Nación* (Santiago) 18 Mar. 1928: 8.

E31 ———. "Poesía en la obra de Marcel Proust—Notas para un estudio." *La Nación* (Santiago) 25 Mar. 1928: 8.

E32 ———. "El humorismo en la obra de Marcel Proust—Notas." *La Nación* (Santiago) 15 Apr. 1928: 4.

E33 ———. "El amor en la obra de Marcel Proust—Notas para un estudio." *La Nación* (Santiago) 22 Apr. 1928: 4.

E34 ———. "El sentimiento de la naturaleza en la obra de Proust— Notas." *La Nación* (Santiago) 6 May 1928: 4.

E35 ———. "La idea de la inmortalidad en la obra de Proust— Notas." *La Nación* (Santiago) 20 May 1928: 4.

E36 ———. "El tiempo en la obra de Marcel Proust—Notas." *La Nación* (Santiago) 17 June 1928: 4.

E37 ———. "El temperamento femenino de Marcel Proust (Notas)." *La Nación* (Santiago) 19 Aug. 1928: 4.

E38 ———. "Atenea." *La Nación* (Santiago) 30 Sept. 1928.

E39 ———. Rev. of *Au bal avec Marcel Proust,* by Princess Bibesco. *La Nación* (Santiago) 28 Apr. 1929.

E40 ———. "Marcel Proust, escritor místico." *La Nación* (Santiago) 17 May 1931: 11.

E41 ———. "Proust y Montesquiou—sus cartas." *La Nación* (Santiago) 31 May 1931: 11.

E42 ———. "Marcel Proust en Estados Unidos." *La Nación* (Santiago) 28 May 1932: 3.

E43 ———. "Décimo aniversario de Marcel Proust 1871–1922." *Lecturas* (Santiago) 1.4 (24 Nov. 1932): 52–54.

E44 ———. "Valery, Gide, Proust, Bergson, Claudel y Peguy por André Maurois." *El Mercurio* (Santiago) 4 Oct. 1942: 3.

E45 ———. "Un atentado contra Marcel Proust." *Nuevo Zig-Zag* (Santiago) 2288 (29 Jan. 1949): 6, 62–63.

E46 ———. Rev. of *A la recherche de Marcel Proust,* by André Maurois. *El Mercurio* (Santiago) 21 Aug. 1949: 3.

E47 ———. "El extraño caso de Painter y Proust." *El Mercurio* (Santiago) 23 Oct. 1966: 3. Rpt. in *Crónica literaria,* 89–93.

E48 ———. "Univers de Proust." *El Mercurio* (Santiago) 28 Feb. 1960: 11. Rpt. in *Crónica literaria,* 85–88.

E49 ———. "El misterio de la creación literaria." *El Mercurio* (Santiago) 6 Nov. 1966: 3. Rpt. in *Crónica literaria,* 94–97.

E50 ———. "Marcel Proust y Marcel Plantevignes." *El Mercurio* (Santiago) 12 Mar. 1967: 3. Rpt. in *Crónica literaria,* 126–30.

E51 ———. "Marcel Proust y Marcel Plantevignes y el juicio literario." *El Mercurio* (Santiago): 26 Mar. 1967: 3.

E52 ———. Rev. of *Marcel Proust.* Vol. 2, by George D. Painter. *El Mercurio* (Santiago) 16 July 1967: 3. Rpt. in *Crónica literaria,* 98–101.

E53 ———. "Al margen del *Proust* de Painter, II tomo." *El Mercurio* (Santiago) 23 July 1967: 3. Rpt. in *Crónica literaria,* 102–06.

E54 ———. Rev. of *Marcel Proust du côté de la médecine,* by Dr. Robert Soupault. *El Mercurio* (Santiago) 7 Apr. 1968: 3. Rpt. in *Crónica literaria,* 131–35.

E55 ———. Rev. of *Marcel Proust et Henry James, Une confrontation* by Bruce Lowery. *El Mercurio* (Santiago) 19 May 1968: 3. Rpt. in *Crónica literaria,* 107–11.

E56 ———. "*Marcel Proust y Henry James* por Bruce Lowery, II." *El Mercurio* (Santiago) 26 May 1968: 3. Rpt. in *Crónica literaria,* 112–16.

E57 ———. "Marcel Proust y Henry James confrontados por Bruce Lowery, III." *El Mercurio* (Santiago) 2 June 1968: 3. Rpt. in *Crónica literaria,* 117–21.

E58 ———. "La querella de Proust contra Sainte Beuve." *El Mercurio* (Santiago) 23 Feb. 1969: 3.

E59 ———. "La música en *El Dr. Faustus* de Mann y en la obra de Proust." *El Mercurio* (Santiago) 9 Mar. 1969: 3.

E60 ———. Rev. of *Jean Santeuil,* by Marcel Proust. *El Mercurio* (Santiago) 1 Feb. 1970. Rpt. in *Crónica literaria,* 122–25.

E61 ———. "Un centenario y un sesquicentenario." *El Mercurio* (Santiago) 16 May 1971: 3.

E62 ———. "Centenario de Proust." *El Mercurio* (Santiago) 4 July 1971: 3.

E63 ———. "Rabelais y Proust." *El Nacional* (Caracas) 11 July 1971, "Papel Literario": 4.

E64 ———. Rev. of *Monsieur Proust,* by Celeste Albaret. *El Mercurio* 5 May 1974: 3.

E65 ———. "De Paul Bourget a Marcel Proust." *El Mercurio* (Santiago) 14 Nov. 1976: iii.

E66 "Alpha." Notes on Proust. *La Nación* (Buenos Aires) 18 Dec. 1921; 21 Jan. 1923: 21; 19 Aug. 1923: 6.

E67 Alponte, Juan María. "Marcel Proust: Entre el padre y el cuerpo indefenso." *Uno más uno* (México), "Sábado" 18 (18 Mar. 1978): 13.

E68 Alvarez, Alfredo Juan. "A propósito del materialismo de Proust." *El Día* (México), "El Gallo Ilustrado" 339 (22 Dec. 1968): 1.

E69 Alvarez, Arturo Jacinto. "Dos personajes de Proust." *La Nación* (Buenos Aires) 17 Dec. 1972, sec. 3: 8.

E70 Anderson Imbert, Enrique. Rev. of *El mundo de Guermantes,* by Marcel Proust. *La Vanguardia* (Buenos Aires) 16 Sept. 1931: 6–7.

E71 ———. "Retrospectiva de la creación literaria." *La Vanguardia* (Buenos Aires) 14 Mar. 1937. Rpt. in *La flecha en el aire,* 209–10.

E72 ———. "El taller de Proust." *Sur* 246 (May/June 1957): 13–20. Rpt. in *Los grandes libros de Occidente y otros ensayos,* 225–41. Expanded version in *Los domingos del profesor,* 226–33.

E73 Andrade, Raúl. "Lecturas de M. Proust." *El Comercio* (Quito) 27 July 1971, sec. 1: 4. Rpt. in *El Sur* (Concepción, Chile) 29 Aug. 1971: 11.

E74 ———. "Memoria de la caracola." *El Comercio* (Quito) 3 Aug. 1971, sec. 1: 4. Rpt. in *El Caribe* (Santo Domingo, R. D.) 25 Aug. 1971: 10.

E75 ———. "Los barrios de Proust." *El Comercio* (Quito) 6 July 1972: 4.

E76 "Las anécdotas: Las propinas de Proust." *Las Ultimas Noticias* (Santiago) 20 Sept. 1948: 3.

E77 Antuñano, Maru. "Proust: una deuda de amor." *Revista Universidad de América* (Bayamón, P. R.) 2 (1 May 1990): 96–98.

E78 A. P. "Crónicas de Proust." *Pro-arte* (Santiago) 1.37 (24 Mar. 1949): 4.

E79 Arana Freire, Elsa. "Marcel Proust, el autor de *Sodoma y Gomorra* murió hace 41 años." *La Prensa* (Lima) 18 Aug. 1963: 22.

E80 Aranda, Alfredo. "Proust y la psicología moderna." *El Mercurio* (Santiago) 31 July 1960: 2.

E81 ———. "De nuevo en la Búsqueda de Proust." *El Mercurio* (Santiago) 24 Apr. 1965: 7.

E82 Aranda Jofre, Alfredo. "Consideraciones de la secuencia analítica en el hedonismo de Marcel Proust." *Cuadernos de Filología* (Antofagasta, Chile) 1 (2d semester 1974): 93–106.

E83 Arconada, M. Rev. of *La musique et l'immortalité dans l'oeuvre de Marcel Proust,* by Jacques Benoist-Méchin. *La Cruz del Sur* (Montevideo) 16 (Apr. 1927): 20–21.

E84 Arias, Augusto. "Proust, el tiempo recuperado." *El Comercio* (Quito) 15 Aug. 1971, sec. 3: 5.

E85   Arreola, Juan José. "Memoria y olvido de Proust." ¡Siempre!, "La Cultura en México" 492 (14 July 1971): x.

E86   ———. "Marcel Proust. Del libro en preparación: Arte de letras menores." El Heraldo de México, "El Heraldo Cultural" 392 (13 May 1973): 3.

E87   "Asteriscos." "André Maurois, francés." Marcha (Montevideo) 719 (14 May 1954): 15.

E88   "Autores y Libros." Novedades, "México en la Cultura" 157 (10 Feb. 1952): 7.

E89   "Los autores y las obras." "Si Marcel Proust viviera . . . " La Nación (Buenos Aires), 19 Aug. 1928, "Suplemento Literario": 16.

E90   Ayala, Francisco. "Proust en la inactualidad." La Nación 5 May 1940, sec. 2: 1. Rpt. in Histrionismo y representación, 133–45.

E91   Azorín (José Martínez Ruiz). Rev. of Marcel Proust, by Léon Pierre-Quint. La Prensa (Buenos Aires) 18 Oct. 1925, sec. 2: 2.

E92   ———. "Las dos ideas de Proust." La Prensa (Buenos Aires) 22 Oct. 1925, sec. 2.: 1.

E93   ———. "El arte de Marcel Proust." El País (Montevideo) 11 Dec. 1925: 12. Rpt. from ABC (Madrid) 4 Nov. 1925.

E94   ———. "Cartas de Proust." La Prensa (Buenos Aires) 5 Apr. 1931, sec. 2.

E95   "Azreal." "Reflecciones: La última dimensión psicológica." La Nación (Santiago) 23 Feb. 1933: 7.

E96   Azuela, Mariano. "Por el camino de Proust." Contemporáneos (México) 6 (Nov. 1928): 291–92. Rpt. in Obras completas. Vol. 3, 1267.

E97   B. (Mario Benedetti?). "Una nueva lectura de Marcel Proust." Marcha (Montevideo) 214 (17 Dec. 1943): 15.

E98   Baeza, Ricardo. "Siluetas de editores y escritores: Los Premios Goncourt, Marcel Proust, Rostand, Zola . . . " El País (Montevideo) 2 Jan. 1928: 122.

E99   "Balcón." "Marcel Proust." Gaceta (México) 141 (May 1966): 3.

E100 Balza, José. "Proust en noviembre: A los 60 años de su muerte." El Nacional (Caracas) 21 Nov. 1982, "El Papel Literario": 9. Rpt. in Transfigurable, 181–88.

E101 Barberena, Miguel. "Prousteana." Rev. of Marcel Proust, by Jean-Yves Tadié. Excelsior (México), "Arena" 102 (14 Jan. 2001): 11.

E102 Barga, Corpus. "Novelistas franceses: Marcelo Proust." El Universal (Caracas) 28 May 1920: 1. Rpt. from El Sol (Madrid) 27 Mar. 1920: 6.

E103 ———. "La vida literaria." El Universal (Caracas) 9 Jan. 1922: 1.

E104 ———. "Marcelo Proust, el finado novelista—moralista y hombre de ideas—un entierro poco literario." El Universal (Caracas) 25 Jan. 1923. Rpt. from El Sol (Madrid) 28 Nov. 1922: 1.

E105 Barón Supervielle, Odile. "Hechas y figuras" (Notes on Proust). La Nación (Buenos Aires), "Suplemento Literario" 9 Oct. 1977; 29 Oct. 1978: 2; 3 Feb. 1980: 3; 8 June 1980: 2; 30 Aug. 1981: 2; 14 Aug. 1983: 3; 11 Sept. 1983; 20 May 1984; 7 Oct. 1984; 3 Jan. 1988; 3 Dec. 1989: 3.

E106 ———. "Pasado, presente y futuro de Proust." La Nación (Buenos Aires) 22 Nov. 1987, "Suplemento Literario."

E107 ———. "Víctima de Proust." La Nación (Buenos Aires) 7 Mar. 1999, "Cultura": 8.

E108   ———. "Proust según Rolando Barthes." *La Nación* (Buenos Aires) 25 July 1999, "Cultura": 3.

E109   ———. "Dos parientes unidos por el tiempo" (Bergson and Proust). *La Nación* (Buenos Aires) 30 July 2000, "Cultura": 3.

E110   "Baulmundo." "Memorar a Proust." *Excelsior* (México) 8 Dec. 1974, "Diorama de la Cultura": 16.

E111   Beccacece, Hugo. Rev. of *El Indiferente,* by Marcel Proust. *La Nación* (Buenos Aires) 6 Aug. 1978, sec. 3: 3.

E112   ———. "El chisme en Proust y Capote: Arte y suicidio." *La Nación* (Buenos Aires) 5 Aug. 1990, sec. 4: 1–2.

E113   ———. "*A la recherche du temps perdu*—Scénario d'après l'oeuvre de Marcel Proust." *La Nación* (Buenos Aires), 17 Mar. 1995, sec. 4: 3

E114   ———. "Un discípulo ruso de Proust: Entrevista con Andrei Makine." *La Nación* (Buenos Aires) 31 Dec. 1995, sec. 6: 1.

E115   ———. "Tiempo y verdad: El Proust íntimo en una admirable biografía." Rev. of *Marcel Proust,* by Ghislain de Diesbach. *La Nación* (Buenos Aires) 2 June 1996, sec. 6: 4.

E116   ———. "Prisionera." *La Nación* (Buenos Aires) 1 June 1997, sec. 6: 1–2.

E117   Benedetti, Mario. "Aproximaciones: Un mundo." *Marcha* (Montevideo) 494 (9 Sept. 1949): 14–15.

E118   ———. "Metáforas y semimetáforas en la obra de Proust." *Marcha* (Montevideo) 494 (9 Sept. 1949): 14.

E119   Benedick, Claude. "André Maurois nos habla de *Jean Santeuil*. . . " *El Hogar* (Buenos Aires) 2195 (7 Dec. 1951): 20.

E120   Benedit, Miguel Alfredo. "Notas de arte." *Fiesta* (Buenos Aires) 1 (10 July 1927): 7–12.

E121   Bereta Anguissola, Alberto. "Albertina entre luces rojas." Trans. Reynaldo González. *La Gaceta de Cuba* 5 (May 1990): 2–3.

E122   Bergmann, A. M. "Marcel Proust y lo pre-racional." *Ideas y Valores* (Bogotá), 3d. ser., 25–26 (Apr.–Sept. 1965): 5–15.

E123   Bianchi, Alfredo A. Rev. of *Proust,* by Pierre Abraham. *Nosotros* (Buenos Aires) 261 (Feb. 1931): 208–09.

E124   Bianco, José. "Stendhal y Proust." *La Nación* (Buenos Aires) 9 Apr. 1933, sec. 2: 3.

E125   ———. "Proust y su madre." *La Nación* (Buenos Aires) 3 June 1956, sec. 2: 1. Rpt. in *Ficción y realidad,* 19–39 and *Homenaje a Marcel Proust.* . . , 11–30.

E126   ———. "El sentido del mal en la obra de Proust" (published lecture). *La Torre* (San Juan. P. R.) 25 (Jan.–Mar. 1959): 75–86.

E127   ———. "El centenario de Proust: Los avatares del 'yo' diferente." *Panorama* (Buenos Aires) 9.22 (13–19 July 1971) Rpt. as "En torno a Marcel Proust" in *Plural* (México) 2 (Nov. 1971): 36–37. Rpt. in Ficción y *realidad,* 41–52 and *Homenaje a Marcel Proust.* . ., 33–44.

E128   ———. "El ángel de las tinieblas." *La Nación* (Buenos Aires) 27 Jan. 1974, sec. 3: 1–2; 3 Feb. 1974, sec. 3: 1–2; 10 Feb. 1974, sec. 3: 1–2. Rpt. in *Plural* (México) 31 (Apr. 1974): 18–22; 32 (May 1974): 34–41 and in *Ficción y realidad,* 59–109.

E129   "Bibliófilo." Notes on Proust. *El Mercurio* (Santiago) 27 May 1928: 13; 3 June 1928: 11; 22 July 1928: 11; 2 Sept. 1928: 13; 23 Sept. 1928: 11; 4 Nov. 1928: 13; 11 Nov. 1928: 13; 11 Oct. 1931: 2.

E130   "Bibliografía." Rev. of *Géographie de Marcel Proust,* by André Ferré. *Romance* (México) 1.4 (15 Mar. 1940): 21.

E131   Bietti, Oscar. "Glosas europeas en el centenario de Proust." *La Prensa* (Buenos Aires) 17 Oct. 1971, "Sección Ilustrada": 1.

E132   "Biografía de Marcel Proust ha publicado en Francia una mujer de 82 años." Rev. of *Monsieur Proust,* by Céleste Albaret. *La Prensa* (Lima) 16 Mar. 1974: 28.

E133   Boisdeffre, Pierre de. "Proust y el amor." *El Comercio* (Lima) 13 June 1971, "Dominical": 25.

E134   ———. "Situación de Proust." *La Nación* (Buenos Aires) 14 Nov. 1971, sec. 3: 1, 3.

E135   Bollo, Sarah. "De Marcel Proust a Thomas Mann." *Hoy* (Santiago) 545 (30 Apr. 1942): 56–62.

E136   Bonnet, Henri. "Grandeza de Marcel Proust." *La Nación* (Buenos Aires) 11 July 1971, sec. 3: 2.

E137   Botton, Alain de. Interview. "Recuperar las horas perdidas." *La Nación* (Buenos Aires) 18 June 2000, "Cultura": 5. Rpt. from *Animus* 3.

E138   Bruch, Jean-Louis. Rev. of *A la recherche de Marcel Proust,* by André Maurois. *Novedades,* "México en la Cultura" 24 (17 July 1949): 3. Rpt. as "Maurois en busca de Proust" in *El Imparcial* (Guatemala) 6 Aug. 1949: 3.

E139   ———. Rev. of *Proust par lui-même,* by Claude Mauriac. *El Caribe* (Santo Domingo, R. D.) 7 June 1953: 15.

E140   Bueno, Manuel. "El amor y el dolor de Marcel Proust." *La Razón* (Buenos Aires) 30 July 1929. Rpt. from *ABC* (Madrid) 4 June 1929: 7.

E141   Bullrich, Silvina. "De Flaubert a Proust." *La Nación* (Buenos Aires) 16 Nov. 1947, sec. 2: 2. Rpt. in *La aventura interior,* 103–08.

E142   ———. "¿Es verdad la verdad? Intimidades de Proust." Rev. of *Monsieur Proust,* by Céleste Albaret. *La Nación* (Buenos Aires) 28 July 1974, sec. 3: 1–2.

E143   Butor, Michel. "Individuo y grupo en la novela." Trans. Enrique Pezzoni. *Sur* 283 (July/Aug. 1963): 27.

E144   Caballero, Antonio. "Centenario de Marcel Proust." *Correo* (Lima), 17 July 1971.

E145   ———. "Con Proust muere la novela asesinada por la literatura." *El Caribe* (Santo Domingo) 28 Aug. 1971: A4.

E146   Caballero Calderón, Eduardo. "El manuscrito de Jean Santeuil." *El Tiempo* (Bogotá) 5 July 1953, "Lecturas Dominicales": 1–2.

E147   ———. "Combray." *El Tiempo* (Bogotá) 8 Aug. 1976, "Lecturas Dominicales": 4.

E148   ———. "Marcel Proust." *El Espectador* (Bogotá) 13 Dec. 1981, "Magazín Dominical": 4.

E149   Cabau, Jacques. "En busca del Proust perdido." *Ercilla* (Santiago) 1880 (28 July–3 Aug. 1971): 83–88.

E150 Cabrera Alvarez, Carlos. "Marcel Proust y el Tiempo Vivido." *La Voz del Interior* (Córdoba, Arg.) 23 Mar. 1969. Rpt. in *Tiempo y literatura*, 21–27.

E151 C. A. G. "Marcel Proust y el amor." *El Tiempo* (Bogotá) 19 Mar. 1939, sec. 2: 4.

E152 ———. "Otra vez Marcel Proust." *Revista de las Indias* (Bogotá) 30 (June 1941): 127–28.

E153 "Calendario." Notes on Proust. *Sur* (Buenos Aires) 34 (July 1937): 98; 47 (Aug. 1938): 92–93; 58 (July 1939): 69–70.

E154 Campbell, Federico and Sergio Sarmiento. "Encuesta: Lecturas de Proust." *¡Siempre!,* "La Cultura en México" 492 (14 July 1971): 10–13.

E155 Campo, Cristina. "Les sources de la Vivonne." Trans. M. L. Bastos and Eugenio Guasta. *Sur* (Buenos Aires) 287 (Mar./Apr. 1964): 24–28.

E156 Campo, Santiago del. "Andre Maurois y el amor: Las heroínas de Proust." *Atenea* (Concepción) 143 (May 1937): 182–99.

E157 Campos, Julieta. "Marcel Proust." *Novedades,* "México en la Cultura," 2d ser., 444 (22 Sept. 1957): 3.

E158 Cantón, Wilberto. "Proust y una pasión que duró 37 años: Cartas a la señora C." *Excelsior* (México) 10 Oct. 1971, "Diorama de la Cultura": 8–10.

E159 Caparroso, Carlos Arturo. "Críticos colombianos: Glosa sobre Proust." *Nivel* (México) 108 (1971): 9. Rpt. in *Novedades,* "México en la Cultura," 3d ser., 1194 (13 Feb. 1972): 3, 6.

E160 ———. "Un novelista sin canas." *Excelsior* (San José) 5 Sept. 1976, sec. 3: 2.

E161 Capetillo, Manuel. "Proust: la escritura y su sentido." *Excelsior* (México) 12 Sept. 1971, "Diorama de la Cultura": 6, 16.

E162 Carballo, Emmanuel. "Conversaciones con Juan José Arreola: Proust, Joyce, Kafka." *¡Siempre!,* "La Cultura en México" 190 (6 Oct. 1965): xv.

E163 ———. "Dos tocayos geniales: Marcel Proust y Marcel Schwob." *El Nacional,* "Revista Mexicana de Cultura," 8th ser., 45 (19 Oct. 1980): 1, 4.

E164 Carleton de Millan, Verna. "Entre los nuevos libros de París." *El Nacional,* "Revista Mexicana de Cultura" 381 (18 July 1954): 10, 15.

E165 Carpentier, Alejo. "Un acontecimiento literario." *El Nacional* (Caracas) 26 Oct. 1951: 4. Rpt. in *Letra y solfa: Literatura. Autores,* 29–30.

E166 ———. "Ha muerto una heroína de novela." *El Nacional* (Caracas) 30 Sept. 1952: 30. Rpt. in *Letra y solfa: Literatura. Autores,* 51–53.

E167 ———. "Novedades acerca de Proust." *El Nacional* (Caracas) 11 Sept. 1953: 30. Rpt. in *Letra y solfa,* 65–67, *El adjetivo y sus arrugas,* 36–38 and *Letra y solfa: Literatura. Autores,* 100–01.

E168 ———. "Un nuevo inédito de Proust." *El Nacional* (Caracas) 5 Jan. 1955. Rpt. in *Letra y solfa: Literatura. Autores,* 151–52.

E169 ———. "Genio y voluntad." *El Nacional* (Caracas) 13 Aug. 1955: 16. Rpt. in *Letra y solfa,* 67–68 and *Letra y solfa: Literatura. Autores,* 189–90.

E170 ———. "Un memorable entre los *Memorables.*" *El Nacional* (Caracas) 14 June 1957. Rpt. in *Letra y solfa: Literatura. Autores,* 266–67.

E171 Carranca y Rivas, Raúl. "¡Detente oh momento! (Marcel Proust *En busca del tiempo perdido*)." *El Día* (México), "El Gallo Ilustrado" 811 (31 Dec. 1977): 17–18.

E172 Carrera, Margarita. "A la sombra de Marcel Proust." *Prensa Libre* (Guatemala) 7 Dec. 1997: 35.

E173 Carsuzán, María Emma. "Proust y la crítica literaria." *La Nación* (Buenos Aires) 20 Nov. 1966, sec. 4: 2.

E174 "Una carta de Marcel Proust." *Marcha* (Montevideo) 119 (12 Dec. 1941): 18.

E175 Rev. of *El caso Lemoine,* by Marcel Proust. *La Prensa* (Buenos Aires) 26 Jan. 1947, sec. 4: 1.

E176 Castagnino, Raúl H. "En torno de Marcel Proust." *La Prensa* (Buenos Aires) 4 July 1971: 1.

E177 Castegnaro, Marta. "El día histórico: Marcel Proust." *La Nación* (San José) 28 Jan. 1982: B2.

E178 Castro Leal, Antonio. "Balzac, Dostoyevski y Proust." *Atenea* (Concepción) 2.4 (30 June 1925): 437–38.

E179 Catania, Carlos. "En busca de Proust nunca perdido." *La Nación* (San José) 10 June 1982: A15.

E180 Catrysse, Jean. "Las cartas de Proust." *Excelsior* (México) 5 May 1957, "Diorama de la Cultura": 4.

E181 "Centenario de Proust." *El Comercio* (Lima) 13 June 1971, "Dominical": 24.

E182 ———. *El Telégrafo* (Guayaquil) 25 July 1971, "Revista Dominical": 2.

E183 Cheiner, Sophie. "Proust y Freud Inventaron una Nueva Manera de Examinar la Conciencia." *Excelsior* (México) 19 Dec. 1971, sec. B: 21, 26–27.

E184 Chibás, Eddy. "Tres genios modernistas (Marcel Proust, Rainer María Rilke y James Joyce)." *Social* (La Habana) 20.12 (Dec. 1936): 11, 59.

E185 Cocteau, Jean. "Relatos breves." *Hoy* (Santiago) 327 (24 Feb. 1938): 72–73.

E186 Coindreau, Maurice Edgar. "La sociedad francesa y la novela contemporánea." *La Nación* (Buenos Aires) 12 Dec. 1937, sec. 2: 1.

E187 Colette. "Cartas." *La Gaceta* (México), new ser., 31 (July 1973): 15–16.

E188 "Con Proust, hasta la mentira." Rev. of *Monsieur Proust,* by Céleste Albaret. *Excelsior* (México), "Revista de Revistas" 149 (9 Apr. 1975): 18.

E189 "Consultorio bibliográfico." *La Nación* (Buenos Aires) 25 June 1922: 9.

E190 "Correo de domingo." "Marcel Proust." *El Espectador* (Bogotá) 18 July 1971, "Magazine Dominical".

E191 "Correo literario." "Otra obra de Marcel Proust: *Du côté de Guermanies* [sic]." *La Nación* (Buenos Aires) 16 Jan. 1921, sec. 2: 5.

E192 "Correo literario francés." *La Nación* (Buenos Aires) 28 June 1936, sec. 2: 4.

E193 Rev. of *Correspondencia con su madre,* by Marcel Proust. *Marcha* (Montevideo) 853 (1 Mar. 1957): 9.

E194 Rev. of *Crónicas,* by Marcel Proust. *La Prensa* (Buenos Aires) 20 July 1947: 2.

E195 "Cosas del Día." "Proust." *El Tiempo* (Bogotá) 4 May 1950: 5.

E196 ———. "Marcel Proust." *El Tiempo* (Bogotá) 3 Aug. 1952: 5.

E197 Coyne, André. "La obra de Marcel Proust." *Letras Peruanas* 4.10 (June 1954): 5–8, 13, 31.

E198 ———. "Marcel Proust y la crítica." *El Comercio* (Lima), "Suplemento Dominical" 239 (1 Dec. 1957): 3, 5.

E199 Crespo, Luis Alberto. "Por el camino de Proust." *El Nacional* (Caracas) 21 Nov. 1982, "Papel Literario": 9.

E200 "Crónica: Una novela inédita de Proust." *Mar del Sur* (Lima) 7.19 (Jan./Feb. 1952): 87.

E201   Cuevas, Rafael. "En el Sexto Aniversario de la Muerte de Marcelo Proust." *Excelsior* (México) 25 Nov. 1928, "Página Literaria" : 5.

E202   Dandieu, Arnaud. "Marcel Proust: Su revelación psicológica." *Sur* (Buenos Aires) 24 (Sept. 1936): 40–79; 25 (Oct. 1936): 25–49; 26 (Nov. 1936): 74–108; 27 (Dec. 1936): 88–104.

E203   Darré, María Celia. Rev. of *Le style de Marcel Proust,* by Jean Mouton. *Revista de Literaturas Modernas* (Mendoza, Arg.) 9 (1970): 236–38.

E204   ———. Rev. of *Marcel Proust romancier,* by Maurice Bardèche. *Revista de Literaturas Modernas* (Mendoza) 11 (1972): 159–60.

E205   Debesa, Fernando. "Con Proust en Illiers." *El Mercurio* (Santiago) 23 May 1979: E6.

E206   ———. "Beckett sobre Proust." *El Mercurio* (Santiago) 6 Apr. 1980: E7.

E207   ———. "Correspondencia General de Proust." *El Mercurio* (Santiago) 14 Nov. 1982: E4–5.

E208   "Dedalus." Notes on Proust. *La Nación* (Santiago) 15 Jan. 1928: 5; 19 Feb. 1928: 5.

E209   Deleuze, Gilles. "Proust y los signos." Trans. Mary Mora de Ducay. *Ideas y Valores* (Bogotá) 38–39 (1971): 3–26.

E210   Delgado, Honorio. "Marcel Proust y la penumbra anímica." *La Moradas* (Lima) 2.4 (Apr. 1948): 1–7. Rpt. in *De la cultura y sus artífices,* 281–93.

E211   ———. "Estudios psicoliterarios." *El Universal* (México), 4 June 1972, "Revista de la Semana": 3, 12, 14.

E212   Descaves, Pierre. "A la busca del tiempo de Marcel Proust." *El Nacional* (Caracas) 15 Dec. 1953: 24.

E213   "Día a Día." "Marcel Proust." *El Espectador* (Bogotá) 10 July 1971: A3.

E214   "El Día Histórico." "Marcel Proust." *La Nación* (San José) 10 July 1949: 2.

E215   Díaz, José Manuel. "Intermitencias de la memoria de Proust." *Novedades,* "México en la Cultura," 3d ser., 888 (27 Mar. 1966): 3.

E216   Díaz Doín, Guillermo. "Marcel Proust y el amor." *La Nación* (Buenos Aires) 13 Nov. 1960, sec. 3: 2.

E217   ———. "Marcel Proust y los celos." *La Nación* (Buenos Aires) 12 Mar. 1961, sec. 4: 2. Rpt. in *El Diario Ilustrado* (Santiago) 21 May 1961: 3.

E218   Díaz Soto de Mazzei, María Leticia. "En el centenario del nacimiento de Marcel Proust: La psicología, la psicopatología, la medicina psicosomática y los médicos en la obra de Proust." *Anales de la Academia Nacional de Ciencias de Buenos Aires* 5 (1971): 205–17.

E219   ———. "Proust y la medicina." *La Prensa* (Buenos Aires) 16 Apr. 1972 : 10.

E220   Dickmann, Max. "Por el camino de Proust." *Nosotros* (Buenos Aires) 215 (Apr. 1927): 24–42.

E221   Disraeli, Federico. "Nuevas revelaciones proustianas." *Las Ultimas Noticias* (Santiago) 2 Sept. 1949: 2.

E222   Domenchina, Juan José. "Marcel Proust en 1933." *Repertorio Americano* (San José) 706 (10 Nov. 1934): 281–82. Rpt. from *El Sol* (Madrid) 12 Feb. 1933: 2. Rpt. in *El Tiempo* (Bogotá) 31 Dec. 1934: 46.

E223   Dotor, Angel. "Actualización de Marcel Proust." *El Nacional* (México) 31 May 1933: 3, 8.

E224   Dumesnil, René. "Marcel Proust y la música." *Novedades,* "México en la Cultura" 354 (1 Jan. 1956): 3–4.

E225   Durón, José Fidel. "Sobre la vida y la obra de Marcel Proust." *Boletín de la Academia Hondureña de la Lengua* 25 (Dec. 1980): 27–36.

E226   Edwards, Jorge. "Cincuenta años de *El camino de Swann.*" *Boletín de la Universidad de Chile* 45 (Dec. 1963): 67–71.

E227   ———. "Marcel Proust y los bárbaros." *Paula* (Santiago) 318 (11 Mar. 1980): 43; 319 (25 Mar. 1980): 37. Rpt. in *El Universal* (México), "La Letra y la Imagen" 30 (20 Apr. 1980): 5–7.

E228   Edwards-Bello, Joaquín. "¿Qué es una novela? Opiniones de Hugo y de Marcel Proust." *La Nación* (Santiago) 4 June 1928: 3. Rpt. in *El País* (Montevideo) 11 Sept. 1928: 12.

E229   ———. "Victor Hugo, Proust, Azorín y los Estados Unidos de Europa." *La Nación* (Santiago) 17 Nov. 1929: 9.

E230   Elizalde, Luis de. "Reflexiones sobre la novela." *Sur* 195–96 (Jan./Feb. 1951): 6–24.

E231   Emeth, Omer (Emilio Vaïsse). "Marcel Proust—¿En qué consiste la novedad de su arte?" *El Mercurio* (Santiago) 11 Apr. 1921: 3.

E232   ———. "Una buena noticia para los admiradores de Marcel Proust." *El Mercurio* (Santiago) 21 July 1921: 3.

E233   ———. "Claudel, Proust y el Simbolismo." *El Mercurio* (Santiago) 1 Sept. 1924: 1.

E234   ———. "Marcelo Proust, sus enemigos y sus admiradores. Inestabilidad de la fama literaria." *El Mercurio* (Santiago) 31 July 1927: 11.

E235   ———. "El esnobismo literario." *El Mercurio* (Santiago) 13 Dec. 1928: 3.

E236   Emmerich, Fernando. "Por el camino de Proust." *La Nación* (Santiago), "Para todos" 26 (6 Jan. 1985): 23.

E237   Rev. of *En busca del tiempo perdido,* by Marcel Proust. *La Prensa* (Buenos Aires) 9 Oct. 1949.

E238   Rev. of *En busca del tiempo perdido. La Nación* (Buenos Aires) 13 Nov. 1949: 9.

E239   Rev. of *En busca de Marcel Proust,* by André Maurois. *La Nación* (Buenos Aires) 26 Oct. 1958, sec. 3: 6.

E240   "En el centenario de Marcel Proust." *La Prensa* (Managua) 25 July 1971, "La Prensa Literaria": 3.

E241   "En el Instituto Popular de Conferencias se disertó ayer sobre Marcel Proust" (lecture by Simone Garma). *La Prensa* (Buenos Aires) 11 June 1949: 6.

E242   Espejo, Miguel. "El tiempo recobrado (Una relectura del gran novelista)." *El Periodista* (Buenos Aires) 95 (4–10 July 1986): 28–29.

E243   Espinosa, Gabriel. "La filosofía imaginativa de Marcel Proust: psicología estática y psicología dinámica." *Revista Nacional de Cultura* (Caracas) 25 (Jan./Feb. 1941): 47–62; 26 (Mar./Apr. 1941): 7–19.

E244   Espinosa, Januario. "El Balzac del subconsciente." *Atenea* (Concepción) 5.8 (31 Oct. 1928): 258–70.

E245   Espinosa Dederlé, Jaime. "Proust: 50 años." *El Tiempo* (Bogotá) 19 Nov. 1972, "Lecturas Dominicales": 2.

E246   Estrada, Genaro. "Por el camino de Proust." *Contemporáneos* (México) 1.6 (Nov. 1928): 292–96. Rpt. in *Obras,* 350–52.

E247 "Las extrañas y morbosas manías de Marcel Proust." *El Universal Ilustrado* (México) 439 (8 Oct. 1925): 13. Rpt. in *Revista de Revistas* (México) 816 (27 Dec. 1925): 24.

E248 Falgairolle, Adolfo. "Marcel Proust." *Sagitario* (México) 4 (1 Sept. 1926): 16.

E249 Fallas Chacón, Lucía. "El personaje, su aparición en la obra de Marcel Proust." *Káñina* (San José) 1.1 (Jan.–June 1977): 119–25.

E250 ———. "La descripción de los personajes en *Por el camino de Swann* ('Combray')." *Káñina* (San José) 1.2 (July-Dec. 1977): 99–106.

E251 ———. "El personaje: su función en la obra de Marcel Proust." *Káñina* (San José) 4.2 (July-Dec. 1980): 97–107.

E252 Fargue, Léon-Paul. "Recuerdos de Marcel Proust." *El Tiempo* (Bogotá), "Lecturas Dominicales" 317 (6 Oct. 1929): 9–10.

E253 Feher, Eduardo Luis. "Cadáver Errabundo: Los ojos de Proust." *Excelsior* (México) 21 Oct. 1981, "Cultura": 1.

E254 Ferber, Betty. "¿Liebestod o élan vital?" Trans. Jorge Arturo Ojeda. *Revista de la Universidad de México* 27. 9 (May 1973): 25–30.

E255 Fernandez, Ramon. "Nota sobre la estética de Proust." Trans. Xavier Villaurrutia. *Contemporáneos* 22 (Mar. 1930): 269–79.

E256 Fernández Molina, Antonio. "La poesía de Marcel Proust." *Educación* (San Juan) 33 (June 1971): 115–17. Rpt. from *Poesía española e hispanoamericana* (Madrid), 2d ser., 219 (Mar. 1971): 8–9.

E257 Fernández Moreno, César. Rev. of *Marcel Proust. Juventud-Obra-Tiempo,* by Léon Pierre-Quint. *Sur* (Buenos Aires) 122 (Dec. 1944): 60–64.

E258 Feuillet, Maurice. "Una venta de cartas de Marcel Proust." *La Razón* (Buenos Aires) 23 Feb. 1929, sec. 2: 1.

E259 Figueras, Marcelo. "El absurdo amor de Swann." *El Periodista* (Buenos Aires) 95 (4–10 July 1986): 28.

E260 Fleury, Annie. "Proust et son masque." *Maldoror* (Montevideo) 3 (3d trimester 1968): 69–70.

E261 Flot, Yonnick. "Marcel Porust [sic]: El éxito póstumo de un escritor de genio." *Listín Diario* (Santo Domingo) 16 Aug. 1971: 6.

E262 Fowlie, Wallace. "La suerte del artista como héroe: Joyce y Proust." *Mercurio Peruano* 217 (Apr. 1945): 143–54.

E263 Franco, Luis. "Máscaras: Proust." *La Nación* (Buenos Aires) 10 May 1931: 5.

E264 Frejaville, Eva. "Marcel Proust." *La Verónica* (La Habana) 4 (14 Nov. 1942): 113–16.

E265 Frenk, Mariana. "Marcel Proust." *Novedades,* "México en la Cultura," 2d ser., 408 (ll Jan. 1957): 3.

E266 Galimberti, Ana. Rev. of *Le signe des temps,* by Michel Raimond. *Revista Universitaria de Letras* (Mar del Plata, Arg.) 1.1 (Apr./May 1979): 127–30.

E267 ———. Rev. of *Proust ou la généalogie du roman moderne,* by Ramon Fernandez. *Revista Universitaria de Letras* (Mar del Plata) 2.1 (Apr./May 1980): 165–68.

E268 ———. Rev. of *Le progrès spirituel dans "La Recherche" de Marcel Proust,* by Henri Bonnet. *Revista Universitaria de Letras* (Mar del Plata) 3.1 (Apr./May 1981): 137–40.

E269 ———. "Materiales y obra de arte en *La Recherche* de Marcel Proust." *Revista Universitaria de Letras* (Mar del Plata) 3.2 (Oct./Nov. 1981): 235–55.

E270   Gallegos Valdés, Luis. "Marcel Proust, reencontrado." *Revista del Maestro* (Guatemala) 5.15–16 (Oct. 1949–Mar. 1950): 66–68. Rpt. in *Tiro al blanco* 181–87.

E271   Gálvez, Manuel. "A propósito de Proust: la literatura y el conocimiento." *La Nación* (Buenos Aires) 4 Nov. 1923, sec. 3: 4, 8. Expanded version in *El espíritu de aristocracia y otros ensayos*, 145–66.

E271   Gamarra, Pierre. "Proust viviente." *El Nacional* (Caracas) 11 July 1971, "Papel Literario": 1.

E273   Gannon, Patricio. "La Exposición Proust." *La Nación* (Buenos Aires) 13 Feb. 1966. Rpt. in *Esqueletos divinos*, 125–29.

E274   Garavito, Julián. "Marcel Proust a los cien años: Cómo lo recuerda Francia." *El Nacional* (Caracas) 11 July 1971, "Papel Literario": 1.

E275   ———. "Una crónica proustiana y una mistificación literaria." *El Café Literario* (Bogotá) 22 (July/Aug. 1981): 48–49.

E276   García Calderón, Ventura. "La literatura de lujo." *La Prensa* (Buenos Aires) 14 Oct. 1934, sec. 2. Rpt. in *Repertorio Americano* (San José) 708 (24 Nov. 1934): 305–07. Rpt. as part of "Literatura de lujo y literatura proletaria." in *Arte de marear*, 131–53.

E277   García Méndez, Javier. "Retrato de Colón por Proust adolescente." *Plural* (México) 264 (Sept. 1993): 40–41.

E278   García Pinto, Roberto. "El mundo de Marcel Proust." *La Nación* (Buenos Aires) 18 June 1961, sec. 4: 2.

E279   García Ponce, Juan. "En torno a Marcel Proust." *¡Siempre!*, "La Cultura en México" 250 (31 Nov. 1966): xx. Rpt. in *Entrada en materia*, 77–82.

E280   ———. "Proust recuperado." *¡Siempre!*, "La Cultura en México" 492 (14 July 1971): xi.

E281   ———. "El lugar de Marcel Proust." *Uno más uno* (México), "Sábado" 97 (22 Sept. 1979): 5–7. Rpt. in *Apariciones*, 343–51.

E282   ———. "Más allá del tiempo (Marcel Proust)." *Diálogos* (México) 91 (Jan./Feb. 1980): 27–33.

E283   ———. "Marcel Proust: Imposibilidad de amor, posibilidad de novela." *Uno más uno* (México), "Sábado" 303 (20 Aug. 1983): 1, 3; 304 (27 Aug. 1983): 3; 305 (3 Sept. 1983): 4–5. Rpt. in *Imágenes y visiones*, 89–104.

E284   Garma, Simone M. de. "Marcel Proust y la personalidad" (published lecture). *Anales del Instituto Popular de Conferencias* (Buenos Aires) 35 (1949): 57–68.

E285   Gay, Peter. "Proust o el afecto problemático." Trans. Evangelina Niño de la Selva. *La Gaceta* (México), new ser., 227 (Nov. 1989): 15–17.

E286   Genette, Gérard. "Metonimia en Proust." Trans. Mirta A. de Fescina. *Maldoror* (Montevideo) 20 (1985): 77–91.

E287   "Gente." "Celeste Albaret: La mujer que cuidó a Proust habla de él." *Paula* (Santiago) 121 (Aug. 1972): 41–42.

E288   Gicovate, Bernardo. "Pedro Salinas y Marcel Proust: Seducción y retorno." *Asomante* (San Juan) 16.3 (July–Sept. 1960): 7–16.

E289   Gillouin, René. "Marcel Proust." *Revista Chilena* (2) 83 (Mar. 1926): 69–73.

E290   Gimferrer, Pere. "En el París de Swann." *Vuelta* (México) 145 (Dec. 1988): 56–58.

E291 Girard, René. "Los mundos de Proust." Trans. Nicolás Suescún. *Eco* (Bogotá) 44 (Dec. 1963): 142–77.

E292 Gómez, Carlos Alberto. "Nueva traducción de Proust." Rev. of *En busca del tiempo perdido*. Vol. I. *La Nación* (Buenos Aires) 7 Feb. 1982.

E293 Gómez Carrillo, Enrique. "El calvario de un gran escritor." *El Diario de la Marina* (La Habana) 3 Sept. 1926: 16. Rpt. in *El Tiempo* (Bogotá), "Lecturas Dominicalas" 171 (17 Oct. 1926): 333–34. Rpt. in *El Universal* (Caracas) 4 Nov. 1926: 8.

E294 Gómez de Baquero, E. "Las prosas líricas de Salinas." *El País* (Montevideo) 23 Aug. 1926: 12. Rpt. from *El Sol* Madrid) 22 July 1926: 2.

E295 Gómez de Aranda, Luis. Rev. of *Monsieur Proust*, by Céleste Albaret. *La Nación* (San José) 20 Oct. 1974: C2.

E296 Gómez Palacio, Martín. "Por el camino de Proust." *Contemporáneos* (México) 1.6 (Nov. 1928): 296–97.

E297 González, Reynaldo. "En busca del tiempo perdido." *La Gaceta de Cuba* 5 (May 1990): 2.

E298 González Rojo, Enrique. "Por el camino de Proust." *Contemporáneos* (México) 1.6 (Nov. 1928): 298.

E299 Grassi, Ernesto. "El problema filosófico del tiempo en Proust." Trans. José Emilio Osses. *Revista Chilena de Literatura* 30 (Nov. 1987): 7–28.

E300 Gringoire, Pedro. "Proust, vencedor de los siglos." *Excelsior* (México) 6 Oct. 1967: A7.

E301 Guerbero, Cito. "El arte sutil de Marcel Proust." *La Prensa* (Buenos Aires) 29 June 1952, sec. 2.

E302 Guereña, Jacinto Luis. "Proust en autodefiniciones." *Imagen* (Caracas) 96 (15–31 Aug. 1974): 107.

E303 "Guermantes: Un nombre que encantó a Proust." *El Mercurio* (Santiago) 26 Sept. 1982: E1.

E304 Guerra, Angel (José Betancourt Cabrera). "El Premio Goncourt: Marcel Proust." *El Universal* (Caracas) 4 Mar. 1920: 4. Rpt. in *La Nota* (Buenos Aires) 249 (21 May 1920): 1812.

E305 Guerra, Guido. Notes on Proust. *La Nación* (Santiago) 1 Jan. 1928: 7; 22 Jan. 1928: 5; 3 June 1928: 4; 5 Aug. 1928: 4; 2 Sept. 1928: 4; 16 Sept. 1928: 4; 4 Nov. 1928: 4; 25 Nov. 1928; 9 Dec. 1928.

E306 Guette, Jean. "Proust y su padre." Trans. María Tavera. *Casa del Tiempo* (México), 2d ser., 8.29 (Feb. 1994): 68.

E307 Guillot Muñoz, Alvaro. "Marcel Proust, essai d'une littérature introspective." *La Cruz del Sur* (Montevideo) 7 (Oct. 1925): 32; 9 (Dec. 1925): 25–28.

E308 ———. "De Rimbaud a Proust." *La Cruz del Sur* (Montevideo) 24 (June/July 1929): 6–9.

E309 Guillot Muñoz, Gervasio. "Una imagen de Watteau evocada por Proust." *La Nación* (Buenos Aires) 19 May 1940, sec. 2: 4.

E310 ———. "El bajo bosque proustiano." *Revista de la Facultad de Humanidades y Ciencias* (Montevideo) 4.5 (June 1950): 211–43.

E311 "Hace 50 años aparecía *Swann* de Proust." *El Diario Ilustrado* (Santiago) 12 Jan. 1964: 2.

E312   Hanssen, Alfonso. "La biografía de Marcel Proust." *Boletín Cultural y Biblio-gráfico* (Bogotá) 7 (1969): 50–56.

E313   Hausenstein, Wilhelm. "Lecturas de Proust." Trans. Ernesto Volkening. *Eco* (Bogotá) 135 (3 July 1971): 244–49.

E314   Henestrosa, Andrés. "La nota cultural." *El Nacional* (México) 3 Apr. 1967, sec. 1: 3.

E315   Henriot, Emile. Rev. of *A la recherche de Marcel Proust,* by André Maurois. *El Nacional,* "Revista Mexicana de Cultura," 2d ser., 114 (20 May 1949): 1.

E316   Henríquez Ureña, Camila. "Ideología literaria de Proust" (published lecture). *Lyceum* (La Habana) 14 (Apr./May/ June 1939): 52–61.

E317   Herrero, Antonio. "La obra de Marcel Proust." *Nosotros* (Buenos Aires) 169 (June 1923): 208–15.

E318   Hoppenot, Henri. "Paul Claudel, Marcel Proust y Paul Valery" (published lecture). *Atenea* (Concepción) 1.10 (31 Dec. 1924): 340–56.

E319   "El Instituto Popular de Conferencias: Marcel Proust" (Lecture by Juan P. Ramos). *La Prensa* (Buenos Aires) 1 May 1926: 19.

E320   Insúa, Alberto. "Apuntes sobre la renovación literaria en Francia: Un psicólogo: Proust." *La Nación* (Buenos Aires) 17 Oct. 1920, sec. 2: 2.

E321   Irazusta, Julio. "Una opinión de Santayana sobre el testimonio filosófico de Proust." *Sur* (Buenos Aires) 26 (Nov. 1936): 121–24.

E322   ———. "Proust, ayer y hoy." *La Nación* (Buenos Aires) 22 Nov. 1936, sec. 2: 1. Rpt. as "Proust" in *Actores y espectadores,* 153–66.

E323   J. A. "Bibliografía proustiana." *Libros de hoy* (Buenos Aires) 1 (May 1951): 72–73.

E324   Jacob, Jean. "La vida de Marcel Proust." Trans. Eduardo Anguita. *El País* (Montevideo) 28 Jan. 1938, "Artes y Letras": 8.

E325   Jaloux, Edmond. "La obra de Marcel Proust." *Nosotros* (Buenos Aires) 165 (Feb. 1923): 258–60.

E326   J. A. M. Rev. of *Proust y los signos,* by Gilles Deleuze. *¡Siempre!,* "La Cultura en México" 721 (2 Dec. 1975): xv.

E327   Jaramillo Escobar, Jaime. "Dios hizo el mundo, pero Marcel Proust lo escribió." *El Tiempo* (Bogotá) 4 July 1971, "Lecturas Dominicales": 5.

E328   Jarnés, Benjamín. "Marcel Proust en España." *La Nación* (Buenos Aires) 10 Sept. 1931: 8.

E329   Jiménez, Darío. "Marcel Proust: el tiempo recobrado." *Ideas y Valores* (Bogotá) 40–41 (1972): 2ll–14.

E330   J. M. F. "Marcel Proust juzgado por Alvaro Guillot Muñoz" (on a lecture). *La Cruz del Sur* (Montevideo) 15 (Nov./ Dec. 1926): 29.

E331   Joseph, Bernard. "Un inédito de Proust *Contre Sainte-Beuve.*" *El Nacional* (Caracas) 4 Aug. 1955, "Papel Literario": 6.

E332   Juin, Hubert. "El mundo de Marcel Proust." Trans. Fernando Vallejo. *Vida Literaria* (México) 14 (Aug. 1971): 10–14.

E333   Kassner, Rudolf. "Paris en 1900: Intelectuales y artistas." *Sur* 234 (May/Jun. 1955): 5–27.

E334   Kirschbaum, Manuel. "Tolstoy en un atajo de Proust" (Part of a lecture). *Claridad* (Buenos Aires) 171 (24 Nov. 1928).

E335   Koremblit, Bernardo Ezequiel. "Proust cumple 90 años." *La Razón* (Buenos Aires) 8 July 1961: 12.

E336   ———. "A la sombra de las muchachas en flor." *Davar* (Buenos Aires) 123
        (Autumn 1970): 97–102.

E337   Labarca, Eugenio. "Literatura francesa actual." *El Mercurio* (Santiago) 1 Jan.
        1922: 11.

E338   Lacretelle, Jacques de. "A la memoria de Marcel Proust." *La Nación* (Buenos
        Aires) 11 July 1971, sec. 3: 1.

E339   Lafourcade, Enrique. Rev. of *Comiendo con Proust,* by Shirley King. *El Mercurio*
        (Santiago) 6 Mar. 1983: D10.

E340   Lago, Tomás. "De Balzac a Marcel Proust." *Anales de la Universidad de Chile,* 3d
        ser., 15 (1934): 130–60.

E341   Lancelotti, Mario A. "Volviendo a Proust." *La Nación* (Buenos Aires) 23 Nov.
        1952, sec. 2: 1.

E342   Larreta, Enrique. "Lo que no pensaba decir todavía." *La Nación* (Buenos
        Aires) 7 May 1939, sec. 2: 2.

E343   La Torre, Alfonso. "El cine en busca de Proust." *El Comercio* (Lima), "El
        Comercio Gráfico" 120 (12 July 1962): 10.

E344   ———. "Exhumación de *Jean Santeuil* de Proust." *El Comercio* (Lima), "El
        Comercio Gráfico" 776 (9 Sept. 1964): 6.

E345   Laval, Jacques. "La metamorfosis entre la vida y la obra de Proust." *Novedades,*
        "México en la Cultura" 696 (15 July 1962): 1, 6.

E346   Lee, Rose. "Marcel Proust, el literato más grande de Francia juzgado por un
        espíritu sajón." *El Universal Ilustrado* (México) 439 (8 Oct. 1925): 12, 42.

E347   Lefevre, Federico. "Una hora con Eduardo Herriot: Un Concepto sobre
        Proust y su obra." *El Espectador* (Bogotá) "Suplemento Literario" 174 (22
        Apr. 1928): 9–10.

E348   "Letras." "Para leer a Marcel Proust." *La Antorcha* (México) 2.3 (Oct. 1925):
        26.

E349   "Letras." "Biblia de los Proustianos." *Hispanoamericano* (México) 1343 (29
        Jan. 1968): 49.

E350   "Los Libros." "Cartas de Marcel Proust." *Hoy* (Santiago) 39 (19 Aug. 1932):
        27.

E351   ———. "Correspondencia por Marcel Proust." *Hoy* (Santiago) 193 (2 Aug.
        1935): 35.

E352   "Libros, comentarios." Rev. of *La vida de Jean Santeuil,* by Marcel Proust. *La
        Prensa* (Buenos Aires) 3 Oct. 1954, sec. 2.

E353   "Libros recientes." Rev. of *Marcel Proust y Paul Valery,* by Ernst Robert Curtius.
        La Nación (Buenos Aires) 28 Dec. 1941, sec. 2: 5.

E354   ———. Rev. of *Correspondencia con su madre,* by Marcel Proust. *La Nación*
        (Buenos Aires) 27 Jan. 1957, sec. 2: 4.

E355   Lillo, Victoriano. "Marcel Proust y la crítica." *Atenea* (Concepción) 378
        (Oct./Nov./Dec. 1957): 164–69.

E356   Link, Daniel. Rev. of *El indiferente,* by Marcel Proust. *Babel* (Buenos Aires) 1.2
        (May 1988): 10.

E357   "La literatura en el mundo" (note on Proust). *La Nación* (Buenos Aires) 28
        June 1970.

E358   Livacic, Ernesto and Betty Rojas. "Descubramos el mundo de Marcel Proust:
        Trayectoria vital y retrato." *Ercilla* (Santiago) Suplemento no. 4 (26 Mar.–1
        Apr. 1980).

E359   Lleras, Alberto. "El submarino mundo de Proust." *El Espectador* (Bogotá) 25 July 1971: A2. Rpt. in *Visión* 39.15 (31 July 1971): 13.

E360   Llerena, José Alfredo. "El tiempo en la novela." *El Comercio* (Quito) 24 June 1946, "Literatura y Arte": 5.

E361   Llosa, Jorge Guillermo. "Una visita por el lado de Proust." *El Comercio* (Lima) 28 July 1967: 2.

E362   ———. "Evocación de Marcel Proust en el escenario de su nacimiento." *El Comercio* (Lima) 28 Nov. 1971: 28.

E363   Loayza, Luis. "Vagamente dos peruanos." *Letras Peruanas* 13 (Apr./June 1962): 18. Rpt. in *El sol de Lima*, 75–82.

E364   López Raygada, Jaime. "Marcel Proust y el concepto del tiempo." *El Comercio* (Lima) 24 June 1971: 2.

E365   ———. "Centenario del nacimiento de Marcel Proust." *El Comercio* (Lima) 11 July 1971: 2.

E366   ———. "Imágenes de la muerte de Marcel Proust." *El Comercio* (Lima) 19 Nov. 1972: 2.

E367   ———. "Celeste Albaret, la criada de Proust, escribe sus memorias." Rev. of *Monsieur Proust*. *El Comercio* (Lima) 3 Jan. 1974: 2.

E368   Lucca, Carlos de. "Trascendencia de Proust." *Marcha* 72 (8 Nov. 1940): 23.

E369   Luna Olivo, Andrés de. "The Proust Screenplay: *A la recherche du temps perdu*." *Revista de la Universidad de México* 32.6 (Feb. 1978): 31–32.

E370   Lunacharski, Anatoli, V. "Sobre Marcel Proust." Trans. Virgilio Piñera. *Unión* (La Habana) 5.1 (1966): 145–52.

E371   ———. "Una existencia casi exclusivamente nocturna." *Pluma* (Bogotá) 1.9 (June/July 1976): 62–65.

E372   Macchia, Giovanni. "Un gran arquitecto llamado Proust." Interview by Benedetta Craveri. Trans. Reynaldo González. *La Gaceta de Cuba* 5 (May 1990): 4.

E373   Makarow, Vera. Rev. of *La vida de Jean Santeuil*, by Marcel Proust. *Sur* 233 (Mar./Apr. 1955): 87–88.

E374   Malagarriga, Carlos. "La música en la obra de Proust." *Nosotros* (Buenos Aires) 258–59 (Nov./Dec. 1930): 189–219.

E375   Maldavsky, José. "Centenario de Marcel Proust." *El Siglo* (Santiago) 28 Feb. 1971, "Revista Semanal": 10.

E376   Mallea, Eduardo. "Nota conjunta sobre los tres mayores novelistas en lo que va del siglo (Kafka, Proust, Joyce)." *Boletín de la Academia Argentina de Letras* 34 (Apr./June 1941): 153–57.

E377   "Manual del perfecto lector de Proust." *Zig-Zag* (Santiago) 1239 (17 Nov. 1928).

E378   "La máquina del tiempo". "Nace Marcel Proust." *Ercilla* (Santiago) 1878 (14–20 July 1971): 66.

E379   "Marcel Prevost [sic], casi salvaje." *Puerto Rico Ilustrado* (San Juan) 681 (17 Mar. 1923): 7.

E380   "Marcel Proust." *El Universal* (Caracas) 17 Dec. 1922: 1.

E381   "Marcel Proust: El enigmático." *El Tiempo* (Bogotá), "Lecturas Dominicales" 238 (26 Feb. 1928): 198.

BIBLIOGRAPHY 397

E382 "Marcel Proust + [falleció] en París." *La Prensa* (Buenos Aires) 20 Nov. 1922: 5.

E383 "Marcel Proust o la lucha contra uno mismo 1871–1971." *La Opinión* (Buenos Aires) 27 June 1971.

E384 "Marcel Proust, poeta: pecado de adolescencia." *Excelsior* (México) 28 Feb. 1971, "Diorama de la Cultura": 6.

E385 Rev. of *Marcel Proust y Paul Valery*, by Ernst Robert Curtius. *Conducta* (Buenos Aires) 21 (July/Aug. 1942).

E386 "Marcel Proust y la personalidad" (on lecture by Simone Garma). *Guía quincenal de la actividad intelectual y artística argentina* 46 (July 1949): 5–6.

E387 "El Marcel que quiso ser Marcela." *El Mercurio* (Santiago) 18 July 1971, "Revista del Domingo": 14–15.

E388 Mariani, Roberto. "Introducción a Marcel Proust" (published lecture). *Nosotros* (Buenos Aires) 215 (Apr. 1927): 16–23.

E389 Martí, Ellú. Rev. of *En busca de sí mismo*, by Betty Ferber. *El Heraldo de México*, "El Heraldo Cultural" 369 (3 Dec. 1972): 11.

E390 Massuh, Gabriel. "Marcel Proust y el 'Fin de Siècle'." *Eco* (Bogotá) 232 (Feb. 19, 1981): 365–70. Rpt. in *La Prensa* (Buenos Aires) 29 Mar. 1981, "Sección Literaria": 5.

E391 Matamoro, Blas. "Una teoría proustiana del amor." *Cuadernos Hispanoamericanos* (Madrid) 359 (May 1980): 346–70.

E392 ———. "Lectores de Proust." *Cuadernos Hispanoamericanos* 495 (Sept. 1991): 95–116.

E393 Matesanz, José Antonio. "Marcel Proust, surmanierista." *Thesis* (México) 1.4 (Jan. 1980): 71–72.

E394 Maurois, André. "Marcel Proust y la memoria involuntaria." *Síntesis* (México) 124 (1 Dec. 1941): 491–96.

E395 ———. "Las heroínas de Marcel Proust." *La Nación* (Buenos Aires) 5 July 1942, sec. 2: 3.

E396 ———. "Marcel Proust y su doctrina sentimental." *La Nación* (Buenos Aires) 12 July 1942, sec. 2: 2.

E397 ———. "Los últimos días de Marcel Proust." *El Nacional*, "Revista Mexicana de Cultura," 2d ser., 108 (17 Apr. 1949): 1–2.

E398 M. A. V. P. Rev. of *Marcel Proust: Les fictions de la vie et de l'art*, by Leo Bersani. *La Nación* (Buenos Aires) 10 Oct. 1965, sec. 3: 5.

E399 Mejía Nieto, Arturo. "Marcel Proust y la realidad." *La Nación* (Buenos Aires) 19 Mar. 1967, sec. 3: 2. Rpt. in *Honduras Rotaria* 236 (July/Aug. 1967): 7–9.

E400 Mendoza Varela, Eduardo. "Reflexiones sobre la novela y los novelistas contemporáneos." *Espiral* (Bogotá): 2.13 (Sept. 1945): 3–5.

E401 ———. "Un año para Marcel." *El Tiempo* (Bogotá) 6 Jun. 1971, "Lecturas Dominicales": 3.

E402 Meneses, Guillermo. Rev. of *Marcel Proust par lui-même*, by Claude Mauriac. *Revista Nacional de Cultura* (Caracas) 106–07 (Sept.-Dec. 1954): 188–89.

E403 Mengod, Vicente. "Sobre la técnica de Proust." *Atenea* (Concepción) 251 (May 1946): 148–57.

E404 Mercier, Lucien. "Proust: una mitología de la era burguesa." *Marcha* (Montevideo) 1556 (13 Aug. 1971): 30–31.

E405 Merger, Clément. "Combray." *¡Siempre!,* "La Cultura en México" 492 (14 July 1971): xi-xii.

E406 Miomandre, Francis de. "Marcel Proust: El Premio Goncourt." *El Universal* (Caracas) 23 Jan. 1920: 5.

E407 ———. "Marcel Proust y la sinceridad psicológica." Rev. of *Le côté de Guermantes II,* by Marcel Proust. *La Nación* (Buenos Aires) 7 Aug. 1921: 3.

E408 ———. "Crónica de la vida intelectual francesa." *Nosotros* (Buenos Aires) 167 (Apr. 1923): 521–25.

E409 ———. "Un juicio sobre dos libros póstumos de Marcel Proust." *La Nación* (Buenos Aires) 11 Mar. 1924, sec. 3: 11.

E410 ———. "La obra primogenia de Marcel Proust." Rev. of *Les plaisirs et les jours.* *La Nación* (Buenos Aires) 24 Nov. 1924, sec. 3: 10.

E411 ———. Rev. of *De Proust à Dada,* by André Germain. *La Nación* (Buenos Aires) 29 Mar. 1925.

E412 ———. Rev. of *Robert de Montesquiou et Marcel Proust,* by Mme. de Clermont-Tonnerre. *La Nación* (Buenos Aires) 7 June 1925.

E413 ———. "Marcel Proust, clásico." *Novedades,* "México en la Cultura" 236 (27 Sep. 1953): 3.

E414 Miranda, Julio E. "La nueva crítica española, del ensayo escolar al discurso desenfrenado." Rev. of *Proust y la revolución,* by Juan Pedro Quiñonero. *Imagen* (Caracas) 88–89 (30 Sept.–31 Oct. 1973), sec. 2: 9.

E415 Miró, César. "A la sombra de Marcel Proust." *El Comercio* (Lima) 5 Mar. 1964: 2.

E416 ———. "Gloria y agonía de Marcel Proust." *El Comercio* (Lima) 3 July 1969: 2.

E417 Miró Quesada S., Aurelio. "La concepción literaria de Proust." *Las Moradas* (Lima) 2.4 (Apr. 1948): 23–30.

E418 Molina, Mauricio. "Marcel Proust." *¡Siempre!* "La Cultura en México" 2364 (8 Oct. 1998): 68.

E419 Montaño, Vicente. "De cómo se supo y cómo se olvidó la existencia de Marcel Proust." *El Nacional* (México) 15 Jan. 1980: 17.

E420 Monteforte Toledo, Mario. "Marcel Proust, profundo superficial." *Cuadernos Americanos* (México) 43.1 (Jan./ Feb. 1949): 245–54.

E421 Monterroso, Augusto. "Fragmentos de un diario: Proust." *Nuevo amanecer cultural* (Managua) 255 (4 May 1985): 4. Rpt. in *La letra e,* 153.

E422 Moral López, Fernando del. "Proust: materia, sentido, forma." *El Heraldo de México,* "El Heraldo Cultural" 498 (25 May 1975): 4.

E423 Moreno, Artemio. "Semblanza de Marcel Proust." *La Prensa* (Buenos Aires) 7 July 1929, sec. 2. Rpt. in *El sentimiento en la vida y en el arte,* 197–210.

E424 Moro, César. "El sueño de la cena de Guermantes." *Las Moradas* (Lima) 4 (Apr. 1948): 17–22. Rpt. in *La tortuga ecuestre y otros textos,* 121–28.

E425 Mottino, Susana. "La música en la obra de Gide y de M. Proust." *Actas: Jornadas de Investigación* (Universidad Nacional de Río Cuarto, Arg.) 1994: 122–23.

E426 "Movimiento Bibliográfico." Rev. of *Los placeres y los días,* by Marcel Proust. *La Nación* (Buenos Aires) 23 Mar. 1947, sec. 2: 3.

E427 Moyano, Bolívar. "Proust: un siglo." *El Universal* (Guayaguil) 11 July 1971, "Revista Dominical": 4.

E428   "La muerte de un personaje de Proust." *La Nación* (Buenos Aires) 26 Oct. 1952, sec. 2: 3.

E429   "La mujer en la vida: Proust." *El Nacional* (Caracas) 27 June 1971, "Suplemento": 1–2.

E430   Mujica Láinez, Manuel. "Recuerdos de Proust." *La Nación* (Buenos Aires) 9 Oct. 1977, sec. 4: 1. Rpt. in *Placeres y fatigas de los viajes.* Vol. 2, 179–81.

E431   Mulder, Elizabeth. "Las últimas moradas de Marcel Proust." *Universidad de Antioquia* (Medellín) 120 (31 Feb. 1955): 147–50.

E432   Muñoz Borrero, Eduardo. "Estampa de Marcel Proust." *El Comercio* (Quito) 29 Aug. 1971, sec. 3: 5.

E433   Mutis, Alvaro. "Marcel Proust." *Cuadernos de Bellas Artes* (México) 3.3 (Mar. 1962): 33–48.

E434   ———. "La Compañía de Proust." *¡Siempre!,* "La Cultura en México" 492 (14 July 1971): xii. Rpt. in *Eco* (Bogotá) 138–39 (Oct./Nov. 1971): 650–51 and in *Poesía y prosa,* 389–90.

E435   ———. "Proust: el orden de las potestades celestiales." *La Gaceta* (México), new ser., 174 (June 1985): 2–4.

E436   Nairne, Cambell. "Evocación del pasado en Paris: Cómo trabajaba Proust." *Pan* (Buenos Aires) 80 (14 Oct. 1936): 37.

E437   Nicchi, Ubaldo. "Las constelaciones iluminadas de la memoria: *En busca del tiempo perdido* de Marcel Proust." *Clarín* (Buenos Aires) 4 Mar. 1970, sec. 4: 6.

E438   "Nos." Rev. of *Marcel Proust: sa vie, son oeuvre,* by Léon Pierre-Quint. *Nosotros* 196 (Sept. 1925): 110–11.

E439   "Notas bibliográficas." Rev. of *Correspondencia con su madre,* by Marcel Proust. *La Razón* (Buenos Aires) 2 Feb. 1957: 6.

E440   "El novelista Marcel Proust gana el premio Goncourt" (notice). *La Nación* (Buenos Aires) 13 Dec. 1919: 3.

E441   Novo, Salvador. "El cesto y la mesa" (notes on Proust). *Revista de Revistas* (México) 992 (5 May 1929): 5; 1006 (11 Aug. 1929): 24.

E442   Nudelstejer, Sergio. "Marcel Proust: La novela de la novela." *Excelsior* (México), "Arena" 2 (14 Feb. 1999): 12.

E443   Ocampo, Victoria. "La alegría de leer a Rabindranath Tacore [sic]." *La Nación* (Buenos Aires) 9 Nov. 1924, sec. 3: 3.

E444   ———. "Palabras francesas." *Sur* 3 (Winter 1931): 7–25.

E445   "Omega." "Noticiario." *Atenea* (Concepción) 3.9 (30 Nov. 1926): 366.

E446   ———. "Noticiario." *Atenea* (Concepción) 4.3 (31 May 1927).

E447   Onetti, Carlos María. "Du côté de chez Proust." *Valoraciones* (La Plata, Arg.) 3.7 (Sept. 1925): 33–46.

E448   Onetti, J. Carlos. "Marcel Proust: Nota para un aniversario." *Clarín* (Buenos Aires) 16 Nov. 1947, sec. 2: 4.

E449   Ortega y Gasset, José. "Tiempo, distancia y forma en el arte de Proust." *La Nación* (Buenos Aires) 14 Jan. 1923: 18.

E450   Ortiz de Montellano, Bernardo. "Por el camino de Proust." *Contemporáneos* 1.6 (Nov. 1928): 298–300. Rpt. in *Obras en prosa,* 200–01.

E451   Ortiz y Ortiz, Raúl. "La luz interior." *¡Siempre!,* "La Cultura en México" 492 (14 July 1971): 12.

E452 Ospina, Uriel. "Celeste Albaret y Proust: En busca del maestro perdido." *El Tiempo* (Bogotá) 4 July 1971, "Lecturas Dominicales": 5.

E453 Ostrov, León. "Marcel Proust y el psicoanálisis." *La Nación* (Buenos Aires) 10 Apr. 1960, sec. 3: 1.

E454 Pacheco, José Emilio. "Marcel Proust 1871–1922: El desierto del pasado." *Excelsior* (México) 10 July 1971, sec. A: 7–8.

E455 Pacheco, León. "Marcel Proust, una sumersión en el tiempo." *La Nación* (San José) 7 Sept. 1971: 15.

E456 Padilla, Alberto G. "Marcel Proust—bachiller en leyes." *La Prensa* (Buenos Aires) 24 Oct. 1971: 8.

E457 Painter, George D. "La muerte de Proust." *El Comercio* (Lima) 13 June 1971, "Dominical": 27.

E458 ———. "La muerte de Proust." *El Tiempo* (Bogotá) 19 Nov. 1972, "Lecturas Dominicales": 1–2.

E459 Palacios, María Fernanda. "Presentes sucesiones de difunto." *El Nacional* (Caracas) 21 Nov. 1982, "Papel Literario": 9–10. Rpt. in *Sabor y saber de la lengua*, 69–73.

E460 Palmiery, René. "A la busca de Marcel Proust." *La Prensa* (Santiago) 9 Jan. 1972: 18, 24. Rpt. in *El Sol de México*, "En la Cultura" 124 (13 Feb. 1977): 12–13.

E461 ———. "El genio profético de Marcel Proust." *Las Ultimas Noticias* (Santiago) 25 July 1973: 15.

E462 Panesso Robledo, Antonio. Rev. of *Marcel Proust 1871–1922*, ed. Peter Quennell. *Boletín Cultural y Bibliográfico* (Bogotá) 13.2 (1972): 99–102.

E463 "Panorama Literario." "Marcel Proust, Andrés Gide, Paul Valery por Paul Souday." *La Pluma* (Montevideo) 5 (Mar. 1928): 135–36.

E464 Paraf, Pierre. "La juventud de Marcel Proust." *El Nacional,* "Revista Mexicana de Cultura," 2d ser., 1004 (26 June 1966): 5.

E465 ———. "Testigos del hombre: De Proust a Camus." *El Nacional* "Revista Mexicana de Cultura," 2d ser., 1045 (9 Apr. 1967): 1.

E466 "Para leer a Marcel Proust." *Antorcha* (México) 2.3 (Oct. 1925): 26.

E467 "Para releer a Proust." Rev. of *Crónicas,* by Marcel Proust. *La Nación* (Buenos Aires) 5 Aug. 1979, sec. 4: 6.

E468 "Paul Morand dio su quinta conferencia en Amigos del Arte." *La Nación* (Buenos Aires) 27 Sept. 1931: 3, 8.

E469 Paz, Octavio. "Un mundo sin herederos." *El Popular* (México) 25 Nov. 1939: 3, 6. Complete version in *Primeras letras (1931–1943)*, 118–28.

E470 Paz Castillo, Fernando. "En torno a Marcel Proust." *El Nacional* (Caracas) 10 July 1971: A4.

E471 Peltzer, Federico. Rev. of *En busca del tiempo perdido I,* by Marcel Proust. *La Prensa* (Buenos Aires) 1 Nov. 1981: 7.

E472 Peña, Ernesto de la. "Proust, dueño del tiempo" (fourteen articles). *¡Siempre!,* "La Cultura en México" 1980 (5 June 1991): 44; 1981 (12 June 1991): 44; 1982 (19 June 1991): 44; 1983 (26 June 1991): 44; 1984 (3 July 1991): 65; 1985 (10 July 1991): 73; 1986 (17 July 1991): 52; 1987 (24 July 1991): 44; 1988 (31 July 1991): 51; 1989 (7 Aug. 1991): 44; 1990 (14 Aug. 1991): 44; 1992 (28 Aug. 1991): 48; 1993 (4 Sept. 1991): 44; 1995 (18 Sept. 1991): 48.

E473   Peña Barrenechea, Enrique. "Presencia de Proust." *Letras Peruanas* 4.11 (Dec. 1954): 34, 53.

E474   Pérez Turrent, Tomás. "Marcel Proust y César Frank." *¡Siempre!*, "La Cultura en México" 2027 (22 Apr. 1992): xvi.

E475   Perroud de Poccadaz, Robert. "Escritores franceses representativos (Baudelaire, Valéry, Proust. . .)." *La Nación* (Buenos Aires) 14 May 1967, sec. 3: 1.

E476   Petit, Magdalena. "El estilo y la composición en la obra de Marcel Proust." *Atenea* (Concepción) 62 (Apr. 1930): 193–96.

E477   ———. "Marcel Proust y Alexandre Arnoux." *Atenea* (Concepción) 64 (June 1930): 440–42.

E478   ———. "Proust, 'snob y servil'." *Nosotros* (Buenos Aires) 282 (Nov. 1932): 208–14. French version in *Les Cahiers du Sud* 164 (Aug./Sep. 1934): 562–67.

E479   ———. "La psicología en las obras de Proust y Dostoiewsky." *Atenea* (Concepción) 95 (Mar. 1933): 139–44. Rpt. in *Ensayos y cuentos,* 29–34.

E480   ———. "Marcel Proust y la literatura." *Atenea* (Concepción) 116 (Feb. 1935): 195–222. Rpt. in *Ensayos y cuentos,* 11–27.

E481   ———. "Con Proust, en Illiers." *Boletín de la Universidad de Chile* 47 (May 1964): 63–65. French version "En retrouvant le Temps Perdu (Une visite à Illiers)" in *Bulletin de la Société des amis de Marcel Proust et des amis de Combray* (Paris) 14 (1964): 166–69.

E482   Petit de Murat, Ulises. "Superposición del destino en la obra de Marcel Proust." *La Nación* (Buenos Aires) 27 Apr. 1930, "Revista Semanal": 38.

E483   ———. "Concepción proustiana de la novela." *Síntesis* (Buenos Aires) 36 (May 1930): 231–34.

E484   ———. "La voluntad artística de Proust." *El Hogar* (Buenos Aires) 1112 (6 Feb. 1931): 14, 64.

E485   Piaza, Luis Guillermo. "Beckett, Proust y la música." *Novedades* (México), "La Onda" 100 (11 May 1975): 3.

E486   Pillement, Georges. Rev. of *Proust,* by Pierre Abraham. *La Nación* (Buenos Aires) 4 Apr. 1931.

E487   Pimentel, Luz Aurora. "Proust y Joyce: lectura y escritura de una realidad." *Diálogos* (México) 98 (Mar./Apr. 1981): 37–42.

E488   Pinto, Mario. "Variaciones sobre Marcel Proust." *Síntesis* (Buenos Aires) 17 (Oct. 1928): 215–19.

E489   Piñera, Humberto. "'Tempo' de Proust en el tiempo de Machado." *La Torre* (Río Piedras, P. R.) 49 (Jan.–Apr. 1965): 137–54.

E490   Piroué, Georges. "Ni perdido ni encontrado." *La Nación* (Buenos Aires) 11 July 1971, sec. 3: 2.

E491   Pla, José. "La aparición de Proust en París (1920–1924) y su apoteósis." *La Prensa* (Managua) 25 July 1971, "La Prensa Literaria": 3. Rpt. from *Destinos* (Barcelona) 15 May 1971: 27–29.

E492   Rev. of *Los placeres y los días, Parodias y miscelánea,* by Marcel Proust. *La Nación* (Buenos Aires) 14 Nov. 1976, sec. 3: 3.

E493   Ponce, Aníbal. "La sensación olfativa en Marcel Proust." *Revista de Filosofía* (Buenos Aires) 11.6 (Nov. 1925): 459–62. Rpt. in *Obras completas.* Vol. 2, 257–60.

E494 Pondé, Adriano. "La enfermedad y los últimos días de Marcel Proust." *La Prensa Médica Argentina* 60.36 (9 Nov. 1973): 1336–45.

E495 Ponte, Antonio José. "Lectura de Proust." *Unión* (La Habana) 3.9 (Jan./Feb./Mar. 1990): 26–36.

E496 Posse, Abel. "Marcel Proust y Hermann Broch: A contraolvido." *Excelsior* (México), "Arena" 41 (14 Nov. 1999): 1–2.

E497 Poulet, Georges. "La obra única." *La Nación* (Buenos Aires) 11 July 1971, sec. 3: 1–2.

E498 ———. "Proust y la repetición." *Eco* (Bogotá) 171 (Jan. 1975): 225–37.

E499 "El Premio Goncourt de Literatura" (notice). *La Nación* (Santiago) 13 Dec. 1919.

E500 "El Premio Goncourt para 1919" (notice). *El Universal* (Caracas) 14 Dec. 1919.

E501 Prévost, Marcel. "La juventud y la novela moderna." *El País* (Montevideo) 3 July 1928: 12.

E502 Rev. of *La prisionera*, by Marcel Proust. *La Prensa* (Buenos Aires) 30 Dec. 1945: 14.

E503 "Proust y el texto subvertido." Rev. of *Proust y la revolución*, by Juan Pedro Quiñonero. *La Nación* (Buenos Aires) 16 Mar. 1997, "Cultura": 2.

E504 Quiñones, Marta Magaly. "El tiempo y los rostros de Albertina." *Sin Nombre* (San Juan) 2.3 (Jan.–Mar. 1972): 56–59.

E505 Rabell, Malkah. "El año Marcel Proust." *El Día* (México), "El Libro y la Vida" 45 (28 Mar. 1971): 15.

E506 ———. "Centenario de Proust: Entre los 'Delirantes' y los 'Antes'." *El Día* (México) 17 June 1971, "Cultura de Hoy": 11.

E507 Ramela, Carlos. Rev. of *Du côté de chez Proust*, by François Mauriac. *Marcha* (Montevideo) 447 (24 Sept. 1948): 14.

E508 Ramón, David. "*Celeste*, recreación fílmica de la vida de Proust." *Punto* (México) 79 (7–13 May 1984): 24.

E509 Ramos, José Antonio. "Marcel Proust, el novelista de intuición." *Social* (La Habana) 13.9 (Sept. 1928): 37, 67, 81.

E510 Ramos, Juan P. "Marcel Proust" (published lecture). *Verbum* (Buenos Aires) 66 (30 Apr. 1926): 227–50. Rpt. in *Anales del Instituto Popular de Conferencias* (Buenos Aires) 12 (1926): 7–25.

E511 Rangel Guerra, Alfonso. "El hombre en la novela del siglo XX." *Armas y Letras* (Nuevo León, Mex.) 2.4 (Oct.–Dec. 1959): 13–25.

E512 ———. "Los caminos de la novela." *La Palabra y el Hombre* (Xalapa, Méx.) 14 (Apr.–June 1960): 117–28.

E513 Rebry, Lidia. Rev. of *Album Proust*, by Pierre-Louis Rey et al. *Imagen* (Caracas) 100.58 (Oct. 1989): 45.

E514 "Recienvenidos." Rev. of *El indiferente*, by Marcel Proust. *Babel* (Buenos Aires) 1.1 (Apr. 1988): 8.

E515 Repilado, Ricardo. "El lenguage y la caracterización en Proust." *Santiago* (Cuba) 13–14 (Dec. 1973–Mar. 1974): 79–104. Rpt. in *Cosechas de dos parcelas*, 11–38.

E516   Requeni, Antonio. "En Illiers, cuyo nombre es Combray." *La Prensa* (Buenos Aires) 29 Apr. 1962, sec. 2. Rpt. in *La Voz del Interior* (Córdoba, Arg.) 15 June 1969 and in *Los viajes y los días*, 33–38.

E517   R. E. S. (Roque Esteban Scarpa?) Rev. of *A la sombra de las muchachas en flor*, by Marcel Proust. *Estudios* (Santiago) 60 (Nov. 1937): 66–67.

E518   "El retrato de Marcel Proust." *El Sur* (Concepción) 11 July 1971: 11.

E519   Revel, Jean-François. "Proust contra Sainte Beuve." Trans. Jorge Ferreiro. *La Gaceta* (México), new ser., 174 (June 1985): 4–7.

E520   "Las Revistas." "Proust y la música." *Atenea* (Concepción) 71 (Jan. 1931): 142–45.

E521   Rey Alvarez, Sara. "Consideraciones a propósito de la novela contemporánea." *Ensayos* (Montevideo) 19 (Aug. 1938): 8–24.

E522   Reyes, Alfonso. "Vermeer y la novela de Proust." *Social* (La Habana) 9.2 (Feb. 1924): 30–31, 77. Rpt. with note in *Monterrey* 14 (July 1937): 1–2. Rpt. in *Grata Compañía*, 68–74 and in *Obras completas*. Vol. 12, 60–65.

E523   ———. "La última morada de Proust." *Valoraciones* (La Plata, Arg.) 11–12 (May 1928): 169–71. Rpt. in *Atenea* (Concepción) 46 (31 Aug. 1928): 68–71. Rpt. in *Grata compañía*, 75–78 and in *Obras completas*. Vol. 12, 66–68.

E524   ———. "Proust y los gusanos de cuatro dimensiones." *Monterrey* (Rio de Janeiro) 6 (Oct. 1931). Rpt. in *Grata compañía*, 79–80 and in *Obras completas*. Vol. 12, 69–70.

E525   Reyes Nevares, Salvador. "De la novela." *Estaciones* (México) 2.7 (Fall 1957): 272–86.

E526   Reyles, Carlos María. "Marcel Proust: artista investigador." *La Nación* (Buenos Aires) 8 Dec. 1935, sec. 2: 2.

E527   Ribeyro, Julio Ramón. "Del espejo de Stendhal al espejo de Proust." *Amaru* (Lima) 10 (June 1969): 69–71. Rpt. in *Diario de Costa Rica* 20 Dec. 1970, "Suplemento Cultural": 9, 16. Rpt. in *La caza sutil*, 127–31 and in *Antología personal*, 139–43.

E528   Riera, Bernardo. "En torno a Proust." *La Nación* (Santiago) 23 July 1971: 3.

E529   Rinaldi, Angelo. "Proust, ese desconocido." Trans. Jorge Ortiz Barili. *La Nación* (Buenos Aires) 31 Jan. 1988.

E530   Roditi, Edouard. "Perspectivas engañosas." *Sur* (Buenos Aires) 128 (June 1945): 58–72.

E531   Rodríguez-Embil, Luis. "La vivencia religiosa en la literatura contemporánea (Una nueva interpretación del caso Marcel Proust)." *Nosotros* (Buenos Aires), 2d ser., 13 (Apr. 1937): 379–91.

E532   Rodríguez Monegal, Emir. Rev. of *Marcel Proust*, by Léon Pierre-Quint. *Marcha* (Montevideo) 249 (8 Sept. 1944): 15.

E533   ———. "Asteriscos" (notes on Proust). *Marcha* (Montevideo) 282 (18 May 1945): 15; 311 (7 Dec. 1945): 15; 367 (7 Feb. 1947): 15; 375 (18 Apr. 1947): 14.

E534   ———. "El recuerdo de Marcel Proust." *Marcha* (Montevideo) 379 (16 May 1947): 15.

E535   ———. "Aspectos de la novela en el siglo XX." *Sur* (Buenos Aires) 166 (Aug. 1948): 86–97.

E536   ———. "Relecturas: Marcel Proust." *Marcha* (Montevideo) 642 (10 Oct. 1952): 14–15.

E537   Rojas, Manuel. "Marcel Proust." *El Clarín* (Santiago) 24 Apr. 1972: 5.

E538   Rojas Paz, Pablo. "Marcel Proust y la noche." *El Hogar* (Buenos Aires) 1190 (5 Aug. 1932): 73, 91.

E539   Rojas Guardia, Pablo. "El cinema y el Tiempo perdido de Proust." *Imagen* (Caracas) 4 (9–16 July 1971), sec. 2: 16.

E540   Romera, Antonio R. "Marcel Proust en sus cartas." *El Mercurio* (Santiago) 19 Mar. 1969: 2.

E541   ———. "Proust-Swann-Vermeer." *El Mercurio* (Santiago) 18 July 1971: 2.

E542   ———. "Proust y el mundo de la pintura." *El Mercurio* (Santiago) 25 July 1971: 4.

E543   ———. "Proust y la pintura." *El Mercurio* (Santiago) 7 Oct. 1973: 2.

E544   Roubaud, André. "Tres grandes novelistas analizados por sus editores: Marcel Proust, por Gaston Gallimard." *Atenea* (Concepción) 172 (Oct. 1939): 90–95.

E545   Roudene, Alex. "La vida laboriosa de un diletante Marcel Proust." *El Nacional,* "Revista Mexicana de Cultura," 6th ser., 212 (18 Feb. 1973): 2.

E546   Rueda, María Helena. "Una ocasión para editar de nuevo a Proust." *Pluma* (Bogotá) 60 (Feb./Mar. 1988): 55–56.

E547   Ruiz, Bernardo. "Nota introductoria a un pastiche de Marcel Proust." *El Heraldo de México,* "El Heraldo Cultural" 523 (16 Nov. 1975): 7.

E548   R. V. "Una evocación de la obra de Proust." *La Nación* (Santiago) 23 Dec. 1928: 4.

E549   S. "Un nuevo Proust: René Béhaine." *Atenea* (Concepción) 4.1 (31 Mar. 1927): 97–98.

E550   ———. Rev. of *Repertoire des personnages d'A la recherche du temps perdu,* by Charles Daudet and *La vie sociale dans l'oeuvre de Marcel Proust,* by Ramon Fernandez. *Atenea* (Concepción) 5.8 (31 Oct. 1928): 314–15.

E551   Saavedra, Mario. "De Bergson a Proust." *Nivel* (México) 290 (30 Sept. 1987): 9.

E552   Sábato, Ernesto. "Calendario: Vigneron." *Sur* 94 (July 1942): 97.

E553   Sainz, Gustavo. "Maestros fundadores." *Excelsior* (México), "Arena" 46 (19 Dec. 1999): 3–5.

E554   Salaverría, José María. "Unas palabras sobre Marcel Proust." *La Nación* (Buenos Aires), "Letras-Artes" 23 (20 Nov. 1925): 16. Rpt. as "Sobre Marcel Proust" in *El Espectador* (Bogotá), "Suplemento Literario Ilustrado" 60 (14 Jan. 1926): 12.

E555   Salazar, Adolfo. "La sinfonía de Marcel Proust." *El Tiempo* (Bogotá), "Lecturas Dominicales," 2d ser., 432 (6 Mar. 1932): 3.

E556   Salazar Chapela, Esteban. "Exposición Proust." *La Nación* (Santiago) 4 Nov. 1955: 4.

E557   Salcedo Silva, Hernando. "Imágenes cinematográficas en Marcel Proust." *El Tiempo* (Bogotá) 11 July 1971, "Lecturas Dominicales": 7.

E558   Sánchez, Luis Alberto. "La ciencia de los topos." *El Tiempo* (Bogotá) 5 May 1951: 5.

E559   ———. "Acorchado, silencioso y lúcido." *Correo* (Lima) 27 Sept. 1967: 8.

E560 Santa Cruz, Mario. "Marcel Proust, detallista y filósofo." *El Universal Ilustrado* (México) 567 (22 Mar. 1928): 16. Rpt. in *Repertorio Americano* (San José) 16.22 (9 June 1928): 349–50.

E561 ———. "Un hallazgo: La novela póstuma de Marcel Proust." *El Tiempo* (Bogotá) 20 Mar. 1953: 5.

E562 Santa-María, Alejo. "Marcel Proust: Cien años." *El Universal* (Caracas) 4 July 1971: 2–9.

E563 Sarasola, Alberto. "Le vocabulaire de Marcel Proust." *Humanidades* (La Plata, Arg.) 36 (1960): 169–79.

E564 Sartre, Jean-Paul. "La temporalidad en Faulkner." *Marcha* (Montevideo) 566 (2 Mar. 1951): 14–15.

E565 Scarpa, Roque Esteban. "Maestro de Permanencias." *El Mercurio* (Santiago) 14 Nov. 1982: E5.

E566 Schavelzon, Guillermo. "En busca de la revolución perdida." *Babel* (Buenos Aires) 1.2 (May 1988): 33.

E567 Seeber, Arturo (hijo). "Marcel Proust y el momento actual." *Fiesta* (Buenos Aires) 4 (30 Aug. 1927): 9–15.

E568 ———. "El artista de la memoria." *Fiesta* (Buenos Aires) 6–7 (15 Oct. 1927): 32–36.

E569 Seferis, Giorgos. "Cuando se está solo, se puede pedir la ayuda de Swann." *La Gaceta* (México), new ser., 10 (Oct. 1971): 17.

E570 Segal, Alicia F. "Proust perdido y recobrado." *El Nacional* (Caracas) 14 Aug. 1971: A4.

E571 Seligson, Esther. "Marcel Proust: la busca del mundo interior." *El Heraldo de México,* "El Heraldo Cultural" 57 (11 Dec. 1966): 2–3.

E572 ———. "El espesor de lo vivido." *¡Siempre!,* "La Cultura en México" 492 (14 July 1971): 12–13.

E573 Selva, Pedro (Hernán Díaz Arrieta, see also Alone). "El fondo místico de Proust." *Atenea* (Concepción) 273 (Mar. 1948): 184–92; 274 (Apr. 1948): 4–14.

E574 ———. "Defensa de Marcel Proust." *El Imparcial* (Santiago) 12 Sept. 1948: 10.

E575 ———. "La clave de Proust." *El Imparcial* (Santiago) 26 Dec. 1948: 12–13.

E576 "Se publicará una novela que Proust quiso 'olvidar'." *Uno más Uno* (México) 123 (19 Mar. 1978): 20.

E577 Severo, Máximo. "Carta de Proust." *La Nación* (Santiago) 27 July 1971: 3.

E578 Sheridan, Guillermo. "Proustiana." Rev. of *Marcel Proust,* by Roger Shattuck. *El Nacional* (México) 24 Oct. 1976, "Revista Mexicana de Cultura": 6.

E579 "Un siglo a la sombra de Marcel Proust." *El Mercurio* (Santiago) 18 July 1971: 4.

E580 Siles Hur, Mauricio. "El tiempo de Proust medido por Beckett." Rev. of *Eh Joe y otros escritos. Imagen* (Caracas) 59 (15–31 Oct. 1969): 6–7.

E581 Silva Castro, Raúl. "Proust y Cremieux." *El Mercurio* (Santiago) 23 Jun. 1929: 13.

E582 ———. "Más sobre la novela." *Atenea* (Concepción) 56 (Aug. 1929): 84–88.

E583   Slochower, Harry. "Marcel Proust: La redención estética." *¡Siempre!*, "La Cultura en México" 510 (17 Nov. 1971): vi–ix. Rpt. from *Ideología y literatura (Entre las dos guerras mundiales)*.

E584   Souday, Paul. "Marcel Proust, íntimo." *El Tiempo* (Bogotá), "Lectural Dominicales" 175 (14 Nov. 1926): 400.

E585   ———. "Alrededor de Marcel Proust." *La Nación* (Buenos Aires), "Letras-Artes" 182 (23 Dec. 1928): 15.

E586   ———. "¿Marcel Proust era un snob?" *El Universal Ilustrado* (México) 621 (4 Apr. 1929): 30.

E587   Souviron, José María. Rev. of *Marcel Proust y Paul Valery*, by Ernst Robert Curtius. *Estudios* (Santiago) 108 (Jan. 1942): 67–68.

E588   Strachey, John. "Literatura y capitalismo." *SECH* (Sociedad de Escritores Chilenos) 1.1 (July 1936): 21–28.

E589   Sujo, Juana. "El Balzac del señor de Guermantes." *El Nacional* (Caracas) 12 Feb. 1953, "Papel Literario."

E590   Symons, Arthur. "Un casuista de almas: Marcel Proust." *Nosotros* (Buenos Aires) 159 (Aug. 1922): 561–66. Rpt. from *Hermes* (Bilbao, Spain) 84 (June 1922): 246–51.

E591   Tejada, Juan. "Centenario de Proust." *La Nación* (Santiago) 22 July 1971: 3.

E592   Téllez, Hernando. "Las cartas de Proust." *El Tiempo* (Bogotá) 21 July 1946, "Suplemento literario". Rpt. in *Textos no recogidos en libro*, 150–52.

E593   Tinaire, Jean. "Marcel Proust: Un gran novelista. Pérdida notable de las letras francesas." *El Universal* (Caracas) 23 Dec. 1922: 1.

E594   Tollinchi, Esteban. "Las perfidias de la conciencia proustiana." *Sin Nombre* (San Juan) 2.3 (Jan.–Mar. 1972): 43–55.

E595   ———. "Proust y la sociedad: Una visión desmitificante de la aristocracia." *Zona de carga y descarga* (San Juan) 5 (May/June/July 1973): 12–13.

E596   ———. "El amor de Proust." *Río Piedras* 5–6 (Sept. 1974–Mar. 1975): 87–101.

E597   ———. Rev. of *Monsieur Proust*, by Céleste Albaret. *Sin Nombre* (San Juan) 7.4 (Jan.–Mar. 1977): 74–77.

E598   Torre, Guillermo de. "Permanencia de Proust." *Clarín* (Buenos Aires) 16 Mar. 1967, sec. 3.

E599   Torre, Manuel. "Proust, Fotógrafo del Tiempo." *La Vanguardia* (Buenos Aires) 4 Oct. 1942: 8.

E600   Torre Campoy, Manuel de la. "El carácter de Marcel Proust." *La Nación* (San José), "Calidoscopio" 72 (17 Feb. 1968): 43.

E601   Torres Bodet, Jaime. "Aniversario de Proust." *Contemporáneos* (México) 1.6 (Nov. 1928): 280–91.

E602   ———. "La fecundidad del olvido." *Excelsior* (México) 16 Apr. 1967, "Diorama de la Cultura": 1, 6.

E603   ———. "La lucha contra el tiempo en la obra de Proust." *Novedades*, "México en la Cultura," 3d ser., 943 (16 Apr. 1967): 1, 6.

E604   ———. "*En busca del tiempo perdido* y la psicología de Proust." *Novedades*, "México en la Cultura," 3d ser., 944 (23 Apr. 1967): 3.

E605   ———. "Proust y la estética del sueño." *Cuadernos Americanos* (México) 63.4 (July/Aug. 1967): 71–84.

E606   Torres Delgado, René. "Impresionismo y Expresionismo en Proust." *Al Margen* (San Juan) 2 (1981): 64–67.

E607   Torres Fierro, Danubio. "Revolucionarios del siglo XX: Proust." *Excelsior* (México), "Revista de Revistas" 98 (17 Apr. 1974): 27–30.

E608   Torri, Julio. "Por el camino de Proust." *Contemporáneos* 1.6 (Nov. 1928): 300–03.

E609   ———. "La epopeya de los celos y el snobismo." *El Nacional* (México) 18 May 1933: 3. Rpt. in *Tres libros*, 129–32 and in *De fusilamientos y otras narraciones*, 129–32.

E610   "Tragaluz." "Proust/Visconti." *El Universal* (México), "La Letra y la Imagen" 21 (17 Feb. 1980): 15–16.

E611   Uboldi, Oscar. "Marcel Proust inédito." *Buenos Aires Literaria* 1 (Oct. 1952): 45–46.

E612   Urtubey, Agustín. "Proust." *La Nación* (Buenos Aires), "Letras-Artes" 138 (19 Feb. 1928): 16.

E613   Uscatescu, Jorge. "Permanencia de las letras: Actualidad de de Proust." *El Espectador* (Bogotá) 7 May 1972, "Magazín Dominical": 6.

E614   Uslar Pietri, Arturo. "El pequeño Marcel." *El Nacional* (Caracas) 18 July 1971: A4. Rpt. as "Marcel Proust" in *El Comercio* (Quito) 2 Aug. 1971, sec. 1: 4–5. Rpt. as "Proust" in *El Imparcial* (Guatemala) 7 Aug. 1971: 13, 17.

E615   ———. "El cine y Proust." *El Nacional* (Caracas) 27 May 1984: A4.

E616   Valadés, Edmundo. "Proust: Una caída de Gide." *Vida Literaria* (México) 15/16: 27–32. Rpt. in *Por caminos de Proust*, 99–116.

E617   ———. "La casa proustiana de Combray." *Revista de la Universidad de México*. 22.4 (Dec. 1967): 17–21. Rpt. as "Combray" in *Por caminos de Proust*, 123–28.

E618   ———. "El ingenio Guermantes." *Revista de Bellas Artes* (México) 31 (Jan./Feb. 1970): 81–96. Rpt. in *Por caminos de Proust*, 75–98.

E619   ———. "Las letras al día (Faulkner y Proust)." *El Día* (México), "El Gallo Ilustrado" 472 (11 July 1971): 15.

E620   ———. "El ingenio francés en la saeta de la prosa y el color de la anécdota a principios de este siglo." *Novedades*, "México en la Cultura," 3d ser., 1163 (ll July 1971): 1, 3, 7.

E621   ———. "La vida y obra de Marcel Proust." *¡Siempre!*, "La Cultura en México" 492 (14 July 1971): 2–6. Rpt. as "Vida singular, obra maestra" in *Por caminos de Proust*, 7–49.

E622   ———. "Alrededor del amor y los celos en Proust." *Revista de Bellas Artes* (México), new ser., 1.6 (Jan.–Dec. 1972): 115–20. Rpt. as "El amor y los celos en Proust" in *Por caminos de Proust*, 51–73.

E623   Valdés A., Abel. "Proust en Doble Aniversario." *El Mercurio* (Santiago) 3 Dec. 1972: 7.

E624   Valente, Ignacio. "Proust: La perfección de la sicología." *El Mercurio* (Santiago) 9 July 1978: iii.

E625   ———. "Los límites de Proust." *El Mercurio* (Santiago) 30 July 1978: E3.

E626   Valenzuela, Abraham. Rev. of *Marcel Proust, sa vie, son oeuvre*, by Léon Pierre-Quint. *Atenea* (Concepción) 2.7 (30 Sept. 1925): 245–55.

E627   Valenzuela, Renato. "Marcel Proust, o la primera gloria de la nueva literatura y su extraño y portentoso destino." *El Mercurio* (Santiago) 1 Apr. 1928: 5.

E628   ———. "Marcel Proust o la primera gloria de la nueva literatura: La singular construcción de su obra gigantesca." *El Mercurio* (Santiago) 8 Apr. 1928: 4.

E629   ———. "Marcel Proust." *La Nación* (Santiago) 28 Apr. 1929.

E630   Valera, Raúl. "Yo no entiendo a Proust." *Cultura Universitaria* (Caracas) 105 (1983): 117–19.

E631   Valverde, Umberto. "Proust y su madre." *¡Siempre!*, "La Cultura en México" 492 (14 July 1971): xiii.

E632   Vargas, César. "Proust, el tiempo y la memoria." *Casa del tiempo* (México), 2d ser., 72 (Feb. 1998): 46–48.

E633   Vargas Llosa, Mario. "Proust en fotos." *Marcha* (Montevideo) 1268 (20 Aug. 1965): 28.

E634   Vaudoyer, Jean Louis. "La morbosidad de Boylesvre y Marcel Proust." *El Tiempo* (Bogotá), "Lecturas Dominicales" 389 (26 Apr. 1931): 4.

E635   Vega Martín, Carmen. "Influencias de Franz Kafka y Marcel Proust en la creatividad literaria contemporánea." *Colmena Universitaria* (Guanajuato) 2 (19) Suplemento 1972.

E636   Velázquez Medina, Fernando. Rev. of *Por el camino de Swann,* by Marcel Proust. *Revolución y Cultura* (La Habana) 8 (Aug. 1988): 80.

E637   "La verdadera inspiradora de la duquesa de Guermantes." *La Nación* (Buenos Aires) 27 Sep. 1953, sec. 2: 3.

E638   Vergara, Marta. "El prisionero de sí mismo." *Atenea* (Concepción) 53 (May 1929): 254–59.

E639   ———. "Nuevos ataques y nueva actualidad de Marcel Proust." *El Mercurio* (Santiago) 13 Dec. 1931: 2.

E640   "La Vida de los Libros." "Rehabilitación de Marcel Proust." *Cromos* (Bogotá) 1922 (22 Feb. 1954): 41.

E641   "La vida de Marcel Proust narra su mucama en libro." Rev. of *Monsieur Proust,* by Céleste Albaret. *La Prensa* (Lima) 16 Dec. 1973: iv.

E642   "Vida y Obra" (lectures by Jaime Torres Bodet). *Hispanoamericano* (México) 1301 (10 Apr. 1967): 57–58; 1302 (17 Apr. 1967): 55–56; 1303 (24 Apr. 1967): 56–60.

E643   "Vida y pasión de Manuel [sic] Proust." *La Nación* (Santiago) 1 Dec. 1939: 5.

E644   "El Vigía." "Todavía Marcel Proust." *El Diario Ilustrado* (Santiago) 27 Jan. 1929: 9.

E645   "Vigilia." "En busca del tiempo perdido." *El Nacional* (Caracas) 11 July 1971, "Papel Literario": 1.

E646   Vigneron, Robert. "Estela de Marcel Proust: Génesis de Swann." *Letras de México* 3.17 (15 May 1942): 9. Rpt. in *Atenea* (Concepción) 244 (Oct. 1945): 58–64.

E647   Villacrés M., Lautaro. "En el centenario de Marcel Proust." *El Comercio* (Quito) 18 July 1971, sec. 3: 5.

E648   Villordo, Oscar Hermes. "El primer Proust." *La Nación* (Buenos Aires) 3 Apr. 1972: 7.

E649   Vistel, Augusto. "Algunos aspectos de la literatura francesa contemporánea." *Atenea* (Concepción) 77 (July 1931): 208–22.

E650   Volkening, Ernesto. "Marcel Proust." *Eco* (Bogotá) 135 (Jul. 1971): 225–38. Rpt. in *Ensayos II*, 187–97.

E651   ———. "El paisaje mítico de la infancia." *Colcultura Gaceta* (Bogotá) 42 (Jan./Feb. 1984): 57–61.

E652   Vozza, Jaime V. "Marcel Proust, los médicos y los enfermos." *La Prensa* (Buenos Aires) 30 Apr. 1967, "Secciones Ilustradas.": 1.

E653   Walsh, María Elena. "La guardiana de Proust." *La Nación* (Buenos Aires) 1 June 1997, sec. 6: 1–2.

E654   Wasserman, Mario. "Marcel Proust o en busca del transparentismo." *Esto es* (Buenos Aires) 65 (22 Feb. 1955): 40.

E655   Weibel Richard, Robert. "De Bourget a Proust" (published lecture). *Conferencias* (Buenos Aires) 2.9 (1 Apr. 1934): 118–26.

E656   Weiss, Alfred J. "Cartas de Marcel Proust." *Sur* (Buenos Aires) 201 (July 1951): 121–22.

E657   Westphalen, Emilio Adolfo. "Extractos de la Correspondencia de Marcel Proust." *Las Moradas* (Lima) 2.4 (Apr. 1948): 8–9.

E658   Wiesse de Sabogal, María. "El dolor de Marcel Proust." *Social* (Lima) 23.404 (Oct. 1953): 15.

E659   Yañez, María Flora. Rev. of *Marcel Proust*, by George D. Painter. *El Mercurio* (Santiago) 16 Oct. 1966: 9.

E660   Zendejas, Francisco. "Multilibros." *Excelsior* (México) 2 Oct. 1972: A22.

E661   ———. "La introyección del tiempo proustiano." *Las Moradas* (Lima) 2.4 (Apr. 1948): 31–34.

E662   Zen-Lis, Francisco M. "El estudio biográfico de Proust de R. Vigneron." *Letras de México* 3.17 (15 May 1942): 9.

E663   Zilboorg, Gregory. "El descubrimiento del complejo de Edipo: Episodios tomados de Marcel Proust." Trans. Matilde W. de Rascovsky. *Revista de psicoanálisis* (Buenos Aires) 1.3 (Jan. 1944): 319–39.

E664   Zuckermann, Lydia. Rev. of *Monsieur Proust*, by Céleste Albaret. *El Heraldo de México*, "El Heraldo Cultural" 441 (21 Apr. 1974): 3.

E665   ———. "En busca de un personaje: Proust y el conde de Montesquiou." *El Heraldo de México*, "El Heraldo Cultural" 463 (22 Sept. 1974): 2.

E666   ———. "Salir del infierno: En busca de Marcel Proust." *El Nacional*, "Revista Mexicana de Cultura" 308 (29 Dec. 1974): 3.

III. STUDIES ON LITERARY OR PERSONAL RELATIONS BETWEEN PROUST AND SPANISH AMERICANS

F. Books, Theses, Essays, and Chapters or a Continuous Discussion in Books

F1   Achury Valenzuela, Darío. *Cita en la trinchera de la muerte*. Bogotá: Colcultura, 1973.

F2   Amaya Castano, M. "Fonction du récit et mythologies romanesques chez Proust et García Márquez." Ph. D. diss., Université Paris X (Nanterre), 1984.

F3   Bendahan, Daniel. *Reynaldo Hahn*. Caracas: Monte Avila Latinoamericana, C. A., 1992.

F4   Bocaz, Sergio Hernán. "La novelística de José Donoso y su cosmogonía a través de dos influencias principales: Marcel Proust y Henry James." Ph. D. diss., University of Colorado, 1972.

F5   Carballo, Emmanuel. *Jaime Torres Bodet y su obra*, 84–85, 102–06. México: Empresas Editoriales, 1968.

F6   Carpentier, Alejo. "Un venezolano amigo de Proust." In *Letra y solfa*, 45–46. Caracas: Síntesis Dosmil, 1975.

F7   ———. "Proust escribe a los Hahn." In *Letra y solfa: Literatura. Autores*, 222–23. La Habana: Editorial Letras Cubanas, 1997.

F8   Chirol, Marie-Madeleine Juliette. "Ruins and Imaginary Ruins in Twentieth Century Novels: Marcel Proust, Alejo Carpentier, Camilo José Cela, Marguerite Duras, Hubert Nyssen, Raymond Jean." Ph. D. diss., University of Maryland, 1991.

F9   Chase, Alfonso. "Marcel Proust en la vida y la obra de Yolanda Oreamuno." In *Relatos escogidos de Yolanda Oreamuno*, 27–31. San José, 1977.

F10   Craig, Herbert E. "The Presence of Proust in Argentine Narrative." Ph. D. diss., University of Wisconsin–Madison, 1983.

F11   ———. "Teresa de la Parra y la introducción de Marcel Proust en Hispanoamérica." In *Ensayos de literatura europea e hispanoamericana*. Ed. Félix Menchacatorre, 115–20. San Sebastián, Spain: Universidad del País Vasco, 1989.

F12   Dorfmann, Ariel. "Sandwiched between Proust and the Mummy: Seven Notes and an Epilogue on Carpentier's *Reasons of State*." In *Some Write to the Future: Essays on Contemporary Latin American Fiction*. Trans. George Shiverd, 100–32. Durham, NC: Duke University Press, 1991.

F13   Estrada Arriens, Ernesto. "Marcel Proust y Reynaldo Hahn." In *Mis recuerdos de Reynaldo Hahn: El crepúsculo de la Belle Epoque*, 99–108. Caracas: Editorial Sucre, 1974.

F14   Farris, Wendy. "¿Proustitución? *Una familia lejana*." In *De la crónica a la nueva narrativa*, 369–82. México: Ediciones Era, 1980.

F15   ———. "'Proustitution'? *Distant Relations*." In *Carlos Fuentes*, 173–84. New York: Frederick Unglar Publishing Co., 1983.

F16   García Simón, Diana. *Paraíso, metamorfosis y memoria: La influencia de Proust y Kafka en la obra de Mujica Láinez*. Frankfurt/M: Peter Lang, 1998.

F17   García Vega, Lorenzo. "Encuentro en la Victoria: Muchacho, lee a Proust." In *Los años de Orígenes*, 181–84. Caracas: Monte Avila Editores, C. A., 1978.

F18   Golden, Carol Anne. "Proustian Elements in the Novels of Carlos Fuentes." M. A. thesis, University of Florida, 1971.

F19   Harvey, Sally. *Carpentier's Proustian Fiction: The Influence of Marcel Proust on Alejo Carpentier*. London: Tamesis Books, Ltd., 1994.

F20   Hernández Arregui, Juan José. *Imperialismo y cultura (La política en la inteligencia argentina)*, 66–67. Buenos Aires: Editorial Amerindia, 1957.

F21   Jones, Julie. *A Common Place: The Representation of Paris in Spanish American Fiction*. Lewisburg, PA: Bucknell University, 1998.

F22   Lemley, Lynn Jane Roberts. "La índole proustiana de *Palinuro de México*." M. A. thesis, Texas Technological University, 1987.

F23   Martínez, Marco Antonio. "Proust y Teresa de la Parra." In *Teresa de la Parra: Ante la crítica.* Ed. Velia Bosch, 145–54. Caracas: Monte Avila Editores, C. A., 1980.

F24   Matamoro, Blas. "Marcel Proust." In *Genio y figura de Victoria Ocampo,* 167–74. Buenos Aires: EUDEBA, 1986.

F25   Molloy, Silvia. *Signs of Borges.* Trans. Oscar Montero, 115–19. Durham, NC: Duke University Press, 1994.

F26   Patout, Paulette. *Alfonso Reyes et la France,* 211–18, 287–301. Paris: Klincksieck, 1978.

F27   Pimentel, Luz Aurora. *Metaphoric Narration: Paranarrative Dimensions in "A la recherche du temps perdu,"* 6–7, 40–44, Toronto: University of Toronto Press, 1990.

F28   Pollmann, Leo. *La "nueva novela" en Francia e Iberoamérica,* 45–50. Madrid: Editorial Gredos, S. A., 1971.

F29   Ribeyro, Julio Ramón. "Notas sobre *Paradiso.*" In *Recopilación de textos sobre José Lezama Lima.* Ed. Pedro Simón Martínez, 175–81. La Habana: Casa de las Américas, 1970.

F30   Rodríguez, Alicia L. "The Concept of Time in Alejo Carpentier and Marcel Proust." M. A. thesis, Florida State University, 1977.

F31   Ruy Sánchez, Alberto. "*Dama de Corazones* de Xavier Villaurrutia." In *Al filo de las hojas,* 83–86. México: Consejo Nacional de Fomento Educativo, 1988.

F32   Sarduy, Severo. "A Cuban Proust." In *Modern Latin American Fiction.* Ed. Harold Bloom, 131–35. New York, Philadelphia: Chelsea House Publishers, 1990.

F33   Schwartz, Marcy E. *Writing Paris: Urban Topographies of Desire in Contemporary Latin American Fiction,* 93–94. Albany: State University of New York Press, 1999.

F34   Sheridan, Guillermo. *Los Contemporáneos ayer,* 132–33, 249, 308. México: Fondo de Cultura Económica, 1985.

F35   Uslar Pietri, Arturo. "Reynaldo, un personaje de Proust." In *Fantasmas de dos mundos,* 135–37. Barcelona: Editorial Seix Barral, S. A., 1979.

F36   ———. "Proust en Turmero". In *Fantasmas de dos mundos,* 67–73. Barcelona: Editorial Seix Barral, 1979.

F37   Valdivieso, Jaime. "Nuestra herencia de Proust o la Desconfianza de la mirada." In *Bajo el signo de Orfeo: Lezama Lima y Proust,* 111–26. Madrid: Orígenes, 1980.

F38   ———. "Proust en nuestra América." *El espejo y la palabra: Mann, Borges, Proust, Lezama Lima,* 93–115. Santiago: Editorial Planeta, 1997.

F39   Vallbona, Rima de. "La huella proustiana en la novela de Yolanda Oreamuno." In *La narrativa de Yolanda Oreamuno,* 65–83. San José: Editorial Costa Rica, 1996.

F40   Varderi, Alejandro. "El camino de Reynaldo Hahn en el tiempo de Proust." In *Anotaciones sobre el amor y el deseo,* 113–22. Caracas: Academia de la Historia, 1986.

F41   Vásquez, Karina. "A propósito de "La Mayor": Algunas reflexiones sobre el tiempo y la memoria en Juan José Saer." In *Segundas Jornadas Internacionales de la literatura argentina/comparatística.* Ed. Daniel Altamiranda, 391–96. Buenos Aires: Universidad de Buenos Aires, 1997.

F42   Zamudio-Taylor, Victor and Inma Guiu. "Criss-Crossing Texts: Reading Images in *Like Water for Chocolate.*" In *The Mexican Cinema Project.* Ed. Chon A. Noriega and Steven Ricci, 45–51. Los Angeles: UCLA Film and Television Archive, 1994.

G. *Articles, Reviews, and Notes on Proust and Spanish America Published in Periodicals*

G1   Abreu Gómez, Ermilio. "Penetración Crítica." Rev. of *Tiempo y memoria en la obra de Proust,* by Jaime Torres Bodet. *Hispanoamericano* (México) 1324 (18 Sept. 1967): 59–60.

G2   Acevedo Escobedo, Antonio. "Un examen de Proust." *El Nacional* (México) 24 Dec. 1967: 3–4.

G3   Achury Valenzuela, Darío. "En el centenario de Proust: Episodios intrascendentes de la amistad de Proust con el poeta-legionario colombiano: Hernando de Bengoechea." *Revista de la Dirección de Divulgación Cultural* (Bogotá) 9 (Sept. 1971): 101–17.

G4   Alone (Hernán Díaz Arrieta). "Las mejores páginas de Marcel Proust." *La Nación* (Santiago) 18 Mar. 1934.

G5   ———. "Alfonso Reyes y Marcel Proust." *La Nación* (Santiago) 5 Sep. 1937: 2.

G6   ———. Rev. of *Un mito proustiano,* by Marta Rivas. *El Mercurio* (Santiago) 21 Apr. 1968: 3.

G7   Armando-Chacón, Joaquín. "En busca de un encuentro." Rev. of *Por caminos de Proust,* by Edmundo Valadés. *Novedades* (México), "La Onda" 77 (1 Dec. 1974): 10.

G8   Aronne de Amestoy, Lida. Rev. of *La conciencia proustiana,* by Esteban Tollinchi. *Señales* (Buenos Aires) 180 (1979): 45–46.

G9   Avilés Ramírez, Eduardo. "Un nuevo Proust." Rev. of *Tiempo y memoria en la obra de Proust,* by Jaime Torres Bodet. *El Sol de México* 7 Sept. 1967: A5.

G10   Barradas, Efraín. Rev. of *Bajo el signo de Orfeo: Lezama Lima y Proust,* by Jaime Valdivieso. *Sin nombre* (San Juan) 13.1 (Oct.–Dec. 1982): 82–83.

G11   Barrios, Eduardo. Rev. of *Las mejores páginas de Marcel Proust,* selection by Alone. *Las Ultimas Noticias* (Santiago) 27 Dec. 1933: 13.

G12   Battistessa, Angel J. "El general Mansilla visto del lado de Guermantes." *La Nación* (Buenos Aires), 28 June 1981 sec. 4: 1.

G13   Benedetti, Mario. "La saga argentina de Mujica Láinez." *Marcha* 814 (25 May 1956): 23.

G14   Bocaz, Sergio Hernán. "La novelística de José Donoso y su cosmogonía a través de dos influencias principales: Marcel Proust y Henry James." *Dissertation Abstracts International* 33/04 (1972): 1714A.

G15   Bradu, Fabienne. Rev. of *Homenaje a Proust seguido de otros artículos,* by José Bianco. *Vuelta* (México) 94 (Sept. 1984): 34–36.

G16   "Buenos Aires busca el Tiempo perdido." *Realidad* 1 (Jan./ Feb. 1947): 128.

G17   Caballero Calderón, Eduardo. "En torno y en el contorno de Marcel Proust." *El Tiempo* (Bogotá) 4 July 1971, "Lecturas Dominicales": 1, 6.

G18   Capistrán, Miguel. "Proust en México." *¡Siempre!,* "La Cultura en México" 492 (14 July 1971): vii-ix.

G19   Carballo, Emmanuel. "Tiempo y memoria." Rev. of *Tiempo y memoria en la obra de Proust*, by Jaime Torres Bodet. *Excelsior* (México) 26 May 1968, "Diorama de la la Cultura": 5–6.

G20   ———. "Marcel Proust, Tiempo y memoria." *El Universal* (México), "Nuevo Siglo" 147 (25 Dec. 1994): 34–35.

G21   Cardona Peña, Alfredo. "Danza de Rostros." Rev. of *Tiempo y memoria en la obra de Proust*, by Jaime Torres Bodet. *El Nacional*, "Revista Mexicana de Cultura" 1067 (10 Sept. 1967): 6.

G22   ———. "Un libro sobre Proust." *La Nación* (San José) 30 Sept. 1967: 43.

G23   Carpentier, Alejo. "Un venezolano amigo de Proust." *El Nacional* (Caracas) 16 Aug. 1951: 12. Rpt. in *Letra y solfa*, 45–46.

G24   ———. "Proust escribe a los Hahn." *El Nacional* (Caracas) 9 May 1956: 12. Rpt. in *Letra y solfa: Literatura. Autores*, 222–23.

G25   ———. "Marcel Proust y la América Latina." *Casa de las Américas* (La Habana) 69 (1971): 227–29. Rpt. in *La Gaceta de Cuba* 12 (Dec. 1989): 10–11.

G26   ———. "Marcel Proust et l'Amérique latine." *Bulletin de la Société des amis de Marcel Proust et des amis de Combray* (Paris) 22 (1972) 1321–26.

G27   Carranca y Rivas, Raúl. "Torres Bodet y Proust." *El Día* (México) 10 Nov. 1968: 13.

G28   Chase, Alfonso. "Yolanda Oreamuno y Marcel Proust: encuentros y deslindes." *La República* (San José) 13 Aug. 1970: 9, 14.

G29   Cheymol, Marc. "Jaime Torres Bodet y la literatura francesa." *Universidad de México* 425 (June 1986): 3–13.

G30   "Consultorio literario y artístico." *La Nación* (Buenos Aires) 5 Aug. 1928: 15.

G31   Craig, Herbert E. Notes on Proust in Spain and Spanish America. *Proust Research Association Newsletter* (Lawrence, KS) 23 (1982): 10–11; 24 (1984): 17; 25 (1986): 10–12.

G32   ———. "Proust y Mujica Láinez: La memoria asociativa." *Cuadernos Hispanoamericanos* (Madrid) 409 (July 1984): 101–06.

G33   ———. "The Presence of Proust in Argentine Narrative." *Dissertation Abstracts International* 45/02 (1984): 533A–534A. Rpt. in *Proust Research Association Newsletter* (Lawrence, KS) 24 (1984): 62–63.

G34   ———. "Alone, Chilean Critic of Proust." *Proust Research Association Newsletter* (Lawrence, KS) 26 (1986): 44–54.

G35   ———. "Ideas de Ortega y Gasset sobre la novela proustiana." *Bulletin Hispanique* (Bordeaux) 88.3–4 (July-Dec. 1986): 445–56.

G36   ———. "La memoria proustiana en *Rayuela* de Julio Cortázar." *Nueva Revista de Filología Hispánica* (México) 37.1 (1989): 237–45.

G37   ———. "Proustian Time in *El amor en los tiempos del cólera*." *Confluencia* (Greeley, CO) 5.2 (Spring 1990): 55–59.

G38   ———. "Proust in Spanish: The Old and New Translations of *Du côté de chez Swann*." *Platte Valley Review* (Kearney, NE) 23.2 (Spring 1995): 34–50.

G39   ———. Rev. of *Carpentier's Proustian Fiction: The Influence of Marcel Proust on Alejo Carpentier*, by Sally Harvey. *Chasqui* 24.1 (1995): 88–90.

G40 ———. "Una sensibilidad paralela: Marcel Proust y Victoria Ocampo." *Asterión* (Caracas) 1.2 (Oct.–Dec. 1996): 4–9. Rpt. http://www.asterionline.com.ve/revistas/numeros/ numero2/marcel.html.

G41 ———. "Proust en España y en Hispanoamérica: La recepción 1920–1929." *Bulletin Hispanique* (Bordeaux) 101.1 (Jan–June 1999): 175–85.

G42 ———. Review Essay: "The French Connection: *A Common Place: The Representation of Paris in Spanish American Fiction*, by Julie Jones; *Urban Topographies of Desire in Contemporary Latin American Fiction*, by Marcy E. Schwartz; *Paraíso, metamorfosis y memoria: La influencia de Proust y Kafka en Mujica Láinez*, by Diana García Simón." *Chasqui* 29.2 (Nov. 2000): 138–41.

G43 Darré, María Celia. "Proust a través de un cuento de Juan José Saer." *Revista de Literaturas Modernas* (Mendoza, Arg.) 24 (1991): 73–83.

G44 De Aguilar, Helene I. F. "Secret Sharers: Memory in Proust and Fuentes." *Southwest Review* 70.4 (Fall 1985): 500–12.

G45 Diez de Medina, Fernando. "Alone, Francia y Marcel Proust." *La Nación* (Santiago) 20 Oct. 1935: 9.

G46 Dorfmann, Ariel. "Entre Proust y la momia americana: Siete notas y un epílogo sobre *El recurso del método*." *Revista Iberoamericana* 114–115 (Jan.–June 1981): 95–128.

G47 Durand, Claude. "Le Proust des Caraïbes." *L'Express* (Paris) 1030 (5–11 Apr. 1971): 129–30.

G48 Echavarría, Jorge. Rev. of *El olvido en la obra de Marcel Proust*, by María Cristina Restrepo López. *Escritos* (Medellín, Colom.) 7.17 (Nov. 1986): 186.

G49 Emeth, Omer (Emilio Vaisse). Rev. of *Las mejores páginas de Marcel Proust*, selection by Alone. *El Mercurio* (Santiago) 8 Mar. 1934: 3.

G50 Estrada, Ernesto. "Reynaldo Hahn y Proust." *Imagen* (Caracas) 74 (1–15 June 1970): 26–27.

G51 Ertze Garamendi, Ramón de. "Proust: Tiempo y memoria." Rev. of *Tiempo y memoria en la obra de Proust*, by Jaime Torres Bodet. *Excelsior* (México) 23 Aug. 1969: A6.

G52 Faris, Wendy B. "Alejo Carpentier à la recherche du temps perdu." *Comparative Literature Studies* 17.2 (June 1980): 133–54.

G53 García Carrillo, Eugenio. "Marcel Proust en Costa Rica." *La República* (San José) 17 July 1971: 9.

G54 García Ponce, Juan. Rev. of *Ficción y realidad*, by José Bianco. *Vuelta* (México) 2.19 (June 1978): 31–32.

G55 Garrido, Luis. "Leyendo a Proust." Rev. of *Tiempo y memoria en la obra de Proust*, by Jaime Torres Bodet. *El Universal* (México) 8 Sept. 1967: 3, 19.

G56 Gimbernat de González, Ester. Rev. of *Bajo el signo de Orfeo: Lezama Lima y Proust*, by Jaime Valdivieso. *Hispamérica* 30 (Dec. 1981): 143–46.

G57 Gómez, Carlos A. "Proust y su influencia en nuestros escritores" (interview of Herbert Craig). *La Nación* (Buenos Aires) 18 Apr. 1977: 5.

G58 Gnutzmann, Rita. "Carpentier y la herencia proustiana." *Revista de Literatura* (Madrid) 88 (July-Dec. 1982): 169–80.

G59 ———. "Alejo Carpentier: Le Lion fait de mouton assimilé." *Hispanófila* 91 (1987): 29–41.

G60 Guillén, Pedro. "Torres Bodet, Lección y Trabajo." Rev. of *Tiempo y memoria en la obra de Proust*. *El Nacional* (México) 23 Sept. 1967: 3.

G61   Illan Bacca, Ramón. "¿Un samario amigo de Proust . . . ?" *El Café Literario* (Bogotá) 9 (May/June 1979): 37–39.

G62   Jaeck, Lois Marie. "The Text and Intimations of Immortality: From Proust's *Recherche* to Fuentes' *Aura*." *Dalhousie French Studies* 38 (Spring 1997): 109–17.

G63   Jaffella de Dolgopol, Sara A. Rev. of *La conciencia proustiana*, by Esteban Tollinchi. *Bibliographie de la philosophie* (Paris) 27.2–3 (1980): 191–92.

G64   Labarre, Françoise. "Proust dans *Le Recours de la méthode* d'Alejo Carpentier." *Recherches et Etudes Comparatistes Ibero-Françaises de la Sorbonne* 6 (1984): 117–26.

G65   Ladra, Luis Antonio. "Poesía en José Lezama Lima." *Nadie Parecía* (La Habana) 8 (Aug. 1943).

G66   Leiva, Raúl. Rev. of *Tiempo y memoria en la obra de Proust*, by Jaime Torres Bodet. *Novedades*, "México en la Cultura" 961 (20 Aug. 1967): 6.

G67   "Libros y autores." Rev. of *Un mito proustiano*, by Marta Rivas. *Ercilla* (Santiago) 1719 (29 May–4 June 1968): 52.

G68   Linares, Horacio (Alberto Prebisch). "Manuel Gálvez y la Nueva Generación." *Martín Fierro*, 2d ser., 18 (26 June 1925); 21 (28 Aug. 1925): 1, 7.

G69   Magaña-Esquivel, Antonio. "Otro inventor de la realidad." Rev. of *Por caminos de Proust*, by Edmundo Valadés. *Hispanoamericano* 1695 (28 Oct. 1974): 57–58.

G70   Martí, Ellú. Rev. of *Por caminos de Proust*, by Edmundo Valadés. *El Heraldo de México*, "El Heraldo Cultural" 480 (19 Jan. 1975): 7.

G71   Martínez, Marco Antonio. "Proust y Teresa de la Parra." *Imagen* (Caracas) 44 (25 Apr.–2 May 1972), sec. 2: 2–3. Rpt. in *Teresa de la Parra: Ante la crítica*, 145–54.

G72   Martínez Peñaloza, Porfirio. Rev. of *Tiempo y memoria en la obra de Proust*, Jaime Torres Bodet. *Lectura* (México) 168.3 (1 Aug. 1967): 85–88. Rpt. in *El Nacional*, "Revista Mexicana de Cultura," 2d ser., 1066 (3 Sept. 1967): 5.

G73   Matas, Julio. "Pirandello, Proust and *El Chino* by Carlos Felipe." *Hispanic Journal* 5.1 (Fall 1983): 43–47.

G74   M. C. G. "Alone." Rev. of *Las mejores páginas de Marcel Proust*, selection by Alone. *Política, Economía, Cultura* (Santiago) 314 (3 Jan. 1969): 23.

G75   McGowan, John P. "*A la recherche du temps perdu* in *One hundred Years of Solitude*." *Modern Fiction Studies* 28.4 (Winter 1982–83): 557–67.

G76   Mendoza Wolske, Antonio. "Reynaldo a fragmentos." *Imagen* (Caracas) 100–6 (Apr./May 1985): 36–37.

G77   Montezuma de Carvalho, Joaquín. "Jaime Torres Bodet y Marcel Proust." *Norte* (México), 3d ser., 267 (1975): 61–65.

G78   Moscoso-Gongora, Peter. "A Proust of the Caribbean." Rev. of *Paradiso*, by José Lezama Lima. *The Nation* 218 (11 May 1974): 600–1.

G79   Ocasio, Rafael and Fiona Doloughan. "Literary Offspring: The Figure of the Child in M. Proust and Reinaldo Arenas." *Romance Quarterly* 41.2 (Spring 1994): 110–18.

G80   Ortíz, María Salvadora. "La parodia a la obra *En busca del tiempo perdido* de Proust y al *Matadero* de Esteban Echeverría en el texto de Alejo Carpentier." *Revista de Filología y Lingüística de la Universidad de Costa Rica* (San José) 14.2 (July-Dec. 1988): 55–61.

G81   Pailler, Claire. Rev. of *Bajo el signo de Orfeo: Lezama Lima y Proust,* by Jaime Valdivieso. *Caravelle* (Toulouse) 40 (1983): 194–96.

G82   Parra, Frédéric. "Tiempo perdido y tiempo recobrado en *Menos Julia.*" *Río de la Plata* (Paris) 19 (1998): 285–92

G83   Patout, Paulette. "Alfonso Reyes, Marcel Proust y la aristocracia francesa." Trans. Adolfo Castañón. *Revista de la Universidad de México* 34.4 (Dec. 1979): 22–28.

G84   Pérez Moreno, José. "Una obra impresionante." *La Prensa* (México) 20 Sept. 1967: 5.

G85   "Proust y don Jaime." *El Universal* (México) 20 Aug. 1967, "Revista de la Semana": 3.

G86   Reyes, Alfonso. "Proust en América." *Libra* (Buenos Aires) 1 (Winter 1929): 87–88. Rpt. in *Monterrey* (Rio de Janeiro) 1 (June 1930): 8.

G87   ———. "Proust en América." *Monterrey* (Rio de Janeiro) 2 (Aug. 1930): 5; 5 (July 1931): 4; 10 (Mar. 1933): 2.

G88   Ribeyro, Julio Ramón. "Marcel Proust y Lezama Lima: Notas sobre *Paradiso.*" *El Heraldo de México,* "El Heraldo Cultural" 174 (9 Mar. 1969): 2–3. Rpt. in *Recopilación de textos sobre Lezama Lima,* 175–81.

G89   Ruiz-Tagle, Carlos. "Proust en Chile." *El Mercurio* (Santiago) 14 Nov. 1982: E4.

G90   Salazar Mallén, Rubén. "Mecanismo de la creación." Rev. of *Tiempo y memoria en la obra de Proust,* by Jaime Torres Bodet. *Mañana* (México) 1252 (26 Aug. 1967): 44–45.

G91   ———. "Proust y la estadística." *El Universal* (México) 29 Aug. 1967. Sec. 1: 3, 19.

G92   Sarduy, Severo. "Un Proust cubain." *La Quinzaine Littéraire* (Paris) 115 (1–15 Apr. 1971): 3–4.

G93   ———. "A Cuban Proust." Trans. Enrico-Mario Santí. *Review* (New York) 12 (Fall 1974): 43–45. Rpt. in *Modern Latin American Fiction,* 131–35.

G94   Scarpa, Roque Esteban. "Marcel Proust y el joven Richard A. Latcham." *La Prensa* (Santiago) 11 July 1971: 2.

G95   Silva Castro, Raúl. "Notas para la bibliografía chilena de Proust." *Monterrey* (Rio de Janeiro) 7 (Dec. 1931): 5.

G96   ———. Rev. of *Las mejores páginas de Marcel Proust,* selection by Alone. *El Mercurio* (Santiago) 10 Dec. 1933: 7.

G97   ———. Rev. of *Un mito proustiano,* by Marta Rivas. *El Mercurio* (Santiago) 30 June 1968: 3.

G98   Solar, Hernán del. Rev. of *Las mejores páginas de Marcel Proust,* selection by Alone. *El Mercurio* (Santiago) 29 Dec. 1968: 5.

G99   Solis, Valencia. Rev. of *Tiempo y memoria en la obra de Proust,* by Jaime Torres Bodet. *El Universal* (México) 30 Aug. 1967: 3, 19.

G100 Souza, Raymond D. Rev. of *Bajo el signo de Orfeo: Lezama Lima y Proust,* by Jaime Valdivieso. *Chasqui* 10.1 (Nov. 1980): 79–80.

G101 Suárez, Eduardo. Rev. of *Las mejores páginas de Marcel Proust,* selection by Alone. *Caras y caretas* (Buenos Aires) 1842 (20 Jan. 1934); 1883 (3 Nov. 1934).

G102   Torriente, Loló de la. "Carta sin sobre a Edmundo Valadés." Rev. of *Por caminos de Proust. El Nacional* 14 Dec. 1975, "Revista Mexicana de Cultura": 2.

G103   Uranga, Emilio. "Proust por Valadés." *La Gaceta* (México) 299 (Nov. 1995): 15–16.

G104   Uslar Pietri, Arturo. "Proust en Turmero." *El Nacional* (Caracas) 30 Apr. 1972, "Séptimo Día": 3. Rpt. in *Cuadernos Americanos* (México) 186.1 (Jan./Feb. 1973): 242–46 and in *Fantasmas de dos mundos,* 67–73.

G105   Valadés, Adriana. "Valadés por los caminos de Proust: ¿dualidad paradójica?" *La Gaceta* (México) 299 (Nov. 1995): 11–13.

G106   Valdivieso, Jaime. "Nuestra herencia de Proust o la Desconfianza de la Mirada." *Revista de la Universidad de México* 32.11 (July 1978): 20–24. Expanded version in *Bajo el signo de Orfeo: Lezama Lima y Proust,* 111–26.

G107   ———. "Proust, un costumbrista universal." *Universidad de México* 492–93 (Jan./Feb. 1992): 74–75.

G108   Vallbona, Rima de. "Yolanda Oreamuno: El estigma del escritor." *Cuadernos Hispanoamericanos* (Madrid) 260 (Dec. 1972): 474–99.

G109   ———. "*La ruta de su evasión* de Yolanda Oreamuno: escritura proustiana suplementada." *Revista Iberoamericana* 138–39 (Jan.–June 1987): 193–217.

G110   Vallejo, Alejandro. "Una hora con Alfonso Reyes." *El Tiempo* (Bogotá), "Lecturas Dominicales" 203 (19 June 1927): 33–35.

G111   Varderi, Alejandro. "El camino de Reynaldo Hahn en el tiempo de Proust (A propósito de *Reynaldo* de Ugo Ulive)." *El Universal* (Caracas) 23 June 1985, "Culturales": 9. Rpt. in *Anotaciones sobre el amor y el deseo,* 113–22.

G112   Vega, Daniel de la. "Lecturas." *Las Ultimas Noticias* (Santiago) 2 Sept. 1948: 3.

G113   Vela, David. "*La ruta de su evasión:* Revelación de Yolanda Oreamuno II." *El Imparcial* (Guatemala) 14 June 1950: 3.

G114   Vicuña Luco, Osvaldo. "Cartas acerca de Marcel Proust." *Atenea* (Concepción) 5.3 (31 May 1928): 224–31. Rpt. in *Correspondencia,* 132–42.

G115   "Vitrina Literaria." Rev. of *Las mejores páginas de Marcel Proust,* selection by Alone. *Zig-Zag* 1498 (8 Dec. 1933): 34.

G116   Volkening, Ernesto. "Reconquista y pérdida de la América arcáica en *Los pasos perdidos* de Alejo Carpentier." *Eco* (Bogotá) 14.4 (Feb. 1967): 367–402.

G117   Yañez, María Flora. "Cómo conocí a un personaje de Proust." *Ars* (San Salvador) 5 (Jan.–Apr. 1954): 58–59.

G118   ———. "Presencia de un personaje de Proust." *La Honda* (Santiago) 3 (Jul./Aug./Sep. 1967): 5–8.

IV. POEMS, PLAYS, PASTICHES, AND PARODIES ABOUT PROUST PUBLISHED IN BOOKS OR PERIODICALS OF SPANISH AMERICA

H1   Azar, Vicente (José Alvarado Sánchez). "El Tiempo (elegía a Marcel Proust)." In *Arte de olvidar,* 21–27. Lima: Palabra, 1942.

H2   Cardona Peña, Alfredo. "Lectura de Proust." In *Cosecha mayor,* 478–80. San José: Editorial Costa Rica, 1964.

H3   Figueroa Navarro, Alfredo. "Loanza de Marcel Proust (1871–1971)." *Revista Lotería* (Panamá) 189 (Aug. 1971): 93.

H4   Fraire, Isabel. "El tiempo vuelto a perder." *La Gaceta* (México) 61 (Jan. 1976): 11.

H5   Melián Lafinur, Alvaro. "Elegía a Marcel Proust." *La Nación* (Buenos Aires) 24 July 1927, "Letras-Artes": 5. Rpt. in *El País* (Montevideo) 13 Oct. 1927: 12.

H6   Merrill, James. "Para Proust." Trans. Manuel Ulacia. *Vuelta* (México) 71 (Oct. 1982): 12–13.

H7   Monesterolo, Oscar. "Combray, 1978." *La Nación* (Buenos Aires) 16 Mar. 1986, sec. 4: 2.

H8   Mora, José A. "Los diez mandamientos para leer a Marcel Proust." *La Cruz del Sur* (Montevideo) 33–34 (Dec. 1931): 12.

H9   Morand, Paul. "Oda a Marcel Proust." Trans. Héctor Castillo. *Martín Fierro* (Buenos Aires), 2d ser., 4 (15 May 1924). Rpt. in *La revolución martinfierrista* by Cayetano Córdoba Iturburu, 69–70. Buenos Aires: Ediciones Culturales Argentinas, 1962.

H10   ———. "Oda a Marcel Proust." Trans. Angel J. Battistessa. *Verbum* (Buenos Aires) 80 (1931): 13–14.

H11   Mutis, Alvaro. "Poema de lástimas a la muerte de Marcel Proust." *¡Siempre!*, "La Cultura en México" 163 (31 Mar. 1965): xiii. Rpt. in *Summa de Maqroll El Gaviero. Poesía 1947–1970*, 90–91. Bogotá: Editorial La Oveja Negra, Ltd., 1982 and in *Antología de poesía hispanoamericana actual*, Ed. Julio Ortega, 185–86. México: Siglo XX Editores, 1989.

H12   Peña, Enrique. "A Marcel Proust." *Letras del Ecuador* 61 (Sept./Oct. 1950): 17.

H13   Ojeda, Jorge Arturo. "La mujer por el camino de Swann." *Revista de Bellas Artes* (México) 18 (Nov./Dec. 1967): 45. Rpt. in *Caminos: Ensayos literarios*, 55. México: Instituto Nacional de la Juventud Mexicana, 1972.

H14   Prieto, Jenaro. "Una víctima de Proust." *El Diario Ilustrado* (Santiago) 18 July 1929. Rpt. in *Con sordina*, 93–101. Santiago: Nascimento, 1931 and in *Antología Humorística*, 74–79. Santiago: Editorial Nacional Gabriela Mistral, 1973.

H15   Recourat, Edith. "Para el centenario de su nacimiento: A la manera de Marcel Proust." *El Imparcial* (Guatemala) 14 July 1971: 3, 9.

H16   Sábato, Ernesto. "Tatarescu es invitado a comer en casa de Marcel (A la manera de Proust)". In *Genio y figura de Ernesto Sábato* by María Angélica Correa, 261–62. Buenos Aires: Editorial Universitaria de Buenos Aires, Rpt. in *La robotización del hombre y otras páginas*, 84. Buenos Aires: Centro Editor de América Latina, 1981.

H17   Sánchez, Osvaldo. "Sabor de té en los labios de Marcelo Proust." *Casa de las Américas* (La Habana) 142 (Jan./ Feb. 1984): 173–74. Rpt. in *Nueva poesía cubana (Antología 1966–1986)*. Ed. Antonio Merino, 255–57. Madrid: Orígenes, 1987.

H18   Ulive, Ugo. *Reynaldo.* In *Teatro*, 43–102. Caracas: Fundarte, 1985.

H19   Vargas Vila, J. M. "Marcel Proust." In *En el Pórtico de Oro de la Gloria*, 89–95. La Habana: Librería "Cervantes," 1927.

V. TESTIMONIALES AND OTHER TEXTS WHICH DEMONSTRATE
A PERSONAL INTEREST IN PROUST (NOT LISTED ABOVE)

I1 Arenas, Reynaldo. Interview with Perla Rozencvaig. "Qué mundo tuvo que vivir." *Vuelta* 181 (1991): 61–64.

I2 ———. "Last Interview." With Perla Rozencvaig. Trans. Alfred Mac Adam. *Review: Latin American Literature and Arts* 44 (Jan.–June 1991): 78–83.

I3 Bryce Echenique, Adolfo. "Confesiones sobre el arte de vivir y escribir novelas." *Cuadernos Hispanoamericanos* 417 (Mar. 1985): 65–76.

I4 ———. *Permiso para vivir (antimemorias)*, 316, 362. Barcelona: Editorial Anagrama, 1993.

I5 ———. "El camino de Proust". In *El hilo del habla: La narrativa de Alfredo Bryce Echenique*, by Julio Ortega, 109–14. Guadalajara: Universidad de Guadalajara, 1994.

I6 Caballero Calderón, Eduardo. "Preludio" to *Caminos subterráneos: Ensayo de interpretación del paisaje*, 9–12. Bogotá: Editorial Santafé, 1936.

I7 ———. *Memorias infantiles*, 164–65. Medellín: Editorial Bedout, 1964.

I8 ———. *Hablamientos y pensadurías*. Bogotá: Tallers Gráficos de Prograff Impresores, 1979.

I9 Carpentier, Alejo. "Autobiografía." *Bohemia* (La Habana) 57. 28 (9 July 1965): 24–27.

I10 ———. *Ensayos*, 116, 171. La Habana: Editorial Letras Cubanas, 1984.

I11 Coll, Pedro-Emilio. "Una carta." *Revista Nacional de Cultura* (Caracas) 61 (Mar./Apr. 1947): 14–21.

I12 Donoso, José. *Historia personal del "Boom"*, 43. Buenos Aires: Sudamericana, 1984.

I13 ———. *Conjeturas sobre la memoria de mi tribu*, 21–22, 100, 136–38. Madrid: Alfaguara, 1996.

I14 ———. *Artículos de incierta necesidad*, 90–91. Santiago: Aguilar Chilena de Ediciones, Ltda., 1998.

I15 Fuentes, Carlos. *Casa con dos puertas*, 58–59. México: Joaquín Mortiz, 1970.

I16 ———. "No More Interviews: A Conversation with Carlos Fuentes," by Regina James. *Salmagundi* 43 (Winter 1979): 87–95.

I17 Gálvez, Manuel. *Recuerdos de la vida literaria*. Vol. 2: *En el mundo de los seres ficticios*, 171, 264–65, 361. Buenos Aires: Librería Hachette, S. A., 1961.

I18 García Márquez, Gabriel. "El fantasma del Premio Nobel [2]." In *Notas de prensa: 1980–1984*, 21–22. Santa Fé de Bogotá: Editorial Norma, S. A., 1995.

I19 Gónzalez Vera, José Santos. "Tres libros (*Alsino, Zurzulita, Por el camino de Swan*)." In *Cuando era muchacho*, 297–98. Santiago: Nascimento, 1951.

I20 Hahn, Reynaldo. "Promenade." In "Hommage à Marcel Proust." *La Nouvelle Revue Française* 112 (1 Jan. 1923): 39–40. Rpt. in *Hommage à Marcel Proust*, 33–34. Paris: Gallimard, 1927.

I21 Larreta, Enrique. *Tiempo iluminados*. In *Obras completas*, 559. Madrid: Editorial Plenitud, 1958.

I22 Lezama Lima, José. *Cartas (1939–1976)*. Ed. Eloísa Lezama Lima, 123, 263. Madrid: Editorial Orígenes, 1979.

123   ———. *Diarios.* Ed. Ciro Bianchi Ross, 49–50, 86–87. México: Ediciones Era, S. A., 1994.

124   Mallea, Eduardo. "Tentativa de novela moderna." *La Nación* (Buenos Aires), "Letras-Artes" 139 (26 Feb. 1928): 12.

124   Neruda, Pablo (Neftalí Ricardo Reyes Basoalto). *Confieso que he vivido,* 137–39. Barcelona: Editorial Seix Barral, S. A., 1979.

125   Novo, Salvador. "Diario de Salvador Novo: Domingo 30 de diciembre de 1945." *Mañana* (México) 124 (12 Jan. 1946): 38.

126   ———. *La vida en México en el período presidencial de Manuel Avila Camacho,* 562–65. Ed. José Emilio Pacheco. México: Empresas editoriales, 1965.

127   ———. *La vida en México en el período presidencial de Miguel Alemán.* Ed. José Emilio Pacheco. México: Empresas editoriales, 1967.

128   Ocampo, Victoria. "Acusador y acusados: Massis y el Oriente." *La Nación* (Buenos Aires) 2 Oct. 1927, "Suplemento Literario": 4.

129   ———. "Lecturas de infancia." *Sur* (Jan. 1945): 7–29.

130   ———. *Autobiografía.* Vol. 3. Buenos Aires: Ediciones Revista Sur, 1981.

131   Oliver, María Rosa. *La vida cotidiana,* 198–99. Buenos Aires: Editorial Sudamericana, 1969.

132   Oreamuno, Yolanda. *A lo largo del corto camino,* 335. San José: Editorial Costa Rica, 1961.

133   Paz, Octavio. *El arco y la lira.* México: Fondo de Cultura Económica, 1956.

134   Ramírez, Sergio. "Más de diez libros de cabecera." *La Prensa Literaria* (Managua) 27 Aug. 1977: 7.

135   Reyes, Alfonso. *Diario 1911–1930,* 85–86. Guanajuato: Universidad de Guanajuato, 1969.

136   ———. *Obras completas.* Vol. 3. México: Fondo de Cultura Económica, 1960.

137   Sábato, Ernesto. *El escritor y sus fantasmas,* 49–55, 168. Barcelona: Editorial Seix Barral, S. A., 1979.

138   Teitelboim, Volodia. *Neruda,* 55, 300. Madrid: Ediciones Michaay, S. A., 1984.

139   Torres Bodet, Jaime. "Refexiones sobre la novela." In *Contemporáneos: Notas de crítica.* México: Herrero, 1928. Rpt. in *Contemporáneos,* 15–24. México: Universidad Nacional Autónoma de Mexico: 1987.

140   ———. "El problema de la novela contemporánea." *La Prensa* (Buenos Aires) 18 Mar. 1928. Rpt. in *Social* (La Habana): 11, 86–87.

141   ———. "Encuentro con Marcel Proust." *Mañana* 520 (15 Aug. 1953): 20–21. Rpt. in *Tiempo de arena.* México: Fondo de Cultura Económica, 1955 and in *Obras escogidas,* 301–04. México: Fondo de Cultura Económica, 1961.

142   Villaurrutia, Xavier. "Paul Morand." *El País* (Montevideo) 17 Dec. 1927.

143   ———. *Obras,* 695–696, 709, 953. México: Fondo de Cultura Económica, 1953.

Works Cited

LITERARY WORKS AND MEMOIRS

Adán, Martín (Rafael de la Fuente Benavides). 1984. *Casa de cartón*. Lima: Promoción Editorial Inca, S. A.

Adoum, Jorge Enrique. 1983. *Entre Marx y una mujer desnuda*. Quito: Editorial El Conejo.

Aguilera Garramuño, Marco Tulio. 1994. *El libro de la vida: Buenabestia*. Santafé de Bogotá: Plaza & Janés Editores (Colombia).

Alemán, Mateo. 1967. *Guzmán de Alfarache*. *La novela picaresca española*. Vol. 1. Barcelona: Editorial Planeta.

Allende, Isabel. 1988. *Eva Luna*. Barcelona: Plaza & Janés Editores, S. A.

Anderson Imbert, Enrique. 1934. *Vigilia*. Buenos Aires: La Vanguardia.

Arenas, Reinaldo. 1991. *El asalto*. Miami: Ediciones Universales.

———. 1967. *Celestino antes del alba*. La Habana: Ediciones Unión.

———. 1990. *El color del verano o nuevo jardín de las delicias*. Miami: Ediciones Universal.

———. 1965. "La punta del arco iris," "Soledad" and "La puesta del sol." *Unión* (La Habana) 4.1: 113–19.

Arlt, Roberto. 1978. *Los siete locos. Los lanzallamas*. Caracas: Biblioteca Ayacucho.

Azuela, Marino. 1941. *La malhora. El desquite*. México, Ediciones Botas.

Balzac, Honoré de. 1966. *La comédie humaine*. Vol. 4. Paris: Editions du Seuil.

Baudelaire, Charles. 1968. *Oeuvres complètes*. Paris: Editions du Seuil.

Benedetti, Mario. 1976. *Gracias por el fuego*. Buenos Aires: Editorial Alfa Argentina.

———. 1974. *Quien de nosotros*. Buenos Aires: Editorial Alfa Argentina.

———. 1974. *La tregua*. Buenos Aires: Editorial Alfa Argentina, S. A.

Bianco, José. 1932. *La pequeña Gyaros*. Buenos Aires: Viau y Zona.

———. 1972. *La pérdida del reino*. Buenos Aires: Siglo XXI Argentina Editores, S. A.

———. 1973. *Las ratas. Sombras suele vestir*. Siglo XXI Argentina Editores, S. A.

Bombal, María Luisa. 1988. *La última niebla. La amortajada*. Barcelona: Editorial Seix Barral.

Borges, Jorge Luis. 1957. *El Aleph*. Buenos Aires: Emecé Editores.

———. 1956. *Ficciones*. Buenos Aires: Emecé.

————. 1953. *Historia de la eternidad*. Buenos Aires: Emecé.

————. 1928. *El idioma de los argentinos*. Buenos Aires: M. Gleizer.

————. 1993. *Inquisiciones*. Barcelona: Editorial Seix Barral, S. A.

————. 1972. *Obra poética*. Madrid: Alianza Editorial.

Bourget, Paul. 1891. *Physiologie de l'amour moderne*. Paris: A. Lemerre.

Bryce Echenique, Adolfo. 1988. *El hombre que hablaba de Octavia de Cádiz*. Bogotá: Editorial La Oveja Negra.

————. 1989. *Magdalena peruana y otros cuentos*. Barcelona: Plaza & Janés Editores, S. A.

————. 1992. *Un mundo para Julius*. Barcelona: Plaza & Janés Editores, S. A.

————. 1985. *La vida exagerada de Martín Romaña*. Bogotá: Editorial La Oveja Negra.

Butor, Michel. 1957. *L'emploi du temps*. Paris: Les Editions de Minuit.

————. 1957. *La modification*. Paris: Les Editions de Minuit.

Caballero Calderón, Eduardo. 1979. *El buen salvaje*. Bogotá: Plaza y Janés Editores Colombia Ltda.

————. 1936. *Caminos subterráneos: ensayo de interpretación del paisaje*. Bogotá: Editorial Santa Fe.

————. 1964. *Memorias infantiles: 1916–1924*. Medellín: Editorial Bedout.

Cabrera Infante, Guillermo. 1983. *Tres tristes tigres*. Barcelona: Editorial Seix Barral, S. A.

Carpentier, Alejo. 1993. *La consagración de la primavera*. Barcelona: Plaza & Janés Editores, S. A.

————. 1969. *Guerra del tiempo*. México: Compañía General de Ediciones, S. A.

————. 1969. *Los pasos perdidos*. México: Compañía General de Ediciones, S. A.

————. 1974. *El recurso del método*. Madrid: Siglo XXI Editores, S. A.

————. 1983. *El siglo de las luces*. Barcelona: Editorial Seix Barral, S. A.

Carrrera, Marco Antonio. 1988. *Diario de un tiempo escindido*. Bogotá: Editorial Oveja Negra Ltda.

Chateaubriand, François-René. 1964. *Atala. René*. Paris: Garnier-Flammarion.

————. 1951. *Mémoires d'outre tombe*. Vol. 1. Paris: Gallimard.

Coll, Pedro-Emilio. 1916. *El castillo de Elsinor*. Madrid: Editorial América.

Cortázar, Julio. 1973. *El libro de Manuel*. Buenos Aires: Editorial Sudamericana.

————. 1960. *Los premios*. Buenos Aires: Editorial Sudamericana.

————. 1986. *Rayuela*. Madrid: Ediciones Cátedra, S. A.

————. 1968. *62: Modelo para armar*. Buenos Aires: Editorial Sudamericana.

Díaz Rodríguez, Manuel. 1982. *Narrativa y ensayo*. Caracas: Biblioteca Ayacucho.

Dickmann, Max. 1930. *Europa*. Buenos Aires: Palacio del libro.

Donoso, José. 1983. *Casa de campo*. Barcelona: Editorial Seix Barral, S. A.

————. 1996. *Conjeturas sobre la memoria de mi tribu*. Madrid: Alfaguara.

————. 1968. *Coronación*. Barcelona: Seix Barral, S. A.

————. 1982. *Cuatro para Delfina*. Barcelona: Seix Barral, S. A.

————. 1968. *Este domingo*. México: Editorial Joaquín Mortíz, S. A.

————. 1982. *El jardín de al lado*. Barcelona: Editorial Seix Barral, S. A.

————. 1975. *El lugar sin límites*. Barcelona: Editorial Euros, S. A.

————. 1972. *El obsceno pájaro de la noche*. Barcelona: Editorial Seix Barral, S. A.

Droguett, Carlos. 1967. *El compadre*. México: Editorial Joaquín Mortiz, S. A.

Edwards, Jorge. 1967. *El peso de la noche*. Santiago: Zig-Zag.

Edwards Bello, Joaquín. 1928. *El chileno en Madrid*. Santiago: Editorial Nascimento.

Esquivel, Laura. 1990. *Como agua para chocolate: Novela de entregas mensuales, con recetas, amores y remedios caseros*. México: Editorial Planeta Mexicana, S. A.

————. 1995. *La ley del amor*. Barcelona: Plaza & Janés Editores, S. A.

Felipe, Carlos. 1979. *Teatro*. La Habana: Editorial Letras Cubanas.

Foguet, Hugo. 1983. *Pretérito perfecto*. Madrid: Editorial Lagasa S. R. L.

France, Anatole (Anatole Thibault). 1954. *Le livre de mon ami*. Paris: Calmann-Levy.

Fuentes, Carlos. 1980. *Una familia lejana*. Barcelona: Editorial Bruguera, S. A.

————. 1958. *La región más transparente*. México: Fondo de Cultura Económica.

Gálvez, Manuel. 1950. *El cántico espiritual*. Buenos Aires: Editorial Tor.

————. 1961. *Recuerdos de la vida literaria*. Vol. 2: *En el mundo de los seres ficticios*. Buenos Aires: Librería Hachette, S. A.

————. 1922. *La tragedia de un hombre fuerte*. Buenos Aires: Biblioteca de novelistas americanos.

García Márquez, Gabriel. 1986. *El amor en los tiempos del cólera*. Buenos Aires: Editorial Médica Panamericana.

————. 1996. *Cien años de soledad*. Madrid: Ediciones Cátedra.

————. 1972. *La increíble y triste historia de la cándida Eréndira y de su abuela desalmada: Siete cuentos*. Barcelona: Barral Editores.

García Ponce, Juan. 1970. *El libro*. México: Siglo XXI Editores, S. A.

Garro, Elena. 1963. *Los recuerdos del porvenir*. México: Editorial Joaquín Mortiz, S. A.

Gide, André. 1968. *Corydon*. Paris: Gallimard.

————. 1925. *Les faux-monnayeurs*. Paris: Gallimard.

————. 1939. *Journal 1889–1939*. Paris: Nouvelle Revue Française.

González, José Luis. 1988. *La luna no era de queso: Memorias de infancia*. Río Piedras?: Editorial Cultural.

González Vera, José Santos. 1961. *Alhué*. Santiago: Nascimento.

————. 1951. *Cuando era muchacho*. Santiago: Nascimento.

Gregh, Fernand. 1896. "Mystères." *La Revue Blanche* 15 Sept.: 259–63.

Güiraldes, Ricardo. 1962. *Obras completas*. Buenos Aires: Emecé.

Gutiérrez Nájera, Manuel. 1946. *Poesías completas*. Vol. 2. Buenos Aires Editorial Sopena Argentina, S. R. L.

Hernández, Felisberto. 1983. *Obras completas*. 3 vols. Montevideo: Arca-Calicanto.

Huxley, Aldous. 1956. *Point counter Point*. New York: Harper & Row.

Huysmans, J.-K. 1968. *A rebours*. Paris: Editions Fasquelle.

Joyce, James. 1972. *A Portrait of the Artist as a Young Man*. New York: The Viking Press.

————. 1961. *Ulysses*. New York: Vintage Books.

Lafayette, Madame de. 1966. *La princesse de Clèves*. Paris: Garnier-Flammarion.

Lange, Norah. 1973. *Cuadernos de infancia*. Buenos Aires: Losada.

Larbaud, Valéry. 1954. *Journal inédit. Oeuvres complètes*. Vol. 9. Paris?: Gallimard.

Larreta, Enrique. 1958. *Obras completas*. Madrid: Editorial Plenitud.

Lezama Lima, José. 1973. *Paradiso*. México: Biblioteca Era.

López de Mesa, Luis. 1977. *La tragedia de Nilse. La biografía de Gloria Etzel*. Medellín: Universidad de Antioquia.

Loti, Pierre (Julien Viaud). 1895. *Le roman d'un enfant*. Paris: Calmann Levy.

Mallea, Eduardo. 1965. *Obras completas*. 2 vols. Buenos Aires: Emecé.

Manrique, Jorge. 1979. *Obra completa*. Madrid: Espasa-Calpe, S. A.

Mariani, Roberto. 1968. *El amor agresivo*. Buenos Aires: Editorial Paidós S. A. I. C. F.

———. 1943. *Regreso a Dios*. Buenos Aires: Sociedad Impresora Americana.

Marqués, René. 1983. *En una ciudad llamada San Juan*. Río Piedras: Editorial Cultural.

Martínez Moreno, Carlos. 1966. *La otra mitad*. México: Editorial Joaquín Mortíz, S. A.

Monteforte Toledo, Mario. 1986. *Una manera de morir*. Barcelona: Plaza & Janés, Editores, S. A.

Monterroso, Augusto. 1993. *Los buscadores de oro*. México: Alfaguara, S. A. de C. V.

———. 1994. *Cuentos*. Madrid: Alianza Editorial, S. A.

Morand, Paul. 1924. "Oda a Marcel Proust." Trans. Héctor Castillo. *Martín Fierro* (Buenos Aires), 2d ser., 4.

Mujica Láinez, Manuel. 1967. *Bomarzo*. Buenos Aires: Editorial Sudamericana.

———. 1954. *La casa*. Buenos Aires: Editorial Sudamericana.

———. 1972. *Cecil*. Buenos Aires: Editorial Sudamericana.

———. 1982. *El escarabajo*. Barcelona: Plaza & Janés.

———. 1979. *El gran teatro*. Buenos Aires: Editorial Sudamericana.

———. 1976. *Los ídolos*. Buenos Aires: Editorial Sudamericana.

———. 1969. *Invitados en "El Paraíso."* Buenos Aires: Editorial Sudamericana.

———. 1975. *Misteriosa Buenos Aires*. Buenos Aires: Editorial Sudamericana.

———. 1955. *Los viajeros*. Buenos Aires: Editorial Sudamericana.

Neruda, Pablo (Neftalí Ricardo Reyes Basoalto). 1979. *Confieso que he vivido*. Barcelona: Editorial Seix Barral, S. A.

Novo, Salvador. 1998. *La estatua de sal*. México: Dirección General de Publicaciones.

———. 1964. *Toda la prosa*. México: Empresas Editoriales, S. A.

Ocampo, Victoria. 1982. *Autobiografía*. Vol. 4. Buenos Aires: Sur.

Oreamuno, Yolanda. 1961. *A lo largo del corto camino*. San José: Editorial Costa Rica.

———. 1984. *La ruta de su evasión*. San José: Editorial Universitaria Centroamericana.

Palacio Valdés, Armando. 1973. *La novela de un novelista*. Buenos Aires: Editorial Losada, S. A.

Parra, Teresa de la. 1991. *Obras (Narrativa-Ensayos-Cartas)*. Caracas: Biblioteca Ayacucho.

Petit, Magdalena. 1948. *Don Diego Portales: El Hombre sin concupiscencia*. Santiago: Zig-Zag.

Pinto, Julieta. 1969. *La estación que sigue al verano*. San José: Antonio Lehmann Librería.

Pliny the Elder. 1991. *Natural History: A Selection*. Trans. John F. Healy. London: Penguin Books.

Proust, Marcel. 1954. *A la recherche du temps perdu*. 3 vols. Bibliothèque de la Pléiade. Paris: Gallimard.

————. 1987. *Albertine disparue*. Ed. Nathalie Mauriac and Etienne Wolff. Paris: Bernard Grasset.

————. 1971. *Jean Santeuil*. Paris: Gallimard.

————. 1924. *Les plaisirs et les jours*. Paris: Gallimard.

————. 1920. "El Premio Goncourt: Las jóvenes, Las flores, Las sirenas." *América Latina* (London-Paris) Feb.: 15.

Ramos, Juan P. 1946. *La novela de una vocación*. Buenos Aires: Editorial Guillermo Kraft, Ltda.

————. 1933. *La vuelta de las horas*. Buenos Aires: Viau y Zona.

Reyles, Carlos. 1939. *A batallas de amor . . . campo de pluma*. Buenos Aires: Editorial Sopena.

Rojas, Manuel. 1982. *Mejor que el vino*. Santiago: Zig-Zag.

Sábato, Ernesto. 1977. *Abaddón el exterminador*. Buenos Aires: Editorial Sudamericana.

————. 1991. *Abaddón el exterminador*. Barcelona: Editora Seix Barral, S. A.

————. 1966. *Obras de ficción*. Buenos Aires: Editorial Losada.

————. 1971. "Tatarescu es invitado a comer en casa de Marcel (A la manera de Proust)." In *Genio y figura de Ernesto Sábato,* by María Angélica Correa. 261–62. Buenos Aires: Editorial Universitaria de Buenos Aires.

Saer, Juan José. 1976. *La mayor*. Barcelona: Editorial Planeta.

Sand, George (Aurore Dupin). 1968. *Les maîtres sonneurs*. Paris: Garnier.

Sarraute, Nathalie. 1968. *Entre la vie et la mort*. Paris: Gallimard.

Sartre, Jean-Paul. 1938. *La nausée*. Paris: Editions Gallimard.

Silva, José Asunción. 1963. *Poesías completas*. Madrid: Aguilar.

Stendhal (Henri Beyle). 1964. *Le rouge et le noir*. Paris: Garnier-Flammarion.

Torres Bodet, Jaime. 1985. *Narrativa completa*. 2 vols. México: Editorial Offset, S. A.

————. 1961. *Obras escogidas*. México: Fondo de Cultura Económica.

Ulive, Ugo. 1985. *Teatro*. Caracas: Fundarte.

Valdés, Zoé. 1997. *Café Nostalgia*. Barcelona: Editorial Planeta, S. A.

Vargas Llosa, Mario. 1984. *La tía Julia y el escribidor*. Barcelona: Editorial Seix Barral.

Villaurrutia, Xavier. 1953. *Obras*. México: Fondo de Cultura Económica.

Villon, François. 1972. *Poésies*. Paris: Le Livre de Poche.

Woolf, Virginia. 1925. *Mrs. Dalloway*. San Diego: Harcourt, Brace, Jovanovich Publishers.

————. 1920. *The Voyage Out*. San Diego: Harcourt, Brace Jovanovich, Publishers.

Yáñez, María Flora. 1949. *Las cenizas*. Santiago: Editorial Tegualda.

Zalamea Borda, Eduardo. 1985. *4 años a bordo de mí mismo*. Bogotá: Editorial La Oveja Negra.

Zapata, Luis. 1994. *En jirones*. México: Consejo Nacional para la Cultura y las Artes.

CRITICAL STUDIES

Afinidades: Francia y América del Sur. 1946. Montevideo: Servicio francés de información.

Ahlstedt, Eva. 1985. *La pudeur en crise: Un aspect de l'accueil d'A la recherche du temps perdu de Marcel Proust: 1913–1930*. Paris: Jean Touzot, Libraire Editeur.

Albaret, Céleste and Georges Belmont. 1977. *Monsieur Proust*. Trans. Barbara Bray. New York: McGraw Hill Book Company.

Albérès, R. M. (René Marill). 1966. *Métamorphoses du roman*. Paris: Editions Albin Michel.

Alboukrek, Aaron and Esther Herrera. 1991. *Diccionario de escritores hispanoamericanos: Del siglo XVI al XX*. México: Ediciones Larousse, S. A.

Alden, Douglas W. 1940. *Marcel Proust and His French Critics*. Los Angeles: Lymanhouse.

Alley, John Newton. 1959. "English and American Criticism of Marcel Proust." Ph. D. diss., University of North Carolina.

Alone (Hernán Díaz Arrieta). 1968. "Ensayo sobre Marcel Proust" and "Bibliografía crítica." In *Las mejores páginas de Marcel Proust*. 9–47. Santiago: Zig-Zag.

Anderson Imbert, Enrique. 1972. *Los domingos del profesor*. Buenos Aires: Gure.

———. 1974. *Historia de la literatura hispanoamericana*. Vol. 2. México: Fondo de Cultura Económica.

Andrade, Ione de. 1975. "Note sur les critiques brésiliens de Marcel Proust." *Bulletin de la Société des amis de Marcel Proust et des amis de Combray* 25: 127–33.

———. 1972. "Proust et le Brésil." *Les Langues Modernes* 66.2: 193–99.

Arenas, Reinaldo. 1991. Interview with Perla Rozencvaig. "Qué mundo tuvo que vivir." *Vuelta* 181: 61–64.

Arrigucci, Davi Jr. 1973. *O escorpião encalacrado (A poética da destruição em Julio Cortazar)*. São Paulo: Editorial Perspectiva, S. A.

Athayde, Tristão de (Alceu Amoroso Lima). 1931. "Marcel Proust." *Revue de l'Amérique latine* 21: 161–71, 257–70.

Ayala, Francisco. 1944. *Histrionismo y representación*. Buenos Aires: Sudamericana.

Bakhtin, M. M. 1981. *The Dialogic Imagination: Four Essays*. Ed. Michael Holquist. Trans. Caryl Emerson and Michael Holquist. Austin: University of Texas Press.

Balderstron, Daniel. 1995. "The 'Fecal Dialectic': Homosexual Panic and the Origin of Writing in Borges." In *¿Entiendes?*. Ed. Emilie L. Bermann and Paul Julian Smith. 29–45. Durham. NC: Duke University Press.

Balza, José. 1969. *Proust*. Caracas: Universidad Central de Venezuela.

Barga, Corpus. 1920. "Libros y estampas: Un letrado chino: Marcel Proust y sus novelas." *El Sol* (Madrid) 27 Mar.: 6.

Beckett, Samuel. 1957. *Proust*. New York: Grove Press, Inc.

Bedriomo, Emile. 1984. *Proust, Wagner et les coïncidences des arts*. Tübingen: Gunter Narr Verlag.

Bell-Villada, Gene H. 1981. *Borges and His Fiction: A Guide to His Mind and Art*. Chapel Hill: University of North Carolina Press.

———. 1990. *García Márquez: The Man and His Work*. Chapel Hill: University of North Carolina Press.

Bendahan, Daniel. 1990. *Reynaldo Hahn*. Caracas: Monte Avila Latinoamericana, C. A.

Benedetti, Mario. 1951. *Marcel Proust y otros ensayos*. Montevideo: Número.

———. 1956. "La saga argentina de Mujica Láinez." *Marcha* 814: 23.

Bersani, Jacques, ed. 1971. *Les critiques de notre temps et Proust*. Paris: Garnier Frères.

Berveiller, Michel. 1973. *Le cosmopolitisme de Jorge Luis Borges*. Paris?: Didier.

Bianco, José. 1977. *Ficción y realidad*. Caracas. Monte Avila, Editores, C. A.

Bloom, Harold. 1997. *The Anxiety of Influence: A Theory of Poetry*. New York: Oxford University Press.

Boldy, Steven. 1980. *The Novels of Julio Cortázar*. Cambridge: Cambridge University Press.

Borges, Jorge Luis. 1964. *Discusión*. Buenos Aires: Emecé Editores.

———. 1953. "Prólogo" to *La invención de Morel*, by Adolfo Bioy Casares. 11–15. Buenos Aires: Emecé Editores.

Bosch, Velia. 1979. *Lengua viva de Teresa de la Parra*. Caracas: Ediciones de la Presidencia de la República.

Bosveuil, Simone. 1978. "Proust y la novela española de los años 30: Ensayo de interpretación." *Studi Ispanici* 87–102.

Bradbury, Malcolm. 1990. *The Modern World: Ten Great Writers*. New York: Penguin Books.

Brée, Germaine. 1966. *The World of Marcel Proust*. Boston: Houghton Mifflin Company.

Bueno, Manuel. 1929. "El amor y el dolor en Marcel Proust." *ABC* (Madrid) 4 June: 7.

Bucknall, Barbara J. 1969. *The Religion of Art in Proust*. Urbana: University of Illinois Press.

Caballero Calderón, Eduardo. 1971. "En torno y en el contorno de Marcel Proust." *El Tiempo* (Bogotá) 4 July: 1, 6.

Carpentier, Alejo. 1976. *Crónicas*. Vol. 2. La Habana: Editorial Arte y Literatura.

———. 1984. *Ensayos*. La Habana: Editorial Letras Cubanas.

———. 1972. "Marcel Proust et l'Amérique latine." *Bulletin de la Société des amis de Marcel Proust et des amis de Combray* 22: 1321–26.

Carter, William C. 2000. *Marcel Proust: A Life*. New Haven: Yale University Press.

Castillo Vega, Marcia and Rosa González Alfonso. 1984. *Indice analítico del Suplemento literario del Diario de la Marina (1927–1930)*. La Habana: Editorial Academia.

Chumacero, Alí. 1953. "Prólogo" to *Obras*, by Xavier Villaurrutia. México: Fondo de Cultura Económica.

Coll, Pedro-Emilio. 1947. "Una carta." *Revista Nacional de Cultura* (Caracas) 61: 14–21.

Compagnon, Antoine. 1997. "Proust recuperado por las vanguardias." *Cuadernos Hispanoamericanos* 562: 13–26.

"Consultorio literario y artístico." 1928. *La Nación*. (Buenos Aires) 5 Aug.: 15.

Coronado, Juan. 1988. "Prólogo" to *La novela lírica de los contemporáneos*. 9–37. México: Universidad Nacional Autónoma de México.

Cortázar, Julio. 1950. "Situación de la novela." *Cuadernos Americanos* 9.4: 223–43.

Craig, Herbert E. 1983. "The Presence of Proust in Argentine Narrative." Ph. D. diss., University of Wisconsin–Madison.

Crémieux, Benjamin. 1924. *XXe siècle*. Paris: Gallimard.

Curcio Altamar, Antonio. 1975. *Evolución de la novela en Colombia*. Bogotá: Instituto Colombiano de Cultura.

428   MARCEL PROUST AND SPANISH AMERICA

Daireaux, Max. 1926. "Un balance de la literatura américo-latina." *El Espectador* (Bogotá), "Suplemento Literario Ilustrado" 81 (15 July): 10.

Dandieu, Arnaud. 1930. *Marcel Proust: Sa révélation psychologique.* Paris: Firmin-Didot, et Cie.

Darré, María Celia. 1991. "Proust a través de un cuento de Juan José Saer." *Revista de Literaturas Modernas* (Mendoza) 24: 73–83.

De Aguilar, Helene I. F. 1985. "Secret Sharers: Memory in Proust and Fuentes." *Southwest Review* 70.4: 500–12.

Deleuze, Gilles. 1970. *Proust et les signes.* Paris: Presses Universitaires de France.

Delgado, Horacio. 1948. "Marcel Proust y la penumbra anímica." *Las Moradas* (Lima) 2.4: 1–7.

Dezon-Jones, Elyane. 1982. *Proust et l'Amérique: La fiction américaine a la recherche du Temps Perdu.* Paris: A. G. Nizet.

Diesbach, Ghislain de. 1991. *Proust.* Paris: Perrin.

Donoso, José. 1984. *Historia personal del "Boom."* Buenos Aires: Sudamericana/ Planeta.

El Escriba (Virgilio Piñera). 1960. "Después de la novela social." *Revolución* (La Habana) 5 Feb.: 2.

Eyzaguirre, Luis. 1985. "Alfredo Bryce Echenique o la reconquista del tiempo." *Revista de Crítica Literaria Latinoamericana* (Lima) 21–22: 215–21.

Farris, Wendy. 1980. "Alejo Carpentier à la recherche du temps perdu." *Comparative Literature Studies* 17.2: 133–54.

———. 1983. *Carlos Fuentes.* New York: Frederick Ungar Publishing Co.

Fernandez, Ramon. 1927. "La vie sociale dans l'oeuvre de Marcel Proust." In *Les cahiers de Marcel Proust.* Vol. 2. vii–xxiii. Paris: Gallimard.

Flores, Angel. 1955. "Magical Realism in Spanish American Fiction." *Hispania* 38.2: 187–92.

Foster, David William. 1991. *Gay and Lesbian Themes in Latin American Writing.* Austin: University of Texas Press.

———, ed. 1994. *Latin American Writers on Gay and Lesbian Themes: A Bio-critical Sourcebook.* Westport, CT: Greenwood Press.

Fuentes, Carlos. 1968. Letter to Gloria Durán. 8 Dec. In *The Archetypes of Carlos Fuentes: From Witch to Androgyne,* by Gloria Durán. 204–5. Hamden, CT: Archon Book.

———. 1990. *Myself with Others: Selected Essays.* New York: The Noonday Press.

Galimberti, Ana. 1992. *Marcel Proust: estudio de antecedentes, materiales estéticos y estilo en "La Recherche."* Mendoza: Universidad Nacional del Cuyo.

Gálvez, Manuel. 1924. *El espíritu de aristocracia y otros ensayos.* Buenos Aires: Agencia general de librerías y publicaciones.

———. 1925. "Manuel Gálvez y la nueva generación." *Martín Fierro,* 2d ser., 20: 7.

García Carrillo, Eugenio. 1971. "Marcel Proust en Costa Rica." *La República* (San José) 17 July: 9.

García Márquez, Gabriel. 1982. *El olor de la guayaba: Conversaciones con Plinio Apuleyo Mendoza.* Bogotá: La Oveja Negra, Ltda.

———. 1995. *Notas de prensa 1980–1984.* Santafé de Bogotá: Editorial Norma S. A.

García Simón, Diana. 1998. *Paraíso, metamorfosis y memoria: La influencia de Proust y Kafka en la obra de Mujica Láinez.* Frankfurt: Peter Lang.

Garma, Simone. 1949. "Marcel Proust y la personalidad." *Anales del Instituto Popular de Conferencias* (Buenos Aires) 35: 57–68.

Genette, Gérard. 1972. *Figures III*. Paris: Editions du Seuil.

Germain, André. 1924. *De Proust à Dada*. Paris: Editions du Sagittaire.

Glenn, Kathleen M. 1994. "Postmodern Parody and Culinary-Narrative Art in Laura Esquivel's *Como agua para chocolate*." *Chasqui* 23.2: 39–47.

Gómez Carrillo, Enrique. 1927. *La nueva literatura francesa*. Madrid: Editorial Mundo Latino.

Gómez-Gil, Orlando. 1968. *Historia crítica de la literatura hispanoamericana*. New York: Holt, Rinehart and Winston.

González Vigil, Ricardo. 1983. Rev. of *Cuatro para Delfina*. *El Comercio* (Lima) 13 Mar.

Graham, Victor E. 1976. *Bibliographie des études sur Marcel Proust et son oeuvre*. Genève: Libraire Droz.

———. 1966. *The Imagery of Proust*. Barnes & Noble.

Gray, Margaret E. 1992. *Postmodern Proust*. Philadelphia: University of Pennsylvania Press.

Graziano, Frank. 1997. *The Lust of Seeing: Themes of the Gaze and Sexual Rituals in the Fiction of Felisberto Hernández*. Lewisburg, PA: Bucknell University Press.

Grossmann, Rudolf. 1972. *Historia y problemas de la literatura latinoamericana*. Trans. Juan C. Probst. Madrid: Revista de Occidente.

Harvey, Sally. 1994. *Carpentier's Proustian Fiction: The Influence of Marcel Proust on Alejo Carpentier*. London: Tamesis Books, Ltd.

Hernández Arregui, Juan José. 1957. *Imperialismo y cultura (La política en la inteligencia argentina)*. Buenos Aires: Editorial Amerindia.

Hindus, Milton. 1954. *The Proustian Vision*. New York: Columbia University Press.

Hodson, Leighton. 1989. *Marcel Proust: The Critical Heritage*. London: Routledge.

Hommage à Marcel Proust. 1927. Paris: Librairie Gallimard.

Huas, Jeanine. 1992. *L'homosexualité du temps de Proust*. Dinard: Ed. Dauclau.

Hutcheon, Linda. 1988. *A Poetics of Postmodernism: History, Theory, Fiction*. New York: Routledge.

———. 1985. *A Theory of Parody: The Teachings of Twentieth Century Art Forms*. New York: Methuen, Inc.

Rev. of *Los ídolos* by Manuel Mujica Láinez. 1953. *La Nación* (Buenos Aires) 31 May.

Irazusta, Julio. 1936. "Una opinión de Santayana sobre el testimonio filosófico de Proust." *Sur* (Buenos Aires) 26: 121–24.

J. A. 1951. "Bibliografía proustiana." *Libros de hoy* (Buenos Aires) 1: 72–73.

Jaloux, Edmond. 1920. "El año literario." *América Latina* (Paris-London) Feb.: 14.

Jones, Julie. 1998. *A Common Place: The Representation of Paris in Spanish American Fiction*. Lewisburg, PA: Bucknell University Press.

Karsen, Sonja. 1971. *Jaime Torres Bodet*. New York: Twayne Publishers, Inc.

Lasarte, Francisco. 1981. *Felisberto Hernández y la escritura de "lo otro."* Madrid: Insula.

Lemaître, Louis Antoine. 1987. *Mujer ingeniosa: Vida de Teresa de la Parra*. Madrid: Editorial La Muralla.

Lezama Lima, José. 1979. *Cartas (1939–1976)*. Ed. Eloísa Lezama Lima. Madrid: Editorial Orígenes.

——. 1994. *Diarios 1939–49/1956–1958.* Ed. Ciro Bianchi Ross. México: Ediciones Era, S. A.

——. 1968. "Discusión sobre *Rayuela.*" In *Cinco miradas sobre Cortázar.* Ana María Simo, et al. Buenos Aires: Editorial Tiempo Contemporáneo.

Linares, Horacio (Alberto Prebisch). 1925. "Manuel Gálvez y la nueva generación." *Martín Fierro,* 2d ser., 18: 7; 21: 1, 7.

Lunacharski, Anatoli, V. 1966. "Sobre Marcel Proust." Trans. Virgilio Piñera. *Unión* (Havana) 5.1: 145–52.

Magny, Claude-Edmonde. 1950. *Histoire du roman français depuis 1918.* Vol. 1. Paris: Seuil.

Mallea, Eduardo. 1937. "Introducción al mundo de Franz Kafka." *Sur* 39: 7–37.

——. 1941. *El sayal y la púrpura.* Buenos Aires: Losada.

——. 1928 "Tentativa de novela moderna." *La Nación* (Buenos Aires) "Letras-Artes" 139 (26 Feb.): 12.

Mariani, Roberto. 1927. "Introducción a Marcel Proust." *Nosotros* (Buenos Aires) 215: 16–23.

Mariátegui, José Carlos. 1959. *El alma matinal y otras estaciones del hombre de hoy.* Lima: Empresa Editora Amauta.

Martin-Chauffier, Louis. 1943. "Proust et le double 'je' de quatre personnes." *Confluences* 21–24: 55–69.

Martínez, Marco Antonio. 1972. "Proust y Teresa de la Parra." *Imagen* (Caracas) 44, sec. 2: 2–3.

Matamoro, Blas. 1991. "Lectores de Proust." *Cuadernos Hispanoamericanos* 495: 95–116.

——. 1988. *Por el camino de Proust.* Barcelona: Editorial Anthropos.

Matas, Julio. 1983 "Pirandello, Proust and *El chino* by Carlos Felipe." *Hispanic Journal* 5.1: 43–47.

Maurois, André. 1949. *A la recherche de Marcel Proust.* Paris: Hachette.

McGowan, John P. 1982–83. "*A la recherche du temps perdu* in *One Hundred Years of Solitude.*" *Modern Fiction Studies* 28.4: 557–67.

McMurray, George R. 1979. *José Donoso.* Boston: G. K. Hall & Co.

Messières, René de. 1942. "Un document probable sure le premier état de la pensée de Proust:'Mystères' par Fernand Gregh." *Romanic Review* 33.2: 113–31.

Meyerhoff, Hans. 1955. *Time in Literature.* Berkeley: University of California Press.

Miomandre, Francis de. 1920. "Marcel Proust: El Premio Goncourt." *El Universal* (Caracas) 23 Jan.: 5.

Molloy, Sylvia. 1994. *Signs of Borges.* Durham, NC: Duke University Press.

Le monde de Proust: Photographies de Paul Nadar. ?. Paris?: Imprimerie Durand S. A.

Monteforte Toledo, Mario. 1949. "Marcel Proust, profundo superficial." *Cuadernos Americanos* 43.1: 245–54.

Montenegro, Nivia. 1978. "Structural and Thematic Elements in *Abaddón el exterminador.*" *Latin American Literary Review* 6.12: 38–55.

Moscoso-Gongora, Peter. 1974. "A Proust of the Caribbean." Rev. of *Paradiso,* by José Lezama Lima. *The Nation* (New York) 218: 600–1.

Moss, Howard. 1962. *The Magic Lantern of Marcel Proust.* New York: Macmillan.

Müller-Bergh, Klaux. 1972. *Alejo Carpentier: Estudio biográfico crítico.* Madrid: Las Américas.

Mujica Láinez, Manuel. 1977. Letter to Herbert Craig. 1 Mar.

Nava, José. 1960. "Brasileiros nos caminhos de Proust." *Revista do Libro* 5.17: 109–26.

Neis, Ignacio Antonio. 1988–89. "A crítica literária brasileira nos caminhos de Proust." *Trevessia* 16–18: 168–208.

"La novela moderna." 1927. *El Comercio* (Quito) 5 Jan.: 2.

Novo, Salvador. 1929. "El cesto y la mesa." *Revista de Revistas* (México) 992 (5 May): 5.

Núñez, Estuardo. 1951. "Martín Adán y su creación poética." *Letras Peruanas* 1.4: 97, 127–31.

"Una obra sobre la revelación psicológica de Proust." 1936. *Sur* (Buenos Aires) 21: 125.

Ocampo, Victoria. 1920. "En marge de Ruskin." *La Nación* (Buenos Aires) 18 Apr.: 3.

———. 1931. "Palabras francesas." *Sur* 3: 7–25.

———. 1977. Response to questionaire on Proust prepared by Herbert Craig. April.

———. 1975. *Testimonios: Novena serie 1971–1974.* Buenos Aires: Sur.

Ocasio, Rafael and Fiona Doloughan. 1994. "Literary Offspring: The Figure of the Child in Marcel Proust and Reinaldo Arenas." *Romance Quarterly* 41.2: 110–18.

Onetti, J. Carlos. 1947. "Marcel Proust: Nota para un aniversario." *Clarín* (Buenos Aires) 16 Nov. sec. 2: 4.

Oreamuno, Yolanda. 1968. Letter to Victoria Urbano. In *Una escritora costarricense: Yolanda Oreamuno,* by Victoria Urbano, 193–94. Madrid: Colección Orosi.

Ortega y Gasset, José. 1925. *La deshumanización del arte e Ideas sobre la novela.* Madrid: Revista de Occidente.

———. 1963. *Obras completas.* Vol. 2. Madrid: Revista de Occidente.

Painter, George D. 1959. *Proust: A Biography.* 2 vols. New York: Random House.

Peltzer, Federico. 1971. *El amor creación en la novela.* Buenos Aires: Editorial Columba.

Petit, Magdalena. 1932. "Proust, 'snob y servil'." *Nosotros* (Buenos Aires) 282: 208–14.

Petit de Murat, Ulises. 1930. "Concepción proustiana de la novela." *Síntesis* (Buenos Aires) 36: 231–34.

Picón Salas, Mariano. 1961. *Estudios de literatura venezolana.* Caracas-Madrid: Ediciones EDIME.

Pierre-Quint, León. 1928. *Comment travaillait Proust.* Paris: Editions des Cahiers libres.

———. 1925. *Marcel Proust: sa vie, son oeuvre.* Paris: Aux Editions du Sagittaire.

Pimentel, Luz Aurora. 1990. *Metaphoric Narration: Paranarrative Dimensions in A la recherche du temps perdu.* Toronto: University of Toronto Press.

Piroué, George. 1971. "Ni perdido ni encontrado." *La Nación* (Buenos Aires) 11 July, sec. 3: 2.

Pogolotti, Graziella. 1974. "Carpentier renovado." *Casa de las Américas* 15.86: 127–29.

Ponte, Antonio José. 1990. "Lectura de Proust." *Unión* (La Habana) 3.9: 26–36.

Prado, Javier del. 1990. *Para leer a Marcel Proust.* Madrid: Palas Atenea Ediciones, S. A.

Prieto, Jenaro. 1973. *Antología humorística.* Santiago: Editorial Nacional Gabriela Mistral.

Proust, Marcel. 1971. *Contre Sainte-Beuve précédé de Pastiches et mélanges et suivi de Essais et articles.* Paris: Gallimard.

———. 1970–1993. *Correspondance de Marcel Proust.* Ed. Philip Kolb. 21 vols. Paris: Plon.

———. 1956. *Lettres à Reynaldo Hahn.* Ed. Philip Kolb. Paris: Gallimard.

———. 1906. "Préface du traducteur: Sur la lecture" to *Sésame et les lys,* by John Ruskin. Paris: Mercure de France.

———. 1984. *Selected Letters: 1880–1903.* Ed. Philip Kolb. Garden City, NY: Anchor Books.

Ramos, Juan P. 1926. "Marcel Proust." *Verbum* (Buenos Aires) 66: 227–50.

Restrepo, María Cristina. 1986. *El olvido en la obra de Marcel Proust.* Medellín: Universidad Pontificia Bolivariana.

Reyes, Alfonso. 1960. *Obras completas.* Vols. 3, 12. México: Fondo de Cultura Económica.

———. 1929. "Proust en América." *Libra* (Buenos Aires) 1: 87–88.

Ribeyro, Julio Ramón. 1970. "Notas sobre *Paradiso.*" In *Recopilación de textos sobre José Lezama Lima.* Ed. Pedro Simón Martínez, 175–81. La Habana: Casa de las Américas.

Ricardou, Jean. 1971. "Modernité proustienne." *Les Nouvelles Littéraires* 11 June: 5.

Ricoeur, Paul. 1988. *Time and Narrative.* Chicago: The University of Chicago.

Rivas, Marta. 1968. *Un mito proustiano.* Santiago: Editorial Universitaria, S. A.

Rivers, J. E. 1979. "The Myth and Science of Homosexuality in *A la recherche du temps perdu.*" *Homosexualities and French Literature: Cultural Contexts/Critical Texts.* Ed. George Stambolian and Elaine Marks. Ithaca: Cornell University Press.

Rivière, Jacques. 1920. "Marcel Proust et la tradition classique." *La Nouvelle Revue Française* 7.77: 192–200.

Rodríguez Monegal, Emir. 1974. *Narradores de esta América.* Vol. 2. Buenos Aires: Editorial Alfa Argentina.

———. 1952. "Relecturas: Marcel Proust." *Marcha* 642: 14–15.

Sábato, Ernesto. 1979. *El escritor y sus fantasmas.* Barcelona: Editorial Seix Barral, S. A.

Sánchez, Luis Alberto. 1934. *Panorama de la literatura actual.* Santiago: Ercilla.

———. 1968. *Proceso y contenido de la novela hispanoamericana.* Madrid: Editorial Gredos, S. A.

———. 1984. "Prólogo" to *La casa de cartón,* by Martín Adán, 7–11. Lima: Promoción Editorial Inca, S. A.

Santa-María, Alejo. 1971. "Marcel Proust: Cien años." *El Universal* (Caracas) 4 July: 2, 9.

Sarraute, Nathalie. 1956. *L'ère du soupçon: Essais sur le roman.* Paris: Gallimard.

Schwartz, Marcy E. 1999. *Writing Paris: Urban Topographies of Desire in Contemporary Latin American Fiction.* Albany: State University of New York Press.

Seeber, Arturo (hijo). 1927. "Marcel Proust y el momento actual." *Fiesta* (Buenos Aires) 4: 9–14.

Shattuck, Roger. 1968. *The Banquet Years.* New York: Vintage Books.

Shaw, Donald L. 1998. *The Post-Boom in Spanish American Fiction.* Albany: State University of New York Press.

Sheridan, Guillermo. 1985. *Los Contemporáneos ayer.* México: Fondo de Cultura Económica.

Silva Casto, Raúl. 1960. *Historia crítica de la novela chilena (1843–1956)*. Madrid: Ediciones Cultura Hispánica.

Souday, Paul. 1927. *Marcel Proust*. Paris: Simon Kra.

Strachey, John. 1936. "Literatura y capitalismo." *SECH* (Santiago) 1.1: 21–28.

Suárez Calimano, E. 1933. "Directrices de la novela y el cuento argentinos (1920–1932)." *Nosotros* 295: 337–70.

Suzuki, Michihiko. 1959. "Le 'je' proustien." *Bulletin de la Société de Amis de Marcel Proust et des Amis de Combray* 9: 69–82.

Todorov, Tzvetan. 1984. *Mikhail Bakhtin: The Dialogical Principle*. Minneapolis: University of Minnesota Press.

Tollinchi, Esteban. 1978. *La conciencia proustiana*. Río Piedras: Editorial Universitaria.

Torre, Guillermo de. 1955. "Libros: Viajeros inmóviles." Rev. of *Los viajeros,* by Manuel Mujica Láinez. *Saber vivir* 112: 34.

Torres Bodet, Jaime. 1928. "Aniversario de Proust." *Contemporáneos* 1.6: 280–91.

Torres-Rioseco, Arturo. 1941. *Grandes novelistas de la América Hispana: Los novelistas de la tierra*. Berkeley and Los Angeles: University of California Press.

———. 1963. "Influencia de la cultura francesa en la literatura hispanoamericana." *Cuadernos* 78: 69–75.

Uslar Pietri, Arturo. 1948. *Letras y hombres de Venezuela*. México: Fondo de Cultura Económica.

Valdivieso, Jaime. 1980. *Bajo el signo de Orfeo: Lezama Lima y Proust*. Madrid: Editorial Orígenes.

Vallbona, Rima de. 1972. *Yolanda Oreamuno*. San José: Ministerio de Cultura, Juventud y Deportes.

Vargas Llosa, Mario. 1971. *García Márquez, historia de un deicidio*. Barcelona: Barral Editores, S. A.

———. 1986. *La orgía perpetua: Flaubert y "Madame Bovary."* Barcelona: Seix Barral.

Vega, Daniel de la. 1948. "Lecturas." *Las Ultimas Noticias* (Santiago) 2 Sept.

Vergara, Marta. 1931. "Nuevos ataques y nueva actualidad de Marcel Proust." *El Mercurio* (Santiago) 13 Dec.: 2.

Vicuña Luco, Osvaldo. 1946. *Correspondencia: Crítica literaria, apuntes íntimos, artículos y divagaciones*. Santiago: Imprenta Universitaria.

Vigneron, Robert. 1941. "Genesis of 'Swann'." *Partisan Review* 8.6: 460–75.

Villena, Luis Antonio de. 1976. "El país Mujica Láinez." Prologue to *Antología general e introducción a la obra de Manuel Mujica Láinez,* 11–33. Madrid: Ediciones Felmar.

Viñas, David. 1954. "Otros tres novelistas argentinos por orden cronológico: Leopoldo Marechal, Manuel Mujica Láinez, Silvina Bullrich." *Contorno* 2.

Williams, Raymond Leslie. 1998. *The Modern Latin-American Novel*. New York: Twayne Publishers.

———. 1995. *The Postmodern Novel in Latin America*. New York: St. Martin's Press.

Wood, Michael. 1974. "Purgatorio." Rev. of *Paradiso* by José Lezama Lima. *The New York Review* 21.6: 14–16.

Zamudio-Taylor, Victor and Inma Guiu. 1994. "Criss-Crossing Texts: Reading Images in *Like Water for Chocolate*." In *The Mexican Cinema Project*. Ed. Chon A. Noriega and Steven Ricci, 45–51. Los Angeles: UCLA Film and Television Archive.

Index

Adán, Martín (Rafael de la Fuente Benavides), 344 n. 15; *Casa de cartón*, 69–71, 164–65
Adoum, Jorge Enrique, 340; *Entre Marx y una mujer desnuda*, 127–30, 326–28, 332, 353 nn. 26–28, 357 n. 20, 366 n. 25
Agostinelli, Alfred, 145, 156–57
Aguilera Garramuño, Marco Tulio, 51, 356 n. 25
Albaret, Céleste, 116, 344 n. 16, 352 n. 15
Albérès, R. M. (René Marill), 45, 56–57
Albertine, 41, 52, 60, 72–73, 75–76, 91, 120, 135, 141–42, 145, 147, 162–63, 166–67, 169, 171, 173, 196–97, 213, 215, 227, 229, 232, 234–36, 243, 246, 278, 306–7, 316, 319, 360 n. 22, 363 n. 25
Alden, Douglas W., 21–22
Allende, Isabel (*Eva Luna*), 366 n. 26
Alone (Hernán Díaz Arrieta), 27, 29–30, 33, 36, 38, 40, 46–47, 54, 101, 343 n. 6, 345 n. 26, 349 n. 29, 352 n. 12
analysis, psychological, 18, 29, 33, 35, 38, 40, 44, 49, 61, 63–65, 70–71, 75–76, 84, 95, 99, 101, 103, 129, 136–38, 143–44, 147–49, 151, 156, 158–62, 165, 168, 170–72, 180, 207, 217, 249, 336
Anderson Imbert, Enrique, 33, 41–42, 45, 105, 199, 217, 354 n. 2, 357 n. 18; *Vigilia*, 145–46
appearances, deceptive, 138, 140, 160, 171–72, 175, 306
Arenas, Reinaldo, 172, 253, 316, 338, 340, 354 n. 10, 357 n. 17, 365 n. 16; *Celestino antes del alba*, 223–24, 335–

36; *El color del verano*, 157–59, 210–11, 329–32, 366 nn. 27, 29
Argentina, 13, 26–29, 31–38, 40–43, 45–46, 50–55, 61–65, 77–80, 84–96, 102–4, 105–12, 125–27, 137–38, 140–42, 145–50, 161–64, 178, 182–89, 199–207, 218–21, 229–32, 234–40, 242–44, 259–60, 266–68, 274–82, 299–305, 307–10, 318–21, 323–26, 329, 343 n. 5, 345 nn. 21–24, 346 n. 36, 349 nn. 19–28, 350–51 n. 2, 354 n. 2, 357 n. 19, 360 n. 23. 363 nn. 24 and 25
aristocracy, 99–100, 105–8, 114–16, 120, 122, 124, 126, 128, 130, 132, 158, 215, 301, 315–16, 327
Arlt, Roberto, 354 n. 2, 359–60 n. 19
art, 17, 51–52, 107–8, 120, 173–211, 303–4, 315, 341 n. 3, 356 n. 7
artist, the, 61, 104, 173, 177–78, 184–85, 189
Atenea (Concepción), 30–31, 33, 38
authenticity, 38, 103, 114, 128, 133, 265, 282, 284–87, 294, 353 n. 28
autobiography, 214, 254, 279, 296
Ayala, Francisco, 36, 101
Azuela, Mariano, 30, 104, 348 n. 15

Bakhtin, Mikhail, 57, 347 n. 2
Balbec, 71–72, 165, 167–68, 174, 179, 242, 246, 291, 355 nn. 18 and 21
Balza, José, 43–45, 51, 54
Balzac, Honoré de, 30, 59–60, 100, 104, 127, 199, 296, 333, 338
Barga, Corpus (Andrés García de la Barga), 25–26
Baudelaire, Charles, 17, 60, 173, 258, 347 n. 5, 350 n. 1, 351–52 n. 9, 356 n. 1, 361 n. 3

434

436   INDEX

consciousness, 17, 19, 30, 60, 81, 89, 97, 100, 109, 129, 136–37, 140, 159, 162, 164–65, 169–70, 176, 180, 213, 239, 258, 283, 297–98, 302, 351 n. 5, 354 n. 2

Contemporáneos, Los (Mexico City), 30–31, 43–44, 54, 71

Contemporáneos group, 71–77, 145, 348 n. 12

Cortázar, Julio, 109, 127–28, 161, 172, 190, 207, 253, 281, 314, 317, 328, 331–32, 337, 355 nn. 13, 15, and 16, 356 n. 8, 357 n. 20, 358 n. 23, 359 nn. 15 and 16; *Rayuela*, 110–11, 161–64, 186–89, 202–5, 209, 218–20, 234–37, 274–79, 285, 292, 294, 307–10, 335, 338, 340, 351–52 n. 9, 362 nn. 17 and 18, 365 nn. 8, 9, and 10, 15

Cuba, 24, 27–28, 35–36, 46, 48–50, 55, 104, 111–14, 120–21, 133, 151, 157–59, 181–82, 189–93, 201, 208, 210–11, 221–22, 223–24, 241–42, 262–65, 282–87, 294, 315–17, 329–32, 343 n. 7–8, 345 n. 29, 346 nn. 34, 36, and 37, 359 n. 13, 364 n. 28

Curtius, Ernst-Robert, 35, 52

Dandieu, Arnaud, 34–35

death, and art, 184–85, 189, 203–4, 215, 221, 313–14, 317, 322, 323–24, 330–31

Deleuze, Gilles, 23, 308

descriptions, impressionist, 76, 81–84, 107, 176–84, 187, 190–91, 196–98, 210, 269

details, use of, 26, 69–71, 84, 90–91, 333–34, 347 n. 9, 350 n. 31

dialogue: narrative, 19, 57–60, 94–97, 113, 116–21, 125–27, 129, 133, 153, 156–59, 161–64, 172, 188, 193, 200, 202–6, 211, 217, 219–21, 223, 225–26, 236, 242–43, 245–48, 251–53, 259–60, 263, 268, 271–73, 274–87, 288–95, 298, 304–11, 314, 317, 319–21, 323, 325, 331–32, 340, 347 n. 1; within a text, 59–60, 151, 199–201, 204, 318–19, 357 n. 19

Díaz Rodríguez, Manuel, 16–17, 342 nn. 9 and 12, 347 n. 7

Dickmann, Max, 28, 347–48 nn. 11 and 17

diégèse, 176, 181, 183, 190, 198, 300, 364 n. 5

Diesbach, Ghislain de, 14, 341 n. 6

Dominican Republic, 47

Donoso, José, 109, 114–20, 130, 152, 262, 336, 338, 340, 357 n. 14, 359 n. 10–11; *Casa de campo*, 115–16, 191, 352 n. 14; *Conjeturas sobre la memoria de mi tribu*, 226–27, 352 n. 15; *Este domingo*, 270–73, 278, 285; *El obsceno pájaro de la noche*, 114–15, 164, 321–23, 331–32, 366 n. 29; "El tiempo perdido," 116–19, 352 nn. 16 and 17

Dostoevsky, Fedor, 60, 84, 199

Dreyfus Affair, 44, 213, 242

Droguett, Carlos (*El compadre*), 362 n. 12

Eco (Bogotá), 47, 54

Ecuador, 31, 47, 49–50, 127–29, 132–33, 326–28, 340

Edwards, Jorge, 119; *El peso de la noche*, 268–72, 294

Edwards Bello, Joaquín (*El chileno en Madrid*), 259

Elstir, 112, 173–74, 191, 242, 302

Emeth, Omer (Emile Vaïsse), 27, 29

Esquivel, Laura, 316, 338–40, 363–64 nn. 26 and 29; *Como agua para chocolate*, 193–98, 263, 288–95, 335, 357 n. 13

Excelsior (Mexico City), 24, 40, 47, 51

Farris, Wendy, 122, 363 n. 23

Faulkner, William, 18, 109, 208, 258, 342 n. 13, 355–56 n. 22

Felipe, Carlos, 359 n. 13

Fernandez, Ramon, 31, 100, 136, 260, 344 n. 16

Fiesta (Buenos Aires), 29, 344 n. 12

Flaubert, Gustave, 59, 134, 168, 207, 296, 347 n. 4

Flores, Angel, 168, 339

Florida group, 28, 33, 77–78

Foguet, Hugo (*Pretérito perfecto*), 363 n. 25

forgetfulness, 43, 52, 156, 160, 162–63, 213–14, 227, 233, 237, 243, 258, 282

Foster, David William, 146, 354 n. 4

fragmentation, 70, 164, 205, 333

France, Anatole (Anatole Thibault), 58, 124, 358 n. 5